Frommer's

1st Edition

Montana & Wyoming

by Melanie Brinkley
& Randy Provence

Macmillan • USA

ABOUT THE AUTHORS

A Montana resident since 1991, **Melanie Brinkley** is a former editor of *Whitefish* magazine. She edited and contributed to *The Valley Outfitter*, a comprehensive regional guide to Montana's Flathead Valley.

Randy Provence has lived and traveled in Montana for the last five years. He is co-founder of *Kinesis*, a Montana-based literary journal, and has contributed to various regional magazines.

MACMILLAN TRAVEL

A Simon & Schuster Macmillan Company
1633 Broadway
New York, NY 10019

Find us online at **http://www.mgr.com/travel** or
on America Online at **Keyword: Frommer's**

ISBN 0-02-860685-X
ISSN 1088-2650

Editors: Lisa Renaud and Erica Spaberg
Contributors: Reid Bramblett and Dave Taylor
Design by Michele Laseau
Digital Cartography by Raffaele DeGennaro
Map copyright © by Simon & Schuster

SPECIAL SALES

Bulk purchases (10+ copies) of Frommer's travel guides are available to corporations at special discounts. The Special Sales Department can produce custom editions to be used as premiums and/or for sales promotion to suit individual needs. Existing editions can be produced with custom cover imprints such as corporate logos. For more information write to: Special Sales, Simon & Schuster, 1633 Broadway, New York, NY 10019.

Manufactured in the United States of America

Contents

List of Maps

AN INVITATION TO THE READER

In researching this book, we discovered many wonderful places—hotels, restaurants, shops, and more. We're sure you'll find others. Please tell us about them, so we can share the information with your fellow travelers in upcoming editions. If you were disappointed with a recommendation, we'd love to know that, too. Please write to:

Frommer's Montana & Wyoming, 1st Edition
Macmillan Travel
1633 Broadway
New York, NY 10019

AN ADDITIONAL NOTE

Please be advised that travel information is subject to change at any time—and this is especially true of prices. We therefore suggest that you write or call ahead for confirmation when making your travel plans. The authors, editors, and publisher cannot be held responsible for the experiences of readers while traveling. Your safety is important to us, however, so we encourage you to stay alert and be aware of your surroundings. Keep a close eye on cameras, purses, and wallets, all favorite targets of thieves and pickpockets.

WHAT THE SYMBOLS MEAN

✪ Frommer's Favorites

Hotels, restaurants, attractions, and entertainment you should not miss.

⑤ Super-Special Values

Hotels and restaurants that offer great value for your money.

The following abbreviations are used for credit cards:

AE	American Express	EU	Eurocard
CB	Carte Blanche	JCB	Japan Credit Bank
DC	Diners Club	MC	MasterCard
DISC	Discover	V	Visa
ER	enRoute		

The Best of Montana & Wyoming

Montana and Wyoming are so far removed from the rest of the country—in so many ways—that the typical list of tourist attractions just doesn't apply. There aren't any metropolitan operas or magnificent art museums or spectacular amusement parks, and the elements that define these two states can't be found in the rest of the country. The ideals of this vast and lonely expanse have been lost forever in most places—even the other Western states.

That's not to say that there aren't any cars, or that everybody wears boots and cowboy hats, or that rodeos are the only spectator sport. But here are the vestiges of a seemingly lost, even-tempered way of life, with rough hands and urbane poets (and even some rough poets). The soaring mountain scenery and blue-ribbon trout streams temper the fuses of residents and lure refugees from urban America. They come, if only for a few weeks, to see for themselves the wonder of places like Yellowstone, Glacier, and the Tetons. Some wind up staying for life.

We've scoured both states and have come up with a very personal, opinionated list of those experiences that truly exemplify Montana and Wyoming at their best, the tried and true as well as the offbeat. To visit Wyoming and not see Yellowstone would, without a doubt, constitute a crime. But skipping Devils Tower, or Montana's Madison Valley, or historic places like Butte and Fort Laramie would also be a transgression. From the fantastic winter and summer recreational possibilites—skiing, snowmobiling, climbing, and hiking—to the compelling and occasionally even tragic recent histories of these two states, Montana and Wyoming are great places to play in a vanishing playground.

1 The Best Travel Experiences

- **Exploring a National Park** (MT and WY): The three national parks found within Montana and Wyoming's borders—Yellowstone, Grand Teton, and Glacier—unquestionably provide the two states with a height and breadth of natural beauty that is unsurpassed, from Yellowstone's burbling mud pots and thundering geysers and the Tetons's Alplike peaks to Glacier's expansive mountain valleys and abundant wildlife. Elegant lodges, rustic cabins, and remote backcountry campsites enable visitors to enjoy as much or as little of their surroundings as they wish. See Chapters 5, 11, and 12.

- **Following the Trail of History** (MT and WY): For history buffs, Wyoming and Montana are ideal places to delve into the West's age of discovery. Wagon ruts and primitive gravestones are visible reminders of the hardships endured by this region's earliest settlers. Crisscrossing both states are the Old West, Mullen, and Oregon Trails, as well as those of explorers Lewis and Clark and the Nez Perce. Sleep under the stars along one of these trails on a longhorn cattle drive or follow the routes yourself by canoe, bike, or car; maps detailing them are available from local chambers of commerce and state park visitor centers. See Chapters 7, 8, 10, and 15.
- **Riding the Rails** (MT and WY): Both Montana and Wyoming offer scenic train excursions by private rail. Climb aboard one of the seven restored vintage cars of the *Northern Parks Limited* for an intimate look at some of Montana's most stunning scenery and most interesting wildlife guided by the Audubon Society (☎ 212/979-3066), or spend a fun-filled afternoon of family fun in Wyoming on the scenic railroad at Wyoming Territorial Park (☎ 800/845-2287).

2 The Best Adventure Trips

Montana and Wyoming were founded on the spirit of adventure, and this spirit continues to define the people who live here as well as those who come to visit. If you're looking for action, you've come to the right place.

- **Participating in Cycle Montana** (MT): Montana's own premier cycling outfitter, Adventure Cycling Association (formerly "Bikecentennial") coordinates this annual bike tour, previously called "Parks to Peaks." The difficult 640-mile route takes you from Glacier Park in the northwest corner to Yellowstone in the south in 13 days, with plenty of opportunities for drinking in the sights along the way. (☎ 406/721-1776).
- **Biking, Riding Horseback, Hiking, and Rafting through Yellowstone** (WY): Backcountry's active vacation offerings include this multi-faceted trek through the wonders of Yellowstone at the height of its summer beauty. Although biking prevails throughout the trip, there are excursions by horseback, foot, and raft, complemented by gourmet food, first-class accommodations within the park, even an early-morning hot spring soak. The 5¹/₂-day trip is rated for beginners to intermediates, with easy to moderate hiking and biking. Contact Backcountry, Ltd., P.O. Box 4029, Bozeman, MT 59772 (☎ 406/586-3556).
- **Climbing the Tetons** (WY): If merely admiring the majesty of the Tetons from afar doesn't do it for you, and you feel you have to conquer the mountains in order to savor their beauty, you'll find kindred spirits in Jackson Hole. Two premier outfitting services will take you to the top of the highest peak in the Tetons. From beginner to expert, from one-day climbs to two-week wilderness treks in the Wind River Mountains, Jackson Hole Mountain Guides and Exum Mountain Guides are unparalleled. Adventure skiing and snowboarding, ice climbing, and hut skiing are additional extreme options. Contact Jackson Hole Mountain Guides, P.O. Box 7477, Jackson, WY 83001 (☎ 307/733-4979) and Exum Mountain Guides, Box 56, Moose, WY 83012 (☎ 307/733-2297).
- **Sea Kayaking Jackson Lake** (WY): Experience the tranquillity of sea kayaking on Grand Teton National Park's Jackson Lake with O.A.R.S., the industry model for river rafters. No previous kayaking experience is necessary on these one-, two-, or

four-day trip with opportunities for hiking and exploring the park. Alpine peaks surround you as you participate in a moonlight paddle, an especially romantic component of this trip, which runs throughout the summer. Contact O.A.R.S., P.O. Box 67, Angels Camp, CA 95222 (☎ 800/346-6277).

3 The Best Learning Vacations

The wildlife and ecology of Montana and Wyoming make for incredible vacations of discovery. Chosen for their variety of enlightening programs and scenic surroundings, the places and organizations mentioned below can provide you with unsurpassed educational experiences.

- **Exploring Pine Butte Swamp Preserve** (MT): Operated by the Nature Conservancy since 1978, Pine Butte has some of the best naturalist guides in the two states and offers weeklong workshops each spring and fall. Located on 18,000 acres along the eastern Rocky Mountain front, Pine Butte not only offers great opportunities to commune with nature, it is also a great place to relax and enjoy the wonderful scenery on the east side of the Divide. Contact Pine Butte Guest Ranch, Box 34, Choteau, MT 59422 (☎ 406/466-2158). See Chapter 8.
- **Joining a Great Plains Wildlife Institute Safari** (WY): Great Plains Wildlife Institute, though based in Jackson, is only a short four-wheel drive away from Wyoming's natural world. The institute will put you to work as an honest-to-goodness researcher, from ear-tagging prairie dogs to radio-tracking elk calves. And you won't sacrifice comfort when you attend the institute's workshops. Leave from the comfort of a hotel before crusading into the outback on these wilderness safaris. Contact the Great Plains Wildlife Institute, Box 7580, Jackson, WY 83001 (☎ 307/733-2623). See Chapter 12.
- **Taking an Offbeat Workshop with the Snake River Institute** (WY): With its array of instructional programs, the Snake River Institute may very well represent the most eclectic program schedules in Montana and Wyoming. From cowboys and landscapes to birds and Native American studies, the workshops have something to offer everyone. All ages are welcome, with especially unique children's offerings: calligraphy, mythology, and ecology are just a few. Contact the Snake River Institute, P.O. Box 128, Wilson, WY 83014 (☎ 307/733-2214).

4 The Best Scenic Drives

Driving is just something you're going to have to get used to if you plan to see even a small part of these two states, which contain over a quarter of a million square miles between them. Getting from Point A to Point B can sometimes seem like an infinite task. We selected these trails, highways, and byways for their spectacular scenery and historical value, not necessarily for their convenience to the interstate.

- **Trail of the Great Bear International Scenic Corridor** (MT and WY): This is an ambitious journey that covers two countries, five national parks, and an overwhelming abundance of Native American culture, wildlife-viewing areas, and Old West sites of interest. Covering just over 2,000 miles, the route extends from northwest Wyoming in Yellowstone National Park to Jasper National Park in western Alberta, Canada. It's a wonderful way to see the Rockies. The trail publishes a helpful guide that illustrates some of the more specific routes, including helpful maps of important historical and cultural sites along the corridor. For information, contact the Trail of the Great Bear, Box 142, Deer Lodge, MT 59722 (☎ 406/846-2670).

- **Going-to-the-Sun Road, Glacier National Park** (MT): From West Glacier to Logan Pass to St. Mary, there's no better way to view Glacier National Park from the convenience of your car than along this magnificent thruway. The 50-mile Going-to-the-Sun Road bisects the park from southwest to northeast, with spectacular views of glaciated valleys, mountain wildflowers, curious mountain goats, and towering peaks. Because of heavy snowfall, the road is generally not open until early June and usually closes in October. Be sure to check with the park service before planning a driving tour (☎ 406/888-5441). See Chapter 5.

- **Beartooth National Scenic Byway** (MT and WY): Regardless of whether you begin this journey in Red Lodge or in Cooke City, the Beartooth is an incredible journey through southern Montana and northern Wyoming. Climbing to altitudes near 11,000 feet, the Beartooth will take you higher than many small planes and offers views of the surrounding mountains like no other place in America. The trip can take a couple of hours, considering the low speeds at which you must travel and the amount of snow that remains along the roadsides year-round. For great views of Pilot Peak, an 11,699-foot spire just south of Cooke City, begin at Red Lodge and travel west. The mountain will come into view on your descent into Cooke City several miles beyond Beartooth Pass. See Chapter 9.

- **American Dream Safari** (WY): Bothered by the winding mountain roads, the summer snow, the wildlife on asphalt at dusk? Then climb into the backseat of Ted Pierson's 1950 Buick Roadmaster for a retro-style cruise along the blue highways of the West without worrying about the fuel tank or the radiator. When the day's driving is done, crawl into the fully equipped 1953 Airstream that's pulled behind every mile of the way for a good 1950s-style night's rest. Though American Dream Safari isn't in the area as often as we'd like, they're unusual, and they do make tours through Wyoming with enough regularity to warrant a mention. Contact American Dream Safaris, Box 556, McPherson, KS 67460 (☎ 316/241-5656).

5   The Best Places for Nature & Wildlife Viewing

Whether you're a professional or an ambitious amateur, Montana and Wyoming can offer you the sights and sounds of grizzly bear, elk, bison, trumpeter swans, and other creatures. Chart your own "watchable wildlife" tour or join one with Joseph Van Os Photo Safaris, P.O. Box 655, Vashon Island, WA 98070 (☎ 206/463-5383), a premier outfitter that offers several trips highlighting the region's unique scenery and wildlife. The following selections are based on the uniqueness of the wildlife, the number of opportunities, and ease of access.

- **Glacier National Park** (MT): Some of the best views in the country are within the confines of this spectacular national park. The dangerous grizzly bear, an endangered species, has found a home here and can be viewed on rare occasions from the car but more often in the backcountry. At higher elevations, mountain goats can be seen with much more frequency than bears. The Logan Pass area is the most accessible vantage point from which to view the animals as they scramble up and down the rocky mountain slopes, sometimes within feet of the trails. See Chapter 5.

- **Yellowstone National Park** (MT and WY): Without question, Yellowstone offers some of the best opportunities for viewing geologic wonders and incredible wildlife in the entire world. Bison walk up to your car, geysers erupt outside the gift shops, hot pots gurgle like massive vats of boiling water, and waterfalls tumble over canyon cliffs to the Yellowstone floor. Elk abound and, like most of Yellowstone's wildlife, are best seen in morning and early evening. If you've come to see the bison, don't fret. In the middle of the day, in rain, in snow, it doesn't matter—the bison are hard to miss. See Chapter 11.
- **National Elk Refuge** (WY): Nearly 25,000 acres were set aside in 1912 for the elk that migrate to this refuge near Jackson, Wyoming, each winter. Heavy snows in the higher elevations of the elk's summer habitat in the Grand Tetons and the southern part of Yellowstone force them into the valleys in search of food. November and December are usually the best times to view the elk from the unpaved roadways throughout the refuge. Moose, bighorn sheep, coyotes, and badgers also live here and can be spotted from the paved turnouts on the west side of the refuge along U.S. Highway 26. See Chapter 12.

6 The Best Guest Ranches

For the total Western experience, there's nothing like a ranch vacation. Daily horse rides along mountain trails, hearty meals served family-style in rustic log lodges, and dusty, whoop-'em-up cattle drives with twinkling stars for a nighttime canopy hearken to the past yet can still be experienced today at the guest and working cattle ranches of Montana and Wyoming. The following ranches were chosen on the basis of their ability to successfully provide first-rate service, accommodations, and amenities to their guests, while maintaining an old-fashioned integrity.

- **Flathead Lake Lodge** (Bigfork, MT; ☎ 406/837-4391): Because it's located on the eastern shore of beautiful Flathead Lake, this guest ranch is able to offer a unique complement to its horse-centered activities. Cozy two- and three-bedroom log cabins dot the carefully manicured property where nearby horse trails crisscross national forestland. The artistic community of Bigfork and Glacier National Park are close by. See Chapter 6.
- **Red Rock Ranch** (Kelly, WY; ☎ 307/733-6288): This working ranch was homesteaded in the late 1800s and has since become one of the finest of its sort in the country. Located near Jackson, the Red Rock is the quintessential family-oriented ranch, with daily horse rides, excellent stream and pond fly-fishing, and cattle drives in the spring and fall. See Chapter 12.
- **Flying A Ranch** (Pinedale, WY; ☎ 307/367-2385 summer; 800/678-6543 winter): This guest ranch, surrounded by the Gros Ventre and Wind River ranges, has some of the best views in the state. Quaking aspens, stream-fed ponds, and curious antelope are just a few of the natural sights you'll see during your stay. Guests here are encouraged to enjoy the ranch at their own pace, whether that means unlimited horse rides or relaxing with a favorite book on their private porch. See Chapter 13.
- **Lost Creek Ranch** (Moose, WY; ☎ 307/733-3435): Visitors are immediately struck by the breathtaking beauty of this Jackson Hole ranch. Scenic vistas surround Lost Creek, and the lodge and cabins on the property complement them with an elegant Western charm. Activities center around horse rides but also include local outings for anglers and rafters. The ranch has been family-owned and -operated since 1968 and most recently began offering high mountain pack trips into the nearby Gros Ventre and Teton Wilderness Areas. See Chapter 13.

- **HF Bar Ranch** (Saddlestring, WY; ☎ 307/684-2487): A classic, it's evolved into a premier Western guest ranch but still holds sight of its old-time Western traditions. You can strike off on your own during the daily horse rides if you demonstrate adequate "horse sense." Guests return here year after year for the HF Bar experience, marked by an unmistakable flair for a no-nonsense, first-rate vacation. See Chapter 14.

7　The Best Hotels & Resorts

- **Grouse Mountain Lodge** (Whitefish, MT; ☎ 800/321-8822): This grand lodge is graced with an elegant river rock fireplace, delicate walls of etched glass, and broad-beamed architecture. The wildlife trophies that preside over the dining room give the hotel a distinctive hunting lodge feel. Fun-loving Big Mountain and the quaint town of Whitefish are nearby, and there's an outdoor hot tub for unwinding under the stars. See Chapter 6.
- **Old Faithful Inn** (Yellowstone National Park, WY; ☎ 307/344-7311): You merely have to step into the lobby of this imposing lodge to get a feel for the sheer magnificence of its architecture. Designed by Robert Reamer and constructed of logs from the area in 1904, Old Faithful Inn is to hotels what Old Faithful is to geysers. Incessantly buzzing with tourists planning trips, browsing the gift shop, or enjoying books on the deck that overlooks the reliable spout, the inn is a remarkable piece of architecture that continues to be the focal point, gathering place, and man-made wonder of the park. See Chapter 11.
- **Spring Creek Resort** (Jackson, WY; ☎ 800/443-6139): This Jackson Hole resort offers plush accommodations, fantastic gourmet food, and unbeatable views of the Tetons. But if that's not enough to lure you to their ridgetop location, they also coordinate horse trips during the summer and provide free shuttle service to the nearby ski area in winter. There are also facilities for swimming, tennis, ice skating, and cross-country skiing in a beautifully landscaped setting. See Chapter 12.

8　The Best Bed-and-Breakfasts

- **The Sanders** (Helena, MT; ☎ 406/442-3309): Built in 1875, this plum-colored brick and shingle Queen Anne–style mansion, located in Helena's historic district, has welcomed guests from all 50 states and 6 continents, including its most famous guest, Archbishop Desmond Tutu. Original furniture and appointments throughout the grand home provide a period elegance that's equally matched by the peerless service and amenities provided by your hosts. See Chapter 7.
- **Copper King Mansion** (Butte, MT; ☎ 406/782-7580): The former residence of Butte Copper King William Clark is the most awe-inspiring and by far the most accessible private mansion in Montana. Listed on the National Register of Historic Places, the Copper King Mansion is outfitted with authentic antique lamps and chandeliers, ornate frescoed ceilings, and etched amber transoms. A third-floor ballroom contains an 825-pipe Estey organ as well as a private collection of clothing and memorabilia dating back to the late 1800s. See Chapter 7.
- **Spahn's Big Horn Mountain B & B** (Big Horn, WY; ☎ 307/674-8150): Enjoy a 100-mile view from a secluded mountain cabin. Tucked amid the Big Horn Mountains, this rustic hideaway features a massive three-story living area and

rooms decorated with country quilts and lodgepole furniture. After dinner, go on a local wildlife safari in search of a glimpse of moose, elk, or ever-present deer. The Eagle's Nest cabin has a distinctive romantic appeal that is perfect for honeymooners. See Chapter 14.

9 The Best Rodeos

Other than buying a ranch and enduring the hardships of the working cowboy yourself on a daily basis, the next best thing is to experience the vicarious thrills of the rodeo. No one knows rodeo better than these two Western states, and the following are the best of the best, chosen for their authenticity and all-around popularity.

- **Miles City Bucking Horse Sale** (MT): For real rodeo aficionados, this is the place to find the future stars of the rodeo circuit. There's a rodeo, of course, but it's the horses that people come to see and buy. Horse racing, barbecues, and a street dance also highlight the weekend event, held annually in May. Contact the Miles City Chamber of Commerce, 901 Main St., Miles City, MT 59301 (☎ 406/232-2890). See Chapter 10.
- **Cheyenne Frontier Days** (WY): Every summer in the heart of Wyoming's capital the "Daddy of 'em All," Cheyenne's Frontier Days, takes place. The 10-day event packs people in from all over the country for the oldest (1996 marks Frontier Days' 100th anniversary) and largest outdoor rodeo anywhere. Pancake breakfasts reward early risers while night owls enjoy a wide variety of country music headline acts during the week. Call 800/227-6336 for details. See Chapter 15.

10 The Best Places to Rediscover the Old West

From the dusty streets of abandoned ghost towns to the preserved memorabilia of the region's most flamboyant characters, the rich history of the Old West continues to thrive in Montana and Wyoming. The places that follow successfully evoke the Old West at its best—and most notorious.

- **Nevada City, Montana:** This re-created Western town will transport you to the days of Montana's vigilantes. Authentic structures, while not indigenous to Nevada City, include a Chinese laundry, blacksmith's shop, and stables. The city's claim to fame is as a setting for various Western dramas, most notably *Little Big Man.* See Chapter 7.
- **Cody, Wyoming:** Namesake of "Buffalo Bill," Cody ensures the enduring appeal of the Wild West by promoting it through the multi-faceted Buffalo Bill Historical Center. The Whitney Gallery of Western Art, the Buffalo Bill Museum, the Plains Indian Museum, and the Cody Firearms Museum all pay tribute to various versions and interpretations of Western history and, along with the ever-popular Cody Nite Rodeo—the longest-running consecutive rodeo in the country—continue to enlighten and entertain their visitors. See Chapter 13.
- **South Pass City, Wyoming:** The epitome of an Old West ghost town, many of its buildings were restored in 1995. Visitors can wander through them during the summer for a glance at authentic artifacts. Once at the center of the fight to pass women's suffrage, South Pass City is now a state historic site and host to a festive Fourth of July celebration with old-fashioned fun and activities. See Chapter 13.

11 The Best Places to Experience Native American Culture

With eight reservations within its borders, Montana and Wyoming share a rich Native American heritage. The following places and events, open to the general public, were chosen for their historical and cultural significance.

- **Attending Crow Fair** (MT): One of the largest gatherings of Native Americans in the country, Crow Fair takes place during the third weekend in August. The fairgrounds are covered with a melange of tepees and campsites. Traditional giveaways, dances, and the haunting songs of tribes from around the country make this one of the great Native American gatherings in the country, and certainly one of the largest. Contact the Crow Tribal Council, P.O. Box 159, Crow Agency, MT 59022 (☎ 406/638-2601). See Chapter 10.

- **Traveling the Nez Perce (Nee Me Poo) National Historic Trail** (MT and WY): A chilling testament to the anguish endured by the Nez Perce during their flight of 1877 and a visible reminder of their struggle for freedom, this historic trail follows the entire route of the Nez Perce War across four Western states. It is maintained by the Nez Perce National Historical Park, which can provide you with an excellent map of the four-state area. To request one, contact the Nez Perce National Historic Trail, P.O. Box 93, Spalding, ID 83551 (☎ 208/843-2261).

- **Touring Battlefields and Treaty Sites** (MT and WY): Sadly, Montana and Wyoming are scarred by battlefields that dot an otherwise beautiful landscape. Visit **Little Bighorn Battlefield**'s sweeping plains to relive the drama of Custer's Last Stand (see Chapter 10) or the **Bear's Paw Battlefield** near Havre where Chief Joseph of the Nez Perce surrendered with the words "From where the sun now stands, I will fight no more forever" (see Chapter 8). Hundreds of Nez Perce were surprised by Army soldiers and forced to flee for their lives at the **Big Hole Battlefield,** near Wisdom (see Chapter 7). In Wyoming, **Fort Laramie** is the most history-rich place in the state. On the south bank of the North Platte River near its confluence with the Laramie River, the fort is famous for the Treaty of 1868, signed here. The treaty—which was shortly thereafter broken—assured the Sioux rights to the Black Hills and Powder River country "as long as the grass shall grow and the buffalo shall roam." See Chapter 14 .

12 The Best Fishing Waters, Guides & Schools

There are few places in the world more ideal for trout fishing than Montana. Its blue-ribbon streams, in combination with the pure fresh mountain air against a vista almost too big to contemplate, make fishing in the West much more than the simple pursuit of fish. The following fishing waters are some of the finest trout streams in the world. The guides noted below were chosen for their vast knowledge of Western streams and rivers and the attendant quality of their instruction.

- **The Madison** (MT): Home to the highest density of native browns, the Madison is Montana's most popular fishery. With headwaters that originate in Yellowstone National Park, the Madison eventually joins up with its "holy trinity" counterparts, the Jefferson and Gallatin, at the Missouri Headwaters near Three Forks. The Madison can be fished year-round, but watch out for restrictions during early spring runoff. See Chapter 9.

- **The Snake** (WY): It seems somehow fitting that the menacing-sounding Snake River is home to a feisty strain of cutthroat trout, making it one of the most satisfying Western rivers to fish. With picture-perfect scenery and the resort town of Jackson within casting distance, this Wyoming river is an angler's paradise. See Chapter 12.

- **The Sunlight Basin** (WY): This picturesque-sounding name belongs to the Sunlight Creek and the Clark's Fork of the Yellowstone, recently designated a Wild and Scenic River. Located between Cooke City and Cody, the Clark's Fork rewards diligent anglers with spectacular scenery and an abundance of rainbows and cutthroats. Sunlight Creek will provide pan-size brook trout, that can be enjoyed on long summer evenings alongside its crystal-clear waters. See Chapter 13.

The following regional shops are well respected locally and provide top-notch guiding service, schools, equipment, and clothing. If you plan to fish in the West, contact them for all the information you need to know. In **Bozeman,** MT: Montana Troutfitters Orvis Shop, 1716 W. Main (☎ 406/587-4707) and The River's Edge, 2012 N. 7th Ave. (☎ 406/586-5373); in **Cody,** WY: North Fork Anglers, 937 Sheridan Ave. (☎ 307/527-7274) and Yellowstone Troutfitters, 239A Yellowstone Ave. (☎ 307/587-8240); in **Jackson,** WY: High Country Flies, 165 N. Center St. (☎ 307/733-7210) and Jack Dennis Outdoor Shop, 50 E. Broadway (☎ 307/733-3270); in **Livingston,** MT: Dan Bailey's Fly Shop, 209 W. Park (☎ 800/356-4052); in **West Yellowstone,** MT: Bud Lilly's Trout Shop, 39 Madison Ave. (☎ 406/646-9570) and Madison River Outfitters, 117 Canyon St.(☎ 406/646-9644).

13 The Best Summer Vacations

Endless daylight hours and cool evening temperatures make Montana and Wyoming super summer destinations, encouraging you to squeeze every exhilarating ray of sun out of each day.

- **Hiking the Highline Trail** (Glacier National Park): This is one of Glacier Park's most popular summer hikes, with opportunities for viewing wildflowers at their peak in midsummer. Definitely not recommended for those with a fear of heights, the narrow trail skirts the Garden Wall, gaining an altitude of 200 feet along the eight-mile route. The trail begins at the Logan Pass Visitor Center and gradually winds its way toward Granite Park Chalet. See Chapter 5.
- **Golfing the Flathead** (MT): No other sport takes better advantage of the West's long summer days than golf, and northwest Montana's Flathead Valley is home to the state's finest courses. Play a round in Whitefish, whose course is laid out against a mountain backdrop, then head over to Bigfork in the late afternoon for another round at Eagle Bend on the north end of the tranquil waters of Flathead Lake. This is a slice of Montana that will have you hooked and eager for more. For tee times, call Flathead Valley central reservations at 800/392-9795. See Chapter 6.
- **Sandshoeing at Killpecker Dunes** (WY): Looking for a unique way to pass a summer day? Pull out your dust-covered snowshoes and head for Killpecker Dune Field, a stark desert landscape east of Eden, Wyoming, in the Leucite Hills. An area dotted with flat-topped buttes, the remains of ancient volcanoes, the dunes make for a good aerobic workout in a setting that is unique in this part of the West. Bring lots of water and a camera: Otherwise rare desert elk and wild horses are not uncommon. Contact the Bureau of Land Management, 1993 Dewar Dr., Rock Springs, WY 82901 (☎ 307/362-6422). See Chapter 15.

- **Llama Trekking** (MT and WY): If you're looking for a unique trip that falls somewhere between an afternoon excursion and a week-long adventure vacation, consider a relaxing three-day pack trip into the wilderness—by llama. These gentle animals will do the work *for* you as you hike into serene backcountry areas with opportunities for fishing, photography, climbing, and watching wildlife. Trips are offered by the Lander Llama Company, 2024 Mortimore Lane, Lander, WY 82520 (☎ 307/332-5624) and Yellowstone Llamas, Box 5042, Bozeman, MT 59717 (☎ 406/586-6872).

14 The Best Winter Vacations

Ski vacations are practically synonymous with winter adventures in the West, but other options are just as exhilarating as a black diamond run. The following winter adventures are alternative ways to play in the snow.

- **Snowcoaching and Snowmobiling in Yellowstone** (MT and WY): While many other national parks enjoy a somewhat slower pace during the winter season, Yellowstone merely switches into adventure gear as an entirely different crowd comes to explore the winter landscape. Go solo on a snowmobile or rent a snowcoach—a van equipped with tank-like treads that glide over the snow—to get up close and personal with the bison that make the park their home. Winter lends a frosty air to the park's mud pots and geysers, which continue their geothermal burbles and eruptions throughout the year. See Chapter 11.
- **Taking a Sleigh Ride through the National Elk Refuge** (WY): If the only sleigh rides you've ever taken have been through a crowded urban park or along a city street, then you're in for a treat at Jackson's National Elk Refuge. Though you'll be sharing the experience with a group, the sleighs travel throughout the refuge all day long, where the only horns you'll hear belong to bugling elk. This is a wonderful way for kids to experience the splendor of nature as they observe these majestic animals. See Chapter 12.

15 The Best Downhill Skiing

Summers may belong to the dudes, but savvy skiers flock to Montana and Wyoming for fantastic winter fun. (You'll never want to ski in the East again.) Smaller and less crowded than other ski areas in the West, the following resorts were chosen for the quality and variety of their skiable terrain as well as their ability to provide a wide assortment of accommodations, dining, and entertainment options for skiers of all ages.

- **The Big Mountain** (Whitefish, MT; ☎ 800/858-5439): It calls itself a family-oriented ski area but don't let that label fool you into thinking that Big Mountain isn't hip. Rad snowboarders and telemarkers are just as likely to be seen on the hill as teal- and fuschia-outfitted preschoolers, and you can be sure that they're all having a great time. Dining and lodging accommodations are conveniently located at the base village, and other resort activities include snowcat powder skiing, Clydesdale-drawn sleigh ride dinners, and a challenging Nordic trail system. See Chapter 6.
- **Big Sky Resort** (Big Sky, MT; ☎ 406/995-5000): Big Sky's "kids ski free" program, its close proximity to Yellowstone, and its recent expansion make it easy to see why visitors consistently rate it one of the country's best, especially for its uncrowded slopes and breathtaking scenery. With the addition of two new lifts in

1995, 1,200 acres of new terrain became skiable, giving Big Sky 4,180 vertical feet—more than any other ski area in the United States. See Chapter 9.

- **Jackson Hole Ski Resort** (Teton Village, WY; ☎ 307/733-2292): If any ski area in these two states could be considered upscale, this is it. The lift tickets are the highest in the two states, and, thanks to its proximity to the trendy Western town of Jackson and both national parks, it's been attracting tourists for years. But it lives up to the hype with legendary black diamond runs. Many die-hard skiers rate Jackson as the best in the country (that's what Jean-Claude Killy thought when he skiied here back in 1967), and it does have an incredible variety of terrain and 4,139 feet of vertical. Although half of the mountain's runs are advanced, an excellent ski school staff ensures an equally satisfying vacation for the novice. See Chapter 12.

16 The Best Nordic & Backcountry Skiing

- **West Yellowstone** (MT): If you want an unforgettable cross-country, backcountry adventure, this is the place. An official training site of the U.S. Nordic and Biathlon ski teams, the town takes pride in its unparalleled terrain: An extensive 30km series of wilderness trails are professionally groomed from early November through March for track and freestyle skiing, or you can head for the backcountry in nearby Yellowstone. See Chapter 9.
- **Lone Mountain Ranch** (Big Sky, MT; ☎ 406/995-4644): A premier 75-km trail system is the centerpiece of this exclusive guest ranch, tucked in Montana's resplendent Gallatin Valley. Sleigh-ride dinners, trailside buffets, and naturalist-led interpretive ski tours into Yellowstone complement your week-long stay. Guided telemark forays into the nearby Moonlight Basin provide adventurous skiers with views into the Madison Range and overnight accommodations in Mongolian yurts. See Chapter 9.

2 Getting to Know Montana & Wyoming

Montana and Wyoming proudly straddle the Great Plains and northern Rocky Mountains with one cocksure foot rooted in their Wild West past and the other firmly fixed in a setting of unparalleled splendor and majesty. Whether you come for the Old West charm of a dude ranch experience or for fine dining in one of the classic lodges in the national parks, you'll experience firsthand nature's magnanimity: from Yellowstone's gap-toothed grin to the dazzling smiles of Glacier National Park and the Grand Tetons.

People come to the Northern Rockies to experience its back-to-basics way of life, an attitude that makes Montana and Wyoming endearing to visitors and enduring to residents. The land seems to hold some magic for modern-day travelers, though today its peaks are first spied from the lofty vantage point of an airplane than from the bumpy vista afforded by a Conestoga wagon.

The residents of both these states are self-reliant, hardy folks. They like to fish with flies, hike with bears, and ride horses that buck. They've tried mining, logging, farming, and ranching and still believe that no matter what they have to do to live here, the mountains and their fellow neighbors make it all worthwhile.

1 The Natural Environment

If you could drive through Montana and Wyoming in a single day—northwest to southeast—you'd cross two of the country's most famous Western physiographic domains: mountains and plains. The Rocky Mountains, which majestically mark this more or less east-west division, thrust themselves upward ostentatiously while the more subdued plains roll in relative obscurity toward the eastern horizon. Even the names of the two states take their origins from this landscape: Montana is taken from the Spanish for "mountainous," and Wyoming is derived from the Delaware Indian word *echeweami–ING*—"big flats" or "place of the big plain."

The Montana you see on the map is a strange shape: a profile of some anonymous head on a square plinth whose boundaries run for hundreds of miles to touch the borders of Wyoming, the Dakotas, and Saskatchewan, Canada. The head portion of the state, the rough face that looks west, touches Idaho to the west and the Canadian provinces of British Columbia and Alberta to the north. Within these boundaries rise the Rockies as they slowly lumber toward

Wyoming's almost perfect rectangle, giving an imperial third dimension to the two states. Various valleys and basins find themselves overshadowed and enclosed by these and other, smaller ranges throughout both states.

The highest peaks in Wyoming are located within the Wind River Range, which stretches through the middle of the state from its western side. Nine of the peaks in the Winds have elevations of over 13,000 feet; Gannett Peak, at 13,785 feet, is the highest in the state. Similarly, the stunning peaks of the Tetons rise sharply from Jackson Hole's valley floor to heights exceeding a mile. Montana's highest point— Granite Peak, at 12, 799 feet—is also in the Rockies.

The Continental Divide enters Montana from Canada and traces a snaking path through the state roughly south toward Butte and then southwest, forming the state's border with Idaho. From there, the Divide straightens up as it heads west into Wyoming, just south of the West Yellowstone entrance to Yellowstone National Park and continues on to the state's southcentral region. The east-west demarcation formed by this twisting imaginary line causes rivers to the west to flow to the Pacific and rivers to the east to flow to the Atlantic. The area west of the Divide is generally heavily forested and features the towering peaks of the Rocky Mountains; east of the Divide stretch the Great Plains, a vast, flat land characterized by native short-grasses and cottonwood-lined river bottoms.

The intricate river systems of the Yellowstone and the Missouri are veins that supply Montana's lifeblood; major rivers that cut through Wyoming include the Snake and Green Rivers to the west of the Divide and the North Platte, Belle Fourche, Yellowstone, Bighorn, and Powder Rivers to the east. The Fort Peck Dam near Glasgow checks the Missouri to form one of the largest lakes in the country—Fort Peck Lake, while Montana also boasts the country's largest freshwater lake west of the Mississippi: Flathead Lake. Yellowstone and Jackson Lakes are Wyoming's two largest natural bodies of water and are both found in that state's northwest corner.

Dramatic natural attractions can be found throughout both states, though Wyoming certainly seems to have been dealt the better hand. Waterfalls, geysers, and other geothermal oddities are synonymous with Yellowstone. Devils Tower, near the state's Black Hills region of the northeast, is a stump-shaped natural landmark of clustered rock columns that rises more than 1,280 feet above the surrounding plains. Wyoming's other national monument, Fossil Butte, contains an unusually large number of fossilized fish.

The states are characterized by unusually long, cold winters and short, hot summers. Temperatures year-round can range dramatically and are largely dependent on elevation. The average annual precipitation for the areas that usually receive the most rain rarely exceeds 25 inches, with most receiving significantly less than that. Average annual snowfall can range from about 20 inches in the state's basin areas to well over 200 inches at higher elevations.

The western side of this area is covered by forests, making lodgepole pine, spruce, and fir dominant features of the landscape, depending on elevation. Shortgrasses cover the uncultivated areas of the Great Plains in the eastern region and vegetation in basin areas is characterized by greasewood and sagebrush.

2 The Regions in Brief

More than a quarter of a million square miles make up the states of Montana and Wyoming—you can be sure that just one vacation won't allow you enough time to experience even a fraction of their natural beauty. With virtually no sprawling urban landscapes, the geography of the Northern Rockies features stunning natural variables: mountains, valleys, plains, and badlands.

Montana

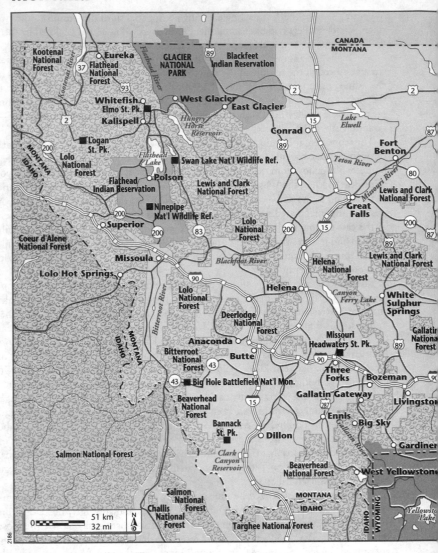

Glacier National Park   Towering peaks, innumerable lakes and streams, and singular wildlife form a natural paradise that millions come to enjoy each summer, especially along the highly accessible Going-to-the-Sun Road, a 50-mile scenic highway that cuts through the heart of the park from southwest to northeast. Created by millions of years of glacial activity, Glacier's rugged peaks seemed carved with dull knives around their icy lakes and streams. Grizzly bears and other creatures—elk, grouse, bighorn sheep, and mountain goats—also abound in the park.

The Flathead and the Northwest Corner   The area's proximity to Glacier National Park, the increasing popularity of Big Mountain as a downhill skier's paradise, and the water sports enjoyed on magnificent Flathead Lake make the northwest corner of Montana a magnet for visitors. One of the fastest-growing areas in the state,

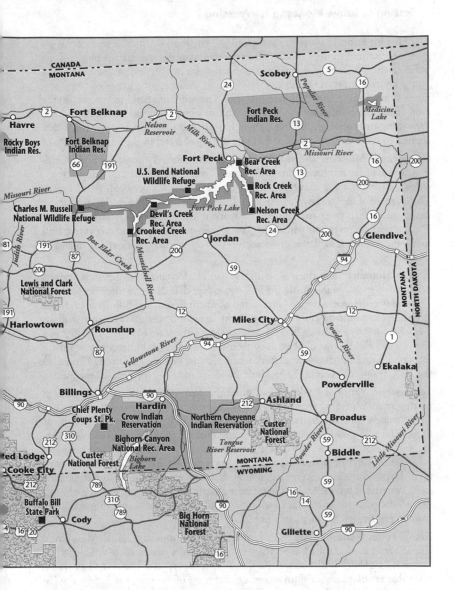

Flathead Valley is home to an interesting mix of residents: Farmers and loggers share ski lifts and trout streams with transplanted urbanites and retro-hippies.

Southwestern Montana   The people of this area in the central part of the state are just as diversified as they were divided more than a century ago. Helena is a town centered around arts and politics, though not necessarily in that order. Butte, on the other hand, seems full of decay. With mining gone, the blue-collar workforce is begging for industry to revitalize the area, a sad state of affairs for a town that once prospered. Other areas in this part of the state are full of lore, though not of the political kind. Vigilantes and corrupt sheriffs dominate the stories of the ghost towns of Virginia City and Alder Gulch, both of which are kept alive today by tourists seeking a lifelike glimpse into the area's past.

The Hi-Line and Missouri River Country   The most distinctive trait of this region, which stretches interminably from the mountains to the eastern border, is its prairies, which roll along in repetitive mundanity for hundreds of miles. One of the least populated areas in the state, the Hi-Line is made up of a series of farms and ranches that perpetuate the homesteader life. New equipment and techniques on the farm and satellite dishes by the house are just modern polish on an old tune. Residents cling to Highway 2 for every means of survival since most of the roads that connect to it are dirt and gravel and hardly worthy of travel in the winter months.

Southcentral Montana and the Missouri Headwaters   Though this region is almost a twin of the northwest part of the state in many ways—a nearby national park, renowned ski resorts, a university, heavy tourism—it has a personality of its own. There's more of the cowboy bearing here, since ranching still thrives throughout the region, and anglers come from all over the world to fish its blue-ribbon trout streams. The main attraction in this part of the state is Yellowstone. Even the valleys that lead to it—the Madison, Gallatin, and Paradise—are spectacular destinations in and of themselves.

Eastern Montana   For the most part, this part of Montana is no different from its neighboring region to the north, the Hi-Line, except that there are more people here. The supply center for eastern Montana and northern Wyoming, Billings is easily the largest city in Montana and has grown in the last half of the 20th century without the helpful hand of tourism that the western side of the state has seen. The Bighorn Canyon and the Yellowtail Dam draw their share of visitors, but this region's main attraction is Little Bighorn Battlefield, where General George Armstrong Custer led the 7th Cavalry to defeat at the hands of the Sioux and the Northern Cheyenne.

Yellowstone National Park   A vast protected ecosystem of two million acres in northwestern Wyoming that crosses over into southern Montana, Yellowstone is a scenic wonderland and literal hotbed of thermal activity year-round. Millions of people annually visit the country's largest and oldest national park to see its towering waterfalls, majestic wildlife, colorful wildflowers, spewing geysers, and bubbling paint pots. The park is best known as the home of Old Faithful and hundreds of bison; but visitors also enjoy fishing, hiking, camping, and boating within its boundaries. The park is busiest during the summer months when all roads in, through, and around the park are open, but snowmobiling and snowcoach tours through select areas during the winter are equally popular.

Grand Teton National Park   As dazzling as Yellowstone is unusual, Wyoming's Grand Teton National Park is regarded by most visitors as scenically superior to its northern neighbor. With shimmering lakes, thickly carpeted forests, and towering peaks that are blanketed with snow throughout most of the year, the Tetons display a magnificent and varied natural topography. Most visitors to the park choose to enjoy its scenery while driving through, but if you leave your car to explore, a vast hiking trail system leads to spectacular views of the surrounding area. The Tetons are equally popular with mountain climbers, who scale its face year-round.

Jackson Hole & Northwest Wyoming   Against the backdrop of the rugged Teton range and thick stands of evergreens, Jackson Hole welcomes visitors year-round and is the region's most visited locale next to the national parks. The valley's unique charm blends a healthy dose of refined elegance with a playful sprinkling of the frontier's Wild West: Tastefully subdued art galleries on Jackson's downtown square rub elbows with the elk-antlered entryways of places hawking chainsaw art. Transplanted urbanites, die-hard skiers, and adventurous yuppies make their home here, whether they live with five roommates in a cramped and overpriced apartment or in a sprawling, million-dollar mansion on the outskirts of the Hole. Recreationists enjoy the Snake River, which provides miles of thrilling whitewater rapids before taking a well-deserved bow near Jackson and exiting into Idaho.

Northcentral Wyoming   Located midway between the state's eastern and western borders, northcentral Wyoming combines two of the state's definitive geographic characteristics: basin and mountains. Today, sheep and cattle ranchers—once plagued by bitter, sometime fatal disputes over grazing rights—peacefully preside over commerce in this part of the state though oil and uranium have blown fortune in both directions for cities like Riverton, situated on the other side of the Owl Creek Mountains from the basin. Highlights include the fun-loving frontier town of Cody, the Bighorn Canyon National Recreation Area, Thermopolis, and the Wind River Indian Reservation, home to the Shoshone and the Arapaho peoples.

Eastern Wyoming   Eastern Wyoming is an expansive land characterized by plains, farmland, and vast protected forests. It is punctuated in the Black Hills region of the extreme northeast by the stump-shaped, 1,280-foot landmark of Devils Tower and in the southeast by the Laramie Mountains. But the region's real claim to fame lies in its history. This is the land of Butch Cassidy and his Hole-in-the-Wall gang, of cattle rustlers, cowboys, and outlaws. History buffs may enjoy exploring historic Oregon Trail sites at Fort Caspar and Independence Rock.

Southern Wyoming   A land rich in history and minerals, southern Wyoming boasts rich deposits of petroleum, natural gas, sodium salts, and oil shale, all important extraction industries to the state. Early settlers traveling westward via the Oregon Trail were some of the first people to see this part of Wyoming, and visible remains of their journey are permanently etched into the existing landscape, with gravestones and wagon ruts marking the historic trail. The citizens of South Pass City, a gold boomtown of the late 1800s, led the cause to grant suffrage to women and the city was once the state's largest settlement. Cheyenne consistently packs in the crowds each summer during Frontier Days, one of the country's biggest rodeos. The recreational highlight of southern Wyoming is the Flaming Gorge National Recreation Area.

3 Wildlife

One of the best places in the United States to view wildlife in their natural habitat, the Northern Rockies are home to a diverse native animal population that includes the badger, bighorn sheep, bison, black bear, coyote, eagle, elk, grizzly bear, hawk, moose, mountain goat, pronghorn, rabbit, and various species of trout. Montana's pronghorn, elk, and deer outnumber its citizens, and trout outnumber the population almost 200 to 1.

The national parks are premier locales in which to view many of these creatures in their natural setting, directly from the roads that loop around or through the parks, though backpackers are often rewarded with glimpses of more elusive animals. Great herds of buffalo do indeed roam Yellowstone unhindered, though their apparent indifference to people shouldn't be construed as veiled friendliness. Glacier happens to be home to one of the highest populations of grizzlies in the lower 48 states.

Wolves have recently been reintroduced into the Yellowstone ecosystem, to the delight of wildlife biologists and the dismay of area farmers and ranchers in both Montana and Wyoming. The debate over whether or not this move will prove to have been worthwhile from an ecological standpoint isn't over; it remains to be seen how the wolves will impact the area as a whole.

Hikers and mountain-bikers exploring higher elevations may find themselves face to face with elk, deer, moose, or bighorn sheep. And though waterfowl and game

Wyoming

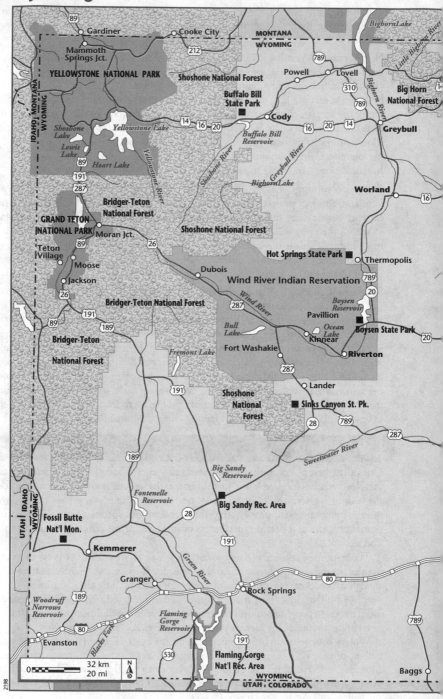

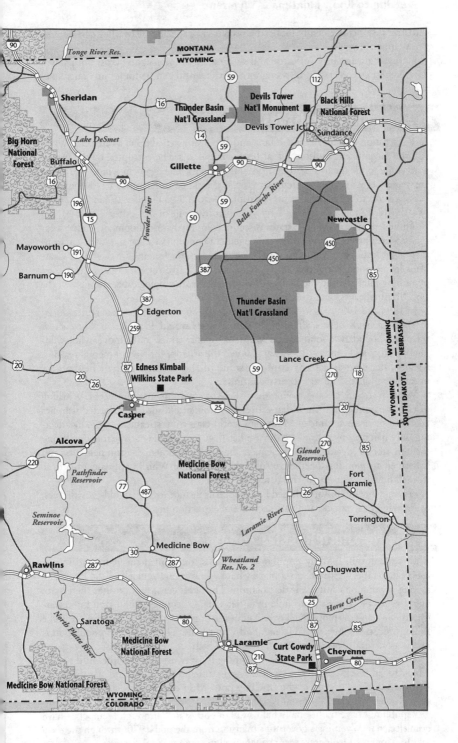

birds refuse to conveniently locate themselves in a specific place, they can be seen pretty much anywhere.

Casually grazing herds of cattle and sheep are common sights across both states. The highest concentration of pronghorn in the world can be found just outside of Casper.

4 Environmental Issues

Any discussion of tourism in Montana and Wyoming is tied up in a catch-22: When will the magnificent landscapes that people come to see be corrupted by the people who come to see them? It's a question national park management would like to see answered, yet it's also something that visitors should consider. Since 1970, the number of visitors to the national parks has tripled—from 80 million to 257 million. Fully two-thirds of America's citizens have visited at least one of these sites.

Though a vast area of both states is secure from further development, concern for roadless area protection and forest management continues to dog statewide environmental groups. Two areas of greatest recent concern in Montana are the Sweet Grass Hills in the northcentral part of the state, sacred Native American land threatened by mining interests, and the Badger–Two Medicine, the biological centerpiece of the Bob Marshall ecosystem, which is threatened by oil and gas leases.

In 1994 and 1995, a new concern swept the region when wolves were reintroduced to Yellowstone. Ranchers, afraid of the damage they would do to livestock just across the park's boundary in southcentral Montana, openly criticized the move, while wildlife biologists and conservationists applauded the attempt for environmental reasons. Meanwhile, unaware of any conflict, some of the wolves left their new home; others were killed. The controversy continues.

Western streams are also having their share of environmental problems. Whirling disease, a parasitical affliction that causes a neurological disorder in affected fish, has begun to show up in some of Montana's world-class trout streams. Originally affecting only hatchery-bred fish, the disease has begun to plague native trout, polluting the blue-ribbon streams where they make their home. Though environmentalists and fishermen are working together to solve the problem of Whirling disease, only time will tell how it affects the native fish population.

Federally owned, privately leased land concerns include logging of old-growth trees, overgrazing by livestock, and various mineral extraction practices.

5 The Northern Rockies Today

Always a colorful, sparsely populated place of strong-willed survivors and rowdy lawbreakers, the West remains a place where you can lose yourself in the landscape as long as you don't mind a little isolation: The latest census found that there were only five people to the square mile in either state. Of course, people don't necessarily settle in one-mile plots. Well over half of the population lives in "urban" areas like Billings, Casper, Cheyenne, Helena, and Great Falls. The rest of the population is in the more rural areas of the states, many of which are nearly roadless.

The population of Montana and Wyoming is overwhelmingly white. Add to that a handful of blacks, Native Americans, Hispanics, and Asians and you have the Northern Rockies' version of the "melting pot." Most of these residents are, predictably, Roman Catholic, Protestant, or Mormon.

Republicans have traditionally held sway in both states, although Democrats have been elected to Wyoming's governor's mansion from the mid-1970s through the early 1990s. Montana Democrats seem to fare well in congressional contests.

Tourism is a driving force in the economies of both states, due to the immense popularity of their premier national parks, ski areas, and dude ranches. Yet, historically, much of their wealth comes from under the ground, with lucrative mines dotting the landscape, particularly around Butte and in the southern part of Wyoming around the Wyoming Basin. While forestry is a relatively small part of Wyoming's economy, it is a dominant force in northwestern Montana. Various agricultural pursuits in both states include ranching—both cattle and sheep—and farming, with hay, sugar beets, barley, and wheat accounting for the greatest crop productions.

6   History 101

MONTANA

The modern history of Montana is a short, violent tale of discovery, gold prospecting, and copper mining that gradually gave way to homesteading and a flourishing agricultural economy.

NATIVES & EXPLORERS   Native Americans were the only people in Montana as few as 270 years ago. Even after Louis-Joseph and Francois Verendrye, the fur-trapping explorers, were sent into the region in 1742 (they soon left), the region remained a vast unknown expanse until the 1803 Louisiana Purchase put much of Montana in the hands of the United States. Shortly thereafter, Meriwether Lewis and William Clark set out on the Missouri River from St. Louis to investigate. It wasn't until reports began filtering back from the expedition that Americans realized what actually existed in the lands west of the Mississippi.

SETTLEMENT   While the rest of the country was getting ready for a bloody civil war, the mineral value of Montana was just being discovered. Though it was nearly impossible to get to Montana from the East, worn-out miners already out West made their way here from other popular gold spots in Colorado, Nevada, and California that were beginning to decline. Word spread and people began taking steamboats up the Missouri. Because of a rough bend just around the corner, Fort Benton was the last stop on the Missouri River for steamboats; from there, people from all over traveled southwest to where gold had been discovered by James and Granville Stuart at Gold Creek. A massive charge followed in Virginia City and the Alder Gulch area, and the rush was on. Placer gold, easily attained surface deposits made obvious by erosion, was discovered in incredible amounts, and the area's population exploded to nearly 10,000.

Over the course of the 1860s, Montana's population grew from a measly 100 curious souls to nearly 20,000 people of every imaginable sort. Shortly

Dateline

- **11,000** B.C. Earliest evidence of man is found in Montana.
- **1500s** Arrival of the Flathead Indians.
- **1620s** Arrival of the Plains Indians.
- **1742** The Verendrye brothers become the first Europeans to enter Montana.
- **1776** United States gains independence.
- **1803** The eastern part of Montana becomes a territory through the Louisiana Purchase.
- **1805–1806** Lewis and Clark journey through Montana on their way to and from the Pacific coast.
- **1846** The Oregon Treaty with England makes northwestern Montana part of the United States.
- **1864** Montana becomes an official territory; gold is discovered at Last Chance Gulch in Helena.
- **1876** Defeat of George A. Custer at the Battle of the Little Bighorn.
- **1877** The surrender of Chief Joseph of the Nez Perce in the Bear's Paw Mountains.
- **1880** The Utah and Northern Railroad enters Montana.
- **1883** The Northern Pacific railroad crosses Montana.
- **1889** Montana, on November 8, becomes the 41st state in the union.

continues

- **1893** The University of Montana in Missoula and Montana State University in Bozeman are founded.
- **1910** Glacier National Park is established.
- **1914** Women's suffrage amendment passes.
- **1917–1919** Missoula native Jeannette Rankin becomes the first woman elected to U.S. Congress and votes against U.S. participation in World War I.
- **1940** Fort Peck Dam is completed; Jeannette Rankin is again elected to the U.S. House of Representatives; she is the only member of Congress to vote against U.S. involvement in World War II.
- **1942** Mike Mansfield, who ultimately becomes Montana's most successful politician since Jeannette Rankin on the national stage, is elected to the U.S. House of Representatives.
- **1952** Mansfield is elected to U.S. Senate; he serves as Senate majority leader from 1961 to 1977.
- **1965** Construction of Yellowtail Dam is completed.
- **1973** Montana's third state constitution goes into effect; it includes the right to a clean and healthful environment and the goal of preserving the cultural integrity of the state's Native Americans.
- **1977** Mansfield is appointed ambassador to Japan by President Jimmy Carter.
- **1983** Anaconda Copper Mining Company shuts down.
- **1986** Montana spends $56 million on environmental protection programs.
- **1987** Montana is ranked fourth in the nation in

continues

after Alder Gulch had been virtually depleted by the placer miners, a group of Virginia City prospectors—later nicknamed the "Four Georgians"—struck gold in 1864 in what they called Last Chance Gulch. This became the second most lucrative gold deposit in the state. Even though gold mining would become less profitable soon, Last Chance Gulch, renamed Helena, hung on and prospered.

After the gold rush died and mining came almost to a standstill, Montana nonetheless moved forward to achieve full territorial status with Bannack as the capital. The railroad, it was thought, would bring new hope to the territory, provide jobs, and link Montanans to both coasts. But Jay Cooke, the major investor in the Northern Pacific Railroad, saw his bank collapse, and a horrible depression in the Panic of 1873 soon swept the country, including Montana. The dream of a railroad immediately seemed far-fetched, if not dead. For years, no one had the funds to extend the line that far west. But just a few years later, the Utah Northern Railroad Company saw an opening and made every effort, however slow, to become the first railroad in Montana. The day after Christmas in 1881, they did: The first train in Montana reached Butte from the south. The Northern Pacific Railroad Company was not to be outdone, and shortly thereafter, began to plan for the laying of an east-west line across the state. With the Utah Northern's presence, Montana had a line from the southwest part of the state to points in Utah and beyond, but a direct line to the East and West Coasts was still unrealized.

Enter the government and its land grant proposals. Once businesses began to recover from the economic collapse of a decade earlier, the Northern Pacific became not only the only intrastate railroad, but the largest private landowner in the territory. Some 17 million acres were given to the railroad for their promise to build a line to the West Coast. Though a power struggle within the Northern Pacific would determine which city, Portland or Tacoma, would be the line's ultimate destination (the ousted president and loser of the struggle, Frederick Billings, would have a town named after him), Montanans were just happy to be a part of it all. Twenty-five years after the first gold had been discovered at Gold Creek, the final spike of Montana's first east-west railroad was driven into place near the same site in 1883.

With tracks laid down across the middle and the southwest part of the territory, the northern part of the state was left wide open for Jim Hill and the Great Northern Railroad. Several railroad companies followed, touching off a war for control of Montana's transportation lines. This was akin to afternoon tea, compared to the real political wars that followed.

INDUSTRIALIZATION & THE 20TH CENTURY When copper was first discovered in the silver mines in Butte, no one could have foretold its effects on Montana's future. This vast territory, full of prospectors and railworkers, soon became the home of some of the richest men in America, who would not only seize political power within the territory, but take complete control of the everyday lives of its citizens. As copper wiring became an integral part of several new electrical technologies, Butte became an important resource for America. One of the first men to profit was Marcus Daly, an Irish immigrant, who came to Butte in his mid-thirties, and purchased his first silver mine. The mine proved to yield incredibly large amounts of the purest copper in the world, instead, and soon a smelter was built near the source at Warm Springs in Anaconda, the town that took its name from the company Daly founded.

- volume of hazardous waste generated.
- **1992** Montana loses one of its two U.S. representatives as a result of the 1990 census.
- **1995** Wolves are reintroduced to Yellowstone. Daytime speed limits are abolished.

William Clark, the other baron of the copper mines, was a Horatio Alger type. An average youth from Pennsylvania, he rooted around in mines until, like many others on the mining circuit, his efforts took him to Montana. His wealth was quickly amassed from a keen business acumen that prompted him to purchase mining operations, electric companies, water companies, and banks. Though his interest in wealth was most assuredly magnificent, it was an inflated ego that drove him to the political arena. His was the major voice in the territorial constitution proceedings in 1884, and when Montana held its last territorial election, Clark was determined to get into public office as Montana's representative.

The war that commenced between these two men was rooted in Clark's determination to hold political office and Daly's unwillingness to see him do it. Montana finally became a state in 1889, after five tough years of appeals to the U.S. Congress, but the bellicose millionaires were so set on controlling the young state's political interests that they bought newspapers or created them just to have a printed voice. They stuffed money into the pockets of voters and agreed on nothing. In Montana's first congressional election, Clark fell three votes shy of his bid, and the legislature adjourned without ever selecting a second senator. So in Montana's embarrassing first years as a state it had but half of its due representation in Washington, all because of two pigheaded millionaires who couldn't accept the victory of the other.

The fight for capital status came along in 1894. Helena had been the capital, but the constitution held that the site must be determined by the voters. Daly wanted his newly created Anaconda to be the capital. Clark, with interests of his own in Helena, wanted that city to remain the capital. Given Clark's record, it seemed that Helena was doomed. But the fact that Anaconda was ruled by the strong arm of the Anaconda Mining Company caused voters to turn to the diversified ways of Helena.

Impressions

We are seduced by our patches of wilderness, the open prairies, the thundering summer waters from the high snowpack, and most of all by our own brief history.
—Patrick Dawson, "Glory Holes" from *Montana Spaces* (1988)

For once in his life, William Clark was not only rich, but appreciated by the masses. Or so it seemed.

Now that his thirst for public office had been revitalized, Clark did his damnedest to buy his way into the U.S. Senate. Though he pulled it off, Daly, infuriated by the way his bitter enemy achieved his seat, demanded an investigation by the Senate. The investigation uncovered a wealth of impropriety on Clark's part, who resigned and went home to Montana kicking and screaming. Down, but for some crazy reason not out, Clark took a deep breath and plunged immediately back into the thick of things. Once when Robert Burns Smith, governor of Montana and hardly an ardent admirer of Clark's, was out of town Clark arranged for his friend, A.E. Spriggs, the lieutenant governor, to accept his resignation and in the stead of Governor Smith, appoint Clark to the Senate. This lunatic act embarrassed the state of Montana, causing Smith to nullify the appointment upon his return. Meanwhile, Daly had sold his Anaconda Copper Company to Standard Oil to form the Amalgamated Copper Company, and Clark was now up against a nameless, faceless opponent.

He chose to link his fate with another, younger copper king, Augustus Heinze, who had a reputation as a briber of courts, hoping to form an alliance that Amalgamated couldn't match. Heinze was more influential at this point than the older, less active Clark was, and soon the two had complete control of the mining world in Montana. It seemed as if Clark's last wish—to garner the Senate post he had been denied for so long—was to be realized with Heinze's help. And rather anticlimactically, it was. Clark served his state as a senator from 1901 to 1907.

Though the discovery of copper in Montana was important, it is now commonly thought of as just another chapter in the history of the state's misuse of natural resources. From the near-extermination of the beaver along the Missouri River to the Berkeley Pit in Butte, an ugly massive hole in the earth that today stands vacant, Montana's copper mining industry has brought its share of unmitigated disaster to future generations. Marcus Daly died in 1900 without control of his beloved Anaconda Copper Company. Augustus Heinze sold his interest in mining in 1906 and lost his fortune on Wall Street. William Clark, who at one time in his life was believed to be earning $17 million a month, died at the age of 86 in New York with an estimated worth near $150 million in 1925.

At the beginning of the 20th century, Montana experienced a boom. Homesteaders came from all over the country to stake a piece of land. The Indian Wars ended, and white settlers declared the land a safe and fertile haven for the farming lifestyle. Lands sweeping across the northern plains were advertised shamelessly by railroad companies and real estate agencies as ideal for farming. The U.S. government helped things along in 1909 when it passed the Enlarged Homestead Act, giving 320 acres to anyone willing to stay on it for at least five months out of the year for a minimum of three years.

Sentiment for the homesteaders was never good, and the generalization that homesteaders were stupid, dirty people became increasingly popular, untrue or not. Even the renowned cowboy artist Charlie Russell, who had no stake in the matter, expressed antifarming sentiments. The truth is, Montana's agricultural backbone was created by these extraordinary people who came West to settle farms. Wheat became—and still is—the major crop in such areas as the Judith Basin in the center of the state and Choteau County north of Great Falls.

As more and more homesteaders came to settle in Montana and farming became a mainstay of the state's economy, women began to emerge from their submissive roles in the home and take part in a suffrage movement on a large scale. In the middle of it all, though isolated by geography, was young Jeannette Rankin from Missoula. In 1914, voters narrowly passed the amendment for women's suffrage; two years later, Rankin became the first woman elected to the U.S. Congress. Though her stay was brief, she was there long enough to vote against United States involvement in World War I. In 1940, she was elected once more to the U.S. House of Representatives. Again, she voted against United States involvement in World War II, the only member of Congress to do so.

When the depression hit Montana, farming was enduring some rather dry difficulties, and jobs were nowhere to be found. Had Roosevelt's New Deal not been passed, there's no telling how bad times would have been for Montanans. The Civilian Conservation Corps and the Works Progress Administration came to the rescue in the early 1930s. But the most tangible salvation came when work began on the Fort Peck Dam in the mid-1930s, employing more than 50,000 workers over the course of its construction. The earth-filled dam, the largest of its kind in the world, took almost five years to complete.

Since the 1950s, the story of Montana has been an evolving one, with tourism and agriculture playing key roles. While farming and cattle-ranching methods have become much more sophisticated, many of the younger generation, expected to carry on the farming tradition, have opted to settle in the larger cities and sometimes outside the state entirely. Agriculture's major competitor, tourism, is the state's leading industry—a huge moneymaker. From small, family-owned ranches willing to let guests help out with the haying to tiny bed-and-breakfasts with roosters for alarm clocks, tourism has developed into a multimillion-dollar business in Montana, with nearly everyone in the state getting in on the action.

WYOMING

Man has been present in the Wyoming area for more than 20,000 years by some estimates; up until the 19th century, Native Americans were the sole residents, constantly fighting amongst themselves for control of a land seemingly without boundaries. The 19th century defined what is now Wyoming, and it's a history best viewed through the bold eyes of the enterprising people who were brave enough to found it, choosing to make a life for themselves in an uncharted land.

NATIVES & EXPLORERS   The original settlers in what is now Wyoming were the Crow, Sioux, Cheyenne, Arapahoe, Shoshone, and Bannock, all living a close if not an entirely harmonious existence before the intrusion of white settlers. Outside of the Verendrye brothers (the same duo that turned back from Montana), John Colter, a trapper and fur trader, was one of the early white men in Wyoming. Colter reached the northwestern part of Wyoming in what is now Yellowstone, traveling alone and sometimes unclothed. He paved the way for other like-minded adventurers who hoped to find fortune in furs and later in gold, but the dearth of mineral

Dateline

- **1807** John Colter explores the Yellowstone area.
- **1834** Fort Laramie is built in eastern Wyoming.
- **1843** Jim Bridger establishes Fort Bridger.
- **1852** The first school in the state is founded at Fort Laramie.
- **1867** The Union Pacific Railroad enters Wyoming; gold is discovered at South Pass.
- **1868** The Territory of Wyoming is created by Congress.
- **1869** Wyoming Territorial Legislature grants women the right to vote and hold elective office.
- **1870** Esther H. Morris becomes the nation's first female justice of the peace.

continues

- **1872** Yellowstone National Park is established; the nation's first national park.
- **1886** The University of Wyoming is founded.
- **1889** The state constitution is adopted.
- **1890** Wyoming becomes the nation's 44th state.
- **1892** The Johnson County War breaks out over a dispute about cattle rustling.
- **1897** The first Frontier Days rodeo is staged.
- **1906** Devils Tower is established by President Roosevelt as the country's first national monument.
- **1910** Buffalo Bill Dam is completed.
- **1925** Nellie Tayloe Ross becomes the nation's first female governor.
- **1929** Grand Teton National Park is established; Teapot Dome Scandal occurs.
- **1965** Minuteman missile sites are completed near Cheyenne.
- **1970** Statewide coal production reaches seven million tons.
- **1986** Wyoming spends over $63 million on environmental and natural resource protection programs; 24 other states spend more.
- **1988** Coal production reaches 174 million tons; gas production totals 509 billion cubic feet; fires rage in Yellowstone, damaging almost one-third of the park.
- **1990** Wyoming ranks 50th among the states in population.
- **1995** Wolves are reintroduced to Yellowstone.

wealth kept Wyoming a rather unsettled, and often unsettling, place.

SETTLEMENT   Major routes like the Oregon Trail cut through the heart of Indian lands, and as the number of white travelers increased, hostilities escalated. Whites, especially travelers along the trails, complained of unwarranted attacks by Indians, and the Indians complained that the lands they called home were being defiled by whites. With discord becoming routine between the whites and the Indians, treaties became necessary to both sides in the 1800s.

In 1851, a gathering of 10,000 Indians and government agents convened to solve the problem of whites trespassing on Indian lands; the government's abstruse mission was to convert the Indians from warriors and hunters into pacific farmers. Boundaries were drawn up for the Indians, and penalties for trespassing were paid to them in annuities. Within the tribes, the agreement with the whites caused dissension and attacks on white settlers became worse than ever.

The Fort Wise Treaty of 1851 virtually repealed the treaty of 10 years earlier. Indians were no longer seen as people with whom the government could negotiate. With the Oregon Trail cutting east to west through the southern portion of Wyoming, and the Bozeman Trail running from the southeast to the north, travelers were finding it necessary but less and less safe to move through the state. In the late 1860s, gold was being discovered by whites in the Black Hills and migration over the trails throughout Wyoming was at its zenith. The government decided it was time to implement an eviction policy.

Though important treaty negotiations had transpired within Wyoming's boundaries, the stage for the demise of the region's Indians would be set nearby in Montana along the Little Bighorn River and in South Dakota at Wounded Knee. The Indians were being forced onto reservations to keep them away from the settlers and the hundreds of thousands of travelers passing through Wyoming. Though conditions were sickening at the forts and on the reservations, many of the Indians stayed, now fearing for their lives on the plains they had once called home. A large group, however, did not.

Sitting Bull and Crazy Horse of the Hunkpapa Sioux, angered by the blatant reneging of the Fort Laramie Treaty of 1868—in which the U.S. government promised the sacred Black Hills to the Sioux—joined forces with members of the Cheyenne and Arapaho tribes along the Little Bighorn River. It was here that the greatest gathering of Indians ever assembled defeated George Custer and his men in certainly the greatest consolidated Indian victory. By 1890, however, with the tragic climax of Indian-American relations at Wounded Knee, South Dakota, the Indians of the West were defeated and removed from their lands. All of their great warriors, spiritual leaders, and negotiators were dead. The rest were sent to small reservations throughout the Northwest. Only one remains in Wyoming, the Wind River Indian Reservation, home to the Shoshone and Arapaho.

INDUSTRIALIZATION & THE 20TH CENTURY   With large numbers of settlers moving into the state and setting up farms and fences, absentee cattle barons began slowly to lose what had always been an open range. Ranchers and farmers began arguing over land ownership, often with fatal or at least illegal results. As a result of this discord, the Johnson County War of 1892 erupted between farmers and ranchers and brought the issue to a head. Hired representatives of wealthy stockowners invaded the county in the Powder River Basin, accusing local farmers of rustling their cattle. Order was finally restored by U.S. troops, though not before many people lost their lives in the conflict.

After the Indian removal of the late 1800s, oil was discovered in Wyoming, and for almost a century it proved to be one of the biggest determinants in Wyoming's rather narrow economic future. Like Montana, Wyoming suffered in the 1980s from exhausted supplies of oil and low energy prices.

For now, the oil boom is over, and the push to diversify the economy in Wyoming has taken the state down new roads. Oil is still present but not to the degree it once was, and an incredible reserve of coal has made the state the leading producer in the country.

Tourism is a large part of Wyoming's economic future. Though the northwest part of the state will always monopolize the tourist trade, places like Devils Tower in the northeast, Flaming Gorge in the southwest, and Cheyenne Frontier Days in the capital city all continue to make significant contributions toward developing tourism into a statewide industry.

7 Life & Culture

Both natives and relative newcomers to the Northern Rockies have found that survival in two of the nation's least-populated states depends on serving the ever-present tourists or carving out their own niche. Many old-timers have found a lucrative business in sharing their ranches with urbanite "dudes," while others choose to continue ranching and farming in remote areas of the state in the way that their forefathers did. A younger generation has found success by working electronically from secluded mountain homes nowhere near either coast; others have discovered that selling snowboards in ski resort towns for six months out of the year is just as profitable. The people who seem to stay here are those who know what they want and how to get it, whether their desires center around a 1,500-acre Swan Valley farm with horses and llamas, or a Jackson Hole condominium with ski-in, ski-out accessibility. One could easily argue that the area's extremes of nature are personified in its citizens: intensely stubborn but harboring a soft spot, cautious yet welcoming, feisty yet lovable. Whatever specific task they choose, Montana and Wyoming residents remain rooted in metronomic pursuits that pay the bills *and* satisfy the soul. Who would have it any other way?

A TRADITION OF STORYTELLING   Montana's oral storytelling tradition is particularly rich, beginning with Native American myths that center around the creation. Amotken, in Salish traditions, created the earth, an island in the middle of

---

Colter's Hell

John Colter, famed mountain man, was the first white man in the Yellowstone and Grand Teton areas, exploring Jackson Hole alone after splitting off from the Lewis and Clark expedition and striking out on his own during the winter of 1807–1808. With Manuel Lisa, a fur trapper, Colter helped establish a fort at the Big Horn River, and from there he embarked on his historic journey. Colter came back the following spring with fantastic tales of gigantic mountains, lakes, wildlife, and an abundance of hot springs. His findings and reports were absurd to the men at the fort, and from then on they referred to the place in which he'd spent the winter as Colter's Hell.

But Colter's real hell came later. Working from the fort near the Big Horn River, Colter foraged into the land of the Blackfeet in order to trade with the Indians. He had experience in moving through the mountains alone, but nothing could prepare him for what happened next. Captured by the Blackfeet, Colter was stripped to nothing. Figuring he was to be killed, he knew that escape was the only way he would survive. So, totally naked, Colter ran through the woods until he could run no more. He hid in some brush and after he was sure the Blackfeet had passed him, began to walk back to the fort of Manuel Lisa. All told, Colter walked more than 300 miles to get back to the fort and once there declared he was done with the West. He moved back to his old Kentucky home and died shortly thereafter.

---

water. The Crow world was created by Old Man, who was brought dirt by a brave duck, then blew it in all directions to create the world.

Visions have also always had great significance in the lives of the Native Americans: Before the Battle of the Little Bighorn, Sitting Bull envisioned the army of Custer dying at the hands of the warriors that gathered along the Little Bighorn River.

A popular Devils Tower legend contends that the landmark was created when seven young Indian princesses found themselves being chased by a ferocious bear; their cries for help elicited a massive uprising from the ground, which became marked with claws as the bear frantically tried to catch the girls. The Indian princesses became the Pleiades constellation and their life-saver, Devils Tower.

The cowboy was a natural subject for popular yarns and tall tales. Shaped by the harsh Western land and weather, the quixotic cowboy was as prone to gunfighting as he was to defending the honor of a woman. Legendary Western figures include Calamity Jane, the sharpshooter and horsewoman who reputedly served as a scout for the 7th Cavalry under General Custer because of her knowledge of the frontier. Frontier showman William Frederick "Buffalo Bill" Cody is best known for his traveling "Wild West Show," which included a mock battle with Indians and demonstrations of his shooting skills, along with those of Annie Oakley. She supposedly could hit the thin edge of a playing card from 90 feet and puncture the same card five or six times before it ever fell to the ground. Once, she even shot a cigarette from the mouth of the German Crown Prince, Wilhelm II—at his behest, of course.

The legend of Rawhide Buttes has become immortalized through an annual production in the Wyoming city of Lusk.

Butch Cassidy and the Sundance Kid, along with other members of the "Wild Bunch"—William Carver, Harvey Logan (Kid Curry), and Ben Kirpatrick (The Tall Texan)—were elusive outlaws who only served to further heighten the rough-and-ready reputation of the frontier.

LITERATURE & THE ARTS   There's no more convincing proof of Montana's rich literary heritage than *The Last Best Place*, a 1988 anthology that comprehensively chronicles the state's writings from its Native American legends to the contemporary stories of its current residents. The University of Montana's creative writing program, the second oldest in the country, has developed a national reputation for excellence with a distinguished staff that has included longtime Montana residents William Kittredge, James Welch, James Crumley, and Richard Hugo. Newcomers are also making a name for themselves, with Montana writers Richard Ford, Thomas McGuane, Deidre McNamer, David Long, Pete Fromm, and Rick Bass heading the top of the list. Wyoming writers of particular note are Gretel Ehrlich, Tim Sandlin, Len Edgerly, Sierra Adare, and Candy Moulton.

Charlie Russell and Frederic Remington are the two most recognized visual artists of the region. Their canvases brought the Western frontier to life during the early 1900s. Though their influences continue to be felt, the new Western art is anything but traditional paintings of the landscape. Russell Chatham of Livingston is one of Montana's most prominent contemporary artists. Visitors will see his paintings displayed throughout the state in banks, hotel lobbies, and galleries. They are easily recognizable—pastels of quiet, lonely landscapes appearing through translucent mists. Even easier to identify are the classic paintings of Conrad Schwiering's beloved Tetons.

If you're looking for contemporary art in Wyoming, Jackson has cornered the market, with nearly 40 galleries making their home in the trendy community. Other artists of note throughout the region include poster artist Monte Dolack, who maintains a gallery in Missoula; Kevin Red Star, whose haunting Native American portraits can be seen in his Red Lodge gallery; Parks Reece, whose wry wildlife and river scenes make their home at Livingston's Murray Hotel; Frederic Joy, a fine art photographer whose large-format prints uniquely capture the spectacular Jackson landscape; Mary-Alice Huemoeller, a weaver whose work combines the weaving traditions of Asians and Native Americans; and Maurice Mayer, whose oil paintings find their inspiration in the coexistence of Native Americans with the settlers who displaced them.

SPORTS & THE GREAT OUTDOORS   With visitors coming West to ski and climb their mountains, raft and fish their rivers, and hike and camp within their national parks, the great outdoors looms large for residents of the Northern Rockies. Luckily for Montana and Wyoming, nearly half of their total land area is protected from development. Fishing, snow skiing, and dude ranching are the big draws. Enthusiastic anglers can fish for numerous trout species—rainbow, brook, brown, mackinaw, golden, and cutthroat—in either state's blue-ribbon streams. Numerous ski resorts, especially those in Jackson Hole and at Big Sky, are covered with millions of acres of powder snow. Guest and working ranches abound, with horseback "commutes" to high mountain lakes and remote mountain vistas. Hiking trails and campsites are hot properties in both state and national parks in the summer, when recreational outings include mountain biking, climbing, waterskiing, and boating. Winter is just as active, with some of the best downhill skiing, snowmobiling, cross-country skiing, and snowboarding opportunities in the Northwest.

Professional and collegiate sports teams are few and far between, but high school sports teams are a different story: You can expect to find entire communities in the stands on the most frigid Friday nights supporting the local team. Since Montana will probably never have a major sports team, the Pioneer League has to take the professional burden upon its shoulders. This minor league (actually a Class Rookie league, lower than Class A ball) has been through changes over the years, but teams in Butte, Helena, Great Falls, and Billings have been mainstays, and Missoula has recently put itself in the market for a team of its own. Cecil Fielder and George Brett both came through the Big Sky state on their way to multimillion-dollar contracts, as did Reggie Sanders.

Hands-down, though, the most popular spectator sport in either state is the rodeo. From small-time, local, daylong events like the wild and raging Augusta Rodeo to summer's highly anticipated Cheyenne Frontier Days, you'll be hard-pressed to find an event that draws as many onlookers as this sport does. Time slows to 8-second increments as grandparents and children sit entranced by bucking saddle broncs, concessions peddlers hawk beer, and dust settles slowly on rickety bleachers. It's a festive blend of form and function that no one manages quite so well as the Cowboy State and its neighbor across the fence.

NIGHTLIFE   When darkness falls, about the only place to go to is the local bars. They probably won't have ferns or a uniformed wait staff, but they will have a great back bar—probably from some abandoned saloon in a ghost town—and some of the most interesting folks you'll ever meet. Western bars are more meeting places than pick-up spots, and you don't have to drink to enjoy yourself.

More sophisticated, first-rate cultural affairs are few and far between, though arts festivals throughout both states manage to bring in a good strong dose of culture from time to time. Particularly noteworthy are the nationally acclaimed Grand Teton Music Festival and Montana's Flathead Festival.

WHAT'S COOKING   By and large, the Flathead Valley and Jackson are welcome oases in the culinary deserts of Montana and Wyoming. Though most are overpriced, restaurants in the above-mentioned locales cater to a more eclectic taste, with creative entrées upstaging more traditional fare. If your travels take you outside of these areas, expect to find supper clubs that feature wild game and steaks, tastefully prepared, but without the artfulness and atmosphere.

Microbrews and espresso have taken hold in the region's trendier locales—ski areas and national parks—but bars in most towns, regardless of their size, still pour the old standbys: Budweiser and Miller. If you're not drinking espresso in one form or another (and you probably won't be), expect the coffee to be thin and weak, served with tiny cupfuls of half-and-half.

8 Recommended Books & Films

BOOKS

Montana is fortunate to have the best of its literature compiled in one volume, *The Last Best Place* (University of Montana Press, 1988), the definitive anthology of Montana writings, from Native American myths to contemporary short stories. If you don't have access to a copy, read Ivan Doig's *This House of Sky* (Harcourt Brace Jovanovich, 1978), the author's memoir of growing up in Montana. Gretel Erhlich's

Impressions

The bars in Montana are like the families of China: Millions upon millions of them, with only a few names. In China, you've got your Hongs and Wongs and, aside from an occasional Sun Yat-sen and Mao Tse-tung, that's about it. In the same way, thirsty individuals throughout Montana are confined to places called the Mint, the Longbranch, and the Stockman. You've got to go out of your way to drink in a classy joint like the Owl Casino or Trixie's Antler Saloon.

—Tim Cahill, "The Killing Season" from *Jaguars Ripped My Flesh* (1987)

The Solace of Open Spaces (Viking Penguin, 1986) is a similar, telling account of Wyoming ranch life that is beautifully written and evocative. Both are real-life illustrations of the experiences many are seeking when they visit the West.

NONFICTION   For people who love obscure facts, *Wyoming Place Names* (Mountain Press, 1988), by Mae Urbanek, and *Names on the Face of Montana* (Mountain Press, 1983), by Roberta Carkeek Cheney, are musts. Both books are A-to-Z compendiums with little-known histories of the smallest of small Western towns.

If your interests lean more toward geography, check out the *Roadside Geology of Montana* (Mountain Press, 1986), by David Alt and Donald W. Hyndman, and the similar *Roadside Geology of Wyoming* (Mountain Press, 1988), by David R. Largeson and Darwin R. Spearing.

HISTORY   For a historical perspective, two especially revealing and well-written books are *Montana: A History of Two Centuries* (University of Washington Press, 1976), by Michael P. Malone, Richard B. Roeder, and William L. Lang, and *History of Wyoming* (University of Nebraska Press, 1978), by T.A. Larson.

The Journals of Lewis and Clark (Houghton Mifflin, 1953), by Bernard De Voto, is the classic volume describing the Corps of Discovery's historic trek into the West.

For an overview of Native American issues, read James Welch and Paul Stekler's recent *Killing Custer* (W.W. Norton and Co., 1994) and *The Indian Frontier of the American West 1846–1890* (Univeristy of New Mexico Press, 1984) by Robert M. Utley.

FICTION   The West's ever-growing literary community makes compiling a fiction list difficult at best, but several books are excellent places for the first-time visitor to start. A.B. Guthrie's *The Big Sky* (Houghton Mifflin, 1947) is now a Montana classic, as is Owen Wister's *The Virginian* (Macmillan, 1929), set in frontier Wyoming. *Fool's Crow* (Viking Penguin, 1986) by James Welch and *Heart Mountain* (Viking Penguin, 1989) by Gretel Ehrlich are fictional stories which revolve around Native American and Asian characters. James Crumley's *The Last Good Kiss* (Random House, 1978) is a fun-loving detective novel set in Montana and, last but not least, there's the classic fly-fishing novella, *A River Runs Through It* (University of Chicago Press, 1976) by Norman Maclean.

TRAVEL   Both **Falcon Press** (☎ 800/582-2665) and **American World and Geographic Publishing** (☎ 800/654-1105) publish series of books pertaining to regional recreation, scenery, and history. Best-sellers among the current lists include hiking and floating guides to trails and rivers in both Montana and Wyoming.

Then, there's the classic *Travels with Charley,* John Steinbeck's tale of his American journey, in which the author pauses to contemplate and critique much of the nation, but falls firmly in love with Montana.

MAGAZINES

Though many Western regional magazines often feature Wyoming destinations, there are no periodicals based in the state that are solely devoted to it. There are, however, three magazines that chronicle the Western experience from a Montana perspective. *Montana Magazine*, based in Helena, presents a wide spectrum of articles pertaining to the state, its residents, history, and landscapes, with scenic photography that's second to none. A relative newcomer to the Montana publishing community, *Big Sky Journal* is an impressive quarterly which makes its home in the Bozeman area. The magazine's masthead is a veritable *who's who* of Montana authors and has a much more literary bent than any other magazine in the state, though its coverage of the great outdoors is also very thorough. *Whitefish*—the smaller, regional "magazine of

Northwest Montana"—provides readers with a glimpse of life in the state's most heavily touristed area.

FILMS

Dorothy Johnson, writer and Whitefish resident, wrote the screenplay for *The Man Who Shot Liberty Valance* long before film commissions were established in either state. In fact, both Montana and Wyoming have been hot properties for film production for a long time. Though any list is necessarily partial, a few films that will illuminate a trip to Montana or Wyoming include *Butch Cassidy & the Sundance Kid, Heaven's Gate, Little Big Man, The Pow Wow Highway, A River Runs Through It, Shane,* and *Son of the Morning Star.* Watch *The River Wild, Far and Away,* or *Return to Lonesome Dove* to relive a Western vacation in all its scenic splendor.

Planning a Trip to Montana & Wyoming

Few things can ruin a much-anticipated vacation more than poor planning. Mid-January is not the time to discover that Going-to-the-Sun Road is closed in winter. Similarly, you don't want to turn up with a suitcase full of shorts and T-shirts during a record-breaking June, when a snowstorm might be close on the heels of the heat.

This chapter has been designed to help you with those details that could make the difference between a trip you'll never forget and one you'd rather not remember.

1 Visitor Information & Money

VISITOR INFORMATION

Travel Montana, P.O. Box 200533, 1424 9th Ave., Helena, MT 59620-0533 (☎ 800/VISIT-MT or 406/444-2654) is the perfect starting point for the traveler who wants to find out more about Big Sky Country. Ask for their current Vacation Guide, which includes information about museums, national monuments and battlefields, scenic driving tours, and more. Their Travel Planner is another invaluable planning tool, with data including statewide car rental companies, state camping information, and descriptions of accommodations throughout the state. Travel Montana will also provide you with separate guides dedicated to some of Montana's more popular sports: snowmobiling, fishing, and winter sports, as well as site-specific guides for each of the organization's six travel regions: Glacier Country in the northwest, Gold West Country in the southwest, Russell Country in northcentral Montana, Yellowstone Country in southcentral Montana, Missouri River Country in the northeast, and Custer Country in the southeast. They'll also give you a free map.

For additional information about attractions, facilities, and services in specific Montana destinations—national parks, cities, or towns—contact the **Montana Chamber of Commerce** (☎ 406/442-2405) for the address and phone number of the nearest chamber office.

The **Wyoming Division of Tourism,** I-25 at College Drive, Cheyenne, WY 82002 (☎ 307/777-7777), distributes the Wyoming Vacation Guide, a comprehensive guide with listings for various types of accommodations and attractions in each of the state's six travel areas. It also includes addresses for each chamber office in the state. Call 800/225-5996 to request a free copy.

The **American Automobile Association** (AAA) will provide its members with a variety of travel planning assistance, including personalized maps and listings of accommodations and restaurants in the state. Call 800/391-4AAA.

For up-to-date information on current weather, contact the **National Weather Service** at 406/449-5204 (Montana) or 307/772-2468 (Wyoming). Statewide **road conditions** are available by calling 800/226-7623 (Montana) or 307/635-9966 (Wyoming).

MONEY

Traveler's checks are accepted throughout both states and can be purchased at any bank for a small fee. Most restaurants and shops will allow you to use your credit cards, although some of the smaller, mom-and-pop establishments still refuse to go to all the trouble (these are usually some of the more interesting places to eat). In Montana, Canadian currency is accepted at the current interest rate although some businesses from time to time offer services or goods at par.

2 When to Go

"If you don't like the weather, stick around five minutes." Native Westerners are fond of this saying and if you stay long enough, you'll soon understand their homespun wisdom. While you'd be hard-pressed to pick a best time of the year to visit—each season has its own special appeal, depending on your interests—remember that no matter what the season, daily temperatures vary widely in highs and lows. Always pack

What Things Cost in Montana & Wyoming	U.S. $
Overnight accommodation (double) in Missoula	$50.00
Overnight accommodation (double) at Old Faithful Inn during the summer	$130.00
Guest ranch vacation (family of four, one week, all-inclusive) on the Rocky Mountain Front	$3,450.00
Weekend fishing trip (three adults, moderately priced, with guide) on the Madison	$885.00
Dinner (for two, without drinks) at O'Brien's in Bozeman	$40.00
Eight-mile float trip down the Snake River near Jackson	$30.00
Adult lift ticket at Big Mountain in Whitefish	$35.00
Adult lift ticket at Grand Targhee	$27.00
Great Falls Symphony ticket	$12.00
Cheyenne Frontier Days Rodeo ticket	$10.00
One pint of Bayern lager, microbrewed in Missoula	$3.00
Topographical map of the Teton Range	$6.00
Average price of one pound of Montana Coffee Traders' whole beans	$8.50
One 10-oz. jar of huckleberry preserves	$5.95
One large can of bear mace	.40¢

Internet Resources

The Internet is rapidly becoming a convenient and sometimes invaluable tool for planning a trip, or for checking very specific local conditions before you drive off into the woods during a rainstorm. World Wide Web sites contain information on everything from geography to population statistics to the latest ski conditions.

For a start, try visiting the Yahoo search engine on the World Wide Web at **http://www.yahoo.com,** especially if you have very specific topics in mind: snowboarding, Bozeman, or Glacier National Park, for example. General information about either state can also be found here.

For Western regional climate summaries by state, try **http://wrcc.sage.unr.edu/climsum.html.** For updated reports listing snow and travel conditions at ski areas nationwide, visit the "Ski Web" at **http://www.sierra.net/SkiWeb.** Adventure Source has a new on-line service called the "Internet Tour Shopper" with links to hundreds of tour operators around the country. Visit their homepage at **http://www.halcyon.com/dclawson/advsource.**

Another interesting site, one with a loose Wyoming tie, but with its ear to the ground of cyberspace, is that of Wyoming cattle rancher and Grateful Dead lyricist John Perry Barlow. He is co-founder of the Electronic Frontier Foundation and is currently on the board of directors of WELL (Whole Earth 'Lectronic Link). His homepage, located at **http://www.eff.org/homes/barlow.html,** is full of links to other like-minded sites, but there is also one linking you to the old Bar Cross Land and Livestock Company, which he started operating in 1971 in Cora, Wyoming.

a jacket and sweaters or sweatshirts even when traveling in the summer; you never know when you might run into a June snowstorm (it happens!). The following charts will give you an indication of the disparate daily temperatures in various parts of Montana and Wyoming year-round.

Montana's Average Monthly Temperatures (High/Low)

	Jan	Feb	Mar	Apr	May	Jun	Jul	Aug	Sep	Oct	Nov	Dec
Billings	36/12	44/17	52/24	63/33	72/42	81/50	89/55	88/53	76/43	66/34	49/23	38/14
Bozeman	33/13	38/18	44/23	55/31	64/39	74/46	82/52	81/51	70/42	59/33	43/23	34/15
Butte	29/5	34/10	40/17	50/26	60/34	70/42	80/46	78/44	66/35	56/26	39/16	29/6
Dillon	32/11	39/16	44/21	55/28	64/36	73/44	83/49	81/48	69/39	58/31	42/21	33/12
Glasgow	20/1	27/8	40/19	57/32	67/43	78/51	85/57	84/55	70/44	59/33	40/19	25/6
Great Falls	31/12	38/17	44/23	55/32	65/41	75/49	83/53	82/52	70/44	59/36	44/24	33/15
Havre	25/4	32/10	43/20	57/31	68/41	78/50	85/54	84/53	71/42	60/32	42/18	28/7
Helena	30/10	37/16	45/22	56/31	65/40	76/48	85/53	83/52	70/41	59/32	42/21	31/11
Kalispell	28/13	35/18	43/24	55/31	64/38	71/44	80/47	79/46	68/39	54/29	38/24	30/16
Lewistown	31/9	36/14	41/20	53/29	63/37	72/45	81/50	80/49	68/40	58/32	44/21	34/12
Libby	29/13	36/17	43/21	52/27	62/33	70/40	78/43	78/42	67/35	54/28	37/22	29/15
Miles City	26/6	33/13	44/22	58/34	69/45	80/54	89/61	87/59	73/47	60/36	42/22	29/9
Missoula	30/15	37/21	47/25	58/31	66/38	74/46	83/50	82/49	71/40	57/31	41/24	30/16
Sidney	24/2	32/8	44/19	60/30	72/42	80/51	86/55	85/53	73/42	61/33	41/19	28/6
W. Yellowstone	24/0	30/4	37/10	46/20	58/29	69/37	79/41	76/39	65/31	52/23	34/12	23/1

Wyoming's Average Monthly Temperatures (High/Low)

	Jan	Feb	Mar	Apr	May	Jun	Jul	Aug	Sep	Oct	Nov	Dec
Casper	33/12	37/16	45/22	56/30	67/38	79/47	88/54	86/52	74/42	61/32	44/22	34/14
Cheyenne	38/15	41/18	45/22	55/30	65/40	74/48	82/55	80/53	71/44	60/34	47/24	39/17
Cody	34/12	40/17	47/23	56/31	66/40	76/49	84/55	82/53	71/43	61/35	45/24	36/15
Devil's Tower	34/4	39/10	48/18	60/28	70/38	80/47	88/53	87/50	76/39	64/28	46/17	35/7
Dubois	35/13	38/14	43/18	52/25	62/32	71/39	80/43	79/41	68/34	58/28	43/19	36/14
Gillette	30/10	36/15	44/21	55/30	64/39	76/49	85/55	84/53	71/43	60/33	43/21	33/12
Jackson	26/4	32/7	41/16	51/24	62/30	72/37	82/41	80/39	70/31	58/23	39/16	27/5
Kemmerer	28/5	32/6	39/13	50/22	62/32	72/39	82/45	79/43	69/34	56/25	40/15	30/6
Newcastle	33/11	38/15	47/23	59/33	69/43	80/52	88/59	86/56	74/46	61/35	45/23	35/13
Rawlins	30/11	33/14	40/20	52/28	63/36	75/45	83/52	80/50	69/41	56/31	41/21	31/13
Riverton	29/-2	37/6	48/18	59/28	69/38	80/46	89/51	87/48	75/38	62/27	43/13	30/0
Rock Springs	30/11	34/14	42/21	53/28	64/37	75/46	83/53	81/51	70/41	57/31	41/20	31/12
Sheridan	33/9	38/15	46/22	57/30	66/39	77/47	86/53	85/52	73/41	62/32	45/20	35/10
Thermopolis	35/6	42/13	51/22	61/31	71/39	82/47	90/54	88/51	76/41	65/31	47/19	36/8
Yellowstone	28/8	33/12	39/16	48/26	59/34	70/42	80/47	78/46	67/37	54/29	38/19	29/10

NORTHERN ROCKIES CALENDAR OF EVENTS

January

- **Montana Pro Rodeo Circuit Finals.** Montana's best cowboys and cattle compete in the final round of this regional competition in Great Falls. ☎ 406/727-8115. Second or third weekend in January.
- **Wyoming State Winter Fair.** Livestock exhibits and evening entertainment highlight this annual event in Lander. ☎ 307/332-3892. Late January.

February

- **Winternational Sports Festival.** A multi-sport competition with tennis, racquetball, speedskating, soccer, swimming, and skiing events held in Anaconda and Butte, Montana. ☎ 800/735-6814. Begins first weekend in February, continuing each weekend into April.
- **Race to the Sky.** The longest continuous dog sled race in the Lower 48, this weeklong event starts in Helena and ends in Missoula. ☎ 406/442-4008. Second Saturday in February.
- **Cowboy Ski Challenge.** Novelty ski races and rodeo events take center stage during this Jackson, Wyoming event, that also includes cowboy poetry readings, Dutch-oven cookoffs, and a barn dance. ☎ 307/733-3316. Late February.

March

- **Big Mountain Doug Betters Winter Classic.** Celebrity ski benefit held near Whitefish, Montana, with proceeds going toward medical care for children. ☎ 406/862-3501. Second Friday and Saturday of March.
- **Ski Joring.** A competition rooted in the Scandinavian tradition of pulling a skier behind a horse that's held in Red Lodge, Montana. ☎ 406/446-1718. Early March.
- **St. Patrick's Day.** Montana's biggest one-day celebration, held in Butte, includes a parade, various musical events, and lots of Irish mirth. ☎ 406/723-5042. Week of St. Patrick's Day.
- ✪ **C.M. Russell Auction of Original Art.** The finest Western art auction in the country with exhibitors and attendees from around the world. Great Falls, Montana. ☎ 406/727-8787. Mid-March.

- **World Snowmobile Expo.** Snowmobile dealerships from around the world display their new sleds in West Yellowstone, Montana, with test rides and demonstrations. ☎ 406/646-7701. Second or third weekend in March.

April

- **International Wildlife Film Festival.** A unique, juried film competition in Missoula, Montana, with more than 100 entries from leading wildlife film-makers. ☎ 406/728-9380. Early April.
- **Pole, Peddle, Paddle Race.** This original race marks the end of the ski season in Teton Village, Wyoming, with a relay that combines skiing (downhill and cross-country), biking, and boating. ☎ 307/733-6433. Early April.

May

✪ **Miles City Bucking Horse Sale.** A "three-day cowboy Mardi Gras," this rodeo and stock sale in Miles City, Montana, features street dances, parades, barbecues, and, of course, lots of bucking broncos. ☎ 406/232-2890. Third weekend in May.

- **Annual Whitewater Festival.** Downriver and slalom kayaking races on the Flathead's "Wild Mile," near Bigfork, Montana. ☎ 406/837-5888. Third weekend in May.
- **Elk Antler Auction.** Nearly 10,000 pounds of bull elk antlers are auctioned off in Jackson's town square. ☎ 307/733-3444. Late May.

June

- **Frontier Festival.** The Buffalo Bill Historical Center in Cody, Wyoming, hosts exhibits of frontier skills—rawhide braiding and blacksmithing, among others—along with competitions and entertainment. ☎ 307/587-4771. Early June.
- **Happy Jack Mountain Music Festival.** Bluegrass and fiddles prevail over this festival of mountain music in Cheyenne, Wyoming. ☎ 307/777-7519. Early June.
- **College National Finals Rodeo.** Five nights of exciting rodeo events in Bozeman, Montana, featuring entrants competing for college scholarships. ☎ 406/585-2215. Week preceding Father's Day.
- **Strawberry Festival.** A one-day celebration of the strawberry in downtown Billings, Montana, with food vendors, arts and crafts, and live music. ☎ 406/259-5454. Mid-June.
- **Chugwater Chili Cook-Off.** Thousands of people gather in Chugwater, Wyoming, for this tasty tribute to a spicy stew. ☎ 800/932-4222. Late June.
- **Lewis & Clark Festival.** Commemoration of Lewis and Clark's journey in and around Great Falls, Montana, with historic reenactments, buffalo roasts, and float trips. ☎ 406/761-4434. Late June.

✪ **Little Big Horn Days.** A four-day festival of ethnic food and performances in Hardin, Montana, featuring Custer's Last Stand Reenactment. ☎ 406/665-1672. Last weekend in June.

- **Shoshone Treaty Days/Eastern Shoshone Powwow and Indian Days.** A celebration of Native American tradition and culture that's followed by one of Wyoming's largest powwows and all-Indian rodeos in Ft. Washakie, Wyoming. ☎ 307/332-9106. Late June.
- **Mountain Man Rendezvous.** A tribute to mountain men, traders, and trappers in Laramie, Wyoming. ☎ 800/445-5303. Late June.

July

✪ **Grand Teton Music Festival.** An all-star orchestra presents a varied classical repertoire, including numerous chamber concerts, in Teton Village, Wyoming. ☎ 307/733-1128. Mid-July through August.

- **Legend of Rawhide Reenactment.** An overeager gold miner comes to an untimely end in this production of the popular Western legend in Lusk, Wyoming. ☎ 307/334-2950. Second weekend in July.

- **North American Indian Days.** The Blackfeet Reservation hosts a weekend of native dancing, singing, and drumming, with crafts booths and games, in Browning, Montana. ☎ 406/338-7276. Second week of July.

- **Flathead Festival.** A two-week concert series in Flathead Valley, Montana, featuring a variety of music from headline musicians in valley-wide settings. ☎ 406/257-0787. Mid- to late July.

- **Bannack Days.** Frontier crafts, music, and drama recreate the Old West in the ghost town of Bannack, Montana. ☎ 406/834-3413. Third weekend in July.

- **Montana State Fiddlers Contest.** A two-day event in Polson, Montana, featuring competitions as well as impromptu and organized jam sessions among the state's best. ☎ 406/883-5969. Third weekend in July.

- **Frontier Days.** One of the country's most popular rodeos, the "Daddy of 'em All" entertains standing-room-only crowds during a full week of rodeo events in Cheyenne, Wyoming. ☎ 800/227-6336. Last full week of July.

August

- **Grand Targhee Bluegrass Festival.** A three-day celebration of music, arts, food, and entertainment in Jackson, Wyoming. ☎ 800/827-4433. Mid-August.

- **Sweet Pea Festival.** A full-fledged arts festival in Bozeman, Montana, with fine art, headline musicians, and various entertainment for all ages. ☎ 406/586-5421. First full weekend in August.

- **Wind River Rendezvous.** A buffalo barbecue highlights this black powder, buckskinner event in Dubois, Wyoming. ☎ 307/455-2556. Mid-August.

- **Crow Fair.** By far one of the biggest and best Native American gatherings in the Northwest, with dancing, food, and crafts in Crow Agency, Montana. ☎ 406/638-2601. Mid-August.

- **Montana Cowboy Poetry Gathering.** A three-day event featuring readings and entertainment from the real McCoys in Lewistown, Montana. ☎ 406/538-5436. Late August.

- **Big Sky Indian Powwow.** A celebration of various Native American tribes and their cultures, with traditional dancing, blanket trading, and authentic Native American food. In Helena, Montana. ☎ 406/442-4120. Last weekend in August.

September

- **Fort Bridger Rendezvous.** A Fort Bridger, Wyoming, celebration that pays tribute to its most famous mountain man and early Yellowstone explorer, Jim Bridger. ☎ 307/789-2757. Labor Day weekend.

- **Nordicfest.** A Scandinavian celebration in Libby, Montana, featuring a parade, juried craft show, headline entertainment, and an international Fjord horse show. ☎ 406/293-6838. First weekend following Labor Day.

- **Oktoberfest.** A celebration of fall, German-style, with live music, good food, and better beer in Livingston, Montana. ☎ 406/222-0850. Late September.

October

- **Flathead International Balloon Festival.** Pancake breakfasts, barbecues, and skydiving center around hot air balloon competitions in Flathead Valley, Montana. ☎ 406/756-9091. Early October.

- **Microbrewery Festival.** Buy a mug and sample beers from various Pacific Northwest microbreweries. On the Big Mountain, near Whitefish, Montana. ☎ 406/862-1900. Mid-October.

December
- **Dog Sled Races.** A week's worth of dog sled racing in Anaconda, Montana, from 15 to 50 miles daily, including poker runs, passenger races, and a stampede race. ☎ 406/563-2675. First week in December.
- **National Elk Refuge Opens.** Wintering herds of elk make their way from the high country down to Jackson Hole, Wyoming. ☎ 307/733-9212. Late December.
- **Christmas strolls and parades,** statewide, Montana and Wyoming. Check with local chambers of commerce for specific dates and locations.

3 The Active Vacation Planner

With adventure travel currently representing the fastest-growing segment of the tourism industry—an annual $2 million is generated solely in the United States—it's evident that more and more people are discovering just how exciting and rewarding an outdoor vacation can be. The following information will help you get a head start on what may be the most memorable vacation of your life.

ACTIVITIES A TO Z

No matter what your interest or physical aptitude, there awaits for you in the West a recreational outing that is just as spectacular as the region's scenery, whether you visit during summer's spectacle of multicolored wildflowers or just as the winter snow has settled on towering stands of tamaracks. A few words of warning, no matter which activity you choose: know your physical limits, be aware of the weather and local wildlife, and make sure that you're acclimated to the local elevation, especially if you will be gaining elevation during your outing.

The beauty of this area is often found in less popular, harder-to-reach places where help may not be readily available. When exploring the backcountry, be prepared for an emergency resulting from equipment failure, a sudden weather change, or exhaustion, no matter your level of fitness.

We'll discuss good places to camp repeatedly throughout the book, but one particularly great lodging value for your backcountry adventures is a **Forest Service lookout or cabin.** The definitive rustic lodging experience, lookouts provide a remote backcountry experience at a fraction of the price you'd pay for a secluded guest ranch. Of course you don't get gourmet meals, a flush toilet, or a selection of planned activities, but if camp food, sleeping bags, and strenuous hikes are more to your liking and budget, check them out. They generally rent for $20 or less per night, though you do have to pack in your food and water, linens, and utensils (sometimes). Firewood is generally provided, though a hike or cross-country ski-in may be necessary. For information on cabins and their availability, contact the Northern Regional Headquarters of the USDA Forest Service at P.O. Box 7669, Missoula, Montana 59807 (☎ 406/329-3511).

And it's been said countless times before, but we'll say it again: please be respectful of this region's wild places. If you pack it in, pack it out.

BACKCOUNTRY SKIING Definitely one of the most challenging and rewarding sports, backcountry skiing requires absolute physical and mental toughness. Wyoming and Montana residents who practice this sport are the best authorities on the local hot spots, although some may give you a guarded response when you ask them about their favorite places. The fear of losing their favorite spots to hordes of people makes residents cautious at times. But if you want to ski the more remote backcountry areas in either state, your best bet is to ask at a local ski shop. **Best place**

for secluded skiing in Montana and Wyoming: Either state's publicly accessible national forests and state lands.

BIKING   Biking is one of the most accessible ways for the average person to experience what recreation in Montana and Wyoming is all about: its pace will serve you well in getting to know the states' people and places intimately. Bring your own bike or rent from one of the many local bike shops around the region; they will usually assist you in planning a local day trip equal to your fitness level and ability. While there are certainly ample opportunities for exploring more mountainous terrain on a bike, there are an equal number of more moderate touring trips that are suitable for travelers who are less fit. If you plan to tour backroads or highways, try to schedule your trip during the spring or fall; you'll appreciate the fact that there are fewer cars on the roads. **Best cycling scenery in Montana:** Going-to-the-Sun-Road, Glacier National Park; **in Wyoming:** Grand Teton National Park and the northwest part of the state.

BOATING & SAILING   Here are two good ways to enjoy the scenic wonders of these two states without having to pay your dues on a Stairmaster before your visit (although seasoned sailors may find local winds somewhat less than ideal). Montana's Flathead Lake is generally considered one of the best places to sail in the state, with fairly consistent winds; other lakes are much less dependable.

Boating is another thing altogether, so if you've got a motor, pack a lunch and cruise any of the many lakes that dot Montana and Wyoming's landscape. Just make sure to check around locally regarding access if you're not sure. All types of boats are available locally for rent, so never fear if you don't have your own. **Best places to set sail in Montana:** Flathead Lake or Fort Peck Lake; **in Wyoming:** Bighorn Canyon National Recreation Area.

CROSS-COUNTRY SKIING   Considered one of the best forms of aerobic exercise and requiring good cardiovascular conditioning, cross-country skiing can be practiced almost anywhere if the snow is deep enough. There are scores of guest ranches that groom trails, and almost every ski resort in the region also includes a cross-country area, though you'll have to buy a ticket. If you don't want to pay to ski, forest service logging roads are typically used for cross-country trails. Many golf courses are also regularly groomed for track skiing; some are even lighted for night skiing. **Best place to cross-country ski in Montana:** West Yellowstone, training ground of U.S. Nordic and Biathlon ski teams; **in Wyoming:** Jackson Hole area and Grand Teton National Park.

DOWNHILL SKIING & TELEMARKING   There are 13 downhill ski areas in Montana and 11 in Wyoming, scattered amid the towering mountain ranges found predominantly in the western parts of both states. Usually operating from late November to mid-April, and with comparatively shorter lift lines and less expensive lift tickets than most other ski areas in the country, Montana and Wyoming ski resorts are great values for the ski enthusiast. Breathtaking summit vistas are standard fare and very rarely are the slopes crowded with people, certainly not when compared with neighboring states to the south and west. But don't fret if you're not skiing black diamond runs; all ski resorts have seasoned instructors available for private or group lessons at extremely affordable prices. **Best ski scene in Montana:** Big Sky Resort near Bozeman is the biggest in Montana, with runs for all abilities, and Whitefish's Big Mountain prides itself on a family atmosphere; **in Wyoming:** Jackson Hole wins hands down, with Jackson Hole Ski Resort, Snow King, and Grand Targhee ski areas all in close proximity.

DUDE RANCHES   One of the most satisfying vacation experiences available in the Northern Rockies is found at any one of the many dude or guest ranches dotted around the two states. This is the fabled Western experience come to life: daily rides by horseback, cowboy coffee beneath an expansive blue sky, campfire sing-alongs with rope tricks, and homemade food served family-style in rustic lodges. Best of all, you need not have any riding experience before your visit; ranch "hands" are trained to assist even the greenest of greenhorns. If you want a taste of what it might feel like to be Gus McCrae for a day, this is the outdoor experience for you. **Best places in Montana:** the Paradise and Gallatin Valleys in the southwest; **in Wyoming:** Anywhere. (They don't call it the Cowboy State for nothing!)

FISHING   From blue-ribbon trout streams to warmwater reservoirs, Montana and Wyoming waters are a fisherman's paradise. Long known for world-class fly-fishing, the streams and creeks of the Northern Rockies are teeming with native trout—rainbow, brook, brown, mackinaw, golden, and cutthroat—as well as kokanee salmon, yellow perch, largemouth bass, and northern pike. Warmwater species include sauger, channel catfish, and smallmouth bass in just as abundant numbers. **Best places to fish in Montana:** On any one of the world-class, blue-ribbon streams in the southwest part of the state; **in Wyoming:** Flaming Gorge National Recreation Area.

GOLF   Golfers not familiar with Montana or Wyoming will be pleasantly surprised at the number of exceptional courses found in both states, particularly in Bigfork and Anaconda, Montana (where there are courses designed by Jack Nicklaus). Summer's long days make this a perfect place to play a round (or two), especially when you take into consideration that average daily temperatures are much lower than in more traditional golfing destinations like Florida or California. This isn't much of a secret anymore, so set your tee times well in advance. **Best Montana courses:** Any in the Flathead Valley; **in Wyoming:** Jackson.

HIKING   One of the most popular summertime activities in the West, hiking gives you the extra added bonus of moderate to strenuous cardiovascular exercise while you're drinking in the area's fabulous scenery. The most important factor to consider when embarking on a hike is the ratio of distance traveled to elevation gained. Make sure you study topographical maps to find this information. The elevation you will gain over the course of the hike, much more so than the actual distance you will travel, is the better indication of how difficult the hike will be. Be sure to wear comfortable hiking shoes that have been broken in or you may spend the rest of your trip limping around with blistered feet. If you plan on hiking in prime grizzly country, be sure to carry bear mace and know what to do in case you actually see one (see the sidebar in Chapter 5, "An Encounter with a Bear"). **Best places to take a hike in Montana and Wyoming:** Any of the three national parks: Glacier, Grand Teton, and Yellowstone.

MOUNTAINEERING: ROCK & ICE CLIMBING   With some of the most breathtaking alpine peaks in the country, the Northern Rockies provide a spectacular setting for climbers in search of a peak experience. There are superb opportunities for climbers to experience the year-round beauty of Montana and Wyoming's mountains through a variety of climbing styles and areas: a daylong rock climb during the height of summer in Montana's Beartooths or a weeklong trek into Wyoming's Wind River Mountains, or the Tetons for unforgettable winter mountaineering. This sport is highly technical and requires extreme fitness and stamina, although most climbing outfitters also offer beginner courses for novice climbers. **Best place to climb in Montana:** Granite Peak, the state's highest; **in Wyoming:** Grand Teton National Park.

SNOWBOARDING   Forget all those stereotypes you've heard about snowboarders: this sport is a simple combination of speed, air, and style, and is rapidly defying any attempts to categorize its most devout practitioners. No longer just for the grunge set, snowboarding is becoming more and more popular on Western slopes. If you've never done it, realize that you may get beat up during your first few days of trying to learn how to ride (although seasoned shredders swear that the learning curve is much shorter than that for learning to ski). If you're not new to the sport, you'll find Montana and Wyoming ski areas to be snowboard-friendly—so strap on your board and catch some big air. If you're *really* into riding, ask around at local ski shops for winter backcountry options or summer snowboarding: Glacier Park's Logan Pass is a popular Fourth of July hike 'n' ride destination. **Best place to shred in Montana and Wyoming:** Any ski resort.

SNOWMOBILING With more than 3,000 miles of trails in Montana and 1,300 in Wyoming, snowmobilers have a vast winter playground to explore. Though sled rental shops are plentiful, they're in high demand: make your reservation well in advance of your trip. Though snowmobiling doesn't require an extreme level of physical fitness, you have to be able to adequately handle the snowmobile and be well-versed in safety measures since avalanches are not uncommon in the areas some of these trails traverse. Though snowmobiles are prohibited in Glacier National Park, there's absolutely no better way to experience Yellowstone's diverse majesty than from a sled during the middle of winter. **Best bet for sledding in Montana:** West Yellowstone; **in Wyoming:** Yellowstone National Park.

WATER SPORTS: CANOEING, KAYAKING, RAFTING From the exciting challenge of whitewater rafting to the calm serenity of a sunset paddle across a perfectly calm lake, paddle enthusiasts can partake in a number of water sports in these two Western states.

By far the most popular summer water sport, whitewater rafting is a thrilling way to spend a morning, day, or entire week on some of the states' fastest rivers and is suitable for nearly any visitor, no matter what your age, so long as you don't mind getting soaked. Kayaking can go either way, with hard-core devotees battling stretches of river with names like the "Wild Mile" and "Big Kahuna," or more leisurely fans crossing glassy lake surfaces with considerably more grace. Canoeing is most popular on rivers, ideal for a daylong excursion and picnic, fishing, or just enjoying the views. **Best places to paddle in Montana:** the Missouri River or any of the three forks of the Flathead River; **in Wyoming:** the Snake River.

OUTFITTERS & ADVENTURE TRAVEL OPERATORS

People looking for the ultimate active vacation should consider their knowledge of a particular sport or activity, their physical condition, and how much money they are willing to spend for an adventure travel experience when choosing whether or not to use an outfitter. If you have no idea what a bivouac is and don't own an avalanche transceiver, you have no business going backcountry skiing in a national park unescorted, especially if you are unfamiliar with the area. Knowing your degree of physical fitness is key in selecting an activity that will allow you to enjoy your surroundings without injuring yourself or others you may be guiding. And while hiring an outfitter will probably cost more than a trip you've planned yourself, don't forget to factor in the comfort gained in knowing that the person guiding you down the river or into a wilderness area has been there before.

HOW TO CHOOSE AN OUTFITTER

Selecting an outfitter doesn't have to be hard, although the task can seem a bit overwhelming at first. With literally hundreds of choices, things can seem doubly difficult when you take into account booking agents, those travel planners who work with several different outfitters in providing customized trips.

First of all, ask yourself what you expect to get out of the trip. Think about things like accommodations, meals, group size, activity level, and guide expertise. Do you mind sleeping in a tent every night? Do you want to travel with a small group or be part of a larger one? Is your fitness level appropriate to the type of trip you want to take? When you think you've isolated these and other factors, choose a few adventure travel companies and start asking them questions.

Make sure that the company is up-to-date with state licenses and forest service permits, if applicable. Although it is a criminal offense to offer outfitting services without a license, it is not an uncommon occurrence. In addition, it is a misdemeanor offense to procure the services of an unlicensed guide. Protect yourself by asking to see a copy of their current license.

Find out exactly how knowledgeable the company is of the area and how long they have been in operation. Do they operate out of the state and, if so, how long have they been conducting trips to your specific destination? Ask for details regarding the trip you've chosen. The answers you receive will give you an indication of how well-versed the employees are in the services their company provides.

Find out what is included in the price of the trip and if you will be required to cover any additional expenses such as airport transfers, meals, or equipment rentals.

Ask the outfitter for names of previous clients who have gone on the trip you're researching. Firsthand information from someone who has been there is more valuable than anything you will read from the company's brochure. It's a good idea to ask how best to contact the trip's guide (although they can sometimes be hard to reach) since someone who shares your priorities will make the experience much more enjoyable. Most reputable companies will be glad comply with these requests; if they aren't, consider that as well.

Above all, don't overestimate your physical capability. If trips are designed for different fitness levels and you are in doubt as to yours, choose the easier. You will enjoy the vacation more and will decrease your chances for injury.

Outfitters

Now that you know which questions to ask, you're ready to make that all-important decision: which one? While we can't make that decision for you, here are some of the more popular and well-respected companies operating in the West.

The Montana Board of Outfitters will provide you with a booklet listing all licensed outfitters and guides in the state for a nominal fee. Request one by writing to the Montana Board of Outfitters and Professional Guides, Arcade Building, 111 N. Jackson, Helena, Montana 59620 or call them at 406/444-3738. A similar Wyoming directory is available by writing to the **Wyoming Outfitters and Guide Association,** P.O. Box 2284, Cody, Wyoming 82414 or calling 307/527-7453. See also "Outfitters and Organized Trips" of each regional section for listings of local outfitters.

Remember that it is customary to tip outfitters (horse wranglers or rafting guides, for example), usually at a rate of 20%.

Adventure Cycling Association
P.O. Box 8308, Missoula, MT 59807. ☎ 406/721-1776

Backcountry
P.O. Box 4029, Bozeman, MT 59772. ☎ 406/586-3556

Backroads
1516 5th St., Suite L102, Berkeley, CA 94710-1740. ☎ 800/GO ACTIVE

Christian Adventures
A-4380 46th St., Holland, MI 49423. ☎ 616/751-5990

Earthwatch
P.O. Box 403, Waterton, MA 02272-9924. ☎ 617/926-8200.
E-mail: info@earthwatch.org or http://gaia.earthwatch.org
Joseph Van Os Photo Safaris
P.O. Box 655, Vashon, WA 98070. ☎ 206/463-5383
OARS (Outdoor Adventure River Specialists)
P.O. Box 67, Angels Camp, CA 95222. ☎ 209/736-4677
Rainbow Adventures
15033 Kelly Canyon Road, Bozeman, MT 59715. ☎ 406/587-3883
REI Adventures
1700 45th St. E, Sumner, WA 98390. ☎ 800/622-2236
Rising Wolf Backpacking Expeditions
6454 Saint Marys Lake Road, St. Ignatius, MT 59865-9638. ☎ 406/
745-3212
Roads Less Traveled
P.O. Box 8187, Longmont, CO 80501. ☎ 303/678-8750
Timberline
7975 E. Harvard, #J, Denver, CO 80231. ☎ 303/759-3804
Wild Horizon Expeditions
5663 West Fork Road, Darby, MT 59829. ☎ 406/821-3747
Wilderness River Outfitters and Trail Expeditions, Inc.
P.O. Box 871, Salmon, ID 83467. ☎ 208/756-3959

ADVENTURE TRAVEL OPERATORS

Unlike some outfitters who specialize in only one type of activity, adventure travel operators are brokers for a variety of outfitters and can arrange more than one type of recreational outing depending on your budget and the preferred activity, area, time of year, and length of your stay. Call them for a tailor-made itinerary but be sure to find out which outfitters will be leading your trip. Make sure that the outfitter(s) your adventure travel operator has chosen measures up to your standards, a factor no less important than if you were choosing the outfitter yourself, even if someone else is making the reservations for you.

Most adventure travel companies have very strict refund policies. Make sure you find out what the policy is if the company cancels the trip, not you.

Adventures
P.O. Box 1336, Bozeman, MT 59715. ☎ 406/586-9942
Adventure Source
1111 E. Madison, Suite 302, Seattle, WA 98122. ☎ 206/328-4426 or
800/249-2885
American Wilderness Experience
P.O. Box 1486, Boulder, CO 80306. ☎ 800/444-0099
Off the Beaten Path
109 E. Main St., Bozeman, MT 59715. ☎ 406/586-1311
Venture West Vacations
P.O. Box 7543, Missoula, MT 59807. ☎ 406/825-6200

TIPS ON INSURANCE, HEALTH & SAFETY

INSURANCE   The cost of your trip will usually include liability coverage for any accidents that may occur as a result of your outfitter's negligence. Ask if you're unsure and check your personal health insurance policy for details regarding medical emergencies. If you'd like to increase your coverage before going on the trip with additional insurance that covers lost luggage, cancellation, and emergency evacuation, check out the short-term travel policies offered by **Access America** (☎ 800/284-8300), **Tele-Trip** (☎ 800/228-9792), and **Travel Guard International** (☎ 800/826-1300).

SAFETY   It goes without saying that life jackets, helmets, pads, and other protective gear are essential when pursuing an outdoor adventure. If you aren't bringing your own, make sure that the shop you are renting from will also provide you with safety equipment.

Winter backcountry explorers should always be equipped with a shovel, a sectional probe, and an avalanche transceiver; if you're exploring during the summer, carry bear mace: avalanches and grizzlies are not uncommon. Though the debate continues to rage between its proponents and those who think it merely cruel, bear mace remains an effective deterrent to bears and is available at local sporting goods stores. Additionally, when camping in bear territory, make sure that any foodstuffs are put well out of their reach and try to avoid preparing strong-smelling foods that may attract bears.

If your wilderness activity takes you to a body of water, have dry clothes available in case you get wet. Many Western streams, rivers, and lakes are glacier-fed, making them extremely cold, even during the warmest summer months.

When driving during the winter months, make sure your car is equipped for a road emergency and throw a few blankets in the trunk. Winter temperatures can become subzero quickly and help may not always be readily available.

HYPOTHERMIA   Hypothermia—an abnormally low body temperature resulting from exposure to cold and aggravated by exhaustion, water, and wind—is a leading cause of death among recreationists and should be taken seriously. This condition is a potentially fatal one that occurs when your body gets so cold that it can no longer warm itself. It's something to keep in mind with temperatures in Montana and Wyoming changing dramatically from hour to hour. It is not limited to cold weather; you can get hypothermia on a summer day that suddenly turns stormy. Always dress in layers and be prepared for bad weather, especially if you will be away from your car or lodgings for an extended amount of time. Remember that many Western waters are glacier-fed and are extremely cold, even during the warmest summer months, making them a potential hazard for improperly dressed visitors.

4 Learning Vacations & Alternative Travel Programs

EDUCATIONAL/STUDY TRAVEL   **Montana State University** offers several different courses of study during the summer for people interested in learning about various aspects of Montana: its history, geology, flora, and fauna, to name a few. See the Bozeman regional section of Chapter 9 for specific details about these programs.

As part of the Montana State University system, the **Museum of the Rockies** offers paleontological trips to various dig sites around the state. Their Egg Mountain site, located next to the Nature Conservancy's Pine Butte Swamp Preserve, is one of the most popular. See the Rocky Mountain Eastern Front regional section of Chapter 8 for more information on Egg Mountain and the preserve. Similarly, the **University of New Orleans** conducts a "Digging for Dinosaurs" expedition to Dragon's Grave, Wyoming, each summer during June and July. Sessions are one or two weeks each at a cost of $695 for one week, $95 for each additional week. To find out more, contact Dr. Carl Drichta at 504/286-7100.

The **Audubon Society** conducts a mountain ecology camp in Wyoming's Wind River Mountains. Based near Dubois at the Whiskey Mountain Wildlife Conservation Camp, participants learn about mountain ecology through observing the interaction of plants and animals with their physical environment. Recreation goes hand-in-hand with education as you hike, fish, raft, and canoe through this spectacular alpine ecosystem. Contact the Audubon Society at 203/869-2017 for more information.

The Jackson Hole area is home to a number of facilities that provide educational programs, often led by a naturalist or wildlife biologist. If you have a limited amount of time, consider a sunrise or sunset excursion with the **Great Plains Wildlife Institute** (☎ 307/733-2623). It also offers more in-depth full-day and six-day expeditions. The **Snake River Institute**'s (☎ 307/733-2214) learning expeditions run the gamut from a course devoted to Thomas Molesworth's "Cowboy High Style" to a multicultural examination of the life and culture of the Arapaho and Shoshone. It also has an extensive list of two- to five-day activity-driven courses for children from ages 6 to 15. The **Targhee Institute** at Grand Targhee Resort, Box SKI, Alta, WY 83422 (☎ 800/TARGHEE), offers programs for all ages in the arts and natural sciences, including an extensive offering of Elderhostel programs as well as a "Science Explorers" day camp for 8- to 12-year-olds.

Earthwatch is an eco-tour company with expeditions that examine and explore environmental issues all over the world. Contact Field Representatives Janne Hayward in Bozeman (☎ 406/587-6124) and Brent Weigner in Cheyenne (☎ 307/635-3316) for more specific information on programs in each state.

The outstanding scenery of Wyoming's Sunlight Basin is the setting for Northwest College's **Yellowstone Jazz Camp,** where students receive both ensemble and individual instruction from the most outstanding jazz artists and teachers in the country. The week-long instrumental camp culminates in a trip to Cody, where participants perform at the Yellowstone Jazz Festival. There is also a vocal camp. Contact Northwest College (☎ 307/754-6307) in Powell for more information.

Glacier, Yellowstone, and Grand Teton National Parks each have learning institutes that conduct field courses, an excellent way to learn more about these spectacular nature preserves. See Chapters 5, 11, and 12, respectively, to learn more about specific course offerings and dates for the three parks.

Travelers over 60 years old can participate in **Elderhostel** programs around the state. See "Tips for Special Travelers" later in this chapter for additional information on these programs.

WILDERNESS SKILLS   The **National Outdoor Leadership School** (NOLS) and **Outward Bound** both offer a series of courses with the wilderness as your classroom. With an emphasis on low-impact wilderness living, expeditions provide the participant with the opportunity to practice wilderness skills while gaining a greater appreciation of the natural world. Trips can last anywhere from eight days to three months. For a detailed course catalog, contact NOLS at 288 Main St., Lander, WY 82520-3128 (☎ 307/332-6973). Course descriptions for the Voyageur School of Outward Bound can be requested from the offices at 111 Third Ave. S., Suite 120, Minneapolis, MN 55401 (☎ 800/328-2943 or 612/338-0565).

NEW-AGE/SPIRITUAL PROGRAMS   The **Feathered Pipe Ranch,** located west of Helena in the Colorado Gulch, offers weeklong summer programs devoted to yoga, holistic medicine, shamanism, Native American spirituality, and astrology. The 110-acre ranch near the Continental Divide has been in operation as a healing center since 1975, with accommodations that include Mongolian yurts, tents, tepees, dormitory rooms in a log lodge, and some private rooms with baths (reservations should be made at least two weeks in advance). Run by the Feathered Pipe Foundation, a non-profit educational foundation devoted to the "healing of the heart," programs usually run from Saturday to Saturday with prices from $1,065 to $1,250. That includes all lodging, meals, and educational programs. For reservations or additional information, contact the Feathered Pipe Foundation at P.O. Box 1682, Helena, MT 59624 (☎ 406/442-8196).

5 Tips for Special Travelers

FOR TRAVELERS WITH DISABILITIES   For general travel information and assistance, contact the **Information Center for Individuals with Disabilities** at Fort Point Place, 27-43 Wormwood St., Boston, MA 02210 (☎ 617/727-5540). The **Montana Independent Living Project** (☎ 800/735-6457) operates an information and referral service for travelers with disabilities, providing information relating to such topics as accessibility, recreation, and transportation. **Amtrak** (☎ 800/USA-RAIL) and **Greyhound** (☎ 800/231-2222) also both provide assistance and discounts for travelers with disabilities.

The Wyoming Division of Tourism, in conjunction with the Department of Vocational Rehabilitation, offers an incredible free guide to disabled persons touring the state. **Access Wyoming** is free and provides readers with important information concerning restaurant and hotel listings complete with visual alarm clock information, TDD numbers, and wheelchair-accessible facilities throughout the state. For a copy of the guide, contact the Wyoming Division of Tourism, I-25 at College Dr., Cheyenne, WY 82002 (☎ 307/777-7777 or 800/225-5996).

D.R.E.A.M. (Disabled Recreation and Environmental Access Movement) is a non-profit organization based in the Flathead Valley that will provide you with an accessibility guide to Glacier Park and northwest Montana. An excellent resource, it includes information for regional restaurants, shops, accommodations, and recreational centers as well as an extensive list of additional resources. For a free copy, contact P.O. Box 8300, Kalispell, MT 59904 (☎ 406/758-5411).

Eagle Mount is committed to creating unparalleled recreational opportunities for people of all ages with disabilities. Adaptive ski techniques and personalized instruction are utilized in Eagle Ski programs at the following Montana ski areas: **Bridger Bowl and the Bohart Ranch** (☎ 406/586-1781), **Red Lodge Mountain** (☎ 406/245-5422), and **Showdown** (☎ 406/454-1449).

FOR GAY & LESBIAN TRAVELERS   Gay and lesbian visitors to the state are most likely to find kindred spirits in Montana's larger cities: Billings, Bozeman, Helena, and Missoula, all of which also happen to be college towns. For the most part, Montana is largely conservative, although the recent influx of transplants to the state from more cosmopolitan areas has begun to effect a more progressive trend.

If you have Internet access, try combing the "Gay and Lesbian Travel Web" **(http:/www.cts.com/~drcarr/gay_travel/index.html)** for regional travel information. Links include "Travel Tours and Cruises Calendar," "Destinations," "Sport Adventure and the Outdoors," and "Parties and Special Events Calendar."

FOR SENIORS   The **American Association of Retired Persons** (AARP), 601 E. St. NW, Washington, DC 20049 (☎ 202/434-2277), and the **National Council of Senior Citizens,** 925 15th St. NW, Washington, DC 20005 (☎ 202/347-8800), both offer members various travel benefits. Similarly, many hotels and attractions in both states offer a discount to senior citizens. Be sure to ask for this discount before you make your reservation or purchase a ticket and have proof of your age (driver's license or passport).

If you are interested in traveling, learning, and meeting new friends with similar interests, an **Elderhostel** program may be the perfect way to spend a week or two in Montana or Wyoming. Geared specifically for seniors, the organization leads educational and recreational field trips and seminars across the country. Inquire about current programs at 75 Federal St., Boston, MA 02110 (☎ 617/426-7788).

FOR FAMILIES   Be sure to ask about family discounts for accommodations before making your reservations. If you plan to stay a week at a ski resort or dude ranch, you may find a better value by renting a condominium or lodge than multiple rooms. Ski areas often offer packages that include accommodations and lift tickets; check with the ski resort's reservation service for current prices. Before booking any type of room, event, or activity, be sure to inquire if there are discounts for children or age restrictions. Know exactly what you're buying before you leave home: does the per-person cost includes meals and activities, for example.

FOR STUDENTS   Students looking for a good lodging value should check out the states' hostels. Though Montana and Wyoming have an unusually short list of statewide hostels, you can usually rent a room for under $10, although you'll probably have to share it. We've listed hostels throughout the regional chapters of this book, or you can contact **Hostelling International-American Youth Hostels,** 733 15th St. NW, Washington, DC 20005 (☎ 202/783-6161). Memberships cost $25 for adults (ages 18 to 54), $10 for youth (under 18), $35 for families (parents with children under 16), $15 for seniors (over 54), or $250 for a life membership. Included in the cost of membership (or $8 for non-members) is a publication titled *Hostelling North America*, a thorough directory of member hostels. If you have Internet access, you can join by contacting "GNN Direct" at **http://gnn.com/gnn/bus/ayh/usa/montana.html.**

With three national parks within their borders, Montana and Wyoming are popular destinations for students, regardless of the season. Many choose to work in a national park during the summer or a ski resort in the winter. If you're interested in obtaining a summer park job, contact Glacier (☎ 406/888-5441), Yellowstone (☎ 307/344-7381), or Grand Teton (☎ 307/739-3399) National Parks directly for more information and applications.

6 Getting There

BY PLANE   Travelers flying into Montana can choose to land in one of the state's six major airports: Billings, Bozeman, Great Falls, Helena, Kalispell, or Missoula. Air service to these airports is provided by the following airlines, although only Billings can boast of service from all three: **Delta and the Delta Connection** (☎ 800/221-1212), **Northwest** (☎ 800/225-2525), and **United** (☎ 800/241-6522). Commuter service is available through **Big Sky** (☎ 800/237-7788), **Horizon Air** (☎ 800/547-9308), and **Skywest** (☎ 800/453-9417).

In Wyoming, Jackson, Casper, Cheyenne, Cody, Gillette, Laramie, Riverton, Rock Springs, and Sheridan all have airports with commercial intrastate airline service as well as a couple of points beyond. **American** (☎ 800/433-7300), **Continental** (☎ 800/525-0280), and **Delta** (☎ 800/221-1212) all serve Wyoming, with **Frontier Airlines** (☎ 800/432-1359) providing several commuter flights.

Though these airlines offer service to Montana and Wyoming, it's not uncommon for some airlines to pull out of smaller markets like Montana and Wyoming with changing seasons. Continental, for instance, recently flew in and out of Billings, but discontinued their service.

BY CAR   In Montana, I-90 runs east-west from St. Regis to Wyola, near the Wyoming border and southeast of Billings. I-94 goes east from Billings to Glendive and the North Dakota border. Highway 2, called the "Hi-Line," is another east-west alternative, stretching across the northern reaches of the state from Bainville to Troy. The major interstate traversing the state from north to south is I-15, from Sweetgrass to Monida. Wyoming is crossed through the southern part of the state by I-80, a huge trucker route from Egbert in the east to Evanston in the west. I-90 begins in the northcentral part of the state near Ranchester and comes out in the northeast near Beulah. Just outside Buffalo is I-90's junction with I-25, a north-south route that runs through Cheyenne. The western part of the state north of Rock Springs is dominated by U.S. highways and secondary state-maintained roads.

BY TRAIN   Amtrak's *Empire Builder* (☎ 800/872-7245) provides rail service along the northern tier of Montana, traveling west from Chicago and east from Seattle. The train stops in the following towns along the Hi-Line (Highway 2, east-west): Wolf Point, Glasgow, Malta, Havre, Shelby, Cut Bank, Browning, East Glacier, Essex, West Glacier, Whitefish, and Libby. In Wyoming, the *Pioneer Line* runs through Evanston, Green River, Rock Springs, Rawlins, Laramie, and Borie (a place Amtrak swears exists—we prefer to call it Cheyenne, the closest city) three times weekly. The train is an unusual and unique way to travel if you've never done it before, but the fact is, train travel in this part of the country is an inconsistent mode of transportation, certainly not anything to set your watch by.

BY BUS   **Greyhound** (☎ 800/231-2222) can provide you with information on specific routes to Montana's and Wyoming's most popular destinations from other cities around the country. Be sure to inquire about discounts on advanced ticket purchases and reduced fares for foreign travelers.

7 Getting Around

BY CAR   There's no better way to see Montana and Wyoming than driving, especially since so much of the best scenery is so far removed (or seems to be) from civilization. Most paved roads are well-maintained, although potholes are abundant, especially on state and county roads. Be forewarned that many of the less-accessible places require driving down dirt or gravel roads; you may want to consider renting a car instead of driving your own if you're planning on exploring these out-of-the-way places.

If you decide to rent a car, make sure it's suitable for your itinerary. A sedan or minivan is perfect for driving Going-to-the-Sun Road but wouldn't be the best choice for exploring backcountry dirt roads. A four-wheel-drive vehicle is a good choice during the winter when weather conditions can make any road treacherous.

Car rentals are available in every sizable city in the state and at airports. Widely represented agencies include **Avis** (☎ 800/831-2847), **Budget** (☎ 800/527-0700), **Dollar** (☎ 800/800-4000), and **National** (☎ 800/227-7368). We give detailed lists of car rental agencies in particular areas throughout the book.

Travel Montana provides an excellent map of Montana for free. Request one at 800/VISIT-MT or 406/444-2654. The Wyoming Division of Tourism is also a fantastic source of information. They can be reached at 800/225-5996 or 307/777-7777.

A copy of the driver's manual for Montana is available at any state licensing bureau office in the state, and the same holds true for Wyoming. While they don't cost anything, you must ask for them in person.

One particular driving fact worth noting: in Montana, the Basic Rule Law, MCA 61-8-303, which states that vehicles "shall drive in a reasonable and prudent manner depending on the conditions at the time and place of operation," took effect in December 1995. Translation: there is now no speed limit during the day;

depending upon traffic patterns, your vehicle's condition, road and weather conditions, and visibility, you can drive as fast as you please. For example, if you're traveling in a blinding snowstorm, driving 70 mph is considered unsafe and will probably get you pulled over and ticketed, but driving a brand-new car on a clear summer day along a straight stretch of highway with no traffic at 80 mph should be fine. The nighttime speed limit in Montana is 65 mph on the interstate and 55 mph on the two-lane highways.

In Wyoming the laws are gentler in some areas and firmer in others, but with the advent of the new interstate speed limit (which also went into effect in December 1995), the window of leniency has been diminished. The speed limit has increased from 65 to 75 mph (day and night, year-round), but driving 76 mph gets you a $60 ticket and driving 85 mph, a $110 ticket. The speed limits for two-lane roads throughout the state are as posted (usually 55 or 65 mph).

For information on current driving conditions in **Glacier National Park**, call 406/888-5441; in **Yellowstone National Park**, call 307/344-7381.

Going-to-the-Sun Road in Glacier National Park is closed in winter, usually from mid-October to early June, although it may open earlier or later depending on current weather and road conditions. Call the park at 406/888-5441 to find when tentative openings and closings are scheduled. During the winter, you can drive Going-to-the-Sun Road for 10 miles from West Glacier along Lake McDonald to the road closure. U.S. Highways 2 and 89—with access to East Glacier and St. Mary, respectively—are plowed regularly.

In the winter, the only access into Yellowstone National Park by car is the northern entrance in Mammoth Hot Springs, near the town of Gardiner, Montana. The west entrance, just outside the town of West Yellowstone, Montana, is open to wheeled vehicles from April to November and during the winter to snowmobiles. The south entrance is the entrance from Grand Teton National Park and is open to wheeled vehicles from May to November and to snowmobile traffic from December to March. The east entrance is 52 miles west of Cody and is open to wheeled traffic from May to September and to snowmobiles from December to March. The northeast entrance, at Cooke City, Montana, is open throughout the year to wheeled vehicles, but in the late fall, when the Beartooth Pass is closed, the only route to Cooke City is through Mammoth Hot Springs.

Take extra precautions when driving in winter, since some highways may be restricted to all-wheel-drive vehicles or those equipped with tire chains or snow tires (these highways will be clearly marked). If the transportation department or highway patrol determines that a road is hazardous, roads may be closed by a barrier. If you encounter a roadblock during winter, choose an alternate route: passing a road barrier is a misdemeanor offense and punishable by fine and/or imprisonment. Make sure your trunk is equipped with the following safety items: a shovel and a small bag of sand or cat litter in case you get stuck in snow or ice; a first-aid kit; jumper cables; wool blankets; and an ice scraper/snow brush.

Above all, drive slower, don't make any sudden turns or stops, and watch for wildlife: some animals gravitate to the warmth of asphalt during cold weather.

BY RV   If you plan to see the state by RV, write to the **Recreation Vehicle Industry Association** at P.O. Box 2999, Reston, VA 22090 (☎ 800/47-SUNNY) for the free planner "Go Camping America" or the $3 booklet titled "Set Free in an RV." The Recreation Vehicle Rental Association publishes a "Rental Ventures" booklet as well as a directory of *Who's Who in RV Rentals*. Both are available for $7.50 from

Montana Driving Distances

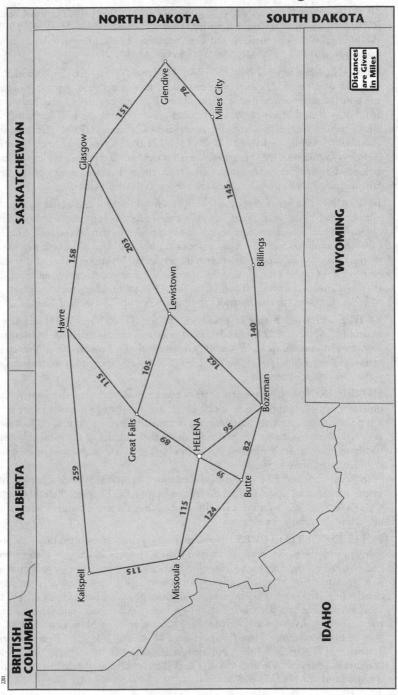

3930 University Dr., Fairfax, VA 22030 (☎ 703/591-7130). National rental RV companies include **Cruise America,** 11 W. Hampton Ave., Mesa, AZ 85210 (☎ 800/327-7799) in the U.S. and **Go Vacations,** 129 Carlingview Dr., Etobiacoke, ON M9W 5E7 (☎ 416/674-1880) in Canada.

BY PLANE   Big Sky (☎ 800/237-7788), **Horizon** (☎ 800/547-9308), and **Skywest** (☎ 800/453-6522) all provide commuter service between popular Montana cities, including the major tourist destinations—Billings, Bozeman, Great Falls, Helena, Kalispell, and Missoula—as well as various points along the Hi-Line: Glasgow, Glendive, and Havre. In Wyoming, **American** (☎ 800/433-7300), **Continental** (☎ 800/525-0280), and **Delta** (☎ 800/221-1212) all have flights, with **Frontier Airlines** (☎ 800/432-1359) providing several commuter flights. Destinations include Jackson, Casper, Cheyenne, Cody, Gillette, Laramie, Riverton, Rock Springs, and Sheridan, with Delta providing the most service to the most cities.

BY TRAIN   The only scenery you'll see by train within Montana's borders is in the northern part of the state, where Amtrak's *Empire Builder* runs east-west from Chicago to Seattle. Though not without its own appeal, this part of the state is decidedly less scenic than the more mountainous regions, and is not the best way to see what Montana is all about. Passenger train service in Wyoming is just as monotonous on the *Pioneer Line,* a route that features none of the natural wonders of the state as it crosses the southern part of the state. For more information on schedules and discount fares, contact **Amtrak**'s reservation line at (☎ 800/872-7245).

BY BUS   Rimrock Stages (a Trailways affiliate, ☎ 800/255-7655) and **Greyhound** (☎ 800/231-2222) provide daily service to locations statewide in Montana with interlinking routes. In Wyoming, **Greyhound** and **Powder River Transportation** (☎ 307/266-1904 or 800/442-3682) offer transportation to destinations within and outside the state.

HITCHHIKING   Unless you're literally on the road—between the painted lines on either side—or happen to be sticking your thumb out in a location where signs are posted to the contrary, hitchhiking is perfectly legal in Montana. For your personal safety, make sure that you are well off the shoulder of the road and watch for those signs: where designated illegal, hitchhiking is a misdemeanor offense and can carry fines of up to $500.

In Wyoming, hitchhiking is illegal and can set you back $750 and/or land in you in the slammer for up to six months. According to the Highway Patrol office in Cheyenne, fines and jail time are unlikely, but they do mean business when they ask you to get off the roadside.

FULLY ESCORTED TOURS   If you're short on time, an escorted tour may provide you with the most thorough trip, even though you'll be traveling in a large group and observing a rigid time schedule. One particular advantage is that tour companies are staffed with knowledgeable operators who will be able to enhance your understanding of the area. The following companies provide escorted tours of specific areas in Montana and Wyoming including Glacier, Yellowstone, and Grand Teton national parks. **Aventours** (☎ 406/587-5226); **Common Man Tours** (☎ 406/446-2329); **Montana's First Connection** (☎ 406/652-8839); **High Country Discovery** (☎ 406/267-3377); **Northwest Passage** (☎ 406/256-9793); **Rocky Mountain Tours** (☎ 406/862-4648); **Tauck Tours** (☎ 800/468-2825); and **Tours by Maitland** (☎ 406/755-8687).

Wyoming Driving Distances

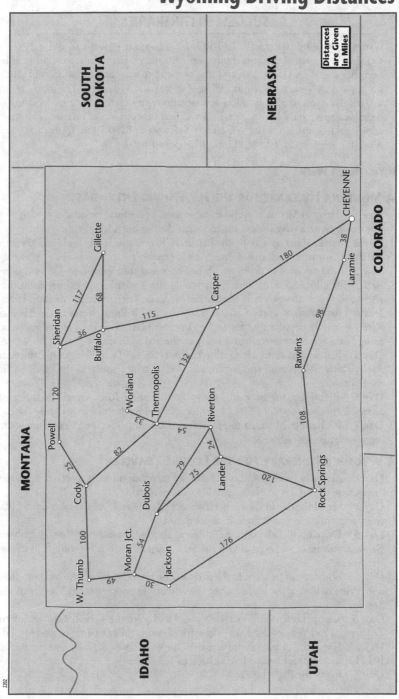

SUGGESTED ITINERARIES

Cartography enthusiasts with CD-ROM hardware may want to use a digitized topographical map as a trip-planning tool. A Rocky Mountain recreation map has been developed on CD-ROM, and it allows you to view any localized land area in portions of six Western states, including Montana and Wyoming. The topographical images allow you to plot distances and elevations and even include information on nearby campgrounds, hot springs, ski areas, and other points of interest. To request additional information, write to **Coldbay Software** at 8200 South Quebec St., Suite A3-0309, Englewood, CO 80112 or call 303/740-5407.

If You Have 1 Week

A MONTANA ITINERARY FOR THE FLY-FISHING ENTHUSIAST

Day 1   Arrive in Missoula; spend the afternoon in the local tackle shops getting the low-down on area river conditions and what the fish are hitting.

Day 2   Find a quiet spot along the Blackfoot River outside Missoula and savor the setting of Norman Maclean's *A River Runs Through It.*

Day 3   Make your way down to Three Forks and stop in at Bud Lilly's Angler's Retreat for information on what's happening along what many fishing enthusiasts refer to as the southwest's holy trinity: the Madison, Jefferson, and Missouri Rivers.

Day 4   Just south of Three Forks on Highway 287 is Ennis, home of the Madison River, an overly popular spot for anglers in these parts. Stop in at any of the shops along Main Street for anything remotely connected to fishing.

Day 5   Just west of Ennis along state Highway 287 is Twin Bridges and the Ruby River, a blue-ribbon trout stream that's not yet quite as popular as the Madison and the Jefferson.

Day 6   Before getting back to Missoula, stop off at Rock Creek. Not terribly accessible, it's just south of I-90 east of Missoula and is a favorite of many fly-fishers.

Day 7   It's back to Missoula to prepare your fables, stories, and lies before boarding your long flight home.

A WYOMING ITINERARY FOR THE LEISURE TRAVELER

Day 1   Arrive in Jackson and spend the day traveling through spectacular scenery: drive along Grand Teton National Park's Teton Road.

Day 2   Spend the day in the park. Hikes along Jenny and Jackson lakes ensure that, weather permitting, you'll grab some good shots.

Day 3   Drive up to Yellowstone and spend the day around the West Thumb and Geyser Basin areas, stopping at Old Faithful. Keep an eye out for wildlife in the late afternoons.

Day 4   This day can be spent in the park driving up to Norris via the Madison Junction. Pause to look at the buffalo along the way before stopping off at Mammoth Hot Springs.

Day 5   Come almost full circle as you head past the Grand Canyon of the Yellowstone and Yellowstone Lake before driving along the east entrance road to Cody.

Day 6   Spend the morning enjoying the Old West flavor of Cody and the Buffalo Bill Historical Center before driving back to Jackson.

Day 7   Enjoy the flight home.

If You Have 2 Weeks

A WYOMING ITINERARY FOR THE CLIMBER AND HIKER

Day 1   Arrive in Jackson, and make your way to the Tetons: check in to a climbing school.

Days 2–4   Spend these days preparing for the climb up the mighty Grand and hiking in and around the Tetons.

Days 5–6   From the Tetons, head down to the Wind River Mountains for some backpacking and climbing in an area that's one of Wyoming's better-kept secrets, before heading to Fossil Butte.

Days 7–8   Spend these two days hiking in Fossil Butte National Monument and Flaming Gorge National Recreation Area in the southwest.

Days 9–10   Spend the day driving to Devils Tower in the northeast part of the state, and the next day climbing one of the country's most unusual formations.

Day 11   Wake up early and catch some of the most magnificent pastels north of the Grand Canyon before returning west to Yellowstone country.

Days 12–13   Spend a couple of days in the Yellowstone backcountry in the mountains along the southern trails crossing the Continental Divide, Two Ocean Plateau, and the Snake River.

Day 14   Head home wearily from Jackson.

A MONTANA ITINERARY FOR THE LEISURE TRAVELER

Day 1   Arrive in Billings and spend the afternoon downtown at the Western Heritage Museum at the old Parmly Library. Shop or take a stroll in nearby Pioneer Park if it's a sunny afternoon.

Day 2   Take a one-hour drive south to Crow Agency and the site of the Battle of the Little Bighorn and Custer's Last Stand.

Day 3   Driving I-94 east to Miles City and visiting the Range Rider Museum is a must, but along the way stop off in Terry and see the photographs of frontierswoman Evelyn Cameron (*Photographing Montana*), or have a milk shake at the immaculate counter at Goplen's Bar and Cafe.

Day 4   Continue along I-94 to Glendive, perhaps the most progressive of eastern Montana's cities. Wander around, then climb back in the car for a drive through the beautiful pastels and badlands of Makoshika State Park.

Day 5   Spend the day driving on Montana Highway 200—a road stretching from one end of the state to the other—stopping off in Circle and Jordan for local color and interesting museums that house more than their share of fossils and dinosaur bones. If you keep an eye out, you may just see some misplaced (or undiscovered) advertisements from Burma Shave days.

Day 6   Continue east on MT 200 to Lewistown for a look at a virtually untarnished Montana town. The architecture isn't awe-inspiring, but neither does it center around the cheap Western facades that seem a part of every town in the new Old West. A stroll through the historic Silk Stocking district, viewing the old homes of the town's early rich makes for an interesting afternoon.

Day 7   Head northwest on Highway 87 to Great Falls and the C.M. Russell Museum Complex. An afternoon in nearby Fort Benton—a 45-minute drive north on Highway 87—is a look back at Montana's beginnings in this Missouri River town which once boasted it was the "bloodiest block in the West."

Day 8   Drive north on U.S. Hwy. 89 through Choteau and Browning to the St. Mary's entrance of Glacier National Park and spend the late afternoon driving through the incredible scenery of the park on Going-to-the-Sun Road.

Day 9   From West Glacier, Whitefish and Kalispell are a little over 30 minutes away. Whitefish is a quaint ski town in winter and a recreational hub in the summer. Whitefish Lake has plenty of room on its city beach, and a gondola ride to the summit of Big Mountain provides views over the Flathead Valley and the west side of Glacier National Park.

Day 10   Bigfork, 15 minutes south of Kalispell, is a cultural oasis in summer. Electric Avenue is full of everything from a bookstore to a playhouse, including great restaurants and a marina for those who wish to spend an afternoon or evening on Flathead Lake.

Day 11   Take state highway 35 to Polson, a shorter, though sometimes slower, route around Flathead Lake. This eastside route is full of shade and you'll see cherry trees along the roadside. From Polson head south on U.S. 93 to Missoula. Once there, spend the day on Higgins and Broadway seeing the eclectic blend of stores, then head over to the University of Montana campus. Take a hike up to the giant M on the side of Mt. Sentinel or go for a ride on the colorful horses at the brand-new carousel on the Clark Fork river's edge.

Day 12   Two hours east on I-90 takes you to Butte. Tour the Copper King Mansion, one of the most spectacular and well-maintained historic homes in the state. A visit to Butte wouldn't be complete without a walk down the tunnel to the largest and ugliest copper mine in either hemisphere, the Berkeley Pit.

Day 13   Before completing the tour, spend a day in Bozeman, the other big college town in the state. Montana State University is the biggest venue in town, and downtown has its hands full keeping up with students and newcomers. The Leaf and Bean coffee house on Main may have more pretensions than roasted beans, but is a good place for gourmet coffee nonetheless, as is the less-inflated Rocky Mountain Coffee Roaster a few blocks down on Mendenhall.

Day 14   A two-and-a-half-hour drive from Bozeman puts you back in Billings. Fly home from here.

If You Have 3 Weeks

With three weeks, of course, you can check out highlights further afield. Northwest Montana is a great place to leave your bags if you want to drive north into Canada and explore Calgary, Banff, Lake Louise, or the Columbia Icefields.

From the southwest part of the state, drive into Idaho, where Sun Valley and Ketchum are equally popular tourist destinations. Eastern Wyoming can provide a starting point for exploring the badlands of South Dakota or making an overnight trip to Mount Rushmore. Of course, from Cheyenne you can always drive into Denver to check out a Rockies game.

A MONTANA ITINERARY FOR THE BACKCOUNTRY CLIMBER & CAMPER

Days 1–7   Get yourself to Glacier National Park and obtain the necessary passes and backcountry permits. Then devote a full week to exploring the park's beautiful backcountry.

Days 8–14   From Glacier, head south and spend the next week in the Great Bear, Bob Marshall, and Mission Mountain Wilderness areas. Access to the Great Bear is easiest from the Spotted Bear Ranger station south of the Hungry Horse Reservoir. The Bob is accessible from the Swan Valley or the eastern front of the Rockies near Choteau and Augusta, but if time is an issue, the west side of the Swan may be the way to enter. The Mission Mountain Wilderness is best entered from Lindberg Lake Road south of Condon in the Swan Valley.

Days 15–21   If you're up for a final week of backcountry hiking, head for the Rattlesnake Wilderness Area and the Welcome Creek Wilderness Area, both located near Missoula. From there, board the plane and put your feet up.

A WYOMING ITINERARY FOR THE LEISURE TRAVELER

Much like the two-week itinerary for Montana, the three-week Wyoming tour takes you on a more detailed loop tour of the state.

Day 1   The first day in Jackson can be spent browsing around downtown, checking out the local color in myriad shops and restaurants.

Days 2–7   Drive north to Grand Teton National Park where you'll pick up a pass for both Grand Teton and Yellowstone National Parks. Spend the entire week in these parks, taking them a section at a time or maneuvering back and forth. Geyser gazing, wildlife photography, and quick and beautiful hikes throughout the parks will easily fill a week.

Day 8   The second week kicks off in Cody, home and namesake of Buffalo Bill Cody, world-famous traveling performer. The Buffalo Bill Historical Center is a must-see.

Days 9–11   From Cody, catch a glimpse of the spectacular Wind River Mountain Range at South Pass City on your way to Kemmerer and Fossil Butte National Monument. Take time to fish at the Flaming Gorge National Recreation Area on your way to Laramie and Cheyenne. If you've timed your trip just right, Frontier Days in Cheyenne is just beginning. Attend a rodeo and a country music concert. If you've never been to a rodeo, this is the one to see.

Days 12–14   Via Casper and Gillette, head north to the Devils Tower National Monument, one of the most inconveniently located landmarks in the country.

Days 15–21   Spend the third week moving slowly across the top of the state through Sheridan, Shell Canyon, the Bighorn Canyon, and Thermopolis (great hot springs!), before heading back to Jackson, where you'll catch your flight home.

FAST FACTS: Montana & Wyoming

American Express   American Express travel service representatives are located across the state. To automatically connect with the nearest agent, call 800/937-2639.

Area Code   The statewide area code for Montana is 406. The Wyoming area code is 307. Intrastate long-distance calls also require these prefixes.

Banks and ATM Networks   Banks in Montana and Wyoming are generally open Monday through Thursday from 9am to 4pm with extended hours to 6pm on Fridays. Some are open on Saturdays from 9am to noon. They are closed on Sundays. Automatic teller machines are generally available for cash transactions at any time of the day; most are compatible with Cirrus, Cash Card, and Plus system networks.

Business Hours   Most businesses in the states operate at least five days each week and many are also open on weekends. Generally speaking, retail shops open around 10am and close at 6pm. During the two peak tourist seasons in summer and winter, many businesses extend their hours. On the other hand, don't be surprised to find a hastily penned note on the door if the snow or sunshine conditions are perfect (and they often are): many business owners have been known to take their share of "powder days" with no advance notice.

Car Rentals See "Getting Around," earlier in this chapter.

Climate See "When to Go," earlier in this chapter.

Driving Rules See "Getting Around," earlier in this chapter.

Emergencies Throughout most of Montana and Wyoming, call 911 for any emergency requiring the police, firefighters, or emergency medical technicians. Where 911 is not available, dial 0 and the operator will connect you to the appropriate emergency service provider.

Gambling You must be at least 18 years old to gamble in Montana. With video gambling machines located anywhere from Pizza Hut to the local bar downtown, you're never very far from a quick game. The two most popular are poker and keno, a game of chance similar to bingo. Although some bars have real poker tables, old-fashioned keno message boards are disappearing and are most likely to be found in bars or restaurants on the eastern side of the state. In Wyoming, gambling is illegal (though the issue seems always on the table).

Information See "Visitor Information & Money," earlier in this chapter.

Liquor Laws The legal age for the purchase or consumption of alcohol is 21. All liquor stores in Montana and Wyoming are state-controlled with minimum hours of 10am to 6pm, although individual stores may be open longer. Most are closed on Sundays and Mondays. Liquor may also be bought at bars with package licenses during their operating hours. Beer is available at convenience stores and supermarkets from 8am to 2am.

Lodging The following companies provide reservation services for statewide lodging options in Montana and Wyoming: **Room Search Network** (☎ 800/869-7666); **America's Lodging Network** (☎ 800/341-8000); **Adventure Connections of Montana** (☎ 800/441-2286); **Adventures in Montana** (☎ 800/473-4343); and **American West Adventures** (☎ 800/952-9996). For a central reservations service representing over 60 facilities in the Flathead Valley, call 406/862-5500. **AHH-West** can book you a room at one of the West's premier historic hotels. Call 303/546-9040 for more information on this lodging option in the Rocky Mountains. **Bed & Breakfast Western Adventure** (☎ 406/585-0557) is a reservation service devoted to bed-and-breakfast inns, homes, and ranches in Montana, Wyoming, and Idaho—each listing has been interviewed and inspected—and is one of the region's most trusted consultants.

Newspapers/Magazines There are three major newspapers in Montana and at least one of them will be available wherever you may find yourself in the state: The *Missoulian,* the *Great Falls Tribune,* and the *Billings Gazette.* Other national and international newspapers are much harder to find. A regional edition of the *Wall Street Journal* is available in most bigger towns and cities but any copy of *The New York Times* you may stumble upon is almost guaranteed to be one week late. In Wyoming, the *Casper Star-Tribune* covers a huge chunk of the state. The *Wyoming Tribune-Eagle* is Cheyenne's daily and in northcentral Wyoming you'll likely have better luck with the *Billings Gazette.*

Pets Pets are sometimes allowed at hotels in these two states—much more often than in the rest of the country. Check out *Frommer's America on Wheels: Northwest & Great Plains* (Macmillan, $14.95), a directory-style guide that uses easily spotted icons to indicate hostelries where Fido is welcome. Dogs are not allowed in many parks and recreational areas, though, and if that's the case, please don't break the rules—it's usually a matter of safety, since many of these areas are in bear country.

Police   Dial 911 or 0 (for the operator) to reach the police.

Safety   While driving through Montana and Wyoming, it is a good idea to carry plenty of water, both for drinking and for your car. Cities are often separated by great distances, although you'll find that people who live in the more remote areas of the state are usually very helpful to stranded motorists. If traveling in the winter, make sure there are plenty of warm blankets in the trunk.

Taxes   There is currently no sales tax in Montana, although the issue is usually debated around election time. There is, however, a resort tax imposed on gift and souvenir-type items in certain resort communities around the state. Wyoming's sales tax is 4% statewide.

Time Zone   Montana and Wyoming are located in the mountain time zone and both states observe daylight saving time from spring to fall.

Weather   See "When to Go" earlier in this chapter.

4 For Foreign Visitors

American fads and fashions have spread across other parts of the world to such a degree that the United States may seem like familiar territory before your arrival. But there are still many peculiarities and uniquely American situations any foreign visitor may find confusing or perplexing. This chapter will provide some specifics about getting to the United States as economically and effortlessly as possible, plus some helpful information about how things are done in Montana and Wyoming—from receiving mail to making a local or long-distance telephone call.

1 Preparing for Your Trip

ENTRY REQUIREMENTS

DOCUMENT REGULATIONS   Canadian nationals need only proof of Canadian residence to visit the United States. Citizens of the United Kingdom and Japan need only a current passport. Citizens of other countries, including Australia and New Zealand, usually need two documents: a valid passport with an expiration date at least six months later than the scheduled end of their visit to the United States and a tourist visa available at no charge from a U.S. embassy or consulate.

To get a tourist or business visa to enter the United States, contact the nearest American embassy or consulate in your country; if there is none, you will have to apply in person in a country where there is a U.S. embassy or consulate. Present your passport, a passport-size photo of yourself, and a completed application, which is available through the embassy or consulate. You may be asked to provide information about how you plan to finance your trip or show a letter of invitation from a friend with whom you plan to stay. Those applying for a business visa may be asked to show evidence that they will not receive a salary in the United States. Be sure to check the length of stay on your visa; usually it is six months. If you want to stay longer, you may file for an extension with the Immigration and Naturalization Service once you are in the country. If permission to stay is granted, a new visa is not required unless you leave the United States and want to reenter.

MEDICAL REQUIREMENTS   No inoculations are needed to enter the United States unless you are coming from, or have stopped over in, areas known to be suffering from epidemics, particularly cholera or yellow fever.

If you have a disease requiring treatment with medications containing narcotics or drugs requiring a syringe, carry a valid, signed generic prescription from your physician to allay any suspicions that you are smuggling drugs. The prescription brands you are accustomed to buying in your country may not be available in the United States.

CUSTOMS REQUIREMENTS   Every adult visitor may bring in, free of duty: 1 liter of wine or hard liquor; 200 cigarettes or 100 cigars (but no cigars from Cuba) or 3 pounds of smoking tobacco; and $100 worth of gifts. These exemptions are offered to travelers who spend at least 72 hours in the United States and who have not claimed them within the preceding 6 months. Foreign tourists may bring in or take out up to $10,000 in U.S. or foreign currency with no formalities; larger sums must be declared to Customs on entering or leaving.

It is altogether forbidden to bring foodstuffs (particularly cheese, fruit, cooked meats, and canned goods) and plants (vegetables, seeds, tropical plants, and so on) into the country. The exception is Canada, from which most foods (except citrus fruits) and plants are allowed to be brought into Montana. However, if you are unsure about a particular item, ask the port official at the Customs Service where you are entering for a publication titled "Know Before You Go" or contact the USDA/ Plant Protection Quarantine at the following address: Federal Building, 6505 Belcrest Rd., Hyattsville, MD 20782 (☎ 301/436-7472).

All visitors from Canada are required to report to U.S. customs when entering the States and to report to Canadian customs when returning. There are three 24-hour service ports of entry into Canada from Montana, located at Roosville (☎ 406/ 889-3865), Sweetgrass (☎ 406/335-2434), and Raymond (☎ 406/895-2664). Additionally, there are 12 seasonal ports, all of which have varying hours and dates of operation. For information on whether or not a specific seasonal port is open, contact one of the above 24-hour service ports of entry.

INSURANCE

Unlike most other countries, the United States does not have a national health system. Because the cost of medical care is extremely high, we strongly advise all travelers to secure health coverage before setting out on their trip.

You may want to take out a comprehensive travel policy that covers (for a relatively low premium) sickness or injury costs (medical, surgical, and hospital); loss or theft of your baggage; trip-cancellation costs; guarantee of bail in case you are arrested; costs of accident, repatriation, or death. Such packages (for example, "Europe Assistance" in Europe) are sold by automobile clubs at attractive rates, as well as by insurance companies and travel agencies and at some airports.

MONEY

The U.S. monetary system has a decimal base: One American dollar ($1) = 100 cents (100¢). Dollar bills commonly come in $1 (a buck), $5, $10, $20, $50, and $100 denominations (the last two are not welcome when paying for small purchases and are usually not accepted in taxis or on buses). There are six coin denominations: 1¢ (one cent, or a penny); 5¢ (five cents, or a nickel); 10¢ (ten cents, or a dime); 25¢ (twenty-five cents, or a quarter); 50¢ (fifty cents, or half dollar; rarely used); and the $1 pieces (both the older, large silver dollar and the newer, small Susan B. Anthony coin; rarely used).

You can telegraph money or have it telegraphed to you very quickly using the **Western Union** system (☎ 800/325-6000).

TRAVELER'S CHECKS   Traveler's checks in U.S. dollars are accepted at most hotels, motels, restaurants, and large stores. Sometimes picture identification is required. American Express, Thomas Cook, and Barclay's Bank traveler's checks are readily accepted in the United States.

CREDIT CARDS   Credit cards are the method of payment most widely used: Visa (BarclayCard in Britain), MasterCard (EuroCard in Europe, Access in Britain, Diamond in Japan), American Express, Discover, Diners Club, enRoute, JCB, and Carte Blanche, in descending order of acceptance. You can save yourself trouble by using plastic rather than cash or traveler's checks in 95% of all hotels, motels, restaurants, and retail stores. A credit card can also serve as a deposit for renting a car, as proof of identity, or as a "cash card," enabling you to draw money from automatic-teller machines (ATMs) that accept them.

If you plan to travel for several weeks or more in the United States, you may want to deposit enough money into your credit card account to cover anticipated expenses and avoid finance charges in your absence. This also reduces the likelihood of receiving an unwelcome big bill on your return.

SAFETY

Though Montana and Wyoming are by no means crime-free, your chance of being robbed in these states is smaller than in most parts of the country. Urban areas are, statistically speaking, the most likely places for you to be robbed, burgled, or pickpocketed—and Montana and Wyoming are noticeably short on metropolitan areas. Common sense is the best weapon against criminals in Montana and Wyoming. Don't stray into dangerous-looking neighborhoods; don't flaunt cash, credit cards, or traveler's checks; and don't leave your car unlocked with items of any significance sitting out in the open.

Safety while driving is particularly important. Question your rental agency about personal safety, or ask for a brochure of traveler safety tips when you pick up your car. Obtain written directions, or a map with the route marked in red, from the agency showing how to get to your destination. And, if possible, arrive and depart during daylight hours.

With the recent change in speed limits, the highways in these two states have become something of an autobahn. In Montana, there are no daylight speed limits on the interstates. Always wear your seat belt, rent cars with airbags whenever possible, and try not to break land speed records.

Recently more and more crime has involved cars and drivers. If you drive off a highway into a doubtful neighborhood, leave the area as quickly as possible. If you have an accident, even on the highway, stay in your car with the doors locked until you assess the situation or until the police arrive. If you are bumped from behind on the street or are involved in a minor accident with no injuries and the situation appears to be suspicious, motion to the other driver to follow you. Never get out of your car in such situations.

If you see someone on the road who indicates a need for help, do not stop. Take note of the location, drive on to a well-lighted area, and telephone the police by dialing **911.** Park in well-lighted, well-traveled areas if possible.

Always keep your car doors locked, whether attended or unattended. Never leave any packages or valuables in sight. If someone attempts to rob you or steal your car, do not try to resist the thief/carjacker—report the incident to the police department immediately.

2 Getting to the U.S.

Travelers from overseas can take advantage of the APEX (advance purchase excursion) fares offered by all the major U.S. and European carriers. Aside from these, attractive values are offered by Virgin Atlantic from London.

A number of U.S. airlines offer service from Europe to the United States. Most major metropolitan airports throughout the country offer nonstop service to and from one another, although each airline has a different hub city through which flights to smaller destinations often are routed, regardless of how out-of-the-way the route seems.

Therefore, regardless where you're flying from, you will inevitably pass through Spokane, Seattle, or Portland if you're traveling to Montana on Northwest; or through Salt Lake City, Utah, if you're traveling to Wyoming on Delta. Getting to Montana and Wyoming is challenging at best, requiring most of a day's travel *after* you've officially arrived in the country.

The airports in these two states are tiny compared to metropolitan airports, but service is dependable and safe, even in winter months when the weather contributes an added amount of travel anxiety. Inquire as to the type of planes you will be traveling on when you make your reservation; some flights connect with small commuter planes that may not be acceptable to some travelers.

There are airports in Montana in Billings, Bozeman, Great Falls, Helena, Kalispell, or Missoula. Air service to these airports is provided by the following airlines, although only Billings can boast of service from all three: **Delta** (☎ 0800/414-767 in or outside the U.K.); **Northwest Airlines** (☎ 0129/356-1000 in or outside the U.K.); and **United** (☎ 0181/990-9900 in or outside the U.K.). In Wyoming, Jackson, Casper, Cheyenne, Cody, Gillette, Laramie, Riverton, Rock Springs, and Sheridan all have airports with commercial intrastate airline service as well as a couple of points beyond. **American** (☎ 0181/572-5555 in or outside the U.K.); **Continental** (☎ 4412/9377-6464 in or outside the U.K.); and **Delta** all have Wyoming flights.

And of course many international carriers serve major cities in the United States. Helpful numbers to know include **Virgin Atlantic** (☎ 0293/747-747 in London), **British Airways** (☎ 0345/222-111 in London), and **Aer Lingus** (☎ 01/844-4747 in Dublin or 061/415-556 in Shannon). **Qantas** (☎ 008/177-767 in Australia) has flights from Sydney to Los Angeles and San Francisco; you can also take United from Australia to the West Coast. **Air New Zealand** (☎ 0800/737-000 in Auckland or 64-3/379-5200 in Christchurch) also offers service to LAX. Canadian readers might book flights on **Air Canada** (☎ in Canada 800/268-7240 or 800/361-8620), which offers direct service from Toronto, Montréal, Calgary, and Vancouver to San Francisco, Sacramento, Los Angeles, and San Diego.

The visitor arriving by air, no matter what the port of entry, should cultivate patience and resignation before setting foot on U.S. soil. Getting through immigration control may take as long as two hours on some days, especially summer weekends, so have your guidebook or something else to read handy. Add the time it takes to clear customs and you will see you should make a very generous allowance for delays in planning connections between international and domestic flights—figure on two to three hours at least.

In contrast, for the traveler arriving by car or by rail from Canada, the border-crossing formalities have been streamlined to the vanishing point. And for the traveler by air from Canada, Bermuda, and some places in the Caribbean, you can sometimes go through Customs and Immigration at the point of departure, which is much quicker.

3 Getting Around the U.S.

BY PLANE   On their transatlantic or transpacific flights, some large U.S. airlines offer special discount tickets for any of their U.S. destinations (American Airlines' Visit USA program and Delta's Discover America program, for example). The tickets or coupons are not on sale in the United States and must be purchased before you leave your point of departure. This system is the best, easiest, and fastest way to see the United States at low cost. You should obtain information well in advance from your travel agent or the office of the airline concerned, since the conditions attached to these discount tickets can be changed without advance notice.

For information about flights around Montana and Wyoming once you're there, see the "Getting Around" section of Chapter 3.

BY CAR   See Chapter 3 for information on rentals and general driving tips.

Auto clubs will supply maps, suggested routes, guidebooks, accident and bail-bond insurance, and emergency road service. The major auto club in the United States, with 955 offices nationwide, is the **American Automobile Association (AAA).** Members of some foreign auto clubs have reciprocal arrangements with the AAA and enjoy its services at no charge. If you belong to an auto club, inquire about AAA reciprocity before you leave. The AAA can provide you with an International Driving Permit validating your foreign license, although drivers with valid licenses from most home countries don't really need this permit. You may be able to join the AAA even if you are not a member of a reciprocal club. To inquire, call 619/233-1000. In addition, some car rental agencies now provide these services, so you should inquire about their availability when you rent.

BY TRAIN   International visitors can also buy a **USA Railpass,** good for 15 or 30 days of unlimited travel on **Amtrak.** The pass is available through many foreign travel agents. Prices in 1995 for a 15-day pass were $229 off-peak, $340 peak; a 30-day pass was $339 off-peak, $425 peak (off-peak is August 31 to June 15). (With a foreign passport, you can also buy passes at some Amtrak offices in the United States including locations in San Francisco, Los Angeles, Chicago, New York, Miami, Boston, and Washington, D.C.) Reservations are generally required and should be made for each part of your trip as early as possible.

Visitors should also be aware of the limitations of long-distance rail travel in the United States. With a few notable exceptions, service is rarely up to European standards: delays are common, routes are limited and often infrequently served, and fares are rarely significantly lower than discount airfares. Thus, cross-country train travel should be approached with caution.

BY BUS   The cheapest way to travel the United States is by bus. **Greyhound/ Trailways,** the sole nationwide bus line, offers an **Ameripass** for unlimited travel for 7 days (for $359), 15 days (for $459), and 30 days (for $559). Bus travel in the United States can be both slow and uncomfortable, so this option is not for everyone. In Montana and Wyoming, where distances are vast, this is not your best choice.

FAST FACTS: For the Foreign Traveler

Business Hours   Offices are usually open weekdays from 9am to 5pm. Banks are open weekdays from 9am to 3pm or later and sometimes Saturday morning.

Shops, especially those in shopping complexes, tend to stay open late: until about 9pm weekdays and until 6pm weekends.

Climate   See "When to Go" in Chapter 3.

Currency   See "Preparing for Your Trip," earlier in this chapter.

Currency Exchange   The foreign-exchange bureaus so common in Europe are rare in the United States. They're at major international airports, and there are a few in most major cities, but they're nonexistent in medium-size cities and small towns. Try to avoid having to change foreign money, or traveler's checks denominated other than in U.S. dollars, at small-town banks, or even at branches in a big city; in fact, leave any currency other than U.S. dollars at home (except the cash you need for the taxi or bus ride home when you return to your own country); otherwise, your own currency may prove more nuisance to you than it's worth.

Drinking Laws   The legal age to drink alcohol is 21.

Electric Current   The United States uses 110–120 volts, 60 cycles, compared to 220–240 volts, 50 cycles, as in most of Europe. Besides a 100-volt converter, small appliances of non-American manufacture, such as hair dryers or shavers, will require a plug adapter, with two flat, parallel pins. The easiest solution to the power struggle is to purchase dual voltage appliances that operate on both 110 and 220 volts; then all that is required is a U.S. adapter plug.

Embassies/Consulates   There are no embassies or consulates in Montana or Wyoming. Most countries have an embassy in Washington D.C., with a consulate in other major cities around the country such Chicago, San Francisco, Los Angeles, Houston, and New York. Make sure to acquire the address and telephone number of your nation's embassy and the address and telephone number of the nearest consulate before your arrival in the United States.

Emergencies   Call 911 for fire, police, and ambulance. If you encounter such traveler's problems as sickness, accident, or lost or stolen baggage, call Traveler's Aid, an organization that specializes in helping distressed travelers. (Check local directories for the location nearest you.) U.S. hospitals have emergency rooms, with a special entrance where you will be admitted for quick attention.

Gasoline (Petrol)   One U.S. gallon equals 3.75 liters, while 1.2 U.S. gallons equals 1 imperial gallon. A gallon of unleaded gas, which most rental cars accept, costs about $1.30 if you fill your own tank (self-service); about 10¢ more if the station attendant does it (called full-service).

Holidays   On the following national legal holidays, banks, government offices, post offices, and many stores, restaurants, and museums are closed: January 1 (New Year's Day), third Monday in January (Martin Luther King, Jr. Day), third Monday in February (Presidents' Day), last Monday in May (Memorial Day), July 4 (Independence Day), first Monday in September (Labor Day), second Monday in October (Columbus Day), November 11 (Veterans' Day/Armistice Day), last Thursday in November (Thanksgiving Day), and December 25 (Christmas Day). The Tuesday following the first Monday in November is Election Day.

Internet Resources   With the increase in popularity of Internet and on-line services, there are more and more places to send and receive documents or buy on-line time to search the World Wide Web or send e-mail. Though there are few in Montana and Wyoming (mainly at universities), data outlets for your laptop computer are becoming more popular in hotel rooms.

Legal Aid If you are stopped for a minor infraction (for example, of the highway code, such as speeding), never attempt to pay the fine directly to a police officer; you may be arrested on the much more serious charge of attempted bribery. Pay fines by mail, or directly into the hands of the clerk of the court. If accused of a more serious offense, it is best to say and do nothing before consulting a lawyer. Under U.S. law, an arrested person is allowed one telephone call to a party of his or her choice. Call your embassy or consulate.

Mail Mailboxes are blue with a red-and-white logo, and carry the inscription "U.S. MAIL." Within the United States, it costs 20¢ to mail a standard-size postcard and 32¢ to send an oversize postcard (larger than 4¹/₄ by 6 inches, or 10.8 by 15.4 centimeters). Letters that weigh up to 1 ounce (that's about five 8-by-11-inch, or 20.5-by-28.2-centimeter, pages) cost 32¢, plus 23¢ for each additional ounce. A postcard to Mexico costs 30¢, a ¹/₂-ounce letter 35¢; a postcard to Canada costs 30¢, a 1-ounce letter 40¢. A postcard to Europe, Australia, New Zealand, the Far East, South America, and elsewhere costs 40¢, while a letter is 50¢ for each ¹/₂ ounce.

Medical Emergencies See "Emergencies" above.

Taxes In the United States there is no VAT (value-added tax) or other indirect tax at a national level. There is a $10 customs tax, payable on entry to the United States, and a $6 departure tax. Sales tax is levied on goods and services by state and local governments, however, and is *not* included in the price tags you'll see on merchandise. These taxes are not refundable.

Telephone and Fax It's not uncommon to see a cluster of pay phones for public use waiting around every corner in Montana and Wyoming. Usually you can find one inside a convenience store, in a bar, at a gas station, in restaurants, or in hotel lobbies. Local calls cost 25¢ and the cost per minute for long-distance calls is graciously given by automated voice when your paid time has expired.

The statewide area code for Montana is 406. The Wyoming area code is 307. Intrastate long-distance calls also require these prefixes. Area codes for other states are found in the front of telephone directories.

In the past few years, many American companies have installed voice-mail systems, so be prepared to deal with a machine instead of a receptionist if calling a business number. Listen carefully to the instructions (you'll probably be asked to dial 1, 2, or 3 or wait for an operator to pick up).

For long-distance or international calls, it's most economical to charge the call to a telephone charge card or a credit card; or you can use a lot of change. The pay phone will instruct you how much to deposit and when to deposit it into the slot on the top of the telephone box.

For long-distance calls in the United States, dial 1 followed by the area code and number you want. For direct overseas calls, first dial 011, followed by the country code (Australia, 61; Republic of Ireland, 353; New Zealand, 64; United Kingdom, 44; and so on), and then by the city code (for example, 71 or 81 for London, 21 for Birmingham, 1 for Dublin) and the number of the person you wish to call.

Before calling from a hotel room, always ask the hotel phone operator if there are any telephone surcharges. There almost always are, and they often are as much as 75¢ or $1, even for a local call. These charges are best avoided by using a public phone, calling collect, or using a telephone charge card.

For reversed-charge or collect calls and for person-to-person calls, dial 0 (zero, not the letter "O") followed by the area code and number you want; an operator will then come on the line, and you should specify that you are calling collect, or person-to-person, or both. If your operator-assisted call is international, immediately ask to speak with an overseas operator.

For local directory assistance ("Information"), dial **411;** for long-distance information dial **1,** then the appropriate area code and 555-1212.

Most hotels have fax machines available for their customers and there is usually a charge to send or receive a facsimile. You will also see signs for public faxes in the windows of small shops.

Time Zones   The United States is separated into six time zones: EST or Eastern Standard Time (New York, Atlanta, Charlotte), CST or Central Standard Time (Chicago, St. Louis, Houston), MST or Mountain Standard Time (Montana and Wyoming, Denver, Phoenix), PST or Pacific Standard Time (Seattle, San Francisco, Los Angeles), AST or Alaska Standard Time, and HST or Hawaii Standard Time. Eastern Standard Time is five hours behind Greenwich Mean Time, Central Standard Time six hours behind, Mountain Standard Time seven hours behind, and so on. Spring travelers should also bear in mind that Montana and Wyoming, like most U.S. states, both observe daylight saving time. On the first Sunday in April, clocks in the United States are turned forward one hour for daylight saving and then turned back one hour the last Sunday in October.

Tipping   Some rules of thumb: bartenders, 10–15%; bellhops, at least 50¢ per bag, or $2–$3 for a lot of luggage; cab drivers, 10% of the fare; cafeterias and fast-food restaurants, no tip; chambermaids, $1 per day; checkroom attendants, $1 per garment; theater ushers, no tip; gas-station attendants, no tip; hairdressers and barbers, 15–20%; waiters and waitresses, 15–20% of the check; valet parking attendants, $1.

Toilets   In big cities, restrooms can sometimes be hard to find and when you do come across one, they're reserved for customers or employees. Not so in Montana and Wyoming. Usually, if there are signs of civilization, a restroom can be found, even though along the interstates these signs can be few and very far between.

5 Glacier National Park

So named because of the 48 slow-moving glaciers that continue to carve valleys throughout its incredible expanse of nearly a million wild acres, Glacier National Park exists because of the efforts of George Bird Grinnell, co-founder of the Audubon Society. Grinnell lobbied for a national park to be set aside in Montana's St. Mary region, and in May 1910 his efforts were rewarded. Just over twenty years later, it became, with its northern neighbor Waterton Lakes National Park in Canada, the world's first international park—Glacier-Waterton International Peace Park—a gesture of goodwill and friendship between the governments of two countries.

The defining characteristic of this vast wilderness preserve is diversity. Majestic and wild, it has overwhelmed visitors for decades. Yet now, years of tourism are taking their toll. While economies in the surrounding areas profit from the park, the park itself does a delicate balancing act to maintain its dual personality as tourist attraction and nature preserve.

Going-to-the-Sun Road, the 50-mile road that traverses the park in slow curves through splendid scenery, has been a concern of park officials over the last few years. In 1995, portions of the road were washed out when avalanches came crashing down, creating early summer season havoc for tourists and park officials alike.

Glacier isn't immune from the congested gateway communities that surround so many of our national parks, but, unlike some of the other major preserves, its environs have not experienced an overwhelming flood of development.

Once you're inside, Glacier is like no other national park in the Lower 48. From the incredible wildflowers that coat the springtime meadows to the astonishing peaks that remain snowcapped even in summer, Glacier is a postcard come to life, one that, for the most part, faithfully continues in the tradition Grinnell started. Moose and elks still roam the land and can be found virtually anywhere. But the unofficial mascot in these parts is the grizzly, a refugee from the High Plains who now inhabits the Montana mountains.

1 Just the Facts

GETTING THERE

The closest cities to the park with airline service are Kalispell, 29 miles southwest of the park; and Great Falls, 143 miles southeast of the park.

Glacier National Park

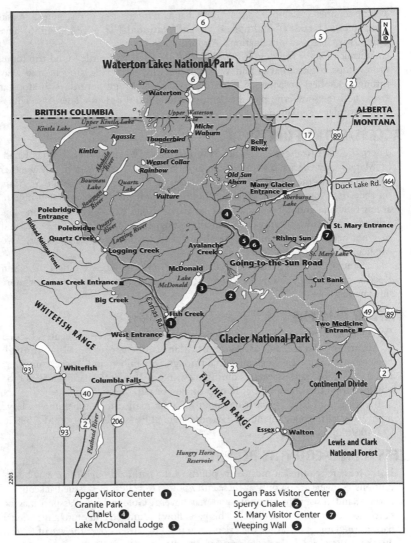

Apgar Visitor Center ❶	Logan Pass Visitor Center ❻
Granite Park	Sperry Chalet ❷
Chalet ❹	St. Mary Visitor Center ❼
Lake McDonald Lodge ❸	Weeping Wall ❺

Glacier Park International Airport, north of Kalispell at 4170 U.S. Hwy. 2 (☎ 406/257-5994), is serviced by **Skywest** (☎ 800/453-9417), **Delta** (☎ 800/221-1212), with daily flights via Salt Lake City, and **Horizon** (☎ 800/547-9308), with daily flights from Seattle, Portland, and Spokane, Washington. **Northwest** (☎ 800/225-2525) has a code-sharing agreement with Horizon, which enables passengers to fly into Spokane on Northwest and connect to a Horizon flight into Kalispell, while earning miles on Northwest.

Great Falls International Airport (☎ 406/727-3404) has daily service on **Delta** through Salt Lake City, **Northwest**, through Spokane, **Horizon,** and **Frontier** (☎ 800/432-1359).

If you're driving, you can reach the park from U.S. 2 and 89. Rental cars are available in Kalispell, Great Falls, Whitefish, East Glacier, and West Glacier. **Avis** (☎ 800/831-2847), **Budget** (☎ 800/527-0700), and **National** (☎ 800/227-7368) all have counters at Kalispell's airport (see Chapter 6 for a listing of discount car rental companies). **Hertz** (☎ 800/654-3131) and **National** (☎ 406/453-4386) have counters at Great Falls International Airport.

Amtrak's *Empire Builder* (☎ 800/872-7245), a Chicago-Seattle round-trip route, makes stops at East Glacier and West Glacier when the park is open (mid-May through October) on Mondays, Wednesdays, Fridays, and Saturdays. It stops at Essex, near the southern tip of the park, year-round, but only on Tuesdays, Thursdays, Saturdays, and Sundays.

ACCESS/ENTRY POINTS

There are six entrances to Glacier National Park: West Glacier, Camas Road, St. Mary, Many Glacier, Two Medicine, and Polebridge. Access is primarily at either end of Going-to-the-Sun Road: at West Glacier on the southwest side and St. Mary on the east. From the park's western boundary, you may enter at Polebridge to access Bowman and Kintla Lakes or take Camas Road to Going-to-the-Sun. The following east-side entrances are primarily designed to access specific places and may not necessarily take you into the heart of the park: Essex, East Glacier, Two Medicine, Cut Bank, and Many Glacier.

Entrance is severely restricted during winter months when Going-to-the-Sun Road is closed. See Section 3, "Driving the Park," later in this chapter for more information.

VISITOR CENTERS

For up-to-date information on park activities, check with the visitor centers located at Apgar, Logan Pass, and St. Mary. St. Mary is open from mid-May through September; Logan Pass, from mid-June through September; and Apgar, from May through October (and weekends during the winter). Park information may also be obtained from the Many Glacier Ranger Station or park headquarters.

If you wish to have information about the park mailed to you before you leave home, contact the Superintendent, Glacier National Park, West Glacier, MT 59936 (☎ 406/888-5441).

FEES & BACKCOUNTRY PERMITS

Entry fees are required at most entry points to the park, although there may be exceptions. Rangers are on duty at these entry points to collect fees, issue backcountry permits, and answer any questions you may have. A Golden Eagle Passport may be purchased for an annual fee of $25. This pass allows unlimited entry into any national park in the United States for the calendar year. U.S. citizens over the age of 62 can purchase the Golden Age Passport, which allows unlimited access to any U.S. national park for a one-time fee of $10. And for travelers with disabilities, there's the Golden Access Passport, which offers the same unlimited access, and is available free of charge. A season pass may be purchased for $15 that allows unlimited entry to Glacier National Park for the calendar year. A daily pass costs $5 and is good for seven days. A pass for walk-ins, bicycles, and motorcycles, also good for seven days, is available for $3. Fees are per vehicle, not per person. A separate entrance fee is charged for visitors to Waterton Lakes National Park.

Backcountry permits must be obtained in person from the visitor centers at Apgar and St. Mary, or the ranger station at Many Glacier. Permits may be obtained no earlier than 24 hours before your trip during the summer months. There is no fee for backcountry camping; trips are limited to six nights, with no more than three nights allowed at each campground. If you plan on camping with a group, keep the group small. Campsites are limited and a single site has a maximum occupancy of four persons. Groups of five have to reserve two campsites, which can be tricky during the crowded summer months.

In winter, due to lower demand, camping permits are available up to seven days in advance. There are a few rules that do take effect beginning each November 20: no wood fires, due to the dead and down fuel covered by snow; party sizes are limited to 12 people with a two-night limit for any one spot; and camping is restricted within 100 feet of any roadway, trail corridor, creek, or lake. Camping is prohibited on vegetation freshly emerging from snow.

REGULATIONS

The following regulations apply. More detailed information about these regulations can be requested from the park superintendent.

BIKES   Bikes are restricted to established roads, bike routes, or parking areas, and are not allowed on trails. Restrictions apply to the most hazardous portions of Going-to-the-Sun Road during peak travel times from around mid-June to Labor Day; call ahead to find out when the road will be closed to bikers. During low-visibility periods such as fog or darkness, a white front light and a back red reflector are required.

BOATING   While boating is permitted on some of Glacier's lakes, motor size is restricted to 10hp on most. The park will provide you with a detailed list of other regulations, available at park headquarters and staffed ranger stations. Park rangers may inspect or board any boat to examine licenses and any permits, if necessary, to determine regulation compliance.

CAMPING   Camping is permitted only at designated locations and is strictly prohibited on the roadside. See also information regarding backcountry permits above.

FISHING   Anglers may be surprised to know that a fishing license is not required within the park's boundaries. Yet there are detailed regulations regarding fishing in Glacier, which are available for free from the park's superintendent. You can also receive daily catch limits and release policies for specific species at no charge. Additional information is available for a small fee.

HORSES   While visitors may bring their own horses and pack animals into the park, restrictions apply to private stock. A free brochure detailing regulations regarding riding horseback is available from the park service.

PETS   All pets must be on a leash no longer than 6 feet, and under physical restraint or caged while in the park. Pets are not allowed indoors at any of the park's gift shops, restaurants, or visitor centers, or on any trails.

VEHICLES   There are vehicle size restrictions for Going-to-the-Sun Road, listed later in this chapter in the section "Driving the Park." No wheeled vehicles are allowed on park trails, and that includes bicycles.

SHUTTLE-BUS SERVICE WITHIN THE PARK

Going-to-the Sun Shuttle Bus Service (☎ 406/862-2539) runs mid-size historic motorcoaches from virtually every major picnic area and campground to other points in the park. Costs for the shuttle service range from $2 for a short distance to $14 for a one-way long-distance excursion. If you plan to use the shuttle extensively, a one-day unlimited pass may be purchased for $28. Unlimited two-day passes may be purchased for $35. Children under 12 ride for half-price, and babies ride free. The maximum price for a family traveling one-way is $50. Reservations are recommended.

CHALETS

Two of the park's most popular destinations, Granite Park and Sperry Chalets—National Historic Landmarks built by the Great Northern Railway between 1912 and 1914—were closed in 1993 because of substandard sewage and water systems. Now the subjects of an extensive restoration project, Granite Park and Sperry Chalets are projected to reopen in 1996 and 1997, respectively.

SEASONS

Glacier is magnificent at any time of the year; the only barrier to enjoying the park during the off-season is limited park access. By far the most popular time to visit is during the summer, when Going-to-the-Sun Road is fully open and the summer sun rises around 5am and doesn't set until nearly 10pm. The shoulder seasons of spring and fall are equally magnificent with budding wildflowers and variegated leaves and trees, but these sights can only be viewed from the park's outer boundaries and a limited stretch of the scenic highway.

In winter, Glacier shuts itself off from the motorized world. Even snowmobiles, which are allowed in Yellowstone, are forbidden here. All unplowed roads become trails for snowshoers and cross-country skiers. Winter sports enthusiasts rave about the vast powdered wonderland that exists here, but again, access is limited. Guided trips into the backcountry are a great way to experience the park in winter, or you can strap on a pair of snowshoes and explore it on your own. Winter weather consists of many overcast days; temperatures sometimes plummet to minus 30 degrees Fahrenheit. Dress as warmly as possible.

AVOIDING THE CROWDS

Most people visiting Glacier National Park don't stray too far from Going-to-the-Sun Road. Therefore, if you want to avoid most of the crowds, either stay away from the road altogether or visit the park just after the road is opened in early summer or just before it's closed in the fall. The more remote areas of the park are usually safe choices for solitude, although the limited number of campsites can still make a place appear to be busy even if it seems to be well-removed from civilization. If you can, visit the park during the week rather than on weekends and take a few hours to get off the road and onto a trail: The park has over 700 miles of maintained ones from which to choose.

RANGER PROGRAMS

"Nature for Kids" activities, evening campfire and slide-show programs, and guided hikes are all offered daily throughout the park. The park's "Nature with a Naturalist" publication—free upon entering the park and also available at visitor centers—is a thorough source for days, times, and locations of various educational programs. Join a naturalist for an easy or strenuous hike and learn about the geology, flora, and wildlife abundant in Glacier. Relax around a campfire and listen to a ranger tell of what life was like in the early days of the national park system or learn about the culture and lifestyle of the Blackfeet people. Most programs are free, although those including boat trips may include a minimal charge.

FOR TRAVELERS WITH PHYSICAL DISABILITIES

Information on facilities and services for those with disabilities is available at any of the visitor centers in the park, although most of the park's developed areas are fully accessible by wheelchair. The park's "Nature with a Naturalist" publication includes current program information for visitors with disabilities.

FOR THE VISUALLY IMPAIRED   Small-scale relief maps, park brochure recordings, and tactile nature items are available at the Apgar, Logan Pass, and St. Mary visitor centers. All other park facilities—restrooms, restaurants, campgrounds, gift shops—are accessible with some assistance.

FOR THE MOBILITY IMPAIRED   The Trail of the Cedars is the park's sole wheelchair-accessible trail, although a bike path at Apgar also provides magnificent views of the park's scenery. Wheelchairs are available for loan at the Apgar Visitor Center and almost all of the park's facilities are fully accessible.

FOR THE HEARING IMPAIRED   Interpreters can provide written synopses of most slide and campfire programs prior to the event. If hiking, five of the park's self-guided nature trails have printed brochures available at the trailhead. General park information is available by TDD at 406/888-5790. An interpreter may sometimes be available by request.

ORGANIZED TOURS & ACTIVITIES

Narrated boat tours from Lake McDonald, St. Mary, Two Medicine, and Many Glacier are offered daily from mid-June to mid-September by Glacier Park Boat Co. These "scenicruises" combine the comfort of an hour-long lake cruise with a short hike or picnic to create an unforgettable Glacier experience. Spectacular views of Lake McDonald sunsets, the awe-inspiring Grinnell Glacier, and the panoramic rugged cliffs ringing St. Mary Lake are just a few of the possible photo opportunities you may have while enjoying a scenicruise. The boats typically depart every other hour, usually five times each day, although schedules are subject to change in late season or if the weather is inclement. For a complete listing of departure times and dates, contact Glacier Park Boat Co. at P.O. Box 5262, Kalispell, MT 59903 (☎ 406/752-5488). Listed below are seasonal phone numbers for cruises at the following locations: Lake McDonald (☎ 406/888-5727), Many Glacier and Two Medicine (☎ 406/732-4480), and St. Mary (☎ 406/732-4430).

Unique coach tours are given aboard a scarlet 1936 "Jammer" coach—so-named because of its standard transmission—along Going-to-the-Sun Road. These coaches, with their roll-back tops, are an ideal means of transportation along this scenic route: their drivers can give you insightful commentary about the park and its history and you don't have to worry about how close you may be to the edge of the often-precipitous road! The tours are conducted by Glacier Park, Inc.; current coach schedules can be requested directly from them at Dial Tower, Phoenix, AZ 85077-0928 (☎ 602/207-6000).

SPECIAL ACTIVITIES

Scenic helicopter tours of Glacier are offered by Eagle Aviation (☎ 406/387-4160), Glacier Heli Tours (☎ 800/879-9310), and Kruger Helicopters (☎ 406/387-4565). Prices range from $60 to $90 for one- to two-hour tours, depending on your destination. All are located within two miles of West Glacier off Highway 2.

The Glacier Institute conducts field classes each summer that examine Glacier's cultural and natural resources. These courses are open to anyone and include instruction, transportation, park fees, and college credit. Instructors are highly skilled in their area of expertise, bringing to each course an intimate knowledge of the region and their subject matter. From these field courses have grown other, additional outreach educational efforts, including Elderhostel programs and one-day exploration courses. Your classroom is the Crown of the Continent Ecosystem, comprised of Glacier National Park and the Flathead National Forest. Previous courses have covered alpine wildflowers, Glacier's grizzlies, weather systems, and nature photography. Contact the institute for a copy of their current catalog at 777 Grandview Dr., P.O. Box 7457, Kalispell, MT 59904 (☎ 406/756-3911).

The institute's **Big Creek Outdoor Education Center**, located on the North Fork of the Flathead River near the park's western boundary, is also used for residential outdoor education and can accommodate up to 38 people. The center, which is open each year from April to October, regularly accommodates school groups, science camps, and Elderhostels. Trained instructors lead the seminars, camps, and classes, which range in price from around $125 for a weekend session to $550 for a two-week course.

A one-week **field ecology tour** of Glacier and Waterton Lakes is conducted through the auspices of the **Audubon Society** in the fall. Led by a team of experts from the Audubon Society and the park, and enhanced by local authorities on such topics as Blackfeet history, environmental concerns, and photography, the course costs $1,150 with accommodations at the park's historic lodges: Lake McDonald, Many Glacier, and Waterton Lakes. To register, contact Audubon Ecology Tours, Audubon Center of the Northwoods, P.O. Box 530, Sandstone, MN 55072 (☎ 612/245-2648).

Guided trail rides have traditionally been offered at Apgar, Lake McDonald, and Many Glacier; inquire at the closest ranger station as to the nearest corral before planning a trail ride.

2 Seeing the Highlights

If you have a limited amount of time to spend in Glacier, the best way to experience the full gamut of the park's beauty is to drive Going-to-the-Sun Road and take one of the many hikes or short walks easily accessible from the parking areas. This 50-mile road bisects the park, going from West Glacier in the southwest portion of the park to St. Mary in the northeast. Points of interest are clearly marked along this road, including plenty of interpretive signage. Numbers appearing in parentheses for the following points of interest indicate mileage from West Glacier as you drive along Going-to-the-Sun Road.

Just a short drive from West Glacier is **Lake McDonald** (10.8 miles), the largest body of water in the park. Numerous turnouts along the way offer opportunities to photograph the panoramic views of the lake with its mountainous backdrop. **Sacred Dancing Cascade** and **Johns Lake** (12.8 miles) are visible from a half-mile hike from the roadside through a red cedar/hemlock forest, often with views of moose and waterfowl. The **Trail of the Cedars** (16.2 miles) is a short, handicapped-accessible boardwalk trail, also through a cedar/hemlock forest, thickly carpeted in vibrant, verdant hues. Almost exactly halfway along Going-to-the-Sun is the **Loop** (24.6 miles), an excellent vantage point for views of **Heaven's Peak**. Just two miles farther is the **Bird Woman Falls Overlook** (26.8 miles), a place for viewing the cascading falls of the same name, which are located across the valley. The **Weeping Wall** (28.7 miles), a wall of rock which does, in fact, weep profusely in the summer, is a popular subject for photographers.

At 32 miles from West Glacier is **Logan Pass**, one of the park's most highly trafficked areas. Sitting atop the Continental Divide at 6,646 feet, the Logan Pass Visitor Center provides free information and naturalist programs, includes a souvenir shop, and is the starting point for one of the park's most popular hikes, **Hidden Lake**.

Jackson Glacier (36.1 miles) is perhaps the most easily recognizable glacier in the entire park; turnouts at the overlook provide you with excellent vantage points for

Impressions

Give a month to this precious reserve. The time will not be taken from the sum of your life. Instead of shortening, it will indefinitely lengthen it and make you truly immortal.

—John Muir, naturalist and conservationist

picture-taking. **Sunrift Gorge** (39.4 miles) and **Sun Point** (40 miles) are two short trails with spectacular views and opportunities for wildlife viewing. **St. Mary** (50.1 miles) is the terminus for this road, with extensive visitor services, including restaurants, places to stay, gas stations, and gift shops.

3 Driving the Park

Going-to-the-Sun Road is by far the most driver-friendly avenue in which to enjoy the park and see some of the more spectacular views if you don't want to actually get out of the car. Accessible from West Glacier and St. Mary, Going-to-the-Sun Road covers 50 gorgeous miles of scenery that stretch above and below the seemingly dangerously high cliffs. It's not uncommon to see the curious wildlife that can wander to the roadside in search of the prohibited food that tourists attempt to dispense. However, the road—which gains an elevation of over 1,400 feet in 32 miles—is very narrow in places and visitors with a fear of heights are likely to experience some anxiety while driving it. An alternative to driving the road yourself is taking a guided coach tour. See the previous section "Seeing the Highlights," for more information on sights along Going-to-the-Sun Road, and "Organized Tours and Activities," for guided coach tour information.

If you prefer to drive around the park, U.S. Highway 2 runs southeast from West Glacier around the park's southern boundary up to Essex and East Glacier. At East Glacier, Highway 49 leads to Kiowa where you connect with Highway 89. A 9-mile paved road from Highway 49, however, will take you to Two Medicine, a magnificent area of the park steeped in Native American tradition and myth. From Highway 49 at Kiowa, travel north on Highway 89 to St. Mary. Here you can take Going-to-the-Sun Road from west to east or you can continue north on 89 to Babb, a small community providing access to the park's innermost center of activity, Many Glacier. You'll find hotels, restaurants, campgrounds, and starting points for a wide variety of hikes here, as well as lots of grizzly activity.

About four miles north of Babb is the junction with **Chief Mountain International Highway** (Highway 17), a 30-mile road that runs northwest and cuts across the park's northeastern boundary as well as the boundary of the United States and Canada. At this point, you are in Waterton Lakes National Park.

If you want to see Glacier's western boundary, take the **North Fork Road** (Highway 486) from Columbia Falls. Though largely gravel and rife with potholes, this road follows the North Fork of the Flathead River, with outstanding views into the park. The road continues on to the U.S./Canadian border 22 miles north of Polebridge, one of the park's most popular areas in which to hike, camp, fish, or cross-country ski. Hugely popular in spite of its outhouses and lack of electricity, the area around Polebridge is perfect for experiencing what Montana and its natural beauty have to offer without modern-day distractions like telephones and TVs.

Camas Road is just inside the park's West Glacier entrance and runs northwest from its junction with Going-to-the-Sun Road to the North Fork Road. It's a popular stretch of highway on which to catch a glimpse of a black bear or moose and provides an alternate route to the park's northwestern entrance at Polebridge.

VEHICLE REGULATIONS Before planning your drive through Glacier, it's important to note that park regulations exclude any vehicles over 20 feet on the 24-mile stretch of Going-to-the-Sun Road between Avalanche Campground and Sun Point on St. Mary Lake. If you are traveling in a vehicle exceeding the 20-foot limit, you may want to park it at one of the parking areas located at Avalanche Campground and Sun Point and take the Going-to-the Sun Shuttle Bus Service (☎ 406/862-2539). See Section 1 of this chapter for more information.

Owing to the narrowness of Going-to-the-Sun Road and its heavy traffic load, oversized vehicles or trailers must use U.S. Highway 2.

WINTER ROAD CONDITIONS Going-to-the-Sun Road is open seasonally, usually from early June to mid-October, although it may be open earlier or later depending on current weather and road conditions. Call the park at 406/888-5441 to find out when tentative openings and closings are scheduled. During the winter, you may drive Going-to-the-Sun Road for 10 miles from West Glacier along Lake McDonald to the road closure, a popular destination for cross-country skiers.

U.S. Highways 2 and 89—with access to East Glacier and St. Mary, respectively—are regularly plowed. The North Fork road to Polebridge has a delayed plowing schedule and may be inaccessible during periods of heavy snowfall. For current road conditions, call ☎ 406/755-4829.

ROAD CONSTRUCTION With the implementation of extensive plans to improve Going-to-the-Sun Road, visitors are advised to check with the park before planning a day trip along this thoroughfare to ensure that points of interest will not be closed to traffic.

4 Sports & Outdoor Activities

See Section 5, "Exploring the Backcountry," for information on camping.

FISHING The crystal-clear mountain streams and lakes of Glacier are home to many native species of fish. Anglers looking to hook a big one should try the North Fork of the Flathead for cutthroat and bull trout and any of the three larger lakes in the park (Bowman Lake, St. Mary Lake, and Lake McDonald) for rainbow, brook trout, and whitefish.

Generally, the park's fishing season lasts from late May through November. A fishing license isn't required for fishing in the park, but many of its rivers and streams cross boundaries where a state and/or reservation permit is required. The park service can provide you with a detailed listing of fishing regulations by request.

Glacier Fishing Charters, 375 Jensen Rd., Columbia Falls, MT 59912 (☎ 406/892-2377 or 800/735-9244) provides full- or half-day charters with lunch and fishing equipment included in the price of the trip.

HIKING With more than 700 miles of maintained trails, hiking is the best way to truly explore the park in depth. One can literally travel through millions of acres of scenery on trails that run sometimes seemingly impossible circuits from one campground to the next.

Trail maps of all kinds are available at outdoor stores in Whitefish and Kalispell as well as at the major ranger stations at each entry point. Before striking off into the wilderness, however, check with the nearest ranger station to determine the accessibility of your destination, trail conditions, and recent bear sightings. This may save you a lot of headache (even, in the summer months) if you're planning a high-country hike and 10 miles into the trip a ranger turns you back.

The Park Service asks you to stay on trails to keep from eroding the fragile components of the park. Also, snowbanks shouldn't be traversed, especially the steeper ones. You should have proper footwear and raingear, enough food, and, most important, enough water, before approaching any trailhead. A can of bear mace can also come in handy when you're in grizzly habitat. See "Exploring the Backcountry" for notable hiking trails and further relevant information.

KAYAKING   If you've taken the trouble to buy a kayak, learned the Eskimo roll without drowning, and have actually gone places with a kayak on top of your car, then you have probably made yourself aware of the places to go. Most kayakers in the park are crossing lakes. Flatwater kayakers make their way across Bowman Lake with regularity. For whitewater voyagers, the North Fork of the Flathead River (Class 2, 3) and the Middle Fork (Class 3) are the best bets. Inquire at any ranger station for details and conditions.

MOUNTAIN CLIMBING   The peaks of Glacier Park rarely climb beyond 10,000 feet, but don't let the surveyors' measurements fool you. Glacier has some incredibly difficult climbs, and you must inquire at the ranger station before setting out. The rangers can answer questions concerning climbing conditions and closures, and can assist in planning climbs. They ask that you keep climbing groups between four and six persons for environmental concerns. Since mountain climbing is one of the most potentially dangerous sports in the world, the park rangers make clear that they do not screen climbers for ability and that you should be prepared to pay for costs relating to search and rescue should anything happen. Efforts begin only after positive information has been received indicating a person is missing. Climbers should complete the Voluntary Climbers Registration form available at any ranger station and at the Apgar Visitor Center.

RAFTING & FLOAT TRIPS   Though the waters that are actually in the park don't lend themselves to whitewater rafting, the boundary forks of the Flathead River are some of the best in the northwest corner of the state. For just taking it easy and floating on your back in the summer sun, the North Fork of the Flathead River stretching from Polebridge to Columbia Falls and into Flathead Lake is ideal. Portaging in Polebridge can be difficult if there's not a good sport waiting for you downstream, however. This goes for the Middle Fork of the Flathead, which forms the southern border of the park, as well.

The Middle Fork is a little more severe and isn't the sort of river you enjoy with an umbrella drink in your hand. The names of certain stretches of the Middle Fork are terror-inspiring in themselves (the Narrows, Jaws, Bonecrusher) and to assuage that terror, several outfitters offer expert and sanctioned guides to make sure you're not floating downstream facedown. **Montana Raft Company** (☎ 800/521-7238 or 406/888-5466) offers Middle Fork expertise and can even arrange for a side trip into the mountains of Glacier. **Glacier Raft Company** (☎ 800/332-9995) has been taking trips since 1976. **Great Northern Whitewater and Chalet** (☎ 800/735-9244 or 406/387-5340) offers summer trips and year-round accommodations if for some reason you decide to hold on through the winter. **Wild River Adventures** (☎ 800/826-2724 or 406/387-9453) also takes river rats on the Middle Fork.

SNOWSHOEING & CROSS-COUNTRY SKIING   Glacier offers several cross-country trails, the most popular of which is the Upper Lake McDonald Trail to the Avalanche picnic area. This 8-mile trail offers a relatively flat route up Going-to-the-

An Encounter with a Bear

Running into a bear on the trail might be the most harrowing experience of your life, and, tragically, it's the last experience of some people's lives. Though you're more likely to see a bear in Glacier than in, say, Los Angeles, it's unlikely you'll see a bear face-to-face while you're in the park. But the possibility exists, so it's important to know what you can do to prevent an encounter and, beyond that, an attack.

The joke among locals is that it's easy to determine the difference between black bear scat and grizzly scat. The grizzly scat is the one with the bear bell in it. But the advice to make as much human noise as possible while hiking is good; if jingling a bell doesn't cramp your outdoor style, by all means do it.

The "nevers" abound and the National Park Service offers some helpful and clear advice concerning the dos and don'ts of bear country. Never approach a bear, never feed a bear, never stay in an area where you see a cub (female bears are fiercely protective), never stay in an area where a bear may be feeding (such as an area where you see or smell a dead animal, or a berry patch), never hike alone or after dark. Sleep in your tent: the tent, though made of material that can be easily shredded in the mouth and claws of a bear, does provide a physical barrier. Don't sleep in the clothes in which you were cooking, but do sleep with a flashlight, noisemaker, or bear spray.

Even when heeding all this advice, there is no guarantee you won't run into one. Should you round a corner and suddenly be confronted by a bear, try to do the impossible and keep calm. Running will likely cause the bear to chase you—and considering the fact that the slowest bear could easily overtake Carl Lewis in his prime, being chased is not the ideal state of affairs. Try to assume a nonthreatening posture, then turn your head (eye contact being a threatening gesture) and talk softly as you slowly retreat.

If the bear attempts to charge you, try to drop something away from your body that doesn't contain food. Climbing a tree may be as foolish as running, considering the time frame. Drop to the ground and assume the fetal position. Play dead and keep quiet if the bear is attacking. Have your pack on at all times to protect your back, and use your arms to protect your head and neck. Tuck your knees to your chest to protect vital organs and remain in that position until you are certain the bear is gone.

Sun Road with views of McDonald Creek and the surrounding mountains looming above the McDonald Valley.

For the advanced skier, the same area offers a more intense trip heading ultimately northwest in a roundabout fashion to the Apgar Lookout. This 10 1/2-mile trip offers great views but may be a little more than the beginner bargains for.

On the east side, the Autumn Creek Trail near Marias Pass is the most popular. Though getting into the park this way doesn't have traditional drive-up window accessibility, the views of the mountains heading west are spectacular. However, avalanche paths cross this area, so, as always, inquire as to current weather conditions before heading into the wild.

Another popular spot is in Essex along the southern boundary of the park at the Izaak Walton Inn (see the "Where to Stay" section of this chapter).

5 Exploring the Backcountry

Getting around the backcountry in Glacier can mean anything from a nice walk in the park to torture beyond your wildest imagination, especially if it's your first experience hiking in the high country. For day hikers, trails can range from 4 miles to 20-mile loops, and campers can cross the park in as many as 70 miles, taking two weeks to do it. The park publishes a backcountry map of sorts that presents the campsites in their proximity to one another and to the major lakes. You can pick it up at any ranger station or visitor center in the park.

If you fish while camping, it's recommended you exercise catch and release so as not to create a problem with wildlife in search of food. If you must eat the fish, be careful while cleaning it; puncture the air bladder and throw the entrails into deep water at least 200 feet from the nearest campsite or trail.

Backcountry campgrounds have maps at the entrance to show you the location of each campground, the pit toilet (some have "urinals only" to keep goats and deer from coming back to the campground for the salt), food preparation areas, and, perhaps most important, food storage areas. The food storage area is usually near the food prep site and is comprised of nothing more than a couple of thin poles shaped at the top like coatracks. These can be a pain to utilize, especially if you're camping alone. Most sites have lines connected at either end by trees over which you toss a rope. Tie one end to the pack and pull it up near the line before tying it off at night to a nearby tree. This instruction may look obvious if you're the second one to the campsite, but it might keep you from looking silly if you're the first.

When backpacking in Glacier, especially in the high country, it's important to remember that all of those 10-pound cans of chili you're lugging around don't get tossed until the end of the trip, outside the park. Pack as lightly as possible (no barbecues or hair dryers) and make sure you're aware of the degree of the ascent or descent your particular trail may have. Some seem to go straight up.

Permits are available at each ranger station and reservations for campsites can only be made 24 hours in advance. Don't be surprised if the park is booked solid on the day you want to camp. It's not an outdoor convention; it's just a popular place to be in the summer. The earlier you start, the earlier you obtain your permit. For everyone's sake, if you have a permit for two days and realize you only want to stay one, notify a ranger so that the park can offer that site to someone else.

NOTABLE HIKING TRAILS

KINTLA LAKE TO UPPER KINTLA LAKE This 12-mile hike skirts the north shore of Kintla Lake above Polebridge for about 7 miles before climbing a couple of hundred feet. This stretch of the Boulder Pass hike is a breeze. However, once you hit Kintla Creek you may want to reconsider going any farther. With 12 miles under your belt at this point, climbing 3,000 feet may not seem like a great idea. The trail, once it breaks into the clear, offers views of several peaks, including Kinnerly Peak to the south of Upper Kintla Lake.

BOWMAN LAKE This trail (14 miles to Brown Pass) is similar to the Kintla Lake hike in difficulty, and, like the Kintla Trail, passes the lake on the north. The growth along the trail once you've passed the head of the lake may seem a bit thick, and it is. After a really wet season, this growth can stay with you on the trail until the true ascent around a western ridge on Thunderbird Mountain, but an occasional glimpse of Hole in the Wall Falls makes it worthwhile. The chute of water on the left spewing out of the mountain wall looks like a bullet-riddled water tank. Like the Kintla Trail, the Bowman Trail then begins to climb out of reach of the heart patient. Jumping 2,000 feet in less than 3 miles, the trail joins the Kintla Trail at Brown Pass. Left takes you back to Kintla Lake (23 miles) and right takes you to Goat Haunt at the foot of Waterton Lake (9 miles).

QUARTZ LAKE   Cross the bridge over Bowman Creek and you're on your way. The entire loop is 12 miles and runs a course up and over a ridge and down to the south end of Lower Quartz Lake. From there it's a level 3-mile hike to the west end of Quartz Lake, then it's 6 miles back over the ridge farther north (and higher up) before dropping back to Bowman Lake. Along this trail you'll probably be able to see evidence of the Red Bench Fire of 1988, which took a chunk out of the North Fork area.

LAKE MCDONALD–TROUT CREEK LOOP   This is a good workout if you're moping around Lake McDonald Lodge sipping coffee and skipping rocks off the lake. This hike is like reliving an Evel Knievel motorcycle experience in slow motion: straight up and straight down. The trail to the foot of Trout Lake and back is roughly 8 miles and begins from the north end of Lake McDonald.

THE HIGHLINE TRAIL   This relatively easy hike, which gains a mere 200 feet in elevation over 7.6 miles, begins at the Logan Pass Visitor Center and skirts the Garden Wall at heights of over 6,000 feet to Granite Park Chalet. It is extremely popular in midsummer, when the wildflowers are in full bloom, though acrophobics may not want to attempt its high, often narrow, snow-covered path. Be sure to allow enough time to make the return hike back to Logan Pass. Alternatively, you can choose to continue on from the chalet to "the Loop," the aptly-named section of Going-to-the-Sun Road where the trail actually terminates (an additional 4.2 miles), although you'll need to plan for a shuttle back to your car. Or you can do what locals who enjoy this hike year after year do: park the car at the Loop, catch a ride to Logan Pass, and then hike the trail.

DAWSON AND PITAMAKAN PASS LOOP   This one's a doozy—3 miles in, you're thinking, Who couldn't do this? Then you climb 3,000 feet in 4 miles. At this point, you can turn around and head back to the Two Medicine campground, but you'd be denying yourself an awesome view of Oldman Lake and its 9,225-foot Flinsch Peak backdrop before returning to the campground. It's a 16.9-mile loop that begins at the Two Medicine campground trailhead.

6 Camping

INSIDE THE PARK

Glacier offers the RV and tent camper seven campgrounds accessible by paved road: Apgar, near the West Glacier entrance; Avalanche Creek, just up from the head of Lake McDonald; Fish Creek, on the west side of Lake McDonald; Many Glacier, in the northeast part of the park; Rising Sun, on the north side of St. Mary Lake; St. Mary, on the east side of the park; and Two Medicine, at the southeast part of the park near East Glacier. Sprague Creek, near the West Glacier entrance, offers a paved road but does not allow towed vehicles. Though utility connections are not provided at these sites, fireplaces, picnic tables, washrooms, and cold running water are located at each campground. The nightly fee is $10 and campsights are obtained on a first-come, first-served basis only. Reservations are not accepted.

For a more rustic camping experience with fewer people and minimal amenities, try the sites located off gravel roads in Cut Bank (on the east side, off Highway 89),

Amenities for Each Campground, Glacier National Park

Campground	# of Sites	Fee	Max RV Length	Flush Toilets	Disposal Stations	Boat Access
Apgar	196	$10	8 sites; up to 35'	Yes	Yes	Yes
Avalanche	87	$10	50 sites; up to 26'	Yes	Yes	No
Bowman Lake *	48	$8	30 sites; up to 22'	No	No	Yes
Fish Creek	180	$10	80 sites; up to 26'	Yes	Yes	No
Kinta Lake *	13	$8	all up to 18'	No	No	Yes
Many Glacier	110	$10	13 sites; up to 35'	Yes	Yes	Yes
Rising Sun	83	$10	3 sites; up to 30'	Yes	Yes	Yes
Sprague Creek	25	$10	no towed units	Yes	No	No
St. Mary	5	$10	sites; up to 30'	Yes	Yes	No
Two Medicine	99	$10	13 sites; up to 32'	Yes	Yes	Yes

* Bowman and Kintla Lakes campgrounds are accessible only by narrow dirt roads. Large units are not recommended. Cut Bank campground is closed.

Bowman and Kintla Lakes (north of Polebridge), and Quartz Creek (south of Polebridge). Stop at any ranger station for information on closures, prices, and availability or consult the chart above.

CAMPGROUNDS IN GATEWAY COMMUNITIES
IN EAST GLACIER

Y Lazy R
Box 146, East Glacier, MT 59434. ☎ **406/226-5573.** 10 tent sites, 30 RV sites. $10 tent, $15 full hookup.

Situated just off Highway 2, this campground is conveniently located within walking distance of East Glacier and is the closest to town with laundry facilities. The campground is grassed, but come early if you want to snag one of the few sites with trees. This place is a great value and an ideal place to plant the RV before heading off for a nearby hike.

IN ST. MARY

Johnson's of St. Mary
St. Mary, MT 59417. ☎ **406/732-5565.** 50 tent sites, 65 RV sites. $12 tent; $15 RV with electricity and water only, $16 full hookup.

From April through September (depending on the weather), this is where you want to camp if you can get a spot. With showers ($2) and a laundromat, campers both inside the park and out come to St. Mary for ablutions and a good meal. Johnson's World Famous Restaurant is a welcome sight if you've been in the backcountry, with offerings such as whitefish trout, homemade soups, and homemade breads (topped with local honey), all served family-style.

IN WEST GLACIER

Glacier Campground
P.O. Box 447, 12070 U.S. Hwy. 2, West Glacier, MT 59936. ☎ **406/387-5689.** 80 tent sites, 80 RV sites. $13 tent; $16 RV.

One mile west of West Glacier (near mile marker 152) lies this heavily wooded property—nicely appointed for tent campers and RV campers alike, though the RV sites don't have individual disposal stations (there's only one on the property). Included in the price, however, are hot showers that the public must pay $3 to use. Each campsite is shaded for the most part and comes with a table and a firepit. A playground is located on the grounds and each night at 5pm, the grills are fired up at the Glacier Barbecue where ribs, chicken, and steaks are the main fare.

BACKCOUNTRY CAMPING

If it's the backcountry you're bent on seeing, Glacier has 63 backcountry campgrounds. Though the inexperienced backpacker may have difficulty getting to many of the higher-elevation campsites, Glacier has many lower-elevation trails of moderate difficulty. Inquire at the ranger station for an accurate depiction of your itinerary's difficulty, and advice on what may be needed. Also helpful are the topographical section maps of the park, available at each ranger station. Perhaps the most terrific, though unlikely, sources of danger are the bears that inhabit the park. Park officials are serious when they say not to feed the bears. Don't try to get the bear to pose for photographs, don't pet it, don't look it in the eyes, or approach it. Backcountry permits are available at ranger stations and requests for sites can be made 24 hours in advance. There is no fee for backcountry camping.

WINTER CAMPING

A good complement to skiing in the park is staying in the park. Though snow camping isn't the activity for everyone, it's a great way to see the park in winter. A free permit is required for all overnight trips and, unlike the summer permits so often in demand, the winter camping permits are available up to seven days in advance. See Section 1 of this chapter for more information.

7 Where to Stay

This section provides listings for accommodations inside the park, plus those in surrounding gateway communities.

INSIDE THE PARK

With only one exception, Glacier Park, Inc. (GPI) operates all lodging options in Glacier National Park, from the park's grand, historic log lodges to its smaller hotels and motels. From Lake McDonald's wood-beamed lodge on the west side of the park to the chalet at Many Glacier on the east, Glacier's inns have been popular destinations from which to explore the park for years (some were built by the Great Northern Railroad during its heyday nearly 80 years ago). Although the lodges have a certain stately charm, don't expect in-room hot tubs or even air-conditioning. While they are adequately comfortable, their greatest amenity is their location in one of the most stunning natural settings in the world. Reservations should be made well in advance. For more information on the following properties or to make a reservation, contact Glacier Park, Inc., Dial Tower, Station 0928, Phoenix, AZ 85077 (☎ 602/207-6000 for reservations).

Apgar Village Lodge

Apgar Village, Box 398, West Glacier, MT 59936. ☎ **406/888-5484.** 28 cabins, 20 motel rms. TV. $69–$210 cabin; $57–$86 motel rms. DISC, MC, V. Closed mid-Oct to Apr.

The Apgar Village Lodge is located on the south end of Lake McDonald and is one of two lodgings located in Apgar Village. A less expensive alternative to the park's

GPI-owned properties, the log and frame cabins have a rustic charm but lack in-room amenities. As with all the other park accommodations, reservations are recommended, usually a year in advance.

✪ Glacier Park Lodge

Glacier National Park, MT 59936. ☎ **406/226-9311.** 154 rms. TEL. $105–$142 lodge; $151–$187 suite. AE, DISC, MC, V.

Conveniently located just inside the southeast entrance at East Glacier, this is the flagship inn of the park. This imposing timbered lodge stands as a stately tribute to the Great Northern Railroad and its early attempts to lure tourists to Glacier. The carefully manicured lawn and ever-blooming wildflowers frame the grounds in colors spectacular enough to rival the mountain backdrop. The interior features massive Douglas Fir pillars, some 40 inches in diameter and 40 feet tall. Each of the rooms has a private bath and telephone and is located either in the main lodge around the balconies or in an annexed building. While there are no elevators, bell service is available 24 hours a day. The lodge includes a dining room, coffee shop, and gift shop. Evening entertainment options include a nightly cabaret performance. Kids will enjoy the outdoor heated pool while adults may opt for the nine-hole golf course next door.

✪ Lake McDonald Lodge

Glacier National Park, MT 59936. ☎ **602/207-6000.** 62 rms in lodge and motel, 38 cottage rms (some without private bath). TEL. $106 lodge room; $75 motel unit; $61–$106 cottage. AE, DISC, MC, V.

This rustic hunting lodge, situated on the shore of the park's largest lake, is a hive of activity in the summer, providing a marvelous central base for exploring the western part of the park. Similar to its counterparts in East Glacier and Many Glacier, Lake McDonald Lodge features an enormous lobby with imposing wood beams, keen reminders of nature's majesty. With its location on Lake McDonald, the lodge is a center for boating activity; scenic cruises depart daily and canoe rentals are popular. The deck faces the lake and is a popular place to hang out with friends, read a book in solitude, or savor a sunset. There are 32 rooms in the main lodge, 30 rooms in Stewart Motel (near the camp store), and 38 rooms in cottages that lie between the two. The rooms are comfortable, though old; be sure to inquire as to whether yours has a private bath; as some do not. As in the other park hotels, there are no elevators, but 24-hour bell service is available. One of the larger complexes in the park, it includes a dining room, gift shop, and lounge; a coffee shop, post office, and sundries store are also on the grounds.

✪ Many Glacier Hotel

Glacier National Park, MT 59936. ☎ **602/207-6000.** 208 rms. TEL. $87–$106 lodge room; $146–$156 suite. AE, DISC, MC, V.

This alpine-style hotel is probably the most-photographed building in the park. When you arrive at Many Glacier after driving along the park's interior road from Babb, it comes slowly into view, as picturesque as a Swiss chalet and almost as inviting as the turquoise blue waters of Swiftcurrent Lake, at whose bank it sits. Built in 1915 by the Great Northern Railway, Many Glacier Hotel is the largest lodging in the park and, though relatively removed from Going-to-the-Sun Road, it is among the most popular. Its chalet-style architecture is a charming complement to the many peaks that surround it (the area isn't called "America's Little Switzerland" for nothing). Rooms are located either in the main lodge around the balconies overlooking the lobby or in the adjoining annex. The walls are extremely thin; if you're a light sleeper, make sure you get a unit that's well away from the exit doors. There are no elevators, although 24-hour bell service is available. A dining room, coffee shop, gift shop, and lounge are all located in the hotel; nightly cabaret performances begin mid-summer.

Rising Sun Motor Inn

Glacier National Park, MT 59936. ☎ **602/207-6000.** 63 rms. TEL. $72–$75 motor inn unit; $61 cottage unit. AE, DISC, MC, V.

Located 6.5 miles from St. Mary, just off Going-to-the-Sun Road, the Rising Sun is a complex made up of a restaurant, a motor inn, cottages, a camp store, a gift shop, and a service station. You would think it would be one of the nicer places to stay in the park. But while the rooms are comfortable enough and you'll be ideally located to explore the eastern side of the park from Going-to-the-Sun, Rising Sun is considerably lacking in appeal when compared with its GPI counterparts: It's a lot of asphalt and plain brown buildings. There are 28 motel rooms, 9 of which are located in the same building as the camp store, and 35 rooms in duplex cottages. The motel seems to attract an older set (of the RV variety) and though it bills itself as being on the north side of St. Mary Lake, keep in mind that Going-to-the-Sun Road runs east to west and the lake is on the other side of the road. It's still a convenient place to be, though, especially if you plan to take a scenic cruise or rent a boat.

Swiftcurrent Motor Inn

Glacier National Park, MT 59936. ☎ **602/207-6000.** 88 rms and cabins (most cabins without private bath). TEL. $66–$75 motor inn unit; $26–$45 cabin. AE, DISC, MC, V.

Though modest in price and decor, the Swiftcurrent is a good choice for active people interested in spending lots of time exploring the backcountry trails of the park. Located in the Swiftcurrent Valley, it's a less expensive alternative to Many Glacier Hotel if you plan to explore this part of the park.

Like Many Glacier, it, too, is beautifully set against a mountain backdrop and is generally considered a hiker's paradise. (But beware of bears: it's not unusual to hear of grizzly sightings on some of the trails in the area.) There are 42 motor inn rooms, 20 motel rooms, and 26 cabins. Each of the motel units includes a private bath; cabins are outfitted with kitchenettes, one or two bedrooms, and perhaps a bath (public facilities are nearby if you don't get a private bath). There's also a coffee shop/restaurant on the premises.

Village Inn

Glacier National Park, MT 59936. ☎ **602/207-6000.** 36 rms. $80–$100 double; $100–$111 suite. AE, DISC, MC, V.

Not to be confused with Apgar Village Lodge (see above), the Village Inn is the smallest of the GPI properties operated in Glacier. Located in Apgar Village, the inn is convenient to the general store, cafes, and boat docks. Like its counterparts throughout the park, the Village Inn is comfortably outfitted with modest furnishings, making it a cozy and convenient place to hang your hat: all 36 rooms are located on two floors of the inn and 12 of them are outfitted with kitchenettes. There are, however, absolutely no amenities: no air-conditioning, no phone, no television. And even though you also won't find a dining room on the property, the restaurants of Lake McDonald and Apgar are all close by. Close to the Apgar corral and the docks of Lake McDonald, not to mention the ubiquitous hiking trails, Apgar Village bustles with activity during the summer and is a great choice for families or people who like to engage in a little people-watching.

IN GATEWAY COMMUNITIES

If the convenience of staying on Glacier's back porch is important to you, the following places are your best bets. However, in surrounding communities not necessarily classified as gateway towns, you'll find a greater variety of accommodations. See "Where to Stay" in the Whitefish, Kalispell, and Columbia Falls sections of Chapter 6 for listings of places that might be more in line with your needs if the park is merely a one- or two-day part of your vacation.

IN EAST GLACIER

⑤ Backpacker's Inn

P.O. Box 94, East Glacier, MT 59434. ☎ **406/226-9392.** 3 cabins, sleeping 20 people. $8 per person. DISC, MC, V. Closed mid-Oct–Apr.

This dorm-style hostel consists of three cabins—one for men, one for women, and one coed—each sleeping up to six people (the coed cabin sleeps eight). At $8 per person, the price is right, but don't expect the rooms to include much more than a bed. The inn is especially popular with hikers and is often used as a pickup spot for people hiking the Continental Divide. Located behind Serrano's, one of the most popular restaurants in the park's vicinity, the Backpacker's Inn may be spartan, but the adjacent dining options are pure indulgence.

⑤ Brownies Grocery and AYH Hostel

P.O. Box 229, East Glacier, MT 59434. ☎ **406/226-4426** or 406/226-4456. 10 rms, 2 family rms (all with shared bath). AYH members $10–$15 or $30 family room; nonmembers $13–$23 or $35 family room. MC, V. Closed Oct to early May, depending on the weather.

Reservations are recommended at this popular combination grocery store/hostel. A good value, Brownies offers comfortable rooms at extremely affordable prices in one of the most traveled areas of the park. Dorm and family rooms are located on the second floor of a rustic, older log building with several common rooms for guests to share, including a porch, kitchen, bathrooms, and laundry. Nearby biking, hiking, and fishing in the Two Medicine area of the park are favorite activities and the grocery store, complete with bakery and deli, is conveniently located downstairs.

East Glacier Motel

P.O. Box 93, East Glacier, MT 59434. ☎ **406/226-5593.** 6 rms, 11 cabins. TV. $66–$69 double; $46–$59 cabin. MC, V. Closed Nov–Apr.

Brand-new motel rooms or remodeled forest service cabins are your two options here. The motel rooms are newer but the cabins certainly have more of a Montana feel (don't worry, they all have bathrooms!), and four of them come with a kitchenette. There are picnic tables available for guests, and as with all the other East Glacier accommodations, recreation opportunities and restaurants are all close by.

Jacobson's Cottages

P.O. Box 216, East Glacier, MT 59434. ☎ **406/226-4422.** 12 cottages. $50–$60 cottage. AE, DISC, MC, V. Closed Nov–Apr.

Located in a nicely wooded area, these quaint cottages are small but comfortable. And while they don't come equipped with either TVs or kitchens (with one exception), entertainment and good food are short walks away with the Restaurant Thimbleberry a half block down the street and Two Medicine a mere 4-mile drive. The cottages are available seasonally, and reservations are recommended.

IN ESSEX

✪ Izaak Walton Inn

P.O. Box 653, Essex, MT 59916. ☎ **406/888-5700.** 30 rms, 3 suites, 4 caboose cottages. $92 double; $126 suite; $425 caboose (three-night minimum). MC, V.

Built in 1939 by the Great Northern Railway, this historic Tudor lodge once served as living quarters for rail crews who serviced the railroad. Located just off Highway

2 on the southern boundary of Glacier Park, the Izaak Walton is now extremely popular with tourists and locals alike, many of whom choose to travel there via the train, which arrives a mere 50 feet from the front door of the lodge. Essex is a beautiful spot in summer, but winter is the really busy time for the lodge, with visitors stopping in for a weekend of cross-country skiing on nearly 20 miles of groomed trails. Before planning a quick trip to the Izaak Walton, keep in mind Amtrak's new truncated schedule: Though it was once a daily occurrence, the train now stops at Essex only four days a week (Tues., Thurs., Sat., and Sun.).

IN POLEBRIDGE

⑤ North Fork Hostel and Cabins
P.O. Box 1, Polebridge, MT 59928. ☎ **800/775-2938** or 406/888-5241. 15 bunks, 2 log homes, 2 cabins. $12 bunk; $35 log home; $25 cabin. No credit cards.

Formerly called the Quarter Circle MC Ranch and located inside the park, this lodge was moved to its present location near Polebridge in the late 1960s.

Now it sits within a stone's throw of the North Fork of the Flathead River. The lodge features complete kitchen facilities for the do-it-yourselfer, as do the log homes, each with three double beds, a fireplace, and a refrigerator. The two smaller cabins (one log, one framed) are behind the lodge and use the lodge's facilities. Propane and kerosene lights brighten the place at night and vault toilets (a rich man's outhouse) are the only way to go.

Polebridge Mercantile and Cabins
P.O. Box 2, Polebridge, MT 59928. ☎ **406/888-9926.** 4 cabins, 1 tepee. $30–$35 cabin; $20 tepee. Children under 12 stay free. No credit cards.

If you can make the trek up the gravelly North Fork Road, then give these bare-bones cabins a try. There is no electricity and no running water. And don't even think about bedding—it's bring your own sleeping bag at the Merc. However, each cabin has propane cooking stoves and lights, and the views out over the west side of Glacier National Park make the $35 price tag a steal, especially if you brought the kids. This may sound like an adventure in hell, but Polebridge is a happening spot in the summer when all the river rats and seasonal residents converge for whopping good times and tall tales about the rapids they've run and the peaks they've bagged.

IN ST. MARY

St. Mary Lodge
U.S. Hwy. 89 and Going-to-the-Sun Road, St. Mary, MT 59417. ☎ **406/732-4431** or 800/452-7275. 57 rms, 19 cottages. $85 room; $225 cottage. AE, DISC, MC, V.

Situated at the St. Mary end of Going-to-the-Sun Road, this lodge is one of only a handful of conveniently located properties that aren't owned by GPI. Once you see it, you'll understand why it is often mistaken as a sister property to those in the park. The main lodge and attendant rooms are standard Montana fare, with the ubiquitous yet tasteful western lodgepole furniture and furnishings. A gift shop, supermarket, and full-service gas station are nearby and entertainment can be found at either the upstairs lounge or downstairs pub, where pizza and movies are the order of the day. The Snow Goose Grille serves up breakfast, lunch, and dinner with specialties that include fresh whitefish and sourdough scones.

IN WEST GLACIER

Glacier Highland Resort
U.S. Hwy 2, West Glacier, MT 59936. ☎ **406/888-5427.** 33 rms. TV. $52–$73 double. DISC, MC, V.

Not necessarily a resort, the Highland is run by locals who know the area and know how to have a good time. It was formerly the Highland Motel; the recent switch in moniker was meant to lend a touch of class to the place. Be that as it may, this ersatz resort with a hot tub is a good place to stay in summer. With its close proximity to a snowmobile rental facility (Canyon Creek Cat House, ☎ 800/933-5133), it's an even better place in winter. The Cat House's rides, available to anyone, not just guests at the Highland, include a backwoods trek to the summit of Big Mountain north of Whitefish.

Glacier River Ranch Bed & Breakfast

P.O. Box 176, Coram, MT 59913. ☎ **406/387-4151.** 5 rms, 1 suite. TEL. $85–$110 double; $405 suite. Three-night minimum stay. MC, V. All rates include a continental breakfast.

This 40-acre ranch, bordered by the Flathead River, 7 miles north of the West Glacier entrance to the park, offers a framed lodge with five bedrooms, a television room (with cable, no less), a hot tub, and a main room. In short, all the creature comforts are at your disposal. The flavor of the West is evident in the no-pets rule (which includes all domesticated animals *except* the horse). Overnight horse accommodations are available. Rates are affordable for the area (for people, anyway). A trout pond is located on the property for anglers who don't feel like walking down to the river. We wouldn't call the breakfast a full breakfast, but the selection of baked items, fruits, and cereals is adequate, and the coffee excellent.

Glacier Wilderness Resort

P.O. Box 295, West Glacier, MT 59936. ☎ **406/888-5664.** 10 lodges. TEL. $130–$150 per lodge per night. Five-night minimum stay. No credit cards.

Surrounded by Forest Service lands, the lodges at this year-round resort are as private as you can get. Each lodge is a "home," complete with a stereo, VCR, and a hot tub on the front porch. Families will find the two-bedroom lodges to their liking, and kids can play outdoors during the day (there are 23 undeveloped acres) and at the Recreation Center at night, which includes foosball, a pool table, and even video games. Hiking trails abound and some even come up on some surprising waterfalls. For a summer stay, reservations should be made before March.

✪ Mountain Timbers

P.O. Box 84, West Glacier, MT 59936. ☎ **406/387-5830** or 800/841-3835. 7 rms (4 with private bath). $55–$85 double with shared bath; $85–$125 double with private bath. MC, V.

Tucked away on the other side of the Flathead River near the south side of the park is this cozy lodge. It's not just another Western hand-hewn log cabin that sleeps an ungodly number of people. Situated on 260 acres, this beautiful 5,000-square-foot lodge offers everything from easy access to the park to more than 10 miles of gorgeous hiking and biking trails of its own. Spend the day hiking and enjoying the magnificent views, and the night in the hot tub or reading a book in the library. In winter the lodge is transformed into an excellent base for cross-county skiers, with over 10 miles of well-groomed trails that even locals frequent.

Vista Motel

P.O. Box 98, West Glacier, MT 59936. ☎ **406/888-5311.** 26 rms. TV. $60–$140 double. AE, DISC, MC, V. Closed Nov–Feb.

Perched atop a hill at the west entrance to Glacier National Park, the Vista boasts the best views of the mountains from anywhere around. There's only one catch—you'll have to visit from March through October to see them.

The motel is nothing special to look at, but the rooms are clean and comfortable, and there's an outdoor heated pool. Golf, raft trips, riding stables and restaurants are all nearby.

8   Where to Eat

INSIDE THE PARK

Food options inside the park—off Going-to-the-Sun Road, rather—are limited to dining rooms operated by GPI and, regrettably, are overpriced and unimaginative more often than not. You will probably enjoy your surroundings more than you'll enjoy your meal. A high chef turnover at the park's lodges makes it hard to assume a certain level of quality and service from season to season. The dining rooms are convenient, however, and you're almost always assured of friendly service from a staff of twentysomething college students from around the country. Credit cards accepted at all GPI properties include Discover, MasterCard, and Visa; traveler's checks are also accepted but personal and business checks are not.

For light snacks or a cold drink, stock up in West Glacier or at Lake McDonald; the next place to grab something quick is Rising Sun, at the other end of Going-to-the-Sun Road.

The following dining rooms open with the park and close sometime in September, depending on the facility. At each dining room, breakfast is served from 6:30 to 9:30am; lunch from 11:30am to 2pm; and dinner from 5:30 to 9:30pm. Coffee and snack shops open either at 7am or 8am and close at 9pm.

Glacier Park Lodge has the Goatlick Steak & Rib House and the Teepee Room; **Lake McDonald Lodge** has the Cedar Dining Room and the Coffee Shop; **Many Glacier Hotel** has the Ptarmigan Dining Room and Heidi's; the **Rising Sun Motor Inn** has the Coffee Shop; and the **Swiftcurrent Motor Inn** has the Coffee Shop. There is no restaurant associated with the Village Inn at Apgar. However, Lake McDonald Lodge and restaurants at Apgar Village are convenient to the hotel.

IN GATEWAY COMMUNITIES

IN EAST GLACIER

⑤ Glacier Village Restaurant

304308 Hwy. 2, East Glacier. ☎ **406/226-4464.** Reservations accepted. Breakfast items $3–$5; lunch $4–$7; main dinner courses $8–$17. MC, V. Daily 6am–10pm. Closed Oct–Apr. CONTINENTAL.

This family-owned, seasonal restaurant is actually two in one: a cafeteria on one side and a full-service restaurant on the other. Glacier Village has developed quite a reputation among locals for fine, dependable food. The cafeteria side dishes up great home-style food with standards that include incredible breakfast waffles and pancakes made from homemade batter, as well as a hearty chicken potpie. The restaurant side is equally impressive, with a menu that includes médaillons of pork with raspberry sauce and a succulent smoked chicken breast spinach salad. Take away the florid decor and you have as fine a total dining experience as any in or around the park.

Restaurant Thimbleberry

112 Park Dr., East Glacier. ☎ **406/226-5523.** Breakfast items $5–$6; lunch $5–$7; main dinner courses $9–$15. No credit cards. Daily 7am–9:30pm. Closed Oct–Apr. AMERICAN.

Locally famous for their incredible pies—the lemon meringue and raspberry are both excellent choices—the Thimbleberry serves a great veggie omelet for breakfast, sandwiches and salads for lunch, and an excellent cornmeal-dusted St. Mary's Lake whitefish for dinner. This is a good choice for vegetarians looking for something other than a Montana steak or hamburger, and the calorie-conscious will find several fat-free choices. If you've never had frybread, which is served instead of rolls, then this is the place to try it.

◆ Serrano's

Hwy. 2, East Glacier. ☎ **406/226-9392.** Reservations recommended. Main courses $8–$10. DISC, MC, V. May–mid-Oct. daily 5–10pm; closed mid-Oct.–Apr. MEXICAN.

This seasonal Mexican restaurant has an outstanding local reputation, so don't be surprised if you encounter masses of people during the height of summer. Though small, Serrano's has large booths and tables that are extremely comfortable, especially after a long day of driving or hiking. The food is authentic and the portions are large, making for a satisfying meal with or without the Cuervo Gold Margaritas. The restaurant also has an ample selection of imported beers and microbrews.

IN POLEBRIDGE

Northern Lights Saloon

Polebridge. ☎ **406/888-5669.** Reservations not accepted. Main courses $5–$9. No credit cards. Daily 4pm–midnight. Closed Labor Day–Memorial Day. AMERICAN.

When people don't mind traveling over 30 miles of bumpy gravel road, when they don't blink an eye as they hit yet another gaping pothole and lose a hubcap or bend a rim, you've got to realize that they must know something you don't about wherever it is they're going: in this case, the Northern Lights Saloon. This small restaurant, located squarely in the middle of nowhere, aka Polebridge, boasts summer crowds that often have to wait patiently outside for a table to clear. Picnic tables, a volleyball net, and the peaks of Glacier Park are there to make the wait as painless as possible. Take a seat at one of the five tables, or find a spot at the bar. Friday night is pizza night and Saturday night features Mexican fare, but daily specials on weeknights are just as tasty and it's often less crowded. You won't find a place with more character or with friendlier staff and customers.

IN WEST GLACIER

Glacier Highlander Restaurant

U.S. Hwy. 2, West Glacier. ☎ **406/888-5427.** Reservations accepted. Breakfast $3–$5; lunch $5–$7; dinner $7–$14. DISC, MC, V. Daily 7am–9pm. Closed Nov 2–Mar 31. AMERICAN.

The restaurant inside the newly renamed Glacier Highland Resort is, as you might expect, a laid-back experience. With a baker on hand, the pies are well worth the stop, and the Highland Burger, though by no means the same one you'll find at the Trumble Creek Hub in nearby Columbia Falls, is, by any standard, a great burger. The cinnamon rolls are breakfast giants and the fresh trout is a dinner specialty.

9 A Side Trip to Browning & the Blackfeet Indian Reservation

According to Native American legend, the Blackfeet were named because their moccasins were blackened with soot from fires or paint. *Siksika,* the "Blackfooted People," became their tribal name, and they eventually grew into four bands: the Blackfeet in Montana and the Kaina, Pikani, and Siksika of Alberta, Canada.

Today the Blackfeet maintain a humble existence near the beautiful lands that were once their own, with about half of the tribal enrollment of 14,000 living on the reservation, located on the east side of Glacier National Park and extending north to the U.S.-Canadian border. Browning, the tribal headquarters, is a gateway town to Glacier, but many visitors pass through quickly in anticipation of the end of the prairies and the beginning of the mountains. Though Browning is not a spectacular place, it does have its redeeming side.

The most anticipated annual event in Browning is mid-July's **North American Indian Days**. This four-day celebration draws visitors from across the region to view Native Indian dance competitions, games, and sporting events at the Blackfeet Tribal Campgrounds, which are adjacent to the **Museum of the Plains Indian.** Be sure to stop in at the museum while you're in Browning for insight into the Blackfeet of yesterday and today.

A **Blackfeet Historic Site Tour** is offered daily through Blackfeet Tours and Encampment. Half- and full-day tours depart from the Museum of the Plains Indian and pickups can be arranged from any of the park's hotels, lodges, or campgrounds in either the St. Mary or East Glacier area.

If you want an authentic Native American experience, consider staying at the **Blackfeet Tipi Encampment**, located south of Highway 89, 2 miles west of Browning. Tepees come equipped with washstands, sleeping platforms, and foam mats, and can accommodate up to four adults. Toilets and showers are nearby, but you need to bring towels and sleeping bags. Prices start at $110 nightly for one person and include all meals, served home-style.

For information on these and other programs—including arts and crafts workshops, Blackfeet Elders Storytelling Campfires, or mini-powwows—contact Curly Bear Wagner or Darrell Norman at **Blackfeet Tours and Encampment,** Box 271, Babb, MT 59401 (☎ 800/215-2395).

If you're looking for a more traditional place to stay, the **War Bonnet Lodge**, with 40 rooms, is Browning's largest motel. It's located at the junction of U.S. Hwys. 2 and 89; reservations can be made by calling 406/338-7610. The **Western Motel**, at 121 Central (☎ 406/338-7572), has 25 rooms. There really isn't anywhere to eat in Browning. It's best to stop in either East Glacier or St. Mary.

The Flathead & the Northwest Corner

6

If it's mountains, lakes, and streams you've come for, then northwestern Montana is without a doubt the place to be. Though the summer can bring millions of tourists through this neck of the woods, spring and fall find the place almost empty but for the locals. From Flathead Lake, with its cumbersome claim that it's the "Largest Natural Freshwater Lake West of the Mississippi," to majestic Glacier National Park, to Missoula, arguably the state's center of culture, the stretches of Montana State Highways 93 and 2 that run through the region glide by some of Montana's better vistas.

Skiing, snowboarding, mountain biking, snowmobiling, golf, windsurfing, boating, and fishing are all important staples for the folks who live here. Flathead Lake is a favorite recreational spot that's big enough to accommodate valley residents and visitors alike, but smaller lakes abound throughout the region. Magnificent Glacier National Park is the area's crown jewel, rich in scenic beauty and year-round recreational opportunities.

1 Scenic Drives

There are really only two major roads that run through the northwest corner: U.S. 93, north to south; and U.S. 2, east to west.

The north-south route runs from the Bitterroot Mountains north through Missoula. From there it stretches up into the Flathead Valley near St. Ignatius and the spectacular Mission Mountains. Continuing past the National Bison Range to the west, the valley opens up and as soon as you reach Polson, Flathead Lake becomes visible. On a clear summer day it's not uncommon to see yachts, waterskiers, and windsurfers enjoying the massive lake, which is 28 miles in length and in some places stretches to an 8-mile width. North of the lake are Kalispell, Whitefish, and Columbia Falls, gateway towns to nearby Glacier National Park, and farther still is the border village of Eureka, just minutes south of the Canadian border.

U.S. 2 runs from Libby to Glacier and passes through downtown Kalispell. The road from Libby to Kalispell is full of trees and wildlife, and offers peeks at some of western Montana's lesser-known mountains. Continuing east from Kalispell, you'll skirt Glacier Park and for a moment enter it near the Isaak Walton Inn. This is the route to East Glacier, Many Glacier, and St. Mary, all within park boundaries.

Without a doubt, when you think "driving tour" in this part of the state, you think Going-to-the-Sun Road, Glacier Park's magnificent 52-mile thruway. While it is spectacular and a route no visitor to this part of the state should miss, there are many other, lesser-known driving routes in the state's northwest corner.

In addition to the following tours, consider spending an afternoon making your way around Flathead Lake, ringed by snow-capped mountains and bright blue skies. One of the largest lakes in the West, it offers a lot of summer pleasures: On the east side, you can stop to pick ripe cherries from the cherry orchards and explore the art galleries and Western boutiques of Bigfork; and on the west side, you shouldn't miss having a creamy huckleberry shake and poking through the antique stores.

DRIVING TOUR 1: THE NORTH FORK ROAD (COLUMBIA FALLS TO POLEBRIDGE)

This is undoubtedly one of the most scenic drives in northwest Montana, taking you from the small community of Columbia Falls to the even tinier town of Polebridge, the only western gateway to Glacier National Park. The entire drive is about 40 miles long, and all you have to do is take Highway 486 northeast out of Columbia Falls. You'll follow along the meandering North Fork of the Flathead River, with amazing views of some of the park's most impressive peaks to the east. Although the road can wreak havoc on your car—potholes are plentiful—just knowing that the Northern Lights Saloon is at the end of the road makes the trip more than worthwhile (see "Where to Eat" in Chapter 5).

With the exception of the saloon, Polebridge facilities are open year-round (as are the mountains), making this a nice drive any time of year, though an all-terrain vehicle or truck is recommended, especially during the winter.

DRIVING TOUR 2: THE BITTERROOT VALLEY

This driving tour takes you south from Missoula into an area rich in natural and historical attractions. Named after the magnificent Bitterroot Range that rises from its western side, the Bitterroot Valley is home to the St. Mary's Mission near Stevensville—the first Catholic mission in the Northwest—and the Daly Mansion near Hamilton, built by one of Montana's early copper kings, Marcus Daly.

If you'd rather concentrate on natural scenery, you can observe nesting osprey and other wildlife at the Lee Metcalf National Wildlife Refuge, where a short loop trail, open from mid-July to mid-September, gives you access to several ponds and blinds that are perfect for observing birds and other wildlife undetected in the refuge's southwest corner. Winter is the best time to view bald eagles; look for white-tailed deer and Canadian geese in spring.

Natural hot springs are also common in this area, with an especially popular destination at Lost Trail Pass, just east of Highway 93.

This is an excellent drive any time of the year, especially for wildlife watching, though some of the historical attractions, like the Daly Mansion, are closed in winter. Allow an afternoon for this three-hour excursion and consider spending the night at Lost Trail Hot Springs (☎ 800/825-3574), covered in Chapter 7 under "A Side Trip to Lost Trail Pass for Skiing and Hot Springs," or return via Highway 93.

2 Missoula

The biggest city in the state's northwest corner, Missoula is by far the most progressive community in all of Montana. Home to the University of Montana, Missoula

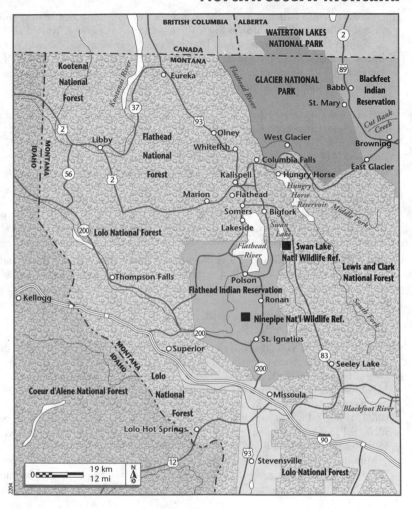

boasts the second-oldest creative writing school in the country, with an ever-increasing literary community of established and emerging writers. A distinctly younger, very hip crowd populates this place, where Birkenstocks outnumber cowboy boots and cars are much more likely to come equipped with sports racks than cellular phones. Though locals sometimes complain about winter's gray skies and fumes from nearby Frenchtown often pervade the clean mountain air, Missoula is an excellent place to explore the outdoors, with skiing at nearby Snowbowl and hiking in various wilderness areas ranking high on the list of things to do.

ESSENTIALS

GETTING THERE   Delta (☎ 800/221-1212), **Horizon** (☎ 800/547-9308), **Skywest** (☎ 800/453-9417), and **Northwest** (☎ 800/225-2525) all have flights into the Missoula County International Airport at Johnson Bell Field, northwest of downtown on U.S. 93.

I-90 leads into Missoula from the west (Washington State and Idaho) and the east (Billings and Bozeman). If you're driving up from Salt Lake City, I-15 leads up through Idaho and intersects with I-90 at Butte. For information on **road conditions** in Missoula, call 406/728-8553. For statewide conditions, call 800/332-6171. Avalanche information can be obtained by calling either the Lolo National Forest Weekend Report (406/549-4488) or the U.S.D.A. Forest Service at ☎ 800/281-1030.

If you want to leave the driving to someone else, the northwestern part of the state has reliable intrastate bus services that have an advantage over bus travel in other parts of the world: They're uncrowded most of the time. The bus terminal, 1660 W. Broadway (☎ 404/549-2339), is served by **Greyhound,** which offers east-west service and usually has considerably more passengers than the other, smaller companies. **Rimrock Stages** (☎ 800/255-7655) can't get you to Seattle or New York but is estimable in its efforts to move you from one part of Montana to the next.

The nearest train station is located 134 miles north at the beautifully restored Whitefish Depot. The schedule recently has been truncated and trains now appear at most four times a week. Call **Amtrak** (☎ 800/USA-RAIL) for details.

VISITOR INFORMATION   The **chamber of commerce,** on Van Buren and Front (☎ 406/543-6623), is full of everything you'd expect to find in the way of brochures, city maps, and area maps for outdoor activities, shopping, dining, and tours for not just Missoula but most of northwestern Montana. If you don't feel like making the trip and just need a quick adumbration of events, a recorded list is updated weekly (☎ 406/728-4636).

GETTING AROUND   If nobody is waiting to greet you at Missoula's airport with open arms, several rental car agencies, including **Avis** (☎ 800/331-1212), **Budget** (☎ 406/543-7001), **Hertz** (☎ 800/654-3131), and **National** (☎ 800/227-7368), maintain counters at the airport. For the truly good deals, however, you have to call **Rent-a-Wreck,** 2401 W. Broadway (☎ 800/421-7253 or 406/721-3833); **Payless,** which has a convenient airport shuttle service to its office at 200 S. Pattee at the Holiday Inn (☎ 800/237-2804 or 406/728-5475); or **U-Save,** 3605 Reserve (☎ 800/426-5299 or 406/251-5745).

Missoula's city bus line is **Mountain Line Transit,** 1221 Shakespeare (☎ 406/721-3333). Forty cents gets you just about anywhere you want to go throughout the city. The only problem is that it doesn't run late at night and on Sundays it doesn't run at all.

Taxi service is available through **Yellow Cab, Inc.** (☎ 406/543-6644).

GETTING OUTSIDE
Sports & Outdoor Activities

Though Missoula is full of progressive bookworms, the community does not live on text alone. Looming above it each and every day in white on dull green and brown is the giant *M* on Mount Sentinel. The trail to the *M,* a steep zigzag that wends a path of certain exhaustion, may for some folks stand for Murder. And given what lies just out the back door—the Rattlesnake National Recreation Area and Wilderness, the Clark Fork of the Columbia, the Blackfoot, and the Bitterroot Rivers, not to mention the Montana Snowbowl, a ski area with more than 30 runs—there's always something to do that requires a little physical exertion.

Missoula

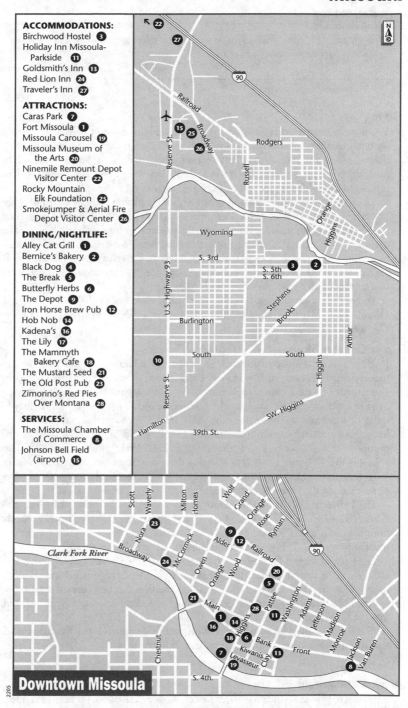

ACCOMMODATIONS:
Birchwood Hostel ③
Holiday Inn Missoula-
  Parkside ⑪
Goldsmith's Inn ⑬
Red Lion Inn ㉔
Traveler's Inn ㉗

ATTRACTIONS:
Caras Park ⑦
Fort Missoula ①
Missoula Carousel ⑲
Missoula Museum of
  the Arts ⑳
Ninemile Remount Depot
  Visitor Center ㉒
Rocky Mountain
  Elk Foundation ㉕
Smokejumper & Aerial Fire
  Depot Visitor Center ㉖

DINING/NIGHTLIFE:
Alley Cat Grill ①
Bernice's Bakery ②
Black Dog ④
The Break ⑤
Butterfly Herbs ⑥
The Depot ⑨
Iron Horse Brew Pub ⑫
Hob Nob ⑭
Kadena's ⑯
The Lily ⑰
The Mammyth
  Bakery Cafe ⑱
The Mustard Seed ㉑
The Old Post Pub ㉓
Zimorino's Red Pies
  Over Montana ㉘

SERVICES:
The Missoula Chamber
  of Commerce ⑧
Johnson Bell Field
  (airport) ⑮

Downtown Missoula

Impressions

---

*With the passage of time, I have become possessive of these surroundings. The beautiful
mountains have become my old friends.*

Edward L. Foss, *A Swan Valley Journal*

Biking

You'll see more mountain bikes on streets than on mountains in Missoula. Though
we don't recommend challenging automobiles to a joust, the unwritten rule here is
that when a cyclist or pedestrian even seems inclined to cross the street (crosswalk or
not), the approaching vehicle courteously pauses and allows the nonmotorized
traveler to cross. It's the city's way of saying, "Thanks for moving fuel-free."

The best place to cycle, however, is not within the bicycle-friendly confines of the
city. The Rattlesnake Recreation Area (mind you, don't strike off into the wilderness
portion of the Rattlesnake; it is forbidden) is a great spot for mountain biking. The
maps available at most outdoor stores that rent bikes show the trails. If you're a
passionate peddler, make sure to stop off at **Adventure Cycling Association,** 150 E.
Pine (☎ 406/721-1776). They publish a touring map of the city, but if you want
to see America on a bike, they can handle that, too.

To rent bikes, contact the **Baxton Bike Shop,** 2100 South (☎ 406/549-2513);
Open Road, 218 E. Main (☎ 406/549-2453); or **New Era,** 741 S. Higgins
(☎ 406/728-2080).

Cross-Country Skiing

If you're not in the mood to go screaming down the mountainside, the Missoula area
has several cross-country trails within 30 miles of town. The absence of gold in nearby
Garnet turned a once-prosperous mining town into a ghost town that's become a
magnet for cross-country skiers at the **Garnet Resource Area.** With more than 50
miles of trails and a remote location, this area offers something approaching a
backcountry experience. Information on camping and maps of the area can be
obtained before you leave town at the Bureau of Land Management office, 3255 Fort
Missoula Rd. (☎ 406/329-3914). Getting there can be an arduous task in winter.
Take I-90 east to Highway 200, turn east for 5 miles to Garnet Range Road, then
go south along the Forest Service Road.

The **Lubrecht Experimental Forest** is operated by the University of Montana's
Forestry Department (☎ 406/243-0211) and has six ski trails. To reach Lubrecht
from Missoula, take I-90 east to Highway 200 to Greenough and make a right just
past the post office. Less than a half mile down is the Lubrecht camp.

The **Pattee Canyon Complex,** 5¹/₂ miles south of town in the Lolo National Forest, is home to several intermittently groomed trails that range in difficulty from a
short 1.6km trail to a longer 5.4km trail. Information can be obtained by contacting the Lolo National Forest Ranger Building, 24-A, Fort Missoula, Missoula, MT
59801 (☎ 406/329-3814).

The **Rattlesnake National Recreation and Wilderness Area** has many trails
available to skiers. Maps are available at most outdoor shops.

Downhill Skiing

Marshall Mountain Ski Area

Take I-90 east to Hwy. 200, and proceed for 7 miles. ☎ **406/258-6000.** Lift tickets $17 adults;
$15 students; $10 children. Open daily Nov–Apr.

If Montana Snowbowl is too extreme, too crowded, or just a bit pricey, check out this smaller facility. The skiing isn't as good as at Montana Snowbowl, but night skiing for $9 is a bargain if you can endure the wind and cold.

Montana Snowbowl

P.O. Box 8226, Missoula, MT 59807. ☎ **800/728-2695.** Lift tickets $23 adults, $10.50 children; senior citizen, student, and half-day rates available. Open Wed–Mon from late Nov to early Apr. From I-90, exit at Reserve Street; head north on Grant Creek Road, and turn left on Snowbowl Road.

A new high-capacity double-chair lift, a T-bar, or a beginner tow will transport you to more than 30 runs and a half-mile vertical drop at the Snowbowl. Located in the Lolo National Forest, this place is well worth the price of a lift ticket. But Snowbowl is not necessarily for the beginner: 80% of the runs are for intermediate, expert, and advanced skiers, with another 700 acres for the extreme skier.

Instruction ranges from a two-hour adult group lesson for $15 and a one-hour adult private lesson for $25 to the Pee-Wee private tutorial for $15. If you prefer one big ski instead of two small ones, PSIA-certified instructors can teach you how to snowboard.

For refreshments you can try the Double Diamond cafe in the base lodge, the Grizzly Chalet at mid-mountain, or the mountain's saloon, the Last Run Inn. Day care for kids two years and older is provided as well as "Pandas" for children ages three to six, which include equipment, lessons, a lift ticket, and lunch for $25.

Fishing

Norman Maclean grew up here, "haunted by waters." His novel, *A River Runs Through It,* is set here. But since the **Blackfoot** just isn't the same pristine, unpolluted water it once was, the river scenes of the movie weren't filmed here. Haunted, indeed.

The **Clark Fork,** which runs through town, has also had its share of environmental problems and concerns over the years. A clean-up effort in the 1970s has gone a long way in cleaning it up, but it's never going to be an angler's first choice.

The **Bitterroot River** and **Rock Creek** may be better bets for trout, the fish to catch in these parts, and though Rock Creek has been known to shut out more than a few anglers, it is a blue-ribbon trout stream. The problem is staying overnight. Rock Creek has a full-service campground at Elkstrom's Stage Station, a mile off I-90 on Rock Creek Road (☎ 406/825-3183), but the RV campground, showers, toilets, store and swimming pool do nothing to contribute to its primitiveness. The Missoula office for the **Montana Department of Fish, Wildlife, and Parks,** 3201 Spurgin (☎ 406/542-5500), makes a habit of being in the know where area fishing is concerned. They can direct you to Siria, a more remote site 30 miles up Rock Creek Road.

Golf

Every town in the northwest corner, it seems, has a golf course. Missoula has three. The nine-hole **Highlands Golf Club,** located on 102 Ben Hogan Dr. (☎ 406/721-4653), may not be a PGA stop, but it is public. Then there's the historic Greenough Mansion clubhouse and restaurant. Another nine-hole course is located on the **University of Montana** campus (☎ 406/728-8629). The **Larchmont Golf Course,** 3200 Old Fort Rd. (☎ 406/721-4416), is the only course within city limits with 18 holes.

Hang Gliding

This sport is most popular on Mount Sentinel, though the **Montana Hang Gliding Association** (☎ 406/721-7546) also sanctions Mount Charrety. The University Golf Course marks the spot where most gliders land, and visitors are always welcome.

Hiking

Though the town has trails running through it like veins, the true test of heart (the muscle) and endurance is sitting against Mount Sentinel in the form of the white *M* overlooking the city. Though the views from up there are astounding, you may not care by the time you've reached the top.

A less strenuous hike follows the **Kim Williams Trail,** along either side of the Clark Fork River through downtown. Outside of town is the **Rattlesnake National Recreational Area and Wilderness.** The beauty of the Rattlesnake is that it's just a stone's throw from the city; drive northeast on Van Buren to Rattlesnake Drive.

NEARBY NATURE PRESERVES & WILDERNESS AREAS

The **Lee Metcalf National Wildlife Refuge** is a wetland habitat of the Bitterroot River and an excellent place to view nesting ospreys in spring. A short loop trail, open from mid-July to mid-September, gives you access to several ponds and blinds in the refuge's southwest corner. Winter is the best time to view bald eagles; look for white-tailed deer and Canada geese in spring. The picnic area allows year-round access with two 1-mile trails. To reach the refuge, take U.S. Highway 93 to Stevensville, then the East Side Highway to Wildfowl Lane. Drive for 1.5 miles to the boundary signs.

There are two state parks in the Missoula area: Beavertail Hill and Council Grove. **Beavertail Hill** is located on the Clark Fork, open May through September, with excellent river access and shady cottonwood trees lining the river banks. There is a day-use charge of $3; campers pay $9 per night. **Council Grove** has some historical significance, its site marking the location where the Hellgate Treaty was signed, establishing the Flathead Indian Reservation. Open for day use only, the park has interpretive displays and picnic facilities. Take the Reserve Street exit from I-90 and drive 2 miles south, then 10 miles west on Mullan Road.

OUTFITTERS & ORGANIZED TRIPS

Venture West Vacations (☎ 406/825-6200) and the **Number for Adventure** (☎ 406/721-3000, ext. 1160) can arrange a number of Missoula-area adventures for you, including parachute jumping, hot air ballooning, bus tours, and much more. Call for information and reservations.

Biking

Adventure Cycling Association

P.O. Box 8308, Missoula, MT 59807-8308. ☎ **406/721-1776.**

Formerly Bikecentennial, Adventure Cycling has been leading bike tours across the country since 1973, with three types of trips to choose from: expeditions, treks, and events.

The expedition trips have an advanced difficulty rating and range from two to three months in length, with riders traveling the "Northern Tier" (Seattle to Maine) or the "Southern Tier" (San Diego to St. Augustine), just to name a couple. The "North Star" trip begins in Missoula and ends up in Anchorage, Alaska.

Treks are shorter than the expedition trips but are just as challenging, with participants exploring a smaller area of the country within a couple of weeks: Anchorage to Denali; Big Sky fly-fishing; "Great Lakes Explorer"; and national parks in northern Montana and southern Alberta, Canada.

Event tours feature catered meals and lots of camaraderie, with participants from around the world. These tours are much larger, often with up to 200 participants on each ride.

Though the prices of individual trips will vary, they range from $500 for a one-week trek to $2,950 for a three-month, trans-America expedition tour. You must join Adventure Cycling in order to sign up for one of their trips. Membership costs are $25 for an individual, $19 for a student or senior (60 or older), and $35 for a family and include a subscription to the *Adventure Cyclist*, a copy of *The Cyclists' Yellow Pages*, and discounts on other Adventure Cycling publications.

Fishing

Grizzly Hackle International Fishing Company

215 W. Front St., Missoula, MT 59807. ☎ **406/721-8996.**

Whether guiding you along Missoula's Clark Fork, helping you pick out the perfect fly, or booking an Alaskan fishing vacation, Grizzly Hackle can help you with your fly-fishing vacation. Seasoned guides take you along the Lower Clark Fork, the Bitterroot, and the Blackfoot Rivers, as well as Rock Creek, in search of native rainbow, Westslope cutthroat, brown, and bull trout. Float trips, wading trips, and overnight horseback trips can all be arranged with the store's guides. Environmentally responsible, Grizzly Hackle advocates catch and release and barbless fishing and donates 5% of all fly sales to Trout Unlimited and the Clark Fork Coalition to help keep rivers healthy, locally and nationally. The store stocks a complete selection of equipment and clothing for the fly fisherman, and includes a full-service travel agency.

Whitewater Rafting & Kayaking

10,000 Waves

Box 7924, Missoula, MT 59807. ☎ **406/549-6670.**

The Clark Fork and the Blackfoot are the settings for whitewater adventure with this Missoula-based outfitter. Half-day and full-day floats feature thrilling whitewater rapids along high mountain rivers and through steep, narrow canyons. Keep your eyes peeled for local wildlife; you may spot a moose, osprey, or eagle. Half-day trips are $30 per person; full-day floats cost $55 (includes lunch). A source of pride are their self-bailing rafts, which enable the paddler to focus on the sport, not survival.

If you want an even bigger thrill, consider renting an inflatable kayak. One- and two-person kayak trips include equipment and a guide and usually accompany the raft trips. Half-day rates are $40 per person; it's $65 per person for a full day (lunch included).

SPECIAL EVENTS   The **International Wildlife Film Festival,** which began in 1977, has become the longest running such film festival in the world. Founded by internationally known bear biologist Dr. Charles Jonkel, the festival recognizes scientific accuracy, artistic appeal, and technical excellence through a juried competition. Highlights of the one-week festival, held each year in early April, include three daily screenings, workshops and panel discussions, a wildlife photo contest, and various wildlife art displays. Contact the festival at 802 E. Front St. (☎ 406/728-9380) for details.

Out to Lunch at Caras Park (☎ 406/543-4238) is a popular summer series featuring live entertainment and numerous food vendors from 11:30am to 1:30pm every Wednesday from June through August. Missoula's carousel is also located at this riverfront park (see below).

Of particular note to music lovers, but only occurring every three years, is the **International Choral Festival**, a weeklong musical extravaganza that brings in talented choral groups from around the world. Call Don Carey at ☎ 406/728-4294 for information on the event in 1996.

EXPLORING THE TOWN

If you want to check out the architectural highlights of the "Garden City," stop by the Chamber of Commerce and pick up their **historical walking/driving tour brochure.** With an economy based on trade, timber, and agriculture, Missoula can trace its past through its historic homes. The tour is organized in four distinct districts: the central business district downtown, residential districts adjacent to downtown, the southside neighborhood, and the university district.

Fort Missoula and Historical Museum

Fort Missoula Road. ☎ **406/728-3476.** Free admission. Tues–Sun 8am–5pm.

Fort Missoula, one of Montana's first military posts, was established in 1877, when Chief Joseph of the Nez Perce led his tribe toward Canada. Now home to the National Guard and Reserve units, Fort Missoula has as its main attraction this museum, which houses rotating art exhibits in its indoor galleries. An outdoor area recreates Western history with numerous buildings.

Smokejumper and Aerial Fire Depot Visitor Center

Adjacent to Johnson Bell Airport, Highway 93. ☎ **406/329-4900.** Free admission. Memorial Day–Labor Day daily 8:30am–5pm. Tours available on the hour beginning at 9am.

Along with the Ninemile Remount Depot Visitor Center, this facility offers a fascinating look into the life of a Western firefighter, from the days when pack animals were an important part of backcountry firefighting to the advent of the smokejumper in 1939 to the present day. The Aerial Fire Depot Visitor Center features murals, educational videos, a reconstructed lookout tower, and exhibits of firefighters to illustrate the history of this hard-working group of rescue workers. Keep your eyes peeled for present-day smokejumpers; "hot shots" are trained here.

Historic Ninemile Remount Depot Visitor Center

22 miles west of Missoula on I-90, 4 miles north of Exit 82. ☎ **406/626-5201.** Free admission. Memorial Day–Labor Day daily 8:30am–5pm.

This visitor center, along with the Smokejumper Center, will educate you in the early-day methods of rugged firefighting in the Northern Rockies, when pack animals were a vital part of a firefighter's "equipment." Listed on the National Register of Historic Places, the depot appears today much as it did when it was constructed by the Civilian Conservation Corps in the 1930s. Unlike those at the Smokejumper Center, all tours are self-guided.

Missoula Museum of the Arts

335 North Pattee. ☎ **406/728-0447.** Free admission. Mon–Sat noon–5pm.

Changing exhibits at this downtown museum feature regional, national, and international art with a special emphasis on art of the Western states. Associated programs include films, concerts, lectures, tours, and children's events.

Rocky Mountain Elk Foundation

2291 W. Broadway. ☎ **406/523-4545.** Free admission. Memorial Day–Labor Day daily 8am–6pm; winter Mon–Fri 8am–5pm, Sat–Sun 11am–4pm.

This wildlife visitor center consists of an art gallery, theater, and gift shop, each dedicated to the majesty of Rocky Mountain wildlife. The gallery is filled with an impressive array of paintings, prints, and bronzes, with trophy mounts of elk, grizzly bear, mountain goat, bighorn sheep, wolf, and lynx. You can view a wildlife film in the theater or browse through the books and T-shirts available in the gift shop. The non-profit wildlife conservation organization is dedicated to conserving, restoring, and enhancing the natural habitat of elk and other wildlife and can provide membership information (☎ 800/CALL-ELK).

Farmers Market

Market Plaza. ☎ **406/777-2636** or 406/549-0315. Tues and Sat mornings from 9am.

Market Plaza is the place to be during summer for organic vegetables, fresh flowers, and a diverse collection of Made in Montana crafts and art objects.

ESPECIALLY FOR KIDS

A remarkable community effort, **the Missoula Carousel** was a project begun with nothing more than unrealistic optimism that sprouted into the first carousel built in decades in the United States. From the planning to the funding to the actual assembly of the structure, Missoula relied on the kindness of others to make it happen. The hand-carved and hand-painted horses are the result of thousands of hours of devotion from volunteer workers, most of whom were novices trained in the art of carving and painting. The result is nothing less than professional, if not downright astounding. This is definitely for kids, but adults will also marvel at this merry-go-round by the river at downtown's Caras Park.

SHOPPING

In a state where souvenir shops are the order of the day and you often have to drive an hour to the nearest mall, Missoula is one of Montana's more refreshing oases for the serious shopper. Granted, in most respects Missoula can't compete with other Western towns its size, like Jackson Hole—whose proliferation of designer boutiques includes a Ralph Lauren factory outlet and a Gap store on the square. But Missoula, a hip town in a decidedly less-than-progressive state, has a much nicer personality.

The diverse collegiate community that makes its home in Missoula is reflected in several downtown shops. **Global Village World Crafts,** 519 S. Higgins, is a project of the Jeannette Rankin Peace Resource Center and sells jewelry, clothing, and musical items from communities around the world. **Butterfly Herbs,** 232 N. Higgins Ave., features an eclectic collection of items, including fresh herbs, jewelry, coffee mugs, teapots, and handmade paper and candles. And if you begin to feel the spirit and suddenly want your own pair of Birkenstocks, just go next door to **Hide & Sole,** 236 N. Higgins, for anything your heart desires in the way of groovy shoes.

Missoula is home to an impressive literary community, and the city's bookstores are among the state's best. Check out offerings from local writers at **Freddy's Feed and Read,** 1221 Helen, and **Fact and Fiction,** 216 W. Main. Both stores host signings and readings from well-known authors, many of whom make their home in Montana. New Age literature is available at **Earth Spirit Books,** 135 E. Main.

A shopping spree in Missoula wouldn't be complete without a trip to **Rockin' Rudy's,** 237 Blaine. Here you'll find the most complete collection of music in the state, as well as a friendly and knowledgeable staff. In addition to CDs and cassettes, the expansive store sells T-shirts, cards, and jewelry in what used to be a bread factory. The listen-before-you-buy policy is more than just a ploy to get you in the store; several portable CD players are located in the listening room toward the back of the store.

If you're looking for clothes, the **Bon Marche,** 110 N. Higgins, is an old standard and Missoula's only downtown department store. **Benetton,** 130 N. Higgins, and **Rattlesnake Dry Goods,** 220 N. Higgins, feature the latest in women's and unisex fashion. **Sylvester's,** 700 SW Higgins, is the place for you if you're low on cash or just looking for a screaming deal. A word of warning, though: Before you buy, make sure the masking tape isn't hiding a snag, stain, or tear.

If you love to hate Martha Stewart, then these stores are for you. **In Good Taste,** 132 N. Higgins, **Red Rooster Trading,** 301 N. Higgins, and **Native Woods,** 517 S. Orange, can outfit you with a living room, kitchen, or bedroom that even the guru of redo would envy.

Original Montana art can be found at the **Monte Dolack Gallery,** 139 W. Front, home to the most complete collection of the artist's paintings, prints, and posters, as well as other fine art from Montana artists. Other galleries include **Art Attic,** 123 S. Avenue West, and the **Paxson Gallery,** University of Montana.

An excellent source for Western souvenirs is the **Rocky Mountain Mercantile** catalog, which makes its home in nearby Ovando. With items that include Gros Ventre buffalo spoons, reproductions of ancient Native American rock art, and huckleberry gift packages, Richard Howe has collected an impressive group of native gifts you'll want to share with your friends. Request a copy of his catalog by writing to Rocky Mountain Mercantile, P.O. Box 6, Ovando, MT 59854.

Finally, if you absolutely have to mall walk, try the **Southgate Mall** at Brooks and South, home to over 100 stores with the requisite department stores, specialty shops, professional services, and restaurants.

WHERE TO STAY
HOTELS & MOTELS

Holiday Inn Missoula-Parkside

200 S. Pattee St., Missoula, MT 59802. ☎ **406/721-8550.** 102 rms, 8 suites. A/C TV TEL. $85 double; $110–$150 suite. AE, DISC, MC, V.

This Holiday Inn isn't much different from any other Holiday Inn in the world, except that none of the others overlook the Clark Fork River. That aside, this is an average downtown hotel (there are others with this same distinction, but lower prices) with king-size beds and coffeemakers in the rooms. Its downtown location makes it convenient for shopping on nearby Higgins and Main.

Lolo Hot Springs Resort

38500 W. Hwy. 12, Lolo, MT 59847. ☎ **406/273-2290.** 34 rms. $42–$69 double. MC, V.

Farther afield from Missoula, this hot springs resort, 25 miles west of Lolo, is an especially popular destination for snowmobilers in winter but is a great place to visit anytime, especially when the summer days turn unexpectedly cool. The Bitterroot Range provides a stunning setting for the rejuvenating powers of the hot springs. Two separate pools retain the mineral waters: An indoor pool is located in a building separate from the lodge and a motel-style unit; the outdoor pool is a short walk across the parking lot.

There are 18 rooms in the lodge, nicknamed the Fort because of the building's layout, and 16 in a motel-style unit. Though the motel rooms are less expensive and have air-conditioning, they are also considerably less appealing in decor. The Eatery and the Saloon provide food and drink for guests, who can enjoy fishing, horseback riding, and hiking in nearby Lolo National Forest.

ⓢ Quinns Hot Springs

Box 219, Paradise, MT 59856. ☎ **406/826-3150.** 24 rms. A/C. $25–$50 double. AE, DISC, MC, V.

Stay overnight or just for a few hours at this hot springs hotel in Paradise (no pun intended). Though the hotel is a far cry from Utopia by nearly any standard, it is comfortable and clean, and four of the rooms include a kitchenette. The mineral hot springs are tapped into a big outdoor pool adjacent to the hotel, as well as into an outdoor Jacuzzi. Two private hot tubs inside the hotel are available for rent by t.. hour. This is a funky little place to soak up some local flavor in addition to the ho springs, and rest your road-weary muscles.

Red Lion Inn

700 W. Broadway, Missoula, MT 59802. ☎ **406/728-3300** or 800/547-8010. 76 rms. A/C TV TEL. $64–$79 double. AE, DC, DISC, MC, V.

A comfortable motel a couple of blocks from downtown, the Red Lion is a sure bet for families. The outdoor heated pool is open year-round and parents can take a dip in the indoor hot tub. The Coffee Garden is a family-style restaurant owned and operated by Red Lion, but since you're so close to Missoula's downtown restaurants, you may want to eat elsewhere. The rooms, though remodeled in 1990, are somewhat bland, and the views aren't necessarily awe-inspiring, but the downtown location and proximity to the university make this place a safe choice. The hotel is a short 5-mile drive from the airport.

Pets are allowed for a $5-per-night fee, but make sure they're at fighting weight when you check in: 15 pounds is the maximum.

Traveler's Inn

4850 N. Reserve, Missoula, MT 59802. ☎ **406/728-8330.** 28 rms. A/C TV TEL. $30–$54 double. AE, DISC, MC, V.

This one-story white stucco building located off the interstate at exit 101 isn't the most exciting place to stay, but it is less expensive than many of the other downtown motels. Basic rooms come with queen-size beds and pets are allowed in some of the rooms, as is smoking (nonsmoking rooms are available, too). The closest place to grab a bite is Rowdy's, a family diner located on the property.

A BED-AND-BREAKFAST

Goldsmith's Inn

809 E. Front St., Missoula, MT 59802. ☎ **406/721-6732.** 7 rms. TEL. $79–$119 double. Rates include full breakfast. AE, MC, V.

Form meets function in this bed-and-breakfast located in the heart of Missoula's university district. Within walking distance of downtown shopping, the inn is located directly across the Van Buren Street footbridge from the University of Montana campus. Combining the elegance of a traditional bed-and-breakfast inn with the amenities of a hotel, Goldsmith's seven rooms each feature a private bathroom and the suites come equipped with a television. The brick bungalow has an interesting history: Built in 1911 for Clyde Duniway, the university's second president and founder of its law school, it served as a fraternity house during the sixties and seventies, a zoology annex during the eighties, and was sawed in quarters and moved in 1989 to its present site on the Clark Fork River. Owners Dick and Jeana Goldsmith operate the locally famous homemade ice-cream parlor and restaurant next door (it also bears their name), which is where guests check in and breakfast is served in the mornings. Complimentary drinks from the restaurant during your stay are included in the price of your room.

GUEST RANCHES

Bruce Spruce Lodge and Guest Ranch

Box 1486, Trout Creek, MT 59874. ☎ **406/827-4762** or 800/831-4797. 8 rms (1 with private bath). $70–$110 double. MC, V.

This guest ranch, located in tiny Trout Creek, was designed by owner Russ Milleson to be completely wheelchair-accessible. Completed in 1986, the Blue Spruce Lodge enables disabled visitors to fully enjoy Montana's scenic Bitterroot Valley year-round through hunting, fishing, cross-country skiing, and other outdoor activities. Lake Pend Oreille and the Noxon Reservoir are both favorite summer destinations for fishing and viewing wildlife. All rooms are located in the main lodge, where the family-style meals are served, and feature rustic hardwood floors and private decks. A TV room, pool table, and upstairs sitting room provide ample indoor diversions.

Lake Upsata Guest Ranch

Box 6, Ovando, MT 59854. ☎ **800/594-7687.** 8 cabins. $165–$195 per person in cabin; $100 tepee. Three-day minimum. Rates include all meals and activities. No credit cards.

This family-oriented guest ranch is located in the Bitterroot Valley, along the southern border of the Bob Marshall Wilderness Area. An emphasis on wilderness education sets this guest ranch apart from others that also offer horseback rides and nearby fly-fishing: The ranch offers wildlife programs and field trips for adults and children, "Evening at the Lake" lectures, and classes at its wildlife educational center. Past Lake Upsata Institute Programs have included those devoted to Montana wolves, fire ecology, waterfowl and wetlands, and the loons of Upsata. An excellent way for families to explore the outdoors is through one of the ranch's wildlife field trips to such locations as the Blackfoot/Clearwater Game Refuge, the Blackfoot River, the Bandy Reservoir, and the Browns Lake/Blackfoot Waterfowl Area. Of course, Lake Upsata itself is the subject of much discussion and exploration, with field trips and programs devoted to it alone. A particularly popular program is the "Evening at the Lake," where visiting experts share their knowledge with guests on subjects ranging from wilderness ethics to Montana ballads. The folks at Lake Upsata clearly love the land and want to teach their guests how it can be preserved and protected for generations to come. This is a great value for families with diverse interests, with a wide spectrum of activities available, most of which are included in the cost. Cabins are lakeside and meals are served family-style in the main lodge.

Triple Creek Ranch

5551 W. Fork Rd., Darby, MT 59829. ☎ **406/821-4664.** 17 cabins. A/C TEL TV. $475 per couple per night. Rate includes meals, drinks, and activities. AE, MC, V.

This guest ranch just outside of Darby caters to adults only, with amenities that include fully stocked refrigerators and a complimentary supply of liquor. Located in the scenic Bitterroot Valley, luxury accommodations are in log cabins complete with a fireplace, small kitchenette, and comfortable sitting area. A pool, putting green, tennis court, and hot tub are available to guests, as is fly-fishing equipment and horses for a leisurely ride amid the mountain splendor.

Although the rates may seem a bit high for Montana, the *Hideaway Report*, a newsletter for the well-heeled traveler, has twice designated Triple Creek a "Hideaway of the Year" as well as one of six "Hideaways of the Decade."

✪ West Fork Meadows Ranch

52 Coal Creek Rd., Darby, MT 59829. ☎ **406/349-2468** or 800/800-1437. 7 cabins. $990–$1,290 per person per week. Minimum stay may be required. AE, DC, MC, V.

A charming blend of Old West and European traditions makes this guest ranch unique. You won't lack for things to do at West Fork Meadows, and chances are you'll meet other interesting people from all corners of the globe. Operated by Guido and Hanny Oberdorfer, themselves transplanted Europeans, West Fork Meadows caters to an international market, with German, French, Italian, and English spoken at the ranch. The main lodge is the picture of rustic Western charm, but its Black Horse Inn is pure international elegance, serving five-course dinners in an intimate setting. The Selway Saloon is open daily until midnight, convenient to the cozy living room and outside deck. Cabins are carpeted, either one-bedroom/one or three-bedroom/two-bath combinations, and are equipped with wood-bur stoves or fireplaces as well as wonderful covered porches. Summer brings with horseback rides, fly-fishing, hiking, and canoeing; winter ranch activities includ snowmobiling, sleigh rides, cross-country skiing, and horse rides.

A HOSTEL

⑤ Birchwood Hostel

600 S. Orange, Missoula, MT 59801. ☎ **406/728-9799.** 22 beds, 2 private rms. $9–$25. No credit cards.

Located just four blocks south of the Clark Fork and 12 blocks west of the university, this traditional European-style hostel opened in 1977. With 22 bunks, it is one of the largest in Montana. The hostel is especially popular with bicycle tours and offers inside bike storage. You can bring your own linens or rent some for $1. Open year-round, the Birchwood is a good value if you don't mind the Spartan lifestyle.

WHERE TO EAT
EXPENSIVE

✪ Alley Cat Grill

125½ W. Main St. ☎ **406/728-3535.** Reservations strongly recommended. Main courses $10–$20. AE, DISC, MC, V. Mon–Sat 5–9:30pm. FRENCH.

Consider yourself lucky if you are able to sit down to dinner at this tiny restaurant without a reservation. Literally tucked into a Missoula alley, the Alley Cat has no problem finding customers, though customers may sometimes have a hard time finding it (look between West Front and West Main). Consistently rated one of the top chefs in the Northwest, owner Pearl Cash has for nearly a decade pleased the palates of discriminating diners at this romantic little restaurant. An eclectic mix of appetizers—Roquefort-pecan wontons, escargot, steamed clams, and French onion soup—is just the beginning of a dining experience like no other in Missoula. Fresh French baguettes complement the mixed baby greens topped with homemade salad dressings, and are preludes to entrées that range from duckling with apricot chutney to chicken with shiitake mushroom sauce to a filet mignon with port and Roquefort or a green peppercorn sauce. The homemade desserts are delectable, with nightly variations on fruit and chocolate: The amaretto mousse with sliced apricots and toasted almonds nicely combines the two. Fine wines, beer, and espresso are all served in this magnificent Missoula restaurant, one no visitor should miss.

The Depot

201 W. Railroad Ave. ☎ **406/728-7007.** Reservations recommended. Main courses $13–$21. AE, DC, DISC, MC, V. Sun–Thurs 5:30–10:30pm; Fri–Sat 5:30–11pm. STEAKS/SEAFOOD.

This bar/restaurant is Missoula's answer to the franchised bar and grill, with food and a clientele that closely resemble those found at an Applebee's or Ruby Tuesday's. There is a festive ambience at the upstairs bar, where twenty- and thirtysomethings gather to sample the region's microbrews and order from an impressively diverse appetizer selection. If you can't get a table at the restaurant (which is likely, especially on weekends), the appetizer menu—available at either bar—includes meal-size portions of filling entrées that include an excellent Caesar salad as well as an enormous open-faced steak sandwich.

The restaurant's pasta dishes are excellent choices, as are the standard cuts of steak: filet mignon and prime rib. The large and tastefully decorated bar area adjacent to

...staurant is complemented by brightly colored paintings from a local artist and ...nice place to spend an evening with friends.

Lily

...o S. Higgins Ave. ☎ **406/542-0002.** Reservations recommended. Main courses $11–$18. ..E, MC, V. Tues–Sat 5–9:30pm. FRENCH/THAI/AMERICAN.

With an in-house bakery, incredible chocolate desserts, and extensive beer and wine lists, The Lily is one of Missoula's more upscale places to eat, and the crowd reflects that. The collegiate crowd is, more often than not, conspicuously absent. Located upstairs, just down from the Wilma Theater, the restaurant is an elegant place to sample Thai cuisine with a "suicide" heat index.

MODERATE

Hob Nob

In the Union Club, 217 E. Main. ☎ **406/728-7980.** Reservations required for parties of six or more. Lunch $5–$9; dinner $9–$16. No credit cards. Mon–Fri 11am–9pm; Sat 5pm–midnight; Sun 5–9pm. AMERICAN.

The word on the street is that there's no word on the street. Since there's no sign for the Hob Nob, this place can be a bit hard to find if you don't know exactly where you're going. It's located in the historic downtown Union Club Building, which should point you in the right direction. A vegetarian's delight, the Hob Nob offers an array of creative menu items that concentrate on fresh vegetables. The place has excelled in its two years of existence and its attempt to be as anonymous as possible has had a reverse effect.

The Mustard Seed

419 W. Front St. ☎ **406/728-7825.** Reservations not accepted. Lunch $4–$8; dinner $7–$12. AE, DC, DISC, MC, V. Daily; call for hours. JAPANESE/AMERICAN.

This restaurant features excellent Asian food in two separate Missoula locations: this one, near downtown; and one at Southgate Mall, Paxson Street entrance (☎ 407/542-7333). Both are extremely popular with the local college crowd, with an extensive menu of vegetarian dishes at affordable prices. The restaurant's "Osaska" sauce—a light and tasty blend of mustard and ginger—tops delicious shrimp and chicken entrées if you happen to eat meat. They also have a wide selection of microbrews on tap as well as a nice wine list.

INEXPENSIVE

✪ Bernice's Bakery

190 S. 3rd St. West. ☎ **406/728-1358.** Most items $2–$5. No credit cards. Mon–Fri 6:30am–5:30pm; Sat–Sun 6:30am–3pm. BAKED GOODS.

This small, out-of-the-way place is known for its sinfully delicious baked goods and is a popular spot to pick up a quick bite to eat in the mornings. In addition to an outstanding crunchy homemade granola, Bernice's sells buttery croissants filled with flavored cream cheeses, an excellent complement to the freshly brewed gourmet coffee also on hand. Though there's no place to sit down, it's the best place in town for coffee and a croissant on the run.

Black Dog

138 W. Broadway. ☎ **406/542-1138.** Reservations not accepted. Lunch $3–$6; dinner $5–$8. No credit cards. Mon–Thurs 11:30am–9pm; Fri 11:30am–10pm; Sat 5:30–10pm. VEGETARIAN.

This vegetarian restaurant, a relatively new addition to the Missoula scene, is small but well worth a visit. Brightly painted tables, chairs, and walls make it a cheery place

to meet your friends. The daily specials feature (almost exclusively) organically g.
ingredients. The hiziki salad, avocado feta roll-up, and potato gordas are highlig
of a refreshingly varied menu. For starters, try the hummus or skordalia, a thick gar.
dip served with pita bread and calamata olives. Desserts are made daily on the
premises.

⑨ Kadena's

231 W. Front St. ☎ 406/549-3304. Reservations not accepted. Lunch $4–$6; dinner $5–$7.
MC, V. Mon–Thurs 11am–7:30pm; Fri 11am–8pm; Sat 11am–6pm. GOURMET DELI.

Come to this gourmet restaurant for one of the most imaginative and affordable meals
in town, then order something to take home with you. Near the downtown riverfront
and carousel, Kadena's is a fresh dining alternative with an extensive selection of
unusual salads, pastas, entrées, and sandwiches, including Cajun chicken with linguini
or eggplant olivada.

Mammyth Bakery Cafe

131 W. Main. ☎ 406/549-5542. Breakfast $2–$6; lunch $4–$10. AE, MC, V. Mon–Sat
7am–6pm. INTERNATIONAL.

Put all preconceptions of the cafeteria out of your head before you enter the
Mammyth. With a great salad bar, delicious cuisine, and outstanding baked goods,
this place offers up some tasty dishes that you've never had in a cafeteria before. Located downtown, this became a local standout because it has great food that doesn't
take all day to get.

Zimorino's Red Pies Over Montana

424 N. Higgins Ave. ☎ 406/549-7434. Reservations not accepted. Main courses $9–$15.
MC, V. Summer Sun–Thurs 5–10pm, Fri–Sat 5–10:30pm; winter Sun–Thurs 5–9pm,
Fri–Sat 5–10:30pm. ITALIAN.

The homestyle Italian meals served up at Zimorino's have been whetting appetites
in Missoula since 1979. Robert Zimorino continued the family restaurant tradition
when he moved from New York to Montana to give the locals a taste of Italy. But
besides being a great spot for pasta, Zimorino's is also a fine place to get a pizza and
a beer.

MISSOULA AFTER DARK
WATERING HOLES FOR ANY TASTE

As with almost any progressive college town, there are plenty of watering holes in
Missoula, whether your buzz of choice is alcohol- or caffeine-induced. Here are some
of the local favorites and their featured beverages.

The Break

432 N. Higgins Ave. ☎ 406/728-7300.

You'll feel as if you've been transported to Seattle in this ultrahip hangout for the
espresso-addicted, dubbed the "home of the velvet foam." Enjoy a savory scone with
your coffee and see what your future holds with their Magic Eight Ball, conveniently
located at the register.

Butterfly Herbs

232 N. Higgins Ave. ☎ 406/728-8780.

This eclectic store has a distinctly retro feel: If you're looking for one-stop shopping
and have incense, earrings, a coffee mug, and fresh thyme on your list, look no
further. Although you can get a hot cup of java or any type of specialty espresso drink
here, check out the juice bar: There's a spirulina shake on the menu called "I Feel

ke James Brown" that's guaranteed to make you feel every bit as good as the godfather of soul himself.

he Iron Horse Brew Pub

00 W. Railroad Ave. ☎ **406/728-8866.**

Home to Bayern, a microbeer brewed next door, the Iron Horse is a local favorite among the college crowd. If you're feeling particularly cocky, ask for a beer in the boot—then see if you can drink it all.

The Old Post Pub

103 W. Spruce. ☎ **406/721-7399.**

The Old Post is a great spot for a draft and generous portions of Mexican food, if you don't mind bar fare. It's also a great place to people watch. Eddie Vedder was rumored to have been seen at the Old Post and some of Missoula's literati are regulars.

CLUBS & MOVIES

The Top Hat, 134 W. Front, is popular with the local college crowd and features area bands for a minimal cover charge. The **UC Ballroom** regularly hosts headline acts and is a great place to see your favorite band in concert. Call 406/243-4051 or 800/526-3400 to find out who's zoomin' who.

If you're in a movie mode, see what's playing at the **Crystal,** 515 S. Higgins. Though the seats aren't cushioned and you actually have to hold your drink, the Crystal is regarded by Missoula—nay, Montana—residents as one of the state's premier big screens. Foreign films are the order of the day, so stay away if you're subtitle-challenged.

THE PERFORMING ARTS

The **Montana Repertory Theater,** located at the University of Montana campus (☎ 406/243-4581), is the state's only Equity company, performing new and classical works. The **Missoula Children's Theater** is the largest touring children's theater in the United States, performing original musical productions and featuring hundreds of talented area children each year. The **Missoula Community Theater** provides a year-round calendar of not-to-be-missed family entertainment. Both the Children's Theater and the Community Theater are located at 200 N. Adams (☎ 406/728-1911). The **Montana Players,** Inc. (☎ 406/728-8293) is an adult group that performs contemporary dramas, usually twice a year.

The **Missoula Symphony Orchestra and Chorale,** 131 S. Higgins in the Wilma Building (☎ 406/721-3194), is composed of university students, Missoula residents, and other regional musicians, often performing with featured guests in the historic Wilma Theater. The **String Orchestra of the Rockies,** P.O. Box 8265 (☎ 406/243-5371), a statewide professional string ensemble, is based in Missoula and performs regularly there. The **University of Montana Music Department,** Music Recital Hall at the University of Montana (☎ 406/243-6880), often brings in outstanding musicians performing in the university's remarkable recital hall. Regularly scheduled recitals include solo and ensemble performances by faculty and students.

A SIDE TRIP TO ST. IGNATIUS & THE MISSION VALLEY

If you travel north from Missoula on U.S. Highway 93, you'll round a hill and suddenly come face to face with the majestic Mission Mountains, often topped with snow even during the warmest summer months. The Mission Valley, which

encompasses the tiny town of St. Ignatius and continues north to Ronan a.
is home to the Confederated Salish and Kootenai tribes. Here U.S. Higr.
the most direct route from Missoula to the Flathead Valley, winds its way
over hills and around sparkling Flathead Lake to end just north of Eureka a
Canadian border. You can easily take a day to explore the National Bison Range,
historic town of St. Ignatius and its mission, the Ninepipe Wildlife Refuge, and mor
of the valley as you drive north along Highway 93. Most of these points of interest
are actually part of the Flathead Reservation; see the section below for details.

3 The Flathead Indian Reservation & St. Ignatius

The Confederated Salish and Kootenai tribes make their home on the Flathead
Indian Reservation, with tribal headquarters for the 1.2 million-acre reservation
in Pablo. The tribes, however, own just over 50% of the land within reservation
boundaries.

Like the other tribes now relocated in Montana, the Salish and Kootenai were not
in agreement with the government's decision to place them on reservations. At one
time, the land base for the tribes was somewhere around 22 million acres, before it
dwindled to its present area.

The change in culture for the tribes came quickly when fur traders, homesteaders, and the missionaries of the Catholic Church headed west. Founded in the early
1850s by Jesuit priests, the town of St. Ignatius is nestled in the heart of the Mission Valley. One of the valley's larger small towns, it contains one of Montana's most
prized architectural treasures, the **St. Ignatius Mission.** Established in 1854, the
mission contains 58 unique murals by Brother Joseph Carignano on its walls and
ceilings and is an enduring testament to the religion and history of the area.

The **National Bison Range,** just west of St. Ignatius and part of the reservation,
is a protected open range for buffalo. Just 7 miles southwest of Charlo on Highway
212, the range protects one of the last remaining herds of bison, numbering from 300
to 500. Drive along the self-guided tour and see how many buffalo, deer, bighorn
sheep, and antelope you can spot within the 19,000 acres. A visitor's center, picnic
area, restrooms, and trail for those with physical disabilities are also available.

If you're more interested in feathers than fur, check out the **Ninepipe National
Wildlife Refuge** located just off Highway 93, 5 miles south of Ronan. This wetland
provides refuge for a waterfowl population that includes nearly 190 different species.
Look for up to 80,000 birds in the fall and 40,000 in early spring, with the most
numerous species including Canada geese, mallards, cormorants, blue herons, and
mergansers.

If you're looking for a dose of culture, call the **St. Ignatius Chamber of Commerce,** 240 Mountainview, St. Ignatius, MT 59865-0396 (☎ 406/745-2190) to find
out who's treading the boards at the **Purple Mountain Theater.** This community
effort is housed in a remodeled turn-of-the-century barn and promises great fun
for all ages. The **Mandorla Ranch Bed & Breakfast** (☎ 406/745-4500) can
provide you with a comfortable place to hang your hat while you explore this
beautiful valley.

Wildlife conservation and land management have played big parts in the lives of
the tribal members. The **Mission Mountain Wilderness,** east of Highway 93,
represents a remarkable feat: It was the first wilderness area officially designated as
such by a tribe in the United States. To hike in the wilderness area, a tribal permit
of $6 is required. These can be purchased in St. Ignatius.

way 93 continues north until you reach Pablo, where the most ambitious
ation project at the moment is the Sqe^{S}lix^W/Aqûsmakni·k^S Cultural Center,
e **People's Center.** Taking its name from the Salish and Kootenai words mean-
g "the people," the center aims to promote, reserve, and enhance the Salish and
Kootenai culture. Constructed after years of planning, the recently opened 6,700-
square-foot facility includes an exhibit gallery, an education room, a learning center,
and a gift shop featuring Native American arts and crafts, books, and music. For more
information on the center, and other activities on the Flathead Reservation, contact
the People's Center, P.O. Box 278, Pablo, MT 59855 (☎ 406/675-0160).

A SIDE TRIP TO HOT SPRINGS

Unlike Columbia Falls, whose name suggests natural attractions that are nowhere to
be found, Hot Springs, Montana, does indeed have hot springs. Situated southwest
of Polson, just off Highway 28, the tiny community is an easy afternoon's drive from
any of the other towns that lie around Flathead Lake. Don't expect world-class
facilities here, though. The **Symes Hotel,** 207 N. Wall (☎ 406/741-2361), is a
funky, art deco establishment that rents the soothing mineral waters by the tub, in
a decidedly old-fashioned manner: Men are on one side and women are on the other.
Rent a room, apartment, or cabin by the day, week, or month here.

If you're traveling by RV, **Camp Aqua Bath House** (☎ 406/741-3480), 5 miles
northeast of town, is a good place to stay if you want to soak. Their private cabins
are each outfitted with a "plunge," toilet, shower, and steam room. The **Hot Springs
Spa,** 308 Spring St. North (☎ 406/741-2283), and **Cabinet Steam Baths,**
405 Central (☎ 406/741-2348), also tap the springs, but you have to call ahead to
make an appointment.

Plans are in the works to refurbish the **Camas Bath House,** and the **Corn Hole**—
outdoor mud baths—is being reconditioned for public use, free of charge. Contact
the **Hot Springs Chamber of Commerce** (☎ 406/741-5642) for information on
these facilities.

4 The Flathead Lake Area: Somers, Lakeside, Polson, Bigfork & Ronan

Home to cherry orchards, stands of evergreens, a sparkling lake, and artists of all
descriptions, the Flathead Lake area can easily be overromanticized. It is, seemingly,
home to all that is beautiful in the northwest corner of a state that has much to
recommend itself.

The scenic beauty of this area is unrivaled in Montana, offering something for
everyone, regardless of whether your interests lie indoors or out. Water sports abound
on the lake and hikes lead to sparkling mountain streams with views, but if you want
to shop or see a play, you can easily spend your day inside the shops, galleries, and
theater of Bigfork.

With much of this area lying within the tribal lands of the Salish-Kootenai, there
is also a long-standing native heritage, especially evident in the summer when
mesmerizing drums beat well into the night.

AREA ESSENTIALS

GETTING THERE The nearest airports are **Glacier International,** north of the
lake between Kalispell and Columbia Falls (see Chapter 5 for airlines), and the
Johnson Bell Airport in Missoula (see Section 2 of this chapter for airlines). Which
particular airport is closer depends upon your destination: Bigfork is just over a

30-minute drive from Glacier International; Polson is roughly midway between
two. For rental cars, **Avis** (☎ 800/331-1212), **Budget** (☎ 800/527-0700), **He.**
(☎ 800/654-3131), and **National** (☎ 800/227-7368) maintain counters at eac.
airport.

VISITOR INFORMATION   Your best bet for information on the west side of the
lake is the **Port Polson Chamber of Commerce,** P.O. Box 677, Polson, MT 59860,
(☎ 406/883-5969). For goings-on east of the lake, contact the **Bigfork Chamber,**
645 Electric Ave., (☎ 406/837-5888). **Travel Montana** (☎ 800/541-1447) and
Glacier Country (☎ 800/338-5072) can supplement this information; call either
number for Glacier Country travel information packages.

GETTING OUTSIDE

The Flathead is one of those places where you see the serious golfer and the serious
backpacker in the same spot, sometimes in the same body. The golfing is incredible
on several courses, and the backpacking, hiking, and fishing are even better. Flathead
Lake is the summer spot for many residents in the valley. Windsurfing and even
yachting are popular sports for those who can afford to practice them, and though
fishing was always good in the past, even pike are now found in abundance. If your
plans take you to one of the lakes or trails on the Salish-Kootenai Reservation, don't
forget to buy a tribal permit on the Salish-Kootenai Reservation.

For fishing gear, fishing licenses, and tribal permits, the leader on the lake is Tom
at **Tom's Tackle** in Polson at 108 E. 1st St. (☎ 406/883-6209). (To rent any other
sort of sports and outdoor equipment, you'll need to drive to Kalispell.)

BOATING

Quiet World Boats (☎ 406/755-SAIL) is the Flathead Valley's source for boat rentals as well as the latest information on the local boating scene on Flathead Lake. They
are located at 15 E. Montana Street in Kalispell, about 15 minutes from the north
end of Flathead Lake. Boat rentals are also available at the **Bigfork Marina and Boat
Center** (☎ 406/837-5556); **Kwa Taq Nuk Resort** (☎ 800/882-6363); and
Marina Cay Resort (☎ 407/837-5861). **Silvertip** (☎ 406/862-2600), a sporting
goods store in Whitefish at 33 Baker Ave. is a good source for kayak and canoe
rentals.

Fixed-keel sailboats can be launched at the state parks around Flathead Lake. Big
Arm, Yellow Bay, and Somers have fishing accesses. Only ballasted boats are recommended on the main portion of the lake. Small boats are usually kept near the shore.

Excursion cruises are an excellent way for visitors to experience the beauty of
Flathead Lake. The 65-foot *Far West* is one of the area's oldest, with daily dinner
cruises and Sunday brunches. Call 406/857-3203 for reservations. One of the
finest charter boats on the lake, *Lucky Too*, is based at Marina Cay. Call 406/
257-5214 to make a reservation with "Shorty" George and this 1995 24-foot Bayliner
Classic. Located just south of Bigfork on Hwy. 35, the Bayview Resort and Marina
at Woods Bay on the east side of the lake (☎ 406/837-4843) provides private
sunset cruises. And if a guided cruise is a little too calm for your taste, consider
parasailing from the dock at Marina Cay with Sky Fly'n Parasail (☎ 406/837-2161).

CRUISES

If you don't have your own boat to drop into one of the ramps surrounding the lake,
contact the **Port of Polson *Princess*** (☎ 406/883-2448). For $16 adults, $8
children, the *Princess* makes the proverbial three-hour tour, leaving the Kwa Taq Nuk
resort marina in the early afternoon and making a loop around Wild Horse Island

.10 stops) before heading back. If it's a Montana sunset you're after, take the two-hour sunset cruise, departing in the late afternoon, and look west. Beware: The sun doesn't truly set in these parts in mid-summer until after 9:30pm. This evening cruise runs $10 for adults, $5 for children.

FISHING

The fishing in Flathead Lake has been strange over the years because they've meddled with the fish. When mysis shrimp were introduced as food for the also-introduced kokanee salmon, a strange thing happened: Intended for the salmon's palate, the shrimp instead began to eat healthy portions of plant life that the salmon had become accustomed to eating. The salmon, rather than prospering, died. Kokanee salmon are now rare, but trout can be found, and largemouth bass and perch haunt the warm, shallow spots.

Fishing the southern half of the lake requires a Salish-Kootenai tribal permit, purchased at stores in Polson or at the tribal headquarters in Pablo.

GOLF

The Flathead Lake area has two outstanding golf courses on its shores. In Polson, the 18-hole **Polson Country Club** public course is situated just off the lake on U.S. 93 (☎ 406/883-2440). A round of 18 is $20, 9 is $12. **Eagle Bend Golf Club,** a challenging Nicklaus-design course with views of Flathead Lake and the surrounding mountains, is located in Bigfork just off the highway on Holt Drive (☎ 406/837-3700). Though the price seems high by valley standards—$35 for 18 holes, $23 for 9—experienced golfers accustomed to bigger city prices will most certainly be impressed by the premier course, praised as one of the country's best by *Golf Digest.* Be sure to call ahead for a tee time.

HIKING

Besides strolling by the lake at one of the marinas or state parks, the best bet for trekking is in the **Jewel Basin,** a designated hiking area north of Bigfork. More than 30 miles of hiking trails make it a great place for day-hiking as well as overnights. Before dropping into the actual basin, you'll get a great look at the Flathead Valley and Flathead Lake. For free maps of some of the more popular trails, inquire locally at one of the Forest Service offices in Kalispell (☎ 406/755-5401) or Bigfork (☎ 406/837-5081). To reach the head of the hiking area, take Highway 83 from either Bigfork or Somers, turn north onto Echo Lake Road, and follow the signs.

RAFTING

The **Glacier Raft Company** (☎ 406/883-5838) runs half of its outfit from Polson at Riverside Park. They operate tours of the South Fork of the Flathead River, including a swing through the Buffalo Rapids and Kerr Dam.

SKIING

There is no downhill skiing around Flathead Lake, especially in summer, but you can take Highway 93 south to **Montana Snowbowl** (see Section 2 of this chapter) or north to the Big Mountain in Whitefish (see Section 8 of this chapter) in less than an hour if road conditions permit.

WINDSURFING

Flathead Lake has a misleading reputation for being a good place to windsurf; the actual windsurfers in the Flathead Valley (we could name them here) aren't even that crazy about the lake as a place to surf. It's not a horrible place, it just isn't

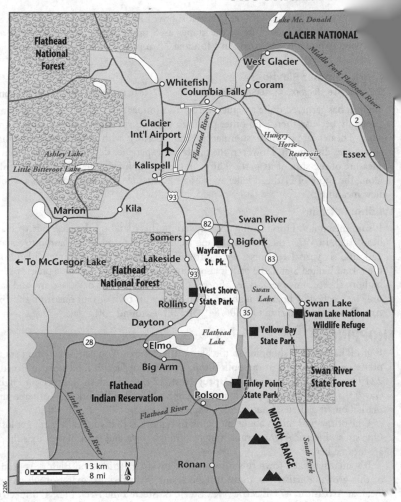

considered one of the nation's best. When the Sportsman and Ski Haus north of the lake in Whitefish stopped renting windsurfing equipment, there suddenly ceased to be any place in the entire Flathead Valley to get a board. Though there are surfing spots on the east side of the valley, they are difficult to predict (wind-wise), and difficult to get to, which has made even the serious windsurfers in the Flathead Valley consider redirecting their obsessions elsewhere. If you have your own board (a necessity) and want to give Flathead Lake a go, try any of the access points at the state parks along the lake (Finley Point on the southeast side of the Lake, Yellow Bay on the west, and Wayfarer near Bigfork are the best). Another good place to put in is on the west side of the lake at Polson, just beyond the golf course.

EXPLORING THE AREA

The Mission Mountain Winery

U.S. Hwy. 93, Dayton. ☎ **406/849-5524.** Tastings daily until 5pm Apr–Oct.

...nery is a popular spot on the west shore of Flathead Lake, just off Highway ...hough more than 97% of the grapes used in the wines are from elsewhere, ... wine is nonetheless "made in Montana." Stop in, visit with the owners, and ...ke a tour.

.gfork Summer Playhouse

...26 Electric Ave., Bigfork. ☎ **406/837-4886** or 406/837-4876 for show times and reservations.

Bigfork has garnered quite a reputation for its summer stock theatrical productions, probably because there's no other program to compete with it in this part of the state. Theater fare is typical summer musical repertory, with hit-and-miss casts that sometimes disappoint. However, the playhouse experience definitely benefits from a measure of the sum of its parts: Throw in dinner at Showthyme and a sunset stroll along the shore of Flathead Lake and "Some Enchanted Evening" takes on a whole new meaning.

Wildhorse Island

It's no misnomer. Horses really do run wild on this island on the west side of Flathead Lake. In 1977, the Bureau of Land Management turned the island into a state park and six years later horses were introduced there. One of the largest islands in the inland United States, the park is also home to an endangered palouse prairie plant, bighorn sheep, and several types of deer. The park is open for day use only, and can only be reached by boat through Big Arm. Take your own or rent one from the **Big Arm Resort and Marina** (☎ 406/849-5622) for around $30 a day.

SHOPPING

Bigfork has the best shopping in the Flathead Lake area. You can usually find some pretty good book buys at the **Folk Shop,** a thrift shop/health food store in Ronan, 221 Hwy. 93 South, and at the **Osprey Nest,** 12 miles south of Kalispell on Highway 93, a treasure trove of antiques and collectibles. But Bigfork has cornered the market on art galleries, boutiques, and specialty shops.

One of the best things about shopping in Bigfork is that you really can't get lost. One street, Electric Avenue, runs straight through town and most of the city's shops are located here.

It's amazing that a town this tiny has so many art galleries. And Bigfork is proud of this growing artistic reputation. Check out the offerings, many of which are local, at **Artfusion,** 471 Electric Ave., **Steele & Steele Fine Arts,** Inc., 470 Electric Ave., and the **Janoff Gallery,** 459 Electric Ave.

If you're looking for an authentic yet unusual gift item with a Western theme, visit the **Great Montana Mercantile and Trading Post,** 469 Electric Ave., **Cabin Creek,** 459 Electric Ave., or **Swan River Trading Company,** 459 Electric Ave.

There are several top-notch specialty stores in Bigfork worth exploring. **Wild Birds Unlimited,** 426 Electric Ave., has an impressive array of bird and birding accoutrements. **Roma's Eclectic on Electric,** 470 Electric Ave., is a gourmet kitchen store that stocks unusual food items and equipment. At **Electric Avenue Books,** 490 Electric Ave., sit down in one of the many rooms and browse through the extensive collection. **Eva Gates Homemade Preserves,** 456 Electric Ave., is locally famous for six gourmet preserves and three syrups, produced since 1949. The **Stone Chair,** 459 Electric Ave., combines tried-and-true Western gift items with artful selections from the East Coast to the Far East, including an extensive selection of unique garden tools. And if you happen to actually be in the market for a stone chair, they've got one of those, too.

Shop for clothes at **Applause!,** 405 Bridge St., or the **Collection,** 549 Electric two shops that feature a mix of women's clothing, fine furniture, antiques, . unusual gift items.

If you need to refuel so you can keep shopping, stop in at **Great Montan.** **Munchies,** 470 Electric Ave., or **Brookie's Cookies,** 191 Mill St., for a quick snack.

WHERE TO STAY

There are five campgrounds in Flathead Lake State Park, each located at a different point around the lake: Big Arm and West Shore on the west side of the lake, and Finley Point, Yellow Bay, and Wayfarers on the east shore. Call 406/755-PARK for specific information on any of these state park campgrounds, open from May through September.

Less expensive options to the ranch vacation or area resorts around Flathead Lake include **The Timbers** (☎ 406/837-6200) and **Woods Bay Motel** (☎ 406/837-5609), both old-fashioned motel units located off the highway in wooded settings near Bigfork. **The Bayshore Resort Motel** (☎ 406/844-3131) in Lakeside is another alternative. Each unit has a kitchenette and some come with a boat slip. In Kalispell, less than 10 miles from the north end of the lake, there are a number of budget accommodations: **Days Inn** (☎ 800/525-2525); **Motel 6** (☎ 406/752-6355); and **Four Seasons Friendship Inn** (☎ 800/545-6399).

✪ Averill's Flathead Lake Lodge

Box 248, Bigfork, MT 59911. ☎ **406/837-4391.** 3 lodges, 20 cabins. $1,350 per person per week (based on one-week minimum stay, includes all meals and ranch activities). AE, MC, V.

By land or by water, this place is the best on the lake. A beautiful log lodge surrounded by thousands of acres of forest is your home base for all activities, whether on horseback or by boat. The Western experience is done up right at this place, complete with sing-alongs, campfires, and barn dances. When the hoe-down is done, take to the water on a windsail, or just relax at the edge of the lake. The location and the atmosphere of this place (the Averills perfectly combine a ranching lifestyle with the summer vacation experience) makes Flathead Lake Lodge not only the best in the area, but quite possibly the best in the state.

Twenty two- and three-bedroom cabins are scattered around the property and feature simple yet tasteful Western-style furnishings. Meals are served family-style in the main lodge.

Kwa Taq Nuk

Hwy. 93, Polson, MT 59860. ☎ **406/883-3636** or 800/882-6363. 112 rms. A/C TV TEL. $89–$104 double. AE, DC, DISC, MC, V.

Built in 1992 right on Flathead Lake, this resort offers a full-service marina, jet skis, and everything else a lake has to offer. Though the resort caters to business travelers, the tourist may find this an expensive but tasteful and accommodating place to stay. The resort has a gift shop, lounge, an art gallery, indoor and outdoor pools, and a hot tub. For food, try the Pemmican Room, offering fine dining in a casual atmosphere overlooking the water.

Marina Cay Resort

180 Vista Lane, Bigfork, MT 59911. ☎ **406/837-5861.** 125 units. A/C TV TEL. Rooms $65–$99, condos $199–$265, suites $145–$275. AE, DISC, MC, V.

Marina Cay is the place for anglers. Though not included in the lodging price, the resort contracts private fishing charters and parasailing adventures on Flathead Lake. This resort has everything: an espresso bar, a pub, lounge, grill, and fine dining at uincy's, the resort's restaurant. Golfers will delight in the proximity to Eagle Bend, ne of the best courses in the state.

he Osprey Inn

5557 Hwy. 93 South, Somers, MT 59932. ☎ **406/857-2042** or 800/258-2042. 5 rms. $90–$110. MC, V. All rates include a full breakfast.

Sharon and Wayne Finney have created a comfortable bed-and-breakfast right on the western edge of the lake. Named for the osprey that frequent the area, the inn is a bird-watcher's dream. A perfect place to relax, the inn provides a couple of vantage points: staring out of your bedroom window to the lake and the mountains to the east, or in a canoe for those wishing to paddle offshore for a closer look. Included in the list of amenities is a hot tub, a nice fireplace, and a player piano. If you plan a summer trip, you'll have no problem making reservations. In winter, however, the Finneys are only open by special arrangement.

WHERE TO EAT

Other than the **Montana Grille** south of Somers, Bigfork has cornered the culinary market for fine dining on the lake. Flathead residents from as far away as Whitefish routinely make their way to Bigfork to eat, shop, and take in a play at the Bigfork Summer Playhouse.

✪ Bridge Street Gallery Restaurant

408 Bridge St., Bigfork. ☎ **406/837-5825.** Reservations recommended. Lunch $4–$9; dinner $10–$19. AE, MC, V. Summer Tues–Sun 11am–2pm and 5:30–10pm; winter Tues–Sat 5:30–10pm. CONTINENTAL/INTERNATIONAL.

Formerly a lunch-only restaurant that was actually more of a gallery, Bridge Street shifted its main focus from art to food in 1991. Though art is still a part of the restaurant—it lends much to the indoor atmosphere—the dining experience is now the center of attention and can be enjoyed on the deck with equal relish. Be sure to try the great appetizers.

The Grill at Eagle Bend

279 Eagle Bend Dr., Bigfork. ☎ **406/837-7305.** Reservations accepted. Lunch $5–$8; dinner $8–$20. AE, DISC, MC, V. Summer daily 11am–11pm; winter Mon 11am–2:30pm, Tues–Sat 11am–2:30pm and 5:30–9pm. PACIFIC RIM/AMERICAN.

A spin-off of the Montana Grille, Eagle Bend offers Pacific Rim and Northwest cuisine every bit as good as what you'll find across the lake. From the lobster stir-fry to the wok-charred ahi and 32-ounce Kootenai grill prime rib, everything about the Grill at Eagle Bend is excellent. The restaurant overlooks the 18th green on the Ridge Course.

✪ Montana Grille

5480 Hwy. 93 South, Somers. ☎ **406/857-3889.** Reservations recommended. Lunch $4–$6; main dinner courses $10–$30. AE, DISC, MC, V. Summer daily 11:30am–2:30pm and 5:30–10pm; winter Tues–Sat 11:30am–2:30pm, 5:30–10pm, Sun 5:30–10pm. SEAFOOD/STEAKS/PASTA.

This is by far the best restaurant of its kind in the Flathead Valley. Exceptionally priced, it serves incredibly fresh Northwest cuisine (every day, the chef receives fish flown in directly from Maui).

Located on the northwest shore of Flathead Lake in Somers, the Grille faces east; from the upstairs dining room you can enjoy views of the mountains and clear skies as reflected in the natural reflecting pool right outside the window. Appetizers include calamari fried in a light batter, very good sushi, and intriguing jalepeño peppers. Our favorite dish is the seafood pasta. Desserts include cheesecake and mousse.

☻ Showthyme

548 Electric Ave., Bigfork. ☎ **406/837-0707.** Reservations recommended. Lunch $4–$6; r dinner courses $10–$20. AE, DISC, MC, V. Mon–Fri 11:30am–2:30pm; Mon–Sat 5–10p AMERICAN.

Located next to the Bigfork Summer Playhouse, Showthyme seems to be the perfect prelude to the drama next door. Dine upstairs or downstairs before taking in a show or stop in afterward for gourmet coffee and the delicious ice-cream crêpes that are sure to satisfy a sweet tooth. Chef Blu's creations have earned quite a following throughout the Flathead Valley. The atmosphere is pleasant, the staff professional, and the food inspiring.

Tiebuckers Pub and Eatery

75 Somers Rd., Somers. ☎ **406/857-3335.** Reservations required for parties of eight or more. Main courses $8–$15. MC, V. Summer Tues–Sat 5–10pm; winter Tues–Sat 5–10pm. AMERICAN.

You won't find better barbecue anywhere in the Flathead than at this (slightly) out-of-the-way restaurant in Somers. With an oil- and vinegar-based sauce, Tiebuckers has created a unique niche in the world of barbecue. Homemade soups, salsas, and desserts complement a diverse menu as well as several nightly specials, which usually include fresh seafood. Entrées each include soup and salad, as well as your choice of pasta or a baked potato.

THE PERFORMING ARTS

In addition to the troupe of the Bigfork Summer Playhouse (see "Exploring the Area," above), Flathead Lake visitors can take in a play by the **Polson Players,** an equally talented group of thespians who take to the stage at the Mission Valley Performing Arts Center. Call the **Port Polson Chamber of Commerce** (406/883-5969) for current information on plays, ticket prices, event dates, and times.

5 The Swan Valley

This is the Montanan's Montana. Hidden from the crowds by the Mission Range, the Swan Valley is a recreational paradise quietly tucked away in beautiful scenery. Though the clearcuts by the timber industry can be an eyesore, the remainder of this thinly populated area is bursting with snowcapped mountains and accessible lakes. The Bob Marshall Wilderness and the Mission Mountain Wilderness Areas are literally within walking distance (at least by Bob Marshall's standards, who sometimes walked 70 miles in a day) and in winter, snowmobiling, cross-country skiing, and even sled-dog mushing are the sports of choice in this remote wonderland. Be sure to watch out for deer year-round along Highway 83, especially at dawn and dusk.

AREA ESSENTIALS

GETTING THERE   Other than being air-dropped like a parcel of supplies, the only way to get into the Swan is by Highway 83. Airports in **Kalispell** (☎ 406/257-5994) and **Missoula** (☎ 406/543-8631) are almost equidistant from the Swan. Though **Glacier International** is undeniably closer, the drive from Missoula to the Swan Valley is more scenic, with remarkable mountain and lake vistas along Highways 200 and 83. Statewide road reports are available by calling 800/332-6171; for weather reports, call 406/449-5204.

VISITOR INFORMATION   The Swan isn't exactly a self-promoter. Though several businesses rely strictly on the tourist dollar, the valley-wide tendency is to remain a small, secretive place for those who either live there or are in the know. If you're ne of those who aren't, however, the **Swan Lake Chamber of Commerce,** Stoney Creek Rd., Swan Lake, MT 59911 (☎ 406/886-2279) can send you information on local happenings. For general information about **Glacier Country,** which includes the Swan Valley, call 406/756-7128 or 800/338-5072.

GETTING OUTSIDE

Densely forested and marked by a sparkling chain of lakes, the Seeley-Swan Valley offers a variety of activities for the outdoor enthusiast, with a vast network of forest service trails marking year-round recreational opportunities for hiking, mountain biking, and fishing. The **Seeley Lake Ranger District,** Bigfork (☎ 406/677-2233), will provide you with a detailed map of these trails upon request.

Highway 83, which runs through the valley, is a scenic route for touring bicyclists, mostly flat, with opportunities for viewing birds and wildlife along the way, especially deer.

Winter sports in the Swan Valley center around cross-country skiing and snowmobiling, along the same forest service trails and logging roads that are popular with bicyclists and hikers in summer.

OUTFITTERS & GUIDES

Situated as it is on the western boundary of the Bob Marshall Wilderness Area, Swan Valley is home to several experienced guides who know parts of this vast territory like the toughened backs of their leathery hands. Guided pack trips on horseback usually run from $165–$200 per person per day with a normal trip into the Bob usually lasting a week. At Holland Lake Lodge, **Holland Lake Outfitters** (☎ 800/648-8859) runs trips from one of the most easily accessed entrances to the wilderness to points beyond. The expertly named **Bob Marshall Wilderness Ranch** (☎ 406/745-4466) operates out of Seeley Lake and offers custom packages for 5- and 10-day trips. One of the best south side outfitters (though they also do incredible outings from the west side), is **Rich's Double Arrow Ranch** of Seeley Lake (☎ 406/677-2317). They've been packing people into the Bob since the late 1950s. Many of the Double Arrow trips are loop outings along the south border where the Bob Marshall meets the Scapegoat Wilderness. **JM Bar Outfitters** (☎ 406/825-3230) of Clinton, a tiny town south of the wilderness area, offer trips into the Bob that range from hunting and fishing to photography and plain old admiring. Good pack trips into the Bob Marshall take at least 5 days, with 10-day trips being a little longer than normal, but certainly worthwhile. Expect to plunk down around $1,000 per person for a trip, with longer trips costing closer to $1,500. All trips come with basic equipment, horses, ground transportation (you're expected to get yourself to the starting point, then back to wherever you came from), and meals. Outfitters aren't the only way to experience the wilderness, but if you're not familiar with the area and you'd rather leave the walking and the backpacking to the horses, guided trips are worth the price.

WHERE TO STAY

✪ The Emily A. Bed and Breakfast

Hwy. 83 (Mile Marker 20), Seeley Lake, MT 59868. ☎ **406/677-3474.** 5 rms, 1 suite (3 with private bath). $85 double; $150 suite. Rates include full breakfast. No credit cards.

If you're not careful, you can miss this bed-and-breakfast home, though as you approach the stunning larch log home along its winding driveway you'll wonder how that was possible: The two-story structure is an imposing sight, set in the middle of a stunning mountain meadow. With views of Swan Valley and the Missior

Mountains in addition to a wide variety of wildlife right outside their door, visit to the Emily A. don't lack for genuine Montana scenery. A strong sense of family evident, with decorations of family heirlooms, rooms named after the owners' children, and grandmother Emily's name above it all. All rooms are located upstairs except for the suite, which is ideal for families, with two bedrooms, a kitchen, and a private deck.

✪ Holland Lake Lodge

SR Box 2083, Condon, MT 59826. ☎ 406/754-2282 or 800/648-8859. 9 rms, 5 cabins. $65 double; $75–$120 cabin. AE, DISC, MC, V. Head south of Condon and 4 miles east of Montana Hwy. 83; look for signs.

Holland Lake is probably not on your road atlas, and if it is, it's probably not labeled. But now that you know it exists, it's worth a visit. Though the current owners have no plans to keep the lodge open in winter, there is the chance that new owners will decide to keep the Holland Lake winter tradition alive. "Race to the Sky," the sled dog race that takes place each winter, has come through Holland Lake in the past, and snowmobilers have found this place to be more than a little to their liking. Summer, though, is the lodge's big season, and this won't change no matter who's in office. The waterfalls are a short $1^1/_2$-mile hike from the main lodge, and 7 miles away is Upper Holland Lake (also hidden from cartographers) and good trout fishing.

The lodge also offers fine dining in the main lodge. The ever popular Cajun cuisine is gone, however, and the new prices are a bit expensive. Also available is a sauna just a few steps from the cabins. Make sure to read the story of Bob Marshall in the main lodge.

Swan Valley Super 8

Between Mile Markers 46 and 47 on Montana Hwy. 83 (P.O. Box 1278), Condon, MT 59826. ☎ 406/754-2688 or 800/800-8000. 16 rms. TV TEL. $50–$55 double. AE, DC, DISC, MC, V.

This is the only chain motel in the Swan, and that's no minor distinction. What other hotel in the valley offers a nationwide reservations service? Though the picnic benches are hardly a selling point for adventurers stopping over on their way to the Bob Marshall Wilderness, the Super 8 in Condon one-ups its chain counterparts by offering (free with the room, mind you) two corrals that can accommodate up to five horses. Adequately priced, the Super 8 is a value, but just not as romantic as other Swan lodgings.

Tamaracks Resort

P.O. Box 812, Seeley Lake, MT 59868. ☎ 406/677-2433 or 800/447-7216. 13 cabins. $55–$120 cabin. DISC, MC, V.

Located off the west side of the highway, Tamaracks started out as a homestead in 1916 and became a resort in 1930. Though not a screaming deal for singles, the Tamaracks is a comfortable place to stay for frugal couples. Four beds in a two-room cabin go for just under $100, and that's not bad, considering the proximity to the Bob Marshall Wilderness. The 1,600 feet of lakefront don't hurt either.

Wilderness Gateway Inn

In Seeley Lake off the west side of Montana Hwy. 83 (P.O. Box 661), Condon, MT 59868. ☎ 406/677-2095. 19 rms. TV TEL. $50 double. MC, V.

Simply put, the Wilderness is simple. All the rooms come with queen-size beds in this rustic wooden structure next to the local grocery store. Not far from the golf course, the Wilderness is a relatively new motel to these parts (construction was completed in 1985). Though it's simple, it does offer a hot tub for the road-weary, and most people passing through here are in fact road-weary. Highway 83 has been known to eat travelers alive, especially when road construction is in full swing. Pets are allowed for a $5 fee per night.

6 The Bob Marshall Wilderness Area

It is the most incredible stretch of wildlands in the Lower 48. It is named for one of the most bizarre and extraordinary conservationists of the 20th century. And it is without a doubt full of the most spectacular wildlands not under the auspices of the National Park Service. Easily the most renowned wilderness area in the United States, the Bob Marshall complex (which includes the Bob Marshall, Great Bear, and Scapegoat Wilderness Areas), has become less of a secret with the passing of each season, and as word spreads, it becomes less of a wilderness.

Just south of Glacier National Park, the Bob complex occupies nearly the entire territory that lies between the boundaries of Hwy. 2. to the north, Hwy. 83 to the west, Hwy. 200 to the south, and Hwys. 287 and 89 to the east. Access points along these roads occur infrequently and are hardly marked for the casual drive-by tourist.

Formed in 1964, the Bob Marshall Wilderness Area was less than a million acres of land appropriated for wilderness. Then 15 years later, over a half-million acres were added to the north (Great Bear) and south (Scapegoat). Perhaps the most spectacular place in the Bob, and certainly the most popular is the **Chinese Wall,** an ominous formation that stands over 1,000 feet tall and stretches for 11 miles through the Bob on the western boundary of the **Sun River Game Preserve,** a haven for elk in the mating season each fall. One of the more well-traveled trails and easy accesses to the Chinese Wall is along the South Fork of the Sun River on the Holland Lake–Benchmark trail (see below). From the east side, reach the Chinese Wall by taking Trail 202 at Benchmark for 5 miles to Trail 203, then stay on this trail for roughly 11 miles before taking the Indian Creek Trail, Trail 211, to the south end of the Chinese Wall at White River Pass, elevation 7,590 feet. The Chinese Wall is unmistakable and is one of the most recognizable geologic formations in Montana.

Towering peaks run great lengths through the Bob and stand as some of the tallest, and certainly the most dramatic, sites in the northwest part of the state outside Glacier National Park. **Holland Peak,** just north of Holland Lake on the wilderness area's western boundary, is a spectacular 9,356-foot giant that can be seen from afar but cannot be accessed directly.

Once inside the wilderness area, **Salmon Lake** is a wonderful destination for the photographer as it captures the length and the beauty of Holland Peak's east face. To reach Big Salmon Lake, take Trail 42 from the Holland Lake Lodge on the west side of the Bob to Trail 110. It's a very long day hike, and a reasonable two-day hike through the Swan Range to Big Salmon Lake.

Located one-third of the way in on the **Holland Lake–Benchmark Trail** (a 60-mile trail that takes roughly a week to traverse the midsection of the Bob), Salmon Lake is simple purity without sight or sound of civilization. This trail also runs just south of the Chinese Wall.

North, in the Great Bear, is the impressive **Great Northern Mountain**. This 8,705-foot peak towers over the northeast part of the Great Bear Wilderness and can be viewed from many different points along the roadsides near the wilderness areas. You'll need a couple of vehicles if you don't have someone who can pick you up where you exit the Bob at the end of your journey. Park one of the vehicles at either end: Holland Lake if you plan on making it your terminus, or Benchmark, west of Augusta, if you plan on ending there.

If you begin on the east side, the trail follows the South Fork of the Sun R. Trails 202 and 203 before moving west along Indian Creek on Trail 211. This you, as mentioned above, to the south end of the Chinese Wall at White River I From there, you'll take Trail 138 along the South Fork of the White River until y. reach the White River and Trail 112. This trail takes you to the South Fork of the Flathead River at White River Park. Across the river is Murphy Flats and Trail 263 along the river to Trail 110. This long trail takes you along Big Salmon Lake, the Swan Range and then to Holland Lake outside the Bob's western boundary. It's a little easier to read than hike.

To reach the summit of Great Northern, you'll have to do some off-trail hiking; eight miles, if you make a round-trip. From Martin City, just northeast of Columbia Falls on Hwy. 2, take the East Side Reservoir Rd. (38) for just over 15 miles to Highline Loop Rd. (1048). Take this road for just over a half-mile across the bridge to the "trailhead." Start along the left side of the creek until the landscape opens up. Trudge up to the ridge, then along it, to Great Northern's summit.

The majestic **Scapegoat Mountain** is the dominating jewel of the Scapegoat Wilderness Area. Surrounded by cliffs, this 9,204-foot summit is easily the most prominent feature in the southern part of the wilderness complex.

Wildlife abounds in the Bob, with grizzly bears being the most feared and the most difficult to spot (see Chapter 5 for tips on what to do if you do run into one). Moose are prevalent, as are deer, which seem to pick inopportune times to cross Highway 83 after emerging from the wilderness. Elk gather each fall for mating at the base of the Chinese Wall in the Sun River Game Preserve on the wilderness's east side. Incredible bird life coexists in the wilderness area, including the ptarmigan, a brown bird resembling the quail, which changes the color of its plumage each winter to snow white.

Hiking is allowed in the wilderness and trails from the west side are the easiest to reach. Though the network of seemingly infinite trails within the Bob is intricate, complex, and difficult to get to, day hikers can enjoy the smaller system of trails emanating from Holland Lake and Upper Holland Lake near the Holland Lake Lodge along the fringe on the Bob without having to load pack horses and march for a week from one side to the other.

Take Hwy. 83 south 61 miles from Bigfork, or north 20 miles from Seeley Lake, to reach the lodge and the trails. Trail 42 from the north side of Holland Lake connects with Trail 110 to reach the Necklace Lakes just inside the Wilderness Boundaries. To reach the Holland Lake Falls and Upper Holland Lake before crossing the wilderness boundary at Gordon Pass, take Trail 415 a short way until it joins Trail 35. This trail, taken to its end, stretches from the western boundary into the center of the park near the South Fork of the Flathead River (not a day-hike).

Though camping is allowed in the Bob, the best way to see it is by hiring a licensed outfitter who knows the rules (for outfitters on the east side, see Chapter 8; for outfitters on the west side, see "Swan Valley" in this chapter.) The rivers that run through the Bob make up the largest scenic wilderness river system in the country, and fishing can be a great experience in the middle of the middle of nowhere.

Though camping isn't discouraged in the Bob Marshall Wilderness, it's not exactly amenable to the RV set, making it difficult for people who are out of shape to enjoy the wilderness without the help of horses. Don't, however, let this fool you. Though there aren't any facilities whatsoever in the complex, you may notice when camping that you certainly aren't in uncharted or unexplored territory. Sites along rivers seem if not crowded then often used, and trails aren't exactly overgrown along the more popular routes. Some things to remember when camping: Before you set

, contact and consult a ranger at one of the district ranger stations mentioned
now about distances, the wisdom of your itinerary, and restrictions. You can also
pick up a topographical map. Carry plenty of water and water containers. Remember when loading up your pack that this is the weight you'll likely endure for a week
or so. Restrictions are few. No vehicles are allowed in the area: it's as simple as that.
This includes bicycles of any kind. To get around in the Bob you either walk or ride
on an animal's back. It might also help to remember, too, that licensed hunting is
not forbidden in the Bob except within the Sun River Game Preserve. This makes
backpacking in the Bob Marshall a little less inviting in the fall months.

For information, maps, and advice about traveling in the Bob Marshall Wilderness complex, contact one of the six ranger stations monitoring the wilderness. In the
Lewis and Clark National Forest: Rocky Mountain Ranger District, 1102 Main
Ave. NW, Box 340, Choteau, MT 59442 (☎ 406/466-5341). In the **Flathead
National Forest:** the Spotted Bear and Hungry Horse Ranger Districts, 8975 Hwy.
2 E., Hungry Horse, MT 59919 (☎ 406/387-5243) or the Swan Lake Ranger District, P.O. Box 370, Bigfork, MT 59911 (☎ 406/837-5081). In the **Lolo National
Forest:** Seeley Lake Ranger District, HC 31 Box 3200, Seeley Lake, MT 59868
(☎ 406/677-2233). In the Helena National Forest: Lincoln Ranger District, Box
219, Lincoln, MT 59639 (☎ 406/362-4265).

7 Kalispell

The center of one of the fastest-growing counties in America, Kalispell is the hub of
the Flathead Valley. Situated ideally between Glacier National Park and Flathead
Lake, Kalispell has grown from being a town spurned by the railroad to a virtual center for culture in northwest Montana. The beauty of Kalispell is that it's a big city
(valley residents sometimes complain that Kalispell, at just under 15,000 residents,
is too overgrown) posing successfully as a small one. With northwest Montana's two
major roads (U.S. Highway 2 and U.S Highway 93) converging in the north part of
downtown, Kalispell may seem downright urban after you've traveled through towns
whose only traffic signals are signs declaring speed zones ahead. Add to the major
roads an international airport with daily flights from Salt Lake City and Seattle, a
passenger train depot 15 miles north, internet access, and cellular phone services, and
Kalispell has become an ideal place for big city businesspeople to operate in a small-town setting, with some spectacular scenery just a few minutes away, where the
mountains border the valley.

ESSENTIALS

GETTING THERE   Glacier Park International Airport is located north of
town at 4170 U.S. Hwy 2 (☎ 406/257-5994). **Delta** (☎ 406/257-1030 or 800 221-
1212), **Horizon** (☎ 406/752-2209 or 800/547-9308), and **Skywest**(☎ 800/
453-9417) have daily flights.

Highway 2 will get you here from the east or west. From Missoula, Highway 93
leads north into town on a scenic 120-mile route that takes you past Flathead Lake.
The drive usually takes a solid two-and-a half hours, no matter the season. RVs amble
along the gradually curving road during summer (to the frustration of most other
drivers!) and icy conditions warrant added caution and reduced speeds during the
winter. Statewide weather updates are available by calling 406/449-5204; for
Kalispell, call 406/755-4829. Call 800/332-6171 for statewide road reports and 406/
755-4949 for road information in the Kalispell area.

Amtrak stops at the Whitefish depot, just 15 miles north of Kalispell. The bus terminal is located at 1301 Hwy. 93 South (☎ 406/755-4011).

VISITOR INFORMATION   Kalispell's chamber of commerce, the **Flathead Convention and Visitor Association,** is located at 15 Depot Park, Kalispell, MT 59901 (☎ 406/756-9091 or 800/543-3105), and offers not only practical information concerning Kalispell, but extensive travel and tourism information for the entire valley.

GETTING AROUND   For rental cars, **Avis** (☎ 800/831-2847), **Budget** (☎ 800/527-0700), and **National** (☎ 800/227-7368) maintain counters at the airport. **Rent-a-Wreck** at 1194 Hwy. 2 (☎ 406/755-4555 or 800/654-4642) and **U-Save** at 1010 Hwy. 2 (☎ 406/257-1900 or 800/272-8728), both offer discount car rentals.

For taxi service, call **Flathead Area Shuttle Transport** at 406/755-2488 or **Kalispell Taxi and Airport Shuttle,** 406/752-4022.

GETTING OUTSIDE

Kalispell isn't exactly a destination for the person looking for outdoor recreation, though it's near Glacier Park (see Chapter 5) and Flathead Lake (see Section 4 of this chapter).

Though tooling around on Highway 2 or Highway 93 is not a great idea, there are backroads that cyclists frequent. Whitefish Stage Road runs parallel to U.S. Highway 93 (from 93, go east on Reserve to reach it) and offers some great views of the mountains in a bucolic environment. For area information, **Alpine Cycle and Sports** at 228 Main (☎ 406/755-2453) and **Bikology** at 155 N. Main (☎ 406/755-6758) are the experts and offer all kinds of bicycle accessories and rentals.

Kalispell doesn't have the golf courses that Whitefish can boast, but the courses in Kalispell aren't as expensive. **Buffalo Hill,** just off Highway 2 north of town at 1176 N. Main (☎ 406/756-4545), has an 18-hole course and **Village Greens** at 500 Palmer Dr. (☎ 406/752-4666), offers 18 holes for a little less.

Lone Pine State Park (☎ 406/ 755-2706) isn't exactly a secret, but it doesn't attract much notice since it's overshadowed by nearby Glacier National Park. To get there, head west on Highway 2. At the intersection with Meridian, you'll see signs for the park sending you left (south). Take this road for about 5 miles (in the curve to your right, the road becomes Foys Lake Road) to the park. Once you're there, take in the views of the valley below or hike on the trails.

SEEING THE SIGHTS

Conrad Mansion
330 Woodland Ave. ☎ **406/755-2166.** Admission $4 adults, $1 children. Open May–Oct. Call for seasonal hours.Turn east from Main on 3rd St. Head east until you reach Woodland.

This incredible home was the residence of Kalispell founder Charles E. Conrad, a remarkable man at best and a wild Missouri River trader around Fort Benton at the least. Though the tour doesn't delve into Conrad's illicit past in Fort Benton before his respectable days in Kalispell, it does give good local history. The guides describing the original furnishings are dressed in Victorian costumes.

Hockaday Center for the Arts
2nd Avenue East and 3rd Street. ☎ **406/755-5268.** Free admission. Tues–Fri 10am–5pm, Sat 10am–3pm.

Five galleries under one unique roof—a former Carnegie library—offer regional works of art that often surprise a lot of locals. The Hockaday is the area's source of cultural awareness and artistic instruction that ranges from paintings and sculptures to resident artists who teach classes and workshops.

Woodland Park
On the east edge of town at Woodland Park Drive.

This little spot offers visitors a place to sit down in the sun and relax if they want to kill a day outside without killing themselves. A lagoon with ducks and a swimming pool make this a nice park. For walkers who shun the mall, walking tracks skirt the park.

SHOPPING

Whether you're a mall shopper or a downtown thrifter, you'll find places to divert your attention in Kalispell. The **Kalispell Center Mall** at 20 N. Main has more than 40 stores and eateries, one of which, the **Powder River Ranch Company,** features Western collectibles and one-of-a-kind wood furnishings. **Sunshine Tapes and CDs** has the latest in music.

Just up the street, downtown Kalispell has a few stores of its own. **Norm's News** has the latest newspapers from around the globe as well as a comprehensive magazine rack and espresso bar. **Books West** is the downtown book shop on 1st and Main. For unusual antiques (and some good used books) try the **Kalispell Antique Market** downstairs at 1st and Main across the street from Books West. **Treehouse Toys,** 228 Main St., displays a wide selection of classic and modern toys, including unique, old-fashioned tin toys.

At the Gateway West Mall on Highway 2 West, **Corral West Ranch Wear** has exactly what its name implies: plenty of cowboy boots, hats, and apparel. **Village Book Shop** is the mall's independent bookseller.

WHERE TO STAY

Best Western Outlaw Inn
1701 Hwy. 93 South, Kalispell, MT 59901. ☎ **406/755-6100** or 800/237-7445. 220 rms, 30 suites. A/C TV TEL. $92 double; $109–$140 suite. AE, DC, DISC, MC, V.

Located on the south side of town, the Outlaw has a crass-sounding name but is actually one of the better hotels in the valley. Though it's not necessarily the best deal in town, the Outlaw does come equipped with all the goodies: two indoor pools, a fitness center, tennis courts, and raquetball courts. The weekend entertainment in summer includes comedy acts from all over. You won't find talent scouts hanging around, but the entertainment line-up is a signature for the Outlaw.

Cavanaugh's at Kalispell Center Mall
20 N. Main (at the Kalispell Center Mall), Kalispell, MT 59901. ☎ **406/752-6660.** 126 rms, 10 suites. A/C TV TEL. $87–$97 double; $100–$180 suite. AE, DC, DISC, MC, V.

The first thing you see coming into downtown from the north is the Cavanaugh's marquee and electronic message board. Just off to the west inside the mall is the hotel where you'll find the Fireside Lodge off from the lobby, a sitting area decorated in a Southwestern theme. Rooms are comfortable, but you have to remind yourself that you're staying in a mall. The more expensive suites include Jacuzzis in the room. The Atrium is the hotel's restaurant and, though it isn't the best in the valley, the skylights are a nice touch on sunny summer days.

Days Inn
1550 Hwy. 93 North, Kalispell, MT 59901. ☎ **406/256-3222** or 800/735-6862. 53 rms. A/C TV TEL. $59–$80 double. AE, DC, DISC, MC, V.

Located right on the highway on the north side of town, this particular Days Inn is not anything spectacular. The rooms are clean and well-maintained and the price is lower than at other hotels around town, but other than a continental breakfast, there isn't anything out of the ordinary. Then again, there also aren't any surprises, and, after driving the Hi-Line, a doughnut, cup of coffee, and cable TV may be all you need.

Four Seasons Motor Inn

350 N. Main, Kalispell, MT 59901. ☎ **406/755-6123**. 98 rms. A/C TV TEL. $45–$75 double. AE, DC, DISC, MC, V.

Four blocks from the center of town, this hotel is affordable, comfortable, and not much different than the Days Inn up the street, except that the second-floor units have balconies. (Mind you, the balcony drapes don't open up to Glacier National Park or anything else spectacular.) But getting a room this comfortable for less than $50 in the Flathead Valley is a steal.

WHERE TO EAT

✪ Alley Connection

22 1st St. ☎ **406/752-7077**. Reservations strongly recommended. Lunch $2–$5; dinner $6–$13. AE, DISC, MC, V. Tues–Sat 11am–2:30pm; Tues–Thurs 5–9pm, Fri–Sat 5–9:30pm. CHINESE.

Unquestionably the best place in the valley for Chinese cuisine, the Alley Connection didn't sprout up overnight, but to many it seems like it did. From a small room operation, the restaurant has come a long way. Now food is served in two tastefully but simply decorated dining rooms. Meals of chow mein, sweet and sour pork, and Szechwan chicken can be ordered separately or in the more popular family style. Lunch is a great deal for less than $6 and service is always quick and dependable.

The Bulldog

208 1st Ave. East. ☎ **406/752-7522**. Lunch $4–$6; dinner $8–$12. AE, DISC, MC, V. Mon–Fri 11am–2am; Sat 4pm–2am. STEAKS/SEAFOOD.

This is a bar, yes, but for a bar, it has an incredible menu. Decorated in the English pub vein, The Bulldog is a popular lunch venue. There are pricier items on the dinner menu, including their famous beer-steamed shrimp. Don't confuse this place with the Bulldog Saloon in Whitefish. Both serve drinks, but The Bulldog in Kalispell has steaks; the one in Whitefish serves burgers.

First Avenue West

139 1st Ave. West. ☎ **406/755-4441**. Lunch $5–$8; dinner $11–$16. AE, DISC, MC, V. Mon–Fri 11am–3pm; daily 5:30–10pm. STEAKS/SEAFOOD.

Formerly Bubbaroni's, First Avenue has taken its street address and turned it into the catchword for good dining in Kalispell. Though the prices aren't the best in town, and the service has been erratic in the past, First Avenue is certainly one of the nicer places to eat in town. The appetizer menu is good and some items (the steamed clams, for example) can serve as a whole meal. Try Blackie's wings, a Cajun-style appetizer served with a honey dip and crudités, for a tasty variation on chicken wings. On the dinner menu, the pasta dishes are excellent. First Avenue serves an excellent variety of microbrews and wines.

✪ Moose's

173 N. Main St. ☎ **406/755-2337**. Reservations not accepted. Most items $4–$14. No credit cards. Daily 11am–2am. PIZZA/SANDWICHES.

If you've just leveled someone outside the scrum, put a header into the corner of the net, or cleared the bases with a gapper, then you'll find compatriots at the Moose. It's not exclusively a bar for the aching amateur athlete, but that's its reputation. The truth is, though, that even with the reputation, the sawdust on the floor, and the crowded weekends, Moose's may quietly make the best pizza in town. For lunch it's quiet and kind of spooky being in an empty Moose's. The sawdust is there, the bar is there, but that's it. Kind of like eating in the middle of a football field in summer.

✪ Norm's News

34 Main St. ☎ **406/752-4092.** Reservations not accepted. Most items $3–$6. No credit cards. Summer Mon–Sat 7am–10pm, Sun 8am–4pm; winter Mon–Sat 7am–6pm, Sun 8am–4pm. SOUPS/SANDWICHES.

The amazing thing about Norm's is that, in a valley where many of the rural residents can't even pick up CNN on the television, you can walk a couple of blocks downtown and buy a copy of the *Sydney Morning Herald*. All of the major Northwest dailies are sold here, too. Grab one from your hometown and sit down to some reasonably priced soups and sandwiches. Norm's is especially great in the mornings when you just want to have a cup of coffee and read the paper—from Australia.

Rocco's

3796 Hwy 2. East. ☎ **406/756-5834.** Most items $9–$17. AE, DISC, MC, V. Daily 5–10pm. ITALIAN/STEAKS/SEAFOOD.

Its location near the airport is but one reason Rocco's has an aviation theme throughout the restaurant. The other, more prominent, reason is printed on the back of the menu. Rocco was an aviator (and Italian chef) shot down in World War II. So not to give away the rest of the "fact or fiction" story, we ask you to read the rest. The fettucine Toscana is a traditional combination of pasta, fresh vegetables, sun-dried tomatoes, and pine nuts that is especially tasty, though rest assured that copious amounts of cream and butter make it so. Like most of the entrées, Rocco's homemade desserts are rich and not for the calorie-conscious. Airplanes suspended in flight are hung throughout the restaurant and windows facing east allow for mountain views.

⑤ Syke's Grocery

202 2nd Ave. West. ☎ **406/257-4306.** Most items $2–$9. DISC, MC, V. Mon–Sat 7am–10pm; Sun 8am–10pm. AMERICAN.

Whenever someone asks where the home of the 10¢ cup of coffee is, you can tell them it's Syke's Grocery in Kalispell, Montana. Though it's not gourmet coffee (it's Hills Brothers, to be precise), it is worth a dime to drink all you want or can. The menu is typical home-style food, but it's the least expensive greasy spoon in the valley and you can grocery shop on the way out.

THE PERFORMING ARTS

Kalispell is home to the **Flathead Festival** (☎ 406/257-0787), an outstanding valley arts organization that coordinates musical events valley-wide. Check with them for any upcoming performances under their auspices. In recent years, the festival has brought world-class operas to the area in addition to their annual summer concert series, one of the state's premier cultural attractions.

A SIDE TRIP TO LIBBY

Located about an hour and a half from Kalispell is the logging town of Libby, reached by a scenic drive that winds through the evergreen forests of northwest Montana and the peaks of the Salish and Cabinet ranges. Libby is not an overly exciting town, but, depending on the time of year you visit, there are things to see and do.

Nordicfest, held in the middle weekend of September each year, is a wonderful fall festival that sees the Kootenai Valley turning yellow in spots with the changing colors of the larch trees. This Scandinavian festival includes a juried crafts show, a parade with full folk costumes, antique shows, and "Norsewest Melodrama." Most of the events are free. Another festival that pays tribute to Libby's heritage, **Logger Days,** is held the middle of each July.

If you want to picnic, try the **Ross Creek Cedar Grove Scenic Area** or **Kootenai Falls.** There is a nice hiking trail that lead to the falls, featured in 1994's *The River Wild.* The tumbling falls and towering evergreens provide a stunning backdrop for afternoon picnics on the rocks. Kids will enjoy the hanging bridge that spans the river, but those afraid of heights should forgo the thrill.

The **Libby Chamber of Commerce** can provide you with additional information. Contact them at P.O. Box 704, Libby, MT 59923 (☎ 406/293-4167).

8 Whitefish

Town prophets continue to forecast impending doom for this hamlet, saying it's only a matter of time before the town is run over by outsiders and the locals go stark raving mad. It will, they say, be another Jackson Hole, Wyoming.

But Whitefish, though it's not what it once was, is still enjoying small-town status. Parking at the post office is becoming increasingly difficult, there is a Denny's and a Wendy's now to complement the McDonald's, and on a bad day it takes 30 minutes to get to Kalispell instead of 20. But if you find yourself in Whitefish in the off-season windows of spring and fall you'll find yourself in a sleepy town.

ESSENTIALS

GETTING THERE   Whitefish is extremely accessible. It's easier to get here than to virtually any other Montana town. It's a quick and easy drive up Highway 93 from Kalispell. Statewide weather updates are available by calling 406/449-5204; for Whitefish, call 406/755-4829. Call 800/332-6171 for statewide road reports and 406/755-4949 for road information in the Whitefish area.

The **Glacier International Airport** is 10 minutes away between Columbia Falls and Kalispell. **Delta** (☎ 800/221-1212), **Skywest** (☎ 800/221-1212), and **Horizon** (☎ 800/547-9308) have daily flights.

The **Amtrak** (☎ 800/USA-RAIL) station is shared with **Burlington Northern** at the edge of downtown in the renovated and charmingly attractive depot. The *Empire Builder* travels west from Chicago and east from Seattle four times weekly.

The bus "terminal" is located at Stump's Pumps, a convenience store on the corner of Baker and Second across from the library and city hall. There are two daily **Trailways** arrivals from Missoula at 6:30pm and 1:20am. Service is also available to other Montana destinations through **Rimrock Stages** (☎ 800/255-7655). Call for cities and departure times.

VISITOR INFORMATION   The **Whitefish Chamber of Commerce's** new location is in the recently refurbished train depot on the north end of downtown. Here you'll find just about everything you need in the way of brochures, area maps, and travel information (☎ 406/862-3501).

GETTING AROUND   **Avis** (☎ 800/831-2847), **Budget** (☎ 800/527-0700), and **National** (☎ 800/227-7368) maintain counters at Glacier International Airport.

Impressions

Here for the first time I heard a definite regional accent unaffected by TV-ese, a slow-paced warm speech. It seemed to me that the frantic bustle of America was not in Montana. Its people did not seem afraid of shadows in a John Birch Society sense. The calm of the mountains and the rolling grasslands had got into the inhabitants. . . it seemed to me that the towns were places to live in rather than nervous hives. People had time to pause in their occupations to undertake the passing art of neighborliness.

—John Steinbeck, *Travels with Charley*

Unless you rent a car from there or a company in Kalispell, the only game in town is **Rocky Mountain Transportation** (☎ 406/862-2539). The local cab outfit is the **Sober Chauffeur** (☎ 406/862-7733).

GETTING OUTSIDE

Whitefish is one of the great recreation towns in the Northwest, and many locals are here because vacations turned into residency. With the Big Mountain and Glacier National Park (see Chapter 5) nearby, Whitefish is both a winter and summer wonderland with an array of outdoor activities to suit the hardcore adventurer and the entire family.

For all kinds of outdoor equipment or apparel, check out **Silvertip** at 33 Baker St. (☎ 406/862-2600), **Sportsman & Ski Haus** at the Mountain Mall (☎ 406/862-3111), or **Ski Mountain Sports,** 200 Wisconsin St. (☎ 406/862-7541).

BIKING

Mountain bikes are as prevalent as cars in the summertime in the north part of the Flathead Valley. With old logging roads abandoned throughout the forestlands of northwest Montana, virtually any side road can become an excellent route for cyclists. Two operations in Whitefish share the expertise for mountain bikers seeking adventure on seemingly undiscovered paths. **Glacier Cyclery,** 336 E. Main (406/862-6446), provides excellent service and maintenance as well as rentals and area maps and up-to-date information for the serious mountain biker. These guys know what they're doing. Just as able are the members of the **Timberwolf Bicycle Company** at 903 Wisconsin (☎ 406/862-7547).

CAMPING

Whitefish Lake State Park is tucked on the outskirts of town in a nicely wooded area near Whitefish Lake. Call the Department of Fish, Wildlife, and Parks (406/752-5501) for additional information. For the RV crowd, or those just looking for a hearty chuckwagon supper during the summer months, there's the Diamond K RV Park on Hwy. 93 (☎ 406/862-4242) which also has a limited number of tent sites, along with an on-site laundry and store.

CROSS-COUNTRY SKIING

The Big Mountain (see below) offers $5 lift tickets for its 6 miles of impeccably groomed trails, which offer varying degrees of difficulty. The **Glacier Nordic Club** maintains 5 miles of trails on the Whitefish Lake Golf Course and another mile across the street near the Grouse Mountain Lodge. A small donation allows skiers to enjoy both sides of the street and yearly passes are available. For information, contact the

Outback Ski Shack at Grouse Mountain Lodge (☎ 406/862-3000), which also rents skis and other equipment, apparel, and offers lessons. They are located in a tiny building behind the hotel and just off the track.

DOGSLEDDING

Dog Sled Adventures (☎ 406/881-BARK) lets you explore the mountains around Whitefish "at the speed of dog." Their guided 12-mile rides in two-person sleds run through Stillwater State Forest, 2 miles north of Olney. Each trip takes about two hours and the sleds come equipped with blankets and elk-hide furs to keep you warm. The dogs pulling the sleds, mostly mixed breeds, were all rescued by the owners from unwanted homes or animal shelters and trained as sled dogs. A sled ride costs $100, or $50 per person, and includes a cup of hot chocolate and homemade cookies, waiting for you at the end of your ride.

DOWNHILL SKIING

✪ The Big Mountain Ski and Summer Resort

P.O. Box 1400 (12 miles north of Whitefish on Big Mountain Road), Whitefish, MT 59937. ☎ **406/862-1900** or 800/858-5439. Lift tickets $38 adult, $20 child; senior citizen, student, and half-day rates available. Open daily late Nov–Apr. From Whitefish, head over the viaduct to Wisconsin for 3 miles until you see the flashing yellow light. Turn right on Big Mountain Road and proceed 9 miles to the Big Mountain Village.

With an annual snowfall of 300 inches, night skiing for $12, nine lifts, a vertical drop of 2,300 feet, and virtually no lines, the Big Mountain is easily one of the best ski resorts in the northwestern United States. Geared for the intermediate skier (terrain difficulty is 25% beginner, 55% intermediate, and 20% advanced), the Big Mountain is the town's pride and joy come winter each year. Everyone in town, or nearly everyone, heads to the hill in the mornings when the powder starts to fall. Though prices have increased with the popularity of the Big Mountain in recent years, the Colorado skier will still be amazed at the price of a lift ticket, the quality of the runs, and the dearth of the crowds that seem to afflict every ski town south of the Flathead Valley.

Ski schools range from the half-day group lessons for kids ($18) to private lessons starting at $50 per hour.

For après ski food and entertainment, the Big Mountain does its share. **The Bierstube** and the **Hellroaring** are easily the best spots on the mountain for food, fun, and beverages.

FISHING

It's not the Madison Valley, but Whitefish does have some hot spots for anglers wanting to try their hand. **Tally Lake** is a massive (in depth) lake located north of Whitefish off Highway 93. Five miles north of town, turn left onto the Tally Lake Road (signs will direct you). You can expect cutthroat, rainbow, kokanee, brook trout, and whitefish.

In town, across the viaduct toward the Big Mountain lies **Whitefish Lake.** If you can handle all the recreationists hovering about like flies, the lake offers some pretty good lake trout. Northern pike can be found here, and rainbow and cutthroat can be nabbed on dry flies in the evening.

The **Lakestream Flyshop,** 15 Central (☎ 406/862-1298), provides full-service fly-fishing, tying, and rod-building services in addition to a variety of sports gifts for outdoor enthusiasts.

GOLF

The **Whitefish Lake Golf Club,** Highway 93 North (☎ 406/862-4000), is the only 36-hole course in the state and provides fantastic and challenging rounds of golf. **Par 3 on 93,** Highway 93 South (☎ 406/862-7273), allows for work on the short game.

HIKING

Probably the most popular trail in town is the hike to the summit of the Big Mountain. The **Danny On Trail** (named for the Forest Service ecologist who was killed in a ski accident on the Big Mountain in 1979) begins in the Big Mountain Village and ascends the south face of the mountain on four different paths. There's a 5.6-mile jaunt and three shorter ones. Snow (it is, after all, a ski resort) can be a problem in late spring and even the early months of summer. In fact, the ground is often still damp in August.

HORSEBACK RIDING

Old West Adventures (☎ 406/862-3511, ext. 453) offers trail rides in the summer, plus winter sleigh rides (with dinner included) for around $40. The rides are one of the most popular alternatives in town for nonskiers, and reservations are required in advance.

SNOWBOARDING

Snowboarders will find kindred spirits—as well as an extensive line of boards and apparel—at **Snowfrog,** in the Alpine Village Center at 903 Wisconsin (☎ 406/862-7547). Ask for Jacques—he'll be happy to fill you in on the local snowboarding scene on the Big Mountain and other spots in the Flathead Valley.

SNOWMOBILING

Contact the **Flathead Snowmobilers Association** (☎ 406/752-2561) for current conditions and reports, then head up to **Loon's Echo Resort** (☎ 406/882-4791) for any and all snowmobile adventures you may want or need; it has access to hundreds of miles of trails from state forestlands.

EXPLORING THE TOWN

Descendants of Henry Weinhard have given birth to Black Star beer, the most recent newcomer to the downtown area of Whitefish. The glass-enclosed brewing "tower" at the **Great Northern Brewing Company,** at Central and Railway (☎ 406/863-1000), is now the tallest edifice in Whitefish. Tours of the facility are offered daily.

Downtown is the hub for shopping in Whitefish, with stores concentrated on Central Avenue and Second Street. For clothing, visit the **Village Shop** and **Indigo Creek** in the Orpheum Building at 201 Central. The Village Shop is an excellent women's clothing company that also sells accessories, leather goods, and footwear. Indigo Creek, upstairs from the Village Shop, features fashionable unisex clothing and accessories. For the latest in music, try the **Sound Garden** at 215 Central. **Bear Mountain Mercantile,** 233 Central, and **A Little Bit Western,** across the street at 240 Central, feature unique gift items with a Western flair. **Bookworks,** 110 Central, is an independent bookstore specializing in nature books, regional writing, and children's literature. Next door to the bookstore, the **Toggery,** at 122 Central, stocks a full line of clothing and shoes for men, women, and children. **Crystal Winters,** at 232 Central, is a funky little souvenir shop with a wide selection of cards, T-shirts, toys, and gifts. One of the town's largest selections of souvenir items—

including T-shirts, local books, and regional jewelry—can be found at **Whitefish Gift and Gear,** 229 Central. **Montana Coffee Traders,** 5810 Hwy. 93 South, carries a full line of Montana-roasted coffees and coffee equipment as well as interesting gift items, including T-shirts and Guatemalan crafts. **3 Bar 2 Western Outfitters,** 221 Central, has authentic Western clothing and riding gear, hand-creased hats, saddles, and tack. **Granny Annie's,** 410 E. 2nd, is a charming country store filled with home accessories, antiques, and gifts. For contemporary women's fashions with an international twist, **Sappari,** at 215 Central, is the place. **One Hour Fast Photo,** 533 E. 2nd, or **Northern Exposure,** 235 Baker, are film developers that offer one-hour service. **Heather Candles,** 505 Wisconsin, creates the perfect souvenir of a Montana vacation with hand-crafted beeswax candles, decorated with wildflowers and leaves. Don't expect to find spectacular shopping at the **Mountain Mall,** 6475 Hwy. 93 S; though anchored by an excellent supermarket, video rental shop, and a sporting goods store, the mall has very few other stores worth mentioning. **Eurodeli,** 905 Wisconsin, is a full-service deli and market featuring gourmet food items. **Bebe Kezar Western Eclectic,** also located at the Alpine Village Center, showcases Montana artists, with a focus on uncommon art, and includes an outdoor sculpture garden.

WHERE TO STAY

Whitefish is peculiar—it has almost enough hotel and motel space for the entire town to spend the night away from home and not leave the city. And yet that's not enough beds for all who visit. In recent years there have been problems accommodating tourists without reservations, and this is evidenced by the recent explosion of lodging options that have cropped up around town and continue to do so. Make your reservations well in advance.

IN & AROUND TOWN

✪ Best Western Rocky Mountain Lodge

6510 Hwy. 93 South, Whitefish, MT 59937. ☎ **406/862-2569.** 67 rms, 12 suites. A/C TV TEL. $55–$109 double. Rates include breakfast. AE, CB, DC, DISC, EURO, JCB, MC, V.

The hotel is easy to spot along the strip heading into town from the south: It's the one on your left with the window boxes. One of the newcomers on the lodging scene in Whitefish, the Rocky Mountain Lodge isn't in the most romantic location, but the interior is beautiful for a Best Western franchise member. The suites have fireplaces in the rooms, with kitchenettes, and some have balconies. Breakfast comes with bagels and cream cheese, fresh fruit, pastries, and gourmet coffee.

Comfort Inn

6390 Hwy. 93 South, Whitefish, MT 59937. ☎ **406/862-4020.** 56 rms, 9 suites. A/C TV TEL. Winter $34–$49 double; summer $89–$109 double. AE, CB, DC, DISC, MC, V.

Reasonably priced and equipped with queen beds, the Comfort Inn is a comfortable place to stay and is located conveniently on the south end of town off the highway. Built in 1991 when there seemed to be virtually nowhere to stay, the Comfort Inn filled a void. Now it's simply another adequate motel. But what separates this hotel from the others is the indoor waterslide, which makes this the ideal place to bring the kids.

✪ The Garden Wall

504 Spokane Ave., Whitefish, MT 59937. ☎ **406/862-3440.** 3 rms, 1 suite. $85–$105 double; $175 suite. Rates include full breakfast. MC, V.

Mike and Rhonda Fitzgerald have created a wonderful bed-and-breakfast on the main drag in Whitefish and have somehow made it seem as if it's nowhere near town.

Overflowing with a bucolic warmth that defies its location, the Garden Wall pays attention to detail. From the truffles on the pillow to the incredible breakfast the following morning (which is sure to have local huckleberries in some divine form or other), the Garden Wall is a home full of country charm. If you plan to participate in activities having anything remotely to do with the outdoors, corner Rhonda or Mike for what's happening. Mike is an avid fisherman and outdoor enthusiast (he's one of the local hockey greats to boot), and Rhonda is the trainer for the Glacier Nordic Club. If it's in the Flathead, these guys know what's happening.

Good Medicine Lodge

537 Wisconsin Ave., Whitefish, MT 59937. ☎ 406/862-5488. 9 rms. TEL. $85–$95 double. Rates include full breakfast. AE, DISC, MC, V.

Another newcomer to Whitefish is this cedar-sided bed-and-breakfast on the way to the Big Mountain. The bedrooms are decorated in a Western/Native American theme and some rooms open out onto decks. With nine rooms, two fireplaces, and vaulted ceilings, the Good Medicine Lodge is a bit larger than the average bed-and-breakfast. The phones in each room also detract from traditional inn standards, but every bit of it is intentional—obviously, if you don't want it, you can always unplug it. Private baths are another welcomed feature of the Good Medicine Lodge, of which most other bed-and-breakfasts seem to be in short supply.

✪ Grouse Mountain Lodge

1205 Hwy. 93 West, Whitefish, MT 59937. ☎ 406/862-3000 or 800/321-8822. 144 rms. A/C TV TEL. $119–$189 double. AE, DISC, MC, V.

This place is right in the middle of it all. Despite being one of the more attractive and accommodating facilities in the Flathead Valley, Grouse Mountain is the hub for sports ranging from golf, soccer, and tennis to cross-country skiing. Grouse Mountain is a great resort with a distinct lodgelike atmosphere. Here is the best big place in the north Flathead to get pampered. Exquisitely designed with Western decor, the main lobby, with a comfortable sitting room warmed by a river rock fireplace, is a great place to relax early in the morning. The mountain goat hanging over the front desk looks to the antlered chandelier that hangs gracefully over the center of the lobby. An indoor pool, outdoor hot tub, and the proximity to the golf course makes Grouse Mountain a great place for leisure. The staff is not only polite but the concierge is a great person to chat with when making plans in the area.

Loon's Echo Resort

1 Fish Lake Rd., Stryker, MT 59933. ☎ 406/882-4791 or 800/956-6632. 3 rms, 2 suites, 5 cabins. $100–$130 double, $90–$215 cabin. Discounts for extended stays. DISC, MC, V.

So you want to get out of the Flathead because suddenly, inexplicably, it seems too crowded. Everything's booked anyway. If that's the case, head north on Highway 93 to the little town of Stryker, less than 30 minutes from Whitefish to Ed and Gayle Hynes' Loon's Echo Resort. Begun more than a decade ago as a retreat for those wanting to steal away from the Flathead Valley to a secret hideaway, Loon's Echo changed its tune in 1995 when a multimillion-dollar renovation transformed some rustic cabins into a full-service resort. The main lodge, finished in 1995, is an unbelievable structure. Not only is it an unexpected sight after traveling down the dirt and gravel road 4 miles from the highway, but the architecture is an unlikely blend, however polished. A Spanish tiled roof covers the Tudor frame on the outside, while inside, the main lodge has a very Western feel (though many of the appointments are English antiques). It's a collision of Europe and the West. But the place exudes comfort. Leather sofas make watching the big-screen television a little too easy. The pool, a short walk below the TV room, is so small it's almost decorative. In the adjacent room is the pool table; this room is also furnished with leather couches.

The restaurant is fantastic and certainly not what you'd expect to find. Chef Neil Carloss turns out some incredible meals in the quaint dining room. His background in Cajun cuisine (check out the jambalaya fettucine) and his flair for preparing game (say, elk tenderloin) come through in impeccably prepared meals.

✪ North Forty Resort

3765 Hwy. 40 West, Whitefish, MT 59937. ☎ **406/862-7740** or 800/775-1740. 22 cabins. TV TEL. Winter $59–$139 double; summer $79–$179 double. AE, DISC, MC, V.

Nestled in the pines along Highway 40 between Whitefish and Columbia Falls, the North Forty is a great place to stay if you don't like being in town but still want to be close to all the shopping. This is one of the newer places to stay in the Flathead. What they've accomplished with this place is nothing short of impressive. A multitude of stripped log cabins can accommodate a couple or a couple of families. Though the cabins are hardly distinguishable from each other, they do have names: The Ponderosa Cabin and the Larch Cabin can lodge up to five people each, and the Aspen Suite can house eight. They all have living rooms with fireplaces, dining areas, complete kitchens (with china) and private bathrooms. Though rustic and private in every way, the North Forty doesn't relegate its clients to complete isolation—each cabin unit comes with telephones and televisions.

Quality Inn Pine Lodge

920 Spokane Ave., Whitefish, MT 59937. ☎ **406/862-7600**. 63 rms, 12 suites. A/C TV TEL. $45–$195 double. AE, DISC, MC, V.

Just south of downtown along the Whitefish River, this Quality Inn was built in a Western vein and the name accurately depicts the structure: It is in fact a pine lodge. Rooms are reasonably priced and more than comfortable, but it's the suites that take the cake. They come with private hot tubs, fireplaces, kitchenettes, and their own balconies.

ON THE BIG MOUNTAIN

Lodging options are diverse on the Big Mountain. With an extensive rental pool of single-family homes, duplexes, and condominiums, in addition to several hotels, the Big Mountain is sure to fit any budget. When making reservations (☎ 800/ 858-5439), be sure to inquire about discounted lift and lodging packages; they are often available for multiple-night stays and during value seasons.

If you're looking for an alternative to hotel accommodations, inquire about **Anapurna Properties** and **Big Mountain Alpine Homes** when making reservations. These properties might be exactly what you're looking for. Some are small condominiums and some are large homes available for rent. The funky structures built 30 years also provide a great a place to stay on the Big Mountain for not a lot of money and may be ideally suited for young couples seeking shelter without forfeiting location. The central reservations number for these properties is 406/ 862-1960 or 800/858-5439.

Alpinglow

Big Mountain Village, Whitefish, MT 59937. ☎ **406/862-6966**. 54 rms. A/C TV TEL. $78–$125 double. AE, DISC, MC, V.

Located in the heart of the Big Mountain village, Alpinglow is an adequate facility whose major redeeming quality is its proximity to the chair lifts. The large windows of the main lobby can offer spectacular views out over the Flathead Valley throughout the year. The large covered deck is a great summer hovering spot when the weather begins to slip up into the 80s.

Edelweiss

3898 Big Mountain Rd., Whitefish, MT 59937. ☎ **406/862-5252.** 52 rms. TV TEL. $80–$120 double. AE, MC, V.

Nicer than many of the hotels in the valley below, the Edelweiss has amenities in most of the rooms that would please even the most discriminating of the von Trapps. Complete kitchens with dishwashers, stoves, and microwaves make this an excellent choice if you live out of a cooler on vacations. These are especially important in winter, when it's not always convenient to shoot down the mountain to Safeway or Food Depot for groceries—and restaurants are expensive and few on the mountain.

Hibernation House

3812 Big Mountain Rd., Whitefish, MT 59937. ☎ **406/862-1981** or 800/858-5439. 42 rms. TEL. $45–$105 double. Rates include breakfast. AE, DISC, MC, V.

This is the Big Mountain's economy hotel. Each room has a queen bed and a set of bunk beds for up to four people. As for amenities, a television is located in the lobby, the hotel has an indoor hot tub, and laundry facilities are available. Breakfast in the private dining room off the lobby is included in the price of lodging.

✪ Kandahar Lodge

3824 Big Mountain Rd., Whitefish, MT 59937. ☎ **406/862-6098.** 50 rms. TV TEL. $82–$274 double. AE, DISC, MC, V.

The most prominent and luxurious hotel on Big Mountain is the Kandahar, whose name has absolutely nothing to do with the ancient city in Afghanistan. This cedar lodge with vaulted ceilings, Russell Chatham prints, and an excellent restaurant (peerless on the mountain) is by far the best place to stay in the Big Mountain village. Seventeen of its rooms come with kitchenettes and all the beds at Kandahar come with luxurious down comforters that make even the most bone-chilling nights cozy. Off to the right of the lobby, the small bistrolike Cafe Kandahar serves elegant European specialties in a romantic setting.

Ptarmigan Village

3000 Big Mountain Rd., Whitefish, MT 59937. ☎ **406/862-3594** or 800/552-3952. 124 condos. TV TEL. $50–$200 condo. MC, V.

As you make one of the last big turns on the seemingly endless road up to the Big Mountain, you'll find the Ptarmigan Village straight ahead. Farthest removed of the accommodations choices on Big Mountain, it is practically a coordinate for estimating distances and giving directions for locals ("you know that turn at Ptarmigan?"). A great facility, it has units featuring vaulted ceilings, loft bedrooms, fireplaces, decks, and fully equipped kitchens. Indoor and outdoor pools and tennis courts round out on-site activities, but don't forget—just up the road is some of the best skiing in the state.

WHERE TO EAT

✪ The Buffalo Cafe

516 3rd St. ☎ **406/862-2833.** Reservations not accepted. Breakfast and lunch $3–$6. No credit cards. Mon–Sat 7am–2pm; Sun 9am–2pm. AMERICAN.

It's crowded, inexpensive, and the food is filling. Besides that, more people visit The Buffalo Cafe each year than the Washington Monument, the Louvre, and the Eiffel Tower combined. Not true, but come on Sunday morning and you'll feel that way as you wait an eternity just to get inside, never mind being seated. Begun in Bigfork, then transplanted to Whitefish so owners Charlie and Linda Maetzold could get in more skiing, The Buffalo has remained a breakfast institution in the valley for more than a decade. The menu features a wide variety of traditional breakfast and lunch items in not-so-traditional combinations, many of which are named after loyal locals. Three or four daily specials round out the offerings. Though no longer on the menu, Jessie's Huevos are worth begging for.

✪ The Bulldog Saloon

144 Central Ave. ☎ **406/862-5601** (kitchen 406/862-4748). Reservations not accepted. Lunch and dinner items $4–$6. MC, V. Daily 11am–midnight. AMERICAN.

This is the place to be if you're craving a burger, regardless of whether or not you're a sports fan, although The Bulldog memorabilia (the local high school mascot), collegiate flags on the ceiling, and lights above the bar (faux basketball hoops) may inspire you to pledge allegiance to some sort of team sport. The menu is expansive, especially for a bar, but centers around hearty theme burgers: garlic, bacon and cheese, and ham (the original Bulldog Burger), just to name a few. The Caesar salad and chicken wings are also excellent choices, but are sometimes heavy on the heat. Most meals come with fries, but unless you don't mind developing an addiction, don't ask for the sour cream variety. Considered the local sports bar, The Bulldog is rarely crowded except during big events and Canadian holidays.

Los Corporales

10 Central Ave. ☎ **406/862-6304.** Reservations recommended during summer. Lunch $5; dinner $6–$11. AE, MC, V. Sun–Thurs 11am–10pm; Fri–Sat 11am–11pm. MEXICAN.

This Mexican restaurant, though authentic, is hit-and-miss. With the bar and restaurant under separate ownership, service is somewhat confusing, and paying for your bill can be even more so. The requisite chips and salsa are homemade, but they preface entrées that may or may not fit their menu description. The portions are large, though, and the deck is a relaxing place to spend a sunny afternoon sipping pitchers of margaritas or sangria.

Out of the Blue Bakery

10 Baker Ave. (at the Two Moon Cafe). ☎ **406/862-7580.** Breakfast $3–$6. No credit cards. Weekends only; call for hours. BREAKFAST/BAKED GOODS.

This is a little unusual, so bear with us. Out of the Blue Bakery built up a steady cult following among locals for outstanding breakfasts and baked goods in their previous location when they needed to move. They couldn't find space, so Two Moon Cafe, a restaurant that only serves dinner, offered them use of their kitchen. It may be only temporary, so get here while it lasts.

Out of the Blue hops on the weekends, which is the only time they're open, so you'd better arrive early if you don't want to wait in the parking lot for a table to be cleared. While previously the clientele was largely composed of the ski bum/granola set, word of their baking expertise has spread and so has their client base. Build-your-own omelets come with fresh fruit or home fries and your choice of a number of freshly baked breads. There are also extensive vegetarian options, many of which include tofu.

✪ The Tupelo Grille

17 Central Ave. ☎ **406/862-6136.** Reservations recommended for large parties. Lunch $4–$5; dinner $6–$11. MC, V. Mon 11am–3pm; Tues–Sat 11am–3pm and 5–10pm; Sun 5–10pm. CONTINENTAL/CAJUN.

Recently opened to a hungry mob of locals, this southern restaurant with a Cajun flair has been welcomed with opened arms. Simply and tastefully furnished with New Orleans Jazz Festival placards and black-and-white photographs, the Grille is the best deal in town for dinner; only The Buffalo Cafe competes for lunch options and value. The pasta dishes may look strictly Italian from a distance, but chef Pat Carloss adds a personal Louisiana touch. The bread pudding could cause your arteries to instantly petrify, but it's a risk you simply must take; it's truly incredible.

✪ Whitefish Lake Restaurant

Highway 93 North (at the Whitefish Golf Course). ☎ 406/862-5285. Reservations recommended. Lunch $4–$7; dinner $10–$20. AE, MC, V. Summer daily 11am–3pm and 5:30–10pm; winter daily 5:30–10pm. CONTINENTAL.

This elegant restaurant is one of the few places in Whitefish where you can go out to eat and really feel as if you've gone out to eat. Crisp linens and table candles lend a romantic atmosphere. Though many of the entrées come drenched in heavy sauces, the peppercorn-studded steaks are delicious. Lunch is a great deal and the perfect place to dine in summer if you enjoy hitting the links in the morning. The golf course (all 36 holes) offers some of the most challenging holes and the restaurant provides a perfect complement to the surrounding mountains.

WHITEFISH AFTER DARK

Nightlife in Whitefish, as in most Montana towns, is centered around the city's downtown bars. Though you'll see people of all ages there, the **Great Northern,** 27 Central Ave., and the **Palace,** 125 Central Ave., are the two most popular bars and seem to attract a younger crowd. The Great Northern has a popular open-mike night mid-week and the Palace brings in regional bands for live music on most weekends. Sports fans of all ages huddle up at the **Bulldog,** 144 Central Ave., where you can catch whatever game is on and eat one of the best burgers in the valley (see "Where to Eat" earlier in this chapter). **Stumptown Station,** 115 Central Ave., and **Jack's Diamond Back,** 6155 Hwy. 93 South, have weekly karaoke but aren't as popular with the locals.

As for the performing arts, the **Glacier Orchestra and Chorale** entertains several times throughout the year around the Flathead Valley with guest performers and conductors, usually from late October through April. Call 406/257-3241 for a current schedule of performances. The troupe of the **Whitefish Theater Company** performs traditional and contemporary plays year-round, ranging from musical comedies to classical dramas. Their office at the Mountain Mall (☎ 406/862-5371) can provide you with a list of upcoming productions.

9 Columbia Falls

Columbia Falls gets a bad rep not only for being the home of Plum Creek, a smoke-billowing institution seen for miles even at night, but for its not-so-subtle lack of spirit. Unlike Great Falls, where the falls are out of town and, gasp, dammed underneath, Columbia Falls goes you one better by not having any falls at all. The redeeming feature and equalizer is the town's proximity to Glacier National Park. The lodging rates are somewhat less expensive, and if you have trouble finding a room in Whitefish (not exactly unheard of), Columbia Falls can often come to the rescue.

It's a blue-collar town that's not necessarily respectful (dare we say resentful?) of local environmentalist efforts. A sign just outside town voiced the opinion of at least a few area residents when it exclaimed that Montana was no place for animal rights activists. The people here are real Montanans, and how the town was spared from the real estate invasion and cultural revolution of the West Coast is an enigma. Columbia Falls is surrounded by beautiful mountains and in some ways has prettier views of the valley than does Whitefish.

ESSENTIALS

GETTING THERE   **Glacier International** is the closest airport, 10 miles away on Highway 2, with daily flights serviced by **Delta** (☎ 800/221-1212) and **Northwest** (☎ 800/225-2525).

The closest **Amtrak** station in is Whitefish, 10 miles to the northwest.

Statewide weather updates are available by calling 406/449-5204; for Columbia Falls, call 406/755-4829. Call 800/332-6171 for statewide road reports and 406/755-4949 for road information in the Columbia Falls area.

VISITOR INFORMATION   The **Columbia Falls Area Chamber of Commerce,** P.O. Box 312, Columbia Falls, MT 59912 (☎ 406/892-2072), can provide you with pertinent area information. Columbia Falls is located in Travel Montana's Glacier Country; request information from them at Box 1396, Dept. 8403, Kalispell, MT 59903 (☎ 406/756-7128 or 800/338-5072).

GETTING AROUND   The only car rental agency actually located in Columbia Falls is **Dollar** (☎ 406/892-0009), but the following companies maintain counters at Glacier International: **Avis** (☎ 800/831-2847), **Budget** (☎ 800/527-0700), **Hertz** (☎ 800/654-3131), and **National** (☎ 800/227-7368).

GETTING OUTSIDE

FISHING

The **Hungry Horse Dam,** northeast of town off Highway 2, is one of the better spots in the area. Roads travel the circumference of the water and several sites along the shores provide fishing access near the tributaries that pour in all around the reservoir. Cutthroat trout are best found in these streams.

The **North Fork of the Flathead River** extends from just east of town to the north along Highway 486. Though there's fishing here, it's not particularly great, but the surrounding scenery is spectacular enough to make up for it.

GOLF

Columbia Falls is home to one of the area's premier golf courses, **Meadow Lake.** To reserve a tee time, call 406/892-7601.

HIKING

Columbia Mountain, Glacier National Park, and the Jewel Basin are nearby, but the **Great Northern** is the grandpappy of 'em all in these parts. If you want a leisurely stroll with moderate difficulty, stick to the Danny On Trail on the Big Mountain in Whitefish. If you want eight hours of hardship, then the Great Northern is for you. To get there, take Highway 2 to Martin City, then turn onto the East Side Reservoir Road 38 for 15 miles. At that point, turn east to Highline Loop Road 1048, and from here you should be able to see the approach route. While there's not an official trail, enough people have beaten a path to the summit that one is clear enough to make out. Again, this isn't a leisurely walk nor is it the most well-publicized hike in the area, but it is the most rewarding for those willing to make the effort. The views of Glacier and the Hungry Horse Reservoir are memorable.

SNOWMOBILING

A popular route is the 20-mile **Canyon Creek Trail,** which leads up the back side of the Big Mountain. To get there, take the North Fork Road (Highway 486) for about 6 miles and look for signs to your left. For rentals and additional trail information, contact **Columbia Saw and Ski-Doo** at 406/892-2195 or 800/221-5098.

KITSCH & CAMP

Every tacky tourist attraction has a franchise in Columbia Falls. If you've always longed to sit astride a rare giant jackalope, ride a go-kart, get sucked into a vortex, or zoom down a titanic waterslide, C'Falls has got your ticket. And if all that's not enough to set your cap a-spinnin', head toward Glacier Park on Highway 2. Along the way you can lose yourself in a life-size maze or view some black bears in captivity at the Great Bear Adventure. Just beware: "Your car is your cage!"

Big Sky Waterslide & Miniature Greens, at the junction of Highways 2 and 206 (☎ 406/892-5025), is the main attraction and a good place to cool off. If you've always wanted to reenact the snow scenes from *The Shining* without the snow (and who hasn't?), then **Glacier Maze and Mini Golf,** at Highway 2 East, Coram (☎ 406/387-5902), is your place. Like rats hunting for an odorless cheese, tourists often enter hours before they emerge. The **Great Bear Adventure,** Highway 2 East, Coram (☎ 406/387-4099), doesn't strike fear into the hearts of men like you'd imagine. It's a drive-through zoo with lethargic black bears rambling about, waiting for their next meal. For the Danny Sullivan in you, **Grizzly Go Kart,** 7480 Hwy. 2 East, Columbia Falls (☎ 406/892-3132), offers a track for those wanting to make a run in an imaginative Grand Prix. The **House of Mystery,** 7800 Hwy. 2 East, Columbia Falls (☎ 406/892-1210), offers complete bewilderment to those curious souls who dare enter. **Just for Fun,** Highway 2, Columbia Falls (☎ 406/892-7750), is that place you passed coming into town from the west with the giant jackalope. It gets worse from there.

WHERE TO STAY

Glacier Inn Motel

1401 2nd Ave. East, Columbia Falls, MT 59912. ☎ **406/892-4341.** 19 rms. A/C TV TEL. $50–$52 double. AE, DC, DISC, MC, V.

Other than the comparatively low price for a room, the best thing about this motel (like the town itself) is its proximity to Glacier National Park. The rooms aren't what you'd expect to find at the resorts in town, but neither is the cost, and the rooms on the south side of the motel are actually pretty quiet. A half-mile from the waterslide, the Glacier Inn is located away from the highway. A hot tub is available.

✪ The Inn at Meadow Lake

100 St. Andrews Dr., Columbia Falls, MT 59912. ☎ **406/892-7601** or 800/321-4653. 24 rms. TV TEL. $79–$99 double. AE, MC, V.

This is the poshest place to stay in Columbia Falls, and the price reflects that. If you enjoy golf and have come to Montana for a resort experience in close proximity to Glacier Park, then Meadow Lake is for you. The 18-hole golf course is one of the area's best. Rooms are tastefully decorated and most look out to the golf course. Tracy's Restaurant is a cozy place to enjoy lunch or dinner after a round or two of golf during the summer or cross-country skiing in winter. If you plan to visit during the summer, ask if the resort is hosting a Flathead Festival concert; past headline acts appearing on the course have included America, the Nitty Gritty Dirt Band, and Emmylou Harris (although you still have to buy a ticket).

Turn in the River Inn

51 Penny Lane, Columbia Falls, MT 59912. ☎ **406/257-0724** or 800/892-2474. 4 rms. $85–$110 double. Rates include full breakfast. MC, V.

This modern farmhouse, designed to look antiquated, is actually an incredible home that offers a remote location and a lovely country atmosphere. Judy and Don Spivey have created a haven for relaxation near the Whitefish River that guests are sure to enjoy. Their ebullience is overwhelming as evidenced by the afternoon snacks and beverages offered in exchange for conversation. Breakfast is a delight, be it an omelet, Belgian waffle, or blintz.

WHERE TO EAT

The Back Room of the Night Owl

Highway 2 East. ☎ **406/892-3131.** Reservations accepted. Most items $6–$13. No credit cards. Mon–Sat 4–10pm, Sun 2–9:30pm. AMERICAN.

Located in the—you guessed it—back room of the Night Owl Cafe, this greasy spoon is off the main drag in Columbia Falls. The Back Room is a pleasant surprise. Broasted chicken, spare ribs, and country ribs (small chunks cooked in barbecue sauce) are all delicious and reasonably priced. The fry bread is the house specialty and comes with meals instead of standard bread items. The pizza and salad buffet each Sunday is a bargain for less than $5.

☺ Trumble Creek Hub

5535 Hwy. 2 West. ☎ **406/892-3424.** Reservations not accepted. Lunch and dinner items $3–$6. AE, DISC, MC, V. Mon–Fri 6am–10pm; Sat 6am–9pm; Sun 7am–8pm. AMERICAN.

You'd be hard-pressed to find a better—well, bigger, at any rate—burger anywhere in Montana than at this inconspicuous grocery store/restaurant located on Highway 2 between Kalispell and Columbia Falls. Massive cheeseburgers and Indian tacos are popular menu items, but stay away if you have a heart condition or are counting fat grams: Hub burgers are definitely not for the faint-hearted or calorie-conscious. Everything is big except the price. A burger and fries is a mere $2.99, a small price to pay for a meal that stays with you all day.

7

Southwestern Montana

If Fort Benton is the birthplace of Montana, then the toddling years belong to the mining towns and camps in the southwestern part of the state. From a historical perspective, this part of the state is as wealthy as the gold, silver, and copper mines that once dotted the region's landscape and brought people from all over the country in search of fortune—sometimes gained, but more often not.

Today, southwestern Montana is an outdoor playground full of fantastic trout rivers and streams and beautiful mountain ranges that never seem to vanish from view. Wildlife rambles through ghost towns in Nevada City, farmers continue to bale hay with old-fashioned beaverslide haystackers in the Big Hole Valley, politicians form state laws in Helena, and those who break them head to Deer Lodge.

If it's isolation and outdoor activity you want, then this is the place. Hiking and camping are popular activities within the Lee Metcalf, Gates of the Mountains, and Anaconda Pintler Wilderness Areas. Mile after mile of rivers and streams makes fishing a lucrative summer pastime with whitewater rafters flocking to Bear Trap Canyon for exciting runs through the rapids.

The Continental Divide National Scenic Trail runs through this part of Montana, a 3,100-mile network stretching along the rocky spine of the Continental Divide from Mexico to the Canadian border.

Treasure hunters should try their luck around the state's ghost towns of Bannack, Virginia City, and Alder, where rich gold mines once dotted the stark landscape and modern-day prospectors still pan for gold.

1 Scenic Drives

U.S. Highways 90 and 15 run north to south through the region, but the best roads to take are the well-kept backroads, the state and county highways that follow unlikely and out-of-the-way paths. Traveling from Anaconda to Dillon could be done via the Interstate in good time, just over an hour. But a better, less-frequented route through the Big Hole Valley runs east of the Continental Divide and the Anaconda-Pintler Wilderness area. A good stopping point is Wisdom, one of the coldest places in the Lower 48 (lows, even in July, can drop into the 30s), and the turnoff for the Big Hole

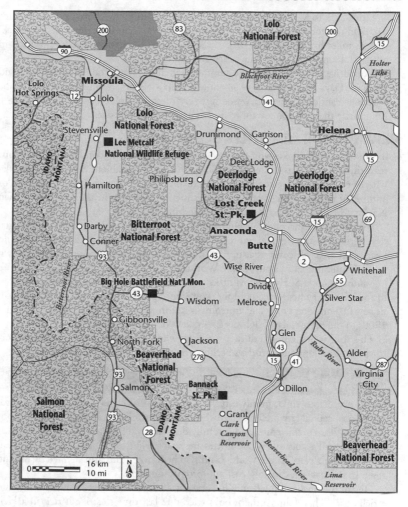

Battlefield. Driving farther south on WYO 278 takes you to Jackson, then Bannack State Park, before ending at U.S. Hwy. 15 south of Dillon. From Dillon, drive north on MT 41 to Twin Bridges and the junction with MT 287. This road runs south through the Old West towns of Sheridan, Laurin, Alder, Nevada City, and Virginia City, before ending in Ennis at U.S. Hwy. 287.

DRIVING TOUR #1: THE BIG HOLE VALLEY

This short loop tour takes you through the Big Hole Valley, nicknamed "Land of 10,000 Haystacks." Begin in Dillon, the largest of the towns in this area, and keep your eye out for whitetail and mule deer in the morning and early evening. Travel north on U.S. Hwy. 15 to Divide, then take MT 43 southwest to Wisdom. This is a tiny town with little other than its residents and the scenery to recommend it, but the Big Hole National Battlefield (described in detail later in this chapter) is a short drive west on MT 43 and is well worth the trip.

Drive back to Wisdom and take MT 278 towards Dillon. Stop off in Jackson for a soak in the hot springs or take a tour of Montana's territorial capitol city, Bannack, just 28 miles further, off MT 278. Walk along the boardwalks and lose yourself in a very real reminder of the state's early history.

This drive is great during the summer, when haystacks dot the landscape and Bannack Days re-create early events in Montana's history. Winter drivers should be especially cautious, however; Wisdom is very often the coldest spot in the nation— not exactly the spot you'd want to find yourself with a flat tire.

DRIVING TOUR #2: PINTLER SCENIC ROUTE

This scenic route takes you from the mining city of Anaconda on a loop tour featuring ghost towns, historic buildings, and wildlife habitat. Start in Anaconda, where you can visit the copper smelting display at the Copper Village Museum or admire an old art deco theater, The Washoe, ranked fifth in the nation by David Naylor *(American Picture Palaces)* for its architectural value.

Northwest of Anaconda on Highway 1 lies Georgetown Lake, a popular tourist destination in summer and winter, when anglers and skiers flock to the lake and nearby ski area, Discovery Basin. Continue on Highway 1 to Drummond, known as the "Bull Shipper's Capital of the World."

Southeast on U.S. Hwy. 90 will take you to Deer Lodge, home to the state prison, historic Grant Kohrs Ranch, and the Towe Ford Museum, featuring a collection of nearly 110 antique Fords and Lincolns—restored, original models from the early 1900s to the present day. Highway 273 takes you back to Anaconda.

This tour is best enjoyed during summer, when area attractions open their doors to visitors and long summer days beckon you to explore forgotten ghost towns.

2 Helena

Like a precocious child, freshly scrubbed and anxious to put his best face forward, Montana's capital city presents itself through beautifully landscaped lawns, historically significant architecture, and carefully designed public places, the kind of places that beg to tell a story and where stories are replete. The exuberance of the city's residents for their place in the world is unmatched, an enthusiasm defined again and again in the state's fascinating past and promising future.

One of the smaller capital cities in America, Helena has a large, resilient heart, and a rich past. When four southern boys tried one last time to strike it rich in a Helena gulch, a town was born. Miners came to rule the emerging community, and some built magnificent mansions on the west side, each following his own architectural whim. During the height of this prosperity, only Manhattan could boast of more millionaires than the small Montana city.

After Helena took capital rights from Virginia City in 1875, Marcus Daly, a Butte copper king with more than just a bystander's interest in the capital location, decided to steal it away from Helena and move it to Anaconda, 25 miles from Butte. This touched off a political war that echoes throughout the state even today. Anaconda went on to have its own dirty little upbringing while Helena had between its teeth the silver spoon of the state and has never let go.

ESSENTIALS

GETTING THERE   **Skywest** (☎ 800/453-9417), a subsidiary of Delta (☎ 800/221-1212), and **Horizon** (☎ 800/547-9308) provide commuter links to larger airports in Montana and other Western states from **Helena Regional Airport** (☎ 406/442-2821), northeast of the city on Skyway Drive off U.S. Hwy. 15.

The bus depot is located downtown at 5 W. 15th St. (☎ 406/442-5860) with service on **Rimrock Stages,** a Trailways affiliate (☎ 800/255-7655).

It's easy to drive to Helena. From the east or west, take U.S. Hwy. 90; turn off and head north toward Helena. From the north or south, U.S. Hwy. 15 leads right into town.

VISITOR INFORMATION   A good starting point for local activities and area maps is the **Helena Area Chamber of Commerce** at 201 E. Lyndale, Helena, MT 59601 (☎ 406/442-4120 or 800/7-HELENA). An even better resource is the state tourism office, **Travel Montana,** the motherlode for brochures and information around the region and the state (Helena is located in Travel Montana's Gold West Country). Contact them at 1424 N. 9th Ave., Helena, MT 59620 (☎ 406/444-2654 or 800/VISIT MT).

GETTING AROUND   Rental car agencies include **Avis** (☎ 406/442-4440), **Hertz** (☎ 406/449-4167), and **National** (☎ 406/442-8620).

GETTING OUTSIDE
FISHING

There are several stretches of prime fishing along this early stretch of the Missouri River. The section from **Toston Dam** downstream to **Canyon Ferry Lake** offers brown and rainbow trout in the 2- to 10-lb. class. Floating with large streamers, wet flies, and lures is the most popular and best way to catch these fish as they make their way upriver to spawn. The fishing gets progressively better from late spring to fall. Motor boats make their way in a 3-mile area below the Canyon Ferry Dam for unusually large trout. The section below **Hauser Dam** to **Beaver Creek** can get exciting, with brown trout up to 20 lbs., sometimes caught in the late fall. Dry fly-fishing is best below Holter Dam in the 30 miles of river extending from there to Cascade, with trout near 20 lbs.

HIKING

Probably the only way to hike the entirety of the massive **Mount Helena City Park**—the state's largest and a prime spot for viewing deer—is to up and move to Helena. Some nine trails, seven of which are easily accessible, cover the park, the easiest of which, the **1906 Trail,** follows the base of the limestone cliffs past Devil's Kitchen to the 5,468-foot summit. **Hogback Trail** may be the steepest and most difficult. It comes from the south along the exposed Hogback Ridge, and, unless you have no plans to walk the next day, may be a more pleasant experience hiking down than climbing up.

ROCKHOUNDING

Born during the gold rush of 1864, Helena is an ideal place to try your hand at rockhounding and mining. Sapphires and garnets are commonly found gemstones, and gold miners often come across nuggets, flakes, and flour gold while prospecting near bedrock. Moss agates, fossils, and hematite are all likely to be encountered by diligent treasure seekers. See the listing for the Spokane Bar Sapphire Mine & Gold Fever Rock Shop below, under "Seeing the Sights."

SKIING

Great Divide Ski Area
P.O. Box SKI, Marysville, MT 59640. ☎ **406/449-3746.** Lift tickets $18 adults, $10 children (5 and younger ski free with adult), $10 seniors; rate reductions at noon, 2pm, and 4pm. Take Exit #200 off U.S. Hwy. 15, then go west on MT 279 to Marysville Road.

It really is impossible to avoid a good ski vacation value in Montana—and Great Divide is just another example of a ski resort featuring dependable skiing at an affordable price. Skiers of all abilities can find runs suitable to their level of expertise amid the 50 runs and 2 open bowls: 15% novice, 30% intermediate, 40% advanced, and 15% expert only.

There are two free ski instruction sessions for entry-level skiers, one at 10am and another at 1pm; KIDSKI is a daily program from 1 to 3pm for children ages four to six, which includes a snack and equipment rental. Private lessons are also available through the ski school. No doubt other ski resorts in the state have better scenery, but none can boast a more favorable location to the capital city and its faithful minions.

SNOWMOBILING

Three major trail systems are all within a 30-minute drive of Helena. The Minnehaha-Rimini area grooms 120 miles of trails and the Marysville and Magpie-Sunshine areas, with views into the Gates of the Mountains Wilderness, both groom 45 miles of trails each. Guided tours can be arranged through the Helena Snowdrifters Snowmobile Club. For details on these tours, as well as specific trail information, contact the Snowdrifters at 1813 N. Oakes, Helena, MT 59601 (☎ 406/449-2685).

WATER SPORTS

Two Helena area state parks center around man-made lakes: Spring Meadow Lake (day use only) and Black Sandy at the Hauser Reservoir. Spring Meadow is a 30-acre, spring-fed lake on Helena's western edge, noted for its clarity and depth. Open to nonmotorized boats only, the lake is popular for swimming and fishing. To reach Spring Meadow Lake, take MT 12 west, then head north on Joslyn to Country Club. One of the only public parks on the shores of Hauser Reservoir, Black Sandy is an extremely popular weekend boating, fishing, and waterskiing take-off point. To get to the Hauser Reservoir, drive 7 miles north of Helena on U.S. Hwy. 15, then 4 miles east on Secondary 453, then follow signs 3 miles north on a county road.

SEEING THE SIGHTS

For a unique look at Helena's colorful past, Last Chance Tours (☎ 406/442-1023) provides guided tour trains throughout the city.

During the height of the summer, the Helena Brewers, a farm team for Milwaukee and Helena's Pioneer League team, plays at the Kindrick Legion Field, behind Memorial Park. Call 406/449-7616 for schedule information.

Montana State Capitol

Montana Ave. and 6th St. ☎ **406/444-4789.** Free admission; no charge for tours. Building open Mon–Fri 8am–6pm. Montana Historical Society gives daily tours on the hour Mon–Sat 10am–5pm, Sun 11am–4pm; call ahead to make group reservations.

Montana's grand capitol building, designed by architects Charles Bell and John Kent in the late 1800s, is a must-see for any visitor to Helena. The estimated cost for the furnished capitol at that time was $485,000. With a Greek neoclassic exterior (constructed of sandstone from Columbus, Montana) and electricity, central heating, indoor plumbing, and elevators on the inside, the capitol building was by far the most magnificent structure in the state and remains so today. A decade after the building was completed, the state added the much-needed wings that now lead to the offices of the governor and the secretary of state at opposite ends.

Helena

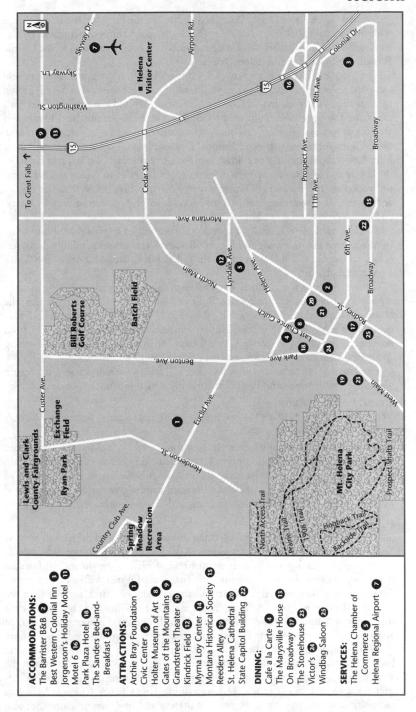

ACCOMMODATIONS:
The Barrister B&B ②
Best Western Colonial Inn ③
Jorgenson's Holiday Motel ⑪
Motel 6 ⑯
Park Plaza Hotel ⑱
The Sanders Bed-and-Breakfast ㉑

ATTRACTIONS:
Archie Bray Foundation ①
Civic Center ⑥
Holter Museum of Art ⑧
Gates of the Mountains ⑨
Grandstreet Theater ⑩
Kindrick Field ⑫
Myrna Loy Center ⑭
Montana Historical Society ⑮
Reeders Alley ⑲
St. Helena Cathedral ⑳
State Capitol Building ㉒

DINING:
Cafe a la Carte ④
The Marysville House ⑬
On Broadway ⑰
The Stonehouse ㉓
Victor's ㉔
Windbag Saloon ㉕

SERVICES:
The Helena Chamber of Commerce ⑤
Helena Regional Airport ⑦

Situated on 14.1 acres, the building is decorated in the French Renaissance design with frescos, stained glass, and murals. The dome, faced with copper, rises 165 feet toward the state's fabled big sky. Inside are murals by noted Montana artists Charlie Russell, Edgar Paxson, and Ralph DeCamp.

The Montana Historical Society (☎ 406/444-4789), located within the capitol complex, gives daily tours of the capitol building. The historical society building features the Mackay Gallery of Charles M. Russell Art and the original governor's mansion. The society—the oldest of its kind in the West—maintains a library and archives, as well as a museum, and publishes a quarterly magazine, *Montana the Magazine of Western History*. Between Memorial Day and Labor Day, the museum is open from 8am to 6pm Monday to Friday, 9am to 6pm Saturday, Sunday, and holidays; the library and archives are open from 8am to 5pm Monday to Friday and are closed on weekends and holidays. During winter, the museum, as well as the library and archives, is open from 8am to 5pm Monday to Friday, 9am to 5pm Saturday, and is closed on Sundays and holidays.

The Mackay Gallery contains a collection of Russell art to rival that of his hometown museum in Great Falls. With over 60 Russell artworks, including oils, watercolors, sculptures, and illustrated letters, the gallery is a showcase for one of the West's most remarkable artists.

Guided tours of the original governor's mansion, located at 304 N. Ewing, are also available through the society. Built in 1888 by a wealthy entrepreneur, the house was acquired by the Montana legislature in 1913 and served as the official residence of nine Montana governors. During summer, tours operate on the hour from noon to 5pm Tuesday to Sunday. After Labor Day, call for information on setting an appointment to view this magnificent "First Family" home.

The grounds of the state capitol building in Helena are a designated state park, with the formal grounds and flower gardens visited by thousands of people each year.

Cathedral of St. Helena
530 N. Ewing. ☎ **406/442-5825.** Unless services are taking place, open to public daily 9am–5pm; call to arrange a free tour.

This exquisite architectural achievement seems misplaced in its Montana setting, but not even the nearby mountains can rival the breathtaking beauty of its 230-foot twin spires. Patterned after a similar cathedral in Cologne, Germany, the Cathedral of St. Helena is decorated with magnificent Bavarian stained-glass windows, hand-carved oak pews, hand-forged bronze light fixtures, and Carrara marble statues.

Last Chance Gulch
So named because a quartet of gold-seeking prospectors declared the spot to be their "last chance" to strike it rich, Last Chance Gulch became one of the richest gold-producing areas in the world and remains one of Helena's main streets. Located downtown, this historic area combines Helena's colorful past with a contemporary freshness. Architecturally significant buildings, many of which are listed on the National Register of Historic Places, house espresso machines and boutiques, while ultramodern sculptures depict historical events. Interpretive markers are scattered along the pedestrian mall, with historical information relating to period construction.

Visitors may note that the street is as "crooked as a dog's hind leg." One historical marker theorizes that the street was laid out in this manner "to restrict the shooting range of impetuous, hot-blooded gents in the roaring days gone by." Whatever the case may be, in typical Helena fashion Last Chance Gulch is Montana personified, a charming blend of past and present and best seen up close. (See also "Shopping," later in this section.)

Reeder's Alley

This quaint shopping area has a distinctly European feel, which lends a romantic atmosphere to its only restaurant, The Stonehouse (see "Where to Eat," later in this section). Its brick streets are home to a tightly packed group of old mining shanties that have been converted into contemporary retail stores, though serious shoppers will find the pickings somewhat slim. Compared to Last Chance Gulch, the shopping at Reeder's Alley is decidedly eclectic, with glass and yarn meriting their own shops. A barber and the Olde Time Photo Shop attest to a bygone era and, like many places in Helena, the past seems to come to life here, and it's described in detail through signs along its winding streets.

Holter Museum of Art

12 E. Lawrence St. ☎ **406/442-6400.** Free admission. Tues–Sat noon–5pm, Sun noon–4pm.

A gallery of contemporary art, the Holter is the home of the Western Rendezvous of Art, an annual summer exhibit spotlighting noted Western artists.

Archie Bray Foundation

2915 Country Club Ave. ☎ **406/443-3502.** Small gallery open Mon–Sat 10am–5pm, Sun 1–5pm, with various items for sale. Visitors may take a self-guided walking tour of the grounds during daylight hours.

Archie Bray, a Helena resident and enthusiastic supporter of the arts, established this artistic colony for potters in 1951, located at the brickyard and kilns of the Western Clay Manufacturing Company. Over the years it has become a premier testing ground for ceramic artists, working together to share ideas and techniques. Like discarded toys, various playful sculptures dot the lawns, some more inconspicuously than others. Of special note are several larger, free-standing monuments by Robert Harrison, most notably *A Potter's Shrine,* dedicated to Bray and incorporating some materials up to 100 years old; *Tile-X,* stacked drain tiles in the shape of a pyramid; and *Aruina,* a monument of brick and tile whose four arches frame the surrounding Helena landscape. Because of the intimate nature of each individual resident's art-making process, visitors are asked to respect their privacy.

Gates of the Mountains

U.S. Hwy. 15 (Gates of the Mountains exit), 18 miles north of Helena (P.O. Box 478, Helena, MT 59624). ☎ **406/458-5241.** Adults $8, seniors $7, children 4–17 $5, under 4 free. June–Sept; call for cruise schedule departures and returns.

Meriwether Lewis, the intrepid explorer who so eloquently wrote of much of Montana in the late 1800s, coined the name "Gates of the Mountains" while plying this portion of the Missouri with his party: At almost every bend in the waterway, the towering rock formations seemed to block their passage, only to magically open up as they drew closer. Visitors can have an experience similar to Lewis's through a boat tour of this scenic riverway on the *Pirogue,* the *Sacajawea,* or the *Hilger Rose.* The 105-minute cruises take you through the mountain "gates" (actually an optical illusion) to a picnic area where wildlife photography opportunities abound. If you'd like, you can choose to return on a later boat and take a hike into the nearby Gates of the Mountains Wilderness Area or explore Native American pictographs on the limestone rocks. Mann Gulch, the setting of Norman Maclean's *Young Men and Fire* and the site where 15 smokejumpers perished, is within hiking distance. Markers indicate where each of the men fell.

Spokane Bar Sapphire Mine & Gold Fever Rock Shop

5360 Castles Dr., Helena, MT 59601. ☎ **406/227-8989.** Daily 9am–5pm; winter hours vary. From U.S. Hwy. 15, take York Road east to Mile Marker 8. Turn right on Hart Lane and left on Castles Road.

If you've come to rockhound, this sapphire mine south of Hauser Lake is the place for you. With a plan for everyone—couples can dig all day for $35 plus concentrate ($1 per bucket, five-bucket minimum)—this sapphire mine will get the entire family into the spirit of Montana's early pioneers. For a quarter a bucket, they'll even haul it out for you. The mine, 150 feet below ancient river levels, is a good source for green-blue sapphires, the most common type found.

SHOPPING

With boutiques, restaurants, and play areas for the kids, Last Chance Gulch is a perfect place to spend a few hours shopping. **Main News,** 9 N. Last Chance Gulch, is a tobacco shop with a decent selection of newspapers from various statewide and regional cities, including Salt Lake City, San Francisco, and Seattle. Next door to Main News is the **Cason Gallery,** 7 N. Last Chance Gulch, an art gallery. Both Main News and the Cason Gallery are located in the **Atlas Building,** one of a group of historically significant architectural structures in Last Chance Gulch. Look for a diminutive Atlas midway up the building as well as a salamander, mythical survivor of fire. Informational kiosks are located in the center of this walking mall and its north end. **Victor's,** the restaurant at Park Plaza Hotel, is a great place to meet your friends. Sit outside on their patio beneath the teal and mauve umbrellas and enjoy contemporary American food (see "Where to Eat" later in this chapter). You'll find **OK Books** at 2 N. Last Chance Gulch in the Livestock Building, a beige structure with colorfully painted accents that belie its crude name. **The Gaslight Cinema,** 5 W. Broadway, shows current movies on three screens every day of the week. **The Panhandler,** 40 S. Last Chance Gulch, is a gourmet kitchen shop. Moms should check out the sartorial splendor of **Kids by Design,** 38 S. Last Chance Gulch, and **Cobblestone Clothing,** 46 S. Last Chance Gulch, a ladies' boutique. Concrete tables with checkerboard tile inlays can be found at the south end of Last Chance Gulch, a great place to play a game of checkers.

ESPECIALLY FOR KIDS

The Parrot Confectionery
42 N. Main. ☎ **406/442-1470.** Mon–Sat 9am–6pm.

Kids and adults alike will love this candy shop, established in 1922. The Parrot continues to dazzle its patrons with cherry phosphates and caramel cashew sundaes served from the shop's original soda fountain and beneath its charming collection of ceramic elephants. The booths here are unusually tall, so indulge yourself with a chocolate fix and don't worry about being found out. Family owned, the Parrot has provided gourmet chocolate and candy to Helena for over 70 years and loyal customers attest that the place and its product haven't changed a bit. Enter at your own risk, though: In addition to a broad-based Helena clientele, the Parrot supplies chocolate to sweets addicts from nearly every state in the country.

WHERE TO STAY
HOTELS & MOTELS

Best Western Colonial Inn
2301 Colonial Dr. (just off U.S. Hwy. 15 at MT 12), Helena, MT. 59601. ☎ **406/443-2100** or 800/422-1002. 149 rms. A/C TV TEL. From $69 double. AE, DC, DISC, MC, V.

This is Helena's biggest and most luxurious hotel. Rooms are tastefully appointed and some even feature fireplaces and hot tubs. All beds are either king or queen size, making it a comfortable place to spend the night. The capitol complex is within easy walking distance, as is downtown. An on-site business center, gift shop, and hair salon make taking care of business effortless. The hotel also features its own restaurant and lounge, as well as two swimming pools: one indoor, one outside.

Jorgenson's Holiday Motel

1714 11th Ave., Helena, MT. 59601. ☎ 406/442-1770 or 800/272-1770 in MT. 117 rms. A/C TV TEL. $45–$85 double. Senior discounts. AE, DC, DISC, MC, V.

A Montana tradition for over 35 years, the Jorgenson is close to two hubs of Helena activity: the capitol complex and the city's biggest indoor shopping mall. Convenient to U.S. Hwy. 15, Jorgenson's has a restaurant and lounge as well as an indoor pool and exercise center. No-smoking and indoor or outdoor room access are two of the options offered guests to this downtown facility. Airport shuttle service is complimentary.

⊜ Motel 6

800 N. Oregon, Helena, MT. 59601. ☎ 406/442-9990. 80 rms. A/C TV TEL. $30–$40 double. AE, CB, DC, DISC, MC, V.

This motel has at least one clear advantage over its competitors: price. It's located across the interstate from the Best Western, and how much you're willing to spend on a room may determine which way you turn. Though it's over 30 years old, it's clean and rooms are comfortable. There is not a restaurant on-site but fast-food options are numerous and close by.

✪ Park Plaza Hotel

22 N. Last Chance Gulch, Helena, MT 59601. ☎ 406/443-2200 or 800/332-2290 in Montana only. 71 units. A/C TV TEL. $62–$130 double. AE, DC, DISC, MC, V.

Seven stories of this downtown hotel overlook historic Last Chance Gulch, a pedestrian mall and a great place to survey distinctive period architecture as you sample its unique specialty shops and restaurants. Shopping, art galleries, restaurants, and theaters are all close by, most within walking distance. The Park Plaza's rooms were last renovated in 1987; its lobby in 1990. Victor's (see "Where to Eat" later in this section) and JD's Nightclub are great places to eat or relax. The lounge has keno, poker, and pool until 2am six nights a week, often with live music. Airport shuttle service is complimentary.

BED-AND-BREAKFASTS

The Barrister Bed and Breakfast

416 N. Ewing (at the corner of 9th), Helena, MT. 59601. ☎ 406/443-7330. 5 rms. A/C TV. $75–$90 double. Rates include full breakfast. MC, V.

Located directly across the street from the cathedral, the Barrister is one of many elegant homes near the original governor's mansion. It's within easy walking distance of downtown shopping and attractions. Built in 1874, the Victorian home showcases original fireplaces (there are six), stained-glass windows, high ceilings, and ornately carved staircases. Many of the house's furnishings are turn-of-the-century, giving it a charmingly nostalgic atmosphere, but all rooms have private baths and the common areas—den, TV room, library, and office—are outfitted with any modern convenience you could desire.

✪ The Sanders

328 N. Ewing, Helena, MT 59601. ☎ 406/442-3309. 7 rms. A/C TV TEL. $60–$98 double. Rates include full breakfast. AE, DISC, MC, V.

To put it simply, there's not a finer bed-and-breakfast in all of Montana. The Sanders is easily the most elegant, comfortable, and interesting place to stay, and its location in Helena—repository of the state's relatively short history—is certainly appropriate. Built in 1875, the plum-colored brick and shingle Queen Anne–style mansion was originally the home of Wilbur Fisk Sanders, Montana's first U.S. senator, first president of the Montana Bar Association, and founder of the Montana Historical Society. Owners Bobbi Uecker and Rock Ringling (whose great-grandfather, incidentally, was one of the original five Ringling Brothers) have meticulously restored the grand home to its original splendor with fully 80% of the original furnishings gracing the rooms throughout the house's three stories. Oak, cherry, and fir woodwork add intricate detail to period furniture, complemented by antique paintings and elaborate appointments. People from all 50 states and 6 continents (Antarctica is the only holdout) have visited the Sanders, including their most famous guest, Archbishop Desmond Tutu. Bobbi and Rock's attention to detail keeps them coming back, too: each of the seven guest rooms includes such thoughtful details as an alarm clock, mini-flashlight, night-light, hair dryer, private bath, a history of the house, and comments from former guests. Some of Rock's gourmet breakfast specialties, served in the wainscoted dining room, include Grand Marnier french toast, orange soufflés, sourdough pancakes, and artichoke-spinach frittatas.

CAMPING

Kim's Marina and RV Resort, 20 miles west of Helena on Canyon Ferry Road (☎ 406/475-3723), has 50 tent and 60 RV sites as well as tennis, volleyball, horseshoes, and boat rentals; it is open from April through September. The Lakeside Resort, 11 miles east of Helena on York Road near Hauser Lake (☎ 406/443-3932), is an RV park that is open year-round with 70 full hookups and an on-site bar, restaurant, beach, and picnic area.

WHERE TO EAT

Ⓢ Cafe a la Carte

48 N. Last Chance Gulch. ☎ **406/442-3936.** Most items $2–$5. No credit cards. Mon–Fri 7:30am–4pm; Sat 9am–3pm. SOUPS/SANDWICHES.

This cozy coffee shop has a great location at Last Chance Gulch. It is decidedly better than the one previously held by its owner, Steve Springmeyer, when he peddled espresso from a cart beneath whatever weather Helena decided to dish up. From his new location—a smallish space adorned by two tables with lots of counter space to keep them company—he has begun selling quick lunch items in addition to Seattle's Best Coffee. The house salad is topped off with a tangy balsamic vinaigrette dressing and his homemade soups are accompanied by a fresh baguette. All items can be bought in half-size portions at extremely affordable prices.

✪ The Marysville House

In Marysville, a 45-minute drive from Helena. Take MT 279 north for 23 miles; turn left at the sign for Marysville for 7 miles to find this living ghost town. No phone. Meals from $10. No credit cards. Open Thurs–Sat year-round; hours vary with the seasons. STEAKS/SEAFOOD.

You're gonna have to trust us on this one. With no phone number and hours that vary with the seasons, the Marysville House is the very model of inaccessibility. Yet Helena residents would surely feel slighted if this unique dining experience wasn't listed among the city's best. Located in what was once a train depot, the Marysville House serves steaks, lobster, and crab legs that are unparalleled, in a rustic setting that only serves to enhance its romantic anonymity. People simply love the fact that they know this place exists, and the place plainly doesn't care if people know or not. The no-nonsense meals—which range upward in price from $10, depending on the market price of seafood—come with corn on the cob and beans, period, and guests have their choice of dining inside or out. And how's this for low-key Americana: Meals are served on paper plates, horseshoes can be found out back, and you can eat at a picnic table in the front yard. Your best bet for more specific details is to ask a local or just head on out.

On Broadway
106 Broadway. ☎ 406/443-1929. Reservations not accepted. Main courses $8–$17. AE, MC, V. Mon–Sat 5:30–10pm. ITALIAN.

Located in an upscale brick building near Last Chance Gulch, On Broadway is the place to go in Helena for good Italian food. It's dressed up like any other fern-laden bar/restaurant, but the food is anything but stereotypical, with artful combinations of meats and vegetables, fresh herbs, and pasta highlighting a menu with Italian subtitles: della casa, pesce, pollo, and contorni. A local favorite is the Petti di Pollo alla Broadway, a chicken breast topped with fresh mushrooms and cheese, then baked in a mornay sauce with mozzarella. The fish (pesce) menu is the most imaginative, headed up by an impressive northern Italian clam sauce—whole baby clams, sweet butter, imported olive oil, white wine, and Italian herbs—served over fresh pasta.

The Stonehouse
120 Reeder's Alley. ☎ 406/449-2552. Reservations recommended. Main courses $11–$17. AE, DC, DISC, MC, V. Sun–Thurs 5:30–9pm, Fri–Sat 5–10pm. STEAKS/SEAFOOD.

Don't be fooled by the country inn ambience you're greeted with as you step in the door of this place. A couple of steps to the right and you're in a funky blue room, which, with its wildlife menagerie of chainsaw art in front of a mountain mural, may appear to be a bit tacky, depending on your mood. If that's the case, another more intimate room is located farther back, though it's somewhere closer to the other end of the spectrum and distinctly lacks ambience of any kind. The food here is exceptional, though. Venison Montana Style, a 7-ounce portion of venison sautéed with onions, mushrooms, and garlic and glazed with a burgundy wine, is an excellent choice. If that's not the game you're looking for, try the Vegetable Wellington, lightly seasoned vegetables wrapped and baked in pastry dough then covered in a mornay sauce. The atmosphere here is like no other in Helena. Just strolling up the red brick walkway of Reeder's Alley throws you into another time.

Victor's
In the Park Plaza Hotel, 22 N. Last Chance Gulch. ☎ 406/443-2200. Breakfast $3–$8; lunch $4–$7; dinner $10–$15. AE, DISC, MC, V. Mon–Thurs 6:30am–9pm, Fri–Sat 6:30am–10pm. CONTEMPORARY AMERICAN.

A faux stained-glass skylight is the centerpiece of this bright and airy restaurant. Located along the walking mall of Last Chance Gulch, Victor's is frequented by the business lunch crowd year-round and tourists during the summer. You can expect fast and friendly service here, whether you dine inside or on the patio. The menus are expansive and are sure to please even the most discriminating of palates. Lunch items include burgers, chicken sandwiches (the "Raging Cajun" is especially tasty), homemade soups and salads, as well as an eclectic collection of Mexican, Asian, and American specialties. The dinner menu is defined by beef and seafood, with a small nod to the pasta family. Servings of the baked raspberry-macadamia nut halibut and the blackened top sirloin with peppercorn sauce are both flavorful and generous. Be sure to have a cup of Victor's specially blended coffee, fresh roasted daily by Helena's Morning Light Coffee.

✪ Windbag Saloon
19 S. Last Chance Gulch. ☎ 406/443-9669. Reservations recommended. Lunch $3–$7; dinner $4–$15. AE, DISC, MC, V. Wed–Sun 5:30–9:30pm; off-season days and hours may vary. CONTEMPORARY AMERICAN.

Helena residents love this restaurant like you'd love an eccentric aunt: She's the most interesting relative you have and you always have a great time at her place. Who cares if she has a checkered past? So what if one of the cleanest and most respected bordellos in all of Montana was once operated in the location where the restaurant now enjoys its own flourishing business? At least it's respectable, continuing in its tradition as a focal part of Helena's nightlife. The main dining room, combining old and new with one wall of exposed rock and another covered in paisley wallpaper, is usually crowded and noisy (acoustics aren't the best in the tin-roofed room) and you may have to wait for a table if you don't have reservations. Try one of a long list of microbrews in the meantime, or order something from their extensive, though mostly french-fried, collection of appetizers. If you usually order the same thing every time you go out to eat, go out on a limb and try one of their daily lunch or dinner specials. They are usually imaginative combinations you won't find anywhere else in Montana for such a great price. If you want to stick to burgers, you get your choice of french fries or pasta salad. Cajun chicken, beef and shrimp kabobs, and grilled salmon are only a few of the dinner highlights, enjoyed with a bottle of wine or a Northwest microbrew: Helena's own Kessler, Red Hook, Norwester Raspberry Weizen, Full Sail, or Portland Brewing Honey Ale, just to name a few.

THE PERFORMING ARTS

Make it a point to visit the **Myrna Loy Center for the Performing Arts,** 15 N. Ewing St. (☎ 406/443-0287). Formerly the Lewis and Clark County Jail, the Myrna Loy (named after one of Helena's most famous residents and a silver-screen legend) is a multidisciplinary cultural center of regional significance. Within its castlelike facade is a 40-seat cinema and a 200-seat performance hall, along with galleries that focus on regional art of all descriptions. The state-of-the-art facilities are second to none in Montana, where you can see the latest foreign films or attend one of the "Helena Presents" programs.

Live theater is also featured at **Helena's Grandstreet Theater,** which makes its home at 325 N. Park Ave. (☎ 406/443-3311). Productions vary widely but occur year-round; call for current information and ticket prices. **The Helena Orchestra and Symphony Chorale** performs seasonally at the Civic Center, located on the corner of Benton and Neill Avenue. Call 406/447-8481 for event information.

3 Butte & Anaconda

This area is strange. It's got to be among the most unusual places on the National Historic Landmark District list—the other places don't have a history of such extremes. Butte has gone from being the "richest hill on earth" to being the home of the Berkeley Pit, a massive hole wrought in the earth by years of mining. Some folks take the "e" off the end of the town's name and call it, among other things, the ugliest town in America. Paul Harvey, for what it's worth, called Butte a "diamond on black velvet," but his observation was made in the dark.

Anaconda was the "company town," formed when copper king Marcus Daly extended his copper empire 24 miles west. The community was spared the name "Copperopolis" but that was about it. Horrible tales would emerge from the workers whose only opportunity for employment came from the toxic smelter.

Historically, Butte's political and economic importance to Montana rose and fell with its mining operations. At first it found success with gold, then with silver. But it was copper on which Montana's most influential town grew in the late 1800s, and on copper that it crumbled. The local economy thrived for almost a century before the need for copper worldwide finally diminished. By the early 1980s, the copper-mining glory days of Butte were gone, leaving a trail of giant blights in the landscape, unemployment, and a suffering economy. Between 1980 and 1990, while most of the cities in the mountain region of Montana were increasing in population, Butte's declined nearly 10%.

If you can look past the depressing and evident signs of decline, Butte is full of rich history (very rich, in fact), colorful citizens, and a sort of blue-collar San Francisco–style charm. Though companies have come in from the outside and virtually raped Butte of its mineral wealth and fled, the town has more pride than it probably has a right to.

Settled for the most part by Irish immigrants working in the mines, Butte retains its Irish heritage and Roman Catholic virtues. St. Patrick's Day turns this mining museum of a town into downtown Dublin each March 17 in one of the biggest celebrations in the state.

ESSENTIALS

GETTING THERE   The **Bert Mooney Airport,** 111 Airport Rd. (☎ 406/ 494-3771), is served by **Horizon** (☎ 800/547-9308) and **Skywest** (☎ 800/ 453-9417).

It couldn't be easier to drive to Butte—it's located right at the junction of U.S. Hwys. 90 and 15. For current road conditions in Butte and Anaconda, call 406/ 494-3666 (statewide 800/332-6171); call 406/449-5204 for current weather information.

The **Greyhound** station in Butte is located at 105 W. Broadway (☎ 406/ 723-3287).

VISITOR INFORMATION   You won't find residents any prouder of their city than those of Butte. Its local chamber office, the **Butte–Silver Bow Chamber of Commerce,** 2950 Harrison Ave., Butte, MT 59701 (☎ 406/494-5595 or 800/ 735-6814, ext. 95) tops the list. The **Anaconda Chamber of Commerce,** 306 E. Park, Anaconda, MT 59711 (☎ 406/563-2400), can give you information on Butte's sister city. Both Butte and Anaconda fall into **Travel Montana's Gold West Country,** 1155 Main, Deer Lodge, MT 59722 (☎ 406/846-1943), where information requests yield brochures devoted to area attractions and driving tours.

GETTING AROUND   Car rental agents in Butte include **Avis** (☎ 406/ 494-3131), **Budget** (☎ 406/494-7573), **Hertz** (☎ 406/782-1054), and **Payless** (☎ 406/723-4366).

The **Butte–Silver Bow Transit System** city buses run from 7am to 5:45pm Monday to Friday; for information on fares and stops, call 406/723-8262. **City Taxi** is located 3 S. Main (☎ 406/723-6511).

SPECIAL EVENTS   If you can't be in Ireland on March 17, Butte is the next best place. The city goes all out for ✪ **St. Patrick's Day** with a celebration that is legendary in Montana, maybe even throughout the West. You won't find anyone in town who doesn't claim to be Irish during the festivities, when corned beef and cabbage and the traditional "wearin' of the green" reign supreme. If you happen to be of Finnish extraction, or simply require a more obscure reason to party in Butte, you may want to visit a few days earlier, when the city takes time off to honor St. Urho, patron saint who reputedly drove grasshoppers from Finland. Contact the **Butte–Silver Bow Chamber of Commerce** (☎ 406/494-5595) for the dates and times of these activities.

GETTING OUTSIDE

Lost Creek State Park is conveniently located just a few miles outside of Anaconda. One of its most scenic views is Lost Creek Falls, which tumble over a 50-foot drop to the stream below. Get out your camera and binoculars, because you just might catch a glimpse of a mountain goat or bighorn sheep, frequently seen on the cliffs. With shaded camping spots, picnicking facilities, fishing access, hiking trails, and access for the disabled, this is a nice location for families or seasoned campers alike. Drive 1¹/₂ miles east of Anaconda on MT 1, then 2 miles north on Secondary 273, then 6 miles west.

GOLF

In a unique Superfund cleanup initiative, the **Old Works** smelter site in Anaconda is being transformed into a world-class 18-hole golf course, which is tentatively scheduled to open to the public in the spring of 1997. A Jack Nicklaus Signature Golf Course, the Old Works (☎ 406/563-5670) rambles between Warm Spring Creek and the neighboring hillside, incorporating many of the former mine site's flues and brick walls. Perhaps the most unusual incorporation of the old smelters is the black slag—a smelting by-product—in the bunkers, giving the course a distinctive, dramatic look. Though the course isn't open until 1997, golf cart tours of the course will be available until then.

There is an 18-hole course at nearby **Fairmont Hot Springs** (see "Where to Stay" later in this chapter) and **Highland View Golf Course** (☎ 406/494-7900), at Stodden Park in Butte, has two separate nine-hole courses, one of which is a par 3.

ROCK CLIMBING

Spire Rock and the **Humbug Spires** are the two most popular routes for rock climbers. Pipestone Mountaineering, at 829 S. Montana St. (☎ 406/782-4994), can give you leads on the local climbing scene.

ROCKHOUNDING

Within the Continental Divide east of Butte and its mountains to the south, diligent rockhounders can find smokey quartz, amethyst, epidote, and tourmalines. Ask the curator at the Mineral Museum ("Seeing the Sights") for leads on local hot spots.

SKIING

In addition to **Discovery Basin,** you're also within range of **Maverick Mountain** (see Section 4, "Dillon and the Big Hole Valley," later in this chapter.)

Discovery Basin

45 miles west of Butte on MT Hwy. 1, off U.S. Hwy. 90 (P.O. Box 221, Anaconda, MT 59711). ☎ **406/563-2184.** Lift tickets $20 adults, $10 children 12 and younger and seniors, half-day $15. Inquire about special group rates.

This is another one of those Montana ski resorts that falls somewhere in the middle if you to make a list in ranking them all in ascending order for nearly any category. The vertical drop isn't the longest, but it's not the shortest, either. In fact, the ski area is noncommital in catering to any one type of skier: All runs on the mountain fall into one of three categories with beginner, intermediates, and experts all enjoying an equal 33% of the total 360-acre resort.

While the scenery equals or exceeds other areas in the state, the real plus here is the resort's proximity to Fairmont Hot Springs, a four-season facility where soaking and swimming are year-round favorites (see "Where to Stay" later in this chapter).

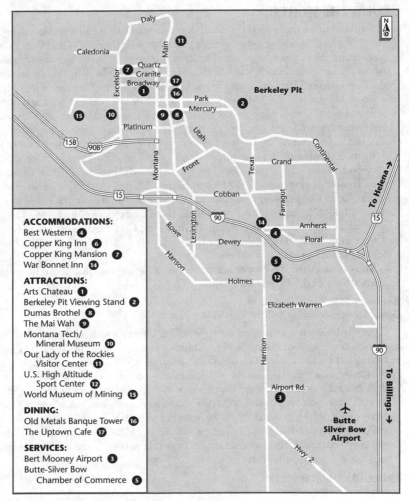

ACCOMMODATIONS:
Best Western **④**
Copper King Inn **⑥**
Copper King Mansion **⑦**
War Bonnet Inn **⑭**

ATTRACTIONS:
Arts Chateau **①**
Berkeley Pit Viewing Stand **②**
Dumas Brothel **⑧**
The Mai Wah **⑨**
Montana Tech/
Mineral Museum **⑩**
Our Lady of the Rockies
Visitor Center **⑪**
U.S. High Altitude
Sport Center **⑫**
World Museum of Mining **⑮**

DINING:
Old Metals Banque Tower **⑯**
The Uptown Cafe **⑰**

SERVICES:
Bert Mooney Airport **③**
Butte-Silver Bow
Chamber of Commerce **⑤**

Ski rentals and instruction are available (private lessons are $25 per hour) as well as cafeteria-style food.

Five kilometers of groomed trails will satisfy the Nordic skier or you can blaze your own trail through untracked snow.

There are no hotels at the ski area; the nearest accommodations are at Fairmont Hot Springs or in Butte and Anaconda.

SNOWMOBILING

The Anaconda Snowmobile Club, 191 W. Park, Anaconda, MT 59711 (☎ 406/563-8182), can point you to the nearest trail or take you on a guided tour, most of which explore the vicinity of Georgetown Lake. The four major trail systems include Carp Ridge, which terminates at the Anaconda-Pintler Wilderness boundary; Echo Lake, at the midpoint of Georgetown Lake and Discovery Basin Ski area; Peterson Meadows, a popular spot for cookouts and picnics; and Red Lion Racetrack Lake, with ridgetop views of surrounding peaks.

SEEING THE SIGHTS

If you want to see Butte's highlights and don't want to take the time to plan an itinerary, take an entertaining and enlightening tour by trolley in the ✪ **Old No. 1 Tour Car.** Along the way you'll be treated to an engaging narrative by a seasoned guide with stops including Butte's National Historic District, its Victorian neighborhoods, the Copper King Mansion, Dumas Brothel, Berkeley Pit, Arts Chateau, World Museum of Mining and 1899 Mining Camp, and Montana Tech. Designed and built in Butte in 1971, the trolley cars are replicas of those used for Butte's original electric trolley system. Drivers are proficient in Butte history and folklore, presented in an entertaining manner during the 1¹/₂-hour tour. Tours depart daily at 10:30am, 1:30pm, 3:30pm, and 7pm from June through Labor Day. The charge is $4 for adults 13 years and older, $2.50 for children ages 4–12, and children under 3 free. Contact the Chamber of Commerce, 2950 Harrison Ave. (☎ 406/494-5595), for details.

The Butte Copper Kings play in Alumni Coliseum, on the campus of Montana Tech (☎ 406/723-8206). They're an affiliate of the Texas Rangers, with home games most nights during the summer at 7pm. Detroit Tiger Cecil Fielder once played here. To get to the field, take the Montana Street exit off U.S. Hwy. 90 north to Park Street, then drive west to the coliseum.

You can also drive the **Pintler Scenic Route,** a driving tour that begins in Butte. See Section 1 of this chapter for details.

Berkeley Pit
Open to the public during daylight hours in Mar–Nov.

Once the largest truck-operated open pit in the United States and rumored to be visible—along with the Great Wall of China—from the moon, the Berkeley Pit is located just off Continental Drive in Butte. Starting in 1955, nearly 1¹/₂ billion tons of material were removed from the pit until mining ceased in 1982—including more than 290 million tons of copper ore. A short walk through a dimly lit tunnel (fully accessible for those with disabilities) takes you to an observation deck where you can view the pit, which is currently filling with groundwater at a rate of about seven million gallons per day. A taped message will tell you these and other facts and the gift shop, open only during summer, will provide you with any kind of copper souvenir you could possibly desire.

Anaconda Smelter Stack
Just off MT 1, on the outskirts of Anaconda.

This 585-foot smelter stack is one of the tallest standing brick structures in the world and is designated a Montana State Park, though there is no public access. Once considered the largest copper-smelting stack in the entire world, all 58 stories of the desolate shaft rise starkly to meet the Montana sky.

Our Lady of the Rockies
Gift shop and information center at 432 N. Main. ☎ **406/782-1221** or 800/800-LADY. Free admission. Summer daily 9am–6pm; winter Mon–Fri 10am–4pm, Sat noon–4pm. Tours depart daily during summer from the Butte Plaza Mall, 3100 Harrison Ave. for $10 adults, $9 children 13–17, $5 children 5–12, under 5 free. For tour reservations call 406/494-2656.

Keep your eyes peeled for this Butte landmark, an imposing 90-foot statue of a woman who gazes out over travelers cruising along the interstate. Though Butte's population is largely Catholic, don't mistake "Our Lady" for the Virgin Mary; she is described as being representative of all women, regardless of religion. Tour buses travel from Butte up to the statue daily (unless weather is inclement), but private travel is restricted. If you don't have time for a tour but are interested in learning more about Our Lady of the Rockies, visit the information center and gift shop for a look at a panoramic mural of the statue. There is also a video detailing the construction: Four hundred tons of concrete were used just for the statue's base.

✪ Arts Chateau

321 W. Broadway. ☎ 406/723-7600. Admission $3.75 adults, $3.25 AAA members, $3 seniors, $1.25 children 10 and under. Summer Tues–Sat 10am–6pm, Sun noon–5pm; winter Tues–Sat 11am–4pm, Sun noon–5pm. Tours available.

Built in 1898 for Charles Clark, son of copper king William A. Clark, the Butte–Silver Bow Arts Chateau is an impressively restored mansion and art gallery. Stained-glass windows, beveled glass, ornate wrought iron, and intricately detailed woodwork contribute to the mansion's turn-of-the-century elegance. The home's magnificent staircase leads to a second-story museum, filled with period furniture, and the gallery, which houses traveling displays by Montana artists in a much more modern setting. Other highlights include the fourth-floor ballroom, which replicates a grand hunting lodge, and the first-floor gift shop, with hundreds of Made in Montana items for sale.

World Museum of Mining & 1899 Mining Camp

Montana Tech Campus. ☎ 406/723-7211. Free admission. Summer daily 9am–9pm; limited hours in spring and fall. Go up the hill to the campus of Montana Tech, past the statue of Marcus Daly. Just beyond the statue, a sign in the middle of the street will direct you. Watch for the Orphan Girl Mine "gallows."

One of Butte's most popular attractions, this museum and re-created mining camp encompasses 12 acres of indoor and outdoor displays at the base of the Orphan Girl Mine, which once produced silver and zinc. Visitors can tour the hoist house of the mine, where huge machines once lowered cages full of miners into the underground tunnels, or they can stroll along the brick streets of the 1899 Mining Camp. The hoist house, full of mining memorabilia, includes historic photos of Butte's heyday as a mining town, as well as a gift shop. Each of the buildings in the mining camp is outfitted with authentic memorabilia and features a walk-through interpretive display that leads visitors step by step through the mining process and its equipment.

Mineral Museum

Montana Tech Campus. ☎ 406/496-4414. Free admission. Summer daily 8am–5pm; winter Mon–Fri 8am–5pm, Sun 1–5pm.

More than 15,000 mineral specimens belong to Montana Tech's Mineral Museum, though its limited space allows display of only a fraction of them in an area that feels much more like a geology lab than a repository of artifacts. Perhaps owing to this academic setting, one display in particular seems plainly didactic in nature: Cases on the museum's balconies contain a systematic collection of mineral specimens based on chemical composition. Another display features a comprehensive display of fluorescent minerals, starkly illuminated by ultraviolet lights. One of the area's most exciting discoveries, a 27.5-oz. gold nugget found in the Highland Mountains south of Butte, is also on display.

Dumas Brothel

45 E. Mercury St. ☎ 406/782-3808. Free admission. Daily 9:30am–5pm.

Opened in 1890 as a "parlor house," the Dumas was once at the heart of Butte's red-light district. Astoundingly enough, it remained so until 1982, at which time it finally became distinguished: not in a manner of refinement, but as the city's longest-running house of prostitution. Today, visitors to the former brothel can view the two-story brick house built by Joseph Dumas, whose distinctive brand of entrepreneurial spirit supplied the impetus for the management of five similar properties, including the famed Windsor Hotel, another house of prostitution, and the Copper Block, a notorious hotel, saloon, and gambling hall.

The Mai Wah

17 W. Mercury St. ☎ **406/494-5595.** Minimal admission fee, children free. Summer only, Mon–Fri 1–4pm.

Adjacent to China Alley, the Mai Wah and Wah Chong Tai buildings stand as tributes to Butte's early Asian population. With a first-floor mercantile and second-floor noodle parlor, the Mai Wah provided a segment of the city's ethnic community with jobs after the mines were exhausted. Today the buildings house exhibits and memorabilia which honor the rich Asian history of the area.

U.S. High Altitude Sports Center

16 E. Granite. Contact the Butte–Silver Bow Chamber of Commerce for information about tours (☎ **406/494-5595** or 800/735-6814).

You may not see any gold medalists during your visit of this world-class training facility, but rest assured they've been here: Of all the speed-skating medals presented to men and women at the 1992 Winter Olympics, only three of the world's best had not either trained or competed in Butte. Quite a record for a facility completed in only 1987. It has since hosted the Ladies' World Speed Skating Championships. Through a training program that includes bicycling, rollerskating, iceskating, running, and weight training—all at a mile-high altitude—the center trains many of the world's best athletes for professional competition.

✪ Washoe Theater

305 Main St., Anaconda. ☎ **406/563-6161.**

This impressive art deco theater still shows current movies weekly but its big screen, though impressive, doesn't begin to compete with the theater's lavish decor (a photograph of it once hung amid photographs of other buildings known for their ornate art deco decor in the Smithsonian). Even if you don't want to see what's playing, you should take a tour of the building, if only to show the kids what a real theater once looked like. Hammered gold and copper moldings frame rich tapestries and faintly glowing lamps lend a gentle radiance to the extravagantly decorated auditorium. Go on Sunday or Monday, when tickets to 8pm shows are $1. Community concerts and plays also take to the stage periodically; call the chamber office for information on any current productions. Movies change weekly and run from Thursday to Monday.

WHERE TO STAY

⑤ Best Western Copper King Inn

4655 Harrison Ave. South, Butte, MT 59701. ☎ **406/494-6666** or 800/332-8600. 150 rms. A/C TV TEL. $60–$70 double. Senior rates and family packages available. AE, CB, DC, DISC, MC, V.

Located just off the interstate on one of Butte's major thoroughfares, the Copper King Inn is the best value in town.

With an on-site restaurant and lounge, a "kids stay free" (and even get free ice cream) policy, extra-large beds, and an airdome fitness center behind the hotel with basketball and tennis courts, this hotel has something for everyone. The Savoy Dining Room prepares great slow-cooked beef ribs in a subdued atmosphere, but if you're looking for a little more action, try the chicken wings or jalapeño poppers from the bar menu. One of the 13 satellite TVs is sure to have your favorite game on.

✪ Copper King Mansion

219 W. Granite St., Butte, MT 59701. ☎ **406/782-7580.** 5 rms (2 with private baths). $45–$95 double. AE, DISC, MC, V.

It's not the Biltmore Estate, but still, words can't fully describe the grandeur of William A. Clark's Copper King Mansion. There are "mansions" throughout Montana, but William Clark's residence is perhaps the most jaw-dropping and by far the most accessible (you can sleep in the man's bedroom, for crying out loud). It took four years (the massive Fort Peck Dam took less than five!) and almost $8 million to complete the home, and when it was finished in 1888, it was the most opulent residence in the Montana territory.

The mansion's stained-glass double doors open into the main hall and the Staircase of Nations, ascending to the second floor where the guest rooms are located. Antique lamps and chandeliers, ornate frescoed ceilings, and etched amber transoms complement the rooms' original furniture, including two matching African mahogany sleigh beds. In the third-floor ballroom is an 825-pipe Estey organ as well as a private collection of clothing and memorabilia dating back to the late 1800s; a small chapel, complete with the stations of the cross, is discreetly located to the side. Listed on the National Register of Historic Places, the mansion conducts tours daily from 9am to 4pm, May to October. This is the only drawback to spending the night in this magnificent mansion: Guests must be up and about before the tours begin, a small price to pay for a night's worth of royalty.

✪ Fairmont Hot Springs Resort

1500 Fairmont Rd., Gregson, MT 59711. ☎ **406/797-3241** or 800/332-3272. 158 rms. A/C TV TEL. $75–$90 double; $100–$275 suite. AE, CB, DC, DISC, MC, V.

Putting it bluntly, Fairmont Hot Springs is the best resort in the area. We add with equal frankness that this doesn't mean much. You'll know you've reached Fairmont when you see a giant intestinal appendage winding its way to the ground. This is the waterslide, one of a slew of activities at the resort. But, like everything else at Fairmont Hot Springs, it costs extra. It's a year-round resort, complete with the requisite horse rides, but the architecture and some of the amenities make it a strange phenomenon in Montana: a 1970s-style structure straight out of Mr. Brady's portfolio with room service and a beauty salon. Golfing is expensive, though the course is one of the better ones in this part of the state. For skiers, Discovery Basin is a short 30-minute drive away. Though there are certainly better finds in Montana in the way of resort facilities, Fairmont is an oasis between Butte and Anaconda with all the characteristics of a mirage.

⑤ Seven Gables Resort

MT 1, Georgetown Lake, Anaconda, MT 59711. ☎ **406/563-5052** or 800/472-6940. 10 rms, all with kitchenette. TV TEL. $36–$50 double. AE, DISC, MC, V.

There's good reason locals call the Seven Gables "the Trap." If the stunning backdrop of the Anaconda-Pintler Wilderness Area doesn't pull you in, a generous serving of the restaurant's mouth-watering buffalo chips will. Located just 4 miles from the Discovery Basin ski area, Seven Gables is an undiscovered haven for anyone with a desire to leave civilization behind and enjoy what Montana is all about: crystal-clear high-mountain lakes, bright meadows of wildflowers, and lots of watchable wildlife. You're almost sure to spy a moose at the pond across the road. The resort is ideally located at the foot of Georgetown Lake, where guests can ice fish or canoe, and can't be missed by skiers traveling up the road to the ski hill (who, incidentally, get a discount off the already low rates). Within easy driving distance of prime fishing at Rock Creek and the Clark Fork River as well as hiking and mountain biking trails,

Seven Gables is even more popular during the summer. Though the restaurant is small, it serves super food with a specialty of roasted chicken and buffalo chips. If you can't bring yourself to try that, though, try the steaks, barbecue ribs, or monster burgers for an equally filling meal. A small grocery sells sundries and boat rentals are available nearby.

War Bonnet Inn

2100 Cornell, Butte, MT 59701. ☎ **406/494-7800** or 800/443-1806, 800/423-1421 in MT. 134 rms. A/C TV TEL. $55–$75 double. Special senior, corporate, and AAA rates. AE, DC, DISC, MC, V.

The War Bonnet is a good choice for families and cowboys, with the largest sleeping rooms in town and a parking lot big enough for cattle trailers. Their location next door to one of Butte's nicest city parks doesn't hurt, either. Baseball diamonds, tennis courts, and a jogging track at Father Sheehan City Park are definite pluses, along with the four-star dining room, the Apache. The hotel has an indoor pool, a sauna, and a hot tub.

WHERE TO EAT

Butte's ethnic tradition is most evident in its food, with pasties (pronounced "PASS-tees" or "PAH-stees," if you're British) ranking high on the list. If you've never tried one of these meat-filled pastries, of Cornish origin, you're in for a treat. Purveyed at nearly every eating establishment in the city, pasties are an essential part of the Butte experience.

✪ Old Metals Banque Tower

8 West Park (at Main). ☎ **406/723-6160.** Reservations recommended, especially on weekends. Lunch $4–$15; dinner $6–$15. DISC, MC, V. Call for days and hours; at press time, they were due to change. CREATIVE AMERICAN.

When restoration began on this deteriorated downtown building in 1989, original marble, African mahogany, solid copper window frames, and an intricate 22-inch vaulted plaster ceiling were discovered and a fine dining establishment was born. Built in 1898 to house the State Savings Bank by Marcus Daly and designed by famous turn-of-the-century architect Cass Gilbert, the Old Metals Banque Tower is today best known for the excellent food found inside its doors. An elegant early San Francisco atmosphere pervades the Old Metals Banque, and it is a charming place to dine, though you'd never realize it's known locally for its Mexican food. Though you'll find a selection of meats on the menu, including steaks and seafood, the emphasis is on "clean" foods and low-fat items. The chef caters to special needs and will prepare food to order if the ingredients are on hand. Espresso and microbrews are also served.

✪ The Uptown Cafe

47 E. Broadway. ☎ **406/723-4735.** Reservations recommended. Lunch $3–$7; dinner $7–$20. AE, DISC, MC, V. Mon–Fri 11am–2pm; Tues–Sat from 5pm. CONTINENTAL.

While this restaurant may no longer be the state's best, it's certainly tops in Butte. Known for its seafood, the Uptown Cafe also serves veal and steaks with equal zeal, accompanied by lavish sauces and dressings. Though the restaurant is strictly cafeteria-style for lunch, it is transformed into a fine dining establishment at night, where changing exhibits of local artists and photographers grace its walls.

THE PERFORMING ARTS & NIGHTLIFE

Under the direction of conductor Matthew Savery, the **Butte Symphony Orchestra,** 1880 Harrison Ave. (☎ 406/723-5590), presents four concerts each year at the Butte–Silver Bow Civic Center, 1340 Harrison Ave. (☎ 406/723-8362 or 723-3055), often accompanied by a featured soloist or chorus. **Troup du Jour,** 646 W. Galena (☎ 406/723-8232) is a local theater group that performs musicals, comedies, and classical dramas at various times throughout the year.

A SIDE TRIP TO DEER LODGE

As home to the state prison, Deer Lodge may seem an odd choice for a vacation destination. Yet it is this very distinction—as home of Montana's criminals—that makes it such a compelling stop off U.S. Hwy. 15. Throw in a collection of old Fords and a ranch that's now a national historic site and you've got an interesting slice of Americana, Montana-style.

Actively used until 1979, the **Old Montana Prison,** at 1106 Main St., Deer Lodge, MT 59722 (☎ 406/846-3111), is a surprisingly ornate brick structure listed on the National Register of Historic Places. Cellblocks, maximum security areas, crenellated guard towers, and the towering arches of the "Sally Port" gate are the attractions here, as well as a tribute to officers killed in the line of duty at the Montana Law Enforcement Museum.

The prison complex also houses the Towe Ford Collection, the Powell County Museum, Yesterday's Playthings, the Montana Law Enforcement Museum, and the Old Prison Players, a summer theater troupe. Call 406/846-3111 for a schedule of upcoming productions and reservations.

The **Towe Ford Museum** currently houses more than 100 exquisitely restored Ford automobiles, from the first production models of the early Alphabet series to the now classic roadsters of the 1950s and 1960s. See a Model A Snowmobile, a World War II Ford Jeep, and a "Bootleggers Special" Lincoln, along with the infamous Edsel. The museum is open to the public year-round. Summer hours: daily, Memorial Day–Labor Day 8am–9pm; winter hours, Sun–Tue noon–4pm, Wed–Sat 10am–4pm. Extended hours in April, 8:30am–5:30pm.

A much broader-based collection is presented at the **Powell County Museum,** 1193 Main St. (☎ 406/846-3294), where visitors can view area artifacts and memorabilia from frontier days when Deer Lodge was an important trading post and center for the state's cattle and farming industries. Free admission. The museum is open Memorial Day–Labor Day, 12–5pm and is closed in winter.

Yesterday's Playthings, 1017 Main St. (☎ 406/846-1480), is a doll and toy museum. The collection of Genevieve Hostetter is displayed here, with dolls of all descriptions: artistic, ethnic, advertising, and Native American. The collection also features dollhouses, toys, and trains and can be viewed from Memorial Day to Labor Day, 9am–5pm; closed in winter.

Set aside by Congress in 1972 for the purpose of providing an understanding of the frontier cattle era of the nation's history, the **Grant-Kohrs Ranch** is a national historic site that spans not only 1,500 acres, but also the early history of ranching, from the late 1800s to the present. The ranch provides an interactive history through an examination of its outbuildings and is open to the public daily except on Thanksgiving, Christmas, and New Year's Day. Adult admission is $1; families, $3.

For additional information on these and other activities in Deer Lodge, contact the **Butte–Silver Bow Chamber of Commerce,** 1171 Main St., Deer Lodge, MT 59722 (☎ 406/846-2094) or Gold West Country, 1155 Main St., Deer Lodge, MT 59722 (☎ 406/846-1943).

4 Dillon & the Big Hole Valley

Nicknamed the valley of 10,000 haystacks, the Big Hole Valley in southwestern Montana is a rambling expanse of cattle ranches, hayfields, and mountain ranges, fed by high mountain lakes and populated with a greater number of animals per square mile than people. With the exception of those who live in Dillon, the area's largest town, the county's 8,000 residents largely choose to spread out around the valley, living in towns with names like Polaris, Wise River, and Wisdom. And why not? There's elbow room in abundance. Beaverhead County, one of Montana's largest, is as large as Connecticut and Rhode Island combined.

The economy here is farm-based, with the county ranking first in the state for hay acres harvested and first in the state for beef cattle production. Haying is done much as it was in the early 1900s, sometimes with beaverslide haystackers, a contraption invented in the Big Hole Valley that resembles a giant mousetrap. You'll still see the giant structures in the fields, though some have long ago been abandoned; if you have the time, stop and ask a local how they work.

The scenic loop that takes you around this valley is one of the state's more popular driving tours and is described in Section 1 of this chapter. A word of warning, though: Before taking off, throw a sweatshirt or jacket in the car. Wisdom, a sleepy little town in the Big Hole Valley, is very often the coldest spot in entire United States, even in summer.

ESSENTIALS

GETTING THERE   The **Dillon Airport** is located at 2400 Airport Road with paved runways for light planes. See Butte and Anaconda "Essentials" earlier in this chapter for information on the closest airport to the Big Hole Valley for commercial flights, car rentals, Amtrak service, and bus schedules.

Since this area is a popular destination for snowmobilers, visitors are encouraged to call the **avalanche advisory** (☎ 406/587-6981) before setting out on a sledding trip. For current road conditions in the Big Hole Valley, call 800/332-6171; 406/449-5204 for current weather information.

VISITOR INFORMATION   The Dillon Visitor Information Center (Beaverhead Chamber of Commerce) is located in the Old Union Pacific Railroad at 125 S. Montana St., Dillon, MT 59725 (☎ 406/683-5511). Horseshoe pits and a branded sidewalk are interesting diversions for the kids while you gather brochures and maps of the area. You can also contact **Gold West Country,** 1155 Main St., Deer Lodge, MT 59722 (☎ 406/846-1943), for information on the entire Big Hole Valley.

GETTING OUTSIDE
Sports & Outdoor Activities

Beaverhead County is home to naturally occurring hot springs, the most popular location of which is at the Jackson Hot Springs Lodge (see "Where to Stay" later in this section). These waters provide a therapeutic complement to various winter activities, most notably snowmobiling, downhill skiing, and cross-country skiing.

Fishing

Big Hole Valley fishermen can find several trout species along the **Big Hole, Red Rock,** and **Ruby Rivers,** including the eastern brook, cutthroat, mackinaw, brown, and golden. **The Clark Canyon Reservoir** provides good fishing for rainbow trout. Arctic grayling, ling, and whitefish also populate the waters of the Big Hole Valley.

For licenses, equipment, and—most important of all—advice on hot spots, check with the locals in Dillon at **Big Buck Sporting Goods,** 125 N. Montana (☎ 406/683-4881); **Blue Ribbon Rivers,** 3535 Hwy. 91 S. (☎ 406/683-5205); **Fishing Headquarters,** 610 N. Montana (☎ 406/683-6660); or **Frontier Anglers,** 680 N. Montana (☎ 406/683-5276). If you're in Twin Bridges, your best bet for fishing equipment and outfitting services is at the **Four Rivers Fishing Co.,** 205 S. Main (☎ 406/684-5651). And if you're not staying at the Montana Trout Club at the Diamond O Ranch (see "Also Worth a Look" below), be sure to stop in at the **Winston Rod Co.,** also in Twin Bridges, at 109 E. 3rd Ave. (☎ 406/684-5674) for a look at some of the finest fly rods in the world.

Hiking

Hike along the **Continental Divide Trail** in the **Italian Peaks** for interesting geologic discoveries, fabulous scenery, and abundant wildlife: elk, moose, mule deer, antelope, and even black bears are all indigenous to the region. **The Wise River Ranger District,** Box 100, Wise River, MT 59762 (☎ 406/832-3178), can direct you to the area's most traveled trails.

Skiing

In addition to **Maverick Mountain,** you're also pretty close to **Lost Trail Powder Mountain.** See the "Side Trip" later in this section for complete details.

Maverick Mountain

Maverick Mountain Road (P.O. Box 475), Polaris, MT 59746. ☎ **406/834-3454.** Lift tickets $17 adults, $10 children 12 and under, kids 5 and under ski free. $8 Thurs ski special. Open late Nov–early Apr Thurs–Sun and holidays 9:30am–4pm. Take MT 287 west off of U.S. Hwy. 15 to the Polaris Road for 13 miles.

Inconspicuously tucked into the Beaverhead National Forest, 35 miles west of Dillon, Maverick Mountain is a snowy playground for local residents, still largely undiscovered by tourists. Its 15 runs and lift capacity of 700 skiers per hour makes it one of the state's smaller ski hills, a fact that can be interpreted as an advantage or an inconvenience, depending on your outlook. With black diamond runs making up nearly half of the trail system, seasoned skiers need not worry that they'll be bored: Wide-open bowls, gladed meadows, winding runs, and steep chutes combine for an unforgettable ski vacation in the magnificent Pioneer Mountain Wilderness Area.

Rentals and lessons are available for downhill skis and snowboards; the mountain's "Ski Starter" package includes ski rental, lesson, and lift ticket for $17. A nursery facility is also available by reservation. There are no lodging facilities at the ski area; see "Where to Stay" later in this chapter for local options. Cafeteria-style meals are available at the base lodge or you can grab a hot toddy at the Thunder Bar.

Snowmobiling

The Wise River trail system features 150 miles of groomed trails in the Big Hole Valley area, including **Anderson Meadows**—which leads to backcountry lakes and a rental cabin—and **Lacy Creek,** with 10 miles of groomed and ungroomed trails to five high mountain lakes. **The Wise River Jackpine Savages,** Box 115, Wise River, MT 59762 (☎ 406/832-3258) are the local sledding authorities; call them for trail specifics.

NATURE PRESERVES & WILDERNESS AREAS

One of the Bureau of Land Management's Backcountry Byways, the **Big Sheep Creek Canyon** offers the opportunity to observe the majestic bighorn sheep in their spectacular natural habitat year round. The 50-mile byway begins in Dell, Montana, on U.S. Hwy. 15, 24 miles north of the Montana-Idaho border, and passes beneath the high rock cliffs of Big Sheep Canyon to the head of Medicine Lodge Creek. From here, it's just a short drive down to the Medicine Lodge Valley to MT 324, just west of Clark Canyon Dam.

Clark Canyon Recreation Area, a man-made lake 20 miles south of Dillon on U.S. Hwy. 15, is the locals' choice for waterskiing or trout fishing, with ice fishing for ling or monster trout during winter ranking high on the list of things to do. Lewis and Clark's Camp Fortunate is located on the northwestern shore of the reservoir, where camping and boat launching facilities are also available.

Two Dillon area landmarks are designated state parks because of the historical significance attached to them as a result of the Lewis and Clark expedition. **Clark's Lookout** (☎ 406/834-3413) provided the explorers with a vantage point from which to view their route and is reached by taking the MT 41 exit from U.S. Hwy. 90. Drive one-half mile east, then another half-mile north on a county road. **Beaverhead Rock,** 14 miles south of Twin Bridges on MT 41 (☎ 406/994-4042), was a tribal landmark recognized by expedition scout Sacajawea. Both parks are day use only.

OUTFITTERS & ORGANIZED TRIPS

Montana High Country Tours
1036 E. Reeder, Dillon, MT 59725. ☎ **406/683-4920.**

Operated by a sixth-generation Montanan, High Country Tours offers year-round guiding services, including fly-fishing, horseback riding, big-game hunting, and snowmobiling. Whether you're a sportsman looking to bag that elusive elk or a family longing for some quality time together, Russ Kipp has plenty of experience in arranging a unique outdoor adventure. His most popular trips center around southwest Montana's classic trout streams, picturesque limestone canyons, and stunning mountain ranges. Prices range from $690 for a three-day/four-night snowmobiling package that includes sled (with fuel), lodging, meals, insurance, and equipment to $2,000 for a five-day bighorn sheep–hunting trip including meals, lodging, and pack service.

Bad Beaver Bike Tours
25 E. Helena, Dillon, MT 59725. ☎ **406/683-9292.**

The Bad Beaver Bike Shop, a full-service facility in Dillon, coordinates forays into the Beaverhead National Forest with customized mountain biking trips. All trips include meals and transportation to and from the ride site, and multi-day trips also include lodging. Their most popular tour is a Lake Powell bike and boat combo, available in March and April and again in October and November. Combine the terrain of the red rock backcountry with the comfort of a fully outfitted houseboat for an unforgettable adventure travel experience. Tour rates begin at $80 per person for a one-day outing and range upwards from $150 per person/day for multi-day tours. Call the shop and have one of their guides talk with you about other trips in the Big Hole area.

SEEING THE SIGHTS

Based in Dillon or elsewhere in the valley, you can branch off to see Big Hole National Battlefield; see Section 5 of this chapter for complete details.

You may also want to drive the **Pioneer Mountain Scenic Byway,** a 27-mile drive that begins on MT 278 west of Dillon or along Highway 43, south of the Wise River. Driving between the east and west Pioneer Mountain Ranges, you'll experience alpine meadows, jagged peaks, and ghost towns with numerous opportunities along

Red Rocks Lakes National Wildlife Refuge: A Haven for the Trumpeter Swan

Often called the most beautiful national wildlife refuge in the United States, the Red Rocks Lakes National Wildlife Refuge was established in 1935 to protect the rare trumpeter swan. It is here that the endangered species has been brought back from near extinction, after a century of being hunted for their meat and feathers (quill pens were a hot item in the 1800s). It was feared that these beautiful creatures, which have massive wingspans of 7 to 8 feet, had been completely wiped out, until biologists discovered several dozen here in 1933. (They're also found along the Pacific coast and in Alaska.) The largest population in the Lower 48 states, 300 to 500 of the rare birds continue to nest and winter at the refuge. They mate for life and often return to the exact same nest each year to tend their eggs and the newborn cygnets.

In addition to the swan population, the 40,000-acre refuge is home to moose, deer, elk, antelope, fox, great blue herons, sandhill cranes, ducks, and geese; more than 50,000 ducks and geese may be seen during times of migration.

The multiuse refuge is a popular spot for hiking, mountain biking, and canoeing; check with the **U.S. Fish and Wildlife Service,** Mountain Prairie Region, P.O. Box 25486 DFC, Denver, CO 80225 (☎ 303/236-7920 or locally 406/276-3536), for regulations concerning these activities within refuge boundaries. The refuge lies just beyond the town of Monida. Off U.S. Hwy. 15 well south of Dillon; you'll take a gravel road the remainder of the way.

the way to camp, fish, or photograph the scenery and wildlife. Plunge into the refreshing mineral waters of Elkhorn Hot Springs or dig for quartz crystals at Crystal Park.

There's not much of a shopping scene in Dillon or the Big Hole Valley but the town's **Patagonia Outlet** store, 34 N. Idaho (☎ 406/683-2580), can easily be compared to Butte's St. Patrick's Day parade in one important respect: You shouldn't miss it if you happen to be in town. If you've never bought a brand-name polar fleece pullover, the prices may not seem to be much of a bargain, but good deals for unbeatable quality are definitely here.

Western Montana College Gallery/Museum

710 S. Atlantic, Dillon. ☎ **406/683-7126** or 800/WMC-MONT. Free admission. Mon–Thurs 10am–3pm.

The most exciting exhibit at this gallery and museum is the Seidensticker Wildlife Collection of big-game trophies. The collection features animals from the far-flung locales of Africa and Asia as well as North American game. Student art is also featured on a rotating basis.

Beaverhead County Museum

15 S. Montana, Dillon. ☎ **406/683-5027.** Free admission; donations appreciated. June–Labor Day Mon–Fri 10am–8pm, Sat–Sun 1–5pm; Sept—May Mon–Fri 10am–5pm, Sat–Sun 1–5pm.

The Beaverhead County Museum is located in the center of town in the depot building, which is also home to the chamber of commerce offices. As a result, there is not a single place in town with more information or history of the Big Hole Valley than this one, whether you're looking for current information on outdoor activities or simply want to admire Dillon's first flush toilet. The museum, like many in smaller Montana towns, is not interactive and therefore may be boring for the kids, but it presents a wealth of information on the history of the area. A small gift shop caters to the local historical scene and also sells Made in Montana items.

WHERE TO STAY

The Best Western Paradise Inn
650 N. Montana, Dillon, MT 59725. ☎ **406/683-4214.** 65 rms. A/C TV TEL. $50–$60 double; $70–$80 suite. AE, DISC, MC, V.

The Paradise Inn is a comfortable two-story facility set back from one of Dillon's busier streets. The basic rooms are moderately appointed and cozy but the penthouse suites are well worth the indulgence, with huge bathtubs and large living areas. There is a heated swimming pool in a separate building to the front of the property along with a hot tub and exercise equipment.

Of course a vacation at the Paradise wouldn't be complete without a trip to the "Garden of Eat'n," the hotel's adjacent restaurant and lounge at 660 N. Montana, open from 6am to 11pm. All meals are moderately priced, with the most expensive item on the dinner menu being the New York cut steak at a whopping $12. Breakfast is served all day.

The Grasshopper Inn
Box 504, Polaris, MT 59746. ☎ **406/834-3456.** 10 rms. TV TEL. $50 double. MC, V.

The Grasshopper is moderately priced and located in a beautifully scenic area, making it a good value for a weekend getaway. It's not in the same league as more ritzy northwest Montana guest inns, but its small-town ambience is refreshing and genuine. Guests can enjoy skiing at nearby Maverick Mountain (located practically next door to the inn), soaking in the inn's hot tubs, snowmobiling, and various other outdoor activities during the summer in the Pioneer Mountains. Similar to the Swan Valley's Holland Lake Lodge, the Grasshopper offers fine dining and cocktails in its restaurant. An antique mahogany bar and fireplace lend a romantic atmosphere. Ask your hosts for tips on local fishing and rockhounding haunts.

⑤ Hotel Metlen
5 S. Railroad Ave., Dillon, MT 59725. ☎ **406/683-2335.** 46 rms (18 with private baths). $15–$30 double. No credit cards.

This downtown Dillon hotel's name is indicative of its carefree sense of style: some days it's the Hotel Metlen; others it's the Metlen Hotel. Ads say one thing; employees say another. Yet it's this same laissez-faire attitude that defines the hotel's success. For nearly 100 years, the Metlen has been a landmark in southwest Montana. Built in 1897 by Joe Metlen, the building was one of the premier hotels of its day, with an opening attended by local and regional dignitaries. Since those grand days, the hotel has fallen into a state of semi-disrepair, though renovations and remodeling occur on an almost daily basis. The huge brick building, listed on the National Register of Historic Places, has three stories and includes two bars, a casino, and a poker room (where you can join in on a live game if you dare), with live country-and-western music on the weekends. Their incredibly low room rates of $15 are for the third-floor rooming house–style rooms, where you walk down the hallway to the bathroom. The hotel is a popular spot for cowboys, hunters, fishermen, and luminaries of almost any description, including President Reagan's son, who stays at the Metlen when he goes fishing. The antique back bar—originally from Bannack, the state's first territorial capital—is the hotel's crowning glory, a gathering place of grand style, complete with dark polished wood, sparkling chandeliers, and an all-pervasive cattle baron elegance. The hotel's restaurant has been closed for a few years, but future plans include reopening the dining room.

GUEST RANCHES & LODGES

⊙ Jackson Hot Springs Lodge

Jackson, MT 59736. ☎ **406/834-3151.** 12 cabins. $60–$70 cabin. MC, V.

Lewis and Clark would have appreciated what commerce has done to the hot springs they first discovered in 1806. A similarly great find for modern-day travelers to the Big Hole Valley, this hot springs facility is a hive of activity year-round. Guests register in the main lodge, the epitome of Western charm, where they can also play shuffleboard or video games, or just relax or read in front of the imposing river rock fireplace. Trophy mounts adorn the walls upstairs and down, with one engraved plate that reads "Barasingh 'Great Deer of Kashmir' Shot by Teddy Roosevelt. James Simpson-Roosevelt Asiatic Expedition. Field Museum of Natural History 1925–6." The 30-by-70-foot hot springs pool, fed by an artesian system that keeps the water fresh daily, has a shallow soaking pool on one end and runs to 8 feet deep on the other. (If you're not staying at the lodge, you can soak for under $5; $2.50 for children 12 and under.)

The cabins are small and Spartan, but each has its own river rock fireplace and bath. If you're looking for a screaming deal, reserve one of the economy units—"rustic hunters' cabins"—for $27. They're basically a shrunken version of the larger ones, with showers and bathrooms in an adjoining building. Telephones and a TV are in the lodge, and the restaurant serves "cowboy gourmet" cuisine for breakfast, lunch, and dinner throughout the week (call for specific hours as it scales back on shoulder seasons and sometimes even during the week). Hiking in summer and cross-country skiing in winter are encouraged; employees can give you the best leads on local trails.

CAMPING

Jefferson River Camp, off MT 41 South in Silver Star (☎ 406/684-5577), offers full RV hookups, tent sites, and tepee rentals. The campground is located on a cattle ranch a short distance from the confluence of the Ruby, Beaverhead, and Big Hole Rivers, which unite to form the Jefferson. Campers have private access to one-half mile of the Jefferson; fly-fishing and fly-tying instruction is available with prior notice.

The Maverick Mountain RV Park & Cabins, P.O. Box 460–516, Polaris, MT 59746 (☎ 406/834-3452), is situated along a National Scenic Byway near Polaris, Montana. Nightly, weekly, and monthly rates are available with full hookups along with a limited number of tent sites.

WHERE TO EAT

Big Hole Crossing Restaurant

Main Street, Wisdom. ☎ **406/689-3800.** Reservations not accepted. Breakfast $2–$7; lunch $4–$6; dinner $9–$18. MC, V. Daily 6:30am–9pm. AMERICAN.

For hot food in a cold town, this is your only bet. But it's a good one. Located in one of the newest buildings on Main Street, the Big Hole Crossing serves up three square meals daily, including a fine-dining experience in the evenings. Decorated Western-style, this restaurant is quite a find in the otherwise vacant valley. For breakfast, try the French toast stuffed with strawberries and bananas, or the buttermilk pancakes. For lunch, you can't go wrong with "gourmet" hamburgers, but the charbroiled chicken sandwich is lighter and just as tasty. Dinner is a meat-lover's dream. Prime rib is served nightly, as is the filet mignon. Though the seafood isn't the freshest you'll find in Montana, it is the best in the Big Hole Valley, hands down.

The Lion's Den

725 N. Montana, Dillon. ☎ 406/683-2051. Reservations accepted. Lunch $4–$6; dinner $7–$17. MC, V. Mon–Fri 11:30am–2pm; daily 5–10:30pm. AMERICAN.

This is another installment in the Montana supper club circuit with lots of red meat. Opened in 1955, this is one of Dillon's oldest eating establishments, but not necessarily the best. With a bar, pool table, and poker machines, the Den can become a lively place when the college kids come around—it may not have quite the atmosphere you're looking for when a quiet evening is what you want most. With its daily specials, the Lion's Den is a good spot for lunch.

The Mine Shaft

26 S. Montana, Dillon. ☎ 406/683-6611. Reservations accepted. Lunch $5–$6; dinner $6–$16. DISC, MC, V. Mon–Thurs 11am–10pm, Fri 11am–11pm, Sat–Sun 4–10pm. STEAKS/SEAFOOD.

This unique restaurant has the best dining atmosphere in Dillon, but it's the antiques that keep people coming in the door. Everything you can imagine having to do with mining can be found under this roof, as well as some incidentals: an old toaster, cameras, and old cans of oil. And they serve food, too. Especially good is the blackened catfish, something you won't find anywhere else in these parts. Also in the Cajun vein is the blackened ribeye. There are a few poker machines in this place, but they've been moved away from the dining room and the machines are silent.

Papa T's

10 N. Montana, Dillon. ☎ 406/683-6432. Reservations not accepted. Pizzas $5–$15. MC, V. Daily 11am–10pm. PIZZA.

A few years ago when the drinking age was lower, Papa T's ruled as one of the biggest off-campus hangouts in Dillon. Now, though, it's a quiet and spacious bar serving up the best pizza in town. There's also a healthy menu for antipizza people. For pizza lovers there's quite an alternative selection: Porky (barbecue pizza with sausage, Canadian bacon, and regular bacon), the Taco Pizza, and the Gourmet Pizza, which substitutes a marinade for a tomato-based sauce.

ALSO WORTH A LOOK:
TWIN BRIDGES & THE MONTANA TROUT CLUB

Just up MT 41 a piece from Dillon, a faded billboard just outside of town proclaims Twin Bridges to be the "platinum capital of the Western world," an odd designation for a town that seems to be much more famous regionally for great fishing. "Floating Flotillas & Fish Fantasies" is the name given to the tiny town's annual summer festival held in mid-July, with highlights that include the extremely popular floating parade on the Beaverhead, dances, and a barbecue. Locals are even given the chance to show their skills at fly-casting, fly-tying, and wader racing.

But perhaps the area's greatest source of pride comes from being the home of the ✪ Diamond O Ranch and the Montana Trout Club.

Owned by the R.L. Winston Rod Company, the Diamond O Ranch is the quintessential private fishing club. The ranch's 6,000 acres are traversed by nearly 11 miles of the Beaverhead River and Albers Spring Creek, waters fished by only a select few over the past 50 years. Set in a magnificent mountain valley, the ranch is surrounded by the Ruby, Tobacco Root, and Pioneer Mountains. Within this spectacular mountain setting, guests stay in refurbished ranch farmhouses, each with a private bath.

Gourmet meals are served at the Main House, either in the dining room or on the veranda, whose wood-paneled walls feature late 19th century oil paintings, reminiscent of the grand era of the Western cattle baron. First-class instruction and guided fishing excursions from senior members of the Winston Rod Company during the stay are unparalleled, whether guests choose to fish the waters at the ranch or explore other nearby blue-ribbon streams. A four-day guided fishing package, including lodging and all meals, is $1,495 per person; a six-day "Skills of Fly-Fishing" school is $2,250 per person. Be sure to inquire well in advance of the time you'd like to visit this exclusive fishing club; a limited number of guests are allowed each week.

For additional information about the Twin Bridges area and scheduled activities, contact the Chamber of Commerce at 406/684-5259.

A SIDE TRIP TO LOST TRAIL PASS FOR SKIING & HOT SPRINGS

Located as it is near the border of Idaho and directly in the nose of Montana's "face," Lost Trail Pass can easily be overlooked, with most of the state's tourist traffic flowing in either direction along U.S. Hwy. 15 to the more touted regions of Montana's north and east. Yet this corner of the state is one of the most scenic, with a unbeatable tandem combo: a ski area and hot springs resort facility. With Lost Trail Powder Mountain, Lost Trail Hot Springs Resort, and Camp Creek Inn, the pass area is an unforgettable winter vacation destination for those who loathe big crowds and the attendant ski scene.

With 60% of the mountain's runs rated for an intermediate ability, Lost Trail Powder Mountain is an incredible value for the average skier and for families. Lift tickets are $16 for adults and $8 for children 12 and younger; kids 5 and younger ski free. The rest of the ski area is equally divided for beginner skiers and experts in the strikingly beautiful Bitterroot Range. After a long day of skiing, relax in the day lodge for surprisingly tasty cafeteria-style food or head for the nearby hot springs.

If you'd like additional information on Lost Trail Powder Mountain, write to P.O. Box 311, Conner, MT 59827. Ski reports are available during the season at 406/821-3211. The ski area is located 90 miles south of Missoula at the Montana-Idaho border, one-eighth mile from U.S. Hwy. 93.

In typical Montana style, the **Lost Trail Hot Springs Resort,** 8221 U.S. Hwy. 93 South, Sula, MT 59871 (☎ 406/821-3574 or 800/825-3574), is a comfortable, unpretentious lodge where fun and friendliness are the watchwords. A variety of Western adventures are at your fingertips, from soaking in the crystal-clear hot springs pool or indoor sauna to summer raft trips on the Salmon and Bitterroot Rivers. Overnight horse-pack trips in the nearby wilderness and blue-ribbon fishing for Dolly Varden on the Big Hole River are other popular resort activities. The lodge's restaurant overlooks the hot springs pool, where you can dine indoors or out, depending on the weather. There is also an on-site casino and lounge. Nightly rates range from $50 to $75 for lodge rooms and are approximately $60 for cabins. Nightly group rates start at $350 for the Clark Lodge, which sleeps 12, and $400 for the Sacajawea, which sleeps 23 in four furnished main rooms with lofts and 20 in a downstairs bunk area. A two-day float trip on the Salmon with a tour of the Big Hole Battlefield and Bannack costs $260; other resort-arranged activities are available with costs ranging from $300 to $500, depending on the activity and length of stay.

The Camp Creek Inn, 7674 U.S. Hwy. 93 South, Sula, MT 59871 (☎ 406/821-3508), a local bed-and-breakfast guest ranch, is also convenient to the ski resort and offers winter packages that include lift tickets, lodging, and breakfast. They can also set you up with excursions centered around horseback rides, hiking, mountain biking, hunting, or float trips in the nearby Bitterroot or Big Hole Valleys. Prices for accommodations start at $35 for one person and $55 for couples. Inquire about the cost of additional seasonal activities.

The closest airport to this undiscovered area of Montana is in Missoula, 90 miles to the north. Rental cars are available there (see Chapter 6).

5 Big Hole Battlefield National Historic Site

The tragic flight of the Nez Perce tribe across Montana in 1877 is memorialized at Big Hole Battlefield. Here you'll learn their story—along with the history of soldiers of the 7th U.S. Infantry and the Bitterroot Volunteers, who also fought and died at the Battle of the Big Hole. A symbol of the strength and spirit of the Nez Perce, the battlefield today serves as a reminder of their heavy losses in their struggle for freedom.

Eastern Washington and Oregon were once the homeland of the Nez Perce people. These rolling hills, covered with lush grasses, were perfect for raising horses (appaloosas were first bred there) and provided fertile ground for hunting and fishing. The Nez Perce befriended explorers Lewis and Clark in 1805 and remained friendly to white settlers when other tribes were waging wars. However, the neutrality of the Nez Perce was rewarded with treaties that twice cut the size of their reservation in half. When some of the Nez Perce bands refused to sign a new treaty and relinquish their land, the stage was set for one of the great tragedies of Northwest history.

In the summer of 1877, several Nez Perce braves ignored orders from the tribal elders and attacked and killed four white settlers in Oregon to exact revenge for the earlier murder of a father of one of the braves. This attack raised the ire of settlers, and the cavalry was called in to hunt down the Nez Perce. The elders decided to flee to Canada, and, headed by Chief Joseph (also known as Young Joseph), 800 Nez Perce, including 400 women and children, began a 2,000-mile march across Idaho and Montana on a retreat that lasted four months.

Skirmishes erupted along the way in Idaho before the Nez Perce entered Montana, fleeing from army troops under the leadership of Gen. Oliver O. Howard. When the Nez Perce reached the Big Hole Valley, they decided to make camp, thinking all the while that they had outrun the army troops, for a short time at least. However, in addition to Howard's troops behind them, a second group of soldiers, under the command of Col. John Gibbon, were advancing up the Bitterroot Valley toward the unsuspecting tribe. On the morning of August 9, 1877, Gibbon's soldiers, along with a contingent of local volunteers, attacked the sleeping tribe in what is today known as the Battle of the Big Hole. Many lives were lost, including many Nez Perce women and children, in the battle that ensued. Less than 48 hours after they'd set up camp, the remaining Nez Perce once again found themselves fleeing for their lives and their freedom. They headed toward Canada, although the U.S. Army troops caught up to them at Bear Paw, a mere 40 miles from the Canadian border.

Begun as a military reserve in 1883, the area became a national monument in 1910 and was designated a national battlefield in 1963. Today, the National Park Service maintains an interpretive center for visitors, where rangers help visitors to understand the significance of the battle that occurred at Big Hole. A museum, exhibits, bookstore, movies, and two self-guided walking trails are open and available to the public.

Trails begin at the lower parking lot and lead to several points of interest. The Nez Perce Camp, where soldiers surprised the sleeping tribe, is considered sacred ground. The Siege Area marks the place where soldiers were besieged for nearly 24 hours as the Nez Perce fought to save their families from certain death. A fairly steep walk will lead you to the Howitzer Capture Site, where soldiers suffered a heavy blow as Nez Perce warriors captured and dismantled the military weapon. A spectacular view of the battlefield and surrounding area can be seen from here.

Significant as it may seem, Big Hole Battlefield represents only a small fraction of the Nez Perce's tragic flight across the West. The 1,700-mile Nez Perce (Nee Me Poo) National Historic Trail follows the entire route of the Nez Perce War, from Wallowa Lake, in northwestern Oregon, to the Bear's Paw Battlefield in northcentral Montana (see Chapter 8). Crossing four states, the trail features several Nez Perce war sites with interpretive markers telling the story of the tribe's fight for freedom. The trail is maintained by the Nez Perce National Historical Park, whose management can provide you with an excellent map of the four-state area. To request one, write to P.O. Box 93, Spalding, ID 83551 (☎ 208/843-2261).

The Big Hole Battlefield visitor center (☎ 406/689-3155) is open daily (except on Thanksgiving, Christmas, and New Year's Day) with summer hours from 8am to 6pm and winter hours from 8am to 4:30pm. Admission is $4 per car, $2 per bike. Picnic tables are located at the lower parking lot, though there are no camping or overnight facilities on the premises. Fishing and hunting are allowed within the battlefield's boundaries as provided by Montana law, but are restricted on private land adjoining the battlesite. Montana laws apply in the adjacent national forest.

The nearest facilities—restaurants, gas stations, grocery stores, and lodgings— are located in Wisdom, 12 miles to the east.

6 The Ghost Towns: Virginia City, Nevada City & Bannack

If you've never seen an authentic Western ghost town, you simply have to include this part of Montana in your vacation plans. There's no better way to appreciate the area's rich history—from gold to sapphires to copper—than to stroll along the deserted streets of the once-bustling mining towns. From the silent, dusty main drag of Bannack to the rowdy Brewery Follies in Virginia City, history continues to thrive, though commerce has not.

If you look closely enough, you can find the remains of many other Montana ghost towns in this part of the state, though information about them is often hard to find and the towns themselves even harder. Start by contacting the **Virginia City Chamber of Commerce,** P.O. Box 218, Virginia City, MT 59755 (☎ 406/843-5377 or 800/648-7588), and **Gold West Country,** 1155 Main St., Deer Lodge, MT 59722 (☎ 406/846-1943). These two agencies can provide you with free information about the historic ghost towns of Montana.

Be forewarned that most of the "tourist" attractions in Virginia City (and all of Nevada City) are run by Bovey Restorations, P.O. Box 338, Virginia City, MT 59755 (☎ 406/843-5377 or 800/648-7588), and they're only open during the peak summer season, from Memorial Day through Labor Day. Before driving in this area during winter, check on weather conditions and road reports statewide (☎ 800/332-6171).

VIRGINIA CITY

With the discovery of gold in the vicinity of Alder Gulch by Bill Fairweather and a party of miners in 1863, Virginia City was born. Scarcely one year later, when the Montana Territory was created by President Abraham Lincoln, nearly 30,000 people were living along the gulch's eight miles. In close competition with Bannack for bragging rights and residents from the start, Virginia City quickly prevailed and reigned as state capital until 1875.

Today the former capital city's biggest distinction is its designation as the county seat. The population dropped off significantly as the mines petered out, but tourism stepped in to provide income for residents, and credit is due Charles Bovey for preserving the town for posterity.

In 1946, along with his wife Sue, Bovey began the painstaking task of preserving and restoring many of the structures you see in Virginia City today. Most of the town's buildings were built during its heyday as the state's second territorial capital, though a seasonal taco wagon is an interesting anachronism. Stroll along the sidewalk or gaze off at the nearby mountains and you'll soon see how easy it is to imagine you are in another time. Rusty, weathered, peeling, crumbling . . . time and nature have been less than kind, yet a sense of magic is undeniably present, especially when you realize that you're looking at some of the oldest buildings in the state.

One main thoroughfare runs through Virginia City, MT 287; historical buildings can be found along both sides of it. One of the oldest, the Montana Post Building, once housed the state's first newspaper. The paper's original press is still used locally for menus, playbills, and placards.

If you're looking for comfortable, authentic Western lodgings, check into the **Fairweather Inn** at 315 W. Wallace (☎ 406/843-5377 or 800/648-7588). Named for one of the founders of Virginia City, the Fairweather is a small hotel located right in the middle of downtown Virginia City with a great upstairs porch, a fun place to sit and people-watch. Though most of the rooms are tastefully decorated in an Old West theme, a few of them are distinguished by odd combinations of bright paint and mismatched quilts. Only five of the hotel's 15 rooms have private baths; the rest are rooming house–style.

If bed-and-breakfasts are more to your liking, try either of these two bed-and-breakfast inns just above Main Street in Virginia City: **the Stonehouse Inn,** 306 E. Idaho, Virginia City, MT 59755 (☎ 406/843-5504), listed on the National Register of Historic Places; or the **Virginia City Country Inn Bed & Breakfast,** 115 E. Idaho, Virginia City, MT 59755 (☎ 406/843-5515 or 800/538-2012), a charming Victorian home.

There aren't many dining choices in Virginia City and there are even fewer down the road. Most of the places where you can find something to eat are only open during summer, from Memorial Day to Labor Day, so be sure to call ahead if you're planning to eat in either of the towns during the off-season. The best bet in Virginia City is the **Wells Fargo,** a former mercantile now serving three squares daily from 8am to 8pm. Soup, salads, and burgers are typical lunch choices. The dinner menu is more elaborate but still falls short of a fine dining experience, although it remains the most elegant place to eat before taking in a show at either the Opera House or the Brewery.

If you *really* want to see the Old West come to life, check out a Brewery Follies or Virginia City Players production. Famous statewide for their cabaret-style revues and entertaining period melodramas, both companies entertain most nights during the summer. Originally intended to entertain the overflow crowds from the Opera House, the Brewery Follies now have a loyal following of their own, with hand-set flyers proclaiming this "A Remarkable Revue in a Cabaret Atmosphere!" The two-hour show is an entertaining song-and-dance revue, peppered with PG-13 humor. The Virginia City Players, the oldest summer stock company in Montana, specializes in presenting authentic 19th-century melodrama and vaudeville in Virginia City's Opera House building. Tickets for the Virginia City Players are $10 for adults,

$5 for children under 12; all Brewery Follies tickets are $8. For information on show times and days for either **the Brewery Follies** or the **Virginia City Players,** call 406/843-5377.

Don't be surprised if you run into someone from either theater company at the Bale of Hay Saloon or the Pioneer Bar. Both are standard late-night spots for high-spirited conversation, homemade pizza, or a quick game of pool.

NEVADA CITY

Easily the state's most interesting and most often photographed open-air museum, Nevada City also exists as the result of Charles Bovey's diligence and dedication to the preservation of history. Though Nevada City was once a thriving mining camp, most of the buildings in town today were originally located elsewhere in the state. In the mid-1950s, like a kindergartner with a set of blocks and with an equal amount of unbridled enthusiasm, Bovey began to re-create an authentic Western town with buildings he'd accumulated around the West, some even from Yellowstone National Park. The result is a reincarnated ghost town that has come to life via Hollywood—parts of *Missouri Breaks, Little Big Man,* and *Return to Lonesome Dove* were filmed here—and one that continues to inspire an appreciation for the region's past.

Though it sounds overly simple, the main attractions in the town of Nevada City are the buildings themselves. You can't see them very well from the highway, but the structures Bovey brought to the town in his efforts to re-create it are arranged as they might have been during the late 1800s. Start behind the Nevada City Hotel, where you can view the state's only double-decker outhouse, and stroll along the streets to see what a Western mining town might have looked like. Boardwalks pass barber shops, homes, a schoolhouse, and even an Asian section. Some of the nearly 100 buildings are closed, but many include period furnishings and wares.

If you happen to hear a cacophony of horns and whistles, follow the noise to the Nevada City Music Hall, located next door to the hotel. There you can see the "famous and obnoxious horn machine from the Bale of Hay Saloon!" A sign on the machine begs visitors not to miss hearing "the machine that has driven 28 changemakers, 72 bartenders, and near a million tourists to the brink of insanity!" Though you'll certainly wonder how anyone could work here all day, the music hall is a fascinating place to spend an hour listening to the many music machines and reading about their history; it's one of the largest collections of its kind on display in the United States today. With player pianos, musical organs, and authentic nickelodeons (they really work, and yes, they really only cost a nickel!), the music hall will entertain visitors of all ages. Notice the huge bronze chandelier near the obnoxious horn machine. Built in 1899, it originally hung in the state capitol; Bovey saved it from being scrapped when the Senate made the switch to fluorescent lighting.

The Alder Gulch Short Line, a gas-powered, narrow-gauge railroad with open-air cars, runs between Virginia City and Nevada City daily from 10am to 5:30pm. The Steam Railroad Museum is actually just a fancy name for its two main attractions: an observation car once used by President Calvin Coolidge, and the last remaining Catholic chapel car in the world.

Though it's certainly not the Hilton, the **Nevada City Hotel and Cabins** (☎ 406/843-5377 or 800/648-7588) exudes a faded frontier grandeur and is run by the friendliest staff in the West. Rooms are simply decorated and are located along narrow hallways upstairs and down in the two-story building. Two Victorian suites, complete with polished burlwood furniture and private baths, are located upstairs and, though they didn't suit Marlon Brando (who, according to the locals, was looking for something closer to a Hilton), they're the nicest the town has to offer. Seventeen renovated miner cabins are located behind the hotel, each with a private bathroom and one or two double beds. One of the cabins, used to depict a Chinese laundry in *Return to Lonesome Dove*, is a charming place to stay if you can tune out the music machines. Just be sure to lock your door: Tourists have no idea that the cabin is actually rented and may try to come inside.

You can believe the Star Bakery's claim to have the best biscuits and gravy in town, though jokers may grin and point out that it's also the *only* restaurant in town. Best known for its breakfasts, the small restaurant begins serving home-style food at 7am in the morning and closes after lunch at 2pm in the afternoon. Though small, the restaurant fairly oozes cozy country charm, and kids will love the old-fashioned soda fountain.

BANNACK

Montana's first territorial capital, Bannack was the site of the state's first big gold strike in 1862. With more than 60 of the town's original buildings preserved for visitors, the tumbledown town is a stark reminder of the heyday of the frontier: vigilantes stalking road agents stalking prospectors, in a favored place where the rivers yielded gold dust.

Born out of the discovery of placer gold in 1862, Bannack quickly grew to a town of 3,000 people, largely comprised of those hoping to strike it rich. Blacksmiths, bakeries, stables, restaurants, hotels, dance halls, and grocery stores rapidly sprang up to complement an expanding mining industry. However, focused as they were around the discovery of gold, many Bannack residents soon left the small Montana town for later and more lucrative discoveries in nearby Alder Gulch (see Virginia City earlier in this section). This touched off a battle between notorious highwaymen and vigilantes, with many an outlaw hanged by his peers for theft and murder.

Visitors can relive this drama during the annual celebration of Bannack Days, staged during the third weekend in July. The two-day event celebrates the history and heritage of Montana's early pioneers with activities centering around frontier crafts, music, hearty pioneer food, and dramas. A black powder muzzle loader shoot, Sunday church services, and horse-and-buggy rides bring the "toughest town in the West" to life and is fun for the entire family.

Designated a state park in 1954, Bannack is open year-round during daylight hours. Although there are no developed facilities in Bannack, there are camping and picnic grounds, as well as a group use area and hiking trails. Other lodging facilities are available in nearby Dillon (see Section 4 of this chapter). Day-use fees are $3 per vehicle, 50¢ per person, and $8 for a campsite ($7 in the off-season).

Bannack is located four miles south of MT 278, 25 miles west of Dillon. To get there, turn west off U.S. Hwy. 15 3 miles south of Dillon. Head west 20 miles on MT 278, then south 4 miles on a gravel road, suitable for all vehicles. For additional information, call 406/834-3413.

The Hi-Line & Northcentral Missouri River Country

8

If you think Montana's landscape is composed solely of crystal-clear mountain streams flowing through towering mountain ranges, think again. While much of the state does fit this description, it by no means covers all that can be found here—especially along the Hi-Line. Though not devoid of a varying topography, northcentral Montana is largely an expansive flat land, characterized by strip farms and a surprising number of badlands. This truly is big sky country, a place endowed with a landscape that seems to sweep outward to the very reaches of the horizon. Few visitors venture off Montana State Highway 2, which traverses the northern part of the state from west to east; and it's a shame: A side trip into the heart of this largely undeveloped region is well worth the time it takes to stray from the beaten path.

Rich in paleontological history (the first T-Rex fossil was discovered here at the turn of the century), this is an area where you can visit small museums with *real* dinosaur bones, hear the best cowboy poets from miles around read from their work, and see the oldest rodeo in the state.

If you're an outdoor sports enthusiast, you'll find plenty to keep you occupied. While less scenic than other parts of the state, largely flat MT 2 is a popular route for cyclists who want to tour Montana. The road provides an ideal east-west alternate to U.S. Hwy. 90, where biking is prohibited. (Just avoid the mosquitoes in summer around Saco, a sleepy town which somehow breeds the largest population of mosquitoes per square inch in the world.)

Fishing waters are abundant as the Missouri and its tributaries meander clear across the region. Walleye, catfish, sauger, and northern pike can be found along the Milk River, and Lewistown's Big Spring Creek is an ideal place to catch native trout. Fort Peck Lake, though man-made, is Montana's largest body of water; it boasts a coastline longer than that of California and teems with trophy walleyes. The site of the annual Governor's Cup tournament, it is also a popular spot for water sports and boating. And the Rocky

Impressions

From the reflection of the sun on the spray or the mist which arises from these falls there is a beautiful rainbow produced which adds not a little to the beauty of this majestically grand scenery.

—Meriwether Lewis, from his journal

Mountain Front offers some of the best fishing in the state with plenty of lakes, rivers, and streams within driving and hiking distance, should you decide to hike out on your own. Think about Pishkun Lake, Eureka Lake, and Freezout Lake, some local haunts, if the idea appeals.

It's not hard to imagine what northcentral Montana looked like a century ago, when cowboys roamed the prairies on horseback. It's a place that remains ideal for this leisurely mode of transportation. The Bob Marshall Wilderness and Scapegoat Wilderness Areas, both accessible from this part of the state, are two of Montana's most vast and pristine places, and a pack trip is a popular and genuine way to experience them.

While hard-core skiers usually flock to Montana's higher elevations in the northwest and southcentral parts of the state, northcentral Montana's ski areas possess their own somewhat rustic appeal. The most remote, Bear Paw Ski Bowl, is located near Havre on the Rocky Boys Indian Reservation. The most popular, Showdown Ski Area, is northcentral Montana's largest and is easily accessible from Great Falls. Rocky Mountain Hi, near Choteau, is much more removed but a treat if you're willing to make the drive.

The 50-mile section of the Missouri River east of Fort Benton, designated Wild and Scenic by the Bureau of Land Management, remains much as it did during the town's heyday as a port city during the rowdy 1800s. Raft or canoe along this historic waterway to catch glimpses of wildlife against an ever-present backdrop of spectacular mountain scenery.

Birdwatchers and those who just want to get away from it all may enjoy visiting the C.M. Russell National Wildlife Refuge, where hawks and other feathered creatures occasionally break the quiet.

The badlands beckon.

1 Scenic Drives

DRIVING TOUR #1: KINGS HILL SCENIC BYWAY

This scenic drive begins at the junction of Montana State Highways 87 and 89, about 22 miles southeast of Great Falls on MT 87. Winding through the Lewis and Clark National Forest and the Little Belt Mountains, the Kings Hill Scenic Byway is a 71-mile, 1¹/₂-hour route with highlights that include opportunities for fishing, wildlife viewing, skiing, hiking, mountain biking, and boating—nearly any summer or winter activity. Allow yourself plenty of extra time to enjoy the myriad sights along the way. In summer, it's definitely worth your time to pull out the binoculars for a chance encounter with the local wildlife or your fly rod for a quick cast for mountain whitefish. Winter brings its own appeal, with opportunities for downhill skiing at Showdown Ski Area, cross-country skiing at the Silver Crest trail system (just north of Showdown), and snowmobiling at Kings Hill, a network of some 200 miles of marked trails northeast of the ski area.

Northcentral Montana

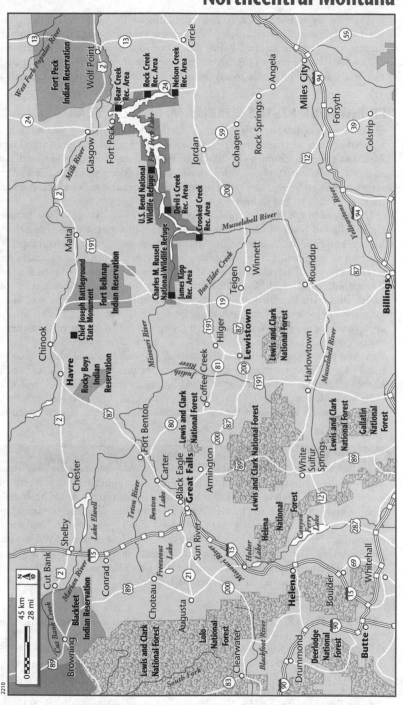

There are ghost towns at Castle Town and Hughesville, and historic mining sites at Glory Hole and Hughesville Star. Take a soak at the hot springs in White Sulphur Springs, the terminus for the 71-mile scenic highway, or explore the backcountry at any one of a number of campgrounds located in the area. For a free detailed map of the Kings Hill Scenic Byway from Travel Montana, call Russell Country at 800/527-5348.

DRIVING TOUR #2: THE CHARLES M. RUSSELL TRAIL

If you're a fan of cowboy artist Charlie Russell, this is the driving tour for you. A wonderfully thorough interpretive guide to the trail, available for free from **Travel Montana's Russell Country** (☎ 800/527-5348), uses reproductions of Russell's art to illustrate the history of the Judith Basin, much of which was the subject of the artist's paintings. Request this guide before you begin your tour for a greater understanding of the area and its history.

Designated by the Montana legislature, the Charlie Russell Trail (MT 87, between Great Falls and Lewistown) provides you with a window to the past. Although the buffalo, mountain men, and miners may have disappeared from the landscape, it's not hard to imagine the artist's experience as you view the places he painted. From Great Falls, you'll travel east along MT 87 through the small communities of Raynesford, Geyser, and Moccasin, learning along the way about Blackfeet in the Judith Basin, the legendary wolves of the Basin in Stanford, and the role of the railroads in Hobson—all through the paintings of Charlie Russell. This drive is appropriate for any time of year, although spring and fall colors are vivid palettes of nature's own artistry.

As you drive along the commemorative trail, you will find roadside turnouts for many of the 25 interpretive sites, including the settings for two of Russell's best-known paintings, "Buffalo in Winter" and "Paying the Fiddler." Yogo Creek Road (#266) and Memorial Way (#487) are two smaller, single-lane gravel roads, also with turnouts, that are included in the tour, even though they're not recommended for RVs.

2 Great Falls

Much of the landscape Charlie Russell painted throughout his life still remains around the prairie lands of Great Falls. What has replaced the rest would likely make Charlie crawl back into the bottle: Minutemen missile silos mar the landscape in fenced-in areas sometimes very near the roadside (don't approach them) and starkly contrasting strip farms now stretch to where the untouched lands once did, as far as the eye can see. Though the city's "great falls" are less impressive than one might expect and its statewide reputation is barely a notch above Butte's, the town has much to recommend itself to the off-the-beaten-path traveler.

ESSENTIALS

GETTING THERE Great Falls is the hub for travel to this portion of Montana with the **Great Falls International Airport** providing daily service on **Delta** (☎ 800/221-1212), **Northwest** (☎ 800/225-2525), **Horizon** (☎ 800/547-9308) and **Frontier** (☎ 800/432-1359). Shelby, located 88 miles to the northwest along U.S. Hwy. 15, provides the closest Amtrak service (☎ 800/872-7245); you can rent a car there with **Ford-Mercury** (☎ 800/823-6737) to drive into town.

Great Falls is located on U.S. Hwy.15 and is easy to reach by car. From Missoula, two routes to Great Falls roughly parallel one another: MT 200, or U.S. Hwy. 90

to U.S. Hwy. 15, via MT 12. Great Falls is 89 miles northeast of Helena on U.S. Hwy. 15, and 153 miles northeast of Butte. From Billings, take either MT 87 all the way or take U.S. Hwy. 90 west to Livingston, then MT 89 and the Kings Hill Scenic Byway (see driving tour earlier in this chapter) northwest to Great Falls. From Bozeman, take MT 287 at Three Forks to Helena, then U.S. Hwy. 15 to Great Falls.

VISITOR INFORMATION   A travel planner for the Great Falls area can be obtained by writing to **Russell Country, Inc.** at P.O. Box 3166, Great Falls, MT 59403, or by calling 800/527-5348 or 406/761-5036. The **Great Falls Chamber of Commerce** is located at 815 2 Ave. S (☎ 406/761-4434). For the Great Falls road report, call 406/453-1605. For statewide weather conditions, call 800/332-6171.

GETTING AROUND   You can rent a car in Great Falls; **Allstar/Practical** (☎ 800/722-6704) has an office downtown. At Great Falls International Airport, **Avis** (☎ 800/831-2847), **Budget** (☎ 800/527-0700), and **Hertz** (☎ 800/654-3131) all operate counters.

While a car provides the best means of getting around Great Falls, the **Great Falls Transit System**'s (☎ 406/727-0382) eight lines are thorough enough to get you around the city from early morning to early evening during the week. (They do not operate on Sundays or major holidays.)

GETTING OUTSIDE
SPORTS & OUTDOOR ACTIVITIES
Biking
The River's Edge Trail, a mostly paved trail system that runs parallel to the Missouri River, was specifically designed for biking, walking, in-line skating, and cross-country skiing. Plans eventually call for nearly 30 miles of connecting trails, linking both sides of the river through an extensive bike/pedestrian network. The trail starts in town at Odd-fellows Park, below the Warden Bridge and follows the Missouri River for 5.5 miles to Giant Springs. There are picnic areas where you can take a rest along the river. The Great Falls Chamber of Commerce can provide you with a map that includes information about various historic sites along the way.

Fishing
The Great Falls of the Missouri is the unofficial dividing line for cold- and warm-water species of fish. You can fish for trout at Giant Springs or hire a guide and tour the Missouri or Smith Rivers.

A Fishing Guide/Outfitter
Montana River Outfitters
1401 B 5th Ave. S. ☎ **406/761-1677.** Half-day float trip with lunch and transportation from Wolf Creek for two persons: $215; full-day, $290. Transportation to and from the Great Falls airport is available at no additional cost. Reservations required well in advance. Forty-five miles south of Great Falls, a half-mile from the Wolf Creek exit off U.S. Hwy. 15.

Whether your ideal fly-fishing trip is a half-day excursion or a 7-day expedition, the knowledgeable guides at Montana River Outfitters can make it happen. Located south of Great Falls near Wolf Creek, Montana River's complex is equipped with cabins, a fly shop, and boat and canoe rentals. Under the capable direction of their guides, you can make your way with confidence through weed-laced water in search of fish ranging from brown trout to pale morning dun. A full-day guided float trip for two people including a drift boat, a hearty lunch, and transportation from Wolf Creek is $290. A weeklong guided trip that accommodates four to eight people and includes gourmet meals, equipment, and camps set up along the river is $1,895 per person.

Also offered is a combination pack/fishing trip that begins by horse packing into the Bob Marshall Wilderness. At the South Fork of the Flathead River, your group floats out on a 5- to 7-day trip—you won't see or use vehicles, not even mountain bikes. The cost: $2,095 per person. A half-day scenic float trip on the Missouri is $33; with lunch, $39. Dinner scenic floats are $49.

Golf

There are two public, 18-hole golf courses in the city: Anaconda Hills, on Smelter Hill northeast of Great Falls (☎ 406/761-8459), and the Robert O. Speck Golf Course at 29 and River Drive, (☎ 406/761-1078).

Skiing

Showdown Ski Area

P.O. Box 92, Neihart, MT 59465. ☎ **406/236-5522** or 800/433-0022; 24-hour snowphone, ☎ 406/771-1300. Lift tickets adult, $23; children 12 and under and seniors, $13. From Great Falls, take MT 89 south to Neihart. Showdown is just south of Kings Hill Pass in the Little Belt Mountains.

Showdown Ski Area, Montana's oldest ski resort, is located in the Lewis and Clark National Forest, 60 miles southeast of Great Falls. It has 34 runs: 30% for beginners, 40% for intermediates, and 30% for experts. Base elevation is 6,800 feet; total elevation is 8,200 feet. The average annual snowfall is 240 inches, and the season lasts from late November to early April. PSIA-certified instructors provide lessons at unbelievable rates: a one-hour private lesson is only $25. Their SKIwee program caters to the three- to six-year-old set and includes rental equipment and a lift ticket, if necessary. The Top Rock Cafe and the Hole-in-the-Wall Saloon are après-ski gathering places.

Snowmobiling

Over 200 miles of groomed snowmobile trails are available through **Montana Snowmobile Adventures** (☎ 406/236-5358) at Showdown Ski Area.

WILDLIFE REFUGES & STATE PARKS

Benton Lake National Wildlife Refuge and Wetland Management District

One mile north of Great Falls on MT 87, take a left onto Bootlegger Trail. Follow the signs to the refuge entrance. ☎ **406/727-7400**.

One of over 450 refuges established to protect, enhance, and restore our nation's wildlife heritage, Benton Lake spans an area of nearly 20 square miles just 12 miles north of Great Falls. Native short-grass prairie dominates the shallow marsh where literally thousands of migrating birds travel each year: Of the nearly 200 species that use the marsh, one-third nest here. A great spot for birdwatching, you're also likely to see rabbits, badgers, ground squirrels, deer, or antelope. Visitors are welcome year-round, though access may be limited in winter. The Benton Lake Wetland Management District also manages over 20 Waterfowl Production Areas that visitors are encouraged to use: Hiking, wildlife observation, and photography are all popular activities; hunting, fishing, and trapping are allowed on some in accordance with state regulations. For a list of these sites, write to the District Manager at P.O. Box 450, Black Eagle, MT 59414.

Giant Springs Heritage State Park

3 miles east of MT 87 on River Drive. The park will be on the left. ☎ **406/454-3441**.

Anyone who wants to follow in the footsteps of Lewis and Clark should make this multi-use facility one of their first stops. Discovered by Lewis in 1805, Giant Springs is the largest freshwater springs in the world, flowing at a measured rate of 134,000

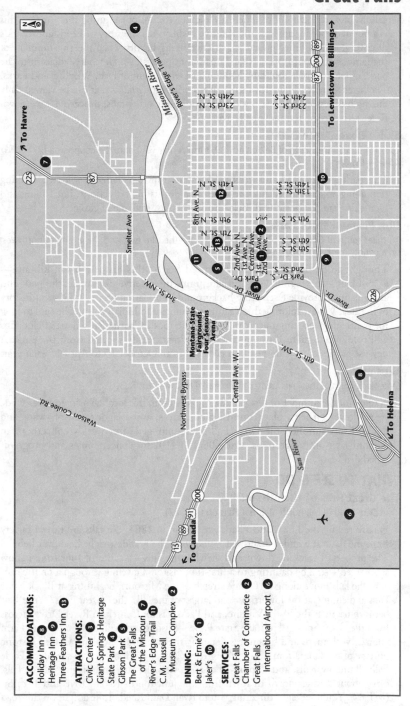

Great Falls

ACCOMMODATIONS:
Holiday Inn **8**
Heritage Inn **9**
Three Feathers Inn **13**

ATTRACTIONS:
Civic Center **3**
Giant Springs Heritage
State Park **4**
Gibson Park **5**
The Great Falls
of the Missouri **7**
River's Edge Trail **11**
C.M. Russell
Museum Complex **12**

DINING:
Bert & Ernie's **1**
Jaker's **10**

SERVICES:
Great Falls
Chamber of Commerce **2**
Great Falls
International Airport **6**

gallons of water per minute. There are picnic grounds open during the summer; this is a popular spot for anglers. Interpretive displays tell the story of Lewis and Clark's discovery, and in June you can experience living history when the encampment of the famous explorers is reenacted. The Giant Springs Fish Hatchery, adjacent to the park, is operated year-round by Montana's Department of Fish, Wildlife, and Parks. The hatchery raises different varieties of trout in rearing tanks that can be viewed daily during business hours. If you want to explore the other falls, proceed 1 mile down River Drive to the Rainbow Falls overlook.

Sluice Boxes State Park
Look for sign 5 miles south of Belt on MT 89, turn ¹/₄ mile west onto the county road. ☎ 406/454-3441.

This park is a beautiful and welcomed respite from the plains. A wilderness hiking trail along an abandoned railroad line is one of its big attractions, but fishing and picnicking are also permitted. Belt Creek is the fishing hole of choice.

Ulm Pishkun State Park
10 miles south of Great Falls on U.S. Hwy. 15, take the Ulm exit, and drive 6 miles northwest on a county road. ☎ 406/454-3441.

Thought to be the largest in the United States, this historic bison kill site—a "pishkun"—has a mile-long buffalo jump. Interpretive displays at the park and along its trails provide fascinating background information on the 1,000-year history of the area. While exploring this historic monument to Indian culture, be sure to look for prairie dogs peeking out from behind the rocks. Charlie Russell art aficionados will recognize Square Butte, a distant landmark easily spotted from the park. A day-use facility only, Ulm Pishkun is closed from October 15 to April 15 each year.

Gibson Park
One block north of the Civic Center along Park Drive in Great Falls.

Named for the founder of Great Falls, Paris Gibson, this local favorite features shade trees, flower gardens, playgrounds, picnic areas, and a lagoon full of swans and ducks. Every summer, the Great Fall Symphony gives free weekly concerts in an amphitheater on the grounds. Call 406/453-4102 for concert times and programs scheduled.

WHAT TO SEE & DO
The Great Falls of the Missouri
Ryan Dam Road (4 mi. north of Great Falls on Hwy. 87).

Discovered by the Lewis and Clark expedition in 1805, the falls are now a far cry from the natural wonder described by Lewis as the grandest sight he'd ever beheld. The process of tracking down and viewing the falls—a series of four (one is now submerged)—can be daunting to a first-time visitor. Traveling through a prairie canyon, the falls move along a 10-mile stretch of the Missouri, beginning at Black Eagle Falls and ending at the lowermost and largest of the falls, the "Great Falls." Your best bet is to begin at the Fish, Wildlife, and Parks Visitor Center on River Drive (across from the Giant Springs Heritage State Park; see listing earlier in this chapter) and arm yourself with maps and brochures detailing the area and Lewis and Clark's historic portage of the falls. From points along River Drive, you'll be able to see Black Eagle Falls, Rainbow Falls, and Crooked Falls. To view the last, and biggest, of the falls, drive about 4 miles north of town from the junction of River Drive and 15th St. (MT 87). You'll see signs directing you to Ryan Dam Road. Take a right on this road and drive 8 miles to the falls.

Though a short walk across a bridge affords the best view, visitors may be disappointed if expecting anything close to the tremendous cascades described by the early explorers. Since the late 1800s, a series of dams have been built along the Missouri, including Morony Dam, just above the Great Falls, and Cochrane Dam, between the Great Falls and Crooked Falls. With the building of each, the falls have decreased in volume. Even though a dam was constructed at the top of Rainbow Falls in 1910, Rainbow and Crooked Falls appear today almost as they did to Lewis and Clark.

C.M. Russell Museum Complex

13th St. and 4th Ave. N. ☎ **406/727-8787**. Admission $4 adults, $3 seniors, $2 students, 5 and under free. Discounts for approved tours. Summer (May 1–Sept 30), Mon–Sat 9am–6pm, Sun 1–5pm; winter, closed Mon; open Tues–Sat 10am–5pm, Sun 1–5pm. The Russell home is closed during the winter season. Group tours by appointment.

This museum complex, dedicated to the art and life of Charles Marion Russell, consists of a museum, the artist's Great Falls home, and his rustic log studio, all of which may be toured for the price of admission to the complex when they are open. (The Russell home is closed during winter.)

Over the course of his lifetime, Charlie Russell completed over 4,000 works of art that depict frontier life on Montana's western plains. In over 46,000 square feet of space, the museum houses the most complete collection of original Russell paintings and memorabilia in the world. The museum's seven galleries also showcase work from a number of other esteemed Western artists, including O.C. Seltzer, Earle E. Heikka, and Joseph Henry Sharp. Paintings of Native Americans dressed in ceremonial clothing by Winold Reiss are particularly riveting for their clarity and bold use of bright colors. The museum's Browning Firearms Collection pays tribute to the world's most famous gun inventor, John M. Browning. Reproductions of Russell works and those of his contemporaries can be bought in the museum gift shop.

Charlie and Nancy Russell's Great Falls home, located next door to his studio, is a National Historic Site, and is remarkable for its unusual construction. A simple log cabin, it was built from telephone poles in 1903, and remains exactly as it did during the artist's life: filled with cowboy gear and Indian artifacts, the props Russell used to ensure his paintings' authenticity.

C.M. Russell Auction of Original Western Art

This annual auction, held at the Heritage Inn each March, has raised over $7 million since its inception, and continues to be one of the biggest events in the Western arts world. With nearly 200 participants each year, it attracts artists and arts enthusiasts from around the world. For additional information, contact the Great Falls Advertising Federation at P.O. Box 634, Great Falls, 59403 (☎ 406/761-6453).

Historic Northside Residential Walking Tour

This walking tour, described in a guide available from the Great Falls Chamber of Commerce, takes you by the historic homes on the north side of the city. Trees planted through the efforts of the city's founder, Paris Gibson, at the turn of the century distinguish this area, a district listed on the National Register of Historic Places. Typical architectural styles of the homes included on the tour are: Second Empire, Prairie, Queen Anne, and Bungalow. Most were built between 1885 and 1945.

Paris Gibson Square

1400 1st Ave. N. ☎ **406/727-8255**. Free admission. Tues–Fri 10am–5pm, Sat–Sun 12–5pm, Tues evenings 7–9pm. Open Mondays 10am–5pm Memorial Day to Labor Day.

Listed on the National Register of Historic Places, Paris Gibson Square is an arts center that hosts contemporary and historical displays. As a community cultural center, it is home to the Cascade County Historical Society and Museum and the local genealogy society, and is available for classes and meetings. Its Conservatory Tea Room serves gourmet lunches Tuesdays through Fridays by reservation but drop-ins are frequently accommodated. Call 406/727-8255 for the day's menu and reservations.

WHERE TO STAY
HOTELS

✪ Heritage Inn

1700 Fox Farm Road, Great Falls, MT 59404. ☎ **406/761-1900** or 800/548-0361. Fax 406/761-0136. 240 rms with executive and bridal suites. A/C TV TEL. $75–$80 single, $85 double, $75–$125 suites. AE, DISC, MC, V.

Decorated New Orleans style, the Heritage is Great Falls' largest hotel and host to the city's annual Charlie Russell Art Auction. With wrought-iron lampposts, brick walkways, and a brightly decorated lounge/casino (complete with a piano-playing alligator you've got to see to believe), the prevailing theme is pure Mardi Gras.

Although the decor of the rooms doesn't contribute much to this festive air, many of them border or overlook the central pool area. You'll want to avoid these rooms if you're looking for peace and quiet, especially since the Heritage is the area's premier convention center. The good news is that, even though they are unremarkable, the rooms are comfortable and it *is* possible to locate yourself away from the daily hustle and bustle at the heart of this property.

The hotel provides valet and guest laundry service, and has a gift shop that sells sundries and espresso. The Mardi Gras Cafe specializes in spicy Cajun dishes and prime rib with a limited bar menu available in the lounge during the day. Not far from downtown Great Falls, the Heritage is considered by most of the city's residents to be the nicest place to stay in town.

Holiday Inn

400 10 Ave. S, Great Falls, MT 59401. ☎ **406/727-7200** or 800/626-8009 (within Montana only) or 800/257-1998. 174 rms with executive and bridal suites. A/C TV TEL. $70 double, $125 suites. AE, CB, DC, DISC, MC, V.

Formerly a Sheraton property, this Holiday Inn wisely chose to retain its upscale accommodations, yet keep its room rates relatively low, so it can promote itself as an affordable hotel. Philly's Restaurant, Lounge, and Casino may seem to contradict the hotel's so-called "family" reputation, but the food is tasty and the gambling well out of earshot while you're dining. Convenient to the Great Falls International Airport and U.S. Hwy. 15, the Holiday Inn is ideal for a single traveler or family looking for a pool, room service, and comfortable beds.

A BED-AND-BREAKFAST

Three Feathers Inn

626 5th Avenue N, Great Falls, MT 59401. ☎ **406/453-5257**. 5 rms, 3 with shared bath. $50–$75. All rates include a full breakfast. AE, MC, V.

This elegant bed-and-breakfast inn is located in the heart of Great Falls' historic district. Owned and operated by Mike and Helen Pluhar, it abounds in distinctive touches that reflect the owners' love of all things British. The plush "Balmoral" suite, located at the top of the three-story house, charmingly incorporates a Scottish theme throughout and the in-room bath (no door) showcases an enormous tin bathtub that has been meticulously restored. The Pluhars' attention to detail and their guests' comfort is underscored through such thoughtful gestures as granting guests full use of their garden (with a fountain and goldfish pond), library, and sunroom. A special area has also been set aside for smokers. Pets are okay by arrangement but, please, no children under 10. Nautical enthusiasts should be sure to check out the antique diving helmets and ship's telegraph in the library.

WHERE TO EAT

Great Falls is not the place to visit if a fine dining experience is what you crave. Almost all of the city's steak houses are good choices, although there is surprisingly little difference among them: all feature standard cuts of Montana beef, served amid the whirling beeps and bells of video gambling machines.

Bert and Ernie's

300 1 Ave. S. ☎ **406/453-0601.** Lunch $3–$5; main dinner courses $8–$13. AE, DISC, MC, V. Mon–Sat 11am–10pm. STEAKS/SEAFOOD/BURGERS.

Don't let the name of this restaurant fool you. Though Sesame Street fans of all ages are just as welcome as anyone else, it's not exactly a "Discovery Zone"–type of establishment. This downtown eatery prides itself on an extensive collection of microbrewed beers, both domestic and imported, and has a fantastic burger menu. The ambience is friendly and casual, as is the wait staff, and the extra-large booths encourage you to sit back and stay a while. With an all-American menu that includes pasta dishes, salads, and steaks, as well as a good downtown location, you're likely to see all types of people here.

Jaker's

1500 10 Ave. S. ☎ **406/727-1033.** Lunch $3–9; main dinner courses $10–18. Mon–Fri 11:30am–2pm, Mon–Thur 5–10pm, Fri–Sat 5–11pm, Sun 4–9pm. AE, DISC, MC, V. STEAKS/ RIBS/FISH.

If you ask a local where to eat, this restaurant will almost surely be recommended. In decor and menu selection, Jaker's is comparable to nearly any bar and grill chain restaurant (Chili's patrons will recognize the "Awesome Blossom" on the appetizer menu), and the crowd reflects the wide variety of food served. The lunch menu is affordable and includes standard burgers as well as lighter sandwiches and salads. You can't go wrong with the C.A.T., a tasty chicken, avocado, tomato, and sprouts combo that comes with soup or salad, but don't believe anyone who tells you that the ostrich burger—a frequent daily special—tastes just like beef; liver would be more accurate. Beef or chicken "A La Jaker's"—a palatable mix of crab, asparagus spears, and béarnaise sauce—are house dinner specialties. The ever-present keno machines are discreetly located near the front of the restaurant where you can play a quick game of video poker undetected on your way to or from the bathroom.

THE PERFORMING ARTS

Great Falls Symphony

Great Falls Civic Center, #2 Park Drive. ☎ **406/453-4102.** Phone for schedule and ticket pricing information.

For nearly four decades, the Great Falls Symphony has been performing for central Montanans through a variety of special events, orchestral concerts, and choral concerts. Their season runs from October to May, with two free concerts for students and seniors as well as a pops concert and weekly outdoor concerts in Gibson Park during the summer. The symphony sponsors the Cascade String Quartet and the Chinook Winds Quartet, both of which perform chamber concerts throughout the state under the direction of Gordon Johnson.

3 The Rocky Mountain Eastern Front

You won't find a more beautiful area of Montana to explore—especially if you are driving through the state—or one with as rich a paleontological history as the Eastern Front of the Rockies. Dinosaur eggs were first discovered here and it continues to be a living classroom for scientists and amateurs alike. The eastern gateway to the Bob Marshall and Scapegoat Wilderness Areas, the Front is also popular with hikers. Elk, pronghorn antelope, deer, and wild birds continue to prevail in copious numbers, despite efforts by environmentalists to turn this region into a protected open range.

Named for the president of the American Fur Co. who brought the first steamboat up the Missouri, Choteau is one of the oldest towns in this part of the state. Although its downtown streets have a distinct abandoned, cast-off look, the town is transformed during summer, when hundreds of visitors make their careful way across the Front in search of precious prehistoric fossils.

While Choteau's nod to the tourist industry is evidenced by the town's handful of gift shops (with tenuous ties to the dinosaur theme at best), Augusta—the only other pocket of civilization along the Front—has stubbornly refused to court the tourist; this is at the core of its irresistible appeal. You can drive completely through this tiny town in well under a minute, but if you do, you'll miss as good an opportunity as you'll ever find to experience a genuine slice of the Old West at its offbeat best.

ESSENTIALS

GETTING THERE   The **Great Falls International Airport** services the Rocky Mountain Eastern Front, Augusta, and Choteau with daily flights on **Delta** (☎ 800/221-1212), **Northwest** (☎ 800/225-2525), **Horizon** (☎ 800/547-9308), and **Frontier** (☎ 800/432-1359). The nearest **Amtrak** (☎ 800/872-7245) station is located in Shelby, 75 miles northeast; car rentals are available there through **Ford-Mercury** (☎ 800/823-6737).

To reach this area from towns in the northeast part of the state, drive along the southern border of Glacier National Park (MT 2) until you reach Browning. At Browning, head south on MT 89. Augusta's position (and that of the Front in general) along MT 287 is roughly parallel with that of Great Falls on U.S. Hwy. 15, which lies to the west about 40 miles. From points south and east of Great Falls, refer to the Great Falls "Essentials" section for appropriate driving directions to this area.

VISITOR INFORMATION   For an information packet, write to the regional tourism office for **Russell Country, Inc.** at P.O. Box 3166, Great Falls, MT 59403, or call 800/527-5348 or 406/761-5036. The chamber of commerce in Choteau does not have a permanent office, but requests for visitor information should be directed to the **Main Connection Travel Agency,** 35 1 Ave. NW, Choteau, MT 59422 (☎ 800/823-3866 or 406/466-5316). Although they do not have a chamber office, several Augusta businesses advertise with the Choteau Chamber of Commerce. The Montana Department of Fish, Wildlife, and Parks (Region 4) is a good source for fishing information. Write to them at 4600 Giant Springs Road, Great Falls, MT, 59406, or call 406/454-3441.

GETTING AROUND   You will need to rent a car in Great Falls to travel around this region; **Allstar/Practical** (☎ 800/722-6704) is downtown at 600 13th St. South. **Avis**

(☎ 800/331-1212), **Budget** (☎ 800/527-0700), and **Hertz** (☎ 800/654-3131), all located at the airport, are just a few of the many companies that provide car rentals.

A reliable four-wheel-drive vehicle is strongly recommended for touring the backroads of the Rocky Mountain Eastern Front: Many are unpaved, gravel roads that turn into a slippery mush locally known as "gumbo." Avis carries the Ford Explorer and Hertz carries the Explorer, the Nissan Pathfinder, and the Toyota 4-runner. Requests for four-wheel-drives should be made a week in advance.

GETTING OUTSIDE
SKIING
⑤ Rocky Mountain Hi

412 S. Main, Conrad, MT 59425. ☎ **406/278-5308** (disconnected during off-season). Lift tickets $17 adult, $13 student, free seniors, children 8 and under. Late November to mid-April, Fri–Sun 9:30am–4pm.

Located 30 minutes west of Choteau and just east of the Bob Marshall Wilderness, this ski run is a small operation with lift tickets topping out at a whopping $17. Though not a world-class run, it is an ideal place for beginners or those who just want to get away from it all. Uncrowded and friendly, Rocky Mountain Hi is not the see-and-be-seen scene you find at larger facilities; Carharts and jeans are the resort wear of choice. There is an average annual snowfall of 300 inches, top elevation is 7,400, feet and base elevation is 6,400. Snowboarders and telemarkers are welcome, so bring your own equipment along or rent it here. Ski instruction is available for everyone from beginner to advanced levels. Quench your thirst or grab a bite between runs at the area's cafeteria or lounge.

OUTFITTERS & ORGANIZED TRIPS
Outfitters
High Country Adventures

Box 5630, Helena, MT 59604-5630. ☎ **406/443-2842** or 701/258-9270.

This wilderness backpacking guide service was founded in 1973 and remains one of the most popular outfitters operating within the Rocky Mountain Front today. Led by an experienced staff of guides with an extensive knowledge of the area, the trips are unforgettable forays into Montana's most pristine lands. A high-country trek into the Bob Marshall Wilderness Area offers you the chance to spot wildlife, fish for native trout, and complete a 40-mile backpack loop through spectacular vistas that include the Chinese Wall, the Continental Divide, and the Sun River Canyon. The cost of a one-week trip is $595 per person if you bring your own gear; if you'd prefer to rent equipment, the total is $630. All food, community gear, travel to and from the trailhead, and a trip video is included in the price of the trip. This company prides itself on providing you with the ultimate in a rugged outdoor experience and, to hear past guests discuss their trip, it seems to be very successful.

K Bar L Ranch

Box 287, Beyond All Roads, Augusta, MT 59410. ☎ **406/562-3589** (winter and spring); 406/467-2771 (summer and fall). Rates range from $1,000–$1,200 per person per week. Reservations should be made at least six months in advance for summer trips.

Three generations of outfitters have run this operation. It is, perhaps, the most respected outfitter along the Front. Not something you can simply drive up to, the K Bar L is the model of inaccessibility. Taking the trek through Sun Canyon is only the beginning. If you drive far enough, you'll notice the K Bar L's lower base camp on your right just before you reach the Gibson Reservoir overlook. Here owners Bill and Nancy Click will haul you and your belongings to the reservoir, and put you in a boat. After you've crossed the Gibson Reservoir, it's off to the Bob Marshall Wilderness. (See also "Where to Stay" later in this chapter.)

Organized Trips

Timescale Adventures

P.O. Box 796, Bynum, MT 59419. ☎ **406/469-2314** or 800/238-6873. 3-hour day tour, $20 adult, $10 child; 2-day dig $125 per person. Reservations required as far in advance of trip as possible.

This company offers a variety of trips designed to explore the history and geology of central Montana. A one-day dinosaur/history tour includes visits to a dig site, the Old North Trail, a Meti Village site, prehistoric tepee rings, and the Old Blackfeet Indian Agency. An alternative sunset dinner tour also explores an archeological digging site with a buffalo jump but includes a Western-style dinner at a local ranch, with opportunities for wildlife and birdwatching. Overnight river trips from five to seven days along the Wild and Scenic Missouri are extremely popular.

Pine Butte Guest Ranch Summer Trips and Workshops

HC 58, Box 34 B, Choteau, MT 59422. ☎ **406/466-2591.** Course rates range from $825–$1,950 per person. Reservations required.

The Nature Conservancy conducts a series of summer trips and workshops in the Choteau area (see also "Where to Stay" in this chapter). Trips have included a five-day llama trek in the Great Burn Wilderness near Missoula, a four-day horsepack trip studying the spring wildflowers along the Rocky Mountain Eastern Front, and a 10-day backcountry trip into the Bob Marshall Wilderness.

SEEING THE SIGHTS

Egg Mountain

From Choteau, go 1 mile south on MT 287, then 13 miles west on Belview Road. ☎ **406/994-5257.** Free tours conducted daily at 2pm from approximately late July to late August.

This "mountain" actually resembles more of a molehill but is the site where Jack Horner of the Museum of the Rockies and Bob Makela discovered dinosaur eggs in the late 1970s. Today it is on a parcel of land owned by the Nature Conservancy next to their Pine Butte Swamp Preserve. Its connection to the Museum of the Rockies continues, however; the site is managed during the summer by museum officials. Visitors are asked to respect this valuable paleontological area by refraining from exploring the site unsupervised.

Sun Canyon

S. of Augusta, on Sun Canyon Road.

The actual canyon is hardly discernible from the roadside, but crossing the bridge below the diversion dam takes you to a lookout point that offers a view of the Gibson Reservoir to the west. To the east, you can see the valley that stretches away from the mountains and into the plains. This is a great scenic drive to take from Augusta, with excellent opportunities for viewing wildlife. Pick up Sun Canyon Road just south of Augusta. Drive west, following the Sun River into the mountains, along the winding gravel road for approximately 15 miles, and then look for the bridge.

AN ECLECTIC SHOP IN AUGUSTA

Latigo and Lace

Main St., Augusta. ☎ **406/562-3665**. Summer, daily 10am–7pm; spring and fall, daily 10am–6pm; winter, Wed–Sun 10am–5pm.

As its name implies, this shop features a mixed bag of gift items. Where else in the world can you purchase a bighorn sheep scrotum dice cup, enjoy a double hazelnut latte, and admire an original bronze by nationally renowned artist Buckeye Blake? Owners Laurie Gilleon and Sara Walsh have collected a remarkable assortment of Made in Montana items and also carry a wide selection of Western-theme books, many by Montana authors. In addition to the antiques for sale, there are unique greeting cards, jewelry, T-shirts, and children's items.

ESPECIALLY FOR KIDS

Pine Butte Guest Ranch offers a variety of two- to three-day summer workshops designed to entertain and educate children of all ages. Want to know what kinds of plants and animals live on the prairie? Learn the stories and music of the Metis culture? Find out how to identify local aquatic life or tie a fly? Workshops are limited to a group of 20 and last from 9:30am to 3pm daily. Participants are asked to bring a sack lunch, water, and day pack as well as good walking shoes and rain gear. To make reservations or find out more about these special programs, contact the Pine Butte Swamp Preserve at 406/466-5526.

WHERE TO STAY
A HOTEL

Ⓢ Bunkhouse Inn

121 Main St. Augusta, MT 59410. ☎ **406/562-3387**. 9 rms. $35 double. AE, MC, V.

This work-in-progress is a history unto itself. Moved by a team of horses from the ghost town of Gilman 5 miles north of Augusta in 1926, the Bunkhouse has retained its Old West appeal without sacrificing simple comforts. You'll find no mints on the pillows here, no air-conditioning, no phones or televisions, and arbitrarily decorated rooms, but you're not likely to find another place as friendly to flop down in. All rooms are located up a steep flight of stairs and guests share two bathrooms, one with a shower and one with a tub. Photography by Gus Wolfe adorns the walls in some rooms, and rooms facing west look out to the Rocky Mountain Front. Located downtown, the Bunkhouse is a good starting point for a quick walk through Augusta.

GUEST RANCHES

JJJ Wilderness Ranch

Box 310K, Sun Canyon Road, Augusta, MT 59410. ☎ **406/562-3653**. 6 cabins. $933 per week, based on 1-week minimum stay. Includes all meals and ranch activities. No credit cards. Transportation from Great Falls Airport is available.

Located in the extraordinary Sun Canyon near the Gibson Reservoir, the Triple J is a guest ranch with everything the outdoorsy type could dream of. Horseback riding, fishing, pack trips into the Bob Marshall Wilderness (not included in price quoted above), and pure and simple relaxation (sitting and enjoying the views) are all here. The cabins accommodate a total of 20 guests, so you're never crowded. Though there are no amenities, it's not due to an oversight. Phones and televisions are forbidden in these parts. That's not to say this ranch isn't amenable to families, however. The Triple J offers horseback riding lessons and there's even a babysitting service available at no additional charge.

✪ Klick's K Bar L Ranch

Augusta, MT 59410. ☎ **406/467-2771,** in summer and fall; 406/562-3589, in winter and spring. 14 cabins. Cabins $810 per person, based on 6-day minimum stay (all meals included); $295 (for a stay of 2 nights, 3 days, all inclusive). No credit cards.

"Beyond All Roads" is the ranch's subtitle and that's not just a catchy sobriquet. Though it implies that the ranch is impossible to reach by car, the fact is, it's only accessible by water, mule, or foot over 7 miles of trails (but don't worry, the Klicks handle getting you there).

Located on the edge of the Bob Marshall Wilderness, the ranch is full of superlative attributes, from the remote location to the Western meals that are more than just stomach filler, though they do that, too. In fact, it's hard to find a more authentic ranch. Cowboy hats and jeans abound on this family operation, owned by the Klicks since 1927.

✪ Pine Butte Guest Ranch

HC 58, Box 34C, Choteau, MT 59422. ☎ **406/466-2158.** 10 cabins. Summer (per week), $975 adults, $750 children; off-season (per week), $775 adults, $575 children; off-season (per day), $115 adults, $85 children. All rates include room, board, naturalist program, riding program (not available in off-season), use of all ranch facilities, and transportation to and from Great Falls International Airport. Group rates also available. No credit cards.

Owned and operated by the Nature Conservancy, the Pine Butte Guest Ranch is a naturalist's paradise. The emphasis here is on education and that's exactly what you'll get, whether you hike with the ranch's resident naturalist, ride horseback through the prairie, or send your kids off to learn how to identify local aquatic life (see "Especially for Kids" above). Your classroom is the Pine Butte Swamp Preserve, a Nature Conservancy wetland complex and the sole surviving Plains habitat of the grizzly. Hike among the wildflowers of towering Ear Mountain or hunker down with the sharp-tailed grouse in the preserve's fen.

Scattered at the foot of the Eastern Front of the Rocky Mountains, each of the ranch's log and stone cabins features imposing river rock fireplaces and is comfortably yet simply furnished with handmade wood furniture. Meals are served family-style in the ranch's lodge, a rustic building furnished with eclectic Western decor: elk antler chairs, a musket-cum-lamp, and bearskins hung open-mouthed on the walls.

CAMPING

Wagons West

Hwy. 287, Augusta, MT 59410. ☎ **406/562-3295.** 50 RV sites (35 water, 15 full); 50 tent sites. RV $13–$15; tent $10. AE, MC, V.

This campground is conveniently located on the outskirts of Augusta next to the motel of the same name and is not necessarily isolated from civilization: It's right off the highway before you enter town from the north. What some campers may find delightful if not peculiar is the very real bidet that rests in the third stall of the women's bathroom—complete with framed instructions on the wall, even offering the campers to, um, take a footbath if they wish.

WHERE TO EAT

Buckhorn Bar

Main St., Augusta. ☎ **406/562-3344.** All dishes $3–$7. Daily 8am–2am. No credit cards. BEEF/CHICKEN.

Roasted beef and chicken are just about the only things available to eat in this downtown establishment. While the food is average, it's the service and the barflies that are the real fare. Dressed much like its neighbor, the Western Bar, across the street, the Buckhorn is a local hangout with plenty of stuffed wild game hanging along the walls. Racks of all shapes and sizes hang on thick wood beams which span the width of the bar. A typical night has local cowboy Jim Lee going from stool to stool to tell a story or offer an opinion of his personal last best place.

Outpost Deli

819 7 Ave. NW, Choteau. ☎ **406/466-5330.** Breakfast items $2–$5; lunch and dinner dishes $3–$6. No credit cards. Summer, daily 7am–10pm; winter, daily 7am–3pm. SANDWICHES.

Decorated like someone's grandmother's house, this little restaurant offers a wide variety of burgers, sandwiches, and wildlife prints. It's a knick-knacked place ideal for getting a sack lunch to go for a day hike. The milk shakes are outstanding.

Wagons West

Main St., Augusta. ☎ **406/562-3295.** Breakfast items $3–$6; lunch $3–$8; main dinner courses $9–$18. Daily 8am–9pm. AE, MC, V. VEGETARIAN.

This is the best bet for vegetarians or those looking for something a little lighter than genuine Montana beef or anything fried. The salad bar is not outstanding, but happens to be the only game in town. Try the veggie sandwich on homemade bread for a tasty and filling lunch.

Western Bar

Main St., Augusta. ☎ **406/562-3262.** Lunch and dinner dishes $4–$13. Daily 10am–2am. AMERICAN.

In a friendly town of friendly bars, this place is a Cheers of the frontier. On the wall to your left as you enter, hunting and fishing seasons are captured in a collage of Polaroid snapshots that some locals are more than proud to discuss. Though not the place to ask for an espresso, the Western is a place for a 16-oz. T-bone and a game of pool or darts with the locals. Tables are located in the back for those not wanting to belly up to the bar for some of the local flavor.

A SIDE TRIP TO FORT BENTON

For a glimpse into the frontier past where once stood the "Bloodiest Block in the West," drive north on MT 87 for 42 miles to Fort Benton, once a bustling trading center where fur traders, miners, cattlemen, and cowboys consorted with one another, with often fatal results, during the earliest settlement of the West. Established in 1850, Fort Benton is one of Montana's oldest towns, and was a hive of activity because of its location at the head of navigation on the Missouri: Steamboats could travel this far but no farther, making it a point of debarkation for thousands of gold-seekers, and a terminus for many overland trails to other early Montana settlements. Although the arrival of the railroad spelled a certain end to Fort Benton's importance as a supply center—there's not a trace of its rough-and-tumble past visible today—ruins of the old fort and blockhouse are staples for the traveler interested in Montana's frontier past.

Start your tour at the farmer's altar of implements past and present, the **Museum of the Northern Great Plains** at 20th and Washington (☎ 406/622-5316). Admission is $2, which also includes admission to the Museum of the Upper Missouri at Old Fort Park and Front St. (☎ 406/622-5316). Three generations of farming are recorded in this collection of farming equipment, cars, and household items. From antique gas pumps to wheat shocking (bundled grains of wheat), it's all here in a museum which should excite not only the septuagenarian but also the little fellow who doesn't know what a Philco looked like. Curator Jack Lepley has amassed implements and descriptions of farming techniques from all over the northern plains to illustrate the evolution of the Montana farmer from homestead days to the depression to the 1960s.

The Museum of the Upper Missouri is equally astounding. If you've ever wondered where in the world the image for the buffalo nickel, the U.S. Department of the Interior's seal, or the old 10-dollar "buffalo" bill comes from, then you'll have to treat yourself to this mecca of taxidermy. Six buffalo set by the renowned Smithsonian taxidermist William Hornaday—including the actual model for the old nickel—have made their way to Fort Benton, Montana, in an incredible posthumous journey. Also included in the collection is the rifle Chief Joseph of the Nez Perce yielded after his surrender at Bear's Paw Mountains, as well as the history and personality of Fort Benton, as expressed by cowboy artist Charlie Russell, his preacher friend, Brother Van, and the woman who really got around, Madame Mustache.

Located at the north end of Front Street, Old Fort Park is built around the last remnant of the actual fort. The park itself is like any other riverside park, but the stucco fort, which still stands from fur-trapping days, is interesting and will serve as the cornerstone for Fort Benton's ambitious project of the future: an exact replica of the fort as it stood in the 1860s.

The story behind the Shep Memorial is an endearing tale of a dog and his master; you can read about it at the base of the statue on Front Street. The statue commemorates a real-life dog, Shep. After his owner died and was carried away by train, Shep returned to the depot to meet each train for six years in hopes of finding his master.

For lodging, the **Pioneer Lodge** at 1700 Front St. (☎ 406/622-5441) has nine units with telephones, television, and air-conditioning, but if you're coming in January or February, call ahead: They may be closed. The 1916 building is located along Fort Benton's scenic stretch of the Missouri River, a view you can appreciate from the hotel's modest, yet comfortable, lobby. The town's rich history has been preserved in the names given each of the hotel's rooms. All are named for a local luminary or give insight into some historical angle.

4 The Hi-Line: Montana State Highway 2

There isn't a whole lot to see on the Hi-Line. Montanans going east for family reunions or business dread the drive across the High Plains into the harsh expanse of prairies that stretch beyond a seemingly endless horizon. This is also the beginning of a very long and seamless range of vacuous, untouristed, and virtually uninhabited property that gets passed over for more occupied sections of the state. However, what does occur with abundance in this level region—if not people, cars, and tourists—are wildlife refuges, immense but virtually unknown recreational playgrounds, and plains which roll for miles. Eastern Montana isn't something to cover in one day, nor is it a place to spend your entire vacation. If you get too far in, there's no turning back to Bozeman, Missoula, or Glacier in a few hours' time (from Wolf Point, Glacier Park is close at 400 miles). Here, you are in the middle of nowhere, which can sometimes be dreadful. But it can also be a very beautiful place.

FROM HAVRE TO FORT BELKNAP

Though Havre (it rhymes with "cadaver") isn't exactly Montana's crowning jewel, there is a lot of history in and around the place. The Bear Paw Battleground south of Chinook, the Wahkpa Chu'gn Archeological Site, Fort Assiniboine, and the Rocky

Boys Indian Reservation lie within a few hours by car of one another and provide an interesting look into this area's past.

An excellent way to drive this region is to start just southwest of Havre on MT 87. Drive north into Havre until you reach the junction with MT 2. Take MT 2 east until it converges with Montana's version of Route 66, a state highway running south through the Fort Belknap Indian Reservation. Take Route 66 through the reservation to the intersection of MT 191. Turn left onto MT 191, and drive 57 miles north to rejoin MT 2.

WHAT TO SEE & DO

Rocky Boys Reservation and the Rocky Boy Powwow

From Hwy. 87, turn east at Box Elder onto Duck Creek Rd. Drive 14 miles to Tribal Headquarters. Call the Havre Area Chamber of Commerce (☎ **406/265-4383**) for precise dates and further information about the Powwow.

Southwest of Havre lies the home of 2,000 Chippewa and Cree Indians on this rather small plot of land at the Western Front of the Bear's Paw Mountains. For years the U.S. government tried to keep the Cree from settling in the States, and the tribe was homeless. In 1911, when Fort Assiniboine was abandoned, the Chippewa and Cree had part of the land set aside as a reservation. Then, as now, employment was difficult to come by. Each July the Rocky Boy Powwow is held near Box Elder.

Fort Assiniboine

3 mi. S. of Havre on MT 87. Weekend tours can be arranged through the Havre Area Chamber of Commerce, ☎ **406/265-4583**. Tours depart from the H. Earl Clark Museum (MT 2 W. at the Great Northern Fairgrounds) at 5pm. Adults, $3; students, $1.50; children under 6, free.

Located 3 miles south of Havre on MT 87 are the remains of one of Montana's most unusual forts. Built in 1879 as a military outpost for troops guarding the border with Canada and monitoring the activities of Indians throughout the region, Fort Assiniboine was by far the most elaborate and grandest outpost ever constructed in Montana. The buildings were at one point surrounded by a half-million acres of undeveloped land, some of which became the Rocky Boys Indian Reservation, a 108,000-acre space, after the closure of the fort. Though many of the original structures are gone, the post in its heyday was a thriving self-contained community where troops saw little or no battle activity and spent a rather cushy time serving out their duty. In 1911 the fort was closed and turned over to the state of Montana and used as an Agricultural Experiment Station. Though the site is not open to the public (it remains as an agricultural research center operated by Montana State University), tours may be arranged through the Havre Area Chamber of Commerce.

Havre Underground Tours

100 3rd Ave, Havre. ☎ **406/265-8888**. Admission $5 adults, $3 children under 12. Mon–Sat 9am–5pm; after-hours and on Sundays upon request. Group rates are available; reservations recommended.

This interesting tour takes you to the bowels of Havre and provides an enlightening look into the city's past, when racism was rampant and the good times were kept out of sight. The Sporting Eagle Saloon, where gambling and drinking were popular pastime, is just down from one of the only opium dens known to have existed in the early history of the west. Also found "down under" are a Chinese laundry and a bordello.

Wahkpa Chu'gn

Behind the Holiday Village Shopping Mall on MD 2. ☎ **406/265-6417** or 406/265-7550. Admission $3.50 adults, $3 seniors, $2 students, children under 6 free. May 21–September 5,

Tues–Sat 10am–5pm; Sun 10am–5pm; closed Mondays. Tickets are purchased inside the south entrance of the mall; this is also where tours venture forth.

Wahkpa Chu'gn, the Assiniboine name for the Milk River which runs through the valley below, is a pishkun, or buffalo jump, located in an unsightly spot behind the mall on the west side of town. Though the spot isn't as isolated (or accessible) as the Ulm Pishkun near Great Falls, the one-hour guided walking tours are worth the price of admission.

FORT BELKNAP INDIAN RESERVATION

This Native American reservation, one of the state's smallest, was established in 1888 as part of an agreement by the Blackfeet (including the Gros Ventre), Flathead, and Nez Perce nations to relinquish over 17 million acres of what was a joint reservation and move to smaller, separate reservations. The almost 700,000-acre home to the Assiniboine and Gros Ventre peoples lies east of Havre and south of MT 2.

The landscape on the reservation is at first glance an extension of the implacable plains that run through the northern part of the state. There are few hills and no trees—that is, until you drive south on Route 66. The road runs straight through the western section of the reservation before halting near Hays. Pine trees and hills emerge as an oasis in the otherwise flat and dreary surroundings. Just outside of Hays lies the St. Paul's Mission, a parochial elementary school built in 1886. The original log structure burned and was rebuilt as the stone structure which still stands. Just up a gravel road leading away from the Mission turnoff is Mission Canyon, a narrow limestone vault of shallow caverns and steep cliffs. In the canyon along the People's Creek are picnic areas and turnouts, though the road is narrow and can be a mess after a heavy rain. While the canyon is a welcome anomaly, the floor is littered with cans and plastic bags. On your right as you progress through the canyon, look up to your right at the Natural Bridge, which crosses a wide, roomlike opening where photographers can perch. From the roadside, the position of the bridge against its rocky background makes it easy to miss. Another fascinating formation with more cultural significance is Snake Butte, an igneous porous rock with direct and indirect Indian ties: The formation is found only in this location and in India. The Snake Butte has been the site for religious and cultural ceremonies for Native Americans for over 2,000 years, but in the 1930s the U.S. Corps of Army Engineers began an effort to quarry the butte for rock used in the construction of the Fort Peck Dam. The effects are, to say the least, noticeable. Tours of Snake Butte may be arranged through the **Fort Belknap Tourism Office** (☎ 406/353-2527).

Annual events the public is invited to attend are the Milk River Indian Days, held the last weekend of July; and the Hays Mission Canyon Dance in the Mission Canyon, held each summer.

A NEARBY WILDLIFE REFUGE

Black Coulee National Wildlife Refuge

Drive north on MT 241 from Harlem for 24 miles. A gravel road right will take you south 3 miles, east for 1 mile, then south again for 1/2 mile. The road sign on your left depicting white binoculars on a brown background indicates the refuge.

Twenty-five miles north of Harlem off MT 241 lies a prairie marsh halfway to nowhere. Though all kinds of fauna exist on the 1,500 acre refuge, the Tundra Swans that often make appearances in late October are a gift. Though the refuge is difficult to get to and access is restricted to those on foot, the opportunity to view

Bear's Paw Battlefield

On County Road 240, 16 miles south of Chinook, is the site where the Nez Perce were engaged in a fierce six-day battle with U.S. troops under the authority of Col. Nelson A. Miles. In 1877, after an increasing appetite for mining and settlement moved whites into the region west of the Salmon River near the Idaho, Washington, and Oregon borders, the Nez Perce were ordered to relocate to a small reservation. About 800 of them refused to comply and began what was to become a 1,700-mile flight, first to Crow country around Yellowstone to seek help, then north to try and make it out of the pursuing U.S. Army's reach and into the safety of Canada.

After several battles fought all along the way, including the army ambush at Big Hole (see Chapter 7), they were finally stopped here at Bear's Paw. Lost in the first day's battle were Chiefs Toolhoolhoolzote, Ollicot, and Lean Elk, leaving Chief Joseph and White Bird to protect the people under seige near Snake Creek. On October 5, 1877, Chief Joseph handed over his rifle (now in the Museum of the Upper Missouri in Fort Benton), and is believed to have delivered his legendary speech of surrender to the U.S. troops:

Tell General Howard I know his heart. What he told me before I have in my heart. I am tired of fighting. Our chiefs are killed. Looking Glass is dead. The old men are all dead. It is the young men who say yes or no. He who led the young men is dead. It is cold and we have no blankets. The little children are freezing to death. My people, some of them, have run away to the hills and have no blankets, no food. No one knows where they are—perhaps freezing to death. I want to have time to look for my children and see how many I can find. Maybe I shall find them among the dead. Hear me, my chiefs. I am tired. My heart is sick and sad. From where the sun now stands, I will fight no more forever.

After the surrender, about 200 escaped in the night and eventually made it into Canada to join Sitting Bull's Lakotas. The rest of the tribe was removed to a reservation in Oklahoma—part of the conditions of surrender had been that they would be put on a reservation on their native Oregon land—and it wasn't until 1885 that they were finally allowed to resettle on reservations in the Northwest. The final battle at Bear's Paw had been fought, and lost, just 45 miles from the Canadian border.

---

wildlife unimpeded in such a remote setting isn't better anywhere. Keep in mind, however, that there are no facilities in the area and the closest town is Turner, 11 miles north.

WHERE TO STAY

El Toro Inn

521 First Street, Havre, MT 59501. ☎ **406/265-5414.** 41 rms. A/C TV TEL. $40–$44 double. AE, DC, DISC, MC, V.

Spanish tiles and stucco walls adorn this comfortable hotel in downtown Havre. The rooms are standard fare, although each also includes a mini-refrigerator and microwave. Coffee is free each morning and laundry facilities are available.

WHERE TO EAT

PJ's

15 Third Ave., Havre. ☎ **406/265-3211.** Breakfast items $2–$6; lunch $4–$8; main dinner courses $7–$17. AE, DISC, MC, V. Mon–Sat 6am–11pm, Sun 6am–10pm. AMERICAN.

This local eatery is conveniently located near the main entrance of the Amtrak station in Havre. You won't find another restaurant that better typifies the rural Montana experience: An overhead electronic keno message board allows you to try your luck within the comfort of a fake leather booth while you enjoy a succulent cut of Montana beef. Portions at any time of the day are hearty and the no-nonsense staff is neighborly.

The Vineyard

1300 1st., Havre. ☎ **406/265-5355.** Lunch $3–$6; main dinner courses $7–$14. AE, DISC, MC, V. Mon–Fri 11am–2pm, 5–10pm, Sat 11am–10:30pm, Sun 11am–9:30pm. AMERICAN.

Everything about this restaurant and the Mediterranean Room next door is overdone, including the size of the menu, but if broad strokes of burgundy—booths, carpeting, silk flowers, linens, skylights—don't bother you, it's one of the nicest places in town to eat. Elaborate place settings and polished wood contribute to the lavish decor but the atmosphere is decidedly casual. Although the food is marginal, it's a safe choice in a town that doesn't have many other options other than fast food.

FROM GLASGOW TO THE FORT PECK INDIAN RESERVATION AND THE C.M. RUSSELL WILDLIFE REFUGE

Glasgow was created in 1887 as a result of the construction of the Great Northern Railroad and remained a sleepy little town of farmers, cowboys, and sheepherders until the construction of Fort Peck Dam began in 1933. The influx of workers needing housing roused the community from its lethargy and it suddenly became one of the busiest towns in northeastern Montana. Today, it remains one of the most important commercial centers on the eastern side of the state, although it is largely dependent on the tourist trade from nearby Fort Peck for much of its income.

Fort Peck is one of the few planned cities in Montana, a result of the construction of Fort Peck Dam, a WPA (Works Progress Administration) project that began in October 1933. Its history began much earlier than the dam, however, as it took its name from a trading post which was located in the same spot in 1867. The old Fort Peck enjoyed a lucrative fur trade with the Assiniboine and Sioux before it was abandoned in 1879 and later swept away by the river.

The federal authorization to build the Fort Peck Dam came in October 1933, as part of Franklin D. Roosevelt's New Deal Program, and it set off an economic explosion in northeastern Montana. This sparsely populated and remote area in dire need of flood control was suddenly transformed into the largest construction site in the country. Roosevelt had hit two birds with one giant dam proposal: The problem of flooding would be alleviated and the depressed area (and nation) would be better off with the creation of 10,000 new jobs, seemingly from thin air. Additional benefits of the dam included an irrigation supply, and eventually, hydroelectric power and a massive lake ideal for recreation.

The immediate reaction to the dam in northeastern Montana was one of ambivalence. Though the benefits were undeniable, the few people living along the banks of the Missouri River were suddenly in jeopardy of losing their homes to the impending lake, a watery equivalent to the highway department running pavement through their property. But due to the Great Depression, these same people were in desperate need of immediate employment, and many went to work on the dam, watching as the lake rose and submerged homes that lay in the way. To further fuel the controversy, much of the rock used in building the dam was quarried from Snake Butte, south of Harlem, Montana, ceremonial grounds for Native Americans for over 2,000 years.

During the construction of the dam, between 1933 and 1940, the population of Fort Peck reached 50,000. Tiny boomtowns sprang up within miles of the site and many of the buildings described below were built. When the dam was finally completed in 1940, a lake 130 miles long and 16 miles wide had been created, the town of Fort Peck and the unfinished dam had been featured on the cover of *Life* magazine, and two massive hydroelectric powerhouses began pumping water through what is still the largest earth-filled dam in the world. What stands today is nothing less than a monument.

Fort Peck Lake is known throughout the northeast part of Montana as an immense recreational site with more shoreline than the California coast. It's recognized as the best spot in the state for walleye fishing, with an annual "Governor's Cup" competition held each spring, and a favorite getaway for campers with sites located all around the shoreline. For detailed camping and boat access information, contact the **U.S. Army Corps of Engineers at Fort Peck Lake,** P.O. Box 208, Fort Peck, MT 59223 (☎ 406/526-3411). Somewhat amazingly, it is still a relatively undiscovered spot.

The tall **Fort Peck Powerhouse** stands high above the river like a confused skyscraper looking out over the river for home. The main plant, besides exhibiting the Missouri River dam system in miniature models, offers a rather surprising display of fossils from the area.

The **Fort Peck Theater** on Main St. is a rather ecclesiastical-looking building that holds over 1,000 people. Built in 1934 for the dam workers, the old cinema is now home to an excellent summer theater company operated by the Fort Peck Restaurant and Welfare Council (☎ 800/828-2259).

For recreational opportunities, the Fort Peck Lake and the surrounding **Charles M. Russell National Wildlife Refuge** are unsurpassed in this part of the state. Turnoffs and campsites skirt the lake on the north and south sides, but the south side of the lake north of Jordan is one of the easier remote locations to get to—if the roads are dry. The Hell Creek campground is right on the south side of the lake and is excellent for viewing the sunset pastels of the breaks and the wildlife which roam throughout the hills. Boat ramps are located around the lake as well. Easiest to reach are the **Flat Creek, Rock Creek,** and **Nelson Creek** boat ramps, located just off Montana State Highway 24, which runs along the eastern side of the lake.

The **Fort Peck Indian Reservation** is home to the Assiniboines and the Sioux. The Sioux, who had been on the reservation by themselves, were joined by the Assiniboine nation after smallpox killed over half of the tribe farther west along the Missouri River and again threatened the tribe after it resettled near Fort Belknap. The exodus from the deadly disease brought them to Fort Peck. Now the reservation is home to many non-Indians, with less than half of the actual reservation owned by Native Americans.

Wolf Point, the supply hub for the Fort Peck Reservation (Poplar is the location for tribal headquarters), has a name with a fascinating history, though the town itself isn't quite so interesting. When fur trappers had a successful winter trapping wolves, they left the animals on the riverbank to keep until they could skin them the following spring. When they came back to complete the job, however, the site was no longer white man's land and they left their kill to rot. The wolves began to stink up the whole place and visitors along the river couldn't help but notice.

Impressions

Something lives on the highline that cannot examine itself. Outsiders recognize its presence but fail to describe it, hurrying instead over the prairie highways at eighty miles an hour to reach the more conventional shadows of the mountains.

—Mary Clearman Blew, "Wahkpa Chu'gn," an essay
from the anthology *Montana Spaces* (1988)

The main attraction in mid-July each year is Wolf Point's Wild Horse Stampede, the oldest rodeo in the state. Toward the end of June each year is the Assinniboine gathering, Red Bottom Day, featuring dancing and singing. For specific dates and times for these events, contact the **Wolf Point Chamber of Commerce** at 201 4th Ave. S. (☎ 406/653-2012).

WHERE TO STAY

In Glasgow

Cottonwood Inn

Hwy. 2 E, Glasgow, MT 59230. ☎ **406/228-8213** or 800/321-8213. Fax 406/228-8248. 92 rms. A/C TV TEL. $54–58 double, $70 deluxe. AE, DC, DISC, MC, V.

This moderately priced hotel is the best in the Fort Peck Lake area, hands-down. Located within minutes of the northeast end of the lake, it is a stopover point for business travelers and tourists alike. Everything reasonable is available, including room service, which is quite a feat for a hotel on the east side.

In Jordan

Hell Creek Guest Ranch

P.O. Box 325, Jordan, MT 59337. ☎ **406/557-2224.** 1 cabin, 1 trailer. $100 per couple (includes meals). No credit cards.

The Hell Creek Guest Ranch is a great spot in the late summer and fall, and the drive out to John and Sylvia Trumbo's place is fascinating. Pines trees scattered over badlands lead up to the place, tucked in the coulees 20 miles north of Jordan. From there it's a short drive in John's truck to Fort Peck Lake. The scenery from here is wonderful. Ranch activities include (besides Mrs. Trumbo's cooking) helping out around the place if you wish, or just heading off to fossil hunt.

Nearby Jordan has the Garfield County Museum and Senior Citizen Center, pardon their pun, where you can check out all of the fossils collected in the area, including some really impressive dinosaur skeletons (some of the best in the state). Dinosaur bones found in the Hell Creek area are scattered in museums throughout the country, including this tiny one in Garfield County.

In Saco

⑤ Big Dome Hotel Bed and Breakfast

Hwy. 2, Saco, MT 59261. ☎ **406/527-3498.** 6 rms, 2 shared bathrooms. $25 single, $40 double (includes full breakfast). MC.

Saco is truly a town that you can miss in the blink of an eye, but if you do, you'll miss out on some great stuff, especially this oasis of a lodging. An area renowned for fossils, Saco has a more infamous claim to fame than simple dinosaur relics. It is the mosquito capital of the world (or so we're told): Apparently, there are more mosquitoes per square inch in Saco than anywhere else in the world.

The Big Dome Hotel, built in 1909 as the grand First National Bank of Saco, has been completely remodeled by owners Mark Zuidema and Jody Menge, with many original items from the bank restored, including the vault. All rooms are located on the second floor and are tastefully decorated (the tin ceiling panels were meticulously hand-painted by Jody) and extremely comfortable. The only knock against the place is the railroad tracks across the street. A train rumbling by can be a less than charming noise at 4 in the morning. But breakfast is wonderful and you aren't going to find this type of service at this type of bed-and-breakfast for this price anywhere.

In Wolf Point

Missouri River Bed and Breakfast

Box 5035, Wolf Point, MT 59201. 2 rms, 1 shared bath. $40–$50 double. No credit cards.

Finding this place can be difficult, and that may be for the best. Located west of Wolf Point on the old Indian Highway, this is not your traditional bed-and-breakfast. There are beds, and you are served breakfast (which is actually quite delicious, a Danish meal of *aebleskivers*), but the place has the feel of a farm. Barnyard animals abound and the grounds are rife with farming implements. This is more of a stay on a farm out in the country. In fact, the place was called the Forsness Farm Bed and Breakfast (a much more revealing name), until the name was changed in 1995 to the present one. A fishing access is south of the farm a mile or so, but it's not the most idyllic spot along the mighty Missouri. Here, it is the Muddy Mo.

WHERE TO EAT

⑤ Elida's

502 Main St., Wolf Point. ☎ **406/653-2681.** Most items $5–$9. MC, V. Tues–Sun 4–11pm. Closed Monday. PIZZA.

This place is relatively new and is located on the site of a former health club. It serves pizza in an open dining room, and though it doesn't necessarily look like a health club, you can tell it was something else in a previous life. The pizza is surprisingly good. Large 15-inch pizzas cost around $11, and dinners (chicken, shrimp, and barbecue plates) around $9.

The Roost

U.S. Hwy. 2 (east of Glasgow, just outside town), Glasgow. Reservations not accepted. Breakfast items $3–$4; lunch $2–$6; main dinner course $4–$13. No credit cards. Daily 6am–2am. STEAKS/BURGERS.

Advertising itself as a fine eating establishment, the Roost falls shy of its claim, though the food isn't as bad as the tacky round table in the middle of the place piled high with magazines. You might mistake the Roost for a bait shop when you drive up, and once you sit down, the casino atmosphere can be a bit much, no matter how well the steak is charbroiled. The Friday night special is coldwater lobster, but if that sounds like it might be too much in a place that doesn't have enough, try lunch. It's a safer bet.

5 Lewistown

Lewistown is, appropriately, the geographic center of the state. After all, it's the hub of an enormous agricultural region of Montana that spans three counties and a lot of capable land. Lewistown is not a tourist attraction for the state, and residents tilt their heads in wonder trying to decide if there's something peculiar or wrong here, something singular that other places have that Lewistown is missing. The truth is,

Lewistown is as remarkable as any other Montana town and matches up in every category.

Lewistown's greatest feature, though, is its humility. It's a comely creature that doesn't quite know how beautiful it is. It's a place you wouldn't kick and scream to visit, but you would do anything to live there. But the attraction goes beyond simple Americana virtues. Lewistown is blessed with mountains, great downtown architecture, stately homes from other eras, and solid and modest citizens who aren't inarticulate agrarian stereotypes. The people in Lewistown are like the land that surrounds them: quiet mountains in the background. And though they welcome you to their "modest" surroundings with open arms and music piped in from the local radio station through speakers downtown, there is probably something in them that's glad to see you leave. There's no blaming them.

ESSENTIALS

GETTING THERE   Big Sky Airlines (☎ 800/237-7788) provides commuter airline service to and from Lewistown daily. A private charter service is available through **Skycraft Inc.** (☎ 406/538-5457) and **Central Air Service** (☎ 406/538-3767). The **Rimrock Stages** depot (☎ 406/538-3380) is located at 102 W. Main and provides service from and to Billings and Great Falls.

Lewistown is connected to other Montana cities mostly by two-lane, U.S. highways that radiate from it. From Billings, the most direct route is northwest on Hwy. 87. From Bozeman, drive east along U.S. Hwy., 90 then north on Hwy. 191. From Great Falls, Lewistown is a short 105-mile drive east along Hwy. 87.

VISITOR INFORMATION   The Lewistown Chamber of Commerce has offices in the Museum of the Central Montana Historical Association in Symmes Park on East Main, Box 818, Lewistown, MT 59457 (☎ 406/538-5436). Contact them for maps from the forest service, Bureau of Land Management, and C.M. Russell Wildlife Refuge, in addition to a number of city and county maps. **Travel Montana's Russell Country, Inc.** includes Lewistown; request information from them at 800/527-5348 or 406/761-5036. Local road reports can be obtained by calling 406/538-7445. Call 406/449-5204 for weather information.

GETTING AROUND   Rental car agencies of Lewistown include **Budget** (☎ 406/538-7701); **Courtesy Chevy, Pontiac,** and **Buick** (☎ 406/538-7417); and **Dean Newton Olds, Cadillac,** and **GMC** (☎ 406-538-3455).

GETTING OUTSIDE

The area around Lewistown has a few parks and lakes that have good local reputations as places for outdoor recreation. **Ackley Lake,** a man-made lake in a state park of the same name, is reputed to be a good source for 10- to 15-inch rainbow trout and is a popular spot for all types of water sports during the summer. To reach Ackley Lake, drive approximately 20 miles west of Lewistown on Hwy. 87 to Hobson, then 2 miles south on 400, then 2 miles southwest on a county road. Call 406/454-3441 for further information.

It's not the most accessible lake in these parts, but **Crystal Lake** is worth the effort it takes to reach it if your plans for visiting Lewistown include a day of fishing and hiking. It lies high in the Big Snowy Mountains on the fringe of a swatch of the Lewis and Clark National Forest, and is easily one of the area's best recreational haunts. Getting there can be a problem if you don't have a vehicle that takes to gravel too well. Take U.S Hwy. 87 west of Lewistown for 8 miles and turn left at the Crystal Lake sign. This is a gravel road—16 miles worth—that runs into Forest

Service Road 275. Take that road for 9 miles to the lake. Overnight tent camping is available.

CROSS-COUNTRY SKIING

With three mountain ranges—the Big and Little Snowies, the Moccasin, and the Judith—surrounding it and a period of snowfall that often begins in early fall and extends through the spring, Lewistown is a great cross-country destination. There are a number of trails (old mining and logging roads, actually) north of town in the Judith Mountains, easily accessible by car. Head north on Hwy. 191 to the Maiden Canyon sign, then take a left and follow the road for 5 miles to the trails. Because snowmobiling is popular in this area, many snowmobilers use these trails, too.

FISHING

Great nearby fishing waters include Big Spring Creek, Crystal Lake, and Flatwillow Creek. **Big Spring Creek** begins south of Lewistown and flows north through the city, where it meets the Judith River. Some of the finest trout fishing in the state is found in these waters. **The Brewery Flats** is one of the easier spots to access on Big Spring Creek and is located about 2 miles outside town on MT 238. A bridge across the creek leads to the access. **Crystal Lake** is most easily accessible by turning south at the Crystal Lake sign on Hwy. 87 about 8 miles west of Lewistown. Motorized boats are prohibited, but there are facilities for picnicking and camping. **Flatwillow Creek,** in the Forest Grove area of the Little Snowies, provides some rainbow and cutthroat trout.

GOLF

Visitors can enjoy limited use of the greens at the **Elks Country Club's** nine-hole course, 2 miles south of town on Country Club Road. Call 406/538-7075 for tee times.

HIKING

Crystal Lake is a nice destination for hikers, with numerous trails originating there as well as on-site camping facilities. The popular **Crystal Lake Loop National Recreation Trail** leads to two of the more popular destinations, Ice Caves and Crystal Cascades. The Judith Resource Area of the Bureau of Land Management, Lewistown District Office, Airport Road, Lewistown, MT 59437 (☎406/538-7461) can give you information on additional hiking trails in the nearby mountains.

WHAT TO SEE & DO

Big Spring
7 miles south of Lewistown on County Rd. 466.

The third largest freshwater spring in the world, Big Spring is located 7 miles south of Lewistown in the foothills of the Snowy Mountains. The spring, which is the water source for Lewistown residents, is considered one of the purest in the country. Capitalizing on this fact is the Big Spring Water Company, which bottles the water and sells it across the northcentral United States. You can buy it at any grocery store, supermarket, or convenience store in Montana. It's very common.

Chokecherry Festival
Held all over town, this celebration honors one of the few indigenous fruits of the prairie. Parades, bake sales, and anything else remotely connected to the chokecherry, including a pit-spitting contest, are held annually on the Saturday following Labor

Day. Though the spitting contest brings bragging rights to the winner, it's the cook-off champion who is most revered.

The Fergus County Courthouse
7th Ave. and Main St., Downtown

Of all the buildings in Lewistown with any architectural or historical significance, the most impressive and certainly the most striking, is this gold-domed courthouse built in the Mission style in 1907. Perhaps the most engaging aspect of the building is that it was ever built in any other fashion than the bland Eastern style for which the West was noted at the turn of the century.

✪ Montana Cowboy Poetry Gathering

The advent of cowboy poetry reading in Lewistown came when the Cowboy Poetry Gathering got to be too big for the saddle it was riding in Big Timber. Now, every year in mid-August at the Yogo Inn, cowboys, ranch hands, and other unlikely members of Montana's literati get together for poetry recitals. Put away any images you may have of cowboys in chaps sipping tea in a parlor. This is a big deal and some serious poets read here each year. The 1995 gathering featured cowboy humorist Baxter Black, a radio personality syndicated primarily in the West, but heard occasionally over NPR's airwaves. Also included each year is an arts and crafts juried show, with booths of leather works and other crafts that takes place poolside. For details on upcoming Cowboy Poetry Gatherings, call the Lewistown Chamber of Commerce at 406/538-5436.

Silk Stocking District

Built during the boom years of 1904–19, this district is one of three neighborhoods in Lewistown listed on the National Register of Historic Places. Located just northeast of downtown on Boulevard (not the section of Boulevard near Symmes Park; if you're here, you're lost), this district was named for its residents, all of whom could afford silk stockings. Prominent figures in the community (mining operators, ranchers, and financiers) owned the homes, whose range in architectural styles extends from gothic arches to Victorian bays. A mix of Georgian, Federal, and Regency styles is seen on the facade of one of the more prominent homes, the Sweitzer residence at 315 3rd Avenue N. Keep in mind that the homes are private residences and are not open to the public.

Symmes Park

Located across the street from the chamber of commerce is Lewistown's civic playground. Picnic tables, a tennis court, and horseshoes are all here to be enjoyed. The park is located on East Main between Prospect and Ridgelawn.

SHOPPING

For a small town, Lewistown offers up some interesting shopping options. **Center of the Universe,** 110 6th Ave. S. (☎ 406/538-2815), has a presumptuous name, but is actually a great shop. Inside you'll find a mix of the latest rock and pop CDs and tapes, as well as an assortment of jewelry, clothing, candles, incense, and interesting cards. **Cottonwood Treasures,** downtown at 219 W. Main (☎ 406/538-5292), has lead crystal, music boxes, little stone figures, and a comprehensive needlecraft section. Across the street at 216 W. Main is **Country Junction,** destination for the coffee lovers. Inside there's fresh coffee and espresso and a gourmet food section. For Western wear, you can find whatever it is you're looking for in the way of boots and hats at **Don's,** 120 2nd Ave. S. (☎ 406/538-9408). If you're in love with the wonderful world of cheese and enjoy sausage and wine, then pencil in **Kitch's Cheese Mart** on Route 2, a mile and a half west of U.S. Hwy. 87 (☎ 406/538-9770). A must-stop is **Poor Man's Books & Coffee and Southwestern Cafe,** 413 W. Main (☎ 406/538-4277), a great place for used books (with a place to read them), green chili cheeseburgers, and a copy of the *Lewistown Free Press,* a little rag with a progressive and off-the-wall take on local happenings.

WHERE TO STAY
A HOTEL
Yogo Inn of Lewistown
211 E. Main, Lewistown, MT 59457. ☎ **406/538-8721** or 800/860-9646. 124 rms. 1 suite. A/C TV TEL. $59–$65 double; $100 suite. AE, DISC, MC, V.

Located downtown, the Yogo is the hotel of choice for most who frequent Lewistown on business. The convention and banquet facilities are impressive, as are the indoor and outdoor pools and indoor hot tub. Though there are other places in town, the Yogo has the most travel-friendly features; it's easily distinguished by its cattle skull logo. The hotel's management claims that the state's precise geological center is located here.

A BED-AND-BREAKFAST
○ The Symmes-Wicks House
220 W. Boulevard, Lewistown, MT 59457. ☎ **406/259-7993.** 2 rms, one with shower, one with half-bath. Shared bathroom. $60–$70 double. All rates include full breakfast. MC, V.

Though the owners are newcomers to the bed-and-breakfast game, their research and attention to detail have paid off. Easily one of the nicer bed-and-breakfasts in the state, the Symmes-Wicks house is an elegant member of Lewistown's Silk Stocking District (see "What to See and Do," above). Though you can see the exteriors of all the homes in the district, a stay here provides a unique opportunity to view the inside of one. Tiffany glass was used in the windows above the landing on the staircase and in living room bookcases, fir beams run the length of entire rooms, and elaborate old heat registers add additional character. Upstairs, the guest rooms are tastefully decorated in two opposing themes: The room facing east, in masculine hunter green tones, has a sleigh bed and a reproduction Degas figure. The bathroom is a wooden work of art and the chain handle of the water closet is a delightful throwback. The room facing south has a more feminine touch: a patina-colored bed with Laura Ashley accents. The bathroom isn't so much a room as it is a tasteful area partitioned off from the main room. Robes are available in both rooms.

A GUEST RANCH
Circle Bar Guest Ranch
P.O. Box K, Utica, MT 59452. ☎ **406/423-5454.** 9 cabins. $980 per week per person (one week minimum stay). Meals and ranch activities included. No credit cards. 33 miles west of Lewistown; take U.S. Hwy. 87 west, turn south at Windham to Utica. 12 miles southwest from Utica on gravel road.

With cross-country skiing, snowmobiling, sleigh rides, and ice skating opportunities on hand during winter, the Circle Bar is one of the few Montana guest ranches that remains open year-round, and is easily one of the oldest. A cattle operation since the late 1800s, the ranch now treats guests to Western activities, including cattle branding in May and remuda (ranch saddle horse) roundups in June and October. Hayrides, horseshoes, and volleyball are popular with kids, as are horse-centered activities, which include trail rides, carriage driving, and pack trips (as long as you give advance notice). The Judith River runs through the ranch, providing fine fishing and photo opportunities.

WHERE TO EAT

Hackamore

U.S. Hwy. 87 (two miles west of town). ☎ **406/538-5685.** Lunch $4–$6; main dinner courses $7–$16. AE, MC, V. Mon–Fri 11am–2pm, 5–9:30pm, Sat–Sat 11am–10pm. AMERICAN.

Make no mistake, Lewistown's restaurant of choice is a casino. And during lunch the casino is where you sit. The lunch menu offers up stirfry, shrimp, burgers, and salads but the chef salad is by far the most appetizing. Dinner moves out of the casino (though strains of the keno machines' winning-hand rendition of the "Hallelujah Chorus" can still be heard) and into the dining room where area cuts of beef are served, including the house specialty, prime rib, seven nights a week. Though only the barest shell of the original building exists, Hackamore remains one of Lewistown's oldest dining establishments.

Howard's Pizza

116 6th Ave. ☎ **406/538-2164.** Reservations not accepted. Most items $6–$15. DISC, MC, V. Tues–Sat 11am—11pm Sun 1–9pm. Closed Mon. PIZZA.

Located a couple of blocks from downtown, this Great Falls franchise offers more than just your ordinary pizza, though pizza is the menu's strong point. Almost everything else is fried: hamburgers, chicken, and shrimp. Barbecued ribs can be had, but they're not the greatest.

❸ The Whole Famdamily

206 W. Main. ☎ **406/538-5161.** Most items $3–$7. AE, DISC, MC, V. Mon–Fri 11am–8pm, Sat 11am–5pm. Closed Sun. SOUPS/SANDWICHES.

By far the best deal in town, this place is a thick cut above a diner. Offering good, original sandwiches named after everybody and everybody's brother (the large Cleo's Club and Aunt Isabell's International Melt are the best choices), the Whole Famdamily is where to go for simple affordable meals. Each night, the dinner menu (it's virtually the same as lunch) offers up two specials.

Yogo Steakhouse

211 E. Main (at the Yogo Inn). ☎ **406/538-8721.** Breakfast items $3–$5; lunch $3–$7; main dinner courses $5–$15. AE, CB, DISC, MC, V. Mon–Sat 6am–10pm, Sun 6am–9pm. AMERICAN.

The Yogo is an average restaurant with a funny name (it's named after the Yogo sapphire, a stone that's prevalent in the area) and all the requisite hotel restaurant items. Though the trout is indeed worth trying, not much else on the menu is eye-catching.

ALSO WORTH A LOOK: WHITE SULPHUR SPRINGS

Though certainly not as popular as Denver, White Sulphur Springs can boast at least two similarities with Colorado's capital. Both cities are exactly one mile high, and both cities have had teams that've won exactly the same number of Super Bowls.

Named for the thermal mineral springs that flow through town, White Sulphur Springs is a small ranching community in the middle of the Smith River Valley.

The pride of the town is the formidable **Castle Museum** at the corner of 2nd Ave. NE and Baker St. on a hill in the north section of town (☎ 406/547-3423). Inside this granite mansion you'll find a wonderful collection of historical objects, mostly from or related to Meagher County (pronounced "mar"). Though the mansion is in need of some minor interior renovation, it is worth the $3 admission fee to look around. Upstairs, if your guide has wrapped up the narrative of Meagher County (the story of Thomas Francis Meagher, the first territorial governor of Montana and county namesake, is actually rather fascinating), you'll find an old soccer game that puts Foosball to shame. It takes nickels and still works.

The Columns, 19 E. Wright (☎ 406/547-3666), just down from the Castle, is the downtown area's bed-and-breakfast, and is a great (and reasonably priced) place to spend the night if you decide to stay in White Sulphur Springs. Owner Dale McAfee (who, incidentally, curates the Castle), will make reservations for you to eat pizza if you wish at **Stageline Pizza and Video** on 210. E. Main (☎ 406/547-3505). Pizzas run around $14 for a large pie, and you can have your pizza brought to your table in the back part of the place, a mid-sized movie theater.

If you're around in winter, snowmobiling in Neihart, 36 miles north on U.S. Hwy. 89, is a big activity. Call Montana Snowmobile Adventures, P.O. Box 5, Neihart, MT 59465 (☎ 406/236-5358) for information on trails and sled rentals.

9

Southcentral Montana & the Missouri Headwaters

Relatively unspoiled, yet one of the most heavily touristed areas in the state, southcentral Montana is a world-class playground for the outdoor recreational enthusiast. Its biggest draw is, without a doubt, the waters of the Madison and Jefferson Rivers for their superb fly-fishing. But as you make your way through this region, following these rivers (and others that run through it), you'll see that water sports, such as rafting, kayaking, and canoeing, aren't far behind in popularity. Other summertime activities include hiking in the Gallatin National Forest, mountain biking in the hills north of Bozeman, and backpacking in Yellowstone National Park.

In winter, downhill skiing takes over at Big Sky and Bridger Bowl—both less than an hour from downtown Bozeman. The region is also excellent for cross-country skiing, with Lone Mountain Ranch and Bohart Ranch, two of the best nordic skiing facilities in the state. And for a change of pace, make your way south to Yellowstone Park for a tour of nature in the tank-treaded snowcoaches, or move at an even quicker speed along the miles of trails on a snowmobile.

Bozeman, home of Montana State University, provides the charm and culture any good college town should—good bookstores and restaurants, charming shops, even a brewpub. Summer brings the Sweet Pea Festival, a celebration of music and the performing arts, and the National Finals Rodeo, the most important competition for high school cowboys in the country.

A few years ago the area around Bozeman bounded by the Bridger, Gallatin, Madison, and Tobacco ranges seemed like an undiscovered bargain for real estate opportunists and others searching for the perfect place to relocate or set up a vacation house. Many who chose to move here, are film and TV actors and personalities. Nearby Three Forks is an easygoing town near the headwaters of the Missouri River where anglers arrive in droves each summer for world-class fishing along the Madison River; the Gallatin Valley, with its preeminent status as a four-season gateway to Yellowstone, is home to Big Sky, Montana's biggest ski resort community; and Livingston, a town undergoing slow change, is southcentral Montana's most renowned ranching community. Full of new faces, new restaurants, and new bookstores, Livingston is becoming a little slice of culture on the banks of the Yellowstone River.

1   Scenic Drives

Interstate 90 runs east to west through this region; and from it, three valley highways extend south. Between Three Forks and Livingston, I-90 is known for its windiness, especially along the stretch of road from Bozeman to Livingston. The first of the region's three valley highways, U.S. Hwy. 287, is picked up in Three Forks, from which it runs 120 miles south through the Madison Valley to the town of Ennis (an angler's dream come true), and West Yellowstone, the western gateway to Yellowstone National Park. U.S. Hwy. 191 runs parallel to Rte. 287 in the east, just across the Madison range in the Gallatin Valley. If you take Rte. 191 from Bozeman to Yellowstone, you'll pass through the resort community of Big Sky, home of some of the best downhill skiing in Montana.

The third highway, U.S. Hwy. 89, runs through the Paradise Valley. From Livingston, it winds its way south for 57 miles to Gardiner and the north entrance of Yellowstone. Along the way, you'll pass through the little community of Chico Hot Springs, as attractive in its own way as Ennis and Big Sky are in theirs.

Red Lodge can be reached a couple of ways. Perhaps the easiest route is east on I-90 to exit 408 then south on MT 78 for 48 miles. The more spectacular route is along the Beartooth National Scenic Byway.

DRIVING TOUR #1: THE BEARTOOTH SCENIC BYWAY

An ideal loop tour is relatively short, runs through lovely scenery, and has excellent roads, facilities, and telephones. By this definition, the Beartooth Byway is not ideal. It is, however, one of the most spectacular drives in America. It passes through exquisite scenery and reaches an altitude of almost 11,000 feet at its peak.

To experience this drive to the fullest, begin in the town of Livingston. Drive south, following the Yellowstone River through Paradise Valley, 53 miles to Gardiner. Once inside the park you can stop off at Mammoth Hot Springs, a geothermal wonderland just inside the park's northern boundary. Then, take the road from Mammoth Hot Springs east to Tower Junction, continuing east to the park's north-east entrance at Silver Gate to pick up Hwy. 212 (this is the Beartooth Byway). Just outside Cooke City, look over your shoulder at the massive spire, 11,699-foot Pilot Peak. From here, the road begins to wind upward along the Montana and Wyoming border for nearly 40 miles until it reaches the Beartooth Pass (elevation 10,947 feet). From that spectacular altitude, you can see an abundance of summer snow and the miles and miles of mountains in Wyoming and Montana. The road then drops for 24 miles as the byway continues on to Red Lodge. From Red Lodge, drive north on Hwy. 78 down into the high plains before heading back to the mountains of Bozeman, west on I-90. The entire trip takes anywhere between six and eight hours, depending on the time of day you choose to drive it, and the condition of the roads. A word to the wise: bring chewing gum.

DRIVING TOUR #2: HWY. 287 FROM THREE FORKS TO WEST YELLOWSTONE

Less strenuous on body and car is the drive along Hwy. 287 from Three Forks to West Yellowstone. As it passes through the beautiful Madison Valley, it allows for some darn good fly-fishing from the many roadside accesses along the way. You'll also pass Quake Lake, which was formed when a massive landslide was triggered by the tragic August 17, 1959, earthquake (in which 20 campers lost their lives). The trip from Three Forks to Yellowstone Park's west entrance at West Yellowstone is 124 miles, a two-hour drive.

To return, you may want to consider making this a loop tour by driving through the Gallatin Valley. This drive offers spectacular views of the Madison range from the east side as you drive through the Gallatin National Forest. Also in sight, on the west side of the highway, is the Gallatin range, which includes two giants: Hyalite Peak at 10,298 feet, and farther north, Mount Blackmore at 10,154 feet. You'll pass by Lone Mountain and the ski and summer resort town of Big Sky along the way. You can grab a bite here at Big Sky's Meadow Village or you can stop off in Gallatin Gateway, a half-hour north of Big Sky, and enjoy the grandeur of the Gallatin Gateway Inn's restaurant.

2 Bozeman

Named for the carousing frontiersman, John Bozeman, this is where you'll find sandaled feet, retro-hippies, bicycles, professors, and ranchers. You may not see them walking the downtown byways arm in arm but they'll be on the same side of the street, nevertheless. This unlikely mixture of lifestyles, along with the surrounding mountains, makes up Bozeman's appeal. As the secret gets out, more and more folks seeking a respite from the hectic pace of urban life choose to resettle here.

As a result, Bozeman finds itself in the middle of a considerable population explosion, with enough growth to make a contractor laugh all the way to the bank. It's not uncommon to hear longtime residents (and even recent transplants who would shut the gate behind them if they could) griping about the good old days when there weren't two houses to be seen along the backroads that lead into town.

Home to Montana State University, an agricultural education center, Bozeman has enough scenery and recreation to keep some of those doctoral candidates washing dishes just to stay near the place. Bozeman isn't what you'd call a trip through time to the Montana days of old, nor is it a microcosm of the Montana of today. But it is a visitor's paradise, filled with a million things to do and see, inside and out.

ESSENTIALS

GETTING THERE   Bozeman's airport, **Gallatin Field,** provides daily service through **Continental** (☎ 800/525-0280), **Delta** (☎ 800/221-1212), and **Northwest** (☎ 800/225-2525); commuter flights between Montana cities are available on **Horizon** (☎ 800/547-9308) and **Skywest** (☎ 800/221-1212).

Bus service into Bozeman is provided by Greyhound, whose terminal is located at 625 N. 7 Ave. (☎ 406/587-3110). **Rimrock Stages** operates an intrastate service from Bozeman with service to Missoula via Helena with continuing service to Great Falls; they also have daily service from Bozeman to Billings and points in between.

Bozeman is easily reached from Montana towns along I-90. From Billings, drive west on I-90 for 140 miles; from Missoula, drive east on I-90 for 120 miles. The quickest route from Great Falls to Bozeman is on I-15 through Helena, south on Hwy. 287 to Three Forks, then east on I-90 to Bozeman. For local road reports, call 406/586-1313; call 800/332-6171 for road conditions statewide.

VISITOR INFORMATION   The **Bozeman Area Convention and Visitors' Bureau** is located at 1205 E. Main (☎ 800/228-4224 or 406/586-5421). A visitor information center kiosk at 1001 N. 7th St. is open from Memorial Day through Labor Day and is a great place to pick up brochures and other city information. For information on **Yellowstone Country** (what Travel Montana calls the region that includes Bozeman), call 800/736-5276 or 406/446-1005.

Southcentral Montana

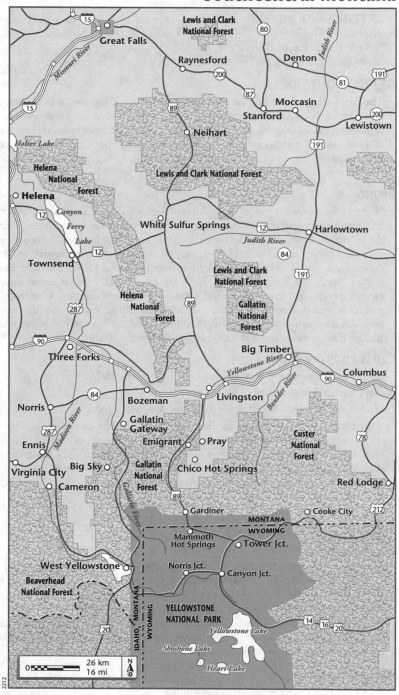

GETTING AROUND   There are many car rental agencies in Bozeman, among them **Avis** (☎ 406/388-6414), **Hertz** (☎ 406/388-6939), **National** (☎ 406/388-6694), and **Rent-a-Wreck** (☎ 406/587-4551).

For a taxi, call **City Taxi** (☎ 406/586-2341), the only cab service in town.

GETTING OUTSIDE

The East Gallatin State Recreation Area is a summertime favorite for local outdoor sports freaks. **Glen Lake,** located inside the recreation area in the northeast corner of Bozeman on Manley Road, is popular with anglers and swimmers, and its 300-foot beachfront is a gathering place for sunbathers. Water sports enthusiasts also can enjoy canoeing, kayaking, and windsurfing on the lake. There is a minimal fee for the day use area; open fires, glass containers, and dogs are all prohibited.

BIKING

Whether you just want to tool around downtown or strike off into the wilderness, Bozeman has plenty of places to mountain bike. However, before you wander off into the hills of the Gallatin National Forest, stop into one of the local downtown shops that make biking in and around Bozeman their business. **Chalet Sports,** located downtown at 108 W. Main across the street from the Baxter Hotel, **the Bike Shop** at 25 S. Black, and **Bangtail** at 505 W. Bozeman, all offer plenty of rental equipment, expertise, and maps covering the trails throughout the region. One map in particular, published by the **Gallatin Valley Bicycle Club,** provides excellent topographical information and charts the most frequented trails northwest of town off Bridger Canyon Road and south of town in the Hyalite Canyon.

CROSS-COUNTRY SKIING

See also Lone Mountain Ranch in Section 4, "The Gallatin Valley."

Bohart Ranch Cross-Country Ski Center

16621 Bridger Canyon Rd., Bozeman, MT 59715. ☎ **406/586-9070.**

Bohart Ranch is the ideal place for the cross-country skier, with its beautiful scenery and wildlife. The ski center has nearly 20 miles of groomed and tracked trails for both diagonal and skating techniques, with a series of looped trails. Cross-country skiers of all skill levels will love this ranch. In summer, it is a perfect vacation destination for hiking enthusiasts and hard-core athletes, with several biathlons held throughout the summer months.

DOWNHILL SKIING

See also Big Sky in Section 4, "The Gallatin Valley."

Bridger Bowl

15795 Bridger Canyon Rd., Bozeman, MT 59715. ☎ **406/587-2111** or 800/223-9609. For snow conditions, call 406/586-2389. December–April. Lift tickets $25 adults ($21 half-day), seniors $15, children 12 and under $10.

Just 16 miles north of Bozeman is one of the better ski areas in the state, though Big Sky, south of Bozeman, is better known and more popular. Bridger Bowl provides excellent skiing without crowds, and the price for a lift ticket is a deal. With a base elevation of 6,100 feet, snow is seldom a problem. A vertical drop of 2,000 feet makes this an excellent place for the expert skier (extreme skiers can have a go at "The Ridge"), and the 2.5-mile run is great for beginners. For the Olympic wannabe, a new NASTAR race course allows you to compare your times with some of the best skiers in the world ($3 for two runs). Bridger Bowl can handle 5,100 people per hour on five double chair lifts and one pony lift, so waiting in line is rare. Rental

Bozeman

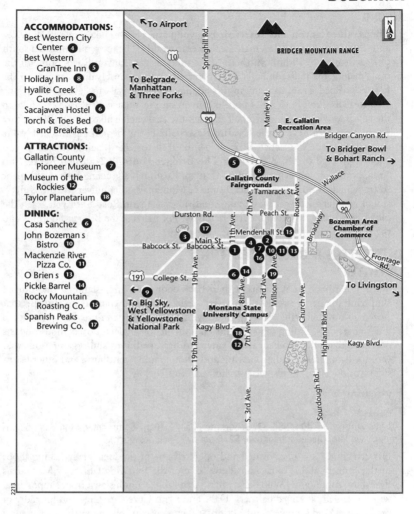

ACCOMMODATIONS:
Best Western City
  Center ❹
Best Western
  GranTree Inn ❺
Holiday Inn ❽
Hyalite Creek
  Guesthouse ❾
Sacajawea Hostel ❻
Torch & Toes Bed
  and Breakfast ❿⁹

ATTRACTIONS:
Gallatin County
  Pioneer Museum ❼
Museum of the
  Rockies ⑫
Taylor Planetarium ⑱

DINING:
Casa Sanchez ❻
John Bozeman's
  Bistro ❿
Mackenzie River
  Pizza Co. ⑪
O'Brien's ⑬
Pickle Barrel ⑭
Rocky Mountain
  Roasting Co. ⑮
Spanish Peaks
  Brewing Co. ⑰

packages are available in the ski shop for $15 and day care is available for around $40. Lessons start at $20 for a class and go up to $45 for one-and-a-half-hour private lessons.

FISHING

For fishing accesses, see "Ennis: Getting Outside," later in this chapter; a list of outfitters and information about fishing regulations can be found later in this section.

GOLF

Bridger Creek Golf Course

1071 Storymill Rd. ☎ **406/586-4866.**

This brand-new public course has nine holes, a practice tee, and a putting green. Like most area courses, it is open from sunup to sundown. Two private 18-hole courses, Riverside Country Club (☎ 406/586-2251) and Valley View Golf Course (☎ 406/586-2145), offer reciprocation with other clubs.

HIKING

The Hyalite Canyon and Reservoir is a wonderful place to hike, scale small peaks, and take in some of the Bozeman area's scenic wealth. The reservoir is located south of Bozeman on S. 19th; from there, it's 7 miles to the Canyon Road. Some of the trails include the **Palisade Falls Trail,** located 12 miles up Hyalite Canyon on the East Fork Road. From the canyon, it's about a half-mile walk to Palisade Falls. The **Grotto Falls Trail** is 13 miles up the canyon on the West Fork Road. The hike to the falls is less than a mile and a half. For a more challenging hike, try the **Blackmore Recreation Area next to the Hyalite Reservoir**. From the parking area at Hyalite you can take the somewhat difficult 5-mile trail to Lake Blackmore and, if you choose, proceed to Mt. Blackmore. **The Bridger Foothills National Recreation Area,** northwest of town on Bridger Canyon Road, has a grueling hike to the giant *M* (much like the one in Missoula, home of Montana's other university, the University of Montana). To get there, take the Bridger Canyon Road until you reach the picnic area just across from the fish hatchery. For maps of the Bridger Foothills and the Hyalite Canyon area, see "Biking" above.

OUTFITTERS & ORGANIZED TRIPS

OUTFITTERS

With blue-ribbon trout steams at their back door and a long-standing tradition of supplying the best gear and even better advice, it should come as no surprise that Bozeman outfitters rank right up there with the very finest in providing top-notch guiding services, fishing schools, and equipment for anglers. Bozeman also boasts outfitters that offer excellent whitewater rafting expeditions and organizations that sponsor llama treks, wildlife viewing and photography workshops, and other learning vacations. (For details, see "Organized Trips" below.)

Fly-fishing

The River's Edge

2012 N. 7th Ave. ☎ **406/586-5373.** Summer, daily 7:30am–6pm; winter, Mon–Sat 9:30am–6pm, closed Sun. Guided trip for two, $275 per day (includes lunch).

His dad, Bud Lilly, once owned and operated one of the premier fly-fishing shops in the country and is today considered one of the founding fathers of Montana's fly-fishing community. Who better than Greg Lilly to run his own trout shop? Along with his equally seasoned partners, Dave and Lynn Corcoran, Greg and his cadre of professional guides provide instruction and guided trips on any of the area streams as well as fly-fishing schools and equipment rentals. And, just like his dad, he'll give you a map detailing area streams and tackle suggestions just for walking in the door. The River's Edge also showcases a wide selection of top-quality outdoor clothing and sporting gifts.

Montana Troutfitters Orvis Shop

1716 W. Main. ☎ **406/587-4707.** Summer, Mon–Sat 8am–7pm, Sun 8am–4pm; winter, Mon–Sat 9am–6pm. Guided trip for two, $270 per day (includes lunch).

This fly-fishing shop, which opened in 1978, is Bozeman's oldest and Montana's only full-line Orvis shop. Owner and outfitter Dave Kumlien, who started guiding in 1974, cites experience and instruction as his shop's two strongest points. The comprehensive Orvis training programs coupled with Kumlien's own "mini" schools are a training combination that's hard to beat. Guides have access to several private streams and also offer instruction for beginners, including a four-day school held at the Gallatin Gateway Inn.

R.J. Cain & Co. Outfitters
24 E. Main. ☎ **406/587-9111.** Summer, daily 8am–6pm; winter, Mon–Sat 9:30am–5:30pm, Sun noon–4pm. Guided trip for two, $260 per day (includes lunch).

In addition to their downtown Bozeman location, R.J. Cain & Co. also operates another shop on the Madison, about ¹/₂ mile south of Ennis on Hwy. 287. Randy Cain and his staff of licensed professional guides provide guiding services on streams that include the Madison, Gallatin, Yellowstone, Big Hole, Jefferson, Bighorn, and Missouri.

Whitewater Rafting

Montana Whitewater
P.O. Box 1552, Bozeman, 59771. ☎ **406/763-4465** or 800/799-4465. Evenings and off-season, ☎ **406/587-1764.** Half-day trips range in price from $32–40; full days from $60–85 (less for children 12 and under). Reservations should be made at least two weeks in advance.

The Gallatin, Yellowstone, and Boulder Rivers play host to Montana Whitewater rafters, through whom you can choose your level of adventure. Want a thrilling half-day trip? Then run the Gallatin through the heart of some of Montana's wildest whitewater. How about a more leisurely pace, where you can take in the stunning scenery of the nearby Absaroka Range? The full-day Boulder trip is just the ticket. Montana Whitewater's kayak school has programs for private and group instruction and they also offer climbing and hiking programs as well as customized trips for special occasions.

ORGANIZED TRIPS

Learning Expeditions

Land Yacht Charters
1765 Alaska Road South, Belgrade, MT 59714. ☎ **800/517-8243.** 4-night, 3-day package (based on double occupancy) is $350 per person; group discounts for 10 or more. DISC, MC, V. All trips include shuttle service to and from Gallatin Field Airport. Reservations should be made at least two weeks in advance.

This company provides a series of trips called Northern Rockies Tours which include customized packages for a wide variety of interests. Participants can choose from packages that explore historic Old West towns, wildlife viewing and photography, history, and geology. The most popular category—wildlife and photography—takes you on a meandering drive from West Yellowstone into Yellowstone National Park and on to the Grand Tetons and Jackson, Wyoming.

Led by knowledgeable, seasoned professionals, the trips include daily driving days, short enough so that you can stray from the pavement and enjoy your surroundings, and hotel accommodations. Although buses are available for large groups, most tours average 6 to 10 people.

Northern Rockies Natural History
P.O. Box 42, Bozeman, MT 59771. ☎ **406/586-1155.** Half-day excursion, $65 per person; Full-day, $125 per person. No credit cards. Reservations should be made three months in advance for multi-day trips.

Who better to guide you through one of the most pristine wildlife habitats in the country than a wildlife biologist with over 20 years of experience in the Rockies? Ken Sinay, owner and outfitter for Northern Rockies Natural History Wildlife Expeditions, is your enthusiastic host for a wide variety of eco-friendly wildlife viewing expeditions and wildland recreation opportunities. Take the personalized "Fur Trade" river float at the Missouri Headwaters and enjoy an ambient discussion of the abundant wildlife and waterfowl as you relive the history of Lewis and Clark and the area's early fur traders, and relax in solitude in a spectacular river setting. Other standard regional adventures include exploring the ecosystems of the Paradise and Gallatin Valleys and Yellowstone National Park, from their wildlife habitats and natural history to their absolutely stunning scenery. Full-day trips include guide, transportation, binoculars and spotting scopes, backcountry tours, and lunch.

Discovery Vacations
MSU Office of Extended Studies, 204 Culbertson Hall, Bozeman, MT 59717. ☎ 406/994-4930. Courses range in length from 2–4 days; prices from $125–$750. DISC, MC, V. Reservations should be made one month in advance.

This summertime weekend program, offered by Montana State University's Office of Extended Studies, gives participants an opportunity to benefit from the university's resident experts. Don't be scared away by unpleasant memories of summer school; these classrooms are definitely outdoors and no tests are given. Recent offerings included "Canoes and Campfires: A Lewis and Clark Adventure" and "Placer Gold, Copper Glance, and Steel Rails: Historic Mining and Railways in Montana." Other enticing subjects are: fly-fishing Montana's Gallatin Valley, identifying southwestern Montana's diverse bird population, and exploring the geologic evolution of the Bozeman area. Participants can choose to stay in the dorms at MSU or at the Comfort Inn at a reduced rate.

Yellowstone Mountain Guides
P.O. Box 3006, Bozeman, 59772. ☎ 406/388-0148. Guided trips from June to October include all activities and meals and start at $240 per person, per day, for a 4–10 day trip. No credit cards. Reservations should be made three months in advance.

Since 1979, Steve and Patty Gamble have been leading pack trips into the Yellowstone backcountry, an area the Gambles like to remind their guests only one-half of 1 percent of the park's visitors ever venture into. Recognized for their low-impact, innovative camps, the Gambles take into account their customers' interests and abilities and plan trips accordingly, including any or all of the following activities: fly-fishing, horseback riding, photographing wildlife and wildflowers, and hiking through pristine mountain wilderness. Full gourmet meals in the kitchen tent might feature grilled leg of lamb or fresh seafood, each planned with their guests' preferences in mind. Ask them to send their "Yellowstone Guide Lines," a seasonal newsletter. It will make you feel a part of their Yellowstone family before you ever arrive and is guaranteed to make you long for their special brand of campfire camaraderie.

Llama Trekking

✪ Yellowstone Llamas
Box 5042, Bozeman, MT 59717. ☎ 406/586-6872. $150 per day, per person. Average length of trip: 3–5 days. No credit cards. 10 departures between July 1–Labor Day; usually fully booked by April.

This unique backcountry adventure combines the simplicity of a rugged hike with the civilization of fine dining and no-impact camping. Treks travel into Yellowstone and other parts of the surrounding area. A typical day begins with a hearty breakfast before heading at a comfortable pace to the next campsite, where the guides set up camp and take care of the llamas. Afternoons are spent at your leisure, exploring alpine surroundings, before a gourmet dinner is served (which includes wine and hors d'oeuvres). A popular 8-mile trip heads for the Black Canyon of the Yellowstone and some of the best trout fishing in the area. Longer trips to Campfire Lake in Montana's Crazy Mountains, or the Thorofare Region of Yellowstone are scenically highlighted by dense lodgepole pines, meadows of wildflowers, and sparkling lakes. No experience with llamas is necessary, but hikers are expected to be able to walk an average of 5 miles each day.

For Women Only
Rainbow Adventures
15033 Kelly Canyon Rd, Bozeman, MT 59715. ☎ 406/587-3883 or 800/804-8686.

This company's location in the Bozeman area makes them ideally situated for many of the trips they conduct, although they also coordinate international excursions to exotic locales the world over. If you want to be a modern-day cowgirl for a week, try the Montana Cowgirl Sampler, a great beginner trip. Accommodations include hotels and ranches (no camping!) and the activities range from exploring old ghost towns to soaking in nearby hot springs. If photography is more to your liking, sign up for the Fall Wildlife Camera Safari, a one-week trip through elk, bison, deer, and moose habitats where the sights and sounds of autumn compete for your attention. Most trips in the Bozeman area cost from $1,300–$1,600, although international trips—and these are equally as spectacular as the forays into Montana and Wyoming—are considerably more expensive. Meals and accommodations vary from trip, to trip, so call for details. There is a no-smoking policy.

EQUIPMENT & SUPPLIES
A four-season recreational center, Bozeman knows sports. If you want to explore the Bozeman area on your own, check out these local shops for gear and advice.

Chalet Sports
108 W. Main. ☎ 406/587-4595. Summer, Mon–Fri 9am–8pm, Sat 9am–6pm, Sun 10am–5pm; winter, Mon–Fri 9am–8pm, Sat–Sun 8:30am–6pm.

One of Bozeman's oldest sporting-goods stores, Chalet Sports is conveniently located across the street from the Baxter Hotel in, appropriately enough, one of Bozeman's oldest buildings. Although they sell top-of-the-line equipment for all sports, they also have a thorough rental program, providing Proflex suspension bikes, in-line skates, skis, and snowboards according to the season. Protective gear is provided at no additional cost.

The Round House Ski and Sports Center
1422 W. Main. ☎ 406/587-1258. Summer, Mon–Thurs 9am–6pm, Fri 9am–9pm, Sat 9am–6pm, Sun 10am–5pm; winter, Mon–Thurs 8:30am–6pm, Fri 8:30am–8pm, Sat 9am–6pm, Sun 8:30am–5pm.

Bicycles and skis are the primary focus here, with bike repair and ski tuning playing a big part in the store's dedication to service. Complete lines of hiking and camping equipment can be found as well as an array of shoes and sports sandals. Ski and mountain bike rentals are available; skis, by the half- and full-day; bikes, by the hour and the day. Eight- to 10-men rafts can also be rented for a mere $50 per day, including life jackets and oars.

Northern Lights Trading Company
1716 W. Babcock. ☎ 406/586-2225. Summer, Mon–Fri 9am–8pm, Sat 9am–6pm, Sun 10am–5pm; winter, Mon–Fri 9am–7pm, Sat 9am–6pm, Sun 10am–5pm.

This high-end outdoor specialty shop will outfit you from head to toe no matter what your interest. Their complete lines of backpacking, skiing, water sports, and camping equipment (you can even rent a tent and a sleeping bag) feature any accessory you might need as well as the complementary clothing required. Canoes and kayaks can be rented for less than $100 a week; daily rates are also available.

SPECIAL EVENTS

College National Finals Rodeo

Brick Breeden Field House, MSU Campus. ☎ **406/994-4813** or 800/447-0507 for more information on event dates and times. Occurs annually in mid-June. Reserved tickets, $10.

Long recognized as Montana's largest city with a proven rodeo tradition, Bozeman pulls in the best collegiate rodeo cowboys from around the country at this annual event. Sanctioned by the National Intercollegiate Rodeo Association, the weeklong event occurs in mid-June with a kickoff parade down Main Street. College scholarships are handed out as prizes once the bucking stops, with 11 regions from across the nation competing.

The Sweet Pea Festival

Throughout Bozeman. ☎ **406/586-4003.** The first full weekend in August.

Begun in the early 1900s, the Sweet Pea Festival was held in honor of the wild sweet peas that grew in and around Bozeman. It was a small, unassuming celebration of local flavor like any other around the country. Over the past few years, however, it has blossomed into one of Montana's premier celebrations of music and the performing arts. The festival has become so big that organizers have ceased all advertising and have made no plans to promote the event outside of Bozeman in the near future. The event itself is an eclectic blend of music, food, and performing arts that takes place all over town. It's not uncommon to hear all kinds of music, from baroque to reggae, and see Montana State's "Shakespeare in the Park" troupe perform one of the Bard's great dramas outdoors. Plenty of food, plenty of fun, and plenty of people.

SEEING THE SIGHTS

As well as being a center for outdoor activities, Bozeman offers a surprising number of indoor educational experiences for people of all ages. Its museums highlight everything from the most massive prehistoric creatures and the tiniest microcomputer chips to the fascinating history of early pioneer life in the West.

Museum of the Rockies

600 W. Kagy Blvd. ☎ **406/994-DINO.** Admission $6 adults, $4 children 5–18, free for children under five; $2.50 planetarium. Winter, Mon–Sat 9am–5pm, Sun 12:30–5pm; summer (Memorial Day to Labor Day), daily 8am–8pm. Closed Thanksgiving, Christmas, and New Year's Day. The Taylor Planetarium is open daily and Friday and Saturday nights; call for a schedule of show times.

This museum on the campus of Montana State University provides an interesting look into the past and continues to be an important center for paleontological research in the West, an area rich in the fossilized remains of prehistoric creatures. Its resident paleontologist, Jack Horner, discovered fossilized clutches of dinosaur eggs in 1978 near Choteau, Montana, and it is this Egg Mountain scene, re-created for museum visitors, that begins your journey through the museum's Berger Dinosaur Hall and its interpretive history from prehistoric times to the present.

A display overlooking Berger Hall includes fossils from current dig sites when available. Native American history is explored in "Enduring Peoples" an exhibit in permanent collection of the museum that includes authentic clothes, tools, and weapons from Montana's indigenous peoples. "Montana on Record," focuses on area and statewide history, with interpretive displays and artifacts ranging from a newspaper account of John Bozeman's murder to a fully-furnished 1930s home. An upstairs gallery highlights art from area residents, and other galleries are devoted to traveling exhibits. Also at the museum and almost as popular as the dinosaurs is **Taylor Planetarium,** a state-of-the-art, 40-foot domed multimedia theater whose computer graphics simulator provides the illusion of flying through space in three dimensions. Programs take you from the evening sky to the farthest galaxies and are enhanced by superb visual effects and sound. Although shows change regularly, popular features include Native American Skies in Winter, a specially designed program for children, and laser light shows combining music with special effects.

This is a beautifully designed facility, obviously geared toward education with fascinating interactive displays. However, you may be surprised at the lack of actual fossils you'll see. Reproductions of different types of dinosaurs give you a perspective on their size and habitat, but if you want to see real fossils, plan to spend a few days exploring the smaller museums of northcentral Montana, most notably those in Jordan and at the Fort Peck Powerhouse (see Chapter 8). Though noticeably lacking in big-budget funding, you will be amazed at the fossils you'll find in these out-of-the-way museums.

American Computer Museum

234 E. Babcock. ☎ **406/587-7545.** Admission $3 adults, $2 children 6–12, free for children under six. Sept–May, Tue–Wed, Fri–Sat 12–4pm, closed Mon, Thu, and Sun; June–August, Mon–Sun 10am–4pm. Closed on major holidays.

This unique museum traces the history of computing technologies from the abacus to the Apple. If you've ever taken electrical tape to the VCR and covered up the flashing clock, this is the place for you. Over 4,000 years of computing circuits are fully explained, from those found in watches and microwaves to automatic bank tellers. Though you won't find any T-Rexs here, you can view computing's dinosaurs: slide rules and room-size computers with a mere fraction of the power of today's superpowered miniatures.

Gallatin County Pioneer Museum

317 W. Main. ☎ **406/585-1311.** Free admission. Oct–May, Tue–Fri 11am–4pm, Sat 1–4pm; June–September, Mon–Fri 10am–4:30pm, Sat 1–4pm. Closed Sun.

This museum gives an excellent perspective on early pioneer life in Montana, from its home in an old jail building—a murderer was hanged here in 1924—to the authentic homestead cabin on the premises. A display model of Fort Ellis, a military fort completed in 1867 and abandoned in 1886, is complemented by photos of the post and artifacts from its original site east of Bozeman. Geneology enthusiasts will enjoy poring over photo and family archives in the Solveig Sales Memorial Library located in the former women's jail on the museum's second floor. The museum's bookstore stocks informative pamphlets and other hard-to-find historical information. Listed on the National Register of Historic Places, the Pioneer Museum also pays tribute to Native American culture and farming practices.

SHOPPING

Bozeman's historic district on **Main Street**—from the intersection at 7th Ave. to I-90—prides itself on an eclectic collection of specialty shops, restaurants, galleries, and retail stores. There's not a finer bookstore anywhere in the state than the **Country Bookshelf,** 28 W. Main, an expansive store with the most complete collection of Montana and Western literature you'll find. Check out the sale books on the second floor for outstanding finds or let your children browse the extensive children's section. **Poor Richard's News,** 33 W. Main, is a used bookstore and tobacco shop.

Locals used to point out with pride that the **Leaf and Bean,** 35 W. Main, was owned by Glenn Close's sister Jessie. She has since sold the chic coffeehouse but it remains one of the best places downtown to hang out and savor an espresso or cup of gourmet tea. For some mountain music, check out **Cactus Records,** 29 W. Main. Satisfy your sweet tooth with homemade confections at the **Candy Store,** 8 E. Main, or **Jonae's Chocolate Factory,** 229 E. Main. **McCracken's,** 131 E. Main, and **Country West,** 137 E. Main, both specialize in traditional Western wear with lines that include Tony Lama, Acme, Woolrich, and the ubiquitous Wrangler. Located at 115 E. Main, **Paisley-Merritt** is an upscale resortwear boutique. **Montana Dry Goods,** 30 W. Main, will dress you in casual Montana fashion without making you look as if you just stepped off the set of *A River Runs Through It.* **Miller's Jewelry,** 2 E. Main, is the downtown source for genuine Montana yogo sapphires. Need a souvenir of your trip to Big Sky country? Check out the offerings at the **Montana Gift Corral,** 237 E. Main, many of them made by Montana craftspeople. Organic cotton casuals, pottery, and body products can be found at **Accents West,** 42 W. Main. **Crossroads,** 27 E. Main, is a combination gourmet kitchen shop and wine purveyor. At **T. Charbonneau's Trading Co.,** 402 E. Main you can browse through furniture, gifts, and clothing with a Montana twist. Blackpowder firearms are for sale at **Wolf Creek Trading Company,** 2 W. Main, along with cowboy collectibles and local art: pottery, jewelry, wall hangings, and more. **Montana Woolen Shop,** 8703 Huffine Lane, has car robes, blankets, sweaters, and other American wool products, all at discount prices. **Main Mall,** at 2825 W. Main, and **University Square,** 200 S. 23rd, are both multipurpose shopping centers with major department stores, restaurants, and specialty shops.

WHERE TO STAY

If you want to make the most of your Bozeman experience, consider staying at one of the area's guest ranches or bed-and-breakfast inns. Unlike most major hotel chains, they are situated in some of the area's most pristine settings and offer a more personal connection to the land and the people who make this area their home. However, if hotels are more your style, Montana's statewide **Room Search Network** provides visitors with a 24-hour reservation service. Call 800/869-7666 to take advantage of this free service.

HOTELS

Best Western GranTree Inn

1325 N. 7th Ave., Bozeman, MT 59715. ☎ **406/587-5261** or 800/624-5865. 102 units. A/C TV TEL. Summer $78–$98 double, winter $58–$66 double. AE, DC, DISC, MC, V.

Located just off I-90 at N. 7th, the GranTree's facility includes a full-service restaurant and coffee shop, Jacuzzi and pool, lounge and casino. Recently refurbished, the hotel's rooms are clean and spacious. Airport shuttle service is complimentary.

Best Western City Center

507 W. Main, Bozeman, MT 59715. ☎ **406/587-3158** or 800/528-1234. 65 units. A/C TV TEL. Summer $65–$80 double, winter $45–$60 double. AE, CB, DC, DISC, MC, V.

Although considerably smaller than Bozeman's other hotels, the Best Western City Center's units are exceptionally comfortable and are all outfitted with queen-size beds. Guests can make use of the facility's indoor pool and Jacuzzi. Although it has no restaurant of its own, the City Center is connected to the Black Angus Steakhouse. The

4B's Family Restaurant, a Montana chain that resembles Denny's, is located across the street, and is open 24 hours.

Holiday Inn

5 Baxter Lane, Bozeman, MT 59715. ☎ 406/587-4561. 178 units. A/C TV TEL. Summer $75–$90 double, winter $60–$80 double. AE, DC, DISC, MC, V.

The Holiday Inn is Bozeman's largest, full-service hotel with 178 guest rooms. Rooms are standard fare, with the exception of two that feature in-room Jacuzzis. There is a large indoor pool and nautilus weights for the health-conscious. The hotel is conveniently located off the interstate at N. 7th Ave., and offers a complimentary airport shuttle.

BED-AND-BREAKFASTS

Hyalite Creek Guesthouse

P.O. Box 4308, Bozeman, MT 59772-4308. ☎ 406/585-0557. 1 guesthouse, 2 bedrooms. TEL. $95 for two persons; $145 for four. Special rates are also available. AE, MC, V. Reserve at least one to two months in advance.

This charming guest house sits back from Hyalite Creek in a landscaped, wooded setting. You'll feel as if you're far removed from the city, yet Bozeman's downtown historic district is a mere five minute drive away. The guest house, though small, has a remarkably spacious feel with its high-ceilinged great room. The master bedroom's bay window looks out onto the creek, a spectacular place to view an early-morning sunrise or listen to the softly running water and windchimes. You'll feel as if you're in a treehouse in the upstairs bedroom or on its private deck, a great place for reading or watching birds or ducks. Though breakfast isn't included, a fully outfitted kitchen enables you to prepare your own food.

✪ Torch & Toes Bed and Breakfast

309 S. Third Ave., Bozeman, MT 59715. ☎ 406/586-7285. 3 suites, 1 carriage house. $75 double, $85 carriage house, based on double occupancy ($10 each additional person). All rates include a full breakfast. Corporate rates available. MC, V.

This unpretentious B&B has a great sense of humor and is conveniently located near downtown Bozeman in the historic Bon Ton district, a quiet residential area. From an eclectic mix of sixties furnishings in the downstairs TV and sitting rooms to the toy crow that hangs on the door of one of the upstairs guest rooms, this is the kind of house where every nook and cranny holds interesting discoveries. It's only natural that the interests of Ron and Judy Hess would be reflected in their home: Sketches of world-famous buildings abound (Ron is an architectural professor at MSU), and handmade rugs and fabrics adorn floors and walls (Judy is a weaver). In addition to the B&B's three upstairs rooms, there is a 1906 carriage house with a galley kitchen in the backyard that is perfect for families or groups of friends.

A HOSTEL

Sacajawea International Backpackers Hostel

405 W. Olive St., Bozeman, MT 59715. ☎ 406/586-4659. 10 bunks. $10 per person. No credit cards.

These bunk-style accommodations are located in a quiet residential neighborhood near the campus of Montana State University. Bunk rooms are co-ed, meaning that couples can stay together. Full kitchen and bath facilities are available to guests. Laundry facilities are on the premises.

CAMPING

The Bozeman KOA (☎ 406/587-3030) is the city's largest campground, with sites for 50 tents and 100 RVs. Amenities include a natural hot springs pool, laundry, and store, along with rental cabins and tepees. It's located 8 miles south of Belgrade on MT 85. **Bear Canyon** (☎ 406/587-1575; exit 313) and **Sunrise Campground** (☎ 406/587-4797; exit 309), though comparable in amenities to the KOA, are scenic public campgrounds within the **Bozeman Ranger District** (☎ 406/587-6920) include Langhor, located in the Hyalite Canyon 11 miles south of Bozeman with handicapped-accessible fishing and fantastic views; Spanish Creek, south of Bozeman with access into the nearby wilderness area; and Battle Ridge, a scenic campground in the Bridger Mountains 22 miles north of Bozeman on Hwy. 86. Other campgrounds in the Bozeman district offer fishing on the Gallatin and hiking trails; contact the ranger district for more information.

WHERE TO EAT

The Bacchus Pub

105 W. Main. ☎ **406/586-1314.** Most items $5–$12. AE, MC, V. Daily 5–10pm. AMERICAN.

Located downtown in the old Baxter Hotel, the Pub features a menu full of salads, sandwiches, burgers, and pastas, with calorie counters below each item so you know what you're getting in the way of sodium and fat grams. But don't think that everything on the menu is a health platter. The Ton O' Cheeseburger is a delicious burger topped with cheddar, Swiss, and mozzarella cheeses, that can also be topped with sautéed mushrooms. For pasta lovers, the scampi pasta primavera is a must: plenty of vegetables and shrimp, without sacrificing your fat intake. The wine list is adequate, but there are plenty of imported and domestic beers to choose from.

Banana Bay Bar & Grill

2825 W. Main (Bozeman Main Mall). ☎ **406/587-0484.** Most items $5–$12. AE, DISC, MC, V. Mon–Sat 11:30am–2:30pm, 5:30–9:30pm, Sun 12–7:30pm. AMERICAN.

Yes, it's located in the mall. But don't let that stop you. Malls can hide some pretty unique places, and this is a case in point. Decorated in a tropical theme, Banana Bay has a casual atmosphere that's abetted by a lively bar. The service is great, the portions are filling, and the beer and wine lists are above average. The Bay's barbecue ribs are some of the best around, and the pasta dishes are mainstays.

Casa Sanchez

719 S. 9th at College. ☎ **406/586-4516.** Most items $6–$9. DISC, MC, V. Mon–Fri 11am–10pm; Sat noon–10pm, Sun 5–9:30pm. MEXICAN.

This crowded house is home to the best Mexican food in Bozeman. If you consider yourself a nacho connoisseur, Ron's Nachos has what you're looking for: a plate full of chips, shredded chicken, salsa, and jalapeños, topped with mounds of guacamole and sour cream. Burritos, enchiladas, chimichangas, and tacos are the basic food groups on the Casa Sanchez menu; the occasional tostado is thrown in for good measure. All dinners come with a plate of refried beans and Spanish rice.

John Bozeman's Bistro

242 E. Main. ☎406/587-4100. Most items $10–$18. AE, CB, DC, DISC, MC, V. Tues–Fri 10am–9:30pm, Sat 8am–9:30pm, Sun 8am–1pm. Closed Mon. CONTEMPORARY AMERICAN.

This is perhaps the most popular fine dining experience in town, largely because of the unabashed zeal with which the resident chefs cook. They're not afraid to prepare anything, and pretension is the only thing they don't do well. The eclectic menu is worth marveling over; it ranges from an innovative Jamaican Jerk chicken breast to a classic London Broil and even includes a few interesting vegetarian entrées. The Santa Fe Setup (a polenta cake with red beans and rice) and the Healthy Happy Bowl (stir-fried vegetables and soba noodles topped with marinated tofu) are just a couple of our favorites. The atmosphere is a cut above casual.

✪ Mackenzie River Pizza Co.

232 E. Main. ☎ **406/587-0055.** Reservations not accepted. Most items $5–$15. AE, MC, V. Weekdays 11:30am–9pm, Fri–Sat 11:30am–10pm, Sun 5–9pm. PIZZA.

Not one of the older establishments in town, Mackenzie River does pizza in a decidedly new way. You've just got to get past the funky, slightly overdone Western-style decor (there's a log structure in the middle of the dining room), to experience it. The tomato-based pizzas are delicious, and there are plenty of old standbys with traditional toppings. But wait till you see the pesto-based pizzas from the "Back Forty" side of the menu. The Athenian is a delicious mix of spinach, tomatoes, feta, and black olives. The Mexican comes with salsa, fajita chicken, and jalapeño peppers. The Angler comes with spinach, sliced almonds, and lightly smoked trout. If you like their pizza and wish you could order it from home, Mackenzie River will overnight it. The delivery charge is $15.

✪ O'Brien's

312 E. Main. ☎ **406/587-3973.** Most items $12–$17. DISC, MC, V. Daily 5–9:30pm. CONTEMPORARY AMERICAN.

Less experimental than John Bozeman's Bistro, O'Brien's is where you'll find such deliciously prepared traditional favorites as pasta with red sauce or filet mignon, as well as a few entrées that are influenced by their Montana surroundings, such as charbroiled breast of pheasant topped with a huckleberry cream sauce, shallots, and mushrooms.

It's the atmosphere and decor (which bears not the slightest resemblance to Western rustic), that separates O'Brien's from other eateries in Bozeman. No saddles or polished pine, just a quiet, dimly lit dining room where strains of classical music can be heard.

Pickle Barrel

809 W. College. ☎ **406/587-2411.** Most items $2–$6. No credit cards. Daily 11am–11pm. SANDWICHES.

For a big sandwich, a bag of chips, and a Coke, this is the place to go. It's no coincidence that the Pickle Barrel is located across the street from the college—the customers are mainly college students on tight budgets. The place is tiny, so most people just grab a sandwich and split, but in the late spring, the benches outside are perfect for eating and spilling condiments on your lap.

Rocky Mountain Roasting Co.

111 E. Mendenhall. ☎ **406/586-2428.** Most items $5 and under. DISC, MC, V. Sun–Tue 6:30am–10pm, Wed–Sat 6:30am–11pm. Closed Mon. COFFEE.

This isn't exactly a restaurant, but it *is* a great quiet spot for freshly brewed gourmet coffee and great pastries. It's similar to the Leaf and Bean in Livingston, but attracts a more laid-back crowd.

Spanish Peaks Brewing Co.

120 N. 19th. ☎ **406/585-2296.** Lunch and dinner items $6–$15. DISC, MC, V. Mon–Sat 11:30am–2:30pm, 5:30–10:30pm, Sun 5–10:30pm. ITALIAN.

Spanish Peaks doesn't serve the best nachos in town, or the hottest fajitas, or anything having to do with refried beans. The name comes from the nearby wilderness area, and the food is Italian. What Spanish Peaks is really known for is its microbrewed beer, Black Dog Ale.

In the Italian Caffe, brick-oven pizzas, pastas, and seafoods are served, but if it's the house beverage you've come for, try the more casual Ale House—it's the ideal spot in which to savor their microbrewed gem.

BOZEMAN AFTER DARK
THE PERFORMING ARTS

The Bozeman Symphony performs year-round at the Willson School, frequently in concert with their Symphonic Choir. Call 406/585-9774 for event information.

Lively Arts produces a variety of cultural events in Bozeman during the year. Past events have featured music by the String Orchestra of the Rockies, as well as contemporary jazz, theater, and ballet performances. For a schedule of upcoming events, call Lively Arts at 406/994-5828.

Shakespeare in the Parks, Montana State University, Bozeman, MT 59717-0400 (☎ 406/994-5881) is a great touring company that all of Montana has come to appreciate. Based in Bozeman, the thespian troupe performs throughout the summer at some 50 communities throughout Montana, Wyoming, Idaho, and Canada. Some summer weekends find them at their Bozeman stage—located on the MSU campus on 11th Ave. near the corner of Grant St.—for "Shakespeare Under the Stars." Parking is available just north of the MSU fieldhouse.

The Vigilante Theatre Company is an upstart theater group that performs more contemporary plays. For information on current shows and venues, call 406/586-3897. **MSU's theater department** takes to the stage from September to May at the Strand Union Theatre and the Underground Theatre, both on the MSU campus. Call 406/994-3904 or 406/994-3901 for ticket information.

The Montana Ballet Company, 221 E. Main (☎ 406/587-7192), produces the Nutcracker and original ballets each season in addition to providing classes locally.

BARS AND CLUBS

Bozeman is a college town, so most of the hangouts are filled with juniors and seniors old enough to drink, or freshmen and sophomores with buddies at the door or fake IDs. **The Molly Brown,** located just off downtown at 703 W. Babcock, and the **Haufbrau,** at 22 S. 8th, are the big college hangouts. **The Cat's Paw,** 721 N. 7th, gets some pretty interesting folks and some pretty groovy acts. Arlo Guthrie has performed here, and when musical groups play relatively small venues in Bozeman, they usually rock the Cat's Paw. **Spanish Peaks,** 120 N. 19th, is a great place for a quiet evening and a Black Dog Ale.

3 The Madison River Valley: Three Forks & Ennis

The Madison Valley is a place almost of myth where anglers the world over come to fish its rivers and streams in a valley full of spectacular mountain scenery. Locals have seen this sparsely settled valley turn into a real estate shrine virtually overnight as those with the wherewithal to stay decide they don't have to leave—at least not for long.

The main attraction is the Madison River, which flows through the valley at the base of the Madison range, a stretch of peaks that runs toward Yellowstone Park. Besides the phenomenal fishing, the historical significance of the Madison Valley makes it a worthy tourist destination. There's Missouri Headwaters State Park at the confluence of the Jefferson, Madison, and Gallatin Rivers, where Lewis and Clark

Streamside Respect: Tips on Environmentally Friendly Trout Fishing

It's little wonder trout fishing in Montana and Wyoming continues to grow in popularity. The scenery is spectacular, the rivers plentiful, the trout abundant and wild. It truly is the Mecca of trout fishing.

Anglers need to revere and respect this special place and its unique natural resources. That means practicing environmentally friendly fishing.

Here are some points to remember while testing your skills on Montana and Wyoming's trout waters:

Practice catch-and-release. If the trout in Montana and Wyoming seem wild, that's because most are wild, the product of naturally reproducing, self-sustaining populations. This makes them stronger, larger, and more genetically superior than their hatchery cousins. The best way to maintain these renowned wild populations is to practice catch-and-release fishing. In other words, let them go alive.

Don't wade through trout spawning beds. Avoid wading into trout spawning areas, known as redds. You'll know a redd when you see it. These trout nests are located in shallow gravel areas, are circular in shape and feature a panlike depression. Often you will see adult fish holding onto a redd, either preparing to spawn, in the act of spawning, or burying eggs in the gravel.

Rainbows and cutthroats spawn in the spring, browns in the fall. Fertilized trout eggs get buried under the surface gravel and take several months to hatch. Wading through redds crushes the eggs, destroying future trout generations.

Respect streambanks and streamside vegetation. Eroding streambanks are one of trout's greatest enemies. Riparian areas—the vegetative zones along streams—represent critical habitats that must be nurtured and maintained. Trees and bushes create shade and help keep water cool. They also harbor insects and other trout foods. Vegetation holds banks and soils in place, curtailing erosion and maintaining water quality. Walk lightly and carefully on streambanks. Stay on trails. If camping, don't cut streamside vegetation for firewood.

Don't litter. Nothing can spoil a great fishing experience like garbage along the stream. Carry out all that you bring in. That's why fishing vests have big pockets. In fact, go the extra mile by carrying a trash bag in your vest and picking up litter that other, less thoughtful anglers have left behind.

Butt out. It's your business if you want to smoke while you fish, but don't fling your cigarette butts in the water or along the bank. Few things are uglier than a cigarette butt swirling around in the eddy of your favorite high-country trout pool. Carry out your butts along with the foil and wrapper.

Support trout resource conservation. Go beyond simply respecting the resource by taking an active role in protecting trout streams. The best way is by joining a conservation organization like Trout Unlimited. At $30, a TU membership is the best investment you can make to protect trout streams. If you've got the time, volunteer for local TU stream restoration projects.

With just minimal effort, you can keep Montana and Wyoming's trout streams running clear, cold, and full of trout.

—*Dave Taylor*

Dave Taylor lives in Boulder, CO., and fishes extensively throughout the Rocky Mountain West. He is chairman of Trout Unlimited's National Resource Board.

paused to name these rivers and take shelter; there's Lewis and Clark Caverns, with its spectacular underground peaks; and there's Buffalo Jump State Park, a Native American site of interest.

ESSENTIALS

GETTING THERE   The Bozeman airport, **Gallatin Field,** is the closest airport to the valley and provides daily service via **Continental** (☎ 800/525-0280), **Delta** (☎ 800/221-1212), and **Northwest** (☎ 800/225-2525). Flights from other Montana cities are available on **Horizon** (☎ 800/547-9308) and **Skywest** (☎ 800/221-1212).

Greyhound stops at the Sinclair station in Three Forks at 2 Main.

Three Forks is conveniently located on I-90, 170 miles from Billings, 30 miles from Bozeman, and 173 miles from Missoula. From Helena, take Hwy. 287. Three Forks is 66 miles away.

VISITOR INFORMATION   The address for the **Three Forks Chamber of Commerce** is P.O. Box 1103, Three Forks, MT 59752 (☎ 406/285-3198). For the **Ennis Chamber of Commerce,** write to P.O. Box 291, Ennis, MT 59729 (☎ 406/682-4388). For information on **Yellowstone Country,** Travel Montana's region that includes the Madison Valley, call 800/736-5276 or 406/446-1005.

GETTING AROUND   As elsewhere in Montana, the best way to get around is by car. If you're flying into Bozeman, you'll probably want to pick up a rental car at the airport. Several companies maintain desks there: **Avis** (☎ 406/388-6414), **Hertz** (☎ 406/388-6939), **National** (☎ 406/388-6694), and **Rent-a-Wreck** (☎ 406/587-4551). For road reports concerning the Madison Valley, call 406/586-1313; for statewide road conditions, call 800/332-6171.

GETTING OUTSIDE

From Three Forks to Quake and Hebgen Lakes along Hwy. 287, there's nothing but blissful stretches of fishing accesses along both sides of the road. Farther south, you can walk alongside stretches of the river that don't cut through private land and take in the magnificence of peaks like Sphinx just east of Ennis; or you can stuff your legs into neoprene waders and waddle out to brave the cold waters of the Madison. The first such fishing access is Cobblestone, just a few miles south of Three Forks on the right side of U.S. Hwy. 287. If you plan to base yourself in Ennis, the Valley Garden, Ennis Bridge, Burnt Tree, and Varney Bridge fishing accesses are within minutes of downtown along Hwy. 287. Between Ennis and Quake Lake, the accesses begin popping up frequently. McAtee Bridge, Wolf Creek, West Fork, and Reynolds Pass are all accessible from the roadside. Hebgen Lake, just south of the dam and Quake Lake, is a great fishing spot, but it's also used for other water sports. Outfitters in the Ennis area include **Jack River Outfitters** at Box 88, Ennis, MT 59729 (☎ 406/682-4948), the **Tackle Shop,** 127 Main St. (☎ 406/682-4263), and **R.J. Cain and Company,** on the outskirts of town (☎ 406/682-7451). In West Yellowstone, **Jacklin's Outfitters,** 105 Yellowstone Ave. (☎ 406/646-7336), "specializes in Madison River trips. Other outfitters can be found under "Bozeman: Getting Outside" above.

SEEING THE SIGHTS

○ Lewis & Clark Caverns

Located midway between Butte and Bozeman on MT Hwy. 2. ☎ **406/287-3541.** Call for additional park information or to make a group reservation. Adults $5.50, children (ages 6–11) $3. Guided tours are conducted daily May–September; weekends April–October.

These Montana caverns, named after the leaders of 1805's "Corps of Discovery," contain underground peaks to rival their aboveground counterparts. Preserved and maintained as one of the state's most interesting state parks, Lewis and Clark Caverns is sure to delight visitors of all ages. Over time, the interaction of water and limestone has created magnificent burled knobs, spear-shaped stalactites, and subterraneous columns of copper-colored dripstone. The caverns are home to a number of plants and animals that thrive in total darkness, among them the Western big-eared bat and the bushytail woodrat. Four rental cabins are available year-round and are perfect for hiking or cross-country ski getaways; they cost $25–$39. Camping and picnic facilities are available for a nominal charge.

Madison Buffalo Jump State Monument

23 miles west of Bozeman. ☎ **406/994-4042.** Free admission. Open year-round. From the Logan exit off I-90, 7 miles south on Buffalo Jump Road.

This day use–only state monument centers around a pishkun, or buffalo jump, a precipice over which Native Americans once drove herds of buffalo. Nothing sets this buffalo jump apart from others in the state, but if you've never seen one, this is a good place to take a look.

○ Missouri Headwaters State Park

Three miles east of Three Forks on I-90; east on County Road 205, 3 miles north on County Road 286. Follow the signs.

You can easily spend an hour just exploring the interpretive signage at this historic state park. Begin by following the Missouri River out from Three Forks. The headwaters themselves are no great shakes—just another river—but the sunsets from the bank of the river are nothing short of breathtaking. From the headwaters, drive back toward Three Forks where, on the opposite side of the road, you'll see a parking area with interpretive markers. Allow plenty of time to read about Lewis and Clark and Sacajawea, the young Shoshone guide, as well as early Native Americans, trappers, traders, and settlers. Camping and RV units are available as well as access to hiking, boating, and fishing.

Quake Lake

Off Hwy. 287, 43 miles south of Ennis. ☎ **406/646-7369.** Free admission. Visitor center open Memorial Day–Labor Day daily 9am–5pm.

Quake Lake is easily one of the eeriest sites in Montana. Just before midnight on August 17, 1969, a massive earthquake measuring 7.1 on the Richter scale jolted Yellowstone and the Madison River canyon, sending large chunks of mountain into the river. Tragically, a campsite just below the mountain was covered with rubble and 19 people were buried alive. Yet the rubble that fanned into the river created a dam and the aptly named Quake Lake. The visitor center off to the left of the highway offers exhibits, a viewing area, and hourly interpretive talks.

WHERE TO STAY
IN THREE FORKS

✪ Bud Lilly's Anglers Retreat

16 W. Birch, Box 983, Three Forks, MT 59752. ☎ 406/285-6690. 3 rms, 2 suites. A/C TEL. $55 double; $75–$145 suite. MC, V.

To have Bud Lilly mastermind your fishing itinerary is reason enough to stay here, but it's not the only one. Formerly a railroad hotel belonging to Mr. Lilly's mother, the Anglers Retreat has been refurbished and is now a cozy lodge. Those who fish will absolutely love it, guaranteed. (Those who don't may be happier at the Sacajawea Inn, however)

The three upstairs bedrooms share a bathroom with a claw-footed bathtub (robes are provided); each of the suites has a full bath with shower, as well as a fully equipped kitchen. Mr. Lilly's thoughtful attention to detail is evident no matter where you look: a shady deck, a backyard vegetable and flower garden (help yourself), a washer and dryer, and a comfortable TV room with an extensive library of fishing and Montana videos. But these are secondary. The big draw here is, of course, the nearby fishing. Every reservation at the Anglers Retreat includes a personalized, detailed itinerary of where to fish locally, based on your preferences and length of stay. Though Bud has surely been a respected guest at much more elegant fishing lodges around the world, his own retreat is refreshingly simple and unpretentious. Much like the man himself.

Sacajawea Inn

5 N. Main, Three Forks, MT 59752. ☎ 406/285-6515. 33 rms. TV TEL. $60–$100 double. All rates include a light continental breakfast. AE, DISC, MC, V.

The sprawling front porch of the Sacajawea is perhaps the best feature of this charming inn. If you've never sat in an oversized rocker on a breezy afternoon and watched the cars go by, this is the place to do it. Listed on the National Register of Historic Places, the Sacajawea elegantly presides over the dusty main street of Three Forks, as it has since 1910. The rooms have been renovated since then, with up-to-date amenities, but an ample amount of Old World ambience can still be found. The hotel's restaurant serves dinner year-round and breakfast and lunch during the busier summer months.

IN ENNIS

9T9 Guest Ranch

99 Gravelly Range Rd., Ennis, MT 59729. ☎ 406/682-7659. 3 rms, 1 with private bath. $45–$65 double. All rates include a full breakfast. No credit cards.

If you've ever wished you had a relative living along the Madison River then make a reservation at the 9T9: Vaughn and Judy Herrick are bound to make you feel at home, and you won't find a more accessible stretch of the Madison anywhere for the price. While comfortable and tastefully decorated, the guest rooms are not spectacular, but the views from the main floor—where you can enjoy television in the living room or just relax on the deck—certainly are. Equally impressive are breakfast and dinner. The latter is only a supper club–type affair only scheduled for certain weekends throughout the year. Reservations are required and entreès usually feature steak, chicken, or ethnic foods. Guided fishing is also available for an additional fee.

CAMPING

Missouri Headwaters State Park is host to some of the most scenic campgrounds in this part of the state, with plenty of fishing accesses. The year-round campground has 20 sites scattered along the river and numerous hiking trails. There is a minimal fee. **Three Forks KOA** is located on Hwy. 287, one mile south of exit 274 at I-90. A swimming pool, rec room, playground, and sauna will keep the entire family happy. There are 20 tent and 50 RV sites available at the seasonal campground, open May through September. **Elkhorn Store and RV Park** (☎ 406/682-4273) is located in Ennis on Hwy. 287 and is open from mid-April through November. You can get gas, purchase a hunting license, or rent a video here, and downtown Ennis is just a short drive down the street.

WHERE TO EAT
NEAR THREE FORKS

✪ Blue Willow Inn
1st and Main, Willow Creek. ☎ 406/285-6660. Reservations not accepted. Lunch $3–$6; main dinner courses $8–$16. DISC, MC, V. Daily year-round, call for hours. AMERICAN.

This place is a find. But finding it can be a problem. Located 7 miles southwest of Three Forks on the Willow Creek Road, the Blue Willow is the best restaurant in the Three Forks vicinity (don't let the bullet holes in the ceiling scare you off). Named for the china that sits over the antique cookstove, it began as the Babcock Saloon, a bar established around 1910. In 1980, the property was restored to what is now a remarkable little shelter for antiques, locals, and those who manage to find it. Montana beef is the big seller at the Blue Willow, but seafood and chicken are also on the menu. The names of the entrées come from the old mines in Pony, a small town up the road. If you plead, you may get to order one of their great burgers off the lunch menu at dinner.

IN ENNIS

Continental Divide
Main St., ☎ 406/682-7600. Reservations recommended. Main dinner courses $12–$22. MC, V. Daily in summer 6–9pm. Call for off-season dates and hours. CONTEMPORARY AMERICAN.

The food is delicious, the atmosphere casual, the service great, and the bistro setting a welcome surprise for a small Montana town. Duckling is prepared in a variety of ways, escargot appears on the appetizer menu, and Sciabica olive oil complements the bread the waiters bring to your table. Outside of the vegetarian platter (basically a stir-fry for $12), nothing on the menu is priced under $15.

✪ Wild Rose Bistro
213 E. Main St., ☎ 406/682-4717. Reservations recommended. Breakfast items $4–$9; lunch $4–$8; main dinner courses $12–$20. DISC, MC, V. Daily in summer 7am–3pm; 5:30–10pm; call for winter hours. CREATIVE AMERICAN.

The Wild Rose Bistro is the newest addition to Ennis' dining scene and not a few things make this place great. The dining room is quaint, not in an old-fashioned way, but in a close-quarters, small private dining rooms, sandstone fireplaces kind of way. An incredible dinner menu includes cappellini with snow crab in a Parmesan cream sauce, fettuccine Bolognese, and, of course, a giant Montana cut of prime rib. If you can find a spot, sit at one of the outside tables during the summer months when vibrant Montana wildflowers complement the delicious food.

4 The Gallatin Valley

Cradled between scenic mountain ranges that rise to its east and west, the Gallatin Valley is Bozeman's gateway to Yellowstone. While the Absarokas and the Gallatin mountains on its eastern border are impressive, the majestic Madison range on its western boundary is the more spectacular.

Nestled into by this lush valley, located almost exactly midway between the flourishing university town of Bozeman and the sprawling natural wonder that is Yellowstone, is Big Sky, Montana's premier resort. Big Sky encompasses three distinct areas: the Canyon, a small portion of the stretch of Hwy. 191 that lays itself out like a red carpet between Bozeman and Yellowstone; the Meadow Village, two miles west of Hwy. 191; and the Mountain Village, 8 miles further along the Lone Mountain Trail.

Its two ski resorts—Big Sky and Lone Mountain Ranch—are phenomenal, yet the great fly-fishing and whitewater rafting available in the summer months are drawing notice.

ESSENTIALS

GETTING THERE   Fly into Bozeman's **Gallatin Field** on **Delta** (☎ 800/221-1212)**, Northwest** (☎ 800/225-2525)**,** or **Frontier** (☎ 800/432-1359) for easiest access to Big Sky; commuter flights from other Montana cities are available through **Skywest** (☎ 800/221-1212) and **Horizon** (☎ 800/547-9308)**.**

From the airport, you can ride to the ski area with the **4X4 Stage,** a company that has a transportation fleet of sturdy four-wheel-drive vehicles (☎ 800/517-8243 or 406/388-6404). The ride is $20 one-way, $35 round-trip. Or you can take a taxi provided by **City Taxi** (☎ 406/586-2341); they have a calling board at Gallatin Field.

If you are traveling with a group of 10 or more people, **Karst Stages** (☎ 406/586-8567) or **Montana Motor Coach** (☎ 406/586-6625) can provide a full-sized, 48-passenger motor coach, which makes a cost-effective means of transportation.

GETTING AROUND   A car gives you the greatest flexibility in getting around this area. The following car-rental agencies are located at the airport: **Avis** (☎ 406/388-6414), **Budget** (☎ 406/388-4091), **National** (☎ 406/388-6694), **Thrifty** (☎ 406/388-3484), and **Rent-a-Wreck** (☎ 406/587-4551).

For service between condominiums, hotels, restaurants, and activities within the ski area, take the **Snowexpress,** Big Sky's local shuttle bus system which operates daily between 7am and 10pm. Skis are allowed and the service is absolutely free. The bus operates along three routes. The first completely covers the Mountain Village—condos, hotels, and restaurants. The second runs from the Mountain Village to the Meadow Village, and the third runs around the Meadow Village and through the Canyon.

WHERE TO STAY & DINE

✪ Big Sky Ski & Summer Resort
P.O. Box 160001, Big Sky, MT 59716. ☎ **406/995-5000.** Central reservations, ☎ 800/548-4486. Snow conditions, ☎ 406/995-5900. Lift tickets adult $34–$38, seniors 50% off adult rate, children 10 and under ski free (two free children's tickets with each paying adult; more than two children per paying adult, 50% off the adult rate).

Big Sky Ski Resort may well be one of the best undiscovered ski areas in the entire country. It has short lift lines, fantastic ski instruction programs for kids (who ski free if they're 10 or younger), and a close proximity to Yellowstone.

With its most recent expansion in 1995, Big Sky gained 1,200 acres of skiable terrain and two new lifts, giving it the most vertical feet of any ski area in the United States. With all this, it's not hard to see why *Snow Country* readers consistently rate Big Sky one of the country's best ski resorts, and single out its uncrowded slopes and breathtaking scenery for particular praise.

The ski area, built in the early 1970s by television news anchor and Montana native Chet Huntley, is designed around two stunning peaks: Lone Mountain and Andesite Mountain. Over 60 named runs traverse the ski area's 3,154 skiable acres and 14 lifts get you to them. One of the newest, the Lone Peak Tram, will take you a scant 15 feet from the very pinnacle of Lone Mountain, affording breathtaking views and extreme skiing, previously only accessible by hiking. Though you may have to stand in line a few minutes to get there (there are only two 15-passenger tram cars), this one is well worth the wait, even for nonskiers: An enclosed observation deck frames the panoramic views of the wide-reaching valley below. Be sure to ask about the ski resort's innovative and highly praised Ski Day Camp for ages 6–14. Kids will have so much fun on the treasure hunt they'll forget they're actually in class! Specialty workshops for snowboarders and telemarkers, a playcare center for infants, and an extensive rental and repair center are just a few more services that will ensure the perfect ski vacation.

And that's just *winter*. Summer finds visitors to Big Sky just as busy golfing, hiking, mountain biking, rafting, or riding horses. The Arnold Palmer–designed Big Sky Golf Course is an 18-hole, par 72 course that follows the meandering Gallatin River. Views abound at the 6,500-foot elevation, a magnificent course for the advanced or beginner golfer. To reserve a tee time, call 406/995-4706. Hike or mountain bike along rutted trails with views of summer's wildflowers—just don't forget to bring your camera. Raft the whitewater "Whacker Wave" along the Gallatin or saunter along a mountain trail by horseback. **Adventures Big Sky** can coordinate these and other activities during your stay. Call them at 406/995-2324.

LODGING   Several lodging choices are yours at Big Sky, ranging from modest hotel rooms and luxury condominiums to Western-style ranch cabins. All room rates are based on double-occupancy and are quoted in parentheses below; if the rates differ from peak to off-season, it is noted. Otherwise, they apply year-round.

The resort's newest facility is the **River Rock Lodge** (☎ 800/995-9966 or 406/995-2295), a well-appointed hotel in the best European boutique-style tradition. Thoughtful touches include a complimentary newspaper and continental breakfast every morning and ski area shuttle service and ski storage during winter months ($150–$250). The 200-room **Huntley Lodge** (winter, $135–$240; summer, $120–$130) and 94-unit **Shoshone Condominium Hotel** (winter, $220–$318; summer, $165–$260) are the cornerstones of the Mountain Village, and pamper the visitor in grand Western style. Weight training centers, saunas, an outdoor pool, gift shops, and ski storage complement the rustic surroundings. Call for reservations (☎ 800/548-4486 or 406/995-5000). Less expensive options include the **Golden Eagle Lodge** (☎ 800/548-4488 or 406/995-4800), in the Meadow Village adjacent to the cross-country trail system ($45–$50); and **Buck's T-4 Lodge** (☎ 800/822-4484 or 406/995-4111), just off Hwy. 191 in the Canyon ($59–$99 double, suites up to $175).

If you'd prefer to rent a condominium, check with the following management companies: **Big Sky Condominium Management** (☎ 800/831-3509 or 406/995-4560), **Golden Eagle Management** (☎ 800/548-4488 or 406/995-4800), or **Triple Creek Realty and Management** (☎ 800/548-4632 or 406/995-4848). In winter, expect to pay anywhere from $103–$706 per double; in summer, $87–$487 per double.

DINING   Big Sky offers a wide variety of dining choices. If you're in the canyon, try a down-home steak dinner for around $20 per person at **Buck's T-4**, just off Hwy. 191. A sleigh-ride dinner ($22 adults, $15 children) of mouth-watering cowboy chili at the **320 Ranch** makes for an unforgettable night out in winter; or you can settle back with the locals at the **Half Moon Saloon**, and maybe even play a game of pool or try your luck at one of the poker machines. The Meadow Village's **Cafe Edelweiss** (main dinner courses: $14–$25) is usually busy and serves great Austrian cuisine in a European atmosphere. For fresh-baked muffins or huckleberry pancakes, try the **Blue Moon Bakery** and the **Huckleberry Cafe,** two breakfast hangouts in this area. Stop off at **Uncle Milkie's** for genuine New York–style pizza and calzones.

Just a few miles up the road you'll find the **Mountain Mall,** where there are a number of affordable eateries. Look for pizza by the slice at **Levinsky's,** cool jazz and drinks at the **Caboose,** takeout Mexican at the **Tumbleweed Connection,** and a fantastic turkey club at **M.R. Hummer's.** There's also great Mandarin and Szechuan food at the **Twin Panda** located in the base village's **Arrowhead Mall.** However, for a fine dining experience to rival the scenery, splurge for dinner at the nearby **Gallatin Gateway Inn** (see below) or **Lone Mountain Ranch** (see below).

✪ Lone Mountain Ranch

P.O. Box 160069, Big Sky, MT 59716. ☎ **406/995-4644.** 24 cabins, 1 lodge, 1 house. Winter rates: cabin, $1,250–$1,800 first person, $700 each additional person; Ridgetop Lodge, $1,775 first person, $700 each additional person; Douglas Fir House, $2,500 first person, $700 each additional person. All rates are per person and include seven nights' lodging, three meals daily, an eight-day trail pass with unlimited access to the ranch's trail system, evening entertainment, a sleigh-ride dinner, a trail buffet lunch, and airport transfers. Summer rates are slightly higher. AE, DISC, MC, V.

Their promotional tag line reads "Discovery is in our nature," and if anything sets Lone Mountain apart from its guest ranch counterparts, it is their commitment to the nurturing of the mind as well as the body. The ranch sits regally between the Mountain and Meadow communities of Big Sky, with views into the Spanish Peaks Wilderness Area, a backyard playground of immense proportions. A dude ranch in summer and a premier cross-country skiing center in winter, Lone Mountain may well be the finest four-season guest ranch in all of Montana and Wyoming. Of particular distinction are its naturalist programs, bird walks, and excursions into nearby Yellowstone, not to mention its incredible food (see "Dining" below).

Summer is the ranch's busiest season with activities that are nearly limitless in number and scope. Horseback rides and guided naturalist hikes are fun ways to gain an appreciation for native plants and animals while you revel in the beauty of the natural world. An Orvis-endorsed private guest ranch, Lone Mountain's cadre of seasoned guides will show you around the area's blue-ribbon streams and high mountain lakes with great expertise.

Winter brings lycra- and wool-clad skiers to the ranch to explore their 75-km trail system. Groomed for track and skate skiing, the trail system will challenge skiers of all abilities, with PSIA-certified instructors available for individual and group lessons. For the adventurous, there are guided telemark forays into nearby Moonlight Basin, with views into the Madison range and accommodations in Mongolian yurts. And if the ranch's massage therapists are booked solid, winter fishing on the Gallatin provides a calming alternative to skiing if you want to give your muscles a break.

Lone Mountain prides itself on a family atmosphere and has put together an impressive list of activities for children of all ages. Llama walks, stream discovery programs, cave exploration, and mammal tracking will not only provide hours of fun for children, it will also help them to develop a respect for nature and wild places. And what kid wouldn't like to sleep in a tepee?

Ruddy-faced guests regale one another with stories in either the Ranch Saloon or the BK Lodge, formerly the ranch's main lodge and once its dining room.

LODGING   Guests stay for one week—Sunday to Saturday—in cabins scattered around the property. Though some are slightly larger than others, all are comfortably furnished and feature large fireplaces and rustic, Western decor. The newer Ridgetop Lodge is perfect for friends who want to vacation together and showcases native logs and river rock from the nearby Madison. Each of its six large suites includes a spacious bedroom and bathroom, a living area, and an outside deck with a fantastic view of Lone Mountain. The lodge also contains a recreation room and an expansive yet cozy living room. The smaller Douglas Fir House has three bedrooms and is ideal for bigger families.

DINING   Lone Mountain is known locally for its fine food, so expect the dining room to be packed even if you visit during the less-touristed spring or fall. Chef Gerard van Mourik specializes in the artful preparation of game, though his vegetarian dishes are equally satisfying in appearance and taste. In addition to the regular daily offerings, favorites among Lone Mountain guests are the weekly Trail Buffet, served along one of the ranch's trails on a snow-carved table, and the sleigh-ride dinners served at the ranch's North Fork cabin, complete with Western entertainment and sing-alongs. The lodge's dining room is a feast for the eyes as well, with enormous elk-antlered chandeliers hanging from the massive beams.

✪ Gallatin Gateway Inn

Box 376, Gallatin Gateway, MT 59730. ☎ **406/763-4672.** 35 rms. A/C TV TEL. $60–$100 double. All rates include a full continental breakfast. AE, DISC, MC, V.

The Gallatin Gateway Inn is a model of historical elegance that recalls the grand old days of luxury railroad travel. The hotel originally opened in the summer of 1927, when visitors from the East were beginning to flock to the nation's grandest park in large numbers. With lavish appointments that include Polynesian mahogany woodwork, decoratively carved beams, and high arched windows, the Gallatin Gateway has maintained its proud history of lavish style and refinement. Guest rooms provide a tastefully understated balance to the regal lobby and dining room, where the seasonally changing menu reflects regional specialties. Chef Erik Carr, formerly of Tra Vigne and Little Nell, prepares hearty, peasant-style dishes with an eye toward imaginative combinations and generous portions. The wine list is extensive and complements the food superbly. Look for the Gateway Inn's specialty foods at their front desk and at various Big Sky and Bozeman gourmet food stores: warm tomato chutney, fennel spice mix, and mixed summer berry jam.

5 Livingston & the Paradise Valley

Livingston is hard to peg. As recently as the early 1990s it was a sleepy town of ranchers, with one bookstore, no trendy coffee shops, and a shortage of fine restaurants. In fact, it really *was* the wild milieu of "Livingston Saturday Night," Jimmy Buffett's song about saloons full of cowhands playing pool in the rear of the bars. But, as the song seemed to predict, "it ain't the same Old West, no that's for sure." Now Livingston has come of age, much like a vibrant miniature Bozeman. This windblown city is catching on, to the delight of the tourism industry and the dismay of longtime residents. It's a problem similar to what Bozeman contends with on a more visible scale. The Paradise Valley south of town is no longer simply another gateway to Yellowstone; it, too, is a popular destination for those who seek a somewhat remote place to live, including some rather famous personalities and even a church whose name sparks instant reaction from residents. The Church Universal and Triumphant, whose headquarters is in nearby Corwin Springs, is comprised of the followers of Elizabeth Claire Prophet and has amassed quite an estate in the Paradise Valley, more than a few properties of which are located in the Livingston area. Though church members aren't a visibly evangelical lot, the community keeps its distance.

ESSENTIALS

GETTING THERE   Like every other community within 50 miles of Bozeman, Livingston's residents use Bozeman's airport, **Gallatin Field,** which offers daily service on **Continental** (☎ 800/525-0280), **Delta** (☎ 800-221-1212), and **Northwest** (☎ 800/225-2525), as well as commuter flights from other Montana cities on **Horizon** (☎ 800/547-9308) and **Skywest** (☎ 800/453-9417). It's also possible to fly into Billings' **Logan International Airport,** however.

Billings is 116 miles east along I-90. Just 26 miles east is Bozeman. Missoula is farther east along I-90 at the 228-mile marker. From the north entrance to Yellowstone National Park at Gardiner, Livingston is 53 miles north on Hwy. 89. For local road reports, call 406/586-1313; call 800/332-6171 for road conditions statewide.

Bus service into Livingston is provided by **Greyhound,** whose terminal is located at 107 W. Park (☎ 406/222-2231), just east of the old depot. Call for schedules and cities serviced.

VISITOR INFORMATION   The **Livingston Convention and Visitors' Bureau** is located at 212 W. Park in the Livingston Depot Center (☎ 406/222-0850). For information on **Yellowstone Country,** Travel Montana's region which includes Livingston, call 800/736-5276 or 406/446-1005.

GETTING AROUND   Car rental agents in Livingston include **Avis** (☎ 406/388-6414), **Hertz** (☎ 406/388-6939), **National** (☎ 406/388-6694), and **Rent-a-Wreck** (☎ 406/587-4551). All have desks at Gallatin Field.

Call for a taxi at **VIP Taxi** (☎ 406/222-0200).

GETTING OUTSIDE

Hiking in the Absarokas and the Crazy Mountains can make for a spectacular day. Some of the more popular hikes include the **Pine Creek Falls** south of town off the East River Road, the **Livingston Peak** (or Mount Baldy) trail east of town off Swingley Road, and the **Big Timber Canyon** east of town and north of Big Timber. The **Livingston District Office of the National Forest Service** is a mile south of town on U.S. 89 (☎ 406/222-1892). It's where you'll find maps and other pertinent backcountry information about all the trails in and around Livingston.

Fishing is one of the main attractions of Livingston, largely due to the bend in the Yellowstone River that causes it to wrap around the town. Dan Bailey's world-famous fly-fishing shop is downtown at 209 W. Park. The staff at this 60-year-old institution can provide information on current river conditions, fly-tying workshops, and, of course, all the outdoor gear you need for a day on the water. **Skiing** is nearby at **Bridger Bowl** north of Bozeman, and **Big Sky** across the Gallatin range, but Livingston proper doesn't have much in the way of winter outdoor recreation. For more on other area activities during the summer and winter months, see "Getting Outside" in the Bozeman, Madison River Valley, and Gallatin Valley sections earlier in this chapter, and the Red Lodge & the Absaroka-Beartooth Wilderness section later in this chapter.

SEEING THE SIGHTS

After you've taken in the amazing view of the Absaroka range that's afforded from almost anywhere in town and gazed at the Crazy Mountains off in the distance, you should be ready to wander around Livingston and get a great feel for a real Montana town. It's no accident that part of *A River Runs Through It* was filmed here. Unlike so many other western towns, the architecture in Livingston isn't made up of tacky false-fronted buildings. Instead, the streets are lined with turn-of-the-century redbrick buildings with still-visible advertisements painted on the sides, bars with vertical neon signs, and old businesses, like Sax and Fryer on W. Callender. The town's primary attraction is the **Livingston Depot Center** at Park and Main, a museum dedicated to preserving the history of the railroad ($3 for adults, $2 for children). Yet the **Park County Museum** at 118 W. Chinnok is also worth a visit. It offers a free glimpse into the area's past with a rather professional archeological exhibit, a railroad room, and Native American artifacts.

For the outdoors-minded, there's **Sacajawea Park,** south on Yellowstone Ave., a fantastic local park with tennis courts, a playground, and a stone bridge that crosses Yellowstone River with the Crazy Mountains in the background.

SHOPPING

The art galleries of Livingston range from the so-so to the truly incredible. For wildlife art, head to **Visions West Gallery** at 104 Main. Inside you'll find hand-crafted wood carvings, bronzes, and original oil paintings. At the Murray Hotel at 201 W. Park, you can see the wild imagination of artist-in-residence Parks Reece come to life in the **Parks Reece Gallery** upstairs. If you can't afford to plunk down the money for an original, the hotel offers T-shirts with Reece prints for $15. The **Danforth Gallery** at 106 Main displays the works of contemporary artists in revolving exhibits that change twice a month. The crowning jewel of Main Street's galleries is the **Chatham Fine Art** gallery at 120 Main, however. The featured artist is of course Russell Chatham, the world-renowned lithographer whose prints are in many establishments across the state.

Coming into town you probably had trouble averting your eyes from the signs advertising **Gil's Gift Shop.** The brazen highway advertising ploy rivals Wall Drug of South Dakota for top honors in the advertising hall of shame. What you'll find is of course a let-down, but you won't forgive yourself if you don't at least peek inside. **Mountunes** at 109 S. Main is the local music shop. For upscale leathers, suedes, and ladies' accessories, check out the **Obsidian Collection** at 105 S. Main. For the best in books, try **Books, etc.** at 106 S. Main. Coffee can be found in a variety of gourmet blends at the Livingston off-shoot of Bozeman's **Leaf and Bean** at 113 W. Park or down the street in the plaza at the **Crazy Mountain Coffee Company,** 1313 W. Park.

WHERE TO STAY
A GUEST RANCH
✪ Mountain Sky Guest Ranch
Box 1128, Bozeman, MT 59715. ☎ **406/587-1244** or 800/548-3392. 27 cabins. $1,650–$1,900 per person/per week. MC, V. Open May–Oct. Reservations required six months to a year in advance. Take Hwy. 89 south from Livingston to Big Creek Road (just past Emigrant). The ranch is located 4¹/₂ miles down Big Creek Rd.

The address is Bozeman, but the ranch is firmly ensconced in the Paradise Valley along the Yellowstone River. It's billed as a guest ranch, but the fact is, Mountain Sky is head and shoulders above the usual guest ranch. This is more of an upscale resort with a Western theme. The main lodge is a refined log structure with vaulted ceilings and beams of lodgepole pine. In the corner is a grand piano for those brave enough to play. Great fishing is one of the assets of Mountain Sky, with the Yellowstone River, Big Creek, and a stocked pond to choose from. Meals are fantastic, with huge gourmet feasts served twice a week, big breakfasts, a lunch buffet, and a barbecue cookout by the pool. If the kids are all but sick of you, the popular children's programs include a riding school, hiking, fishing, and swimming.

HOTELS

✪ Chico Hot Springs Lodge

Old Chico Rd., Pray, MT 59065. ☎ **406/333-4933.** 50 lodge rms, 24 motel rms, 4 cabins, 4 cottages. Lodge rms, $40–$70 double; motel rms $60–$85 double; cabins $60–$75 double; cottages $100–$300 double. DISC, MC, V.

Just off Hwy. 89 between Livingston and Yellowstone is a small town called Pray, near which is a bizarre, distinctly Montanan resort. It's attracted notice not for its fancy ways, incredible amenities, or Olympic-size pool, but rather for its saloon with a bar on the ceiling, its bare-bones rooms, and its hot springs pool. This place is filled with a charm you're not going to find anywhere else in Paradise Valley, and something about Chico lets you know it's aware of this. It's funky, but comfortable. The food, however, is another story and The Chico Inn's reputation is perhaps better known than the lodge's (see "Where to Eat" below).

⑤ The Murray Hotel

201 West Park, Livingston, MT 59047. ☎ **406/222-1350.** 41 rms, 29 with private bath; 1 suite. TV TEL. $35–$55 double; $65–$150 suites. AE, DISC, MC, V.

You can't find a place with more style, more history, more stories, more personalities, or more bullet holes than this hotel. Quite frankly, a night here is worth the money, unless you're given the room above the bar when the band is playing. If you ask, the desk clerk will be happy to take you and your bags up to your room in an old elevator that is a ride back in time. The rooms are all tastefully decorated (the Rose Room on the fourth floor is a nice room for couples) and the rooms on the east side look over the Crazy Mountains or the Masonic Lodge.

Paradise Inn

Box 684, Livingston, MT 59047. 406/222-6320 or ☎ **800/437-6291.** 43 rms. A/C TV TEL. $42–$89 double. AE, DISC, MC, V.

Just off the interstate, the Paradise Inn is a comfortable place to stay. The rates are fair, especially considering the inn's proximity to Yellowstone, and the most expensive room comes with a hot tub. There are other places to stay in Livingston with more charm, but for a quiet and convenient place to sleep, this is a safe bet. An average restaurant and a lounge full of gambling machines is located at the front of the parking lot.

CAMPING

The Forest Service's **Pine Creek campground** is open from late May to mid-September with 24 tent sites, a series of hiking trails, and fishing access. The campground is located 4 miles south of Livingston on Hwy. 89, and 6 miles east on Pine Creek Road. Also south of town, the **Paradise Valley/Livingston KOA**

(☎ 406/222-0992) is 9 miles south on Hwy. 89 and is open from May through October. Located right on the Yellowstone River, this campground, with 27 tent sites and 52 RV spaces, has plenty of room and is the only one in the area with a heated indoor pool.

WHERE TO EAT

Amadeus Coffee House

102 N. 2nd. ☎ **406/222-7423.** Lunch $3–$6; main dinner courses $7–$12. MC, V. Mon–Fri 7am–5pm, Sat 9am–3pm, closed Sun. CONTINENTAL.

This little spot on the corner with its unmistakable green and red trim may bill itself as a coffeehouse, but it's also a quiet little lunch spot. Located right next door to the Empire movie theater, the Amadeus Coffee House serves a typical soup, salad, sandwich menu along with daily specials and mouth-watering, made-from-scratch desserts. Mornings and afternoons, locals depend on Amadeus for its tasty coffee cakes and creamy flavored lattes.

✪ The Chico Inn

Old Chico Rd., Pray. ☎ **406/333-4933.** Reservations recommended. Main dinner courses $16–$25. AE, DISC. Daily 5:30–10pm in summer; Sun–Thu 6–9pm, Fri–Sat 5:30–10pm in winter. CONTINENTAL.

This quietly understated restaurant located at Chico Hot Springs Lodge may be more popular than the lodge itself. Depending on what you order, entrées can be pricier than a stay at the lodge might suggest, but they're well worth it. Celebrities can often be spotted enjoying local wild game or traditional French dishes (rumor has it that Jack Nicholson is a big fan), and although dress is casual, reservations are encouraged. If you own your own plane, you might want to fly into Pray for this fine dining experience—just be advised that the highway and the runway are one and the same.

The Pickle Barrel

113 W. Park. ☎ **406/222-5469.** Reservations not accepted. Most items $4–$10. No credit cards. Daily 10:30am–8pm. SOUPS/SANDWICHES.

The Pickle Barrel of Livingston is just as good, just as inexpensive, but not as crammed with college students as its sister branch 26 miles west in Bozeman. The hoagies are great. This place is ideal if you want a quick but filling lunch.

The Sport Restaurant and Bar

114 S. Main. ☎ **406/222-3533.** Lunch $3–$6; main dinner courses $9–$13. MC, V. Mon–Sat 11am–9pm, closed Sun. AMERICAN.

Full of old newspaper clippings from other cities and different eras, the centrally located Sport serves decent food in a great atmosphere. When we first sat down and looked this place over, we found its self-promotion overdone. But by the time we left, we were calling it quaint and full of antique charm. The most popular item on the menu is the Name Your Own burger, but the barbecue chicken and ribs are definitely worth a try. Formerly the Beer Hall, the place was renamed the Sport in 1909 and has never looked back.

✪ Uncle Looie's

119 W. Park. ☎ **406/222-7177.** Lunch $5–$11; main dinner courses $15–$23. DISC, MC, V. Mon–Thu 11:30am–2pm, 5:30–9:30pm, Fri–Sat 11:30am–2pm, 5:30–10pm, Sun 5:30–9:30pm. ITALIAN.

Run by virtually the same crew that steers the ship at the Chico Inn, Uncle Looie's was still getting the kinks worked out when we visited. The first serious restaurant to open in Livingston, Uncle Looie's doesn't have far to go before it becomes the best place in town. Previously the Longbranch Saloon, Looie's has transformed itself from a smoky pool hall to a first-class restaurant, absolutely unrecognizable from its former incarnation. And although residents may miss their old hangout, this one is sure to become just as popular. The entrées are sometimes too heavy on the olive oil, but come in large portions. The ambience is nicer than anywhere else in Livingston.

6 Red Lodge & the Absaroka-Beartooth Wilderness

Red Lodge is a tiny progressive town with an interesting mix of folks. At one time, its ethnic diversity rivaled Butte's. Yet unlike those who settled Butte, the international community that's thrived in Red Lodge since the railroad brought them down the tracks at the turn of the century couldn't have picked a more beautiful place. Situated at the edge of the Absaroka-Beartooth Wilderness, Red Lodge is surrounded by the spectacular scenery of the Beartooth Mountains. It's a stopping point on the impressive Bearthooth National Scenic Byway that climbs up and down the Beartooth range to Cooke City, a small but popular ski resort on the brink of a $17 million expansion project, and each August it hosts the Festival of Nations, a celebration that honors the nationalities of the miners who founded the town.

ESSENTIALS

To reach Red Lodge, you'll have to fly into **Logan International Airport** in **Billings** (see Chapter 10, "Billings: Essentials"). Rental cars are rare in town, but **Anderson's** (☎ 406/446-2720) at 210 N. Broadway offers limited rentals. For road conditions concerning the Red Lodge area and closures of the Beartooth National Scenic Byway, call 406/252-2806 or 307/237-8411. For statewide weather conditions, call 800/332-6171. For visitor information, contact the **Red Lodge Area Chamber of Commerce**, P.O. Box 998 Red Lodge, MT 59068 (☎ 406/446-1718).

GETTING OUTSIDE
GOLF

Red Lodge has two courses, both of which are open to the public. **Red Lodge Mountain Golf Course** (☎ 406/446-3344), is exceptional—there are few better places to play on this side of the state. The par-5 18th is one of the longest in the world—680 yards. **The Elks Club** (☎ 406/446-1812) runs the other, a more laid-back nine-hole course with sand greens.

HIKING

The Absaroka-Beartooth Wilderness area is a million-acre wonderland that is easily one of the more spectacular wilderness areas in Montana. One of the largest and most often-used wilderness sites in the country, the Absaroka-Beartooth is full of great hikes, incredible overlooks, and pristine lakes. It's home to Montana's highest mountain, **Granite Peak**. At 12,799 feet, it's one of 28 peaks over 12,000 feet in the Absaroka-Beartooth. **East Rosebud** and **Mystic Lakes** are two more popular hiking and camping destinations in the wilderness. The Beartooth Ranger District office of the Custer National Forest, at the south end of town along U.S. Hwy. 212 (☎ 406/446-2103), can provide you with helpful information including topographical maps, cabin sites, and trail conditions.

SKIING

Red Lodge Mountain

Box 750, Red Lodge, MT 59068. ☎ **406/446-2610** or 800/444-8977. Dec–Apr. Lift ticket adults $24; children $10.

One of the smaller ski resorts in the state, Red Lodge Mountain is peaceful, uncrowded and affordable. Full-day lift tickets cost less than $25, lines are nonexistent and runs, such as the Lazy M, a fantastic 2½-mile run for intermediates and experts, allow for nonstop cruising without breaking for the chair. Early weekday discounts—lift tickets are less than $15—make skiing on Monday or Tuesday an incredibly sweet bargain.

SEEING THE SIGHTS

You're probably in Red Lodge because you're either beginning or ending a drive along the **Beartooth National Scenic Byway.** This 64-mile stretch runs along U.S. Hwy. 212 from Red Lodge to Cooke City over the Beartooth Pass, an incredible piece of road that puts your car at almost 11,000 feet. Make sure a camera is handy when Pilot Peak, the giant spire just outside Cooke City, comes into view. The **Beartooth Nature Center** (☎ 406/446-1133), formerly the local zoo, is located on Hwy. 212 just ¼ mile north of town; it's a good spot for families with young children since it's basically a petting zoo. Admission is $2.50 for adults and $1 for children.

During the summer you can visit the **Carbon County Historical Museum** on U.S. Hwy. 212, known more for being the cabin of "Liver Eatin'" Johnson than anything else. The story of who he is and how he came by such a lovely nickname is told here.

There are also a number of **special events** that take place in Red Lodge at this time of year.

Classical music lovers may want to take in a concert during June's **Red Lodge Music Festival,** which brings professional musicians to town and gives local high school students the opportunity to study with them. During the nine-day session, students and faculty perform together in at least two chamber music ensembles. Faculty members perform five evening recitals during the nine days, and students end the week with a final concert.

August brings the **Festival of Nations,** an annual get-together of townsfolk from different cultural backgrounds. A weeklong extravaganza, it devotes days to exploring each of the nationalities—Scottish, Scandinavian, Finnish, Italian, Slavic, English, Irish, and German—of Red Lodge's original settlers.

During winter's last blast in early March, the **Red Lodge Winter Carnival** opens each year with a theme parade on Friday night. The carnival includes a ridiculous fireman's race and often surprisingly good ice sculptures. Call the chamber of commerce (☎ 406/446-1718) for dates and information about events.

SHOPPING

The truth is, Red Lodgers head to Billings when they want to do some serious shopping. For those who are just passing through, there are nonetheless a few places where you can take care of basic needs and pick up a souvenir of two. For one-hour photo developing or vintage postcards of Yellowstone and Montana, head to **Flash's** at 21 S. Broadway. **Moosely Tees,** 14 S. Broadway, has souvenir T-shirts, jackets, hats, shorts, sweatshirts—and new age music. At 111 S. Broadway is the **In Step,** a groovy shoe and sandal shop. At **Native American Trading,** 19 S. Broadway, you'll find an assortment of jewelry, rugs, dolls, and pottery. The **Montana Candy Emporium** and fifties soda fountain, located upstairs, is at 7 S. Broadway. The **Merida Gallery** showcases Native American artist Kevin Red Star's work at 15 S. Broadway.

WHERE TO STAY

Best Western Lupine Inn

702 S. Hauser, Red Lodge, MT 59068. ☎ **406/446-1321.** 46 rms. A/C TV TEL. $40–$60 double. AE, DISC, MC, V.

Located a block west of downtown, the Lupine is a great place for families, especially those not looking to spend a small fortune. It isn't as comfortable as some of the other accomodations in the area, but it is reasonably priced, and amenities aren't in short supply. Each room has a queen-size bed and some have kitchen units. There's an indoor pool and sauna as well as a ski wax room.

The Pollard

2 N. Broadway, Red Lodge, MT 59068. ☎ **406/446-0001** or 800/765-5273. 36 rms. A/C TV TEL. $60–$175 double. AE, DISC, V, MC.

Built in 1893 by the Rocky Fork Coal Company, the Pollard was visited by such Western legends as Buffalo Bill, Calamity Jane, and Jeremiah "Liver Eatin'" Johnson before it fell into a long period of disrepair. In 1991, the Hotel Company of Red Lodge purchased it and undertook a complete renovation. When it reopened in June 1994, the Pollard was an immediate success. The hotel has a three-story gallery with a wood-burning fireplace, which six of its rooms overlook. The entire facility is nonsmoking and features a club with aerobic and strength training equipment, a sauna, a hot tub, and two raquetball courts.

✪ Rock Creek Resort

Route 2, Box 3500, Red Lodge, MT 59068. ☎ **406/446-1111.** 33 rms, 40 condominiums. A/C TV TEL. Rms $80–$200 double, condominiums $60–$260 double. AE, DISC, MC, V.

Before Rock Creek was built, Red Lodge had only moderately priced, family-style accommodations. A resort complex that caters to business travelers, Rock Creek hosts conferences, seminars, and reunions, and provides all the expected amenities: a nearby golf course, restaurant, indoor pool, sauna, hot tub, and tennis court.

The cedar-sided Beartooth Lodge is the main building on the grounds. It boasts a giant corner fireplace made of river rock and windows that offer mountain views. Old Piney Dell is the restaurant on the premises, and while the food is remarkable, expect to pay about twice as much as you would in town. The European cuisine and views of Rock Creek make dining here worth every penny, however.

CAMPING

There are 16 Forest Service campgrounds available in the Red Lodge area, with sites for over 700 campers. Closest to town are **Sheridan** and **Ratine,** just 5 miles away via a gravel road. **Parkside, Limberpine,** and **Greenough** are all within a mile of each other and are reached by paved roads. Sites are more developed, with hand pumps for drinking water, picnic tables, and fire pits.

Basin campground, 6 miles from Red Lodge, is located 1 mile from Wild Bill Lake, a day use area popular for its fishing access and hiking trails. All of its facilities are wheelchair-accessible. There are also eight Forest Service campgrounds along the Beartooth National Scenic Byway. For information on any of the above-listed campgrounds, contact the **Beartooth Ranger Station** at 406/446-2103. Their office is at the south end of town on U.S. Hwy. 212, and they can inform you of seasonal closings and locations.

For a much less isolated experience, try **Perry's RV Park & Campground** (☎ 406/446-2722), just 2 miles south of town off U.S. Hwy. 212 along Rock Creek. Perry's has 20 tent sites and 30 spots for RVs, along with a store and laundry. **The Red Lodge KOA** (☎ 406/446-2634) is at the other end of town, 4 miles north of Red Lodge on Hwy. 212. Somewhat bigger than Perry's, the views here aren't quite as nice, but it's a great place for kids with a swimming pool, rec room, playground, and sauna on-site. Both of these private campgrounds are open seasonally, from mid-May through September.

WHERE TO EAT

Bogart's

11 S. Broadway. ☎ **406/446-1784.** Reservations not accepted. Most items $5–$10. V, MC. Daily 11am–9pm. AMERICAN.

In a town that claims it has more restaurants per capita than any other community in Montana, Bogart's is the most popular and the safest choice in town. The menu is full of great sandwiches, Mexican entrées, and pizza. The place, as you might have guessed, is named after Humphrey himself; but other than the humble homage of naming sandwiches after some of his movies, don't expect much more of a tribute.

10 Eastern Montana

There isn't a place in the state with better collective self-esteem than Eastern Montana. There are no mountains, just badlands; the grass has a scorched look almost year-round; and driving distances stretch on so infinitely that only the road signs seem to change. Yet the people are proud of where they live. And though it seems to repeat itself mile after mile, Eastern Montana has an eerie, paradoxical beauty. It's a desolate place, stretching into the horizon without a trace of the mountains for which the state is named, and yet it is this very quality of wide-openness, where wheat and sky seem to touch, that is so compelling.

It also occupies a seminal place in American history, for this is where Gen. George Armstrong Custer and 260 men were wiped out by Sioux and Cheyenne warriors in a mysterious battle near the Little Bighorn River.

The most accessible roads in eastern Montana are Interstates 94 and 90, which join 7 miles east of Billings. Along I-94 from Glendive, the wide expanses of rolling hills and badlands give way to the softer hills of pine trees as you follow the Yellowstone River into Billings. But south of Billings, from MT 416, begins a series of well-maintained backroads that provide a silent and lonely look into the lands of the Crow people. You can reach Pryor by turning south when 416 ends; in Pryor, head east for 33 miles to St. Xavier, then southeast 22 miles to Lodge Grass. From Lodge Grass, you can reach I-90 1 mile to the east.

1 Billings

If there is a bona fide city in Montana, then Billings, without question, is it. From shopping malls and buildings that actually climb above 10 floors, to traffic at five o'clock on weekday afternoons, Billings has an urban feeling that no other Montana town can boast. Lying as it does in the middle of an area that would otherwise be nowhere, Billings has evolved since its 1880s development as a railroad town by Frederick Billings into the economic hub for much of the eastern portion of the state and parts of northern Wyoming.

Though the city has an intrastate reputation for being a blight in the middle of beauty, Billings is not without its own outdoor charm. From the Beartooth Mountains, which peek at the city from the southeast, to the rimrocks that line the northern edge of the city, to the Yellowstone River, which cuts through the south, Billings has its share of splendor. Combine that with a rich Native American tradition that continues to thrive in and around the city and you have one of Montana's most complex and diverse areas.

ESSENTIALS

GETTING THERE   Billings is home to the busiest airport in Montana, **Logan International,** located on the rimrocks two miles north of downtown. Daily intrastate service is provided by **Big Sky Airlines** (☎ 406/245-2300 or 800/237-7788), and regional daily service is provided by **Delta** (☎ 800/221-1212), **Frontier** (☎ 800/432-1359), **Horizon** (☎ 800/547-9308), **Northwest** (☎ 800/225-2525), and **United** (☎ 800/241-6522).

From the west, Interstate 90 cuts through the south part of the city and can be used to reach the west end of the city at exit 446, or downtown, farther east at exit 450. From the east, coming from Hardin, I-90 meets the end of I-94 7 miles from town. Heading west from Glendive and Miles City, I-94 ends and becomes I-90 before taking you south of town. From the north, coming from Roundup, U.S. Highway 87 turns into a four-lane road before heading west into the Heights, the northeast part of the city. Follow this road into downtown, or turn right at Airport Road across from **MetraPark** to reach Logan International Airport.

The bus terminal for **Greyhound** (☎ 406/245-5116) and **Rimrock Stages** (☎ 406/245-5392 or 800/255-7655) is located downtown at 2502 1st Ave. North.

VISITOR INFORMATION   The **Billings Area Chamber of Commerce,** 815 S. 27th St., Billings, MT 59107 (☎ 406/245-1111 or 800/735-2635), is open Monday through Friday and has brochures, maps, and area information. It's part of **Travel Montana's Custer Country;** request a free vacation guide from Rt. 1 Box 1206A, Hardin, MT, 59034 (☎ 406/554-1671).

GETTING AROUND   There are many car rental companies in Billings, with **Avis** (☎ 406/252-8007 or 800/831-2847), **Budget** (☎ 406/259-1800), **Hertz** (☎ 406/248-9151 or 800/654-3131), and **National** (☎ 406/252-7626 or 800/227-7368) maintaining counters at Logan International Airport.

The city bus service is **Billings Met Transit** (☎ 406/657-8218).

GETTING OUTSIDE
SPORTS & OUTDOOR ACTIVITIES
Biking

Beartooth Bicycle and Sports (☎ 406/656-2453 or 800/310-2453) offers detailed trail guides for the Billings area and southcentral Montana, from casual rides at Riverfront Park off South Billings Boulevard to the scenic Zimmerman Trail on the rims. Bike rentals are available. The shop is open Monday through Saturday 9am to 7pm, and Sundays 1 to 5pm.

Fishing

Though the Yellowstone runs through Billings, you may want to inquire locally before casting below the oil refinery. The Classic Angler, 1901 Broadwater Ave. (☎ 406/652-2001), offers up-to-date information on local conditions, fly-tying classes, and everything the fisherman needs for a day on the water.

Golf

Lake Hills Golf Club (☎ 406/252-9244) and the **Peter Yegen, Jr., Golf Club** (☎ 406/656-8099) are the two 18-hole public courses in Billings. Two private courses, the 18-hole **Briarwood Country Club** (☎ 406/248-2702) and the 27-hole **Pryor Creek Golf Course** (☎ 406/256-0626), offer limited public play. Call ahead for availability and tee times. **Circle Inn Golf Links** (☎ 406/259-3351) and **Par 3 Exchange City Golf Course** (☎ 406/652-2553) are public par-3 courses.

Hiking

Lake Elmo State Park, located north of town, and **Riverfront Park,** south of town, offer casual hiking trails. See below for details.

NEARBY PARKS & NATURE PRESERVES

Lake Elmo State Park is a year-round favorite. With 1.3 miles of shoreline, swimming, picnicking, fishing, and volleyball are all popular summer activities; you can cross-country ski or check out the wildlife during winter. Yellow perch, black crappie, channel catfish, and largemouth bass can all be found in Lake Elmo, though motorized boats are prohibited. Windsurfing and kayaking are also popular water sports. The park is open from sunrise to sunset, except during peak summer months, when it opens at 11am and closes around 8pm. Boat rentals, windsurfing lessons, and concessions are available from June through August. Fees are $1 per person, 50¢ for children 10 and under. From Billings, take Main east to Highway 87 and drive north for 10 miles to Lake Elmo Drive.

Nestled at the base of sandstone cliffs, **Pictograph Caves State Park** features ancient rock paintings and encompasses an area that was once home to generations of prehistoric hunters. Explore Ghost Cave, Middle Cave, and Pictograph Cave, the largest, for pictographs depicting shield-bearing warriors, humanlike figures, and animals. Trails and interpretive signs add to the visitor's enjoyment of this area. From Billings, take I-90 to the Lockwood Exit, no. 452. The park is open mid-April to mid-October from 8am to 8pm. Overnight camping is prohibited, but picnic facilities are available. There is a $3 fee.

Also nearby is the **Crow Reservation.** Take I-94 just out of town and you'll reach the turnoff to Chief Plenty Coups State Park, an easy day trip from Billings. See Section 2 of this chapter for complete details.

SEEING THE SIGHTS IN & AROUND TOWN

The Moss Mansion

914 Division. ☎ **406/256-5100.** Admission $3. Guided tours scheduled Mar–Dec; tours may be arranged by phone in Jan–Feb.

This three-story, fully furnished mansion has remained virtually unchanged since its construction in 1903 for prominent Billings banker Preston B. Moss. European touches are manifest throughout the house, most notably in the arched entryway inspired by Spain's Alhambra Palace, the custom-designed formal French parlor, and the lavish wood and fabric appointments in the upstairs bedrooms.

Avenue of the Sculptures

Along 27th St. from exit 450 off I-90 to Logan International Airport.

This drive through the middle of downtown offers an array of artwork. You'll have to look pretty closely to see some of the pieces amid the buildings. The *Cattle Drive Monument* is first and the easiest to spot: It's on your right as you approach the Visitor Center from the south. The contemporary piece that resembles a dislocated fragment of concrete building fallen to the ground, also on your right in front of Norwest Bank at 175 N. 27th, is *The Trough*. At the corner of 2nd Avenue North and North 27th is the Sheriff Webb memorial marker, which sits on the courthouse lawn, followed

Eastern Montana

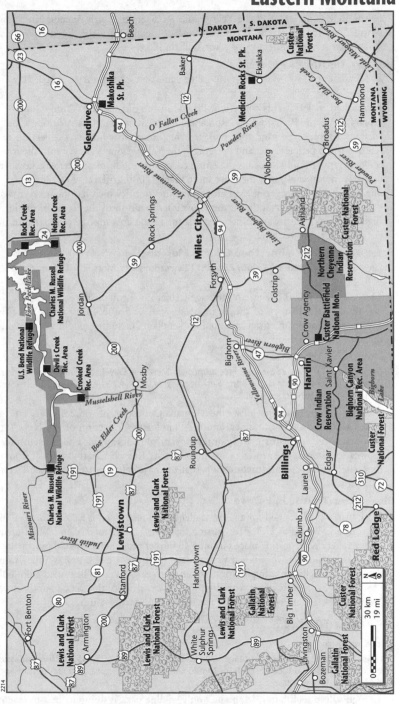

243

by the Reineking statue at the Yellowstone Art Center at 4th Avenue North and North 27th. Finally, up to the rims in front of the airport is the *Range Rider of the Yellowstone* statue, in memory of actor William Hart.

Western Heritage Center

2822 Montana Ave. ☎ **406/256-6809.** Free admission; donations accepted. Tues–Sat 10am–5pm; Sun 1–5pm.

Established in 1971, this collection, located in the old Parmly Billings Memorial Library, belies the Richardsonian Romanesque style in which the structure was built. Made of rubble-faced sandstone in 1901, the library now houses a collection that represents the peoples, past and present, of the Yellowstone Valley. From the interactive computer and videos on the entrance level to the homesteader checkerboard below (yes, you can play), there are more than 16,000 artifacts. The museum also offers an outreach program, "Museum Without Walls," which has included trips to the Crow Indian Reservation for the Crow interpretation of the Battle of the Little Bighorn. Books, shirts, and other gifts relating to the area may be purchased in the gift shop on the lower level.

Peter Yegen, Jr., Yellowstone County Museum

Logan International Airport. ☎ **406/256-6811.** Free admission. Mon–Fri 10:30am–5pm, Sun 2–5pm.

This museum, like the Western Heritage Center downtown, strives to preserve the legends and the history of the Yellowstone Valley. Some 4,000 artifacts of the cowboy and Native American traditions are kept here, including an old steam engine, the last in Billings to operate.

Yellowstone Art Center

401 N. 27th St. ☎ **406/256-6804.** Free admission. Memorial Day–Labor Day, Tues–Wed and Fri–Sun 10am–5pm, Thurs 10am–8pm. Rest of the year, Tues–Wed and Fri–Sat 11am–5pm, Thurs 11am–8pm, Sun noon–5pm.

This regional art museum houses the Montana Collection of contemporary art, the Snook Collection of Will James, and the Poindexter Collection of the New York School as well as historic and contemporary photography. The museum also showcases some of the works of Montana artists Russell Chatham and Deborah Butterfield. There is a museum shop that offers jewelry, pottery, and children's gift items.

Black Otter Trail Scenic Drive

Black Otter Trail, named for a Crow leader buried near here, is a scenic drive along the rims and begins at U.S. 318, passing the Boot Hill Cemetery and Monument. The cemetery is the resting place for some 40 former residents of the old nearby town of Coulson, most of whom died violent deaths. Farther up the trail is Yellowstone Kelly's grave. Kelly, an intrepid frontiersmen and scout, asked to be buried atop Kelly Mountain. From this point, the Bighorn, Pryor, Beartooths, Crazy, and Snowy Mountain ranges are visible looking left to right and facing south.

ESPECIALLY FOR KIDS

ZooMontana

Exit 446 off I-90; head west on Frontage Road to Shiloh Road. ☎ **406/652-8100.** Admission $3 adults, $2 children under 16. Mid-Apr to mid-Oct, daily 10am–5pm; mid-Oct to mid-April, weekends only 10am–4pm.

Though still in its infancy, Montana's only wildlife park is doing its best to emerge as a full-fledged zoo. Current exhibits include the river otters, a homestead, and a

Billings

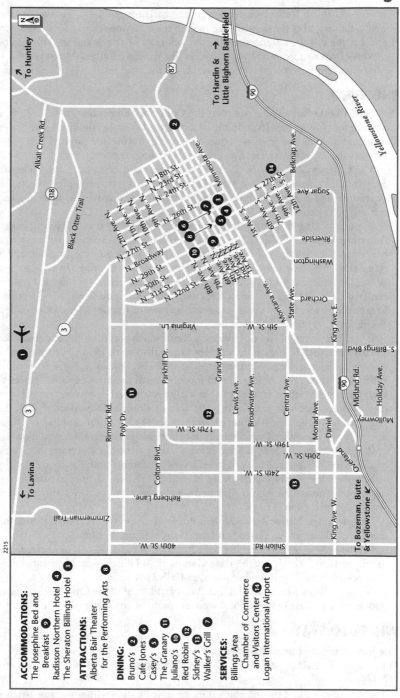

ACCOMMODATIONS:
The Josephine Bed and Breakfast 9
Radisson Northern Hotel 4
The Sheraton Billings Hotel 3

ATTRACTIONS:
Alberta Bair Theater for the Performing Arts 8

DINING:
Bruno's 2
Cafe Jones 6
Casey's 5
The Granary 11
Juliano's 10
Red Robin 12
Sidney's 13
Walker's Grill 7

SERVICES:
Billings Area Chamber of Commerce and Visitors Center 14
Logan International Airport 1

245

2215

waterfowl habitat. Under construction is the Siberian tiger exhibit. Though small at home, the zoo takes the show on the road in the ZooMobile. An education center and petting zoo are also on the 70-acre facility. The zoo is still in the ongoing process of raising money, with fund-raisers like the ZooMontana Music Festival at MetraPark, the largest outdoor music festival in the state.

SHOPPING

A giant 14,000-foot antique complex, the **Collectors Emporium,** 114 N. 29th, is a haven for (you guessed it) collectors. Furniture, glassware, primitives, and Native American artifacts and jewelry are just a sampling of what you can find here. This downtown shop is the largest of its kind in the Billings area.

The **Crafters Mall,** 114 N. 29th, is located on the mezzanine of the Collectors Emporium. This place is stuffed with Made in Montana crafts and has an assortment of ceramics and textiles. The Fireside room features wall decorations, porcelain, and soft-sculpture dolls.

If you're looking for original art or reproductions, there are several Billings galleries. **American West Art Gallery,** 2814 2nd Ave. North, specializes in Western art and contains a wide selection of original paintings and prints, along with a full-service frame shop. The jewelry by Ken Real Bird and the array of prints, including those of Bev Doolittle, are worth browsing. The **Toucan Gallery,** 2505 Montana Ave., is centered in the Billings Historic District and offers an unusual mix of oils, prints, handmade furniture, and ceramics as well as custom framing. This gallery is less Western and features more contemporary fine art.

If you're in search of eclectic fashions, some of which border on the eccentric, then **Cactus Rose,** 202 N. 29th, is the store for you, with clothing from all over the world. A more traditional alternative, **Herberger's,** at 200 N. Broadway, is just what you'd expect to find in a department store. Probably one of the more expensive places to shop for everyday items, Herberger's has a conservative feel. If you are looking for a dress shirt for six bucks, then head to **Sylvester's Bargain Emporium** at 2901 1st Ave. North. Though the selection can sometimes be thin and frustrating, the finds are here to be had. Watch out, though: not all the clothes are in mint condition.

Rimrock Mall, 300 S. 24th West, offers a more eclectic blend of stores than you'd expect to see in Billings. A tobacco store, several restaurants (including one especially good one, Sidney's, which is described later in this section), a cineplex, and several department stores. Though it's located on the west end of town, this is where serious shoppers go in Billings.

Center Lodge Native Arts, 121 N. 29th St., features Native American arts and crafts, specializing in Kevin Red Star framed and unframed prints.

For the latest in outdoor clothing and equipment or to simply rent some active gear for the weekend, check out the **Base Camp,** 1730 Grand Ave.; **Big Bear,** in the Rimrock Mall; or **Play it Again Sports,** at 1005 24th St. West.

Global Village, located at 2910 7th Ave. North (behind the Castle), sells unique gifts items from developing nations, with an emphasis on Guatemalan crafts.

WHERE TO STAY

The Josephine Bed and Breakfast

514 N. 29th St., Billings, MT 59101. ☎ **406/248-5898.** 5 rms (3 with private bath). $48–$78 double. MC, V.

The great thing about the Josephine is its strategic location within walking distance of downtown, the summer farmers' market, and the Met, Billings' rapid transit bus system. Named after a steamboat that once plied the nearby Yellowstone River, this bed-and-breakfast offers a good night's rest in the center of urban bustle. Owners Doug and Becky Taylor have equipped the Captain's Room with a four-poster, mahogany queen-size bed and an unusually large private bathroom whose centerpiece is an antique clawfoot tub. The Garden Room has a more feminine feel with Victorian touches, and the well-lighted Courtyard Room overlooks the church where the Taylors were married. Though there is no smoking in the house, the wraparound porch is an inviting spot to read or people-watch.

Radisson Northern Hotel

Broadway and 1 Ave. North, Billings, MT 59101. ☎ **406/245-5121** or 800/333-3333. 160 rms (including 47 mini-suites and 7 parlor suites). A/C TV TEL. $94 double; $89–$109 suite. AE, DC, DISC, MC, V.

This downtown hotel exudes a contemporary Western flair: From the lobby's magnificent river rock fireplace to the bar's somber wildlife trophies, the Radisson is distinctly Montana-made. From its humble beginnings in 1902—a fire in 1940 facilitated the first renovation, completed in 1942—the Radisson Northern has grown to a ten-floor facility complete with bar and restaurant, both of which are quite popular with the locals. Suites feature a sitting room and bedroom, both with telephones and televisions.

Dine at the Golden Belle, where the Monte Cristo is a perennial lunch favorite and the French pancakes are a sure bet for breakfast. The Saloon, located on the ground floor just off the lobby, bills itself as an old-time watering hole and is a comfortable place to visit with friends without having to yell over lots of other noise.

✪ The Sheraton Billings Hotel

27 N. 27th St. (at Montana Avenue), Billings, MT 59101. ☎ **406/252-7400** or 800/325-3535. Fax 406/252-2401. 282 rms, 10 suites. A/C TV TEL. $72 double; $130–$190 suite. AE, DC, DISC, MC, V.

At 23 floors, the Billings Sheraton has the singular distinction of being Montana's tallest building, a fact many big city visitors may find downright humorous. Located in the heart of downtown, the Sheraton is within walking distance of a variety of shopping, dining, and entertainment options and affords views of the city from each of its rooms; you can even see the spectacular Beartooth Mountain Range from higher-floor rooms facing west. The Lucky Diamond Restaurant and Lounge is conveniently located on the 20th floor, but is decidedly second-rate in comparison to other fine dining options in Billings. Airport shuttle service is complimentary.

WHERE TO EAT
EXPENSIVE
The Granary

1500 Poly Dr. ☎ **406/259-3488.** Reservations recommended on weekends. Main courses $15–$35. AE, DISC, MC, V. Mon–Sat 5:30–10pm. STEAKS/SEAFOOD.

This dimly-lit establishment is one of the more overrated restaurants in Billings. Though the food is certainly well-prepared, the chef lacks imagination in presentation and, more important, the portions are stingy for the price. In recent years, national and Montana beef councils have bestowed their highest honor to the Granary, and it must be said, the steaks are excellent. But in Billings there are other places to eat an excellent steak. The outside deck is a favorite haunt for many locals just wanting to quaff late-afternoon beers and cocktails. Owing to next-door neighbors, however, there is no live music, and the deck usually closes down before the summer sun does.

✪ Juliano's

2912 7th Ave. N. ☎ **406/248-6400.** Reservations appreciated but not required. Lunch $5–$7; dinner $13–$22. AE, DC, DISC, MC, V. Mon–Fri 11:30am–2pm, Wed–Sat 5:30–9pm. PACIFIC RIM/CONTEMPORARY AMERICAN.

This quaint Victorian house was originally a livery stable but now serves as one of Billings' finest restaurants, due in large part to the efforts of owner and chef Carl Kurokawa. The elegant atmosphere of the restaurant—its two dining rooms on the main floor and two smaller upstairs rooms seat 65—is enhanced by crisp white linens and darkly polished wood set against a backdrop of leaded windows. Chef Carl is clearly enthusiastic about what he does, changing his menu monthly and striving to accommodate his guests in every way possible. The grilled seafood risotto is a mouth-watering combination of shrimp, scallops, salmon, and halibut atop a creamy asparagus risotto. The fettuccine with grilled marinated lamb is flavorful but very rich, made with cream and goat's cheese. A smoked salmon appetizer comes with fiddlehead ferns, an early summer delicacy that closely resembles tentacles. A chef's table is available by reservation where you actually sit in the kitchen and watch your food (and everyone else's) being prepared. During the summer, the second-floor balcony can be reserved for intimate occasions. Chef Carl takes great pains to accommodate the tastes and whimsy of his clientele: If you have a wine preference, call ahead and he will make every effort to procure a bottle for you.

MODERATE

⑤ Sidney's

Rimrock Mall. ☎ **406/652-6000.** Lunch $5–$9; dinner $6–$10. AE, DC, DISC, MC, V. Mon–Thurs 11am–10pm, Fri–Sat 11am–11pm, Sun 11am–9pm. PASTA/PIZZA.

You absolutely cannot go wrong at this restaurant. With the freshest possible ingredients, including their own handmade pasta, Sidney's has created a menu of matchless taste, in every sense of the word. The coconut chicken from their pasta selection is a feast for the palate and eyes, with vegetables and angel hair pasta highlighted by subtle flavors of coconut, lime, and red curry. Popular pizza choices include the Mediterranean and the fajita chicken. The decor is Southwest fresh, with stucco walls painted in an adobe-colored wash and teal umbrellas covering the patio tables outside. The location at the mall makes this place even more popular, so if you don't want to wait, be sure to come early.

✪ Walker's Grill

301 N. 27th St. ☎ **406/245-9291.** Reservations recommended. Main courses $7–$18. AE, DISC, MC, V. Mon–Sat 5–10pm. AMERICAN BISTRO.

Trained at Jack's Firehouse in Philadelphia, James Honaker, along with brother Bill and Irish-born Michael Callaghan, have created what is quickly becoming known as the finest restaurant in Montana. The tastefully understated decor, with walls highlighting the artwork of friends, gives Walker's a reserved self-assurance found only in well-known establishments. Though the menu changes seasonally, locals have become accustomed, if not downright dependent, on the arrival each spring of morels, which are served in a port-cream reduction. The simplicity of the meals is intentional. The pastas are excellent and well priced, and the small but exotically adorned pizzas are a meal unto themselves. The thoroughness of the place is evident, right down to the bread: Walker's sent the baker to Paris to learn the art of bread-making. The wine list is virtually French by Montana standards, with almost half of the selections coming from France.

INEXPENSIVE

Bruno's

1002 1st Ave. N. ☎ **406/248-4146.** Lunch and dinner $5–$10. DISC, MC, V. Mon–Thurs 11am–9pm, Fri 11am–10pm, Sat 5–10pm. ITALIAN.

Located at the huge stucco building east of downtown, this was once a little Italian place hidden in a strip mall until it just couldn't handle the crowds. Now in its larger, dark-green setting, Bruno's thrives. The white pizzas are excellent here and most of the pastas are delicious, with the possible exception of the ones heavily covered in marinara.

Cafe Jones

2712 2 Ave. N. ☎ **406/259-7676.** Lunch $2–$6. No credit cards. Mon–Sat 7am–10pm, Sun 8am–10pm. AMERICAN.

A distinctly bohemian atmosphere is as pervasive as the smell of coffee in this art deco cafe, making the Western scenics hung on the wall seem oddly out of place against their backdrop of teal and chartreuse. The walk-up counter, covered in a funky mélange of broken glass and mirror, contains fresh muffins and biscotti and is the showpiece in a room already drenched in bright color. An eclectic and extremely affordable lunch menu includes a tasty artichoke-heart sandwich, a Cafe Jones original, and costs less than what you'd pay for a pocket-size *Dharma Bums*. You're likely to see almost anyone here, since its downtown location is convenient for businesspeople, college students, and visitors alike. Expect a more progressive crowd on Wednesdays, when open-mike night features poetry readings.

Red Robin

West Park Plaza, Grand Ave. ☎ **406/248-7778.** Most items $4–$7. AE, DISC, MC, V. Mon–Fri 11am–10pm, Sat–Sun 11am–10:30pm. BURGERS.

The Red Robin's menu is full of every sort of burger you can imagine, along with large sandwiches and salads. Though the place has a distinctly juvenile feel, with its burger-and-fry menu and silly logo of a giant bird flying a plane, the full bar and the gambling machines keep it from being strictly wholesome. Prices are reasonable, especially if you like to eat lots of fries: They keep coming at your request.

BILLINGS AFTER DARK
A GREAT LOCAL WATERING HOLE

Casey's

109 N. Broadway. ☎ **406/256-5200.**

This bar rocks on Monday nights, when the locals come downtown to jam. They're an unusually talented crew, but don't expect to be able to carry on a conversation with your companions. Neon arcs make an interesting contrast against the mirrors of the 1870s back bar, a structure almost as impressive as the arched ceiling where Bob Dylan, Michael Jackson, and Beethoven (among other musical luminaries) stare down in shadowed relief. Their self-described Cajun food—"classic American with Mexican accents"—is best enjoyed before the music starts around 8:30 or 9pm. Pool tables and video gambling machines are located in the back, as well as a shop specializing in Native American beadwork and unusual T-shirts. A temperature-controlled wine cellar boasts the largest selection of fine wines in the region.

THE PERFORMING ARTS

Alberta Bair Theater for the Performing Arts

Broadway and 3rd Ave. N. ☎ **406/256-6052.** Call for events and ticket pricing information.

The Alberta Bair, named in honor of the eccentric philanthropist who funded it, is the home to the Billings Symphony Orchestra and all things theatrical and musical. Located in the middle of downtown, the Alberta Bair has welcomed a variety of performers and is one of the largest performing arts centers on the plains.

The Writer's Voice

402 N. 32nd St. ☎ **406/252-0898.**

Produced by the YMCA, this reading series has brought some interesting writers to Billings. Though it's rare to find a best-selling author in town, well-known readers have included poet Allen Ginsberg and novelist Ken Kesey.

A SIDE TRIP TO POMPEY'S PILLAR: FOLLOWING IN THE FOOTSTEPS OF LEWIS & CLARK

This sandstone butte, 29 miles west of Billings, just off I-94, bears the only remaining physical evidence along the trail of the Lewis and Clark expedition: Captain William Clark's signature, carved in 1806. Now under a locked glass cabinet, the signature is surrounded by the graffiti of youngsters who've managed to climb and scrawl their own names. A short walk up planked stairs takes you to the famous inscription, and farther up, to the summit of the butte. Though the view from the top isn't particularly awe-inspiring, the preserved signature is worth seeing. Trails branch off to the Yellowstone River to the right, leading past antlers and replicas of canoes from the explorers' era. The name of the butte comes from a nickname for Baptiste, the son of expedition scout Sacajawea, whom they called "Pomp," a Shoshone name for "chief." Summer interpretive tours are available and off-season tours are available by request. Admission is free. The visitor center is open from Memorial Day through September daily from 8am to 5pm, but you can make the 1-mile walk from the entrance gate year-round.

2 The Crow Reservation

It is on Crow land that the Battle of the Little Bighorn, site of Custer's Last Stand, took place (see Section 4 of this chapter for complete details on the site itself). The battlefield itself, discernible from I-90 only if you happen to know what you're looking for, is a vast prairie of velveteen hills that gently forms a valley near the Little Bighorn River. Though the battlefield site is unmistakably the most historically significant point of interest from a U.S. perspective, shrouded as it is in mystery concerning the movements and intentions of the ill-fated Gen. George Armstrong Custer, the traditions and culture of the Crow people are the reservation's real attraction for us.

Though the beauty of the Crow people isn't exactly an experience the outsider can behold on any given day, their pageantry and magnificence can be witnessed at Crow

Impressions

The Crow country is good country. The Great Spirit has put it in exactly the right place; while you are in it you fare well; whenever you go out of it, whichever way you travel, you fare worse.

— Arapooish, "My Country"

Fair, where Crow life (and other tribes as well) is on public display: the haunting music of the drums and songs, the women in colorful elk teeth dresses, the synchronized dances of the men. For information on the Crow Reservation, contact the Tribal Headquarters in Crow Agency (☎ 406/638-2601).

Their very name is a topic for controversy among whites and Native Americans alike; the word itself, according to one Crow oral historian, is untranslatable. Everyone, it seems, gets it wrong. Absaroka, Absorkee, Crow, and Children of the Large-beaked Bird are some of the names given the tribe, but Apsaalooke (which doesn't translate as Crow, or Children of the Large-beaked Bird) is perhaps the closest and most recently accepted spelling to the traditional pronunciation of the tribal name.

Witness the pageantry, color, and culture of one of the nation's largest Native American powwows during Crow Fair, held annually the third weekend in August. Natives and visitors alike gather from around the country for daily grand entries, fancy dancing competitions, stick games, and food booths.

Driving northeast from Billings along I-94, you'll first reach the turnoff to Highway 416, which leads to Chief Plenty Coups State Park. Last chief of the Crows, Plenty Coups deeded his home and land in 1928 to be used for a park, "not to be a memorial to me, but to the Crow Nation." Today Chief Plenty Coups State Park includes the chief's home and a museum, which houses the Crow leader's personal items, as well as interpretive displays of Crow culture and a gift shop. There are picnic facilities on the grounds, but overnight camping is prohibited. The park is located 35 miles south of Billings, 1 mile west of Pryor off Highway 416. It's open May 1 through September daily from 8am to 8pm; there is a $3 entrance fee. The museum is open daily from 10am to 5pm, May 1 through September, but tours can be arranged during the off-season by appointment.

Fishing on the reservation is not recommended. The Bighorn River and Bighorn Canyon provide excellent nearby fishing opportunities and fishing supplies and guide services are available in Fort Smith (see below). Interstate 90, the major road that runs through Hardin and Crow Agency, provides very few dining options. For the typical diner and things chicken-fried, try the **Purple Cow** (it's hard to miss) just east of the interstate at the Hardin exit on the edge of the reservation. For Indian tacos (cheese, ground beef, and veggies piled high), head 15 miles south where I-90 meets Hwy. 212 and stop off at the **Custer Battlefield Trading Post** just across from the Little Bighorn Battlefield.

3 Bighorn Canyon National Recreation Area

After driving through the rolling praries of the Crow Reservation, it's hard to imagine a giant canyon sitting in wait just over the Bighorn Mountains. But the Bighorn River has cut between the Pryor Mountains to the west and the Bighorns on the east to create sheer canyon walls that run wicked paths through the valley.

Like Yellowstone Park, the Bighorn Canyon National Recreation Area is a shared resource between Montana and Wyoming, but access is limited on the Montana side—at some points it's easier to reach a Montana destination by traveling through Wyoming.

FROM THE MONTANA SIDE

For visitors on the go, the **Yellowtail Dam** at the northern part of the recreation area is the largest dam in the Missouri River drainage. The completion of the dam in 1968 created a giant serpentine lake that stretches 71 miles from the top of the recreation area to the bottom. After the creation of Bighorn Lake, Congress designated the site as a national recreation area and outdoor enthusiasts have never looked back. A history of the dam, its components, and the influence the dam has had on the area are all found at the **Yellowtail Visitor Center** (☎ 406/666-2443) near the dam itself. The visitor center is open 9am to 6pm daily from Memorial Day to Labor Day. From the visitor center you can look over the 1,480-foot-wide dam at the 525-foot drop to the river below.

The **Fort Smith Visitor Center** (☎ 406/666-2339), on Hwy. 313 and Afterbay Road, shows the film *Land of the Bighorn* each day and is open 9am to 6pm June through August, 9am to 5pm in spring and fall, and from 10am to 4:30pm December 15 to March 1.

Recreational opportunities abound throughout the park. The **Ok-A-Beh Boat Landing** (☎ 406/665-2216) offers a marina, boat rentals, a gas station, and fishing supplies. To get to the boat ramp and fishing access site, turn left after Fort Smith but before the park headquarters and head 11 somewhat treacherous miles over the Bighorn Plateau.

Fishing regulations are tricky in these parts since the Crow Reservation encompasses nearly all of the Montana portion of the canyon. State fishing licenses are required; though you have a Montana fishing license for fishing on the north end, you have to purchase a Wyoming license to fish on the Wyoming side of the park. One state does not honor the license of the other.

Hikers may be a little disappointed to discover that there are few trails in the park. The park ranger can direct you to the Om-Ne-A Trail, a short but steep 3-miler that skirts the canyon rim, and the Beaver Pond Trail, a five-minute walk from the Visitor Center along Lime Kiln Creek. Fishing, on the other hand, is excellent along the Bighorn River. Brown and lake trout can be found in abundance and there are several fishing outfitters in Fort Smith eager to please. Angler's Edge (☎ 406/666-2417); Bighorn Angler (☎ 406/666-2233); Kelly George J Bighorn Outfitters, just north of Fort Smith (☎ 406/666-2326); Phil Gonzalez's Bighorn River Lodge (☎ 406/666-2368); and Quill Gordon Fly Fisher's (☎ 406/666-2253) all operate out of Fort Smith and offer tailor-made trips in the canyon on the Bighorn River.

Camping can be as simple or as difficult as you choose. Afterbay, a rather large conglomeration of campsites just beyond the Visitor Center, is excellent for drive-up campers as is Cottonwood Camp (☎ 406/666-2391), the privately-owned RV park in town. Those with boats will want to cruise up the canyon to either Black Canyon (accessible from the Ok-A-Beh boat ramp), or Medicine Creek (accessible from Barry's Landing in the southern part of the park).

As far as accommodations are concerned, Fort Smith doesn't approach resort status. The **Big Horn Trout Shop** (☎ 406/666-2375), the **Bighorn Angler Motel** (☎ 406/666-2233), **Polly's Place** (☎ 406/666-2255), **Quill Gordon Fly Fisher's Motel** (☎ 406/666-2253), and the **Kingfisher Motel** (☎ 406/666-2326) all have rooms for less than $40 but should not be mistaken for anything other than places for anglers to rest weary heads.

FROM THE WYOMING SIDE

At the very south end of the park in Wyoming is the **Mason-Lovell Ranch** house, built as ranch headquarters in 1883 by A.L. Mason and H.C Lovell. These early ranchers were of the free-range school, letting their cattle roam throughout the Bighorn Basin. Still on site are the log structures the blacksmith worked and the cabins where married employees lived.

The **Bighorn Canyon Visitor Center** (☎ 307/548-2251) is located just east of Lovell, Wyoming, on Highway 10 and Highway 14A and is open daily from Memorial Day to Labor Day 8am to 6pm and the rest of the year from 8am to 5pm. As you walk up to the center, check out the unusual solar panels on the building's sloping roof. Inside, the visitor center is full of information on the area.

Heading north on Wyoming Highway 37 you'll pass **Horseshoe Bend,** where a southern section of the river becomes lake again. Not only does the south side of the park offer some of the more sensational views of the canyon, it also is home to some of the last wild horses that run free in North America. The **Pryor Mountain Wild Horse Range** extends from Crow land into the recreation area on the Wyoming border. The herd, which now has reached numbers over 120, has roamed about the range since 1968 when it was established. Also just off Highway 37 (just across the Montana border) is the **Devil Canyon Overlook,** with dizzying and incredible views where the Bighorn River is joined by Porcupine Creek.

Barry's Landing, with a boat ramp and fishing access, is located at the end of the highway and is the focus for most of the recreational opportunities in the southern part of the park. But before you reach the landing, check out **Hillsboro,** a ghost town that came about after G.W. Barry (of Barry's Landing fame) failed as a miner and rancher and fell into the tourist business.

Used by Native Americans and later fur trappers to sidestep the dangers of the Bighorn Canyon, the Bad Pass Trail is a no-trespassing trail and is now closed to tourists (though there is very limited access as the trail actually follows the road from the Wyoming line to the Layout Creek ranger station). Another site with limited access is the Lockhart Ranch, the abandoned home of Carolyn Lockhart, an East-coast journalist who left the good life to move West. It can be reached by turning left off Hwy. 37 onto Dryhead Road and hiking roughly 3 miles until you reach the ranch. Camping access in the south end of the park can be found at two drive-up facilities, Horseshoe Bend, the first turn-off along Hwy. 37, and Barry's Landing, at the very end of the road. Medicine Creek is another campground on the south end of the park and can only be reached by boating or hiking in.

For accommodations on the south side of the park, travel to Lovell, 3 miles west of the intersection of Hwys. 37 and 14a. Boaters can get all the supplies they need from the Horseshoe Bend Marina (☎ 406/548-7766), a full-service marina that rents boats, sells fishing supplies, and operates the southernmost boat launch ramp in the park at the head of Bighorn Lake (the other boat ramp on the southern end is north on Hwy. 37 at Barry's Landing). For views of the Bighorn Canyon from the water, give the people at S-S Enterprises in Cowley, Wyoming, a call (307/548-6418). Boat tours of the Bighorn Canyon run roughly $15 for 90-minute trips. Hiking trails, again, are limited, even in the south end of the park. The Canyon Creek Nature Trail (self-guided, quarter-mile) and the trail from Barry's Landing to the campground at Medicine Creek (2 miles) are the only hiking trails on the southern end.

4 Little Bighorn Battlefield National Monument

Perhaps there is no phrase in the English language that serves as a better metaphor for an untimely but deserved demise than "Custer's Last Stand." It was on this battlefield, on the dry sloping prairies of southeastern Montana, that George Armstrong Custer met his end. Though the details of the actual battle that took place on June 25, 1876, are sketchy at best, much remains for the visitor to explore and ponder in this mysterious place.

Some 3,000 people of the Sioux and Cheyenne, including 800 warriors, lay in wait for Custer on that summer Sunday, and though many accounts of what actually happened have been told and retold, written, and filmed, the truth lies buried.

With the Fort Laramie Treaty of 1868, a reservation was set aside in eastern Wyoming and the western Dakotas for the Sioux and Cheyenne. For a few years, there was an uneasy peace—until gold was struck in the Black Hills, setting off a rush that prompted prospectors from all over to come streaming through the region. Fed up with the intrusions, many Indians left the reservation for a spot near the Rosebud and Little Bighorn Rivers. With yet another government treaty broken, the warriors, under the leadership of Sitting Bull and the enigmatic Crazy Horse, began gathering on the plains away from the reservation, reviving their culture and their hunting traditions. When the warriors began harassing settlers, the United States gave notice. The Indians were to return to the reservation in the Black Hills. When there was no response, the government resolved to send them back by force.

Among the troops sent to the area was the Seventh Cavalry under the command of one of America's most fascinating military leaders. Fascinating not for his brilliant tactics or his nerves of steel, Custer was one part genius and one part profound dimwit—and he may have even bordered on insanity. Custer's life up until that point had been an adventure in extremes. He graduated last in his class at West Point, yet became the youngest general in the history of the U.S. Army when General Robert E. Lee surrendered to him during the Civil War. He was court-martialed for issuing an order to shoot army deserters in Kansas, and later fought his way back up the military hierarchy to become commander of the Seventh Calvary, and fancied himself a tamer of savages in the West.

As the battle erupted, Custer, armed with information from his scouts about the location of the Indians' camp, sent three of his companies, headed by Major Marcus Reno, ahead to attack. The men were immediately beaten back, forced to retreat to the top of a ridge where they hung on desperately against a constant onslaught for 48 hours, before the Indian attack mysteriously subsided. It was only then that the troops were able to learn what had happened to Custer and his men.

Not wanting the Sioux to catch wind of the troops' arrival, Custer had marched the troops out at midnight and begun a surprise attack, going on the offensive at a spot only a few miles away from where Major Reno was trying to defend his position. Custer and every one of his 265 men perished, defeated by the thousands of Sioux and Cheyenne warriors that they had planned to round up and relocate.

The history of the park is also intriguing. It was formerly known as Custer Battlefield and was originally meant to honor Custer and his men. Congress wisely changed the name to the Little Bighorn Battlefield National Monument in 1991, only after activists complained that the battlefield was recognizing only a portion of what happened and was slighting the Indian perspective. Currently, the park is in the process of completing a monument commemorating the Native Americans who fought for their homelands.

The sites on the battlefield include the eerie tombstone marking Custer's death on **Last Stand Hill.** A driving tour takes you on a 7-mile paved road through the grounds and culminates on the hill at the **Reno-Benteen Battlefield.**

The Visitor Center is located just past the entrance and is an excellent starting point for a park tour. Visitors can view actual uniforms worn by Custer, read about his life, and see an eerie reenactment of the battles on a small-scale replica of the battlefield as dotted lights trace the movements of each unit. Available in the souvenir and gift shop at the visitor center are books proposing every imaginable theory on what actually took place, including the recently published book, *Killing Custer* (W.W. Norton and Co., 1994), by Montanan James Welch and Paul Stekler, which pieces together the battle from a Native American's perspective.

Touring the park on your own can be an extraordinary way to recapture some of what took place during those 48 hours, and the park offers brochures for self-guided tours through the battlefield. Private group tours are available through the Custer Battlefield Preservation Committee (☎ 800/331-1580) for $200. A private hourly service is also available for $25 an hour. During Little Bighorn Days, an annual event in Hardin held in late June, the Battle of the Little Bighorn is reenacted for the public. The reenactment takes place 20 miles from the original battlesite 6 miles from Hardin. For information on specific dates, call 406/665-1672.

There is a $4 admission fee per vehicle. The park is open daily from 8am to 8pm from Memorial Day to Labor Day. Spring and fall hours are 8am to 6pm and winter hours are 8am to 4:30pm. To reach the battlefield, head 15 miles south of Hardin off I-90. Turn east for 1 mile on U.S. Hwy 212.

5 The Northern Cheyenne Reservation

Wohehiv, the Morning Star, is of great spiritual significance to the Cheyenne people and has evolved into the Northern Cheyenne official emblem, appearing on craft items and even the tribe's cattle herd. Juxtaposed to the massive Crow Reservation, the Northern Cheyenne Reservation lies on less than a half-million acres of arid prairielands and a massive coal deposit. There are nearly 5,600 tribal members on the reservation, most of whom live in small towns, principally Lame Deer, Busby, and Ashland, a town on the western border near the Tongue River. Forced west by the Sioux, who themselves were being pushed west by white settlement, the Cheyenne were driven onto prairies that couldn't support their agricultural way of life. The tribe eventually split, the Northern Cheyenne moving into the Black Hills, the Southern Cheyenne into Colorado.

In 1988, the Cheyenne Depot in Lame Deer became the first tribal-owned convenience store in the state, providing one of the few opportunities for employment. Though the tribe has tentative plans to begin mining the massive coal deposit underneath them (oil exploration proved fruitless), nothing has been decided; economic opportunities on the reservation remain scarce. U.S. Highway 212 cuts a path through the reservation and through the towns of Busby, Lame Deer, and Ashland, and is known locally as the shortest route from Billings to the Black Hills, though the unimproved roads don't always make it quicker. There's very little of interest to the tourist in this area. It is, unfortunately, an incredibly depressed area, even when compared to other Montana reservations.

6 Miles City

Named after Col. Nelson A. Miles, the commander of the 5th Cavalry who was ordered to return bands of Indians to reservations in the summer of 1876, Miles City has retained its Western flair for over a century. In the early days, as portrayed in Larry McMurtry's *Lonesome Dove,* Miles City was a cowboy town on the verge of becoming a leading cattle market; the market came with the arrival of the Northern Pacific Railroad in 1881.

Today, Miles City continues its cowboy traditions with its annual Bucking Horse Sale—attracting thousands of stock contractors from all over the country—and the Range Riders Museum, a thorough collection of photographs and firearms from the old days. It's where remote ranchers go when they need barbed wire or tractor axles, and it's the closest business and agricultural center to Billings.

Miles City isn't lost in the 19th century, but its citizens take an active pride in the town's lack of parking meters—just one indication that it isn't exactly leading the 20th century's technological revolution. Nonetheless, Miles City is a lifeline to its surrounding communities. There is still a traditional Main Street with a saloon and lunch counter, and local merchants make conscious efforts to keep up this city's Old West appeal.

ESSENTIALS

GETTING THERE It's an easy drive up I-94 from Billings.

Like other airports throughout eastern Montana, Miles City's Frank Wiley Field is serviced by **Big Sky Airlines** (☎ 800/237-7788), which provides service to other eastern Montana communities and parts of North Dakota.

The **Greyhound** station is located at 18 S. 6th St. (☎ 406/232-3900).

VISITOR INFORMATION The **Miles City Chamber of Commerce,** located at 901 Main St., Miles City, MT 59301 (☎ 406/232-2890), provides tourists with city maps and guides to virtually everything in the area (including telephone directories). Complete tourist information may be received by writing or calling **Custer Country,** Rte. 1, Box 1206, Hardin, MT, 59034 (☎ 406/554-1671).

SPECIAL EVENTS Every fourth weekend in June, Miles City gets full of hot air with the **Miles City Hot Air Balloon Roundup,** when balloons color the sky above the city from dawn to dusk. The balloons take off from an open field on South Haynes Avenue.

GETTING OUTSIDE
FISHING

Miles City is surrounded by badlands that are interrupted by rivers and streams. To make them accessible (perhaps overly so), the Montana Department of Fish, Wildlife and Parks has created river accesses every 12 miles along the Yellowstone. The **Kinsey Bridge,** a boat access located 10 miles east of Miles City, is a 27-acre site on the Yellowstone and can be reached from a county road north of town that intersects the Kinsey highway.

Though the fishing isn't exactly world-class, the **Twelve-Mile Dam,** 11 miles south on MT 59, then 1 mile south on Tongue River Road, is the source for walleye, smallmouth bass, and sauger, and even has a catfish fishery. There are camping facilities, toilets, and a boat launch.

Roche Jaune, actually within city limits at Truscott and N. 6th Streets, is another boat ramp on the Yellowstone. Every spring it's full of anglers casting for shovelnose sturgeon, ling, and (though it's rare) paddlefish.

Pirogue Island, north of town and off a gravel road, is a bit harder to find, and there are no camping facilities or boat accesses—this is for bank anglers. Stop by **Red Rock Sporting Goods,** 2900 Valley Dr. E (☎ 406/232-2716 or 800/367-5560), Miles City's largest outdoor retailer with extensive selections of camping, fishing, and hunting gear.

GOLF

The private nine-hole **Town and Country Club** course is situated on the east bank of the Tongue River southeast of downtown. The course is open to the public. For fees and tee times, call 406/232-1800.

SWIMMING

The undercurrents and the swiftness of the Yellowstone River preclude safe swimming, but there's a **public pool** on the **west end of Main Street**—it's actually a pond surrounded by late-blooming cottonwood trees and it's a local favorite.

THE JAYCEE BUCKING HORSE SALE

Many of the horses seen in rodeos around the country get their start in Miles City at this annual stock contractors' gathering, held every year during the third weekend in May. Begun as the Miles City Roundup in 1914 to provide bucking stock, the Bucking Horse Sale became a full-fledged event when the Jaycees took over in 1963 and has since blossomed into one of the largest rodeo horse proving grounds in the country. Various asides complement the event, from barbecues to gun shows to a downtown parade. Tickets for the actual rodeo are $7 on Saturday and $7 to $10 for weekend shows. General admission tickets for children under 12 may be purchased for $5. Call the **Miles City Area Chamber of Commerce** (406/232-2890) for specific scheduling information.

SEEING THE SIGHTS

Range Rider Museum

Highway 12 (on Main Street, just outside of town). ☎ **406/232-4483.** Admission $3.50 adults, $3 seniors, 50¢ children, children under 6 free. Apr 1–Oct 31 daily 8am–8pm. Closed rest of the year.

As far as Old West memorabilia is concerned, this collection has it all. The Wilson Photo Gallery is especially charming; it's a sort of cowboy Hall of Fame, with more than 500 portraits exhibited throughout the hall. The museum ranges from a truly spectacular display of firearms, some of which date back more than 100 years, to an almost nonsensical collection of old telegraph insulators. Strolling through the indoor Miles Town replica is almost like walking onto a movie set: a barber shop, bank, saloon, and hotel are all there.

Custer County Art Center

Water Plant Road (just over the Tongue River bridge west of town). ☎ **406/232-0635.** Free admission. Tues–Sat 1–5pm. Take Main Street west out of town to the Fish and Wildlife office and turn right.

This former water plant has found a new identity as an art museum specializing in Western pieces. Listed on the National Register of Historic Places, the museum is actually a piece of work itself. In 1979, the structure was awarded the governor's trophy for best adaptation of a historic structure. Now the building is the home to the Western Art Roundup, an annual show that features the works of Western artists around the time the Bucking Horse Sale is in full swing.

WHERE TO STAY

Best Western War Bonnet Inn

1015 S. Haynes, Miles City, MT 59301. ☎ **406/232-4560.** 54 rms. A/C TV TEL. $50–$80 double. Rates include continental breakfast. AE, DC, DISC, MC, V. Take exit 138 off I-94.

Not as bellicose as the name might imply, this Best Western installation is conveniently located off I-94. It's primarily a businessperson's motel—the War Bonnet offers free continental breakfasts and airport shuttles—but it's also a great place to head when the kids are screaming for you to please get off the highway. An indoor pool, hot tub, and sauna are provided for motel guests.

Motel 6

1314 S. Haynes, Miles City, MT 59301. ☎ **406/232-7040.** 113 rms (52 in winter). A/C TV TEL. $34–$40 double. AE, DC, DISC, MC, V.

Across the street from the War Bonnet is this option for more frugal travelers. The light will, as they say, be on, and the rates are as they promise: lower than the competition's. The drawback is that while it is less expensive than others, it is also a hotel built around the time Reagan was first elected president.

Olive Hotel

501 Main St., Miles City, MT 59301. ☎ **406/232-2450.** 59 rms, 1 suite. A/C TV TEL. $45 double. AE, CB, DC, DISC, MC, V.

Built in 1898, the Olive Hotel has for almost a century been a landmark in eastern Montana. The hotel was originally called the Leighton, after a leading Miles City businessman, but the name was changed to the Olive when the new owners renamed it after their daughter. Added to the National Register of Historic Places in 1988, the hotel features such architectural signatures as curvilinear beveled glass, multicolored tile floors, and high arched windows. Though the hotel got an overhaul in the seventies, the original look of the place has remained (this is especially true of the exterior). An interesting sidenote is the hotel's claim that the Olive is "where Gus slept" (they're referring to Gus McRae of *Lonesome Dove* fame). Though this is simply not true, the Olive, had it existed in the 1880s, would most assuredly have been the ideal place for Gus to lose that leg.

CAMPING

The safest bet is the **KOA Campground,** 1 Palmer (☎ 406/232-3991), which is literally in town. Shaded by giant cottonwoods in summer, the site offers full hookups, sites for tents, a heated pool, and laundry facilities. To get there, take exit 135 off I-94 and drive a little over 2 miles to 4th Street. Take a left and go four blocks.

WHERE TO EAT

The New Hunan

716 N. Earling St. ☎ **406/232-3338.** Reservations recommended. Lunch $4–$5; dinner $6–$8. DISC, MC, V. Daily 11am–9:30pm. CHINESE.

Though the menu is inclusive enough to satisfy even the most ardent admirer of Chinese cuisine, burgers make appearances too. (This is, after all, Miles City.) However, you just can't find a better deal than the all-you-can-eat buffet. For $4.95, the lunch buffet offers eight different items that vary daily, and the dinner buffet, for $7.95, includes 10 items. With one of the more elegant dining rooms in Miles City, the New Hunan is a good place to eat in a town where beef rules.

600 Cafe and the Hole in the Wall

600–602 Main St. ☎ **406/232-3860** or 406/232-9887. Reservations not accepted. Breakfast $2–$6; lunch $5–$7; dinner $8–$20. No credit cards. Daily 5am–10pm. AMERICAN.

Though the Hole in the Wall is perhaps the nicer of the two (these restaurants use the same kitchen), it doesn't much matter since you'll experience both. If you order a buffet dinner at the Hole in the Wall, you'll have to walk through the door to the 600 Cafe to get your food. Though these aren't great places for sophisticated cuisine, they are great places to get a feel for Miles City.

MILES CITY AFTER DARK

About the only thing to do in the evenings in Miles City is to head out to one of the bars. There are no symphony orchestras, comedy clubs, or dance clubs in Miles City, but you can hear some good country-and-Western music, swap a few jokes, and mingle with the townsfolk in the **Montana Bar** at 612 Main St., or at the **Range Riders,** a few steps down at 605 Main St.

A SIDE TRIP TO TERRY

If you get a chance to slide down the interstate to Terry, a small town situated against the badlands of the Yellowstone River, make sure you stop in at two places: Goplen's, and the Prairie County Museum.

To get to **Goplen's Bar and Cafe,** follow the signs from the interstate to downtown. Don't be fooled into thinking this is a cheap little tourist haunt that dwells on self-promotion. This is a great little malt shop in the mornings and early afternoons and the cleanest bar you'll ever see. Come Sunday afternoon, Goplen's serves up the town's best meal buffet-style, but a morning spent just talking with owner Bud Goplen over one of his delicious milk shakes is a morning well spent. Up until a few years ago, Bud and his wife Bette actually made the ice cream that went into every shake, but a stroke a few years ago has kept Bud from continuing the tradition. In addition to the great shakes and entertaining conversation, Bud also boasts one of the largest collections of Jim Beam bourbon decanters in the world. The rumor went that Bud would pop the caps on the decanters New Year's Eve, 1999, but he confesses that since the day is fast approaching, he may change his mind. And Cal Ripken Jr., take note: Bud and Bette have been working seven days a week—since 1947.

At the **Prairie County Museum** on Logan, a block from Goplen's, are the Evelyn Cameron photographs that were published in Donna M. Lucey's *Photographing Montana.* Cameron's photographs were shot in the early days of Terry and chronicle the life of pioneer women like herself. The photographs are remarkable, especially when you consider that Cameron was an amateur photographer who spent her early years in England, a long way from the Wild West she eventually grew to love.

7 Glendive

Situated on Montana's eastern plains, Glendive is a friendly town that boasts no towering mountain ranges, but is nonetheless extremely proud of its natural resources and community spirit. The town took shape along with the Northern Pacific Railroad during the late 1800s and soon became a ranching center, although present-day agricultural pursuits mostly produce sugar beets, grain, and forage crops. The area is known for its abundance of Yellowstone moss agates, and visitors strolling along the banks of the Yellowstone, which flows through town, should keep their eyes peeled for the favored gems.

Nearby Makoshika State Park, Montana's largest, is a treasure unto itself, site of the town's annual "Buzzard Days," a weekend that pays tribute to turkey vultures and gives residents an opportunity to share their enthusiasm for their town. But most famous of Glendive's attractions is its corner on the paddlefishing market, a season enthusiastically ushered in every May as thousands of anglers attempt to snag one of the prehistoric big fish, which can weigh upwards of 100 pounds.

ESSENTIALS

GETTING THERE   **Big Sky Airlines** provides daily flights to and from Billings at the Dawson County Airport (☎ 406/687-3360 or 800/237-7788).

Glendive is an easy drive up from Billings on I-94.

The **Greyhound** bus depot is located at 1302 W. Towne St. (☎ 406/365-2600).

VISITOR INFORMATION   Not only does the **Glendive Chamber of Commerce** provide visitors with information about the city and the surrounding area, it also produces paddlefish caviar, with the profits going to local organizations for cultural, recreational, and historical uses. Order some by mail or drop by their office at 200 N. Merrill, Glendive, MT 59330 (☎ 406/365-5601). Glendive is part of **Travel Montana's Custer Country;** to order a free vacation guide to this eastern section of Montana, write or phone: Rte. 1, Box 1206A, Hardin, MT, 59034 (☎ 406/554-1671).

GETTING AROUND   Glendive operates a senior citizens bus seven days a week (☎ 406/365-5024).

GETTING OUTSIDE

PADDLEFISHING

It's hard to enter Glendive without seeing something to do with the paddlefish. The best spot to snag a paddlefish is the Lower Yellowstone Diversion Dam near Intake off of Highway 16 northeast of town. The word "snag" is not used figuratively here: To catch the ever-elusive paddlefish, the angler must plunk his large treble hook into the water and yank. Paddlefish, like wild game, have seasons that differ depending on where you are—or aren't—catching them. The Intake season on the Yellowstone runs from May 15 to June 30, and fishermen must purchase tags in order to try their luck. Several places in town, including the Cenex Supply and Marketing filling station, at exit 213 off I-94 (☎ 406/365-8381), sell paddlefish tags. The limit? One fish.

ROCKHOUNDING

The river beds throughout Dawson County have provided residents and tourists with a fair crop of Yellowstone moss agates. One of the better places to stumble upon the gem is near the Intake diversion dam 15 miles northeast of town on Highway 16, with the best season occurring in spring after the ice has broken up on the Yellowstone River. Equipment you may want to bring along on your prospecting adventure should include a rock hammer, a bucket or bag for the gems you find, and, as always, a comfortable pair of shoes. The chamber of commerce can give you information on guided boat tours for agate-hunting.

MAKOSHIKA STATE PARK

Makoshika, the Lakota-Sioux word meaning badlands, is a few blocks from town via the railroad underpass. The amazing thing about this state park is not necessarily the uncanny resemblance to Badlands National Park in South Dakota, but the abundance of dinosaur bones that have been removed from under the loess. Erosion has done wonders with the park's upper and most malleable layer, forming magnificent spires in some places and coulees that cut deep into the multicolored valleys in others. Over much of the park are scattered stunted ponderosa pine. Inside the visitor center is an actual skull, not a replica or cast, from a young triceratops that was uncovered from the park.

A drive of switchbacks, paved, then unpaved, wends its way to the top of a scenic overview, and is as well-kept as Montana Fish Wildlife and Parks can afford to make it, but the feasibility of taking an RV or mobile home on such a road is not good. And any vehicle attempting the road after a hard rain may want to have a tow truck follow—the road can become a gumbo that offers little or no traction.

Though a small campground can accommodate campers and RVs just up the road from the entrance, the park also allows for campers to strike off on their own. A fee is still required for backcountry use.

EXPLORING THE TOWN

Many of Glendive's downtown buildings, most notably those on Merrill Avenue from Douglas to Clement Street, are listed on the National Register of Historic Places. If you enjoy and appreciate period architecture, ask the chamber of commerce for their guide brochure. It gives an abbreviated summary of Glendive's history over the last century.

Frontier Gateway Museum

Belle Prairie Frontage Rd. ☎ 406/365-8168. Free admission. Summer, Mon–Sat 9am–noon and 1–5pm, Sun 1–5pm; the rest of the year, daily 1–5pm.

You might not expect to find a brief history of time in Glendive, Montana, but this museum north of town does its darndest. Some of the fossils on display date back 200 million years. From there the museum skips a couple of thousand millennia to the railroad days when Glendive sprouted up with the Northern Pacific Railroad. A small town behind the museum offers a peek into Dawson County's residential past, including a transplanted log home that came piece by piece from Paxton, and a schoolmarm's delight, a rural schoolhouse that has the seating capacity of a large living room.

WHERE TO STAY

Best Western Holiday Lodge

222 W. Kendrick, Glendive, MT 59330. ☎ 406/365-5655 or 800/824-5067. 100 rms. A/C TV TEL. $50–$75 double. AE, DISC, MC, V.

Sharing the same lobby with the Jordan Motor Hotel is unusual, but the Holiday Lodge has offerings for the whole family. The outside pool has a courtyard and the recreation area has a pool table, a Ping-Pong table, and video games. Inside the hotel there's another pool, a lounge and casino, and a gift shop. But the legend at the Holiday Lodge is a meal at the hotel's restaurant, the Blue Room Steak House. Included in the price of a meal is a gander at one of the largest paddlefish of all time, and a look at the murals of J.K. Walstron.

Days Inn

2000 N. Merrill, Glendive, MT 59330. ☎ 406/365-6011 or 800/325-2525. 59 rms. A/C TV TEL. $50–$40 double. AE, DC, DISC, MC, V.

Built in 1982, this relatively new hotel offers easy-on, easy-off access to the interstate for the traveler racing the clock or the dad trying to make the best time ever recorded in the history of I-94. Though there are no dining facilities on the premises, CC's is within a block (see "Where to Eat" later in this section). Pets are okay.

Hostetler House Bed and Breakfast

113 N. Douglas, Glendive, MT 59330. ☎ **406/365-4505.** 2 rms. $45 double. No credit cards.

Craig and Dea Hostetler operate this bed and breakfast (built in 1912), and it truly feels like a home. There's probably not a more accommodating couple on the planet. Stay here if you need a good pampering and want to know what is what and where is where. Though the Hostetler House isn't necessarily full of Old-World style and charm, the tasteful decorations exude a country coziness. Their house is your house and there's always ice water in the rooms.

WHERE TO EAT

Bacios

302 W. Towne, Glendive, MT 59330. ☎ **406/365-9664.** Main courses $6–$16. MC, V. Mon–Sat 5–10pm. ITALIAN.

A gutted and refurbished former Kentucky Fried Chicken, this place may offer the finest dining experience you can have beneath the late colonel's roof. Though the Victorian wallpaper is a nice touch for Glendive, it's not what you'd call Italian. No matter. This hunter-green-and-mauve eatery is elegant enough, the food is more than well-priced, and it comes in plentiful portions. A fettuccini Alfredo is served with alfredo a touch too thick, but the lasagna is a reward and the black forest cheesecake is an excellent dessert. The meals here are definitely worth the price.

CC's

I-94 and N. Merrill, Glendive, MT 59330. ☎ **406/365-8926.** Reservations not accepted. Breakfast $3–$6; lunch $5–$10; dinner $5–$15. No credit cards. Daily 6am–10pm. AMERICAN.

At this little family-style restaurant by the highway you can get the average meal in an average atmosphere. The food may taste better after a long day. Even though the prime rib is probably the best item on the menu, it's been prepared better. A former chain restaurant before it was purchased and remodeled in 1984, CC's is the oldest and, sadly, one of the wisest choices in town.

Yellowstone National Park 11

At the mere mention of Yellowstone, many visions spring to mind: magnificent geysers, steaming hot springs, thundering waterfalls, pristine forests, blue-ribbon trout streams, great herds of bison and elk, giant silvertip grizzly bears, trees sparkling under a fresh blanket of snow. The superlatives are endless. As the world's first, most famous, and most treasured national park, Yellowstone stands proudly alone. The very birthplace of conservation and natural preservation, Yellowstone has served as an example for parks around the world for well over 100 years.

Yellowstone's diversity accounts for the mulititude of reactions it provokes in visitors. Each of us has our own favorite part, our own favorite season. Whether it's your 1st or 21st visit, you don't have to look far to find extremes and drama in this ever-evolving park. The most famous of its traits are its signature geological wonders, which tell the story of a tumultuous volcanic past. The Yellowstone area has a long history of tremendous and catastrophic volcanic activity. Approximately 600,000 years ago the most recent eruptions created the 28-by-47-mile volcanic crater, or caldera, which is central to Yellowstone's present geography. This ancient volcanism still powers the park's famous spouting geysers, boiling hot springs, steaming fumaroles, and bubbling mud pots. The thermal activity in Yellowstone is so intense that the geysers here account for more than half of all the geysers on earth.

From a geological perspective, human history within the Yellowstone ecosystem is a very recent occurrence. Although nomadic foragers traveled the region as early as 4000 B.C. and prehistoric peoples have been documented in the area as early as 11,000 years ago, the only known year-round inhabitants of the area were a small band of the Native American Shoshone tribe, the Sheepeaters. These people, so named for their hunting of and reliance upon bighorn sheep, remained in the park until 1871, when they were moved to the Shoshone Wind River Reservation.

European influence in the Yellowstone area began in the early 1800s when the strange stories of a land of boiling cauldrons of mud and spewing steamholes found their way to the American Midwest. But these fur trappers' wild stories were quickly dismissed. It was not until 1871 that these stories were taken seriously, when Montana's surveyor general, Nathaniel P. Langford, having visited this strange land himself the previous year, convinced the director of the U.S.

Geological Survey, Dr. Ferdinand Hayden, to mount an official exploration. It was through the findings of Hayden's exploration, aided greatly by the work of landscape artist Thomas Moran and photographer William Henry Jackson, that Congress was convinced to declare some 2.2 million acres as Yellowstone National Park on March 1, 1872.

1　Gateway Towns: West Yellowstone, Gardiner & Cooke City

West Yellowstone is the biggest and gaudiest of the park's gateway communities; in many ways, its in-town amusements that shamelessly promote the park keep people from being able to see the real thing. Compared to West Yellowstone, Gardiner and Cooke City seem more like authentic small Montana towns that just happen to have great locations—simple towns with regular folks, places that haven't changed much over the years.

For information about the whole Montana portion of the region, call **Travel Montana** at ☎ 800/736-5276 or 406/446-1005. Ask for brochures and information about Yellowstone Country, Travel Montana's term for this region. Statewide weather reports can be obtained by calling 406/449-5204. For road conditions, call 800/226-7623 or 406/444-6339.

Remember, if you're visiting Yellowstone in winter, the north entrance at Gardiner, Montana, is the only access point open to cars. You can enter the park via snowmobile from the other towns in winter.

WEST YELLOWSTONE

A major gateway into the national park whose name it shares, West Yellowstone is located just outside the park's western entrance. Incorporated in 1966, it only became an official park entrance in 1907—nearly four decades after Yellowstone was declared a national park. A town of sorts, consisting of a hotel, a general store, and a restaurant, grew up a year later, but it took the arrival of the town's first train—the Oregon Short Line's *Yellowstone Special*—in 1909 to lure folks in larger numbers. Mass tourism came with the automobile, and by 1915, cars could be seen pulling into town.

Originally called Riverside, then Yellowstone, the name was officially changed to West Yellowstone in 1920 when Gardiner residents grudgingly complained that people would assume that the town was the park.

The years since then have proved that there's plenty of commerce to go around, especially during the summer months when literally thousands of people find their way along the town's ordered streets, all named after the natural treasures that await visitors just through the gate: Geyser, Firehole, Canyon, Grizzly, Cascade. Summer breezes make shopping and strolling its streets a pleasant alternative to spending the day in the car and there are plenty of treasures (some tacky, some trendy) to keep you interested.

Despite the large numbers of tourist-oriented businesses that have sprung up over the years and the increasingly large crowds to whom they cater, somehow West Yellowstone has managed to retain a personality that is distinctly Montanan. To experience it at its fullest, come after the first good snowfall.

Nicknamed the "Snowmobile Capital of the World," West Yellowstone is absolutely transformed in winter. A mostly male set of snowmobilers returns to "West" to kick up some snow and the family demographic is once again outnumbered—until next summer.

ESSENTIALS

GETTING THERE The **West Yellowstone Airport,** Hwy. 191, 1 mile north of West Yellowstone (☎ 406/646-7631), provides commercial air service seasonally, from June through September only, on Delta's commuter service, **Skywest** (☎ 800/453-9417 or 406/646-7351).

If you're driving to West Yellowstone from Bozeman (91 miles), take Hwy. 191 south to its junction with Hwy. 287 and head straight into town.

From Billings, drive 126 miles west to Livingston on I-90 and take Hwy. 89 south 53 miles to the Gardiner entrance of the park. Drive south 21 miles to Norris Junction, then west another 21 miles to Madison Junction. From Madison Junction it's 14 miles to West Yellowstone.

If you're visiting the park in the summer, a spectacular drive along the Beartooth National Scenic Highway is a must (see Driving Tour #1, Chapter 9). From Billings, drive southwest along I-90 to Laurel and take Hwy. 212 west to Red Lodge. At Red Lodge, continue west on Hwy. 212 to Cooke City. Along the way, you'll be sure to see some of the most stunning mountains in all of the West. If you're visiting in late spring or early fall, be sure to check with the locals to see if the pass is open.

VISITOR INFORMATION Contact the **West Yellowstone Chamber of Commerce,** 100 Yellowstone Ave. (P.O. Box 458), West Yellowstone, MT 59758 (☎ 406/646-7701).

GETTING AROUND Cars can be rented in West Yellowstone through the following agencies: **Avis** (☎ 406/646-7635), **Budget** (☎ 406/646-7882), and **National** (☎ 406/646-7670). **Big Sky Car Rental,** at 429 Yellowstone Ave. (☎ 800/426-7669 or 406/646-9564), is locally owned and located at Randy's Auto Repair.

GETTING OUTSIDE

Obviously, you've come here because of the town's proximity to the national park, so that's where you'll be headed for hiking, boating, wildlife viewing, and more. The sections that follow in this chapter will tell you all about the park itself. But there are a few notable things to do in the immediate environs of the town as well.

West Yellowstone ranks among the best fishing locales in all of Montana—and considering all the sublime fishing waters with which the southern part of the state is blessed, that's some compliment. The following tackle shops offer the full gamut of guided fishing trips and schools, from one-day trips to weeklong excursions: **Arrick's Fishing Flies,** 128 Madison Ave. (☎ 406/646-7290); **Bud Lilly's Trout Shop,** 39 Madison Ave. (☎ 406/646-9570); **Eagle's Tackle Shop,** 3 Canyon St. (☎ 406/646-7521); **Jacklin's,** 105 Yellowstone Ave. (☎ 406/646-7336); and **Madison River Outfitters,** 117 Canyon St. (☎ 406/646-9644).

You can't explain the appeal of West Yellowstone in winter until you've actually seen for yourself how thoroughly the town enmeshes itself in **snowmobile culture.** Downtown streets are traveled by cars and sleds in equal numbers as visitors return year after year for the rugged, yet pristine experience afforded by this mode of travel. Also popular are **Yellowstone snowcoach tours,** offered in vans equipped with tanklike treads that move effortlessly over the snow. The following companies can provide you with the latest snowmobiles, snowcoaches, and other equipment and give you leads on local trails: **Ambassador Snowmobile & Snowcoach Rentals,** 315 Yellowstone Ave. (☎ 800/221-1151); **Backcountry Adventures,** 224 Electric St. (☎ 406/646-9317); **Lone Rider Snowmobiles,** 8 miles west of West Yellowstone on Hwy. 20 (☎ 800/884-1844); **Rendezvous Snowmobile Rentals,**

429 Yellowstone Ave. (☎ 800/426-7669); **Two Top Snowmobiles,** 645 Gibbon Ave. (☎ 406/646-7802); **Westgate Station Snowmobile Rentals,** 11 Yellowstone Ave. (☎ 800/255-3417); **Yellowstone Adventures,** 131 Dunraven St. (☎ 800/231-5991); **and Yellowstone & Old Faithful Snowmobiles,** 215 Canyon St. (☎ 406/646-7614).

Additionally, nearly every hotel and motel in town offers snowmobile packages that include your room and a sled rental. Whether you procure your sled with or without a room reservation, be sure to book well in advance because of the popularity of this winter activity.

West Yellowstone has also made a name for itself in **cross-country skiing.** Designated an official training site of the U.S. Nordic and Biathlon Ski Teams, West Yellowstone plays host to aspiring racers of all ages every November. The **Rendezvous Trail System** is made up of a 30km series of premier wilderness trails, professionally groomed from early November through April 1 for track and skate skiing. The gently rolling, deeply forested terrain will invigorate all your senses, making for—what else?—a wilderness outing of Olympic proportions. **Yellowstone Nordic Guides,** 511 Gibbon Ave. (☎ 406/646-9333), offers the area's premier guide service. Weekly departures lead to hidden geyser basins and powder slopes and are designed for skiers of all abilities. Travel by snowcoach to their skiers' yurt in Yellowstone for a memorable Nordic outing.

If you'd rather strike out on your own, unguided, check with the tackle shops listed above for a complete line of cross-country ski rentals. Lone Mountain Ranch is nearby, too (see "Where to Stay" in the The Gallatin Valley section of Chapter 9).

SEEING THE SIGHTS

Yellowstone IMAX Theatre

101 S. Canyon St. ☎ **406/646-4100.** Admission $6 adults, $3 children 3–11, under 3 free. Daily May–Sept 9am–9pm, Oct–Apr daily 1–9pm. Call for information and reservations for groups.

This IMAX theater is just one of several attractions that make up West Yellowstone's new Grizzly Park complex (see below). If you're unfamiliar with the concept, IMAX is the world's largest motion picture format, with six-channel stereo surround sound; theaters equipped with it have super-sized screens. (This particular theater claims the screen is six stories tall, but we're a little skeptical.) One of the specially designed feature films, *Yellowstone: Grizzlies, Geysers, Grandeur,* occasionally dazzles you with innovative photography, but more often than not it simply plods along the Yellowstone timeline with no clear purpose or destination. Though the theater itself is comfortable, with seating for nearly 350 people during each hourly showing, take our advice: spend your $6 on a park ticket and go see Yellowstone for yourself.

Grizzly Discovery Center

Grizzly Park. ☎ **406/646-7001** or 800/257-2570. Admission $6.50 adults, $3 children 5–15, children under 5 free. Year-round daily 9am–6pm.

As part of the greater Grizzly Park complex, the Discovery Center shares the ignoble designation, along with the IMAX theater, of promoting a plastic and secondhand version of nature. On entering the brand-new facility—captive home to a set of grizzly bears named Toby, Fred, Kenai, Max, and Lewie—the visitor is welcomed to a somewhat interactive interpretive area that illuminates the history and current plight of the grizzly. From here, doors lead to the grizzlies' outdoor home, a carefully

Yellowstone National Park

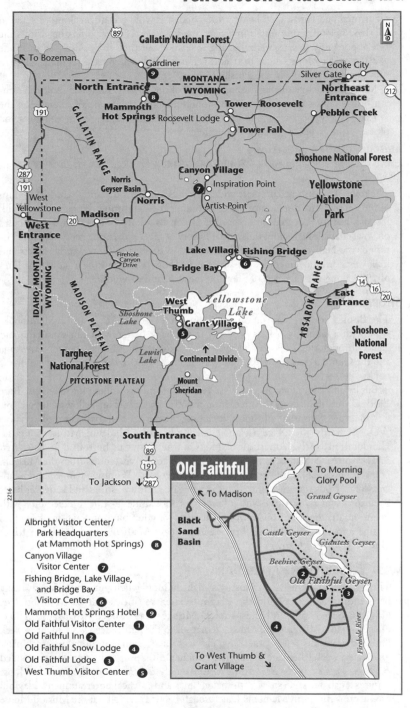

Gallatin National Forest

↖ To Bozeman

MONTANA
WYOMING

Gardiner

North Entrance

Mammoth
Hot Springs

Roosevelt Lodge

Tower—Roosevelt

Tower Fall

Cooke City
Silver Gate

Northeast
Entrance

Pebble Creek

Shoshone National Forest

GALLATIN RANGE

Norris
Geyser Basin

Norris

Canyon Village

Inspiration Point

Artist Point

Yellowstone
National
Park

West
Yellowstone

Madison

West
Entrance

Firehole
Canyon
Drive

Lake Village Fishing Bridge

Bridge Bay

MADISON PLATEAU

Shoshone
Lake

West
Thumb

Grant Village

Yellowstone
Lake

ABSAROKA RANGE

East
Entrance

IDAHO
MONTANA
WYOMING

Lewis
Lake

Continental Divide

Shoshone
National
Forest

Targhee
National
Forest

PITCHSTONE PLATEAU

Mount
Sheridan

South Entrance

To Jackson ↓

2216

Old Faithful

↖ To Morning
Glory Pool

↖ To Madison

Grand Geyser

Black
Sand
Basin

Castle Geyser

Giantess Geyser

Beehive Geyser

Old Faithful Geyser

Firehole River

To West Thumb &
Grant Village ↘

Albright Visitor Center/
Park Headquarters
(at Mammoth Hot Springs) 8

Canyon Village
Visitor Center 7

Fishing Bridge, Lake Village,
and Bridge Bay
Visitor Center 6

Mammoth Hot Springs Hotel 9

Old Faithful Visitor Center 1

Old Faithful Inn 2

Old Faithful Snow Lodge 4

Old Faithful Lodge 3

West Thumb Visitor Center 5

manicured and landscaped living area. Though it will be heartbreaking to some to see these magnificent animals in a cage, the Discovery Center offers its visitors the rare opportunity to watch grizzlies and to learn about their lives. Also located inside is a screening room where bear and other wildlife videos are regularly shown; souvenirs are available in the gift shop.

Make it a day by cruising through the rest of the Grizzly Station complex: Northern Bear Trading Co., Silvertip Station (a restaurant), Michone's Candies, and the Grizzly Gallery. Because you're stamped as you enter the center, come and go as you please—your ticket is good for the entire day.

Museum of the Yellowstone

Canyon St. and Yellowstone Ave. ☎ **406/646-7814.** Admission $5. May–Sept daily 8am–10pm.

The town wouldn't be complete without a museum, and the aptly named Museum of the Yellowstone does a nice job of recording and exhibiting the region's colorful, if short, history. Located in the historic Union Pacific Depot, the museum focuses on what shaped the region: the natural history of the Yellowstone ecosystem, the history of the Native Americans of the Plains, and the history of the early settlers and their westward movement. An on-site theater shows a video of the Yellowstone Fires of 1988 along with footage of the park, the area, and its wildlife.

SHOPPING

The Book Peddler, Canyon Square Shops, 106 Canyon St., is an excellent bookstore with a fabulous espresso counter in the back (where you can sip a latte and glance through the *Times Book Review*). The store features books about Yellowstone and the Grand Tetons as well as old West standards and a vast selection of children's books.

But by and large, shopping in West Yellowstone means trolling for souvenirs. **Rare Earth Unlimited,** across the street from the Visitors Center on Yellowstone Ave., offers an array of unusual gift items, including meteorites and fossils as well as native Western items—local gems, antler products, and Made in Montana crafts. Handcrafted Native American blankets and jewelry can be found at **Lost Art,** 32 Canyon St. **Smith & Chandler,** 121 Yellowstone Ave. (across from the Museum of the Yellowstone), is the town's Western clothier, with Woolrich flannels and hand-creased Stetsons for sale along with the requisite cotton T-shirts and souvenir baseball caps. Anglers, or those who just want a cool fishing T-shirt to take home with them, should check out these two tackle shops for good buys on anything from flies to fine apparel: **Bud Lilly's Trout Shop,** at 39 Madison, and **Madison River Outfitters,** at 117 Canyon St.

WEST YELLOWSTONE AFTER DARK

Though it may seem hard to justify a night indoors when you could just as easily be spending it in the park, the **Playmill Theatre,** located at 29 Madison Ave. (☎ 406/646-7757) and the **Musical Moose Playhouse,** 124 Madison Ave. (☎ 406/646-9710), are can't-miss alternatives to the nature scene. Six nights a week during the summer season, the Playmill stages three separate productions, each playing twice a week (there are no shows on Sunday). Recent productions have included *Barnum, Fiddler on the Roof,* and *You Can't Take it With You.* The Musical Moose features a cabaret-style show with melodramas and musical entertainment. Playmill productions run from Memorial Day through Labor Day; folks at the Musical Moose perform from December through March and June through October. Advance reservations are recommended for both.

WHERE TO STAY

West Yellowstone may seem like a small town with plenty of hotel and motel space, but during the summer months rooms become scarce items. Winter can also be difficult. Snowmobilers converge with even more zeal than families in summer, turning West Yellowstone into one giant party. The least expensive times to lodge in West Yellowstone are the fall, when there's not enough snow for winter recreation, and spring, before the summer masses arrive. Rates for rooms often reflect the season, and prices can fluctuate enormously. Prices quoted below are for doubles.

Best Western owns a large portion of the lodging market in West Yellowstone, with four different motels located around town. The **Best Western Desert Inn** at 133 Canyon (☎ 406/646-7376 or 800/528-1234) has 57 rooms. In season, a double room goes for $52–$102 per night; in winter, the rates drop to $38–$57 per night. The **Best Western Executive Inn** at 236 Dunraven (☎ 406/646-7681 or 800/528-1234) is by far the largest Best Western property in West Yellowstone with 82 rooms. Its winter rates are $54–$84 per night, only slightly higher in summer. The **Best Western Weston Inn** at 103 Gibbon (☎ 406/646-7373 or 800/528-1234) has 55 rooms. In summer, rates range from $35–$95 per night, and in winter, they drop to $50–$70 per couple. The **Best Western Pine Motel** at 234 Firehole Avenue (☎ 406/646-7622 or 800/646-7622) has 46 rooms which range in price from $65–$95 in summer to $47–$69 in winter.

Other choices include the **Brandin' Iron Motel** at 201 Canyon (☎ 406/646-9411 or 800/217-4613) with 84 rooms (summer rates start at $60; winter rates from $39) and the **City Center Motel,** 214 Madison Ave. (☎ 406/646-7337 or 800/742-0665), whose 25 rooms go for $46 to $97 year-round.

Stage Coach Inn

209 Madison Ave. (at the corner of Dunraven), West Yellowstone, MT 59758. ☎ **406/842-2882.** 88 rms. TV TEL. $55–$115 double. Sightseeing, snowmobiling, and snowcoach packages available upon request. AE, DISC, MC, V.

The Stage Coach is a West Yellowstone classic. Its crisp Tudor-style exterior is offset by the warm Western decor of the spacious pine-paneled lobby. Rooms feature furnishings in muted tones with subtle bear-and-moose motifs; the walls are accented by mounted fishing trophies instead of sketches or paintings.

The Coachman Restaurant serves savory fresh seafood entrées and other gourmet entrées. The Coachroom Lounge dispenses drinks to the accompaniment of keno machines and live poker. There is a spa facility and gift shop on the premises, as well as an underground parking lot.

Three Bear Lodge

217 Yellowstone Ave., West Yellowstone, MT 59758. ☎ **406/646-7353.** 43 rms. TV TEL. $70–$95 double. Snowmobile and cross-country skiing packages available in winter. DISC, MC, V.

The cozy pine-furnished rooms of this family-style inn are located less than three blocks from the park entrance. With an outdoor heated pool, indoor whirlpools, and a youth activity center, it is especially suitable for families. Like every other lodging in West Yellowstone, the Three Bear offers snowmobile and cross-country ski packages with or without licensed guides, however, unlike elsewhere, their snowcoaches are brand-new. Three Bear Lodge's restaurant and lounge are great spots for refueling and relaxing after a long day of playing in the snow.

✪ West Yellowstone Conference Hotel Holiday Inn SunSpree Resort

315 Yellowstone Ave., West Yellowstone, MT 59758. ☎ **800/646-7365** or 800/HOLIDAY. 123 rms and suites. A/C TV TEL. $70–$130 double; $90–$200 suite. Special snowmobile/snowcoach packages available during winter. AE, DISC, MC, V.

The wordy name of West Yellowstone's newest hotel says it all—and a little bit more. Though their conference facilities are first-rate, tourists will be more interested in the last half of their appellation, Holiday Inn. The hotel's designation as a SunSpree Resort, a four-season active tourist destination, makes it a bit more expensive than the average Holiday Inn, but the extra amenities that come with the SunSpree name are well worth the difference.

Because it's a brand-new facility, the rooms are particularly welcoming, with lush carpeting and polished appointments, as well as coffeemakers, hair dryers, mini-fridges, microwaves, and sofas. The king spa suites are especially popular with snowmobilers in winter; they feature a king-size bed and an in-room Jacuzzi along with standard room features. The hotel's mini-mall layout is home to the Oregon Short Line Restaurant, a great place to sample regional and international cuisine for breakfast, lunch, and dinner, as well as the popular Iron Horse Saloon. The Eagle's Crossing Gift Shop sells a fine assortment of souvenirs and unique gift items. A heated indoor pool, exercise area, and guest laundry facilities round out the amenities. All things considered, there is no finer hotel in West Yellowstone.

Guest Ranches & Resorts

✪ Firehole Ranch

11500 Hebgen Lake Rd., West Yellowstone, MT 59758. ☎ **406/646-7294** in summer or 307/733-7669 year-round. 10 cabins, each sleeps up to 6. Daily rate: $200–$290 per person, based upon occupancy. Rate includes all meals, airport transfers, and activities (except guided fishing). Four-day minimum stay required. No credit cards.

The Firehole Ranch was one of the area's first fly-fishing guest ranches and it's one of the only such lodgings endorsed by Orvis in the state. Built in the 1940s, the main lodge is where meals are served and guests are encouraged to relax and get to know one another. Though fishing is certainly the main attraction along the area's blue-ribbon streams and high mountain lakes, guests can also go horseback riding, mountain biking, or hiking along the ranch's many trails. Canoeing is equally popular. Nearby Hebgen Lake, Mt. Baldy, and Yellowstone provide inexhaustible scenic vistas. Gourmet meals, prepared by a French chef, are an added bonus. Specialties include fresh grilled seafood and innovative pasta dishes.

The Hibernation Station

212 Gray Wolf Ave., West Yellowstone, MT 59758. ☎ **800/580-3557.** 18 cabins. TV TEL. $75–$135 per cabin. AE, DISC, MC, V.

These brand-new luxury cabins are an excellent example of the principles of supply and demand at work in a tourist town. Though the deluxe Western furnishings in the hand-built cabins are top-notch, with down comforters atop queen-size log beds and enormous bathrooms, the cabins' presence in Grizzly Park makes them seem as displaced as the bears. The single and double cabins are no doubt as comfortable as any you'll find in the area, but they don't have the atmosphere you'll find in older, more authentic places. Like a fancy saddle, they haven't had enough time or use to become broken in; they're nice, they're just not the first ones you'd reach for. The Gallatin National Forest, Yellowstone, and a multitude of snowmobile trails are all nearby, though, making for a spectacular setting.

Camping

There are three Forest Service campgrounds in the West Yellowstone area. They all accommodate RVs and tent campers and are open throughout the summer. Reservations can be made for any of them by calling 800/280-CAMP. **Bakers Hole** is just 3 miles north of West Yellowstone on Hwy. 191. It's popular, so reservations should be made before driving up. It's open from late May to mid-September. The second Forest Service campground is **Lonesomehurst,** 8 miles west on Hwy. 20, then 4 miles north on Hebgen Lake Rd. This campground is about one-third the size of Bakers Hole and fills up quickly in summer; reservations are strongly advised. **Rainbow Point** is 5 miles north of West Yellowstone on Hwy. 191, 3 miles west on Forest Service Rd. 610, then north 2 miles on Forest Service Rd. 6954.

In addition, there are a few RV parks in town. **The Hideaway RV Campground** at the corner of Gibbon St. and Electric Ave. (☎ 406/646-9049) has cable TV hook-ups for those who simply cannot bear to live without their favorite TV programs, and is open from May 1 through October. **The Yellowstone Park KOA** (☎ 406/646-7606) is 6 miles west on Hwy. 20 and offers a pool, a hot tub, and a game room for kids. It stays open from May 1 through September.

WHERE TO EAT

✪ Cappy's Bistro & Country Store

Canyon Square, at the Bookpeddler. ☎ **406/646-9537.** Reservations not accepted. Most items $3–$6. Tues–Sun 11am–4pm. AE, DISC, MC, V. SOUPS/SALADS/SANDWICHES.

It may be a contradiction in terms, but Cappy's is a great little Western bistro. The woven leather chairs are huge and the tables for two are small, giving it an atmosphere that manages to be both spacious and intimate at the same time. Locals are addicted to the black bean soup, which is served daily along with the soup of the day. All sandwiches are served on your choice of croissant, whole-grain roll, or whole-wheat pita pocket, and come with either a cup of soup or coleslaw. The Targhee is a tasty combo of dilled shrimp, avocado, salsa, mayonnaise, mozzarella, chives, and crunchies that tastes great with a cup of the black bean soup. This is one of those places where sprouts show up in unlikely places and daily specials feature tasty and unique combinations.

Adjoining the cafe, extending into the bookstore, is an espresso counter also run by Cappy's. An unfinished log "fence" separates the cafe from the country store, where you can find such items as Montana Coffee Traders coffee by the pound, birch bark birdfeeders, Bodum bistros, and novelty teapots. Stop by in summer for delicious homemade ice cream.

⊝ Eino's Tavern

8955 Gallatin Rd. ☎ **406/646-9344.** Reservations not accepted. Most items $3 and up. No credit cards. Daily noon–8pm. Closed first two weeks of Dec. AMERICAN.

You're in for a unique experience at Eino's, where locals snowmobile out (there's a trail that follows Hwy. 191 from West Yellowstone) just to have the opportunity to pay for grilling their own food. Sound unusual? It's certainly a novel concept, but one that keeps people coming back for more. If you want to blend in with the locals, go up to the counter and place your order for a steak, teriyaki chicken, hamburger, or hot dog—just don't gasp when you're handed an uncooked piece of meat. Simply drop your drink off at the nearest available table and head for the grill room like you've been there before. Stand around and shoot the breeze with other patrons until your food is exactly the way you like it, and enjoy. Steaks and chicken come with your choice of a baked potato or a garden salad, and hamburgers come with chips. Though it's not exactly a fine dining experience, it's a lot of fun and the views of Hebgen Lake are spectacular. Snowmobilers can purchase gas and oil here, too.

GARDINER

Gardiner and West Yellowstone are studies in contrast. West Yellowstone is almost like a wildlife Las Vegas, with its grizzly bear complex; and Gardiner, though it provides the only year-round access to Yellowstone at the park's northern entrance, is a small town that could easily suffer from an inferiority complex. But it doesn't. Though its position as the only year-round entry point to Yellowstone gives it something the other gateway communities can't boast, Gardiner still remains a lazy little town that, oh, by the way, has a world-famous national park next door.

There's no fanfare, no precise street addresses, and no enormous signs (until you leave town and meet Roosevelt Arch, the marker for the park's entrance—it was named for Theodore Roosevelt, who dedicated it in 1903). Deer and elk and other animals meander in from the park to graze on town land. There are always hoofed creatures hanging around, waiting for a little attention and a lot of food. Tourists oblige, though this is bad for the animals and certainly not condoned.

In fact, wildlife straying by from Yellowstone is hardly remarkable to folks around here anymore and is sometimes even considered a nuisance or a danger. A few years back, Gardiner became known for bison hunting. Because bison can carry brucellosis, a bacteria that when transmitted to cattle causes them to abort, ranchers, private hunters, and wildlife officials began to gun down bison found wandering outside the park. Naturally, a brouhaha transpired, culminating in state and federal agencies turning their attention to the question of how bison are managed in and around the park; as yet, no conclusion has been reached. Until then, rangers continue to shoot bison caught damaging private property or otherwise causing a disturbance.

If you need additional information on the town, contact the **Gardiner Chamber of Commerce,** Box 81, Gardiner, MT 59030 (☎ 406/848-7971).

LOCAL OUTFITTERS

A few adventure travel outfitters are based here. The **Yellowstone Raft Company,** on Hwy. 89, just north of the bridge, makes its home in Gardiner (☎ 406/848-7777 or 800/858-7781) and offers guided whitewater paddle trips down the Yellowstone River. The **Wilderness Connection** on Cinnabar Basin Road (☎ 406/848-7287) is operated by Gary Duffy, who has spent a couple of decades packing people by horse in and out of the park.

SHOPPING

The **Town Cafe, Motel, Lounge, Casino & Gift Shop** is a good place to start the souvenir spree. It's open year-round in downtown Gardiner on Park St. **Out West T-Shirts & Sweats** offers quality designed Yellowstone and Montana shirts at the Yellowstone Outpost Mall (Hwy. 89). **Yankee Jim's Trading Post,** also right downtown on Park St., is a complete clothing store and one-stop shopping source for all your pre-Yellowstone needs: film, T-shirts, jewelry, and other souvenirs.

WHERE TO STAY

Be sure to make lodging reservations well in advance of your trip to Gardiner, a small town whose few rooms are often hard to come by. Call ahead and ask about promotional rates, since many properties provide seasonal discounts and can be considerably less expensive than the in-season rates quoted in the listings below.

In addition, there are a few chains in town, all of which recommend advance reservations. When we checked, all of them were offering the same deal: $40 for a double in winter, $80 for the same room in summer. The **Super 8,** located on Hwy. 89 S (☎ 406/848-7401 or 800/800-8000), is open year-round and has 64 simple, yet clean rooms. The **Yellowstone Village Motel,** 808 Scott St. (☎ 406/848-7417 or 800/228-8158), has a heated pool and 43 rooms. The **Absaroka Lodge,**

U.S. Hwy. 89 at the Yellowstone River Bridge (☎ 406/848-7414 or 800/755-7414), is a 41-room facility. All accept major credit cards for payment.

Best Western by Mammoth Hot Springs

Hwy. 89 (P.O. Box 646), Gardiner, MT 59030. ☎ **406/848-7311** or 800/828-9080. 85 rms. A/C TV TEL. Summer, $84–$94 double; winter, $47–$57 double. Snowmobiling and cross-country skiing packages available. AE, DISC, MC, V.

One of several hotel chains in the Gardiner/Mammoth area, the Best Western, like its competitors, offers winter rates that are about half its summer rates.

But even during peak season, this Best Western is reasonably priced when you consider its location and amenities. Just a mile from the north entrance to the park, the Best Western offers an average restaurant (see "Where to Eat" below), a casino and lounge, an indoor pool, and a whirlpool. They also have cross-country skiing and snowmobile equipment rentals and winter packages are available.

Comfort Inn

107 Hellroaring, Gardiner, MT 59030. ☎ **406/848-7536** or 800/221-2222. 80 rms. $95–$145 double. AE, DISC, MC, V.

A 3,000-square-foot lobby is the centerpiece of this Gardiner motel. With balconies featuring stunning mountain views and dining and shopping options across the street, the Comfort Inn is a great base from which to explore this tiny Montana town and to appreciate the natural beauty of the national park next door.

Maiden Basin Inn

No. 4 Maiden Basin Drive, P.O. Box 414, Gardiner, MT 59047. ☎ **406/848-7080.** 2 rms, 3 suites, 1 cabin, 1 studio unit. Summer, $70–$90 rm (double), $125–$155 suite, $90–$105 cabin, $85–$100 studio; winter: $42–$60 rm (double), $75–$110 suite, $60–$80 cabin, $55–$75 studio. MC, V.

The Maiden Basin Inn sets itself apart from other accommodations in Gardiner in more ways than one. In addition to being 5 miles north of town off Hwy. 89, it provides luxury inn–like accommodations that surpass any of the chain options nearby. A handsome ranch house with scenic views of the Yellowstone River, it offers a variety of choices: The Maiden Basin is a spacious studio unit with a kitchenette; the La Duke is wheelchair-accessible; and the Yellowstone Suite caters to romantic couples, with a whirlpool bath and panoramic views. The Big Sky and Montana suites are perfect for families, with full kitchens, a laundry, living room, and one or two bedrooms. The "cabin" is interesting in that it is actually a part of the inn, even though the inside looks exactly like a remote mountain hideaway. Nearby Yellowstone National Park and the Absarokee Beartooth Wilderness provide numerous options for outdoor recreation, including fishing, hiking, cross-country skiing, and snowmobiling.

Camping

If you'd prefer to camp, there are two choices in Gardiner, one public, one private. The Forest Service's Eagle Creek campground is 2 miles northeast of Gardiner on Jardine Road. It's rather small—only 10 tent sites—but is open year-round. Call the Forest Service in Gardiner at 406/848-7375 for directions to this campground and information on local recreational opportunities nearby. The town's private campground, **Rocky Mountain Campground** (☎ 406/848-7251), is open year-round with 97 sites for RVs or tents and 13 mobile-home spaces. There are 30 full hookups and 34 with electricity and water only. A complete grocery store, laundry, game room, and mini golf course round out the amenities. To get there, drive one block east of U.S. Hwy. 89 on Jardine Road.

WHERE TO EAT

The Yellowstone Mine

In the Best Western by Mammoth Hot Springs, Hwy. 89. ☎ **406/848-7336.** Reservations not accepted. Breakfast items $4–$6; main dinner courses $10–$20. AE, DISC, MC, V. Daily 6–11am and 5–9pm. AMERICAN.

The old-time mining atmosphere may not spark your appetite, but the meals come in healthy portions and the prices are, like the hotel's, reasonable. Steaks and seafood are the restaurant's specialty. There's also a lounge and casino known as the Rusty Rail. Inside you'll find live poker, machine poker, keno—whatever you need for a fix before you head into gambling-free Wyoming.

Outlaws

Yellowstone Outpost Mall. ☎ **406/848-7733.** Reservations not accepted. Most items $6–$15. MC, V. Daily 11am–11pm. ITALIAN.

You really don't have to be hungry when you stop in at Outlaw's. The views are incredible and the wait staff doesn't mind if you just sit and look at the park over a cup of coffee (especially in winter). The gourmet pizza is the local favorite and there's also a salad bar that's not only the best in town, but one of the few.

COOKE CITY

This little tourist community finds itself smack-dab in the middle of it all. From its mile-and-a-half elevation, Yellowstone is to the west, the Beartooth Highway to the east, and mining controversy is to the north. The local politics are a miniature version of all Montana's: There are those who wish mining would return; and those who want nothing to do with it. If Cooke City's small-town political agenda holds no interest for you, never mind; you'll be occupied with the almost hypnotically spectacular mountain scenery. Nearby **Pilot Peak** is without a doubt one of the more dramatic peaks one can see from Montana (it actually lies within Wyoming's boundaries).

Cooke City is full of outdoor enthusiasts in the summer and the winter. Bicyclists can find a helping hand at the **Bike Shack** where maps and advice—such as where to go and where not to—are plentiful (not to mention rental bikes and other equipment).

If you choose to spend the night in Cooke City, you have several options, although none of them include modern facilities complemented by gourmet dining and valet parking. Rooms here are clean and comfortable, but that's about all lodgings in Cooke City offer. Expect to pay from $50–$65 for a room, regardless of the season, at each of the properties listed below.

The 32-room **All Seasons Inn** on Main St. (☎ 406/838-2251), is Cooke City's largest, with a restaurant, lounge, and heated pool. The somewhat smaller **Alpine Motel,** also on Main St. (☎ 406/838-2262), is a bare-bones operation, but it accepts pets. The **High Country Motel,** Main St. (☎ 406/838-2272), has 15 rooms.

For a meal or a beer (the selection of imports is amazing), try the **Beartooth Cafe** right downtown on the north side of Main St. (☎ 406/838-2475). Reservations are accepted and midday meals range from $3 to $7; a dinner can be had for anywhere from $9 to $14. Call ahead for hours.

For more information on the town, contact the **Cooke City Chamber of Commerce,** Box 1146, Cooke City, MT 59020 (☎ 406/838-2272 or 406/838-2244).

2 Just the Facts

GETTING THERE

The closest airports to the park are in Jackson, Wyoming, and West Yellowstone and Bozeman, Montana and Idaho Falls, Idaho.

The Jackson Airport at Grand Teton National Park is served by **American Airlines** (☎ 800/433-7300), **Continental Express** (800/525-8280), **Delta** (☎ 800/221-1212), **Skywest** (☎ 307/733-7920 or 800/453-9417), and **United Express** (☎ 800/241-6522). From here you can easily rent a car and head north 45 miles toward Yellowstone on Highway 89/191. (See Chapter 12 for additional details.)

See Section 1 of this chapter for details on how to get to West Yellowstone.

Bozeman's airport, **Gallatin Field,** provides daily service via **Continental** (☎ 800/525-0280), **Delta** (☎ 800-221-1212), and **Northwest** (☎ 800/225-2525) as well as **Horizon** and **Skywest** commuter flights. Car rentals are a snap from here (see Chapter 9 for details). From Bozeman you can take Highway 191 91 miles to West Yellowstone, or you can proceed east 26 miles toward Livingston on I-90, turning south on Highway 89 for 53 miles to Gardiner, the northern gateway to the park.

From Cody, it's a gorgeous 53-mile drive west along Highway 16/14/20 to the east entrance of the park.

The Idaho Falls Airport, **Fanning Field,** is located 2 miles northwest of Idaho Falls off I-15 and provides daily service on **American** (☎ 800/433-7300), **Continental** (☎ 800/525-0280), **Delta** (☎ 800/221-1212), **Northwest** (☎ 800/225-2525), **United** (☎ 800/241-6522), and **USAir** (☎ 800/428-4322). Car rentals are also available at the airport through the following companies: **Avis** (☎ 800/831-2847), **Budget** (☎ 800/527-0700), **Dollar** (☎ 800/800-4000), **Hertz** (☎ 800/654-3131), and **National** (☎ 800/227-7368).

To reach Yellowstone from Idaho Falls, take I-15 south from the airport 1 mile to exit 119 and head east (actually northeast) on Hwy. 20. It's a roughly two-hour, 107-mile drive to the park's entrance at West Yellowstone.

ACCESS/ENTRY POINTS

Throughout the summer, Yellowstone is accessible through five major entrances.

The North Entrance is located at Mammoth Hot Springs, just south of Gardiner, Montana In the winter, this is the only access into Yellowstone by car.

The West Entrance is just outside the town of West Yellowstone. This entrance is open to wheeled vehicles from April to November and during the winter to snowmobiles. The South Entrance is the entrance from Grand Teton National Park and is open to wheeled vehicles from May to November and to snowmobile traffic from December to March. The East Entrance is 52 miles west of Cody and is open to wheeled traffic from May to September and to snowmobiles from December to March. The Northeast Entrance, at Cooke City, Montana, is open throughout the year to wheeled vehicles, but in the late fall, when the Beartooth Pass is closed, the only route to Cooke City is through Mammoth Hot Springs.

Check road conditions before entering the park by calling the visitor center number at 307/344-7381. An ongoing construction project will delay summer travelers for at least a half-hour in some places, and as winter approaches, early snows can close roads temporarily.

VISITOR CENTERS & INFORMATION

There are five visitor centers and each has something different to offer. The **Albright Visitor Center** at Mammoth Hot Springs provides visitor information, publications about the park, exhibits depicting park history from prehistory through the creation of the National Park Service, and a wolf display on the second floor. The **Old Faithful Visitor Center** offers publications, a movie on geysers, and up-to-date geyser predictions. The **Canyon Visitor Center** and **Fishing Bridge Visitor Center** dispense visitor information and publications. The **Grant Village Visitor Center** has information, publications, a slide program, and a fascinating exhibit that examines the effects of fire in Yellowstone. Other sources of park information can be found at the Madison Information Station, Museum of the National Park Ranger, and the Norris Geyser Basin Museum.

If you wish to have maps and information mailed to you before you leave home, contact the Superintendent, Yellowstone National Park, WY 82190 (☎ 307/344-7381).

When you enter the park, you'll be given a good map and up-to-date information on facilities, services, programs, fishing, camping, and more.

FEES

The cost to enter the park is $10 per vehicle for a seven-day period, $4 per person (over age 16 and under age 62) for those entering the park by other means. Those 16 and under or 62 and older are admitted free. The entrance permit is good for both Yellowstone and Grand Teton National Parks.

If you plan on visiting Yellowstone more than once in a calendar year, you may want to purchase the annual pass for $15. The Golden Eagle Passport, available for $25, allows the holder and accompanying passengers in a private, noncommercial vehicle to enter all of the national parks for one year from the date of purchase. The Golden Age Passport is available to all persons over the age of 62 for a one-time $10 fee; it allows all holders and their accompanying passengers entrance to all national parks indefinitely. The Golden Access Passport for the disabled is offered free of charge.

REGULATIONS

The following regulations apply. More detailed information about these rules can be requested from the park rangers or information offices.

Defacing park features, picking wildflowers, or collecting natural or archeological objects is illegal.

BIKES Though it's not uncommon to see bicyclists touring Yellowstone, bikes are prohibited on backcountry trails and boardwalks. Cyclists ride along the roadside in the park where currently no bike paths exist. This can be harrowing, especially along the many curves in the park where drivers may not be prepared for suddenly coming upon a cyclist. Visitors centers throughout the park can give specific guidelines and safety recommendations. In addition to safety regulations, the visitors centers also provide lists of trails throughout the park.

BOATING Boating permits are required for all vessels. Motorized boating is restricted to designated areas. Boating is prohibited on all of Yellowstone's rivers and streams except for the Lewis River Channel, where hand-propelled vessels are permitted. Coast Guard–approved personal wearable flotation devices are required for each person boating. Boating fees for motorized craft are $20 for annual permits and

$10 for seven-day permits. Nonmotorized fees are $10 for annual permits and $5 for seven-day permits.

CLIMBING Rock climbing is prohibited in the Grand Canyon of the Yellowstone.

FIREARMS Firearms are not allowed in Yellowstone National Park. However, unloaded firearms may be transported in a vehicle when cased, broken down, or rendered inoperable. Ammunition must be carried in a separate compartment of the vehicle.

FISHING Anglers 16 years of age and older must purchase a special-use permit to fish in the park. The permit costs $5 for seven days and $10 for the season. Those 12 to 15 years of age may obtain a nonfee permit. Anglers under the age of 12 may fish without a permit, but should be accompanied by an adult who is familiar with the regulations. Permits are available at any ranger station, visitor center, or Hamilton store in the park.

LITTERING Littering in Yellowstone National Park is strictly prohibited—remember, if you pack it in, you have to pack it out. Throwing coins or other objects into thermal features is illegal.

MOTORCYCLES Motorcycles, motor scooters, and motor bikes are allowed only on park roads. No off-road or trail riding is allowed. Operator licenses and license plates are required.

PETS Pets must be leashed and are permitted only within 25 feet of roads and parking areas and may not be left unattended. Pets are prohibited in the backcountry, on trails, on boardwalks, and in thermal areas for obvious reasons.

SWIMMING Swimming or wading is prohibited in thermal features or in streams whose waters flow from thermal features. Swimming is not recommended because of the low water temperature in Yellowstone.

WILDLIFE It is unlawful to approach within 100 yards of a bear or within 25 yards of other wildlife. Feeding any wildlife is illegal.

SEASONS

Yellowstone National Park is open daily but in November, December, March, and April, access is limited. Summer finds the park populated with millions of visitors, unbelievable wildlife, and spectacular bursts of thermal activity. But during the winter, when access by car is possible only through the north entrance, most winter devotees arrive in the park via snowmobiles or snowcoaches. Winter images can be even more spectacular than those in summer: steam cutting through frigid winter air or the snow beards of the buffalo. Cross-country skiing is also a major winter sport during the uncrowded winters and a great way to see the winter face of Yellowstone.

Spring can be a roll of the dice in Yellowstone. If you have plenty of patience and time, it can be an excellent time to visit. The problem is, road openings can be delayed for days and sometimes weeks at a time (especially at the higher altitudes), and heavy spring storms can cause restrictions or lengthy delays on roads. Couple this with the massive road project already in progress and you have a frustrating experience waiting to happen. However, there are no crowds in spring, and during a good year, most roads are open throughout the park by Memorial Day. Plowing begins during the first part of March and the Old Faithful area is usually cleared by the middle of April. If everything goes well with the roads, you can almost have Yellowstone to yourself in spring. Wildflowers are beginning to bloom and the Yellowstone wildlife are still at lower elevations, waiting to return to the high country for summer.

AVOIDING THE CROWDS

The best way to avoid the majority of Yellowstone's more than two million annual visitors is to avoid the busy summer season (July and August). From May through mid-June and September into early October the crowds are greatly diminished and the park's attractions are much more accessible.

Another method of distancing yourself from the crowds is to plan a backcountry camping trip as part of your vacation. Only a very small percentage of Yellowstone's visitors venture past the roadside attractions—and that's their loss. With a backcountry permit you can experience the essence of Yellowstone's wilderness without having to crawl over the tourists in front of you.

RANGER PROGRAMS

National Park Rangers are present not only to make sure you stick to the 45 mph speed limit and store your food properly, but also to carry out their role as naturalists. Activities include demonstrations and talks at visitors centers, guided walks and hikes, and evening programs at the park's many amphitheaters (many of these activities are accessible to the disabled). Be on the lookout for "roving" ranger/naturalists at major park features—they are there to help you appreciate your park.

Children between 7 and 12 years of age are encouraged to become Junior Rangers. This program introduces children to the wonders of Yellowstone and teaches the importance of its preservation. There is a $1 donation requested; information on the program is available at any ranger station or visitor center.

SERVICES & SUPPLIES

In 1915, when Charles Ashworth Hamilton purchased the general store at Old Faithful, today's oldest privately owned and family-run concessionaire in the National Park system—Hamilton Stores, Inc.—was born. The stores offer a wide array of items such as groceries, souvenirs, photo supplies and processing, clothing, outdoor gear, and food and beverage service. Especially worth checking out is the original store at Old Faithful and the new Nature Shop at Mammoth Hot Springs. Most of the hotels and lodges have gift shops as well.

Automatic Teller Machines   There are 24-hour cash machines—compatible with Cirrus and Plus systems—available at the Old Faithful Inn, Lake Yellowstone Hotel, and Canyon Lodge during regular operating hours.

Medical Facilities   The three medical facilities in Yellowstone National Park are: Mammoth Clinic, open year-round (☎ 307/344-7965); Old Faithful Clinic, open early May to mid-September (☎ 307/545-7325); and Lake Hospital, open late May to mid-September (☎ 307/242-7241). For emergencies dial 911.

Service Stations   The Yellowstone Park service stations have been serving park visitors since 1947. Today there are seven service stations throughout the park, with towing service from Old Faithful, Canyon, Fishing Bridge, and Grant Village.

FOR TRAVELERS WITH PHYSICAL DISABILITIES

A large number of Yellowstone's roadside attractions, including the Grand Canyon of the Yellowstone's south rim, West Thumb Geyser Basin, much of the Norris and Upper Geyser Basins, and parts of the Mud Volcano and Fountain Paint Pot areas are negotiable by wheelchair. For a complete listing, pick up a copy of "Guide to Accessibility for the Handicapped Visitor" at any visitor center. TDD access for the hearing impaired can be reached at 307/344-2386.

ORGANIZED TOURS & ACTIVITIES

Like many of the other services and activities in Yellowstone, organized tours are spearheaded for the most part by **TW Recreational Services, Inc.** (☎ 307/344-7311 for tour reservations).

Motorcoach tours are available from all of Yellowstone's villages. Offered are the Upper Loop, Lower Loop, and Grand Loop Tours. The tours stop at all major points of interest and short guided walks are conducted. Drivers provide interesting facts and stories along the way and answer any specific questions you may have. All of these are full-day tours and children under 12 ride free. Fares for adults are $23; children between 12 and 16 are $12 each.

At Bridge Bay Marina, one-hour **scenicruiser tours** are conducted throughout the day. The tours explore the northern part of Yellowstone Lake and the narrative is interesting and entertaining. Fares are $7 for adults and $4 for children (those under 2, held on lap, are free). **Yellowstone Guidelines** (☎ 800/314-4506), based in Bozeman, provides private, customized itineraries with prices that start at $125 per person, per day. Some of the highlights of their trips include excursions to the lesser-known Echinus geyser (as well as you-know-who), exploring backcountry waterfalls, and soaking in the natural outdoor hot springs of Boiling River. Although camping is encouraged (and all equipment is supplied), hotel and cabin accommodations can be arranged at additional expense. Rates include transportation within the park with guide, park and camp fees, customized activities (such as rafting or horse rides), hearty meals, and use of all camping gear and binoculars. Their season runs from June through September and advance reservations are required.

For a memorable wildlife expedition that is both educational and fun, check out Ken Sinay's Northern Rockies Natural History tours (☎ 406/586-1155). See the "Learning Expeditions" in the Bozeman section of Chapter 9 for details on these specialized nature adventures.

SPECIAL ACTIVITIES

Guided horseback trail rides are offered for those in search of a Western-style tour. Trail rides are available at Mammoth Hot Springs, Roosevelt Lodge, and Canyon Village Corrals and are offered in one- or two-hour tours. Children must be 8 years old and at least 48 inches tall. Tour prices are $15 for a one-hour ride and $24 for a two-hour ride. Check any activity desk for times and dates. Reservations are recommended.

For those interested in a Western experience without the saddle sores, a **stagecoach ride** from Roosevelt Lodge is just the thing. Rides leave throughout the day and fares are $6 for adults and $5 for children 2 to 11. The Lodge's Old West cookouts combine a trail ride and a hearty dinner for a genuine Western experience, with old-fashioned entertainment.

Self-guided car audio tours are a great way to get the most out of a drive through the park in your own vehicle. The system plugs into your vehicle's cigarette lighter and plays through your FM radio. The system, which costs $25 for a full day or $16 for a half day, is available through activity desks and is highly recommended.

The **Yellowstone Institute** was established in 1976 by the Yellowstone Association, a group that assists with educational, scientific, and historical programs for the benefit of the park and its visitors. Basically, the Yellowstone Institute offers educational seminars and classes for the public. Courses offered cover such topics as birding, wolf tracking, canoeing, fly-fishing, backpacking, history, and many others. Headquarters are at the historic Buffalo Ranch in Yellowstone's Lamar Valley but courses are conducted throughout the park. For a detailed course listing, call the Yellowstone Institute at 307/344-2294.

3 Seeing the Highlights

If your time in Yellowstone is limited, you'll want to plan carefully, so below we've compiled a rundown of the park's major attractions and features, starting from the north entrance and moving roughly counterclockwise in a loop around the park. All are easily accessible along the major loop roads (see also Section 4, "Driving the Park," below), though we strongly advise you to plan some time to get out of your car and walk. If you venture even a short way beyond the major roads, you'll lose most of the crowds and get a real feel for the unspoiled side of Yellowstone.

MAMMOTH HOT SPRINGS

At the park's north entrance, 5 miles south of Gardiner, Montana, Mammoth Hot Springs is home to spectacular limestone terraces, historic park buildings, and the Mammoth Hot Springs Hotel. This may be the best entrance to the park for the first-time visitor because of its history as park headquarters and traditional entry point. From Gardiner you pass through the Roosevelt Arch, dedicated by President Theodore Roosevelt in 1903, and follow the winding road along the Gardiner River to Mammoth. Many of the old stone buildings here date back to pre–Park Service days when the U.S. Army was stationed here at Fort Yellowstone. Watch for **pronghorn antelope** near Gardiner, **elk** as you approach Mammoth, and, for the alert traveler, **bighorn sheep** on the cliffs along the Gardiner River. Before reaching Mammoth from the north, you may want to stop at the 45th parallel parking area, where a short hike leads you to the **Boiling River hot spring.** Here you may take a dip, during daylight hours, where a hot spring empties into the Gardiner River.

Once at Mammoth Hot Springs, a stop at the **Albright Visitor Center** will provide exhibits of the park's history as well as wildlife exhibits.

One of Yellowstone's most unique and beautiful attractions are the **Mammoth Hot Springs Terraces.** Mineral-rich hot waters flow to the surface at an unusually constant rate, resulting in the remarkable succession of limestone terraces. The flow of these springs brings with it up to 2 tons of limestone daily, and these deposits form the ever-changing terraces.

The restaurant at **Mammoth Hot Spring Hotel** serves one of the park's finest dinners, which you may enjoy while viewing the resident **herd of elk** that frequents the hotel lawn. You may wish to rent one of the **hot tub cabins** that are available on an hourly basis. **Guided horseback rides and sightseeing tours** are available or you may want to take one of the **day hikes** in the immediate area.

NORRIS GEYSER BASIN

Traveling south from Mammoth Hot Springs, the first major geyser basin is located at Norris Junction: Norris Geyser Basin, home to the park's highest concentration of thermal features. It's the hottest, most dynamic area in Yellowstone. At Norris, three faults in the earth's crust intersect and any movement in any of these faults can change the face of the geyser basin. A walk of less than 2 miles will take you past both the northern Porcelain Basin and the southern Back Basin. At the right time of day the haunting music of Porcelain Basin is an experience not soon forgotten. These basins contain a great variety of geysers and if you're lucky, you may witness a rare eruption of Steamboat Geyser, which has been known to shoot up to 400 feet and is the world's largest. The nearby Norris Geyser Basin Museum explains geothermal features and the Museum of the National Park Ranger tracks the history of the park's most recognized employee.

From Madison Junction south to Old Faithful, there are several geyser basins to explore in the Lower Loop Tour (see later in this chapter).

OLD FAITHFUL

Old Faithful is synonymous with Yellowstone National Park for millions of people around the globe. Undoubtedly the world's most famous geyser, Old Faithful is aptly named. Over the last 100 years, its eruptions have been remarkably consistent— 21 to 23 times daily with a column averaging about 134 feet and a duration of about 40 seconds.

A National Historic Landmark, the **Old Faithful Inn** is the most unique and impressive structure in Yellowstone. This log hotel was completed in 1904 and narrowly escaped destruction during the Yellowstone fires of 1988. Longtime village employees may be willing to share with you stories of the inn's reported "haunting"!

GRANT VILLAGE/WEST THUMB AREAS

Grant Village, named for President Ulysses S. Grant, was completed in 1984 and is the newest of Yellowstone's villages—so, logically, it's home to the park's most modern facilities. Located on the southern shore of Lake Yellowstone, Grant Village offers dramatic views of summer squalls and one of Yellowstone's most inspiring sunrises. Watch for **otters and cutthroat trout** in the old marina's waters or dine at the **Marina Steakhouse** at the water's edge: the view from the steakhouse is worth the walk. For a full-service dining experience, try the beautiful main dining room and lounge.

The **Grant Visitor Center** offers an exhibit exploring the history of fires in Yellowstone. There is also a Kodak-sponsored slide presentation of the park worth checking out. West Thumb, just two miles north of Grant Village, is the home of one of the park's **self-guided walking tours.** The boardwalk takes you through a wonderfully concentrated collection of thermal features on the shore of Lake Yellowstone.

YELLOWSTONE LAKE

At 7,733 feet, Yellowstone Lake is the country's largest lake at so high an altitude. The lake, reaching depths of up to 320 feet, has more than 100 miles of shoreline and is roughly 20 miles long by 14 miles wide. **Wildlife** abounds in and around the lake area. Watch for osprey, bald eagles, white pelicans, cormorants, moose, and grizzly bear, which are especially prevalent during the trout spawn runs in spring.

Yellowstone Lake has the largest population of native cutthroat trout in North America and makes an ideal **fishing** spot during the summer. Be advised of catch limits and general fishing regulations, available at any visitor center or ranger station, before you stake your claim to a part of the lake. While you're out there, keep an eye out for the "Yellowstone Lake Monster," reported to surface occasionally in the deep waters. Some marina employees may even regale you with stories of Jacques Cousteau's submarine exploration of the lake's depths.

Lake Village, on the north shore of the lake, offers a large range of amenities including fine restaurants at either the rustic Lake Lodge or the majestic 100-year-old Lake Yellowstone Hotel. Just south of Lake Village is the park's water activity center, the **Bridge Bay Marina.** You may enjoy taking an hourlong **scenicruiser tour** of the northern part of the lake. The views are magnificent and your captain will share fascinating facts about the area's natural, geological, and cultural history. The

Trial by Fire

In 1988, something terribly magnificent happened in Yellowstone. It wasn't car-bound tourists flocking in for another typical season at America's first and most beloved national park. Anyone over the age of 15 probably remembers the violent conflagrations that whipped through Yellowstone in firestorms and canopies that scorched more than 700,000 acres, exploding boulders, charring wildlife, and, in one instance, killing a firefighter when a snag fell from above.

When Yellowstone Park is mentioned it's hard not to recall the brilliant images of the park during the raging fires in late summer of 1988. Every night on the evening news, anchors from the major networks focused their reports on the massive blazes, eight in all, that were sweeping through Yellowstone in a way no one had ever seen, damaging more than one-third of the park in the process. Afterward, the fires provided fodder for an intense debate concerning the government's policy of land management in national parks.

Until the 1970s it was thought that fires were bad under any circumstances, especially in the eye of the public. Then the National Park Service quietly established the Wildlife Fire Management Plan for Yellowstone, which allowed fires ignited by natural causes, such as lightning, to burn freely. All fires started by humans were still put out, and even the lightning fires were to be closely monitored. But the policy of letting fires burn was hardly tested until 1988. By that time, at least 100 years of dry wood and unburned kindling lay on the park floor, waiting for incineration. When the fires of 1988 started, small blazes that were usually put out by rains turned into bigger, almost uncontrollable ones. The most devastating of the fires, the North Fork Fire—which mounted a furious attack on September 8—was in truth a man-made fire begun just east of park boundaries in Idaho's Targhee National Forest. In the end, the park suffered massive cosmetic damage, some of which is still visible today, but the forest's life cycle is right on schedule. Few buildings were destroyed by the fire (though some, like the Old Faithful Inn, escaped in legendary close calls) and a giant swath from the southwest to the northeast side was virtually untouched. What you can expect to see now is a park on the mend. Yellowstone is doing nicely, thank you. The trees from the serotinous seeds of the lodgepole pine are reborn, the undergrowth that was scorched has returned, and though there are still visible scars on thousands of trees throughout Yellowstone, they serve as a visible reminder of the devastating power of fire.

The exhibit *Yellowstone and Fire* is a wonderful treatment of the fires of 1988 and can be seen at the visitor center at Grant Village throughout the summer season.

marina also offers guided fishing trips, small boat rentals, dock rentals, and a store and tackle shop.

CANYON VILLAGE AREA

The **Grand Canyon of the Yellowstone River** arguably provides the park's most breathtaking views. The intense thermal forces here have colored the canyon walls with many hues of reds, oranges, yellows, tans, and browns. Watch for telling plumes of steam along the canyon's rock spires, where viewing opportunities are extensive and varied. The canyon, 24 miles long and up to 1,200 feet deep, begins at a dramatic waterfall that's more than twice as tall as Niagara Falls—the **Lower Falls,** at 308 feet. The **Upper Falls,** just upstream, stand 109 feet tall. There are trails and roads along both rims of the canyon, offering an incredible array of spectacular views. It is necessary, and well worth it, to walk some trails for the best views. **Inspiration Point** and **Artist Point** (handicapped-accessible) are especially noteworthy.

For the more adventurous, a hike 500 feet down **Uncle Tom's Trail** provides an amazing vantage point for viewing the Lower Falls, though it will be challenging for out-of-shape visitors. Before striking out on any of the trails in this area, consult one of the area maps (available for free or for a nominal fee) to decide which views of the area are best suited to your party's time constraints and physical abilities. You'll be well rewarded with some of the most spectacular photographic opportunities in all of Yellowstone. While you're hiking, be sure to watch for osprey fishing the river or nesting along the canyon walls.

Canyon Village itself, though overdeveloped, provides lots of useful services—a hotel-style lodge, cabins, a snack shop, cafeteria, dining room, bar, gift shop, horseback trail rides, guided tours, and park exhibits.

ROOSEVELT/TOWER AREA

Roosevelt Lodge gives Yellowstone's visitors an opportunity to get a taste of the Old West. This is the most relaxed of the park's villages, a great place to take a break from the more crowded park attractions. You can get into the cowboy spirit by taking a **guided trail ride, a stagecoach ride,** or **a wagon ride.** A more adventurous alternative to the rustic dining-room atmosphere is an **Old West cookout** to which you will arrive by either horseback or wagon for a hearty meal. The nearby 132-foot **Tower Falls** is named for the towerlike volcanic pinnacles at its brink and provides an excellent photo opportunity. While in the area, take time to view the petrified forests on **Specimen Ridge,** where a wide variety of fossilized plants and trees date back millions of years. All things considered, Roosevelt is a great place to leave your car for a day or two and "rough it"!

4 Driving the Park

Touring Yellowstone by car is a great way to see what you want, when you want, at your own pace. Be patient and enjoy the views: Traffic can literally proceed at a slow crawl at times. The main roads in Yellowstone form a kind of "figure eight," commonly divided into the Upper Loop, Lower Loop, and Grand Loop. While it is recommended to spend at least a full day on each loop, the Grand Loop is useful if you have only one day to drive Yellowstone. Taking a "Loop Tour" is also a good way to identify sites you would like to investigate further in days to come.

It is highly advisable to visit the visitor centers and/or ranger stations at all of the major sites. The literature available is invaluable and the exhibits change regularly.

WINTER ROAD CONDITIONS   Due to the high elevation and the abundance of snow, the roads in Yellowstone during winter are closed to all vehicles except those that have commercial agreements with the park. The only ranger station open during the winter months is one located at the north entrance at Mammoth Hot Springs; cars are allowed to drive around the town of Mammoth Hot Springs. Signs will alert you as to how far into the park you can actually go from here (usually to Tower Junction, 18 miles away). From there, the northeast entrance is 29 miles away (the northeast entrance is open, but not accessible from Red Lodge, since the Beartooth Highway is closed in winter). Snowcoaches, snowmobiles and cross-country skiers, however, use the roads regularly throughout the winter. For up-to-the-minute information on weather and road conditions, call the visitor information center at (307/344-7381).

ROAD CONSTRUCTION   Currently Yellowstone is in the throes of an eight-year construction project begun in 1994 and designed to drastically improve driving conditions throughout the park. In the meantime, visitors should expect to suffer delays, sometimes up to 30 minutes, and nightly sectional road closings. Even without delays, some of the roads being repaired are chewed up and barely passable: In 1995, the east side of the park was being repaired and the road was almost impassable without a four-wheel-drive vehicle. Check with the visitor information center (☎ 307/344-7381) before entering the park to determine the best times and the best routes to reach your destination in or outside of the park. Yellowstone's extreme conditions take their toll on the roads constantly.

THE UPPER LOOP

This tour is 70 miles long and passes through the major sights of Mammoth Hot Springs, Roosevelt Lodge, Tower Fall, Dunraven Pass, the Grand Canyon of the Yellowstone, and Norris Geyser Basin.

At Mammoth Hot Springs, you should take the one-way **Upper Terrace Loop** drive. The terraces here are some of the most spectacular anywhere and the only of their kind in Yellowstone. Enjoy a ranger-guided tour or pick up a self-guiding trail map. Those interested in the history of Yellowstone should take time to explore the **Albright Visitor Center.**

Heading east from Mammoth, drive six miles to the **Children's Fire Trail,** perfect for the family. Relatively flat and easy, the walk was built after the fires of 1988 to show the effects of forest fires.

A few miles ahead, **Blacktail Plateau Drive** is a very pleasant alternative to the main road. The one-way dirt road exits to the south and offers great wildlife-viewing opportunities and a bit more solitude. Shortly after returning to the main road, there is a short spur road that leads to one of northern Yellowstone's many ancient **petrified trees.**

Roosevelt Lodge is a good stop to get a taste of the Old West. Perhaps a one-hour guided horseback or stagecoach ride appeals to your sense of adventure. If so, this is the place.

Heading south toward Canyon Village, make a stop at **Tower Falls,** a 132-foot waterfall surrounded by volcanic pinnacles. Continuing south, the road climbs Mount Washburn to **Dunraven Pass** (elevation 8,859 feet), where keen eyes might be rewarded with a glimpse of a grizzly bear in an open meadow—this is one of their prime habitats. South of the pass is an **overlook** that provides views as far as the Teton Mountain range to the southeast on a clear day.

Stop next at Canyon Village and choose one of the many observation points into the **Grand Canyon of the Yellowstone:** Inspiration Point, Grandview, Artist Point, and Lookout Point are all excellent scenic vantages. The **Lower Falls** are nothing short of awe-inspiring and the canyon's shapes and colors will astound.

On the 12-mile drive west from Canyon Village to Norris Geyser Basin, we suggest taking the alternate road, the **Virginia Cascades Drive,** which is well worth the extra few miles. The road doesn't generally see much traffic and the cascades are beautiful. Plan to spend some time walking and exploring the **Norris Geyser Basin** area (see Section 3, "Seeing the Highlights," earlier in this chapter for details). It's the most fascinating and varied thermal area in the park, and there's lots to see.

From Norris Geyser Basin, drive back north towards·Mammoth Hot Springs. You will first pass **Obsidian Cliff,** a source once tapped by ancient peoples of North America. Obsidian is a black volcanic glass used for weapons and tools; through trade, it traveled great distances across the continent (please remember that it's unlawful to remove any natural features from a national park). Further ahead there is a picnic area at the turn-off at **Sheepeater Cliff,** named for the only native people ever to inhabit Yellowstone year-round. Continuing north, watch for **moose at Swan Lake Flats** on your left.

The final few miles into Mammoth take you through a small canyon and along the unusual formations of limestone boulders called the "hoodoos" on your left.

THE LOWER LOOP

Using Old Faithful as the starting point for this tour, the Lower Loop is 96 miles long and can easily take up most of your day. Stop first at the visitor center at Old Faithful and pick up the Yellowstone Association's guides for Old Faithful and the surrounding geyser basins: Fountain Paint Pots, Norris Geyser Basin, Canyon, Mud Volcano, and West Thumb Geyser Basin. These are well worth the 25¢ donation.

Old Faithful, the geyser, is certainly one of the park's most reliable thermal features. It has not missed a periodic eruption in over 120 years, with a current average interval of eruption of 74 minutes. After viewing Old Faithful, visit the visitor center for predictions of nearby geyser eruptions or stop in at the **Old Faithful Inn** (see also "Where to Stay" and "Where to Eat" later in this chapter). The log structure, finished in 1904, is a National Historic Landmark and an impressive attraction in itself.

Accessible by walkways from Old Faithful Village is the **Upper Geyser Basin.** Among the attractions here are Beehive Geyser, Grand Geyser, Castle Geyser, Riverside Geyser, and the beautiful Morning Glory Pool.

Leaving Old Faithful Village toward Madison Junction you may wish to stop at **Black Sand Basin** to view **Emerald Pool.** A little further up the road is **Biscuit Basin,** so named for the biscuit-shaped formations later destroyed by natural causes. A short stop here will allow you to see Jewel Pool, Sapphire Pool and Mystic Falls on the **Little Firehole River.** The **Midway Geyser Basin** is a must-see stop. The major attractions here are the **Grand Prismatic Spring,** Yellowstone's largest hot spring, and the **Excelsior Geyser,** once the park's most powerful geyser.

On your way to the Lower Geyser Basin, you may wish to take the one-way **Firehole Lake Drive** to Firehole Lake, **Great Fountain Geyser,** and **Three Senses Trail.** At the Lower Geyser Basin view the **Fountain Paint Pots** and **White Dome Geyser.** The small detour of **Firehole Canyon Drive** is worth the time spent: there are great views of the canyon and the **Firehole Falls.**

Before turning north at Madison Junction, take a 9-mile detour to the west to **Two Ribbons Trail,** which winds its way through the burned forest along the Madison River, providing a fascinating look at fire ecology. North from Madison to Norris, follow the Gibbon River, which runs along the volcanic caldera's rim. About half-way to Norris is **Gibbon Falls,** where the river tumbles over the caldera wall.

In the Norris area is **Norris Geyser Basin,** the **Norris Geyser Basin Museum,** and the **Museum of the National Park Ranger,** all described above in the first tour and in Section 3, "Seeing the Highlights."

Heading east towards Canyon Village, take the **Virginia Cascades Drive** alternate road along the Gibbon for some lovely views. This is a one-way road traveling west to east and exiting from the main road to the south. Located near Canyon Village

Wolves in Yellowstone

When Yellowstone became a national park in 1872, no one would have dreamed of the likelihood of outrage over certain animals found wandering into the parks. But that was more than 100 years ago, before ranches began springing up along park boundaries. Now every move the park makes is held up to microscopic scrutiny. In the not-so-distant past, buffalo strayed outside the park with cattle-killing diseases. And now wolves that have crossed over the boundaries of Yellowstone to southern Montana and Wyoming have caused the latest uproar.

The new controversy first erupted in January 1995, when 14 wolves were captured in the Canadian Rockies and transported to the United States to be prepared for a March release into Yellowstone. The park was (and still is) reeling from a lack of predators, since wolves, wolverines, and mountain lions were hunted down decades ago. Grizzly bears and coyotes still survive here and they do their share of hunting, but with the population of elks soaring up over 35,000, they simply cannot do enough to thin the herds and strike a natural population balance. In March 1995, when the wolves were finally released, ranchers all around Montana and Wyoming wanted to know why the reintroduction of wolves was so important. Cattle all over the two states would again be in danger—not from disease this time, but from new predators.

Of the three packs of wolves released in Yellowstone, two got along nicely, staying within park boundaries. But a male and his mate from the third group, the Rose Creek pack, affirmed the fears of every rancher in Montana and Wyoming when they crossed the border into Montana and began loitering very close to Red Lodge. Before members of the Yellowstone Restoration Project team could get to Red Lodge and assess the situation, a local allegedly shot and killed the male wolf. The person then skinned and beheaded the wolf. What made matters worse, in the eyes of wildlife biologists, was that the mate was pregnant. She was captured, along with her eight pups, and penned in a facility back in Yellowstone. When the wolves were released in October 1995, another male stepped in as leader of the pack and replaced the wolf that had been killed.

Though disaster was averted, relations are still strained between the two sides of the restoration argument and ranchers still question the logic of Yellowstone officials (as does the Montana state legislature, which half-humorously tried to introduce a bill to put wolves into New York City's Central Park and Washington, D.C.). The park staff, in the meantime, hopes to improve the image of the wolf in and around the park before they reach their goal of maintaining 10 packs (roughly 100 wolves) in Yellowstone.

Educating the tourist is another immediate goal of the park. Though wolves may look like coyotes from a distance, they should be easily distinguished from the coyote by their size. A coyote can reach somewhere close to 45 pounds soaking wet, while the wolf weighs closer to 125 pounds. Visitors to the park are encouraged to report any wolf sighting to rangers so that the park can continue to successfully monitor the progress of this restoration project.

is the magnificent **Grand Canyon of the Yellowstone** (see details in Section 3), where there are vantage points along both rims with marvelous views of the canyon, the Upper Falls, and the breathtaking Lower Falls. There are also some nice day hikes here; make the time for walking if you can. The **Brink of the Lower Falls** and **Uncle Tom's Trail** offer a close-up look at the mighty power of the Lower Falls.

Driving south from Canyon Village, the road follows the Yellowstone River from the Upper Falls to Yellowstone Lake. **Hayden Valley** is a wide sprawling former extension of Yellowstone Lake. Here a 6-mile section of the river has been closed to fishing, thus leaving the natural state of the valley relatively undisturbed. **Herds of bison** roam the area and can be seen occasionally fording the river. Watch the marshy areas for **trumpeter swans, white pelicans,** and **Canadian geese. Moose** also frequent the area, as well as **river otters** and the occasional **grizzly bear.**

Ten miles south of Canyon Village is the **Mud Volcano** area, which is full of unique thermal activity. The trail is only ²/₃ of a mile long and includes such attractions as Mud Geyser, Black Dragon's Cauldron, Dragon's Mouth Spring, and Sulfur Caldron. The major features here are all handicapped-accessible.

A little more than 2 miles on the road to Yellowstone Lake is **Le Hardy Rapids.** Here you can enjoy a shaded stroll in the trees and perhaps a glimpse of **spawning cutthroat trout** in the early summer. Fishing Bridge is located in prime grizzly bear habitat due to the cutthroat trout spawn. Though now closed to fishing, the bridge was once commonly packed elbow-to-elbow with fishermen. Today it provides an excellent vantage point from which to view the trout spawn in early and mid-summer. The **museum** here features exhibits of Yellowstone's birds and animals, which can help you to put names to the wildlife you will spot in the park.

Yellowstone Lake is North America's largest high-altitude lake, at 20 miles long, 14 miles wide, and up to 320 feet deep. Take a one-hour narrated boat tour of the northern lake, leaving from Bridge Bay Marina, for great views and informative and entertaining narrative. The 185-room **Lake Yellowstone Hotel** has been beautifully restored and is a nice place to stop for a relaxing break in its sunroom.

From the Lake Village area, the road follows the lake's western shore to the **West Thumb Geyser Basin.** The bay of West Thumb is a caldera, or volcanic crater. West Thumb was a major center of activity in the park's early history and the log structure that functioned as the original West Thumb Ranger Station still stands here. The existence of these geysers, hot pools, and mud pots on the lake's shore makes for great vistas.

The final leg of this tour leads east over the **Continental Divide** at Craig Pass and back to Old Faithful. At **Shoshone Lake Overlook** there are pleasant views of the lake and valley below as well as a unique view of the distant Tetons.

THE GRAND LOOP TOUR

The Grand Loop Tour encompasses most of the sights included in the Upper and Lower Loop Tours but does not allow the visitor as much time to enjoy the more subtle aspects of each area. This tour is a good idea if you have only one day to spend in Yellowstone. Highly recommended is the rental of a self-guided audio tour unit. The unit plugs into your car's cigarette lighter and plays through your FM radio. Inquire at a hotel activity desk for rental information.

5 Summer Sports & Activities

There are many activities, outfitters, and rental shops in the park's gateway towns; see Section 1 of this chapter for details.

BICYCLING   Bicycling in Yellowstone is permitted on established public roads, campgrounds, parking areas, and designated routes, such as those trails in the Old Faithful area that permit bicycles. Inquire at a visitors center for information on bike trails. The park roads themselves are usually narrow and winding and can be quite dangerous, as the traffic is heavy and there are no bike lanes. Bicycles are not allowed on backcountry trails and boardwalks. Gateway communities usually rent bicycles and can recommend rides. Try Bill Blackford's **Cooke City Bike Shop** (☎ 406/838-2412), located in Cooke City, near the northeast entrance of the park, for rentals, excellent advice, and a darned good espresso.

BOATING   The best place to enjoy boating in the park is on Yellowstone Lake, which has easy access and beautiful, panoramic views. The lake is also one of the few areas where power boats are allowed; rowboats and outboard motorboats can be rented at Bridge Bay Marina (☎ 307/344-7381).

For a fully guided three- or four-day paddling/camping experience on the lake, call **Far and Away Adventures** at 800/232-8588.

Permits are required for any type of boating in Yellowstone. See Section 2, "Just the Facts," earlier in this chapter for details on regulations and fees. Inquire at a ranger station for more detailed boating restrictions and permits.

FISHING   The fishing season in Yellowstone begins as early as late May and continues into early November. See Section 2, "Just the Facts," earlier in this chapter for details on permits and regulations. Permits are available at any ranger station, visitor center, or Hamilton store in the park.

The large population of native cutthroat trout in the park's lakes, rivers, and streams provides a challenging and exciting angling experience. You can rent fishing equipment and/or a small boat at the Bridge Bay Marina; fishing tackle is available at any Hamilton Store in the park. Also at Bridge Bay Marina you can arrange a guided fishing trip on one of the available cabin cruisers, including tackle, on an hourly basis. If you want a guided river-fishing experience in the area, refer to Section 1 of this chapter for guides based in West Yellowstone, Wyo., and Gardiner, Mont. You may also contact Yellowstone Visitor Services at 307/344-2107 for more information on fishing guides.

HIKING   The vast majority of Yellowstone National Park is accessible only by leaving your car behind and hitting the trail. There are more than 1,200 miles of walking and hiking trails (Yellowstone is, after all, more than two million acres of wilderness). You don't need to hike great distances to enjoy Yellowstone country; the park takes on an entire new identity just out of sight of the road. The roads of Yellowstone can be very busy and even hectic at times, and to escape to the park's true essence is a highlight of any Yellowstone vacation.

The park's many trails vary greatly in length and level of difficulty. It is always important to check with the nearest ranger station before using any of the park's trails. Bear activity, damaged bridges, or weather may affect a trail's accessibility. Rangers also conduct various guided walks or may be able to suggest hikes suitable to your expectations and ability.

See also Section 7, "Exploring the Backcountry," for longer, more demanding backpacking trips.

HORSEBACK RIDING   Viewing the stunning landscapes of Yellowstone from the back of good trail horse is a Western experience you should not pass up. Throughout the summer season, Canyon Village, Roosevelt Lodge, and Mammoth Hot Springs offer one- and two-hour guided trail rides daily. Roosevelt Lodge also offers evening rides from June into September. If you are looking for a more extensive horseback experience, sign on with **Yellowstone Mountain Guides** (☎ 406/388-0148) for a great backcountry adventure. For recommendations of other guides, call Yellowstone Visitor Services at 307/344-2107.

6 Winter Sports & Activities

In the winter, Yellowstone is transformed into a surreal wonderland of snow and ice. The landscape is blanketed with a glistening cloak of powdery snow. The geyser basins take on a more dominant role, with the air's temperature in stark contrast to their steaming waters. Nearby trees are transformed into "snow ghosts" by frozen thermal vapors. Bison become frosted shaggy beasts, easily spotted as they take advantage of the more accessible vegetation on the thawed ground surrounding the thermal areas. Lake Yellowstone's surface freezes to an average thickness of 3 feet, creating a vast ice sheet that sings and moans as the huge plates of ice shift warily. Ice forms up the sides of waterfalls; sometimes a complete ice-cone builds around the falling waters of the Lower Falls of the Yellowstone. Snow-white trumpeter swans glide through geyser-fed streams under clear-blue skies of clean, crisp mountain air.

These scenes are all but unimaginable to Yellowstone's two million summer visitors, but if you're fortunate enough to experience a Yellowstone winter, the memories will stay with you forever. An average of 4 feet of snow provides the perfect backdrop for a multitude of winter activities.

Transportation into the park is accomplished mainly by over-the-snow-tracked vehicles. The exception to this is the plowed road from Gardiner, Montana, into Mammoth Hot Springs, which is kept open for cars across the park's northern section through Cooke City, Mont., outside of the park's northeast entrance. During the winter season, the Mammoth Hot Springs Hotel and Old Faithful Snow Lodge provide accommodations and restaurant services. While the Mammoth area may be reached by car, the Snow Lodge may only be reached by snowmobile or snowcoach and is a getaway destination unrivaled anywhere.

For additional information on all of the following winter activities and accommodations, contact **TW Recreational Services, Inc.** (☎ 307/344-7311). There are also many activities, outfitters, and rental shops in the park's gateway towns; see Section 1 of this chapter for details.

CROSS-COUNTRY SKIING Yellowstone's light, powdery snow is a skier's dream. Whatever your level of expertise, there are backcountry and skied-in trails suitable for you. Whether gliding through a forested trail or striding past grazing elk and bison on the 40-plus miles of trails surrounding the Old Faithful Geyser area, the experience is unparalleled. Equipment rentals (about $12 per day), ski instruction, ski shuttles to various locations, and guided ski tours are all available at the park's two winter lodging options: the Old Faithful Snow Lodge and the Mammoth Hot Springs Hotel. Discounts are available for multi-day rentals of skis or snowshoes. Ski instructions costs $17 per person for a two-hour group lesson. A half-day guided excursion (two-person minimum) is around $32 per person; a full day is $69 per person. If your group has three or more people, the cost is considerably lower: $21 per person for a half day, $48 per person for a full day. See West Yellowstone's "Getting Outside" section earlier in this chapter for other guide services to this area, one of which—Yellowstone Nordic Guides, 511 Gibbon Ave. (☎ 406/646-9333)—maintains a yurt in the park.

If you want an enlightened workout, contact the **Yellowstone Institute** (☎ 307/344-2294) for information on their winter programs. Past offerings have included three-day classes devoted to "Backcountry by Ski," "Yellowstone's Winter World," and "Tracking Yellowstone's Wolves."

For a unique ski experience, try the **Cooke City Bike Shop** (☎ 406/838-2412), located in Cooke City near the northeast entrance to the park. For those who are not comfortable on skis, there are also snowshoe rentals, which offer a fun way to explore Yellowstone's winter.

Yellowstone Nordic Guides, 511 Gibbon Ave., in West Yellowstone (☎ 406/646-9333), offers cross-country tours and maintains a yurt in the park.

ICE SKATING   Located behind the Mammoth Hot Springs Recreation Center is the Mammoth Skating Rink. On a crisp winter's night you can rent a pair of skates and glide across the ice while seasonal melodies are being broadcast over the PA system. It's cold out there, so you can enjoy a hot drink by the warming fire at the rink's edge.

Hot tubs, complete with private heated changing rooms, are available hourly at the edge of the rink. This is a great way to relax after a long, cold day of skiing or snowmobiling ($15/hour for 1–6 people) and isn't nearly as corny as it sounds.

SNOWMOBILING   An excellent way to winter sightsee at your own pace is by snowmobile. There are roads that are groomed specifically for snowmobile travel throughout the park. A driver's license is required for rental ($130 per day for two riders at Mammoth Hot Springs Hotel or Old Faithful Snow Lodge) and a quick lesson will put even a first-timer at ease. Also for rent is a snowmobiler's clothing package for protection against the bitter cold. At Mammoth, Indian Creek, Canyon, Madison, West Thumb, and Fishing Bridge are warming huts, most of which offer food, beverages, and an excellent opportunity to stretch your legs in warm surroundings. Half- and full-day guided snowmobile tours are available as well.

Snowmobile rentals are also available in the gateway communities of Gardiner and West Yellowstone, Montana (see Section 1 of this chapter for lots of operators and their phone numbers) and Flagg Ranch (south of Yellowstone, heading toward the Tetons). It's not impossible to get a snowmobile to rent the day you want to go, but reservations are accepted by most rental shops weeks in advance, and reserving at least a day or two weeks ahead of time is a good idea.

SNOWCOACH TOURS   You don't have to be a skier or a snowmobiler in order to enjoy Yellowstone's winter. Why not sit back and enjoy one of the scenic snowcoach tours available to various locations in the park (about $12)?

If you've never seen a snowcoach, you're in for a treat. Don't be fooled into thinking that this distinctively Yellowstone mode of transportation is merely a fancy name for a bus that provides tours during winter. Imagine instead an Econoline van with tank treads for tires and water skis extending from its front, and you won't be surprised when you see this unusual-looking vehicle. The interiors are toasty-warm, with seating for a large group, and they usually allow each passenger two bags.

Your guide will provide interesting and entertaining facts and stories of the areas you explore. Be sure to bring your camera along to catch the scenery and wildlife. Snowcoaches aren't the most comfortable mode of transportation, but they do allow larger groups the option of traveling together in the same vehicle. They are also available for rent at most snowmobile locations if you want to do the coaching yourself.

7 Exploring the Backcountry

Not even 1% of Yellowstone's more than 2.2 million visitors ever stray more than 3 miles from the roadside. But for those visitors interested in the park's essential wildness, a venture into the backcountry will be just the ticket. Escaping the crowds and spending a night or two of solitude under a star-filled sky—with no other sounds but a coyote's cry and the murmuring of a snow-fed stream—is what the Yellowstone experience is all about.

The park has an extensive array of hiking trails to suit whatever style hike you might have in mind. Whether you're interested in searching out particular wildlife, reaching a mountain's peak, or exploring Yellowstone's thermal wonders, there's a hike for you here.

The Bechler Region, in the park's southwest section, was not scarred by the fires of 1988 and offers great examples of cascades, waterfalls, and thermal features. Many backpacking routes cut through this region—you could hike from here to Old Faithful on the **Bechler River Trail,** for example, passing several waterfalls along the route, which extends for more than 30 miles. Check in at the Bechler Ranger Station (drive into the park from Ashton, Idaho). You'll be far from the madding crowds in this part of the park.

The **Thorofare Trail** is a hike that covers over 70 miles through the most isolated and pristine wilderness in the Lower 48 states, rounding Lake Yellowstone's southern and eastern sides, where the cutthroat trout fishing is phenomenal in the early summer. It extends south, following the Yellowstone River and heading into the Teton Wilderness. The Thoroughfare Ranger Station lies in the southeast corner of the park.

Electric Peak, named for its uncanny ability to attract lightning in a storm, is located in the park's northwestern corner and is one of the park's most scenic backcountry attractions. Take the **Sportsman Lake Trail,** which begins near Mammoth Hot Springs and extends west toward Highway 191.

The spectacular sights to be seen in Yellowstone's backcountry are numerous, and though only a few places are listed above, you could spend a lifetime exploring it. To delve more deeply, consult a specialized travel guide such as *Yellowstone Trails: A Hiking Guide,* by Mark C. Marschall (Yellowstone National Park, WY, the Yellowstone Association, 1990). It covers more than 1,000 miles of trails, has a useful backcountry guide, and provides tips for hiking through bear country.

The best plan for an expedition is to decide what your objectives are, bring all of the necessary supplies and equipment, and be sure not to overstep the limits of your experience and knowledge. If you are unsure of your capabilities, you should employ the services of a backcountry guide; call Yellowstone Visitor Services at 307/344-2107 for leads on local experts. If you are prepared for a backcountry adventure, the most important step is to see a park ranger. A ranger can suggest the best hike for you, advise you of any closed or restricted areas, and grant you a backcountry permit and campsite assignment. This free permit is mandatory.

Camping in the backcountry can be an activity enjoyed year-round with the proper equipment. In winter, obviously, you need much more than the simple tent and sleeping bag that suffices in summer. Check with the nearest ranger station before setting out into the backcountry during winter to get weather information and to determine trail conditions and any hazards of which you ought to be aware. During winter, fires are forbidden in Yellowstone's backcountry. You must carry a stove and fuel to cook food and melt snow while camping there in winter. However, during summer, campfires are allowed in the backcountry, but only in established firepits. Not all campsites allow wood or ground fires, so a gas stove is recommended for cooking at these sites. Before setting out to a particular campsite, check at the nearest ranger station to determine whether or not the site allows wood fires.

Bears, though not the threat they are in Glacier National Park, are certainly creatures you ought to think about when in Yellowstone. Though it's unlikely you'll see a bear, it's not impossible. Make plenty of noise when hiking trails to make the bear aware of your presence and lessen the chance of a surprise encounter. For information about bears in Yellowstone and what to do in case of a confrontation, contact the nearest ranger or read the "Yellowstone Guide," the brochure distributed by the park service when you enter the park.

8 Camping

Of the 12 campgrounds in Yellowstone, 7 are operated by the National Park Service, and these sites are available on a first-come, first-served basis. These campgrounds are located at Indian Creek, Lewis Lake, Mammoth, Norris, Pebble Creek, Slough Creek, and Tower Fall. If you arrive before noon, you run the best chance of getting a campsite for the evening.

TW Recreational Services, Inc. (☎ 307/344-7311), accepts reservations for campgrounds at Canyon, Grant Village, Madison, and Fishing Bridge. The **Fishing Bridge RV Park** is the only campground offering water, sewer, and electrical hookups and accepts hard-sided vehicles only (no tents or tent trailers).

Reservations for **Bridge Bay Campground** may be made no more than eight weeks in advance by calling MISTIX reservations at 800/365-2267.

Camping is allowed only in designated areas and is limited to 14 days between June 15 and Labor Day, and to 30 days the rest of the year. Check-out times for all campgrounds is 10am. Quiet hours are strictly enforced between the hours of 8pm and 8am. No generators, radios, or other loud noises are allowed during these hours.

Amenities for Each Campground, Yellowstone National Park

Campground	# Sites	Fee	Showers/ Laundry	Flush Toilets	Disposal Stations	Generators Permitted
Bridge Bay*	434	$12	Yes	Yes	Yes	Yes
Canyon**	273	$12.50	Yes	Yes	Yes	Yes
Fishing Bridge	345	$20	Yes	Yes	Sewer	Yes
Grant Village**	428	$12.50	Yes	Yes	Yes	Yes
Indian Creek	75	$8	No	No	No	No
Lewis Lake	85	$8	No	No	No	No
Madison**	281	$12.50	Yes	No	Yes	Yes
Mammoth	85	$10	Yes	No	Yes	No
Norris	116	$10	Yes	No	Yes	No
Pebble Creek	36	$8	No	No	No	No
Slough Creek	29	$8	No	No	No	No
Tower Fall (RV hookups)	32	$8	No	No	No	No

* Reserve through Mistix (summer only) ☎ 800/365-2267.
** Reserve through TW Recreational Services, ☎ 307/344-7311 or TDD 307/344-5395.

9 Where to Stay

To book lodgings in Yellowstone itself, you must go through TW Recreational Services, Inc., the company that operations all accommodations, restaurants, and snack bars in the park. Yellowstone accommodations are normally open from early summer to late September, however snowmobilers and cross-country skiers can stay at either Mammoth Hot Springs from mid-December to early March or Old Faithful Snow Lodge and Cabins, which opens for its winter season at the beginning of December and stays open all winter long.

Rooms throughout the park are often difficult to come by as summer approaches, so reservations should be made well in advance. For information or reservations at any of the following locations, contact **TW Recreational Services, Inc.,** at P.O. Box 165, Yellowstone National Park, WY 82190 (☎ 307/344-7311).

Many other alternatives exist outside the park (see Section 1 of this chapter for lodgings in gateway communities). For accommodations listings south of the park, in Grand Teton National Park, see Chapter 12. Places to stay in and around Jackson, Wyoming, can also be found in Chapter 12.

Canyon Lodge and Cabins

In Canyon Village (P.O. Box 165), Yellowstone National Park, WY 82190. ☎ **307/344-7311** for reservations. 37 rms, 572 cabin units. $93 double; $48–$84 cabin. AE, DISC, JCB, MC, V.

Located in unsightly and overdeveloped Canyon Village, the Canyon Lodge and Cabins isn't the place to get away from it all—just count the number of cabins at the village. The rooms at the Canyon Lodge are located in the three-story lodge building, while the cabins are scattered throughout the village. Cabins are just as comfortable as the Lodge rooms (but less expensive). However, any notion of originality you may have had concerning your evening's stay is wiped away when you drive by the endless units of identical cabins and campers on the way to your own site.

Grant Village

On the West Thumb of Yellowstone Lake (P.O. Box 165), Yellowstone National Park, WY 82190. ☎ **307/344-7311** for reservations. 300 rms. $68–$84 double. AE, DISC, JCB, MC, V.

The southernmost of the major overnight accommodations in the park, Grant Village was completed in 1984 and is one of the more contemporary choices in Yellowstone—it's not a grand old historic lodge. Prices are reasonable considering it's one of the few places where you're going to find a private bath with a shower. Other guest services located at Grant Village include a dining room, lounge, a marina steak house, a gift shop, and a laundry facility.

Lake Lodge Cabins

On Lake Yellowstone (P.O. Box 165), Yellowstone National Park, WY 82190. ☎ **307/344-7311** for reservations. 186 cabins. $43–$84 double. AE, DISC, JCB, MC, V.

These cabins, surrounding Lake Lodge, are located just down from the Lake Yellowstone Hotel and Cabins. The lodge, with its cafeteria dining room facing Lake Yellowstone, serves as home base for the cabins, which are designated either Western or Frontier, with the Western accommodations being considerably larger and twice as expensive. Both offer at least a bath, unlike some of the other cabins in Yellowstone with names like "Roughrider."

Lake Yellowstone Hotel and Cabins

On the north side of the lake (P.O. Box 165), Yellowstone National Park, WY 82190. ☎ **307/344-7311** for reservations. 194 rms, 102 cabins, 1 parlor suite. $84–$125 double; $63 cabin; $342 parlor suite. AE, DISC, JCB, MC, V.

In 1991, the Lake Yellowstone Hotel was placed on the National Register of Historic Places. In addition to its many hotel rooms, this recently restored 1920s hotel has comfortable, rustic cabins. The main lodge has a beautiful sunroom and bar, and sits on the edge of the north side of the lake, just south of the Yellowstone River. Some of the most expensive hotel rooms in the park are located at this hotel's annex, directly behind the main building. The parlor and bedroom suite goes for $342 per night—easily the most expensive room in Yellowstone.

Mammoth Hot Springs Hotel and Cabins

P.O. Box 165, Yellowstone National Park, WY 82190. ☎ **307/344-7311** for reservations. 96 rms, 126 cabins. $47–$65 room; $34 cabin. AE, DISC, JCB, MC, V.

This is the only place to stay year-round in the north part of the park. In fact, the Mammoth Ranger Station is the only station open throughout the year. Mammoth Hot Springs is one of the older park settlements, dating back to the late 19th century when Fort Yellowstone was still around. The actual lodge was built in 1937, but a hostelry dating from 1911 didn't fare as well. It's been incorporated into the Mammoth Hot Springs Hotel as a wing. The rooms are hotel-style and the cabins are cottage-style (a few units have private hot tubs).

✪ Old Faithful Inn

P.O. Box 165, Yellowstone National Park, WY 82190. ☎ **307/344-7311** for reservations. 359 rms. $68–$210 double. AE, DISC, JCB, MC, V.

Built of local logs and stone in 1904, the Old Faithful Inn is the greatest treehouse you've ever imagined, with the most splendid backyard fort a child could ever dream up. Designated a National Historic Landmark in 1987—a year before the fires threatened the old structure—the Old Faithful Inn is a remarkable gabled mansion that rivals its namesake in popularity and greets visitors to the park's most renowned site with style. The central lobby towers six stories high (you can visit the roof) with small windows and intricate logwork from nearby trees. A magnificent fireplace stands just off the dining room entrance. The rooms are comfortable, especially in the recently remodeled East Wing, where views of the geyser are best from the third floor. As with all the other rooms in Yellowstone, the family will either curse or enjoy the respite from television. Phones are available in most of the motel-style rooms.

⑤ Old Faithful Lodge and Cabins

P.O. Box 165, Yellowstone National Park, WY 82190. ☎ **307/344-7311** for reservations. 122 cabins (some without private bath). $22–$38 double. AE, DISC, JCB, MC, V.

If you want a dirt-cheap geyser view, a nearby cafeteria, and a snack bar, these rustic and economical cabins will fit the bill, and they'll suit the tightest of budgets. The Frontier cabin units are a cut below the Western cabins you'll find at the Canyon Lodge, but here they are the most expensive units and still come with a full bath. The next step down is the Economy cabin unit, which has a toilet and sink but no bath and costs only $4 less. The Budget units are short on conveniences, save the kitchen sink (but alas, there is no kitchen). These don't cost much more than a tent site, but then again, you're not getting much more than a tent site. Showers and restrooms are located nearby.

Old Faithful Snow Lodge and Cabins

Old Faithful, P.O. Box 165, Yellowstone National Park, WY 82190. ☎ **307/344-7311** for reservations. 65 rms, 34 one-bedroom cabins. $47–$53 double; $64–$83 cabin. AE, DISC, JCB, MC, V.

Winter puts a new face on Yellowstone and the views can be as pleasurable in winter as they are in summer. The Snow Lodge and Cabins offers a remarkably inexpensive way to stay inside the park during winter and enjoy the many trails of cross-country skiing the Old Faithful area has to offer. And don't worry, the giant geyser continues its famous eruptions throughout winter with an even more dramatic effect than in summer. The crowds have dispersed, a fresh blanket of powder is on the ground, and an eerie steam rises continuously from the gaping hole, even when the geyser has died down. Rooms at the lodge are comfortably furnished, although they don't begin to compare with their charming counterparts at the Old Faithful Inn. Perhaps owing to the romance of staying in a national park during winter, the cabins seem more cozy than cramped and are tastefully furnished in Western motifs.

Roosevelt Lodge Cabins

P.O. Box 165, Yellowstone National Park, WY 82190. ☎ **307/344-7311** for reservations. 80 cabins (none with private bath). $24–$63 cabin. AE, DISC, JCB, MC, V.

This lodge and its accompanying cabins are named for President Theodore Roosevelt, who camped in and loved this area. The cabins called Roughriders have purely descriptive names, though—they really are bare-bone cabins of frame construction. There are no bathrooms or showers in the rooms (there are facilities nearby), and the Rustic Shelters are even more basic because they're smaller. However, since the cabins are just north of the Grand Canyon of the Yellowstone and Tower Falls, Roosevelt can be the ideal spot for exploring the northeast part of Yellowstone without having to pay through the nose for accommodations.

10 Where to Eat

Eating in the park can be a nightmare if you're trying to save money—lines in the cafeterias can sometimes be extraordinarily long if you decide to eat at normal mealtimes. On the other hand, if you dine in some of the nicer restaurants, you may find that you're paying *a lot* for not standing in line. Being the executive chef for millions of people in the nation's premier national park is an unenviable and seemingly impossible task, but on the whole the food is well prepared, though the menus are similar from place to place. Cafeterias and fast food are convenient—if less appetizing—alternatives to the more formal dining rooms and are located in Mammoth Hot Springs, Canyon Village, Grant Village, Old Faithful, and West Thumb. Also see "Where to Eat" in Section 1 of this chapter for places to eat outside the park in gateway communities.

Grant Village

At Grant Village. ☎ **307/242-3899.** Dinner reservations required. Summer daily 6:30–10am, 11:30am–2:30pm, and 5:30–10pm. Breakfast items $2–$6; main lunch courses $5–$7; main dinner courses $11–$17. AE, DISC, JCB, MC, V. STEAK/SEAFOOD.

In many ways Grant Village is much like the other restaurants in the park for breakfast and lunch, but it occasionally offers some interesting items that stray from the norm. For lunch, the pan-fried trout covered with toasted pecans and lemon butter is delicious and costs less than $7. For dinner, Grant offers a vegetarian dish of cannelloni filled with spinach, carrots, and onions and covered in a tomato tarragon sauce. The New York strip and prime rib are still tops, but the swordfish steak and orange roughy are delicious deep-sea items that also shine.

✪ Lake Yellowstone Hotel

On the north side of the lake. ☎ **307/242-3899.** Dinner reservations required. Summer daily 6:30–10am, 11:30am–2:30pm, and 5:30–10pm. Breakfast items $2–$6; main lunch courses $5–$7; main dinner courses $8–$17. AE, DISC, JCB, MC, V. PASTA/STEAK/SEAFOOD.

At most of the TW restaurants in the park, expect the breakfast buffet every day. But at the Lake Yellowstone Hotel, breakfast is made a touch nicer. The view over the lake in the mornings as you watch the sun come up can be exceptional, though a late sunset dinner can be just as spectacular. The food is much the same as the other restaurants in the park; many of the menu items, in fact, are identical.

Mammoth Hot Springs Hotel

At Mammoth Hot Springs. ☎ **307/344-5314.** Dinner reservations required. Summer daily 6:30–10am, 11:30am–2pm, and 5:30–10pm. Breakfast items $2–$6; main lunch courses $5–$7; main dinner courses $8–$17. AE, DISC, JCB, MC, V. STEAK/SEAFOOD.

At Mammoth, the breakfast buffet features scrambled eggs, French toast, and muffins. The omelets are delicious and all come with home fries and toast. Lunch is an array of sandwiches, including teriyaki chicken breast, Wyoming cheese steak (beef covered in red and green peppers with jack cheese), and grilled German bratwurst. Dinner is a bit more substantial, and the menu has something for everyone—from the 12-ounce New York strip to the shrimp and scallops served over linguine and topped with a curry sauce.

Old Faithful Inn

Near Old Faithful. ☎ **307/545-4999.** Dinner reservations required. Summer daily 6:30–10am, 11:30am–2:30pm, and 5:30–10pm. Breakfast items $2–$6; main lunch courses $5–$7; main dinner courses $8–$17. AE, DISC, JCB, MC, V. STEAK/SEAFOOD.

It's difficult not to be overcome completely by the architecture of the Old Faithful Inn as soon as you enter the magnificent central lobby. The knotty logs wrap around the center as if it were an elegant fortress, and toward the center of it all, the massive stone fireplace leads you to the restaurant. The food at Old Faithful is much the same as the other restaurants throughout the park. What you had on Tuesday at Grant Village, you can enjoy again on Wednesday in another part of the park. What is different at Old Faithful is the atmosphere. The dining room is always filled with interesting people, and the wait outside the dining room can offer a chance to meet fellow travelers or to marvel silently at the surroundings.

Jackson Hole & Grand Teton National Park

This part of the state has a lot going for it, even minus its marquee attraction, Yellowstone (see Chapter 11). Jackson Hole and its surroundings dish out their share of breathtaking scenic beauty, as well as skiing, all kinds of outdoor recreation, Old West cookouts, trail rides, art galleries, and activities to help the kids unwind. The northwestern section of Wyoming draws more tourists than any other. It's no wonder Jackson Hole has reaped incredible rewards (and curses) just from sitting so close to the edge of Grand Teton National Park, and within an easy drive of Yellowstone. Though not as expansive as either Glacier or Yellowstone, Grand Teton National Park is a major draw as well. Some three million people visited the region last year, and the bets are that number will only increase.

From rodeo to rock climbing, the northwest corner has Wyoming's widest selection of outdoor recreation and activities. Often the best (and most extreme) athletes can be found pushing their limits in and around the Tetons. Summer brings a wealth of choices—climbing, hiking, boating, waterskiing, ballooning, backpacking, pack trips, and whitewater rafting, for starters. But come winter, Jackson Hole becomes a paradise for skiers of every skill level, from the novice who's just learning to maneuver through the powder to the extreme skiers who brave the dangers of the Tetons. Jackson is a viable contender for the title of America's best ski resort.

1 Jackson Hole

When John Colter traversed through these parts in the winter of 1807, Jackson was a pristine mountain valley called Teewinot by the Shoshone. It was teeming with wildlife. Looking at today's population figures—fewer than 5,000 residents actually live here full-time—you might even venture to guess that Jackson, Wyoming, has barely grown since those early days. But think again. This village, which 20 years ago was a quiet little infant town on the fringe of Grand Teton National Park, has grown into the poster child of Western tourism, with more than two million annual visitors, three major ski resorts, and enough hotel space to accommodate everyone in Cheyenne (and that's *still* not enough).

The real estate boom in Jackson Hole has driven a lot of people off their property and some out of their minds. Locals will compare the phenomenon to something from Kafka: One morning the sleepy town awoke and was amazed to discover it was a full-fledged resort. The telltale sign of Jackson's metamorphosis (for those not convinced by the affairs of last decade) was the day when Fred's Super Market, an ancient mom-and-pop downtown institution, went out of business in 1995. In its stead went up another real estate office.

Today Jackson Hole is on the verge of becoming more and more like a few other Western resort towns that on the fly-by seem indistinguishable from each other. The Vails, the Aspens, the Tellurides. Celebrities have crept in (it's not uncommon to catch a glimpse of Harrison Ford in town) and the President of the United States has even held press conferences here, indications to many that Jackson Hole's days as a quaint Western town may be numbered.

ESSENTIALS

GETTING THERE   The **Jackson Airport at Grand Teton National Park** is located north of town and just south of the park. **American Airlines** (☎ 800/433-7300), **Continental Express** (☎ 800/525-8280), **Delta** (☎ 800/221-1212), **Skywest** (☎ 307/733-7920 or 800/453-9417), and **United Express** (☎ 800/241-6522) all have flights in and out of Jackson Hole.

If you're driving, Highway 189/191 leads here from the north or south before intersecting with Highway 89, which runs the length of the national park and right through town. For up-to-date weather information and road conditions, contact the Chamber of Commerce (see below), or the Wyoming road and travel hotline for the Jackson area at ☎ 307/733-9966.

VISITOR INFORMATION   The **Jackson Hole Visitors Council and Chamber of Commerce** is a fantastic source of information concerning just about everything in and around Jackson. You can't miss the chamber if you're heading through downtown on your way to the national park. Just about three blocks north of the Town Square on your right is the chamber building at the Wyoming Information Center at 532 N. Cache; the mailing address is P.O. Box E, Jackson, WY 83001 (☎ 307/733-3316 or 800/443-6931). Here they can give you brochures for every imaginable activity, as well as up-to-date information on what's happening in the park, road closures, and weather reports.

GETTING AROUND   Once you're on the ground, **Alamo** (☎ 307/733-0671 or 800/327-0400), **Avis** (☎ 307/733-3422 or 800/831-2847), and **Budget** (☎ 307/733-2206 or 800/527-0700) offer car rental service at airport counters. South of town on U.S. Highway 89 is a gauntlet of car rental companies. **Dollar** (☎ 307/733-0935 or 800/800-4000), **Rent-a-Wreck** (☎ 307/733-5014 or 800/800/637-7147), and **Ugly Duckling** (☎ 307/733-3040 or 800/843-3825) all have offices in this area. Downtown at 375 N. Cache is **Eagle Rent-a-Car** (☎ 307/739-9999 or 800/582-2182). These guys rent everything from mini-vans to RVs to snowmobiles and even have vehicles outfitted with locking ski racks. They also provide free pick-up and delivery.

Taxi service is available from **A-1 Taxi** (☎ 307/733-5089), **All Star Taxi** (☎ 307/733-2888 or 800/378-2944), **Buckboard Cab** (☎ 307/733-1112), **Jackson Hole Transportation** (☎ 307/733-3135), and **Tumbleweed Taxi** (☎ 307/733-0808).

Jackson Hole & Grand Teton National Park

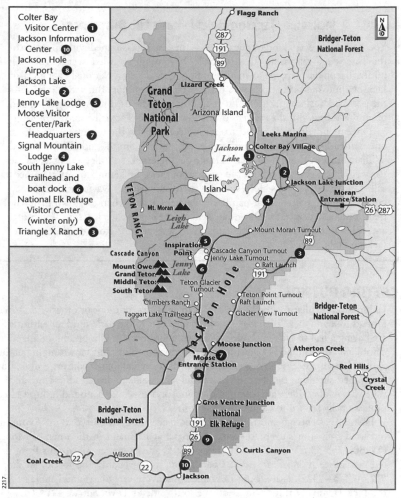

Colter Bay
  Visitor Center **1**
Jackson Information
  Center **10**
Jackson Hole
  Airport **8**
Jackson Lake
  Lodge **2**
Jenny Lake Lodge **5**
Moose Visitor
  Center/Park
  Headquarters **7**
Signal Mountain
  Lodge **4**
South Jenny Lake
  trailhead and
  boat dock **6**
National Elk Refuge
  Visitor Center
  (winter only) **9**
Triangle X Ranch **3**

Flagg Ranch
287
191
89
Bridger-Teton
National Forest
Grand
Teton
National
Park
Lizard Creek
Arizona Island
Leeks Marina
Jackson Lake
Colter Bay Village **1**
2
Jackson Lake Junction
Moran
Entrance Station
26 287
4
Mt. Moran
Leigh Lake
Elk
Island
Mount Moran Turnout
89
5
Cascade Canyon Turnout
Jenny Lake Turnout
Raft Launch
191
3
Inspiration
Point
Cascade Canyon
Mount Owen
Grand Teton
Middle Teton
South Teton
Jenny Lake
6
Teton Glacier
Turnout
Climbers Ranch
Taggart Lake Trailhead
Teton Point Turnout
Raft Launch
Glacier View Turnout
Jackson Hole
Bridger-Teton
National Forest
Moose Junction
7
Moose
Entrance Station
8
Atherton Creek
Red Hills
Crystal
Creek
Gros Ventre Junction
National
Elk Refuge
191
26
9
Curtis Canyon
Bridger-Teton
National Forest
89
10
Jackson
Coal Creek
22
Wilson
22
2217

Before you call a cab, remember that many of the hotels and car rental agencies in the Jackson area offer free shuttle service to and from the airport.

It's not just any town of 5,000 souls that has a mass transit system. The **Southern Teton Area Rapid Transit (START)** service offers bus transport from Teton Village to Jackson, daily (every other hour) on the Green Line for $2. The Blue Line runs daily (also every other hour) from Jackson to Hoback throughout the summer for $1 each way. A season pass may be purchased for $35. Senior citizens and children eight and under ride free. Winter service runs as frequently as the summer (usually between 7am and 10pm), but during the off-season months in spring and fall, START slows down with the rest of the town. For specific schedule information, contact START at 307/733-4521.

Jackson or Jackson Hole: What's the Difference?

You'll likely see every kind of merchandise imaginable fashioned with an image of the Tetons and the words "Jackson Hole, Wyoming" scrawled over it. You *may* notice that on the map, the town just south of Grand Teton National Park is called Jackson. But your plane ticket says Jackson Hole, Wyoming. But wait a minute— the postmark just says Jackson. The names seem to be used interchangeably, and often this is true. But the mystery of the town's name is actually pretty simple.

Three mountain men ran a fur trapping company in these parts in the 1800s: one named David Jackson, another named Jedidiah Smith, and a third named William Sublette. Mountain men in those days referred to a valley as a hole. As the story goes, Sublette (for whom the county southeast of Teton County is named) called the valley Jackson's Hole, since his friend and partner David Jackson spent a great deal of time in it. That name was shortened, and when the town materialized, it was also named for David Jackson. So the city itself is Jackson, Wyoming, and it lies in the great valley that runs the length of the Tetons on the east side, Jackson Hole.

GETTING OUTSIDE

Jackson is a peculiar town when it comes to activities, outdoor or otherwise. While tourists tour and make their way by overloaded cars to the park, outdoor enthusiasts are having a ball in Jackson Hole's wilderness. From mountain biking, hiking, and climbing in the summer, to downhill skiing, snowboarding, and snowcamping in the winter, Jackson Hole is full of serious intermediates and all-but-insane extremists. But first-timers shouldn't fret. For the brave soul who wants to dive headfirst into all the valley has to offer, there are plenty of outdoor specialists in and around Jackson Hole professionally trained to handle all your desires.

Jackson has enough sporting equipment places to keep everyone in Wyoming outfitted a few times over. **Adventure Sports,** at Dornan's in the town of Moose (☎ 307/733-3307), has mountain bike, kayak, and canoe rentals. Across from the old post office at 245 Pearl is the **Boardroom,** a snowboard shop to end all shops (☎ 307/733-8327). Jack Dennis can handle just about everything and handle it well; the **Jack Dennis Outdoor Shop** on the south side of Town Square (☎ 307/733-3270) has all the fishing supplies, skis, and outdoor clothing you can possibly need. The branch in Teton Village (☎ 307/733-6838), along with **Pepi Steigler Sports** (☎ 307/733-4505) can accommodate winter and summer outdoor enthusiasts with guides, lessons, and the best in equipment. **Hoback Sports,** 40 S. Millward (☎ 307/733-5335) is the automatic teller of ski shops and has two more locations around town (Snow King, ☎ 307/733-5200; the Aspens, ☎ 307/733-4664). **Skinny Skis,** at 65 W. Deloney off Town Square (☎ 307/733-6094), is a year-round specialty sports shop and has excellent equipment. It's probably the best shop in town for free recreational literature. For a great supply of fresh hand-me-downs, head to **Moosely Seconds** in Moose (☎ 307/733-7176). They also have a great selection of mountain-climbing equipment (not used).

SUMMER SPORTS & ACTIVITIES

Biking

Just grab your bike off the rack and head into the park; it's simple enough. There are plenty of backroads to cruise in the Tetons. But for detailed information, rentals, maps, and reliable information about trails and equipment, drop by **Teton Cyclery** at 175 N. Glenwood (☎ 307/733-4386) and **Wilson Backcountry Sports,** 5 miles west of Jackson in Wilson, at the Fish Creek Center (☎ 307/733-5228). Closer to the park, **Adventure Sports** at Dornan's in Moose (☎ 307/733-3307) offers hourly, daily, weekly, and even monthly rentals.

For rentals and tour information, both guided and unguided, contact **Fat Tire Tours** at Hoback Sports, 40 S. Millward (☎ 307/733-5335) or **Teton Mountain Bike Tours** at 430 S. Cache (☎ 307/733-0712).

Climbing

Just the sight of the mighty Grand Teton towering over Jackson Hole at 13,770 feet stirs the imagination and determination of climbers from all over the world. A couple of excellent climbing schools in Jackson take guided climbs to the summit each summer. **Exum Mountain Guides,** P.O. Box 56, Moose, WY 83012 (☎ 307/ 733-2297), has been around since 1931 and offers guided climbs to the top of the Grand for $320. Group preparation classes run from $65 to $85. **Jackson Hole Mountain Guides,** 165 N. Glenwood St., Jackson, WY 83001 (☎ 307/733-4979), offers advanced climbing courses for $125 and a Grand Teton summit climb for $465. Those who need to practice their moves on a rainy day should try the **Teton Rock Gym,** 1116 Maple (☎ 307/733-0707).

Fishing

Yellowstone and Grand Teton National Parks have incredible fishing in their lakes and streams; see the park sections for details.

The Snake River is also a fantastic place for fly fishermen. You can either fish from the riverbanks or hire a guide. In either case, several outdoor shops in Jackson will be able to provide you with all the tackle you need and more information on fishing conditions in the area than you can likely process. **High Country Flies,** 165 N. Center St. (☎ 307/733-7210), has all the goods and offers guided fishing trips and schools as well as the best in angling fashion. The most renowned fishing experts assemble at the **Jack Dennis Outdoor Shop,** downtown on the Town Square at 50 E. Broadway (☎ 307/733-3270). There's another version of the store in Teton Village (☎ 307/733-6838). **Westbank Anglers,** 3670 N. Moose-Wilson Rd. (☎ 307/733-6483), is another full-service fly shop offering everything from flies to guides and fishing trips in Jackson Hole.

Golf

Though there are plenty of other ways to spend time in Wyoming without playing golf, there's probably no better place in the state to break out your clubs than in Jackson Hole.

The **Jackson Hole and Tennis Club** (☎ 307/733-3111) north of Jackson off U.S. 89 has an 18-hole course that's one of the best in the country. The Teton Pines Resort, 3450 N. Clubhouse Dr. (☎ 307/733-1005 or 800/238-2223), has a course that was designed by Arnold Palmer (it becomes a cross-country ski center in winter). Both courses are open to the public.

Hiking

This is the favorite pastime of just about everyone in the area. Anyone can do it and just about everyone does. The obvious destination in the spring and the fall is Grand Teton National Park just north of town (for details, see Section 2 of this chapter).

You may want other, less-traveled alternatives when the **park trails** fill up with out-of-towners, though, and then you can check out the **Bridger-Teton National Forest** just east of Jackson. A visitor center is located in the log cabin at 340 N. Cache in downtown Jackson (☎ 307/739-5500) and includes all the hiking and access information you'll need for the national forest as well as the Gros Ventre and Teton Wilderness Areas.

The **Wind River Range** is also a popular destination for Jackson area residents. The "Winds," as they're called by locals, are southeast of Jackson and lie in the Bridger-Teton National Forest. The actual range stretches from just southeast of Jackson near Pinedale to the South Pass area. Information on the peaks and trails can be obtained by contacting the U.S. Forest Service at the Bridger-Teton office in Jackson mentioned above.

For expert advice on trails in and around Jackson, stop by **Skinny Skis** at 65 W. Deloney just off the Town Square in downtown Jackson (☎ 307/733-6094). Not only do they have all the hiking equipment you'll need, they publish an outdoor guide (with plenty of self-promoting ads, of course) written for the most part by the store's staff. The guide is free at both Skinny Skis and Moosely Seconds (north of town in Moose), and covers favorite day hikes, climbing techniques, and Teton and Bridger excursions on foot.

Horseback Riding

In and around Jackson there are innumerable companies that offer trail rides. Many hotels, especially those in Grand Teton National Park, have stables and operate trail rides for their guests. A few of the places ready to put you in the saddle are **Bridger-Teton Outfitters** (☎ 307/739-4314 or 307/733-7745), **Green River Outfitters** in Pinedale (☎ 307/733-1044 or 307/367-2416), **Jackson Hole Trail Rides** (☎ 307/733-6992), **Snow King Stables** (☎ 307/733-5781), and the **Mill Iron Ranch** (☎ 307/733-6390).

Kayaking

Between the Snake River, Yellowstone Lake, Lewis Lake, and Shoshone Lake in Yellowstone National Park, both river and sea kayaking are popular sports. The Snake can be pretty treacherous in spots; beginners won't want to brave the river if they haven't had proper training or experience. The lakes of Yellowstone are relatively calm waters and ideally suited for the sea kayak. Those willing to strike out their own should first be aware of the park's boating regulations (see Section 2 of Chapter 11).

Several operators in Jackson run schools and guide services for beginners, intermediates, and advanced kayakers as well as for the kayaking photographer. Greg Winston's **Wilderness Exposure Expeditions,** P.O. Box 505, Wilson, WY 83014 (☎ 307/733-1026), offers specialized custom trips into the Yellowstone backcountry on Lewis and Shoshone Lakes. **Greater Yellowstone Sea Kayaking,** P.O. Box 9201, Jackson, WY 83001 (☎ 800/733-2471) has similar trips to the lakes of Yellowstone. The **Snake River Kayak and Canoe School,** P.O. Box 3482, Jackson, WY 83001 (☎ 307/733-3127) offers the touring sea kayak experience on Yellowstone Lake, but they also have incredible one-day classes for canoes and inflatable kayaks, as well as an indoor kayak school in their 45,000-gallon teaching facility.

Rafting

The Snake River has made itself famous by doling out ignominy to people like Evel Knieval, whose death-defying malfunction over and into the Snake River Canyon makes flipping in a raft seem downright safe. And though launching yourself over the Snake in a rocket is strictly prohibited, whitewater rafting is not. In fact, we recommend it. There are a couple of ways to see the Snake River and enjoy it on the level and speed you choose.

You can mosey, fish, and take your time on the many scenic floats because there are more than a few outfits offering trips along the Snake: **Barker-Ewing,** P.O. Box 100, Moose, WY 83012 (☎ 307/733-1800); **Flagg Ranch,** in the north part of Grand Teton National Park, P.O. Box 187, Yellowstone, WY 82190 (☎ 307/543-2861 or 800/443-2311); **Fort Jackson River Trips,** P.O. Box 1176, Jackson, WY 83001 (☎ 307/733-2583 or 800/735-8430); **Grand Teton Lodge Company,** P.O. Box 250, Moran, WY 83013 (☎ 307/543-2811); **Lewis and Clark Expeditions,** at Snow King Ski Resort, P.O. Box, Jackson, WY 83001 (☎ 307/733-4022 or 800/824-5375); **O.A.R.S.,** Jackson, WY 83001 (☎ 307/733-3379); **Signal Mountain Lodge,** in Grand Teton National Park, P.O. Box 50, Moran, WY 83013 (☎ 307/543-2831); and Triangle X Ranch with **Osprey,** in Moose (☎ 307/733-5500).

But the most popular way to experience the Snake River is whitewater rafting. Several other companies (some are, of course, the same as the scenic trip companies), offer adrenaline-pumping day trips down the Snake with not much opportunity to remark on riverbank wildlife: **Barker-Ewing** (☎ 307/733-1800); **Charlie Sands Wildwater,** P.O. Box 696, Jackson, WY 83001 (☎ 307/733-4410 or 800/358-8184); **Dave Hansen Whitewater,** P.O. Box 328, Jackson, WY 83001 (☎ 307/733-6295); **Jackson Hole Whitewater,** P.O. Box 3695, Jackson, WY 83001 (☎ 307/733-1007 or 800/648-2602); **Lewis and Clark Expeditions** (☎ 307/733-4022 or 800/824-5375); and **Mad River Boat Trips,** P.O. Box 222, Jackson, WY 83001 (☎ 307/733-6203 or 800/458-7238).

Costs for trips vary depending on the kind of trip you want to take, and the length of the trip.

If you have all the equipment you need for a scenic trip (most of the relaxed stretches of the Snake lie within the confines of Grand Teton National Park), contact the National Park Service at 307/739-3300 for information on rafting in the park. Once you get outside the park, you're in the jurisdiction of the National Forest Service. The Bridger-Teton supervisor's office is in Jackson at 340 N. Cache (☎ 307/739-5500).

DOWNHILL SKIING

This is it, folks—you've come to one of the premier destinations for skiers in the entire country, and has it ever got an array of choices for you.

✪ Jackson Hole Ski Resort

7658 Teewinot, Teton Village, WY 83025. ☎ **307/733-2292** or 307/733-4005, or 307/733-2291 for snow conditions, 800/443-6931 for central reservations. Lift tickets $42–$45 adults, $21–$24 seniors and children 14 and under.

Yes, the prices approach those of Colorado resorts. Management troubles have plagued Jackson Hole in the past, and everything on the hill is expensive. To top it off (literally), Big Sky in Montana's Gallatin Valley just replaced Jackson Hole as the ski resort with the longest vertical drop—by a measly 41 feet.

What, then, is all the fuss about? Well, even with all of the problems Jackson Hole has had in keeping its status as the number-one ski area in this part of the country (which it is), it keeps people coming back for more. Olympic medals are tossed around the place like spare change: U.S. Olympic gold medalist Tommie Moe is a spokesperson for the resort and Pepi Steigler, the Jackson Hole Ski School's director, won gold, silver, and bronze for the Austrian team at the 1964 winter games.

This is a place of extremes, a place for beginners, *and* a place for intermediates— it's not just a challenging mountain with a couple of easy runs set aside for beginners. It's actually two separate mountains that serve two different needs entirely. The novice skier will find solace on 8,481-foot Aprés Mountain, which is a network of beginner and intermediate slopes. The truly deranged will find pleasure on the sometimes insane slopes of 10,450-foot Rendezvous Mountain, fraught with black diamond and double–black diamond runs that head straight for the bottom of the mountain.

There's also plenty of elbow room at Jackson Hole with 2,500 acres of skiable terrain, 62 named runs, 9 lifts, and an aerial tram (which you can use for just $3 more than the price of a lift ticket; you can get an unlimited day-pass to ride the tram for $14) to reach the top of Rendezvous. If you want an orientation to the mountain, join the Ski Hosts, who gather a group together at the top of the Rendevous lift every hour on the hour and will take you on a tour.

If you're a powder-hound, get out there early—The Hobacks zone, just under Cheyenne Bowl, is set aside for perfect powder mornings and the ski patrol closes it off as soon as the snow gets tracked out.

LODGING   McCollister Drive in the Village is lined with places to stay that can range in price from $100 per night to well over $300. But staying on the mountain in winter simply isn't the economical way to spend your vacation. Property management companies offer several lodging options in Teton Village. **Jackson Hole Property Management** (☎ 307/733-7945 or 800/443-8613) has 85 condominium units and **Teton Village Property Management** (☎ 307/733-4610) runs the Village Center Inn (see "Where to Stay" later in this section) and the Crystal Springs Inn. The **Jackson Hole Racquet Club** (☎ 307/733-3990 or 800/443-8616) has a resort with 120 condominium units.

DINING   There's no shortage of places to eat in Teton Village. Besides the restaurants covered in the "Where to Eat" section, like Steigler's and Beaver Dick's, the Alpenhof hotel has a couple of nice restaurants. The **Alpenhof Dining Room** (☎ 307/733-3462) has an excellent reputation and specializes in local trout and wild game. **Dietrich's Bistro** has a sun deck for the summer visitors and a cozy fireplace for the aprés ski crowd.

✪ Grand Targhee Resort

Hill Rd, Alta, WY 83422. ☎ **307/353-2300** or 800/827-4433, 307/353-2300 or 800/ 827-4433. Lift tickets $30 adults, $15 seniors and children over 5.

Less than 10 years ago, Grand Targhee was *not* rated as a great place to ski, a good place to ski, or even just a decent place to ski. It simply wasn't rated at all. But then this little resort on the other side of the mountain started giving Jackson Hole a run for its money.

In fact, Targhee became one of the better places to ski in this part of the country. The average snowfall of over 500 inches certainly hasn't hurt the publicity campaign. It's 40 miles from Jackson, and when Teton Pass gets snowed on heavily, it can be pretty impossible to get there, but when you can make it to Targhee, you're going to find great powder and plenty of opportunities to ski as much as your legs will allow.

Targhee is not really a place for extreme, straight-down-a-cliff skiing, but it doesn't need to be. It's a powder mountain. Not only does it actually have a beginner's powder area and hundreds of acres of wide-open powder slopes for intermediates and other cruisers, but it also offers such rich, open-mountain wilderness powder navigation that you can explore all day without ever crossing your, or anyone else's, ski tracks. The Lost Groomer Chute, a run that takes full advantage of the weather moving west to east, can provide even the most insatiable powder hound with enough dust.

Two pieces of advice: The mountain gets a lot of snow because it is wide open to the coming weather, but this means that storms hit it full blast, so the most open areas can get a crusty, wind-whipped surface and be uneven in quality and unpredictable. Steer for the more sheltered areas, and the shady forest zones, where the powder stays soft, fine, and deep. Also, be sure to reserve at least one day with the snow cat to slip your skis through the soft crystalline wilderness of Peaked Mountain's ungroomed slopes.

What makes Grand Targhee such a hit with families is the Powderbuster program for kids, a $30 per half-day program for little ones five and up. Babysitting programs offer in-room care for $3 per hour.

Targhee's drawbacks, when compared to the area's other ski hills, is the lack of accommodations, dining options, and after-dark fun. Grand Targhee offers a range of units, though none have cooking facilities, for a range of prices. Skadi's is Grand Targhee's top restaurant, and it's been rated as one of the best in the country at a ski resort.

Snow King Resort

100 E. Snow King, Jackson, WY 83001. ☎ **307/733-5200** or 800/522-7669 (within Wyoming), or 800/533-5464 (outside Wyoming); ☎ 307/734-2020 for snow conditions. Lift tickets $25 adults, $16 seniors and children under 16.

Third fiddle to the other ski resorts in Jackson, Snow King has the distinction of being the oldest of the three (and the oldest in Wyoming). The drawback with Snow King is that it's incredibly steep—first-timers don't have a prayer when they come here. In addition to the grade, the wind and cold can be a problem on this hill more so than others. The number of black diamond runs outnumbers the beginner runs almost 3 to 1. "Town Hill" as it's known, has 500 acres of skiable terrain, two double chairs, and a Poma lift. The Innovative Great Ski School is directed by Bill Briggs, supposedly the first person to ski the Grand Teton.

OTHER WINTER SPORTS & ACTIVITIES

Cross-Country Skiing

Though they're not the rave that the downhill resorts are, cross-country and backcountry skiing are still pretty hot tickets in Jackson Hole. With five Nordic centers and a couple of national parks at your feet, this part of Wyoming is hardly just for the downhill crowd. The people who cross-country ski around Jackson vary in expertise from one extreme to the other. If you're not familiar with cross-country skiing on any level, a trip to one of the Nordic centers is in order. If, however, you feel like you have a good idea of what's going on, then visit or call the National Park Service in Grand Teton National Park (☎ 307/739-3300) or the National Forest Service in downtown Jackson at 340 N. Cache (☎ 307/739-5500) before you go.

For the unofficial scoop on things, the local ski shops more often than not keep up with what's happening in the backcountry. Also keep in mind that many of the trails used by cross-country skiers are also used by snowmobiles.

The **Jackson Hole Nordic Center,** 7658 Teewinot, Teton Village (☎ 307/733-2629), is a small part of the giant facility that includes some of the best downhill skiing around (see above). Not that you'd actually cross-country ski after a full day of downhill or snowboarding, but the price of a downhill pass does include the price of skiing on the cross-country trails—it's kind of like offering you free refills on that vat-sized popcorn at the movies.

Teton Pines Cross Country Skiing Center (☎ 307/733-1005) has 13km of groomed trails that wind over the resort's golf course. Rates are $5 (see also "Where to Stay" later in this section). **Spring Creek Resort,** 1800 N. Spirit Dance Rd., Jackson (☎ 307/733-1004) has an excellent facility—14km of groomed trails, and you don't have to be a guest to enjoy them. The fee for skiers (guests or non) is $7 per day.

At **Grand Targhee** (☎ 307/353-2304), you can get anything you need in the way of cross-country ski equipment and take off on the resort's 12km of groomed trails.

For those seeking some guidance, **Teton Parks and Recreation** (☎ 307/733-5056) has instructional programs for those who want to ski all day and have brought their own equipment.

For cross-country information in **Grand Teton National Park,** call 307/739-3300 or 307/739-3611 (for recorded weather information) or see Section 2 of this chapter.

Dogsledding

If you've never actually driven a dogsled before, here's your chance. **Jackson Hole Iditarod,** P.O. Box 1940, Jackson, WY 83001 (☎ 800/554-7388), offers both half- and full-day trips in five-person sleds (only four passengers; the fifth companion is your guide) and—as promised—you, too, will get a chance to drive. The half-day ride costs $125 per person, gives the dogs an 11-mile workout, and includes a lunch of hot soup and cocoa before you turn around and head back to the kennels. For $225 a head, you can take the full-day excursion out to Granite Hot Springs, a 22-mile trip total. You get the hot lunch, plus your choice of freshly barbecued trout or steak for dinner.

These trips book up pretty quickly, so call three to four days in advance to reserve a spot; you can charge it to Visa or MasterCard. When you call, set up a time for them to come pick you up in Jackson and take you right to the kennels. If you want to drive out yourself, head south out of Jackson to Hoback Junction, then south on Highway 189/191 about 12 miles to the wide spot in the road with a green "snow-mobile parking" sign and turn left.

Snowmobiling

Though West Yellowstone is the best place in the area to snowmobile, that doesn't mean Jackson doesn't have facilities and trails that allow you to do it there. Several operators rent snowmobiles by the day and will also conduct one-day and multi-day tours of Jackson Hole and the surrounding area. High Country Snowmobile Tours, at 3510 S. Hwy. 89 in Jackson (☎ 307/733-5017 or 800/524-0130) offers touring service for Jackson Hole, Yellowstone, and the Gros Ventre Mountains. Rocky Mountain Snowmobile Tours, 1050 S. Hwy. 59 (☎ 307/733-2237 or 800/647-2561) offers one-day trips in Yellowstone and multi-day trips along the Continental Divide. Wyoming Adventures also takes trips along the Continental Divide as well as Grey's River. Typical one-day outings run $150 with pick-up and drop-off service, equipment, fuel, a continental breakfast, and lunch at Old Faithful included. Multi-day trips run anywhere from $220 to $275 per day per person (including all equipment, guide, meals, lodging, and fuel), depending on the destination.

COMPLETELY OFFBEAT BUT MEMORABLE WAYS TO SEE THE TETONS

AERIAL TOURING

For a high time, call **Grand Valley Aviation,** Driggs Airport, Driggs, ID 83422 (☎ 208/354-8131 or 800/472-6382). This is a great way to experience the immensity of the Grand Teton without actually climbing it, and you'll get a perspective no climber will ever have. The Super Teton Ride is an incredible glider ride that takes you to 11,800 feet on the west side of the Grand. The one-hour ride is $125, the 45-minute ride is $105, and the half-hour glider ride is $90. You'll never forget the incredible silence. For smoother rides, ask about the early flights.

BALLOONING

Early in the morning, when the rest of the valley is still sound asleep, the folks at the **Wyoming Balloon Company,** P.O. Box 2578, Jackson WY 83001 (☎ 307/739-0900), are preparing themselves for another one of their "ultimate float trips." Cruising over the valley in a beautiful multicolored balloon with a gorgeous mountain scene emblazoned on the side, the ride glides past wildlife and offers great early-morning views of the Tetons. Since 1989, Wyoming Balloon has been waking up at the crack of dawn to fly tourists over the Jackson Hole Valley. After you touch down, a champagne breakfast is served to celebrate the flight. Flights are $175 per adult, $120 for kids, and reservations should be made a month in advance.

EDUCATIONAL ADVENTURES

Rarely can the average person hike in the mountains and accurately identify all the curiosities found along the trailside. Sure, every now and then a cardinal might slip into view to relieve your sense of ignorance, but for the most part it's a mysterious journey. Naturalist vacations are popular in this area because of the wealth of the surrounding natural world and the experience and expertise that has followed it here. Several organizations in and around the valley have done wonders for travelers with a thirst for learning.

The **Great Plains Wildlife Institute,** P.O. Box 7580, Jackson Hole, WY 83001 (☎ 307/733-2623), has been providing full-day and six-day trips through the area since 1986. The GPWI allows guests to participate in the active research of the institute, doing everything from ear-tagging small mammals to radio-tracking elks.

The **Snake River Institute,** P.O. Box 128, Wilson WY 83014 (☎ 307/733-2214), is not so much oriented toward active research as it is toward ecological and cultural awareness. Programs of the past have included dinosaur digs in northcentral Wyoming and classroom discussions that explore the literature of the Jackson Hole area.

The **Teton Science School,** P.O. Box 68, Kelly WY 83011 (☎ 307/733-4765), offers summer classes dealing with the wildlife in and around the Jackson Hole Valley. (See also Section 2 of this chapter.)

Educational vacations are so popular that even the Grand Targhee Ski Resort is in on the act. The **Targhee Institute** (☎ 307/353-2233) is a nonprofit organization located in the middle of Yellowstone and the Tetons that features ecological classes on the delicate balance of man and the surrounding ecosystem, but there are also some interesting alternative classes like the music and dances of the Basque peoples of Wyoming. Targhee also offers kids ages 8–12 the "Science Explorers" program.

The **Audubon Ecology Workshop in the Rockies** (☎ 612/245-2648) conducts classes in and around the Tetons and the Wind River range and uses 20 rustic cabins at the Whiskey Mountain Wildlife Conservation Camp as its base of operation.

EXPLORING THE AREA

Jackson is what you make it. It can, of course, be your jumping-off spot for exploring Grand Teton and Yellowstone National Parks, but it also offers a variety of other things to do, from rodeos to gunfights in the streets. Jackson is a kid's town (a rich kid's town, actually) and the activities here reflect a charmingly innocent, fun-loving spirit. It's easy to drive north and spend the day looking at the mountains, but it's even easier to stay put and "do Jackson."

Jackson Hole Aerial Tram Rides

At Jackson Hole Ski Resort, 7658 Teewinot, Teton Village. ☎ **307/739-2753.** $14 adults, $12 seniors, $5–$7 children; ages 5 and under free. Late May–Sept daily 9am–5pm, extended hours to 7pm mid-June through August. Tram runs approximately every half hour.

Here you can see the Tetons from an elevation above 10,000 feet—but don't expect a private tour. The trams can carry up to 45 people and in the summer they're often almost filled to capacity. The top of Rendezvous Mountain can get pretty chilly, even in the middle of summer, so bring a light coat if you're not used to cool weather in July.

National Museum of Wildlife Art

2820 Rungius Rd. (3 miles north of town on U.S. Hwy. 89, across from the National Elk Refuge). ☎ **307/733-5771.** Admission $4 adults, $3 students and seniors, children under 6 free. Mon–Sat 10am–5pm, Sun 1–5pm.

This museum was recently transplanted from downtown Jackson to a beautiful new location north of town, on Rungius Road, which is named after wildlife artist Carl Rungius. The museum is a 50,000-square-foot castle that houses some of the best wildlife art in the country, and it may very well be the only museum of its magnitude devoted to wildlife art exclusively. Formerly the Wildlife of American Art Museum (and then the National Wildlife Art Museum), the museum has 12 exhibit galleries, a 200-seat auditorium, an incredible collection of Rungius's works, and a repository of internationally acclaimed wildlife films. Memberships are available.

Jackson Hole Museum

105 N. Glenwood (at the corner of Deloney). ☎ **307/733-2414.** Admission $3 adults, $2 seniors, $1 students and children. Mon–Sat 9:30am–6pm, Sun 10am–5pm. Closed May 28–Sept 30.

This quirky museum stands downtown (it's truly hard to miss with a wagon on its rooftop), and it's a strongbox of early photographs, artifacts, and other items of local historical significance. It's well worth the price of admission if you're at all interested in the olden days of Jackson Hole. Some 3,000 square feet of floor space is smothered with fur-trading artifacts from the early to mid-1800s, an eclectic mix of guns, and a tribute to the homesteading days.

Teton County Historical Center

105 N. Mercill St. ☎ **307/733-9605.** Free admission. Mon–Fri 9am–5pm and by appointment.

The Historical Center, just a couple of blocks north of the Jackson Hole Museum, doesn't attract as many visitors as the latter. But this is the place for arcane tidbits like the beard-trimming habits of area residents in the late 1800s, or ancient page 2 newspaper headlines. The center, though, does welcome the public, and can provide an interesting and in-depth history lesson for the rained-out scholar or the exceedingly curious traveler.

NEARBY WILDLIFE WATCHING

National Elk Refuge

U.S. Hwy. 26, P.O. Box C, Jackson, WY 83001. ☎ **307/733-9212.** Headquarters hours Mon–Fri 8am–4:30pm.

This spectacular expanse of land, in the shadows of the Grand Tetons, is the winter home to the largest gathering of elk in North America. The thinly timbered stretches along the Gros Ventre River that roll into grassy meadows and sagebrush, and the outcroppings of rock along the foothills form an ideal habitat for not just elk, but moose, bighorn sheep, and more than 175 species of birds. Though wildlife viewing is excellent on the refuge throughout the year, winter is the best time to catch glimpses of the migrating elk herd. During the first snows of late autumn, the elk move from the higher elevations of the Tetons and Yellowstone National Park to the valley floor of the refuge in search of vanishing food.

Each winter the Fish and Wildlife Service offers wonderful **horse-drawn sleigh rides** that provide up-close glimpses of the 8,000 elk. Rides early in the winter will find young energetic bulls playing and sparring harmlessly, while late winter visits (when the Fish and Wildlife Service begins feeding the animals) allow for looks at the rest of the herd. Tickets for the 45-minute rides ($8 for adults and $4 for children 6–12) can be purchased at the National Museum of Wildlife Art on Highway 26 across from the refuge. Ask about a combination pass for the sleigh ride and the museum.

OLD WEST COOKOUTS

So you don't have time for the full guest ranch experience or the money to stay for the entire week? What do you do? In Jackson, you make for the nearest guest ranch around mealtime and enjoy Western cuisine served up to the strains of yodeling cowpokes.

Before you run up hungry to the ranches, you may want to make reservations. The **A/OK Corral,** 10 minutes south of town at 9600 U.S. Hwy. 191 S. (☎ 307/733-6556), offers up a steak dinner and a covered wagon ride for $22 ($14 for kids ages four to seven; kids under age four eat free). The **Bar-J Ranch** (head for Wilson and turn right toward Teton Village and watch for the ranch about a mile down the road on your left; ☎ 307/733-3370) has an incredibly complete $13 meal with a real Western show. Even though the place can seat up to 600 people and rain and cold weather don't stop these Western singers, reservations are recommended. The **Bar-T-5,** 790 E. Cache Creek, Jackson (☎ 307/733-5386 or 800/772-5386), offers one heck of a covered wagon ride through Cache Creek Canyon to the "dining room" for an evening of Western victuals and after-dinner songs from the Bar-T-5's singing cowboys. The covered wagon dinner runs around $24 for adults, $16–$19 for kids, and children under three can enjoy the night free.

ESPECIALLY FOR KIDS

If your childrens' eyes are glazing over at the mention of words like "geothermal," haul 'em off to **Snow King's Alpine Miniature Golf Course and Alpine Slide** (☎ 307/733-5200). The golf course is actually pretty amazing if all you're used to is the broken windmill back home (and you can still see the Tetons). A round of 18 holes is $4 for kids, $5 for adults (junkies may purchase the shameful 10-round punch card for $30).

If the miniature golf is somehow not the thrill you anticipated, then head next door to the **Alpine Slide,** the golf course's untamed neighbor. The Alpine Slide is a wild ride down the 2,500 ophidian highway running from the top of the Rafferty chairlift to the bottom of Snow King Mountain. It's a waterslide without the water. You don't actually slide down the mountain; you more or less glide.

SHOPPING

Pretend for a moment that you have time to enjoy the many clothiers and curio merchants in and around Jackson. Town Square alone would eat up your entire vacation—and you'd hardly seem like a savvy traveler when you got back home and announced (with a new wardrobe and Western art collection) that you somehow completely missed the Tetons. Souvenirs are everywhere and extremely hard to miss. Photo shops, T-shirt outlets, jewelry stores—they're all here.

Town Square is a good place to begin and end the shopping spree without having missed much. For T-shirts and such, **Jackson Tee Party** at 120 E. Broadway, **Thomahawk Athletic Outfitters** at 135 N. Cache, just north of the Town Square, and **Sirk Shirts** on the square at 10 W. Broadway, all have selections of souvenir shirts for a wide range of budgets. Jackson is full of factory outlet stores: **Benetton** at 48 E. Broadway, **J.Crew** at 50 Center St., and **Polo** at 75 N. Cache, are all in the Town Square vicinity and advertise discounts off their normal prices. For quick turn-around on the whitewater photos, try **Sure Shot Photo,** upstairs on the northeast corner of the square at 90 N. Center.

GALLERIES

It would be difficult to be an artist here and not paint, sculpt, draw, or mold some image of the mountains that run the length of Jackson Hole. Inspiration has touched the muse of everyone from Ansel Adams to the fumbling novice, and sometimes the results are profound. Jackson is a town of creative minds and nowhere is that fact more evident than in the galleries that cover the town like wildflowers. There are more than 20 galleries in downtown Jackson alone. The emphasis, of course, is on the West, the land, and the people, but there are pieces not categorically Western to be found in some of the galleries. Besides these avant-garde stragglers, the town boasts a number of collections that include some of the finest Western art in the country.

The **American Legends Gallery,** at 365 N. Cache, has a massive array of bronze sculptures and features the works of several local artists. **Images of Nature Gallery,** 170 N. Cache, exhibits Tom Mangelson's excellent wildlife photography; a number of his photographs are signed and numbered—not something you'll find browsing through his mail-order catalog. The **Center Street Gallery,** 172 Center St., has the lock on abstract Western art in Jackson. The **Moynihan Gallery,** at 120 E. Broadway, displays some of Russell Chatham's landscapes (Chatham's gallery is in Livingston, Montana). A mile north of town at 1975 U.S. Hwy. 89, towards the park, is the **Wilcox Gallery,** which showcases more than 20 painters and sculptors from across the nation.

WHERE TO STAY

If you'd come to Jackson 20 years ago you'd have had a limited range of lodgings from which to choose—but you probably wouldn't have had any trouble getting a room at last minute's notice. But be advised that times have most certainly changed. There is some strange mathematical property at work, causing the number of hotels to increase dramatically while the availability of these places in summer still significantly decreases (to nil, if you're trying to find a place the day of your arrival).

Prices are becoming increasingly exorbitant—you shouldn't be surprised to find a decent hotel room costing $100 (that's why you'll find an inexpensive category in other chapters of this book, but not here).

But that's if you can even *find* a room. One woman standing at a hotel counter was incredulous when she found out there wasn't a single room available in early June. She'd been, she said, to every other hotel in the valley. "What is going on? Is there a convention or something in town?" Yes, ma'am. Something to do with the National Park Service, most likely.

If you would like to have someone else handle the headache of finding lodging for you (as well as handling other parts of your vacation planning), try one of the destination management companies in Jackson. **Business and Vacation Planning** (☎ 800/733-6431) will handle all the reservation making; the fee depends on what kind of planning they do for you. **Conference Consultants** (☎ 800/645-5380) makes arrangements for businesses planning to visit Jackson Hole.

VERY EXPENSIVE

✪ Flying A Ranch

Rte. 1 (P.O. Box 7), Pinedale, WY 82941. ☎ **307/367-2385.** 6 cabins. $1,500–$1,575 per person per week. Rates include all meals and ranch activities. No credit cards.

This guest ranch, surrounded by the Gros Ventre and Wind River ranges of Wyoming, has one of the best views in the state. Quaking aspens, stream-fed ponds, and curious antelope are just a few of the natural sights of this high mountain valley (keep in mind that you'll be 50 miles southeast of Jackson). Built in 1929, the ranch cabins have been carefully restored, with evocative touches that include wood-burning stoves, handmade furniture constructed of native pine, and regional artwork. A minimum guest capacity of 12 and intentional lack of children's activities ensures a low-key ranch experience for adults, complemented by gourmet meals, excellent sightseeing and shopping in nearby Jackson Hole, and unparalleled opportunities for fly-fishing and exploring the outdoors. Guests are encouraged to enjoy the ranch at their own pace, whether that means unlimited horse rides or relaxing with a favorite book on their private porch.

✪ Spring Creek Resort

P.O. Box 3154 (on top of the East Gros Ventre Butte), Jackson, WY 83001. ☎ **307/733-8833** or 800/443-6139. 116 units. A/C TV TEL. $200–$950 per unit per night. AE, MC, V.

Spring Creek masquerades as a secluded resort since it sits atop the Gros Ventre Butte, a sheltering formation that keeps the Tetons invisible to downtown Jackson. But the fact is, Spring Creek is only a short 4-mile drive from Jackson's Town Square. Since the early 1980s, this resort has been a standout choice in the Jackson Hole area. Prices are colossal compared to other places in the valley, but there are few opportunities around here to enjoy a four-bedroom million-dollar property.

The free-standing units (homes actually) can sleep eight people comfortably and come equipped with all the amenities, as they should: a fireplace, an enormous kitchen, and plenty of living space. The condominiums all come with fireplaces, accommodate fewer people, and are a few hundred dollars less than the homes. Even with all the amenities, we'd still say that the resort's best attribute is that nearly every single room has a view of the Teton range.

Dining/Entertainment: The resort's restaurant, the Granary, offers great food and, like the guest rooms, excellent views of the Tetons. Lunch is a great way to enjoy both the food and the view with items like rabbit bratwurst and seafood quiche. Prices for main dinner courses run from $14 to $25, and include a wide variety of seafood as well as buffalo tenderloin. Reservations for the restaurant should be made by calling 307/733-8833.

Services: The resort offers shuttle service to the Jackson Hole Ski Resort. Dry cleaning is available, and the Conference Services department can accommodate group needs. There is a computer service to preplan activities in and around Jackson and a fax service is also available.

Facilities: Summer facilities include a swimming pool, outdoor hot tub, and tennis courts. In winter, the cross-country center opens as soon as there's adequate snow.

Teton Pines Resort

3450 N. Clubhouse Dr., Jackson, WY 83001. ☎ **307/733-1005** or 800/238-2223. 16 suites. A/C TV TEL. Summer $250–$360 suite; rest of year $125–$195 suite. Closed Nov.

This is not only a luxury resort, it's also a resort with a country club conveniently attached, along with an 18-hole golf course designed by Arnold Palmer and Ed Seay (not a course to improve handicaps). The Teton Pines is definitely one of the most upscale places to stay in Jackson and the rooms are by themselves worth the grand price. And that's good, because that's about all you get in the way of extras. A continental breakfast is laid out each morning and a tennis complex is available to guests, but everything else on the premises is not included and expensive.

Dining: The dining room, The Grille at the Pines, is in the incredible Teton Pines Clubhouse. The restaurant is one of the better places to eat in Jackson (though prices are somewhat higher than average) and looks out over the Teton Pines golf course. The menu is impressive and includes an array of well-prepared pasta dishes. Steak and seafood and a veal du jour round out the heavier side of the menu. The chef has fresh seafood flown in daily.

Services: Free shuttle service to and from the airport; ski shuttle.

Facilities: Besides the 18-hole golf course, Teton Pines also offers guests 8 miles of groomed Nordic trails at the Teton Pines Nordic Center (see "Getting Outside," earlier in this section).

EXPENSIVE

✪ Days Inn of Jackson Hole

1280 W. Broadway (just off the junction of Hwy. 22 and U.S. Hwy. 191), Jackson, WY 83001. ☎ **307/733-0033** or 800/329-7466. 91 rms, 13 suites. A/C TV TEL. $149 double; $159–209 suite. Off-season rates considerably lower. Rates include continental breakfast. AE, DC, DISC, MC, V.

It's easily one of the nicer hotels on this side of town, but it's incredibly expensive. In fall and spring, though, you'll pay less than half of the summer rates. What you can expect is an above-average Days Inn, an extremely helpful staff, a free continental breakfast that is exceptional (if you don't mind filling up on coffee, a wide variety of muffins, and fresh orange juice), and beautiful and spacious suites with fireplaces and hot tubs. This Days Inn would be a great place to stay even if it wasn't located in Jackson.

Red Lion Wyoming Inn of Jackson

930 W. Broadway, Jackson, WY 83001. ☎ **307/734-0035** or 800/844-0035. 73 rms. TEL TV. $179–$219 double; $369 suite. Rates include buffet breakfast. AE, DISC, MC, V.

In the "hotel chains getting a piece of the pie" complex, a mile from downtown, the Red Lion is one of the newest members of the team assaulting tourists with outlandish rates. There is nothing particularly amazing about this Red Lion—no secret passageways, no lavish appointments, no acrobats flying across the entrance. This is just a chain motel built on expensive real estate with the original artwork and bronze sculptures in the lobby. The breakfast bar is complimentary and is stacked with cereals, pastries, fresh fruit, and juices. Coffee is complimentary 24 hours a day.

Rusty Parrot Lodge

175 N. Jackson, Jackson, WY 83001. ☎ **307/733-2000** or 800/458-2004. 31 rms, 1 suite. TV TEL. $98–$215 double; $300 suite. Ratse include full breakfast. AE, DISC, MC, V.

It might sound like an out-of-practice jungle bird, but since 1990, the Rusty Parrot has been one of the most finely tuned places to stay in Jackson. If it weren't right slap in the middle of town, you'd think it was a country lodge. Located across from Miller Park, the Parrot is decorated in the new-Western style of peeled log, with an interior appointed with pine furniture and river rock fireplaces. If you're going to spend this kind of money and not stay at a guest ranch, the Parrot is a good idea. Rooms are gigantic and several have private balconies. The suite is an incredible apartment with fireplaces in both the living area and the bedroom. The location is a bit unusual for this sort of place, but if you've come to enjoy the shops and ski hill a couple of blocks away, then the Rusty Parrot has an ideal location. If you came to wake up to breathtaking views of the Tetons, you'll have to drive farther up the road.

Wort Hotel

50 N. Glenwood, Jackson, WY 83001. ☎ **307/733-2190.** 55 rms, 5 suites. TV TEL. $145 double; $190–$295 suite. AE, DISC, MC, V.

You can burn it alive, but it still comes back. The Wort was all but destroyed in a fire that preceded Yellowstone's by eight years, and when it returned, it was as popular as ever. Located in the heart of Jackson's downtown district, a few steps from Town Square, the Wort is an institution with plenty of character to go around. Opened in the early 1940s by the wife and son of Charles Wort, an early 20th-century homesteader, the Wort's Tudor exterior belies its location and the major design elements of its interior—Western artwork and taxidermy. In 1989, the Wort underwent major surgery to replace the Wild West look with something a little less hokey. Now you'll find in your rooms more of a Tudor feel rather than a Western atmosphere.

MODERATE

Alpine Motel

70 S. Jean, Jackson, WY 83001. ☎ **307/739-3200.** 18 rms. A/C TEL TV. $48–$74 double. AE, DC, MC, V.

You won't be taking any glamour shots in front of the Alpine. This small white U-shape motel offers a heated pool, a decent location (three blocks from downtown), and a relatively recently remodeled section (1989). The older part of the motel, though, is actually worth a stay. For less than $70 (bargain basement in Jackson Hole), you get minimal cooking facilities (some utensils, a refrigerator, stove, oven, table, and chairs). Keep also in mind that when they refer to the older section, they mean *older*. The Alpine has been around since the 1950s.

Trapper Inn

235 N. Cache, Jackson, WY 83001. ☎ **307/733-2648** or 800/341-8000 for reservations. 54 rms, 1 suite. A/C TEL TV. $85–$105 double; $195 suite. AE, DC, DISC, MC, V.

The location is worth a gold mine, and the staff here are some of the best you're going to find in Jackson. They know all the good deals and they're not afraid to share. Based here, just two short blocks from town square, you can walk anywhere in downtown within minutes. The Trapper is hard to miss if you're walking north on Cache from the Town Square. On the left side of Cache you'll notice the crazy Trapper guy on the sign. Though the decor of the rooms is average, the space is not. In the newest building, erected in 1991, the rooms are larger than normal. Many of the hotel rooms come with miniature refrigerators. Laundry facilities and an indoor/outdoor hot tub are also on hand.

Village Center Inn

3275 W. McCollister, Teton Village, WY 83025. ☎ **307/733-3155.** 16 rms. TEL TV. Winter $102–$132 double. AE, MC, V.

It's a bit out of the way if you're planning to stay in the heart of Jackson, but if you don't mind the 15-minute drive into town, this place can be a lot more affordable for summer travelers. The winter rates quoted above are higher because of the proximity to the ski resort (the units are at the base of the hill next to the Jackson Hole tram). The units are a step up from your average motel room. Resembling efficiency apartments, the units come with cable television, small kitchens, and a living area.

The Village Center Inn is run by Teton Village Property Management (☎ 307/733-4610), a rental company with condominiums and homes also available.

Virginian Lodge

750 W. Broadway, Jackson, WY 83001. ☎ **307/733-2792** or 800/262-4999. 135 rms, 12 mini-suites, 11 suites. A/C TV TEL. $95–$105 double; $110 mini-suite; $115–$155 suite. AE, DC, DISC, MC, V.

With its overhaul in 1995, the Virginian is truly one of the best hotels in Jackson. It's not brand-new; it's not a resort; it doesn't have a golf course; and the highway is right outside the door. You will not, however, find yourself swearing when you get the bill, as you would in most of the other accommodations in Jackson. That's right, there is actually a hotel whose rates are less than the age of the town. Since 1965, the same owner has run the Virginian, and before he ran it into the ground with ancient policies, the hotel came alive with fresh coats of paint, new carpet, and a hot tub. In a questionable call, he did keep the nightmare of taxidermy that adorns the walls of the lobby and the bar. But the hotel's Old West flavor is charming. If they charged what a lot of other places did in Jackson, we'd have to say the place was tacky. But they don't, and it's not. The Virginian also has an outdoor heated pool, an average family-style restaurant on the premises, an arcade for the youngsters, and laundry facilities. No-smoking rooms are also available after 30 years of not having any.

NEARBY GUEST RANCHES

They're everywhere in this part of Wyoming. You can't find a list of accommodations in the Jackson Hole area that doesn't include guest ranches. They give vacationers the real flavor of the West—with cookouts, horseback riding, and a slew of other activities. Though Jackson certainly has its share of ranches, see the Grand Teton National Park chapter for a short list of other ranches in and around the park.

Gros Ventre River Ranch

About 18 miles north of Jackson (P.O. Box 151), Moose, WY 83012. ☎ **307/733-4138.** 8 cabins. $945–$1,854 per person/week. No credit cards. The ranch is actually pretty close to Kelly, but call for complete directions.

Just outside Kelly, the Gros Ventre River Ranch is a year-round guest ranch devoted to keeping the Old West alive—but nonetheless, the emphasis here is on rest and relaxation. It's a great spot to spend a week in Jackson Hole. Horseback rides and fly-fishing dominate the program of events, but just taking a few hours out of the day (or a couple of days out of the week) staring at the Tetons can be a worthwhile way to while away the time. Four log cabins and four log lodges (lodges are larger and have living rooms) are spread out on this property, which looks straight out to the Teton Range.

Since taking over in 1987 (the ranch has been around since the 1950s), Tina and Karl Weber have put their own imprint on Gros Ventre. A new lodge built the year they arrived looks out to the Tetons and the Gros Ventre River, which runs past the ranch. The lodge includes a living room, bar, game room, and a small library, as well as the main dining room, but meals aren't served exclusively indoors: They also have great cookouts. The atmosphere is of the Old West, but the comforts of home (down comforters adorn the beds) aren't lost and the activities are seemingly endless: canoeing, bike riding, horseback riding, and fishing in stocked ponds (for lazy anglers). In winter you can cross-country ski or go snowmobiling.

✪ Heart 6 Ranch

Five miles outside Grand Teton National Park (P.O. Box 70), Moran, WY 83013. ☎ 307/543-2477. 15 cabins. $1,072–$1,265 per person per week. MC, V.

A little more than an hour north of Jackson, just east of the Moran Junction, is the Heart 6, a fistful of fun for families looking to spend some time together in the West. The Heart 6 isn't the fanciest of the guest ranches in and around Jackson Hole, but it's certainly not short on entertainment for the young at heart. The Heart 6 is dedicated to providing every member of the family—including the kids. Fishing, horseback riding, hiking, or just sitting and talking around the ranch lead the long list of outdoor activities for the short of breath and the long-winded. A naturalist from the park service is also on hand for many of the activities to educate guests on the local wildflowers. The ranch has an airport shuttle system, Saturday trips to the rodeo in Jackson, and extensive children's programs: counselors take care of the kids while parents ride. Babysitting service is also available for infants and children up to four. In fact, Heart 6 is the only ranch in the valley that takes care of young infants. On rainy days, kids and adults alike can enjoy the recreation center, with bumper pool, foosball, and Ping-Pong.

✪ Lost Creek Ranch

P.O. Box 95, Moose, WY 83012. ☎ **307/733-3435.** $3,960–$8,980 per cabin per week. Call for discounted group and off-season rates. Corporate rates available. No credit cards. Closed mid-Sept to May.

Decisions, decisions . . . whether to buy a brand-new car or take a weeklong vacation. If you're leaning toward the vacation, then consider Lost Creek Ranch. Yes, it's possible for a family of four to spend $9,000 in a week's time at Lost Creek, but it's also the most breathtaking vacation spot in northwest Wyoming. That picture of the Tetons in your cabin isn't a picture, it's a window. The riding program with group instruction, the Snake River float trips, the food (truly incredible), the dances, the campfire songs—it's all part of the trip. It's hard to describe exactly how spectacular the scenery is and how friendly the staff is at Lost Creek, but we really feel it's worth the price.

✪ Red Rock Ranch

P.O. Box 38, Kelly, WY 83011. ☎ **307/733-6288.** 9 cabins. $1,085 per week. Minimum seven-day stay (Sun to Sun). No credit cards. Closed Oct–May.

This working cattle ranch is one of the best family vacation spots in either state. With excellent fly-fishing on the ranch's private stretch of Crystal Creek, horseback riding in the mountains, and activities that include overnighters for the kids and weekly trips to the rodeo in Jackson, this wonderful family-oriented guest ranch northeast of Jackson is a great spot to bring the whole bunch. Since 1972 the MacKenzies have operated Red Rock Ranch, a late 19th-century homestead surrounded by the mountains of this remarkably remote valley east of the Tetons. Guests can expect to enjoy some of the area's most spectacular scenery by horseback or they can just while away the lazy days in the atmosphere of the Old West.

All nine cabins are comfortable log structures built in the 1950s. Each comes equipped with a small refrigerator and charming wood stove (electric heat is also available). The ranch's list of amenities includes a pool hall and bar, an activities room to square dance the night away, and a recreation room for the kids. You'll also find a heated pool to warm your body on chilly Wyoming nights, and if that doesn't do the trick, try the giant hot tub that seats eight people. The kids will have a blast here.

The Children's Riding Program (for those 6 and older) is a great learning experience and takes kids all over the ranch by horseback, but the overnight campout is the real Western treat. After a horseback ride to the upper end of the ranch, the kids (with the help of a couple of wranglers) set up camp and cook supper over an open fire. The night is spent playing games, telling stories, and looking up at a million stars. In the morning they fix their own breakfasts, break down the camp, then mosey on back for a well-deserved rest at the ranch.

CAMPING

There are several places to park the RV around Jackson Hole and a few of them are reasonably priced and not too far away. Most are going to charge around $20, though prices seem to change at the drop of a hat, rising just like local motel prices.

Some of your best bets are either out of town or way out of town. Most campgrounds are open from late spring to early fall. **Astoria Mineral Springs,** also known as Astoria Hot Springs, is at 12500 S. Hwy. 89 (☎ 307/733-2659), and has 110 tent and RV sites. It's located about 17 miles south of town towards Pinedale. The **Snake River Park KOA Campground** is also on U.S. Hwy. 89, 10 miles south of town (☎ 307/733-7078). In town, the **Wagon Wheel Campground** is about five blocks north of Town Square at the Wagon Wheel Motel and has sites for less than $20. The **Teton Village KOA** (☎ 307/733-5354), 12 miles northwest of Jackson, has some sites for $15.

See also Section 2 of this chapter for details on camping in Grand Teton National Park.

WHERE TO EAT

Jackson has more dining options than most of the other towns in this book combined. In fact, the Jackson area has more restaurants than most towns *10* times its size. You can find lots of different kinds of cuisine, though, of course, there's a more than adequate amount of game and beef served around town. There are, however, some pleasant surprises. Though the prices at some of the places may seem offensive, you have to keep in mind the costs of running a restaurant in a tourist town like Jackson, where the real estate market is untethered to reality.

EXPENSIVE

✪ The Blue Lion

160 N. Millward. ☎ **307/733-3912.** Reservations recommended. Main courses $15–$26. AE, DC, MC, V. Daily 6–9:30pm. Closed Tues off-season. CONTINENTAL.

The menu at the Blue Lion, a quaint restaurant off the Town Square downtown, is filled with a delicious array of creative entrées that reflects the restaurant's flair for rich foods. Rack of lamb, beef tenderloin médaillons, and wild game, including elk loin grilled and served in a peppercorn sauce, are specialties of the Blue Lion. But for every item of beef, there is a vegetarian entrée prepared with zest. The pasta primavera is a delicious mixture of veggies sautéed in olive oil and served on a bed of fettucine with a delicious basil-walnut pesto.

The Cadillac Grille

55 N. Cache. ☎ **307/733-3279.** Reservations recommended. Lunch items $5–$8; main dinner courses $15–$25. AE, MC, V. Daily 11am–3pm and 5:30–9:30pm. CONTINENTAL.

If presentation is everything, then the Cadillac has it all. It's a trendy California-influenced restaurant. The art deco restaurant, with a liberal use of neon, jumped right out of the 1940s and into the 1990s with its award-winning wine list and nationally acclaimed cuisine. The Cadillac is Jackson's premiere see-and-be-seen restaurant. The menu changes seasonally, but has included some delicious entrées in the past. Stuffed Dakota pheasant, bleu cheese tournedos, and steamed Alaskan halibut are just a few of the creative items the Cadillac has dished up.

Stiegler's

Teton Village Road (at the Jackson Hole Racquet Club), Teton Village. ☎ **307/733-1071.** Reservations recommended. Main courses $14–$24. AE, MC, V. Tues–Sun 5:30–10pm. AUSTRIAN/CONTINENTAL.

People often wonder where the Von Trapps eat on vacation. I mean, Austrian cuisine isn't exactly lurking beyond every street corner waiting to be summoned with a Julie Andrews yodel. But in Jackson, the discerning Austrian has two options: Steigler's Restaurant or Steigler's Bar. Since 1983, Steigler's has been confusing, astonishing, and delighting customers with such favorites as the Bauern Schmaus for two and the less-perplexing venison filet mignon morel. Peter Stiegler, the Austrian chef, invites you to "find a little *gemutlichkeit*." Tyrolean leather breeches are, of course, optional.

Sweetwater Restaurant

At the corner of King and Pearl. ☎ **307/733-3553.** Reservations recommended. Lunch items $5–$7; main dinner courses $13–$18. DC, MC, V. Daily 11am–3pm and 5:30–10pm. AMERICAN.

Though this little log restaurant serves American fare, it does so in a decidedly offbeat way. Lunch is soups and sandwiches, but the Greek phyllo pie is a delicious diversion, as is the Mediterranean, a French roll stuffed with grilled eggplant, red peppers, tomatoes, and Provolone. The tables outside are a great way to enjoy a summer lunch. The dinner menu is just as quirky and starts off with an incredible appetizer called the Angel of Death, an artery-closing snack of Armenian crackers served with a bleu cheese and garlic spread topped with walnuts. Or, for another starter, try the unique smoked buffalo carpaccio before diving into the giant salmon fillet smoked on the Sweetwater's mesquite grill. Vegetarians will want to try the spinach-and-feta casserole topped with a cheese soufflé.

MODERATE

✪ Acadian House

170 N. Millward. ☎ **307/739-1269.** Reservations recommended. Lunch items $3–$7; main dinner courses $9–$17. AE, DC, MC, V. Tues–Fri 11:30am–2pm; daily 5:30–10pm. CAJUN.

Formerly located at the junction of U.S. Hwy. 89 and WY 22 as you came into town from the west, the Acadian House has since moved, but its loyal following has not. Serving up some of the best flavors from the swamplands of southern Louisiana, this Cajun restaurant is Jackson's finest in the cayenne department. Traditional dishes like boudin—a sausage-and-rice bratwurst lookalike—next to red beans and rice, and shrimp etouffée make appearances with continental-style creations like the crawfish fettucine. There is, too, an abundance of seafood and fish. The catfish, if you've never treated yourself to the South's most delicious bottom-feeder, is delicious when blackened to perfection and topped with almonds, pecans, and white wine.

Anthony's

62 S. Glenwood St. ☎ **307/733-3717.** Reservations not accepted. Main courses $10–$17. MC, V. Daily 5:30–9:30pm. PASTA.

Just south of the Wort Hotel is one of Jackson's two most notable downtown Italian restaurants, with dishes like fettucine with heavy cream, broccoli, and mushrooms. Though Anthony's is one of Jackson's mainstays, it's not by any stretch the finest restaurant in town. It is, however, the place to dine if you're looking for a strictly Italian menu with plenty of pasta options.

✪ Lame Duck

680 E. Broadway. ☎ **307/733-4311.** Most dishes $9–$17. AE, MC, V. Daily 5:30–10pm. CHINESE/JAPANESE.

You wouldn't think that a visit to the Wild West would yield good sushi prospects, but the Lame Duck is the only game in town for decent Japanese and Chinese cuisine. Some of the Lame Duck favorites include the Samurai Chicken, otherwise known as the Oriental fajita, and the Six Delicacies, a dish of duck, lobster, shrimp, snow peas, and mushrooms served with a secret sauce. For something to provoke the fire alarm, try the Fireworks Shrimp: shrimp, snow peas, and bamboo shoots mixed with an incredible hot sauce that warrants a beware sign. The Lame Duck also offers private tearoom seating for those who want to enjoy the sit-down, shoes-off experience of the restaurant's more authentic side.

✪ Nani's Genuine Pasta House

240 N. Glenwood (two blocks north of Broadway at the El Rancho Motel). ☎ **307/733-3888.** Reservations recommended. Main courses $8–$14. MC, V. Tues–Sat 5:30–9:30pm. ITALIAN.

It's a quaint spot just off the square, but its cuisine is truly from another continent. Each month Nani's takes you to another place to explore the regional cuisine. Other than the fresh handmade ravioli (one of the reasons the residents of Jackson call it one of the best restaurants in town), there isn't much to say about the menu at Nani's, because it changes so frequently. One minute you can enjoy the white sauces of northern Italy, the next you're on the east coast in Puglia.

⊜ Nora's Fish Creek Inn

5600 W. WY 22, Wilson. ☎ **307/733-8288.** Reservations not accepted. Breakfast items $3–$7; lunch items $4–$6; main dinner courses $8–$14. DISC, MC, V. Daily 6am–9:30pm. AMERICAN.

This little place outside Wilson is a great spot for a weekend breakfast because it's all-you-can-eat pancakes. Locals have enjoyed it for years and the place has achieved status as one of Jackson Hole's institutions. The food isn't gourmet, and that's precisely why a lot of folks keep coming back. Prices are inexpensive compared to those at any of the other restaurants in town. Coffee isn't brewed in a Bodem and you still get as many refills as you like. Dinner is fish, fish, and more fish, like fresh Idaho trout.

✪ Vista Grande

Teton Village Road, Teton Village. ☎ **307/733-6964.** Reservations not accepted. Main courses $9–$17. AE, MC, V. Daily 5–10pm. MEXICAN.

Since the late 1970s, the Vista Grande has been a crowd-pleaser. It's a reasonable place in a town full of sometimes unreasonable restaurants. The food is great south-of-the-border cuisine (there are others in town, but this is one of the best), and the portions are plentiful. What separates the Vista Grande from a lot of other Mexican restaurants is the variety of the menu: You have a choice of the requisite fajitas, burritos, chimichangas, and enchiladas, but you'll also find chicken asados (grilled chicken on a bed of rice with pico de gallo), blackened tuna, and a vegetarian plate that makes no excuses for the fat grams.

INEXPENSIVE

⑤ Beaver Dick's Saloon

3345 W. McCollister, Teton Village. ☎ 307/733-7102. Reservations not accepted. Most items $3–$6. AE, DISC, MC, V. Daily 11am–2am (closes earlier in off-season). BURGERS.

This is the place for the burger-eating sports fan, the beer drinker, and the crazy beaver man with the coonskin cap tapping a frying pan with a giant spoon. There's nothing world-class about the place except for the burgers: They are truly something to behold. The Mountain Man Burger, for instance, is not a $^1/_4$-pound burger, nor is it a $^1/_3$-pound burger. It's a $^5/_8$-*pound* burger. Yes, at Beaver Dick's your entire family can split one of these creations and have some left for the dog. Whether or not you want to bring them here is another question.

⑤ The Bunnery

130 N. Cache St. ☎ **307/733-5474.** Breakfast items $3–$6; lunch items $5–$6. MC, V. Daily 7am–3pm and 5:30–9:30pm. Closed for dinner except in summer. SANDWICHES/SOUPS/SALADS.

A Jackson mainstay, this bakery and restaurant is a great place to have one of the famous Bunnery breakfasts outside on a cool morning, or to drop by around 11:30am before the crowds inundate the place for a sunny-day lunch. Sandwiches are reasonably priced and the portions are larger than most other trendy sandwich places. For a peek at the other side of the Bunnery, have a look at all the baked goods when you go inside to pay your bill.

Jedidiah's House of Sourdough

135 E. Broadway. ☎ **307/733-5671.** Reservations not accepted. Breakfast items $4–$8; lunch items $3–$7. AE, DC, MC, V. Daily 7am–2pm. AMERICAN.

Though they get uppity and serve dinner in the summertime, Jedidiah's is known throughout the valley for its breakfast and its log-cabin atmosphere. It's not a good idea to come here unless you're really hungry. The sourjacks are a stack of sourdough pancakes, served with blueberries if you like, and the 'Diah's omelet is a big three-egg concoction stuffed with bacon, onions, and cheddar cheese and served with a side of potatoes. The old photographs give customers a great excuse for staring at the wall while waiting for the food.

JACKSON AFTER DARK

For family fun in an Old West atmosphere, head down to **Dirty Jack's Wild West Musical Theatre** on the north side of downtown at 140 N. Cache (☎ 307/733-4775). The jokes are run-of-the-mill, but the cast loves telling them anyway and the audiences love listening.

Throughout the summer, the **Grand Teton Music Festival,** 4015 N. Lake Creek (☎ 307/733-3050), brings in some world-class musicians (like the Moscow String Quartet) to play classical music.

The **Jackson Hole Playhouse,** 145 W. Deloney (☎ 307/733-6994), and the **Lighthouse Theatre,** 49 W. Broadway (☎ 307/733-3670), always have something in production during the summer months. Tickets for all shows should be reserved.

Those less impressed with dramaturgy should head down to the **Silver Dollar Bar** at 50 N. Glenwood in the Wort Hotel for a drink with one of the real or imagined cowpokes who are bellied up to the bar. And, yes, those 1921 silver dollars are authentic. The very famous **Million Dollar Cowboy Bar** down the street also packs in the Western crowd for cocktails.

If you're a little younger and not as Western, say, as the people in the Silver Dollar or the Million Dollar, you may want to socialize with the **Mangy Moose** crowd at 3285 W. McCollister in Teton Village. The Moose is where itinerant up-and-coming bands play when they stop in Jackson Hole. For Sunday night drink and merriment, the **Stagecoach** on WY 22 in Wilson is where you'll likely find the Moose crowd you saw the night before.

2 Grand Teton National Park

The Rocky Mountains do interesting things as they move from Montana into Wyoming. And there's no better view of the massive range than what you'll see in Grand Teton National Park—on a clear day the views are simply not to be believed. Formed by the massive jolts of earthquakes, the Tetons rose from the depths of the earth at a typically geologic pace. Some nine million years ago, enormous faults began fracturing formations in the earth and set the Tetons on their path to greatness. The mountains themselves seem to shoot straight out of the earth at odd angles, stretching toward the sky. No fewer than six peaks tower over 12,000 feet.

Native American tribes that have haunted the place include the Blackfeet, Crow, Gros Ventre, and Shoshone. In the winter of 1807, wilderness man extraordinaire John Colter made his way into the region and began the white man's intrusion into this spectacular area of the West. Park status was achieved after Pierce Cunningham, a rancher near Spread Creek, began spreading a petition around the valley in an attempt to get government officials to set the area aside much the way Yellowstone and Glacier had been preserved.

Witness what has become a wonderful wildlife testimonial to Cunningham's efforts. Everything from yellow-bellied marmots (a creature you'll become familiar with if you spend any time at all in the backcountry) to bugling elk. The Tetons are extraordinary, not only for their raw visual power, but as an enduring wildlife habitat. Gliding blue herons, bald eagles, and osprey can all be seen flying sorties around the Oxbow Bend area, feeding on trout in the slow-moving waters. Pronghorn, bison, and moose are occasional sights you can witness as they graze along the Snake River. And, of course, anywhere there's a picnic table, ground squirrels are sure to be there begging for forbidden morsels that some tourists dole out—against park regulations.

JUST THE FACTS
ACCESS/ENTRY POINTS

There are really only three ways to enter the park: the Yellowstone South entrance through the John D. Rockefeller Jr. Memorial Parkway; the Moran entrance station; and the Moose entrance station. The Moran entrance station is located on the east side of the park. To get there from Dubois, take Highway 287 west and turn right at Moran Junction. The Moose Entrance station is located 15 miles north of Jackson. There are park rangers at each of the entrance stations to answer any questions you may have.

VISITOR CENTERS

There are now three visitor centers in Grand Teton National Park: the Moose Visitor Center in Moose, the Jenny Lake Visitor Center (eight miles north of Moose), and the Colter Bay Visitor Center on the north side of the park. All three are wheelchair-accessible.

The **Moose Visitor Center** (☎ 307/739-3399), 8 miles north of the park's southern boundary, is a half-mile west of Moose Junction on the Teton Park Road. From May 15 through June 4, the visitor center is open daily from 8am to 6pm; from June 5 through September 5, the visitor center stays open from 8am to 7pm. Winter hours (8am to 5pm) begin September 6 and continue through May 14.

The **Colter Bay Visitor Center** (☎ 307/739-3594) is a half-mile mile west of Colter Bay Junction on Highway 191. From May 13–20, it's open daily from 9am–5pm; from May 21–June 4, its hours extend to 8am to 7pm. From June 5 through September 5, the center is open from 8am to 8pm.

The **Jenny Lake Visitor Center** is open daily from 8am to 7pm June 5 through September 5. It's closed the remainder of the year.

FEES & BACKCOUNTRY PERMITS

Though it's possible to view the park without ever having to pay a dime (Highway 191 runs north to south through the park from Moran Junction to Moose Junction on beyond), a $10 fee is required to enter at Moose or Moran and is good for seven days.

If you enter from the north, the park assumes you've paid in Yellowstone. A season pass for both Yellowstone and Grand Teton National Parks is available for $15.

A Golden Eagle Passport is available for $25 and entitles the holder to enter any national park for the calendar year. The Golden Age Passport (for citizens over 62) is available for a one-time fee of $10. The Golden Access Passport is available to travelers with disabilities free of charge.

Bicyclists and walk-throughs must pay a $4 fee, which allows them access to the park for seven days.

A backcountry permit is required for all hikers planning to spend the night and may be obtained at the Moose Visitor Center in the south part of the park, the Colter Bay Visitor Center in the north, or at the Jenny Lake Ranger Station at South Jenny Lake.

REGULATIONS

BIKES   Bikes are allowed on all major roads throughout the park, on the right side of the road. Groups of cyclists should ride single file. Bikes are never allowed on trails throughout the park, nor are they allowed in the backcountry. Cyclists entering the park on bicycle are required to pay a $3 entry fee.

BOATING   Motorboats are permitted on Jenny Lake (7.5 horsepower or less), Jackson Lake, and Phelps Lake.

"Human powered vessels" are permitted on Jenny, Jackson, Phelps, Emma Matilda, Taggart, Bradley, Two Ocean, Bear Paw, Leigh, and String Lakes. Waterskiing, windsurfers, and jet skis are only permitted on Jackson Lake. Boats permits are required ($10, motorized, $5 nonmotorized) and may be obtained at Moose Visitor Center at the south entrance of the park, or Colter Bay Visitor Center near the north end.

CLIMBING   Registration is no longer required by the park service for those climbing in the park. However, backcountry permits are required for all overnight climbs.

FISHING   Fishing conforms with Wyoming and park service rules and regulations. Detailed fishing regulations may be obtained at Moose, Jenny Lake, or Colter Bay Visitor Centers. A Wyoming fishing license is required for fishing anywhere in the park or at the Rockefeller Parkway and may be purchased at the Moose Village store, Signal Mountain Lodge, the Colter Bay Marina, or at the Flagg Ranch Village. Fishing in Yellowstone requires a separate permit.

PETS   Pets are allowed in the park, but must be restrained on a leash at all times. Pets are not allowed on trails, or in the backcountry, in boats on the Snake River, in boats on lakes (except Jackson Lake), in visitor centers, or on ranger-led activities. Pets are never to be left unattended in the park. Kennels are available in Jackson.

SWIMMING   Swimming is allowed in all lakes, although there are no lifeguards on duty. Due to the swift nature of the Snake River, swimming there is not recommended.

SEASONS

In May and June, mild days and cool nights intersperse with occasional rain and snow. Depending on snowpack, snow level remains just above valley elevation until mid-June. In July and August, warm days and cool nights prevail, with afternoon thundershowers common. Snow level in the late summer gradually retreats; divides between mountain canyons are usually free of snow by August. In September, sunny days and cooler nights alternate with rain and occasional snowstorms, and by the middle of the month, fall colors are beginning to make their way across the landscape.

Spring is an excellent time to drive through the park. On clear days, the snow-encrusted Tetons are a striking contrast to the deep-blue skies. Wildflowers bloom along the southern part of the park in great numbers throughout late spring on into summer. One of the more spectacular places to see some relatively new Teton wildflowers is along the Rockefeller Parkway between Yellowstone and the Tetons, where the Yellowstone fires of 1988 literally blazed the way for fireweed (little red flames reminiscent of the Indian paintbrush), purple asters, and yellow groundsel. Trails are almost devoid of fellow hikers, making spring an excellent time of year to enjoy the Tetons, but these paths are not always clear of snow in the higher elevations and checking in at one of the ranger stations for trail conditions is advisable, especially in early spring and even as late as Memorial Day.

AVOIDING THE CROWDS

If you're one of the three million visitors in the park, chances are you're going to need a plan to avoid the summertime masses. If you absolutely must come in the summer months, early June or mid-September are the ideal times to visit. Rates at most of the lodges surrounding the park have dropped, roads are less traveled, and the temperature is cool or has cooled off. The advantage of the early summer is the remaining snow at the higher elevations. The best piece of advice, however, would be to avoid the crowds by coming to the Tetons in winter. Elk have returned to the refuge south of the park, snow covers the mountains, and no one is around.

RANGER PROGRAMS

Ranger-led activities in the park run from early June to early September. A complete guide for activities can be found in the park newspaper, *Teewinot.* Most of the activities are hourlong programs scheduled from 9am to 9pm and are free, though some programs charge a nominal fee.

FOR TRAVELERS WITH PHYSICAL DISABILITIES

As even the park service will admit, not a lot has been done to make the Grand Tetons an easily navigable environment for the physically disabled. The Moose Visitor Center, Colter Bay Visitor Center, and Jenny Lake Visitor Center are all wheelchair-accessible, and some of the lake side trails are partially paved, but other than that, the park is a near bust. Ranger-led activities, such as campfire talks and tours, are excellent interpretive programs that are available, but many of the programs involve hikes along thin trails, along which it is nearly impossible to maneuver. Inquire at one of the visitor centers to determine which programs are wheelchair-accessible.

The park's telecommunication device (TDD) for the deaf can be reached at 307/739-3400.

ORGANIZED TOURS & ACTIVITIES

If you've always wanted to pretend you were homesteading from some big city east of the Mississippi, the Colter Bay Village Corral offers **wagon rides** in the summer. Each ride is different in view and length and some come with breakfast or dinner. The Jackson Lake Lodge Corral offers similar adventures for the sodbuster wannabe. However, if the kind of coach you had in mind is on wheels, the Grand Teton Lodge Company offers bus tours and charters to and from Jackson as well as through Yellowstone and Grand Teton National Parks. All can be reached at the Grand Teton Lodge Company (☎ 307/543-2811).

Founded in 1967, the **Teton Science School,** P.O. Box 68, Kelly, WY 83011 (☎ 307/733-4765), has evolved into one of the nation's more unique naturalist institutions. Located in the southwest part of the park north of Kelly, the school offers an array of programs that discuss the ecology of the park and the surrounding area. "The Nature of Jackson Hole," a five-day program, studies the geology, plants, and wildlife of the mountains for a fee of $50 per day or $225 for the week. The school uses an old dude ranch for headquarters, has two dorms, a library, and a main building that houses the Murie Collection of birds, skulls, and animal tracks. Though the public is invited to visit the school, it's a good idea to call ahead to make sure classes aren't in full swing.

SEEING THE HIGHLIGHTS
VIEWING THE PEAKS

The Cathedral Group is comprised of Grand Teton, Middle Teton, and Mt. Owen.

The name Grand Teton is worth a lift of the eyebrow, and it's certainly provoked a red face or two, perhaps a dozen jokes, and the occasional bit of puritanical outrage. French-Canadian fur trappers of the 1800s are the wags responsible for coining the name for the West's most famous range, an act comparable to dubbing the Eiffel Tower the Great Phallus of Europe. However one reacts to the translation of the Grand Tetons (Big Tits, pardon the French), the name remains inappropriate. As Nathaniel Langford, the first superintendent of Yellowstone Park, penned in 1870: "He indeed must have been long a dweller amid these solitudes who could trace in these cold and barren peaks any resemblance to the gentle bosom of a woman." That said, the Grand is the largest peak in the park, standing 13,770 feet and towering over the other nearby peaks—only Mt. Owen to the north can compete in altitude.

The **Middle Teton,** not as glamorous as the Grand, plays second fiddle in contributing to the massive range. Just to the left, the Middle isn't quite as perky, shall we say, and has a more rounded quality.

Though **Mt. Owen** is impressive, its relationship with the Grand is an ironic juxtaposition. It's named for William Owen, the man who owns the official record for having been the first to scale the Grand Teton in 1898. But the records tell quite a different tale in truth. Nathaniel Langford and John Stevenson, two members of the 1872 Hayden Expedition, actually made it to the top well before Owen and his party. Before the record could be set straight—Owen actually accused Langford of talking an author into crediting him as first—Owen went to the state of Wyoming and had it declared officially that his party was, in fact, the first. And so stands the peak, memorializing Owen while Langford and Stevenson languish in the shadows of history.

As a peak, **Signal Mountain,** situated east of Jackson Lake, is far from impressive. But as a lookout point, it's the best. A narrow winding road wends its way to the summit, where you'll have a fabulous view over Jackson Lake and the Tetons. A word of caution to the RV traveler, however: The road is too narrow to allow any large vehicles or trailers to make it up to the summit.

North of the concentration of peaks near Jenny Lake is **Mt. Moran,** the 12,605-foot peak you first encounter if you're driving south from Yellowstone. Mt. Moran is the fourth largest of the Tetons (behind the Grand, Mt. Owen, and Teewinot Mountain). On a clear day, you can take a great photograph of this peak all the way from Colter Bay to North Jenny Lake Junction.

OTHER PARK HIGHLIGHTS

MENOR'S FERRY & THE CHAPEL OF THE TRANSFIGURATION A half-mile north of Moose, a side road off Teton Park Road leads to Menor's Ferry, named for William Menor, a homesteader near the Tetons shortly before the turn of the century. You'll come across a country store and a replica ferry, similar to the ingenious contraption used in Menor's day to ferry passengers (including horses and wagons) across the river.

The nearby Chapel of the Transfiguration is a log church built in 1925, and the rear window frames the Cathedral Group of the Tetons. The church is still in operation; the park service asks visitors to be respectful of this place of worship.

JENNY LAKE Named after the Shoshone wife of Beaver Dick Leigh, who was one of the first white settlers in the area, this is the most popular lake in the park. Set amid spruce, pine, and fur, Jenny Lake is a natural reflecting pool for the Cathedral Group of the Grand Tetons. Teewinot in the foreground, the Grand behind it, and Mt. Owen just off the right are the more spectacular peaks of the range and can be easily viewed from this point.

A **hiking trail** surrounds the shore of the lake to provide hikers with a multitude of perspectives to enjoy. The loop is relatively simple and can be easily done in a day; other good trails for day hikes are found in this area as well. There's also good **fishing** at the lakes.

A **scenic drive** begins at North Jenny Lake and heads southwest with a stop at the Cathedral Group Turnout, a terrific stop for photographers. The one-way road then goes past Jenny Lake Lodge before joining the north end of the lake. The road then continues its one-way path to the south end of the lake before rejoining the two-way Teton Park Road.

At the South Jenny Lake area, those who wish to forgo a hike around the lake can hop aboard a shuttle boat for a trip to the other side. The shuttle leaves daily approximately every half-hour from 8am to 6pm June 3 through mid-September. A round-trip ride costs $5. The season's closing date depends upon the water level at the lake. Short "cruises" are also available. Call Teton Boating Company (307/733-2703) for more details.

COLTER BAY Colter Bay, located near the north entrance, is one of the more unsightly places in the park, with everything material under the sun at your fingertips. It's a township of sorts with all the amenities and services. Unless you're in dire need of a postcard, a stamp, or a T-shirt, the only real attraction worth seeing is the **Colter Bay Indian Arts Museum** in the Colter Bay Visitor Center (☎ 307/543-2467). Open daily throughout the summer, the museum is not only a free spot to cool off from the mid-summer sun; it's a remarkable collection of Native American crafts, clothing, and beadwork covering rooms on two floors of the visitor center.

JACKSON LAKE   This is the least pristine of the Teton lakes, but it's also the biggest and accommodates more recreation than do any of the others. A controversial dam is located just west of the Jackson Lake Junction; a stop at the Jackson Lake Dam Overlook seems silly when you have views of the Tetons towering all around you, but it lets you get a look at the dam nonetheless. Though the lake was formed by a glacier that flowed south from the Yellowstone, man is solely responsible for the increase in the lake's size.

In the Jackson Lake area, there are a few things that are worth a look. **Willow Flats,** just north of Jackson Lake Junction, is a freshwater marsh and playground for some of the park's diminutive inhabitants—marmots, squirrels, and coyotes—as well as the occasional moose. South of Jackson Lake Junction is the Signal Mountain Road, which takes a curvy route to the summit of **Signal Mountain.** RVs are not recommended on this road. North of Colter Bay is the Leeks **Marina** (☎ 307/543-2494). The marina offers overnight buoys and gas docks and is open throughout the summer. Though the Snake River and majority of the lakes in the park are free of motorized boats, Jackson Lake allows motor boats to move on the lake. Check with the ranger at the Colter Bay Visitor Center for maximum horsepower. If you want to slip indoors for a spell, check out the murals in the **Jackson Lake Lodge Mural Room,** a dining room with murals of Old West trappers.

The Grand Teton Lodge Company (☎ 307/543-2811) offers three daily 90-minute cruises (dependent on fair weather) of Jackson Lake at 10am, 1pm, and 3pm. The 1pm cruise, "Fire and Ice," is a ranger-led cruise during which the story of how the Grand Tetons were formed is told, as the boat makes its way around the lake. All cruises are $10 for adults, $6 for children. Call ahead, as these prices are likely to change.

KELLY   At the Gros Ventre (pronounced grow vont) Junction 6 miles south of Moose Junction, turn right and drive 10 miles. You've reached Kelly. There's not much here besides some funky yurts, a couple of log homes, and the memory of a young boy shouting, "Shane, come back!" Just up the road is the dilapidated shack in which the sodbusters dwelled in the classic Alan Ladd film.

DRIVING THE PARK

Though it's not laid out like the giant loop in Yellowstone, Grand Teton National Park is much easier to navigate because of its smaller size and somewhat centrally located main features. Driving every mile of the Teton Park Road and Highway 191 within the park may take a little over three hours with traffic and no stops. The roads cut through the east part of the park, leaving the west side—the backcountry trails and the Tetons themselves—virtually untouched by cement.

Take **Highway 191** north from Jackson; the road forks near Moose at the Moose Junction. There you have the opportunity of closing in on the Tetons by making a left onto Teton Park Road, or staying your course north to Moran Junction, another 18 miles away.

Teton Park Road is the most heavily traveled by tourists: All of the major lodges, restaurants, and trailheads are either on it, or emanate from it. Heading north from Moose, the Chapel of the Transfiguration and Menor's Ferry Historic Site are almost immediately to your right. From there, the Taggart Lake Trailhead, the Lupine Meadows Trailhead Road, and several turnouts pop up before you find yourself at South Jenny Lake. Four miles north is the North Jenny Lake Junction, which offers a road to the left that takes you on a one-way tour through the dense pine shoreline of Jenny Lake, before connecting with Teton Park Road at South Jenny Lake.

Teton Park Road then moves past the Mt. Moran turnout, a great spot for photographing Mt. Moran and the north end of the Teton Range, the Signal Mountain Road, and the Chapel of the Sacred Heart, before rejoining Highway 191, 5 miles west of Moran Junction.

U.S. Highway 191 cuts a friendlier, less traveled path to Jackson Lake. If you have no plans to stay in the park, or if you're in a hurry and staying at the north end at Colter Bay, Lizard Creek, or Flagg Ranch, you may want to consider this route. It's shorter, the speed limit is 50, and the traffic isn't as bad, but it does run away from the Tetons. You'll still get a great look—you just won't be on the front row. Also, the turnouts, attractions, and facilities are scarce on this road.

SUMMER SPORTS & ACTIVITIES

There are many independent activities, of course, but if you'd like a more structured outing, everybody and their brother runs some sort of outdoor adventure operation in and around Jackson Hole.

BICYCLING   Cyclists will enjoy the park's wide shoulders and bike-friendly approach to road design. Several companies in nearby Jackson (see Section 1 of this chapter) offer casual rides through the park, including the **Antelope Flats–Kelly Loop,** which runs through the southwest part of the park on secondary roads. Bicycles are allowed throughout the park where cars can go legally, but are not allowed on trails or anywhere in the backcountry.

Teton Mountain Bike Tours in Jackson (☎ 307/733-0712) offers trips along the Snake River Road, a five-hour summer ride for $45 per person, and an Antelope Flats tour, a four-hour ride for $40. Both rides include bicycle and helmet and transportation to and from Jackson.

BOATING   If you've got a motor on your boat you have three choices: Jackson Lake, Jenny Lake, and Phelps Lake. Check with the ranger at any of the entrance stations or visitor centers to obtain a permit, rules and regulations, and horsepower requirements. Jackson Lake is the only lake in the park designated for sailboating, waterskiing, windsurfing, and jet-skiing. Nonmotorized boats are allowed on Jackson, Jenny, Phelps, Emma Matilda, Two Ocean, Taggart, Bradley, Bear Paw, Leigh, and String Lakes. For a permit ($10 motorized, $5 nonmotorized) contact the Moose Visitor Center at the south entrance or the Colter Bay Visitor Center at Jackson Lake. The **Leeks Marina** (☎ 307/543-2494) is located on Jackson Lake, two miles north of Colter Bay, and offers gas docks and overnight buoys.

CLIMBING   Though youngsters and oldsters alike have ascended the peaks in the park, taken photographs, and lived to tell about it, we certainly don't recommend that you survey the peak, grab a bottle of water, and set off to bag the Grand Teton without first enrolling in at least a one-day basic climbing course at one of the local climbing schools.

The park's policy is noncommittal these days concerning climbers. You are expected to sign in before you climb, and though you are not required to sign out, it is recommended. The park does not check on climbers who have not signed out, and a search-and-rescue attempt is begun only after the park is certain you are missing in the mountains and not at the some local watering hole.

The park is staffed with climbing rangers at the **Jenny Lake Ranger Station** at South Jenny Lake from June until the middle of September. Here climbers are asked to register, are required to get a backcountry permit if the climb is an overnight trek, and can obtain up-to-date weather information and conditions. Since the park service doesn't keep tabs on climbers, solo climbing is not advised.

The **Jackson Hole Mountain Guides and Climbing School** (☎ 307/733-4979) offers daily climbing instruction ranging from a basic one-day course for $60 to the advanced one-day course for $125. They also offer guided climbs of the Grand Teton for $465. The school is an accredited member of the American Mountain Guides Association.

Exum Mountain Guides in Moose (☎ 307/733-2297) has been around since 1931 and offers guided climbs to the summit of the Grand Teton with a high-altitude base camp near 11,600 feet. Basic and intermediate one-day group classes range from $65 to $85. After an evaluation, if instructors feel you've got the goods, a guided climb to the top of the Grand (four climbers to a guide) runs around $320.

FISHING It's not world-class angling like other parts of Wyoming and Montana, but it's hard not to enjoy a sunny day spent casting about for trout, considering the milieu. The park works in conjunction with the state of Wyoming, so a permit and license are required from both and may be purchased at the Moose Village store, Signal Mountain Lodge, the marina at Colter Bay, or at the Flagg Ranch Village, where the folks aren't as well versed in angler-speak as some, but they're happy to point you in the right direction.

HIKING If it's a free outdoor experience you're after without all the heart-stopping frenzy of whitewater rafting or Teton cliff-hanging, day hikes in the park may be the outdoor activity you need. Self-guided trails, from the half-mile Menor's Ferry Trail north of Moose to the Snake River Trail, off the Parkway north of the park, run throughout. Self-guided trail information is available at each visitor center in the park, and some have short paved access for wheelchairs.

North of Menor's Ferry are trailheads leading to Taggart Lake and Bradley Lake. There are lots of good trails for day hikes around Jenny Lake as well. Near Jackson Lake Lodge is a trail leading to Emma Matilda and Two Ocean Lakes; it's a beautiful route that is excellent for wildlife watching, but it's 14 miles round-trip, so either be prepared for a good workout, or double back before you've gone the whole way.

See "Exploring the Backcountry," below, for details.

RAFTING & FLOATING The Snake River is the place to be when it comes to swift water; most of its relaxed stretches lie within the confines of the park. If you have the equipment, the guts, and the know-how, simply register at the Moose Visitor Center in the south part of the park, or the Colter Bay Visitor Center in the north. A $5 nonmotorized boat fee is required and the park service encourages individuals to complete the registration for trip permits and to read the launch site bulletins for the current river conditions.

If you don't have the goods to go it alone, several companies run river-rafting trips on the Snake. Most of the companies offer 10-mile interpretive scenic trips down the Snake for less than $50 per person, and whitewater trips can be done for as little as $30. A number of qualified whitewater guides run trips outside the park (see Section 1 of this chapter).

Inside the park, interpretive scenic trips are the norm. **Solitude Float Trips** of Moose (☎ 307/733-2871) offers 5-mile and 10-mile scenic trips as well as guided fishing trips, and operates throughout the summer. **Triangle X Ranch** in conjunction with Osprey (☎ 307/733-5500) runs similar trips down the Snake, as well as breakfast, lunch, and dinner floats for groups. One of the most experienced groups operating in the park, **Barker-Ewing** (☎ 800/365-1800 or 307/733-1800), offers early summer whitewater deals for as little as $26 per person; the extended 16-mile trip, which includes breakfast, is $56. **Grand Teton Lodge Company** (☎ 307/543-2811), **Flagg Ranch** (☎ 307/543-2861), and **Signal Mountain Lodge**

(☎ 307/543-2831) are other operators within the park who run raft trips on the Snake. Other operators abound in Jackson, with a multitude of trip options and prices (see Section 1 of this chapter).

WINTER SPORTS: CROSS-COUNTRY SKIING

If you want to cross-country ski in the park, you're in luck. The crowds have dispersed, the highways are closed, and the roads in the park become trails for skiers. Though downhill skiing can be found at three different hills outside the park (see Section 1 of this chapter), cross-country is the way to tour the park itself in winter. Though snowmobiling is allowed, it is discouraged; most snowmobilers find Yellowstone a much more accommodating place to play.

The most popular place to embark on a cross-country trip is from the south part of the park near Moose. The roads north are closed and are excellent trails for seeing the Tetons in winter.

EXPLORING THE BACKCOUNTRY

Getting around in the backcountry can be one of the greatest pleasures in the park, if you're prepared. The inclination is to plunge right in and start climbing around, but without proper training and equipment, climbing in the Tetons is not recommended. A backcountry permit is required for all hikers planning to spend the night and may be obtained at the Moose Visitor Center in the south part of the park, the Colter Bay Visitor Center in the north, or at the Jenny Lake Ranger Station at South Jenny Lake.

Bears are rare Teton phenomena, but should you encounter one on the trails in the park, don't run. This causes an otherwise uninterested bear to attack. Shouting, singing, and using any sort of noisemakers (within reason, of course) is recommended, despite the mockery it elicits from other passersby. For additional information on hiking in bear country see Chapters 5 and 11.

More than bears, snow is a Teton hazard, especially for those hiking in the spring. As summer progresses, obviously, snow becomes less and less a concern for hikers and climbers at the higher altitudes. But even in late May, snow can be a problem at elevations as low as 8,000 feet. If you plan on camping higher than 9,000 feet in spring, be prepared to sleep on cold, wet, snowy ground. The ranger stations (especially the Jenny Lake Ranger Station, where climbers check in) should be visited before setting out to hike in the park at any time, but especially in the spring and early summer.

An excellent guide to hiking the park is *Teton Trails* by Bryan Harry (Grand Teton Natural History Association, 1987). This is a locally published guide to the trails throughout the park and is widely available at most area bookstores and at the visitor centers throughout the park.

NOTABLE HIKING TRAILS

LUPINE MEADOWS   This arduous climb to Amphitheater Lake takes you to the edge of the cliffs for spectacular views of the Jackson Hole valley. It's not recommended for the faint of heart, especially if you're carrying a 50-pound backpack to the top. Once you've switched back, and switched back again, $4^1/2$ miles worth, a look over the ridge to the south reveals pristine Delta Lake. Around the bend to the northwest is the Teton Glacier.

TETON CREST   This is the main trail in a system of trails that starts from south of the park near the Teton Pass west of Wilson on Highway 22 and runs miles and miles to the center of the park near Cascade Canyon. Though these hikes aren't necessarily the easiest, they do provide access to parts of the park you wouldn't normally see. The Death Canyon, Granite Canyon, and Open Canyon Trails are all branches of the Teton Crest.

CASCADE CANYON LOOP   By far the most popular of the backcountry hikes, the Cascade Canyon Trail forms a loop (or not, depending on your sense of direction) that begins and ends at the String Creek Trailhead north of Jenny Lake. The trail runs north to Leigh Lake before turning west into Paintbrush Canyon, up to Holly Lake and Lake Solitude before heading south. The trail then connects with the Teton Crest Trail, but the Cascade Canyon Trail is the one to stay on. This takes you through the canyon and back to the west shore of Jenny Lake. All told, the trail runs around 20 miles, depending on how often you wish to stray. Inspiration Point and Hidden Falls is a good destination if you're interested in truncating the marathon. From South Jenny Lake head west toward the Cascade Canyon Trail, where you'll find Inspiration Point, with incredible views and a phalanx of lazy admirers who didn't earn the vistas the hard way like you did.

CAMPING

Jenny Lake is the most popular of the five campgrounds and fills up faster than the others; the maximum stay is seven days. All others have 14-day maximums. National Park Service campgrounds operate on a first-come, first-served basis, so the earlier you set out on finding a spot, especially in mid-summer, the better.

If you're camping with a group, and you know in advance when you would like to visit, think about looking into the Colter Bay Campground, which has sites ranging in capacity from 10 to 75 people. The attraction of Colter Bay group sites is that reservations are accepted between January 1 and May 15 for the summer by writing to the Permits Office at Grand Teton National Park, Moose, WY 83012. Another attraction is the price: only $2 per person per night.

Flagg Ranch and Colter Bay also run RV sites with hookups; reservations are advised.

Amenities for Each Campground, Grand Teton National Park

Campground	# Sites	Fee	Flush Toilets	Disposal Stations	Approx. Filling Time
Colter Bay	350	$10	Yes	Yes	12noon
Gros Ventre	360	$10	Yes	Yes	Evening
Jenny Lake	49	$10	Yes	No	8am
Lizard Ck. (restricted to tents)	60	$10	No	No	2pm
Signal Mtn.	86	$10	Yes	Yes	10am

WHERE TO STAY
EXPENSIVE

Jackson Lake Lodge
Grand Teton National Park, WY 83012. ☎ **800/628-9988** or 307/543-2811. 388 rms, 4 parlor suites. Open May 26–Oct. 15, closed rest of year. TEL. $89–$162 double; $300–$450 parlor suite plus $162 for additional connecting room. AE, DC, MC, V.

A Grand Teton Lodge Company property (as are Jenny Lake Lodge and the Colter Bay Cabins), this accommodation offers views out to Willow Flats from the gigantic windows of the main lodge, a brownstone structure that's actually sits nowhere near the lake, despite the name (Signal Mountain Lodge and the Colter Bay Cabins are closer). The lodge building itself, though large in stature, is not the best place to spend the night on Jackson Lake: Rooms in the nearby unattached buildings are done in better taste.

Dining/Entertainment: The Mural Room menu reflects a flair for local game. The breakfast menu runs from $2 to $6 with such oddball dishes as the smoked trout omelet. Lunch is standard burgers, soups, and salads and goes from $5 to $8, but dinner is the Mural Room's dining forte. Depending upon the night's menu, they serve everything from well-presented pasta dishes to local trout to prime rib (of buffalo!). All this in front of the 60-foot picture windows that never fail to offer great views of the Tetons. The room gets its name from the giant murals of the late-1800s trappers who got together to exchange wares in the fall after trapping season.

Jenny Lake Lodge

Grand Teton National Park, WY 83012. ☎ **800/628-9988.** 37 cabins. Open May 27–Sept. 24, closed rest of year. $255–$322 one-room cabin; $455–$465 two-room cabin. Rates include breakfast, dinner, bicycles, and horseback riding. AE, DC, MC, V; but no credit cards accepted for deposit.

Of the Grand Teton Lodge Company properties, this is the best. That early and late meals, bicycles, and horseback riding come included with the package is a bonus. The setting at Jenny Lake Lodge is ideal: It's surrounded by pine trees and a meadow of wildflowers—a captivating riot of color when they're in bloom. The rooms are rustic and comfortable, and though there are no cabins with kitchens, the inclusion of breakfast and lunch makes up for it. Like any other place to stay in the park, Jenny Lake fills up rapidly; February is the best time to call for summer reservations.

Dining/Entertainment: Easily the best place for fine dining in either national park, the dining room at Jenny Lake may even be one of the best in the entire national park system. Though pricey (most things are in the park), the experience at this four-star restaurant is worth it. Breakfast and dinner are fixed-price for nonguests. For $12, you can sit down to whatever breakfast item you want, all you can eat. Lunch is an array of salads, sandwiches, soups, and even hearty bowls of venison chili. Dinner, again, is a fixed-price menu for nonguests—$36 for a seven-course dinner, and seven choices of entrées including roast breast of pheasant, Rocky Mountain lamb chops, and venison cutlets. For nonguests, reservations are required.

MODERATE

Colter Bay Cabins

Grand Teton National Park, WY 83012. ☎ **800/628-9988** or 307/543-2811. 208 cabins. Open May 12–Sept. 24, closed rest of year. $55–$77 one-room cabin; $79–$99 two-room cabin; $22 tent cabin; $23 RV site. AE, DC, MC, V.

The proximity to Jackson Lake, incredible views, quaint cabins, and access to the rest of the park make these cabins charming in the daytime. But the cabins at Colter Bay can turn into a communal hell at night. The walls are so thin that you may want to pass notes if you're discussing private matters. The tent cabins are a steal for the park, but they're bare-bones. However, if you are a boat enthusiast, Colter Bay offers a full-service marina.

Flagg Ranch and Riverside Motel

Grand Teton National Park, WY 83012. ☎ **800/443-2311.** 50 cabins, 54 motel rms, 4 suites. Open May 15–Oct. 15, Dec. 15–Mar 15; closed rest of year. $104 queen cabin; $114 king cabin; $88 motel room; $98 two-room suite; $23 RV site; $17 tent site. MC, V.

Located north of the park on the John D. Rockefeller Jr. Memorial Parkway, Flagg Ranch bills itself accurately as the jumping-off point for two national parks. What's great about Flagg, if you can get a room, is its incredible location. It's five minutes from Grand Teton National Park, two minutes from Yellowstone, and it sits on the Snake River. The casual observer would call it a ranch, but in reality, Flagg Ranch is a hotel located in the middle of a tiny town. A gas station, grocery store, gift shop, restaurant, and saloon are all on the premises. They even have 100 spots for RVs complete with electricity, sewer, and water. The best deal at Flagg Ranch has to be the incredibly affordable two-room suites for $98; the cabins are adequate (and unlike the rooms, they come with phones) and brand-new, but the suites are hard to match. It's not a five-star hotel (the prices might seem like it), but it is a more than adequate place to lodge while spending time in the parks. A word of caution: If you arrive without reservations, you may not even find a tent site. It's best to call Flagg Ranch at the first of the year to make reservations for the summer.

Signal Mountain Lodge

Grand Teton National Park, WY 83012. ☎ **307/543-2831**. 79 units. TEL. Open May 13–Oct. 15, closed rest of year. $69–$155 cabin; $140 lakefront cabin; $87–$125 country room. AE, DISC, MC, V.

Though not as expensive as Jenny Lake and Jackson Lake Lodges, Signal Mountain is one of the best places to stay in the park. The lakefront cabins, each with a kitchenette, offer the best value at Signal Mountain and, as you might suppose, they sit on the shore of Jackson Lake. The lodge itself is decorated in a comfortable Western style with a large fireplace for those less than balmy nights. The actual cabins are located away from the main lodge.

Spur Ranch Cabins at Dornan's

P.O. Box 39, Moose, WY 83012. ☎ **307/733-2522**. 12 cabins. Open year-round. $125–$150 one-bedroom cabin; $175 two-bedroom cabin. Lower winter rates available. MC, V.

With an incredible wine shop (some 1,500 labels), a service station, and a gift shop, Dornan's is an esoteric wonderland. Every cabin on the place is a winner. All are situated near the Snake River and all have wonderful views of the Tetons. Located on a swatch of private land, the cabins at Spur Ranch are great if you can book by February in time to get one for the summer. The complete kitchens make it a great bargain if you happen to feel like cooking. If not, the popular Chuckwagon restaurant is a stone's throw away in Moose. For the penny-pincher who'd rather see the Tetons up close without forking over the $10 National Park entry fee, take note. The cabins are actually located a quarter mile before the Moose entrance station, so the scenery is free from the Spur Ranch side. Though the cabins are sturdy log structures, their history dates back only to 1992, making them some of the newer units in the park. Another advantage Spur Ranch has over other lodges in the park is winter availability.

The park all but shuts down (the summer throngs are gone) and cross-country skiing is as easy as driving north for a few minutes, strapping on the skis, and heading off into the wild white yonder.

GUEST RANCHES

Triangle X Dude Ranch

Box 120 Moose, WY 83012. ☎ **307/733-2183**. 19 cabins. $785 per person per week for one-bedroom cabin; $785–$980 per person per week for two-bedroom cabin; $785–$890 per person per week for three-bedroom cabin. All meals and horseback riding included.

Since 1926, the Turner family has had an agreement with the park service to operate this dude ranch just off Highway 191 on the east side off the park. If you love horseback riding, or the kids want to learn, then this is the place. If you hate horses, it's not. They've emphasized simplicity here, from the schedule to the cabins, and honed the art of providing a good family vacation down to a science. Children 5 to 12 can ditch the parents for the day, eat with others their own age, and hang out with the wranglers as part of the ranch's Young Wrangler Program. The individual porch-fronted log cabins, though rustic, are equipped with modern baths remodeled in 1991.

Making reservations for Triangle X can be like trying to win the lottery. There's not a decade-long waiting list, but visitors often re-book for the next year, making it difficult for the newcomer to reserve a week for the family. The ranch recommends calling a year in advance.

WHERE TO EAT

There's also first-rate dining at the Jenny Lake and Jackson Lake Lodges (see "Where to Stay," above).

IN JACKSON LAKE

Pioneer Grill

Jackson Lake Lodge, Grand Teton National Park, Wyoming. ☎ 307/543-2811. Breakfast items $2–$6; lunch items $3–$7; main dinner courses $7–$9. AE, DC, MC, V. May 26–Oct. 15 daily 6am–10:30pm, closed rest of year. AMERICAN.

This little eatery offers a casual counter service that differs remarkably from the lavish environs of the Mural Room at nearby Jackson Lake Lodge. Breakfasts are standard fare, but the lunch menu offers a lean Buffalo Burger that's worth trying if you've never experienced ground beef's distant cousin. Dinners are a lot like Mom used to make (meatloaf and fried chicken), just not as good.

IN COLTER BAY

The Chuckwagon

In Colter Bay. ☎ 307/543-2811. Breakfast buffet $4–$6; lunch buffet $5–$7; dinner buffet $10–$14. AE, DC, MC, V. May 12–Sept. 24, daily 7am–10pm; closed rest of year. AMERICAN.

Not to be confused with the Chuckwagon at Dornan's, this is the all-you-can-eat establishment. The menu is middle-of-the- road, basic breakfasts and lunches, but the dinner takes it up one notch. Turkey dinners, prime rib, and seafood are not uncommon on the nightly buffet, and if you have no use for that, you can order off the menu.

John Colter Grill

In Colter Bay. ☎ 307/543-2811. Breakfast items $2–$5; lunch items $4–$6; dinner items $5–$7. AE, DC, MC, V. June 4–Sept. 4, daily 6:30am–10pm; closed rest of year. AMERICAN.

Not substandard, but definitely a place to go when all else fails. Counter seating lends itself to the diner atmosphere, and the menu settles it. The breakfast menu includes omelets and pancakes; lunch consists of hot and cold sandwiches; and dinner is chicken fingers and shrimp-in-a-basket.

IN SIGNAL MOUNTAIN

Aspens Dining Room

In Signal Mountain. ☎ 307/543-2831. Breakfast items $4–$8; lunch items $4–$8; main dinner courses $12–$22. AE, DISC, MC, V. May 7–Oct. 16, daily 6:30am–10pm; closed rest of year. CONTINENTAL.

Dinners are the specialty at this rather drably decorated, open-beamed restaurant sitting across the lake from the Tetons. The breakfast menu is fairly ordinary, other than the buffalo sausage omelet, but even that is standard in these parts. Lunch is soups and salads with a touch of Mexican thrown in. Dinners features local wild game, with the elk médaillons being the best—and most expensive—item on the menu.

IN MOOSE

The Chuckwagon at Dornan's

In Moose. ☎ **307/543-2811.** Breakfast items $2–$5; lunch items $3–$5; main dinner courses $5–$11. MC, V. Jun 10–Sept. 4, daily 6:30am–10pm; closed rest of year. AMERICAN.

Located next door to Spur Ranch Cabins, this a great place for breakfast. It's not pricey and the portions are adequate—that adds up to a screaming deal for any place near the park. Lunches are what you might expect: burgers, French dip, and barbecue. Dinner gets a little fancier and a little more expensive with steaks, barbecued short ribs, and roast beef. What's nice at Dornan's is the conveniently located wine shop. If you can't find it in here, it probably doesn't exist.

3   A Side Trip to Dubois & the Wind River Range

Visiting Dubois is like visiting someone in the middle of plastic surgery. The old is giving way to the new right before your eyes. In this case the new face of tourism is being laid on top of the old lumber industry that's fallen flat. Dubois, perhaps tragically, is a gateway town waiting to happen, and it needs only a decade or so more before it can realize its full potential. The number of ranches (now guest ranches) that used to accommodate only friends and relatives is staggering.

Summer pack trips and winter snowmobile tours, both into the nearby Shoshone National Forest and along the Continental Divide Trail, are staples at each of the following Dubois ranches: **Brooks Lake Lodge,** Box 594, Dubois, WY 82513 (☎ 307/455-2121); **Mackenzie Highland Ranch,** 3945 U.S. Hwy. 26, Dubois, WY 82513 (☎ 307/455-3415); **Timberline Ranch,** 4127 U.W. Hwy. 26/287, Dubois, WY 82513 (☎ 307/455-2513 or 455-2215); and the **Triangle C Ranch,** Box 691, Dubois, WY 82513 (☎ 307/455-2225).

A Western house party atmosphere is pervasive at both the **CM Ranch** (Dubois, WY 82513, 307/455-2331) and the **Lazy L&B Ranch** (Dubois, WY 82513, ☎ 307/455-2839), where evening activities center around cookouts and square dances. A more upscale western experience is offered by the **Bitterroot Ranch,** (Dubois, WY 82513, ☎ 800/545-0019) where guests can practice their English-style riding skills on purebred Arabian horses.

So what is it that makes Dubois such a great place to visit? Well, for starters, to see Dubois you have to drive there. There's no flying in and flying out. And the vistas that unfold as you drive along the Wind River range from the west side are beautiful, to say the least. After you make it across the nearly 10,000 foot Togwotee Pass, leaving Jackson Hole and the park, you'll find yourself on the other side of the Continental Divide, staring at the strange Pinnacle Buttes, large spires cut from volcanic rock and ash. This is a great introduction to the Upper Country, the 6,000-foot nook in which Dubois is settled.

Once you've made it to town, try pronouncing the name without sounding like a pompous city slicker. There are many ways to pronounce it but only DO-boys is correct. Sure, there is the inclination to say doo-BWAH, but it is good to quell that urge.

The **Chamber of Commerce,** 616 Ramshorn (☎ 307/455-2556), can answer any questions you may have and there's plenty of Yellowstone and Grand Teton literature here to fill the glove compartment.

The **National Bighorn Sheep Center** is next door to the chamber and provides some interesting information on the nimble creatures that haunt the area. For a look into the past of Dubois, the Sheepeater Indians, and other interesting artifacts with local flavor, stop by the **Dubois Museum** just across and down from the Chamber at 906 W. Ramshorn. The museum is open 9am to 5pm daily from May through September. Each July the museum hosts **Tie Hack Days,** a celebration of food and festivities to honor the international woodsmen who laid the railroads in the 1800s. The **Wind River Rendezvous,** also known as the Whiskey River Buckskinners Barbecue, is held in the middle weekend of each August and attracts plenty of mountain-men types who converge on the town for a giant weekend that culminates with a buffalo barbecue.

Five miles east of Dubois on U.S. Hwys. 287/26, you'll see the access to the **Whiskey Basin Habitat Area** and the road heading south to Ring, Trail, and Torrey Lakes. Above Trail Lake you can climb around on the boulders in search of Native American petroglyphs. For the lowdown on the Dubois outdoor scene, contact the **U.S. Forest Service** ranger station at 1404 Ramshorn (☎ 307/455-2466). For a big ol' slice of great down-home barbecue, try the **Rustler's Roost** downtown on Ramshorn, and for a little slice of local night life, head down the street to the **Rustic Pine Saloon.**

Northcentral Wyoming 13

Like much of the American Southwest, northcentral Wyoming is composed of a series of dry pockets surrounded by mountains. In its case, these mountains are the Big Horns, which form a backward-C-curve in the east; and the Absarokas, which form a western boundary. The Owl Creek Mountains, a smaller range to the southwest, break off from the Absarokas to join the Big Horns below Thermopolis.

The desertlike conditions of these valleys east of Yellowstone are especially evident in the Wapiti Valley east of Cody, where chimney rock formations appear intermittently along the picturesque roadsides between Cody and Yellowstone's east entrance. Though temperatures can hardly be considered any more extreme than in the rest of the state, the level of precipitation here is almost abnormal. With over 300 days of sunshine per year, this region gets less than 10 inches of rainfall a year and the average snowfall barely tops 2 feet. Combine this with a notorious wind and you have the ingredients for a wasteland.

Nevertheless, these negatives have, over the years, been transformed almost miraculously into positives. Since dry lands mean irrigation problems, the Bureau of Reclamation commenced building the Buffalo Bill Dam in 1905, a project which took five years to complete and cost nearly a million dollars, but resulted in the tallest dam in the world and a new body of water, the Buffalo Bill Reservoir. It was named after Buffalo Bill Cody, since the rights to build a canal and irrigate some 60,000 acres of land near Cody were originally acquired by him back in 1899, before the Reclamation service took over. The dam turned eastern Park County into a place capable of agricultural growth, where grains and sugar beets still contribute to an economy that is now grounded in tourism. And the swift winds that sculpted the geological shapes throughout the valley are now used by windsurfers on the Buffalo Bill Reservoir, who rank it one of the best windsurfing spots in the country.

Rich in Native American history, geology, and scenic wonders, northcentral Wyoming attracts visitors on their way to and from Wyoming's national parks, with highlights that include the fun-loving frontier town of Cody (the second most popular destination in the state, after Jackson), the Bighorn Canyon National Recreation

Area, which straddles the Montana-Wyoming border, the healing hot springs of Thermopolis, and the Wind River Indian Reservation, home to Wyoming's Shoshone and Arapaho peoples.

There are very few places in Wyoming where you can't practice the recreational standbys most often associated with the state: horseback riding, fly-fishing, and rafting. Northcentral Wyoming is no exception, with ample opportunities for all of these activities and more. The Sunlight Basin, an hour's drive northwest of Cody, and Yellowstone National Park (see Chapter 12), are excellent destinations for snowmobiling, fly-fishing, and hiking, and are both within easy driving distance of each other. The fishing along the Clark's Fork of the Yellowstone in Sunlight Basin is considered to be among the best in the region.

The Bighorn Canyon National Recreation Area (see Chapter 10) rivals Yellowstone as a premier spot for viewing spectacular scenery in central Wyoming. Located northeast of Lovell, the canyon's array of attractions include breathtaking views of colorful canyon walls, thundering herds of free-ranging wild horses, and towering cliffs. A paved road takes you through the area and a visitor center near Lovell houses interpretive displays.

As one of the state's most important ranching centers, this region is home to many guest ranches that provide horseback riding and cattle driving activities, often throughout the year. There are ample opportunities to raft the Shoshone from Cody, but experienced paddlers may find the Class II waters a bit too tame for their liking.

By far the most popular outdoor event in this part of the state is the rodeo. Though Cody hosts the greatest number, with one staged every night during the summer, almost any town with at least one resident cowboy enjoys this distinctly Western tradition.

1 Scenic Drives

Unlike the cities of eastern and southern Wyoming, which are somewhat evenly spaced and seem to gravitate toward the interstates, the towns of northcentral Wyoming are far removed from major thoroughfares and are linked by secondary roads in a much more random fashion. U.S. Hwy. 14-16-20 runs from Yellowstone to Cody and Greybull and is the primary west-east route used to traverse this region. The loop tours described below cover most of this region via less-traveled roads that radiate from smaller Wyoming towns.

DRIVING TOUR #1: BIGHORN MOUNTAIN LOOP

This moderately easy day trip explores the upper reaches of central Wyoming and takes you east from Cody in a loop that encompasses the towns of Powell and Lovell, as well as the scenic Shell Canyon area. Begin in Cody by taking U.S. Hwy. 14A northeast to Lovell and the Bighorn Canyon National Recreation Area. A side trip north along Wyoming State Hwy. 37 provides views of the wild horses of the Pryor Mountain Wild Horse Range and Bighorn Lake from the Devils Canyon Overlook (see Chapter 10 for more information on this recreation area). The gradually climbing U.S. 14A continues on to Burgess Junction, passing the Medicine Wheel, a 74-foot stone circle with 28 spokes that is believed to be an ancient Native American relic which predates the Crow tribe, earliest known inhabitants of the area.

At Burgess Junction, take U.S. Hwy. 14 southwest toward the towns of Shell and Greybull and Shell Canyon. Shell Creek tumbles down a steep granite path at Shell Falls, making for a nice photo opportunity. Wildlife and farmland prevail here, as did the dinosaurs; some of the world's first fossils were found in this area. U.S. Hwy. 14-16-20 takes you back to Cody as the rugged Absaroka Range leans in from the west. This driving tour can be enjoyed year-round, though winter drivers should exercise caution as they gain and lose elevation around Burgess Junction. Recreational opportunities in the Bighorn Canyon Recreational Area are greatest during the summer months.

DRIVING TOUR #2: BIGHORN BASIN LOOP

This all-day trip rewards travelers with a taste of undiscovered Wyoming: hot springs, badlands, and open ranges. It begins in Cody, where you travel south along Wyoming State Hwy. 120 to the tiny town of Meeteetse, an almost perfect example of the small towns you'll find scattered all over the state.

From here, continue on WYO 120 to Thermopolis, home of the world's largest free-flowing hot springs, where the temperature is a constant 135 degrees Fahrenheit. After a relaxing soak and a quick look at the bison herd that roams the city's state park, travel northeast to Worland, an important agricultural center. From Worland, drive east along Hwy. 16 to Ten Sleep for an impressive view of the Bighorn Mountains and excellent trout fishing on Ten Sleep Creek.

Here, take the Nowood Road north which joins Wyoming State Hwy. 31 to Manderson and follows the base of the Bighorns. From Manderson, follow Hwy. 16-20 north to Basin, take Wyoming State Hwy. 30 west to the junction of Wyoming State Hwy. 120, and north to Cody. Along the way, you'll enjoy views of the Bighorn River and the Greybull River Valley. This trip is great any time of year, though a leisurely dip in the hot springs at Thermopolis is particularly soothing during the cold winter months. Cross-country ski enthusiasts can combine this driving tour with a quick loop of their own at the Wood River Ski Touring Park, a series of trails located at the head of the Wood River Valley. To reach the trails, drive southwest along Wyoming State Hwy. 290 from Meeteetse toward Pitchfork. Once you've had your fill of skiing, load those skis up, retrace your steps back to WYO 120 and drive south on the state highway to Thermopolis' famous hot springs for a rejuvenating soak.

2 Cody

Named for its founder, the grand showman, scout, and sage William F. "Buffalo Bill" Cody, Wyoming's most colorful cowtown comes to life each summer as throngs of visitors from Yellowstone drift 52 miles eastward to experience the cowboy lifestyle, past and present, here. Located at the western edge of the Bighorn Basin and bordered to the west by the rugged Absaroka Range, Cody is one of the most beautifully situated towns in Wyoming. The drive from the east entrance of Yellowstone to Cody cuts through the magnificent East Yellowstone (or Wapiti) Valley, a drive Teddy Roosevelt once called the most scenic 50 miles in the world.

The town fairly oozes with Western charm year-round, but it's at its best during the summer, when the longest running rodeo breaks from the gate every night. Museums, a re-created Western town, retail shops, and residents preserve and promote Cody's particular brand of Western heritage to visitors the world over. And it's not too hard of a sell: Other than Jackson, Cody was the only Wyoming town to see its number of visitors increase during the dramatic energy bust of the late 1980s, while other less-frequently touristed regions in the state were hard-hit by the demise of the state's oil industry. Though certainly not the resort-laden mountain paradise Jackson is, Cody's Western charm seems much more authentic.

ESSENTIALS

GETTING THERE   **Cody's Yellowstone Regional Airport,** 3001 Duggleby Dr., Cody, WY 82414 (☎ 307/587-5096), serves the Bighorn Basin as well as the east and northeast entrances of Yellowstone National Park with year-round commercial flights via **United** (☎ 800/241-6522) and **Delta** (☎ 800/221-1212).

If you're driving from Cheyenne, travel north on I-25 to Casper, then west on U.S. Hwy. 20 to Thermopolis. From there, it's another 84 miles to Cody. From Jackson, take U.S. Hwy. 191 to the West Thumb Junction in Yellowstone. Drive east along the southern boundary of the park and continue on U.S. Hwy. 14-16-20 to Cody. The 280-mile drive from Rock Springs to Cody follows U.S. Hwy. 191 to Farson, WYO 28/U.S. Hwy. 287 to Lander, WYO 789 to Thermopolis, and WYO 120 to Cody. Call 307/635-9966 for road and travel information.

VISITOR INFORMATION   For printed information on this area of Wyoming, contact the **Cody Country Visitors Council**, 836 Sheridan Ave., P.O. Box 2777, Cody, WY 82414 (☎ 307/587-2297) or the **Wyoming Division of Tourism,** I-25 at College Dr., Cheyenne, WY 82002 (☎ 307/777-7777).

GETTING AROUND   Once you've arrived, the only way to get around Cody is by car. **Avis** (☎ 307/587-5792 or ☎ 800/331-1212) and **Hertz** (☎ 307/587-2914 or ☎ 800/654-3131) maintain desks at Yellowstone Regional Airport.

GETTING OUTSIDE

Because of its close proximity to Yellowstone, the best place to get outdoors near Cody is the park itself. Guided Yellowstone National Park day trips are available locally through **Grub Steak Expeditions,** P.O. Box 1013, Cody, WY 82414 (☎ 307/527-6316) and **Pan-O-Rama West,** 1814 Central Ave., Cody, WY 82414 (☎ 800/227-8483 or 307/527-5618). Once you're outside the park, Cody doesn't have the plethora of activities Jackson Hole does, but there's still plenty to do both in and around town. Popular summertime activities include float trips, windsurfing, and fishing, but mountain-biking trails and golf courses are also available. **Buffalo Bill State Park,** located along the Shoshone Canyon 6 miles west of Cody, is a hot spot for local recreationists, with opportunities for hiking, fishing, and a variety of water sports. Its **Buffalo Bill Reservoir** is regarded as one of the premier spots for windsurfing in the United States. The park also has facilities for camping and picnicking.

In winter, cross-country and downhill skiing and snowmobiling are easy to pursue in the Cody area.

BIKING

If you want to explore the Cody area on your own, mountain bikes and local trail information is available at **Olde Faithful Bicycles,** 1362 Sheridan Ave. (☎ 307/527-5110). Though there isn't an established network of trails in the Cody area, the Forest Service trails west of town off U.S. Hwy. 14/16/20 in the Shoshone National Forest are available. For specific trail information, call Olde Faithful Bicycles or the Forest Service at 307/527-6241.

CROSS-COUNTRY SKIING

Cody's proximity to Yellowstone makes cross-country skiing a fun and easily accessible winter pursuit. Other than those in Yellowstone, some of the most

Northcentral Wyoming

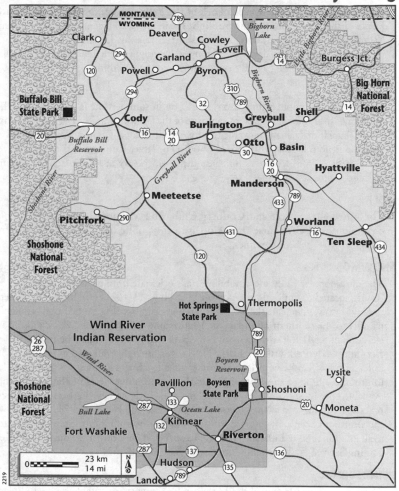

popular cross-country trails lead from the **Pahaska Teepee,** near the east entrance of Yellowstone, into the Shoshone National Forest.

DOWNHILL SKIING

Skiers should check out **Yellowstone Ski Resort,** 50 miles west of Cody and a scant 4 miles from Yellowstone Park. Though the resort boasts a new chairlift and a bigger lodge, if you're really into skiing, you'd be better off heading to Red Lodge Mountain, a popular Montana ski area one hour north of Cody (see Chapter 9).

FISHING

Two premier Cody fishing outfitters—**North Fork Anglers,** 937 Sheridan Ave. (☎ 307/527-7274) and **Yellowstone Troutfitters Fly & Tackle Shop,** 239A Yellowstone Ave. (☎ 307/587-8240)—are your sources for an unforgettable fly-fishing excursion. **The Clark's Fork of the Yellowstone, the North and South Forks of the Shoshone,** and **the Sunlight Basin** area are all gems of local rivers and Yellowstone's legendary trout rivers are a short drive away. Guides are available from either outfitter for short day trips or longer, overnight excursions. Both shops also offer a full line of fishing and fly-tying equipment and clothing.

FLOAT TRIPS

One of the most popular things to do in Cody in summertime is to float along the Shoshone River, the major eastern drainage of the Yellowstone River. The mild Class I and II rapids make it an enjoyable trip for almost anyone. Contact **Wyoming River Trips,** Buffalo Bill Village (☎ 307/587-6661) or **River Runners,** 491 Sheridan Ave. (☎ 307/527-7238) for prices for these trips, which vary in length from 1½ hours to full-day floats.

GOLF

The Olive-Glenn Golf and Country Club, 802 Meadow Lane, is an 18-hole championship PGA course that is open to the public daily from 6am to 9pm. Call 307/587-5551 for tee times.

SNOWMOBILING

The most popular Cody snowmobiling trails originate from nearby Pahaska Teepee Resort, located 51 miles from Cody on U.S. Hwy. 14-16-20 (see listing in "Where to Stay" below). The Pahaska Teepee Trail is a short, 3-mile groomed trail—roughly parallel to the southern boundary of Yellowstone—that crosses Sylvan Pass at an elevation of 8,541 feet with views into the park that include Avalanche Peak (10,566 feet) and Cody Peak (10,267 feet). The longer Sunlight trail system is located 36 miles north of Cody, with four separate trails totaling 41 miles: 29 groomed, 12 ungroomed. One of these provides absolutely stunning views of the Beartooths, available only by snowmobile or sled. This trail, aptly named the Beartooth, originates at a parking area at the junction of WYO 296 and U.S. Hwy. 212 and follows the Beartooth Scenic Byway east for 16 miles to a warming hut. Snowmobiles are available for rent at **Pahaska Teepee Resort** and in Cody at **Mountain Valley Engine Service**, 422 W. Yellowstone Ave. (☎ 307/587-6218).

WINDSURFING

Outside magazine has named the Buffalo Bill Reservoir a "veritable high wind playground," including it in their list of Top 10 windsurfing destinations in the continental United States. The 8 mile-long, 4-mile-wide reservoir receives wind from three mountain gorges; it's best experienced from June through September. The boat ramp on the north side of the reservoir is a prime spot for putting in.

SPECIAL EVENTS

There are a few unique events that happen every year in Cody. Every June, the town resonates with the bright colors and dignified pageantry of the **Plains Indian Powwow.** Held at the Robbie Powwow Garden on the south end of the Buffalo Bill Historical Center parking lot, this powwow features grand entries and traditional dance competitions, along with Native American food and crafts. Visitors can experience the richness of this culture by participating in the Round Dances. Call the Cody Country Visitors Council at 307/587-2297 for exact dates. In mid-June, there's the **Frontier Festival,** sponsored by the Buffalo Bill Historical Center, which revisits the Old West with crafts and entertainment from the turn of the century. Western skills competitions are held for modern-day cowpokes, including a pack horse race, camp cook-offs, and demonstrations of frontier life. Call 307/587-4771 for further information.

Every July 1–4 in City Park the **Cody Stampede** takes place, when the streets are filled with parades, rodeos, fireworks, street dances, barbecues, and entertainment in anticipation of the rodeo, the event's capstone. Call 307/587-5155 for tickets. For one day in mid-July, the cool sounds of modern jazz and the gentle rhythms of big-band and swing music take over the lawn of the Elks Club at 1202 Beck Ave. (next to the Cody Convention Center) during the **Yellowstone Jazz Festival**. A stellar lineup of musical talent—from swing to big band to blues—plays from 11am 'til dark. Food and drink tents contribute to the festive picnic atmosphere. Call 307/587-3898 for further information.

For a few days in late August, one of Cody's newest annual events kicks up some dirt. A benefit for the Buffalo Bill Historical Center, it's the **Buffalo Bill Shootout**, where celebrities and local marksmen test their skills in trap, skeet, sporting clays, and silhouette shooting. Call the Historical Center (☎ 307/587-4771) for exact dates and details.

SEEING THE SIGHTS

✪ Buffalo Bill Historical Center

720 Sheridan Ave. ☎ **307/587-4771.** Admission $8 adults, $6.50 seniors, $4 students (13–21), $2 youth (6–12), free for children under 6. Admission is good for two consecutive days. Group tour rates available by request. Open daily, call for seasonal hours.

This museum complex—The Whitney Gallery of Western Art, the Buffalo Bill Museum, the Plains Indian Museum, and the Cody Firearms Museum—has been called the "Smithsonian of the West," and justly so. From its humble beginnings in a single log building to its present structure, which includes over a quarter of a million square feet of exhibition space, the Buffalo Bill Historical Center's four separate museums are unequaled in the Western United States.

The Whitney Gallery showcases pieces from some of the West's most famous artists—including Frederic Remington, George Catlin, Charlie Russell, Albert Bierstadt, and Carl Rungius—from the 1820s to the present. The Buffalo Bill Museum pays tribute to one of the most fascinating Western pioneers and its most famous showman, illustrating Buffalo Bill's multifaceted career as scout, hunter, guide, showman, and entrepreneur. Kids will love watching the continuously running footage from actual "Wild West" shows, complemented by authentic memorabilia.

The Plains Indian Museum is devoted to the history of each of the seven Plains tribes—Arapaho, Blackfeet, Cheyenne, Crow, Gros Ventre, Shoshone, and Sioux—as depicted through their art and artifacts, including cradle boards, ceremonial dresses and robes, pipes, and beadwork. If you're in Cody in late June, attend the Plains Indian Powwow for a firsthand look at the rich traditions of these Native Americans (See "Special Events" above).

Featured within the Cody Firearms Museum are the Boone and Crockett exhibit of world record game trophies, a stagecoach stop, and an arms manufacturing facility. Site of the world's foremost collection, the museum showcases thousands of firearms from various countries and manufacturers, encompassing the entire development of firearms from the early 16th century to the present.

In addition to their permanent collections and programs, the center features changing exhibits and hosts a wide variety of educational events throughout the year. Late September's annual Plains Indian Seminar brings in scholars and students for an in-depth examination of Native American issues.

❍ Cody Nite Rodeo

Stampede Park. ☎ **307/587-5155.** Admission $7 adult, $4 child, free for children under 6. Jun-Aug, nightly at 8:30pm.

If you need to attend a rodeo to make your vacation complete, Cody's the place to be: This town has one taking place every night, beginning in June and continuing through the last Saturday in August. The longest-running consecutive rodeo in the country, Cody Nite Rodeo performances are enjoyed from covered grandstands that seat up to 6,000 spectators for various rodeo events (the Buzzard's Roost is worth the extra two bucks). With a chance to mingle with performers and special children's events (look out for the calf scramble!), Cody Nite Rodeo is Western entertainment at its best and it's fun for the entire family. Equally thrilling is the annual Cody Stampede (See "Special Events" above).

Trail Town

1831 Demaris Dr. ☎ **307/587-5302.** Admission $3. May-Sept, daily 8am–8pm.

Trail Town is a re-created frontier village that's actually located on the original townsite of old Cody City, west of present-day Cody. More than 20 historically documented buildings show the history of the West, from the rutted wagon trail that runs in front of the faded boardwalks to the authentic exhibits inside many of the buildings. Though the on-site Museum of the Old West houses a respectable collection of Western relics, the real attractions at Trail Town are its buildings. The cabin that housed Butch Cassidy and his Hole-in-the-Wall Gang is here, as is the Rivers Saloon, still marked by bullet holes in the door.

While you're here, check out the Trail Town cemetery for a view of the final resting place of Jeremiah "Liver Eat'n" Johnson and other colorful frontier characters.

The Buffalo Bill Dam Visitor Center

In Buffalo Bill State Park, 6 miles west of Cody along Shoshone Canyon. ☎ **307/527-6076.** Free admission. May 1–Sept 30, daily 8am–9pm.

Located in Buffalo Bill State Park, a terrifically popular spot for anglers, hikers, and windsurfers, this impressive new structure was completed in 1993 as a result of a $132 million fundraising project. The octagonal building, perched more than 300 feet above the river, provides a dizzying view through its glass walls of the Shoshone River rushing west through the deep Shoshone Canyon to the basin beyond. Other great vantage points are found along the open walkway that follows the top of the dam. Facing east, look for the old Shoshone Power Plant along the canyon wall far below.

Construction began on the Buffalo Bill Dam in 1905 and was completed in 1910. In 1946, the name of the dam was changed from Shoshone to Buffalo Bill, who tirelessly worked for years to raise money for the original project. Over the years, it has turned the desertlike Big Horn Basin into one of Wyoming's most productive farming areas.

Featured inside are interpretive areas and various interactive displays relating to the construction of the dam, local history, and scenic attractions.

Cody Wildlife Exhibit

433 Yellowstone Ave. ☎ **307/587-2804.** Admission $3 adults, $2 children over 6. Group rates available. May-Oct, daily 9am–8pm.

This taxidermical collection includes over 400 fully mounted animals from all over the world, displayed in their natural habitats. It's an interesting concept, but Yellowstone is only 53 miles away and the animals there are still breathing.

WHERE TO STAY
HOTELS

Buffalo Bill Village Resort: Comfort Inn, Holiday Inn & Buffalo Bill Village

17th and Sheridan Ave., Cody, WY 82414. ☎ 800/527-5544. Comfort Inn: 75 rms. A/C, TV, TEL. $50–$130 double. AE, DC, DISC, MC, V; Holiday Inn: 189 rms. A/C TV TEL. $50–$130 double. AE, DC, DISC, MC, V; Buffalo Bill Village: 83 cabins. TV TEL. $40–$90 double. AE, DC, DISC, MC, V. Buffalo Bill Village is only open from May through Sept.

Blair Hotels of Wyoming operates these three downtown Cody lodgings, and though the term resort is hardly appropriate, the central grouping of two chain motels and a set of Western cabins (Buffalo Bill Village) is certainly convenient for travelers without advance reservations. In addition to the lodging options, the complex houses four restaurants, a swimming pool, and shops at the Ol' West Boardwalk, where you can even book a local rafting trip to complete your Cody experience.

The Comfort Inn and Holiday Inn are priced identically, and have virtually identical amenities (the rooms at the Comfort Inn, built in 1993, are slightly newer). The rooms at Buffalo Bill Village are simpler and a little less expensive. Carpeted but with a cabin exterior (an odd combination for a downtown motel), each has just a bed, a phone, and a TV.

A good choice for the sheer variety of options it offers, the Buffalo Bill Village Resort is also convenient to downtown Cody.

The Irma

1192 Sheridan Ave., Cody, WY 82414. ☎ 307/587-4221. 40 rms. A/C TV TEL. $35–$85 double. AE, DC, DISC, MC, V.

Named for Buffalo Bill's daughter, The Irma is considered a tourist attraction in its own right because Buffalo Bill himself built it. An imposing brick structure on the corner of 12th and Sheridan downtown, the Irma is just as popular today as it was when it was built at the turn of the century (largely because it's still the first hotel travelers come across after miles of driving). The 15 suites are part of the original hotel and have been refurbished with a mixture of Victorian elegance and Wild West flamboyance not soon forgotten. Prime rib is the local specialty at the Irma's restaurant. Although its colorful legacy as Buffalo Bill's hotel doesn't hurt, the staff is friendly and accommodating, and the rooms are clean and comfortable, making it a very popular place to stay during the summer.

GUEST RANCHES & RESORTS

✪ Castle Rock Ranch

412 County Rd., 6NS, Cody, WY 82414. ☎ 307/587-2076 or 800/356-9965. 12 cabins. $805–$1,200 per person, per week (four-night minimum stay). No credit cards. Rates include all ranch activities.

The picturesque Southfork Valley of the Shoshone River is the setting for this ranch getaway. Designed for adults—singles or couples—who want a truly active ranch vacation, Castle Rock coordinates a variety of seasonal activities for its guests. In summer, horseback riding in the surrounding Shoshone National Forest is the prime draw; winter finds visitors exploring nearby Yellowstone National Park via snowmobile. Other guided adventure options are available, including climbing, kayaking, and mountain-biking excursions. Accommodations are in comfortable log cabins decorated in Western and Native American themes. Family-style dinners are served in the ranch's main lodge, where there is also a game room and lounge area.

Pahaska Tepee Resort

183 Yellowstone Hwy., Cody, WY 82414. ☎ **307/527-7701** or 800/628-7791. 48 rms. $65–$90 double. DC, DISC, MC, V.

Established in 1904, Buffalo Bill's original hunting lodge is located 1 mile from the east entrance to Yellowstone. The Native American name—Pahaska (long-haired) Tepee—has been retained and simply means that it was named after the Indians' long-haired friend, Buffalo Bill.

Accommodations are in either log cabins or A-frame houses. Both the cabins and the A-frames are best described as "mini-hotels" and contain anywhere from two to five rooms; each room has its own separate entrance. The interiors are spartan, with no TVs, phones, or air-conditioning, although the deluxe units boast a shower *and* a tub in the private bathroom (all others have either one or the other). The cabins are scattered on a hill behind the property and are only available in summer, while the A-frames are lined up in an ordered row near the main lodge and are open year-round.

A dining room, grocery store, gas station, lounge, and gift shop can provide you with food and sundries while you make plans for an outdoor adventure: Trail rides ($48 per person, for a half day), overnight pack trips ($125 per person, steak dinner and breakfast included), snowmobiling ($95–$145 per person), and cross-country skiing ($10 per day for rentals) are offered seasonally.

The resort is located in the Wapiti Valley, along Hwy. 14-16-20, providing convenient and comparatively inexpensive lodgings. It is closed in November and April.

A GUEST HOUSE

✪ Cody's Victorian Guest House and Western Cottages

1401 Rumsey Ave., Cody, WY 82414. ☎ **307/587-6000.** 3-bedroom guest house, 4-bedroom lodge, 1 bedroom suite, 3 one-bedroom cottages. TV TEL. Lodge and guest house rates during peak season (Jun 1–Sept 30): $250 double, $1,575 week; off-season (Oct 1–May 30): $150 double, $945 week. Suite and cottages during peak season: $85–$125 double, $535–$787 week; off-season $35–$55 double, $220–$345 week. AE, DISC, MC, V.

These charming accommodations are located in the heart of downtown Cody and provide a spectrum of lodging options for those with different needs and interests. The Victorian guest house, circa 1900, has been lovingly restored and showcases period antiques and tasteful appointments. Shiny hardwood floors set off antique dressers and end tables in rooms with touches of lace and romantic floral drapings. The homey four-bedroom Western lodge is comfortable and sleeps up to eight people. The renovated Western cottages are small enough to feel cozy yet equipped with a living area, kitchen, bedroom, bath, and patio—perfect for romantic getaways. The Executive Suite is equally comfortable and even comes with a carport and car heater plug-in should you find yourself driving through Cody during the winter. Lodgings are located on either Rumsey or Beck Avenues; check-in is at the office between 3–8pm.

WHERE TO EAT

✪ Franca's

1374 Rumsey Ave. ☎ **307/587-5354.** Reservations recommended. Fixed-price dinner $20–$25. No credit cards. Summer, Wed–Sun 6–10pm; off-season (Nov–May), Thurs–Sat 6–10pm. ITALIAN.

You might not expect matchless northern Italian cuisine in the heart of one of the West's biggest cowtowns, but that's exactly what you'll find at Franca's, Cody's finest dining establishment.

Everything about this restaurant is first-rate, from the intimate atmosphere to the meticulously prepared and presented food. There is also an expansive wine list numbering 106 bottles. Chef/owner Franca is unswerving in her devotion to using the finest and freshest ingredients: the lettuce and herbs she uses are grown on the property. Highlights of the seasonal menu are her ever-popular raviolis and tortellinis, along with her personal favorite, focaccine Genovesi, a specialty bread from the town where she was born that is served with every meal.

Seating is limited so reservations are highly recommended, especially during summer.

✪ La Comida

1385 Sheridan Ave. ☎ **307/587-9556.** Lunch $4–$10; main dinner courses $4–$15. AE, DISC, MC, V. Daily 11am–10pm. MEXICAN.

A crowded patio area along Cody's main street signals this celebrated Mexican restaurant. Lauded by *Gourmet* and *Bon Appetit*, La Comida serves a local specialty called Pechuta Chicken that will have you begging for more. Spinach enchiladas and fajitas are perennial favorites, as are the homemade desserts that include praline tostados, an almond flan, and a Margarita mud pie. Gourmet Mexican food has never tasted so good.

Silver Dollar Bar & Grill

1313 Sheridan Ave. ☎ **307/587-3554.** Reservations not accepted. Most items $4–$6. No credit cards. Mon–Sat 11am–9pm. BURGERS.

If you're looking for locals, the Silver Dollar is where you'll find them. Located on Cody's main street, the restaurant makes its home in what was once the town's first post office. Though their claim to world-famous burgers may be stretching the truth a bit, the food is hearty and the occasional live entertainment makes for a fun night of music and dancing. Expect a mixed crowd at this Cody standard; the Silver Dollar has been around since 1960.

3 A Side Trip to Powell & Lovell

There's a certain symmetry to these two Wyoming towns that extends beyond the fact that both their names end with the letters "ell." They occupy opposite positions on either side of the upper reaches of the Bighorn Basin near the border with Montana, and both are easily reached from Cody and Sheridan.

Lovell, the first of the two to be settled, chose the banks of the Bighorn River for a townsite and established itself as a cattle ranching community. Powell evolved as a direct result of the Shoshone Reclamation Project begun around the turn of the century; today it's located near the campsite where the workers for the reclamation project lived.

The **Powell Valley Chamber of Commerce,** located downtown at 111 S. Day, Powell, WY 82435 (☎ 307/754-3494), can send you information about local events and attractions, as well as hot spots to look for fossils. The **Homesteader Museum,** across the street from the chamber's log cabin, is a repository of relics from the early settlers of the area. Its offerings are comparable to most small-town museums throughout the West, though the museum's documentary about nearby Heart Mountain is touching and informative. The museum is open during the summer Tues–Fri from 1–5pm; admission is free.

Every summer, Powell's Northwest College hosts **Yellowstone Jazz Camp.** Open to qualifying high school, college-age, and adult musicians interested in the study of instrumental or vocal jazz, it is taught by outstanding jazz artists and teachers from around the country. The weeklong camp culminates with a trip to Cody where students perform at the **Yellowstone Jazz Festival** (See "Special Events" under Cody.)

Eight miles west of Powell on Hwy 14A is the Heart Mountain Relocation Center, where 11,000 Japanese-Americans were interned during World War II. Today, abandoned buildings and a monument to those who lived and died here are the only reminders of this sobering chapter in American history. Lovell, which calls itself the "Rose City," is a short 22-mile drive east of Powell and is the Wyoming gateway into the Bighorn Canyon Recreation Area. The Bighorn Canyon Visitor Center is located just east of town on Hwy. 10 and Hwy. 14A and is open daily year-round. Stop into the unique solar-paneled building for a quick history of the area and information on recreational opportunities within the Bighorn Canyon. The Lovell Chamber of Commerce can also assist you with a calendar of events: 287 E. Main, Lovell WY 82431 (☎ 307/548-7552).

ALSO WORTH A LOOK: GREYBULL & THE SHELL CANYON

Named for a legendary albino bison sacred to Native Americans, Greybull sits amid fascinating clusters of exposed and eroded red bedrock. Follow the red devil signs from town to **Devil's Kitchen**, one of the area's unique geologic formations. Unusual rocks and fossils have been found here, including one of the largest fossil ammonites in the world, now on display at the **Greybull Museum** on Main Street. Just north of town you'll find a spectacular 15-mile-long, 1,000-foot-high natural fortress named **Sheep Mountain**, a textbook example of a "doubly plunging anticline," geo-lingo for a natural arch folded into layered rock. The lower ridges that bend around each other (the double plunges) were formed as a result of the erosion of sandstone layers from the top of the fold.

Heading east out of Greybull on U.S. Hwy. 14, you'll encounter scenic Shell Canyon along with a few noteworthy sites. First is the **Stone Schoolhouse**, listed on the National Register of Historic Places, just 7 miles outside Greybull. A former one-room schoolhouse—built in 1903 of locally-quarried sandstone—is now an outstanding bookstore/gallery, with hundreds of regional history titles, permanent photographic exhibits of Native American petroglyphs, and special readings throughout the summer season.

For a glimpse at the picturesque Shell Canyon's scenic wonders, stop in at the visitor center at **Shell Falls**, where you can see the falls tumble down a steep granite slope and become the much more subdued Shell Creek. Antelope Butte Ski Area is just 38 miles east of Greybull, but don't expect world-class schussing here: The ski area measures its terrain in feet, not acres; nonetheless, the views are nice and the lift lines short. **Medicine Lodge State Archeological Site,** located about 50 miles east of Greybull, is considered one of the most significant archeological sites in the world. View petroglyphs on sandstone cliffs as you canoe Medicine Lodge creek or picnic along its shore. Thick groves of trees create serene campsights alongside the river, where you can fish for trout. Although RVs are welcome, there are no hookups. The campground is open from May to November and there are no fees. To reach the site and campground, take WYO 789/US Hwy. 16-20 for 20 miles from Greybull to Manderson, then drive 22 miles along WYO 31 to Hyattville. In Hyattville, drive north and turn right onto Cold Springs Road. Drive 4 miles, following the signs.

4 Thermopolis

German-born Julius A. Scuelke is responsible for giving this unassuming Wyoming town its lofty-sounding name, a word whose Greek and Latin roots literally translate into "hot city." Part of the Wind River Reservation in the late 1800s, the land on which Thermopolis sites was purchased by the U.S. government from the Shoshone and Arapaho peoples in 1896 with one stipulation: that a portion of the springs would always be open—free of charge. This promise continues to be honored at the Bath House at Hot Springs State Park, making this small Wyoming community one of the most popular tourist destinations in the state, second only to its national parks.

ESSENTIALS

GETTING THERE   If you're flying into the Thermopolis area, the closest airports are in **Riverton** (55 miles south of Thermopolis, just off Hwy. 26 west on Airport Road): Riverton Regional Airport, 4700 Airport Rd., Riverton, WY 82501 (☎ 307/856-4801); and **Cody** (84 miles northeast on WYO 120 to U.S. Hwy. 14-16-20, north on Duggleby Dr.): Yellowstone Regional Airport, 3001 Duggleby Dr., Cody, WY 82414 (☎ 307/587-5096).

United's **Mesa Airlines** (☎ 800/241-6522) is the sole provider of air service into Riverton, with six flights daily, most of which arrive from Denver. Two exceptions are a morning and an afternoon flight, both of which arrive from nearby Worland (88 miles to the north).

There is a county airport in Thermopolis for private use, which overlooks the city from the north.

To reach Thermopolis from Cody, drive 84 miles southeast along WYO 120. From Cheyenne, drive north on I-25 to Casper (178 miles), then west on U.S. Hwy. 20-26 to Thermopolis (130 miles). The 196-mile drive from Rock Springs to Thermopolis follows U.S. Hwy. 191 to Farson, WYO 28/U.S. Hwy. 287 to Lander, and WYO 789 to Thermopolis. Call 800/442-2535 for current road conditions.

VISITOR INFORMATION   The **Thermopolis–Hot Springs Chamber of Commerce,** 111 N. Fifth, Thermopolis WY 82443 (☎ 307/864-3192 or 800/SUN-N-SPA) will send you a comprehensive package of information related to the area and the hot springs upon request, including a particularly engaging treatise on the "Springs of Healing." This typewritten article sings the praises of Thermopolis and its hot springs as only a devoted senior citizen could; one particular passage boasts that "there is not the fear of the HOODLUM ELEMENT that frequents larger Metropolis places." This priceless piece is alone worth the time it takes to call for information and actually has some useful details mixed in with its hyperbolic homilies.

GETTING AROUND   If you've arrived by plane to one of the area airports, you'll need to rent a car to get around. **Avis** (☎ 800/331-1212) and **Hertz** (☎ 800/654-3131) maintain counters at both the Riverton and Cody airports.

GETTING OUTSIDE

The town's hot springs provide the greatest excuse to head outdoors in Thermopolis; you can enjoy them from a pool, a private tub, or while sliding down a waterslide. See the Hot Springs State Park listing under "What to See & Do" for more detailed information on how to access these healing waters.

Boysen State Park, just a short 20-minute drive south of town, is a popular spot among locals for year-round recreation. Fishing, boating, sailing, and skiing abound on the Boysen Reservoir, which is ringed by 11 separate campgrounds and numerous fishing accesses: The world ice-fishing record for a winter catch was earned here in 1991 when a 17.42-pound walleye was caught by a Casper native. The 76 miles of shoreline also include public use beach areas, located near the park's northeast entrance. For more information on the park, contact Boysen State Park, Boysen Route, Shoshoni, WY 82649 (☎ 307/876-2796) or call Wyoming State Parks and Historic Sites headquarters in Cheyenne at 307/777-6323.

FISHING

Looking for a trophy walleye or brown trout? Fishing accesses are abundant in this part of the state, but be sure you have the correct permits, especially if you plan to fish in the Wind River Reservation, which requires an additional tribal permit. Two of the more popular summer spots to fish are a couple of piers on the east side of the Bighorns by the Holiday Inn. The community has wheelchair-accessible boat ramps at Wedding of the Waters, just south of town, and in the state park. Late spring, fall, and winter are the best times of year to drop a line, when water temperatures are lower and algae levels are down. If you'd prefer to hire a guide, Reggie Treese at **Wind River Canyon Outfitters**, P.O. Box 1216, Thermopolis, WY 82443 (☎ 307/864-5309 or 800/828-7102), is one of the area's best. A full-day fishing excursion, with boat and guide, is $250; multiday fishing packages are also available.

GOLF

The Legion Golf Course is a nine-hole course that overlooks the city from Airport Hill. Call 307/864-5294 to book a tee time at the extremely affordable price of $8 for nine holes or $14 for 18. The club provides a pro shop with cart rentals, driving range, and lessons. A fine steak and seafood house, the Legion Supper Club (see "Where to Eat," below) is adjacent and open daily for lunch and dinner from 11am–10pm.

HIKING

Ready to stretch those cramped legs? Take a hike around Thermopolis's own **Volksmarch Trail**, a 6.2-mile (10K) trek that begins at the state park (marked by the trademark brown and yellow volksmarch insignia) and winds its way downtown. Locals also like to hike **T Hill**, accessible by gravel road off U.S. Hwy. 20 or from the airport. At the top you'll be treated to a bird's-eye view of Thermopolis, the Wind River Canyon, and the Owl Creek Mountains.

ROCKHOUNDING

You don't have to be interested in rockhounding to appreciate the incredible geologic history of this area of the state, but those who are will be wowed. Prehistory takes an in-your-face approach as you view four billion years of geological time—from pre-Cambrian to the present—in the exposed Wind River Canyon. It would only follow that fossils and rocks are abundant here, especially in the hillsides surrounding the city and in streamside gravel beds. If you decide to explore, take care not to trespass: Rockhounding is illegal on nearby reservation land.

WHITEWATER RAFTING

Prohibitions were in effect for many years along the portion of river that flows through the Wind River Canyon, but tribal officials have recently granted permission to **Wind River Canyon Whitewater,** 907 Shoshone, Thermopolis, WY 82443

(☎ 307/864-9343 in season; P.O. Box 592, Crowheart, WY 82512, ☎ 307/486-2253, during off-season) to guide rafting trips down this thrilling section of whitewater: Screamin' Lizard and Sharpnose Chute are only a couple of the rapids you'll encounter, whether you choose a half-day trip, dinner excursion, or overnight adventure.

WHAT TO SEE & DO

✪ Hot Springs State Park

220 Park St., Thermopolis, WY 82443. ☎ **307/864-2176.** Free admission. Open Mon–Sat, 8am–6pm; Sunday 11am–6pm.

Located in the center of town, Wyoming's first state park defines Thermopolis. The town grew up around the hot springs, for which the park was established, a gift from neighboring Shoshone and Arapaho tribes in the late 1800s. And, today, the Thermopolis Hot Springs is the state's third largest tourist attraction, surpassed only by Yellowstone and Grand Teton National Parks.

Hot Springs State Park is a collection of various noteworthy sites, most important of which is Big Springs, the source of the mineral-rich water. At a rate of 2,500 gallons per minute, the springs provide water for a series of pools, all of which maintain a constant temperature of 104° F. They include the state-operated **State Bath House,** a facility open to the public free of charge Mon–Sat 8am–6pm, and Sundays and holidays 12–6pm; and two commercial pools that flank the State Bath House.

Star Plunge (☎ 307/864-3771) has three waterslides. One, called "Star Plunge," is a 300-foot enclosed "Blue Thunder" slide that wraps itself around a 60-foot tower for an unforgettable, freefalling black hole experience. The second, called "Super Star 500," features an open-air tube that curves for 500 feet before dumping into the pool. The third, designed for small children is a 60-foot chute called the "Li'l Dipper." Star Plunge is open daily from 9am–9pm. Admission: $6 ages 5 and up; $2 ages 4 and under; $5 seniors (65 and over). The other commercial operator, **Hot Springs Water Park** (☎ 307/864-9250), has two slides: one indoor, one outdoor, both significantly shorter than those at Star Plunge, though the recently added snack bar and patio are definite assets. The park is open daily from 9am–9pm (Wednesdays until 8pm). Entry fees: $6 ages 6–61; $2.50 ages 4–5; and $5 seniors (62 and older).

Look for the **Terraces,** easily recognized natural formations composed primarily of lime and gypsum, that are created as Thermopolis' mineral water cools. Their unusual colors are caused by algae, which flourishes in the warm water.

And for a surprising natural attraction of an entirely different variety, look for the **Wyoming state buffalo herd** that makes its home in a large range area just east of the Big Springs.

✪ Gift of the Waters Historical Indian Pageant

This annual Thermopolis production commemorates the sale of the hot springs by the Shoshone and Arapaho peoples to white settlers at the turn of the century, with a reenactment of the historical event. With the signing of the April 21, 1896 treaty, Chiefs Washakie and Sharp Nose gave up the mineral waters with one important provision they fought hard to retain: One-quarter of the hot springs would always be free to the public. The State Bath House, part of Hot Springs State Park, was set aside under this provision in 1899, and thousands of people have enjoyed its soothing waters since then free of charge. Written in 1925 by a local resident, this heartwarming pageant enjoyed a limited local run before it was revived in 1950. It has been performed annually during the first weekend in August ever since. Contact the

Thermopolis Chamber of Commerce (☎ 307/864-3192 or 800/SUN-N-SPA) for information on other events during Pageant week.

Hot Springs County Museum and Cultural Center

7th and Broadway. ☎ **307/864-5183.** Admission $2 adult, $1.50 senior, $1 children under 6, $10 family pass. Mon–Sat 10am–5pm, Sun 1–5pm; June–Aug daily until 6pm.

The original cherrywood bar from the Hole-in-the-Wall Saloon is the biggest draw at this local museum, which does a good job of presenting the area's history. Various modes of transportation are represented: highlights include a turn-of-the-century stagecoach, a caboose, and a touring wagon used in Yellowstone. Local commerce is amply represented, with exhibits dedicated to the coal mining, petroleum extraction, and agricultural industries. Native American artifacts and a history of the hot springs add a multicultural element. Memorabilia is displayed on the lower level where there is a fully outfitted print shop, general store, and dentist's office. The museum's cultural center features local artwork and crafts on a rotating basis, so call for information on current exhibits.

✪ Legend Rock Petroglyph Site

Near Hamilton Dome, about 30 miles northwest of Thermopolis. Call the Thermopolis Chamber of Commerce (☎ **307/864-3192** or 800/SUN-N-SPA) to arrange for access to the site.

This petroglyph area dates back nearly 2,000 years, has nearly 300 pictures scattered among 92 rock panels, and is believed to have been sacred to early Native Americans. Animals dominate the sandstone canvasses, some more easily recognizable than others, including a bird glyph ("ghost dance" bird) and numerous depictions of Kokopelli, the humpbacked flute player. The impressive display is well worth the trip but be sure to get a key to the gate before you leave, or you won't be able to access the site. Call the chamber of commerce or park headquarters at Hot Springs State Park (see listing above) from 9am–5pm Monday through Friday to arrange to pick up a key.

To get to Legend Rock, take WYO 120 from Thermopolis toward Meeteetse for 21 miles. Turn left at the second Hamilton Dome turnoff (Cottonwood Creek) and drive west for approximately 5 miles. At the Cottonwood Creek turnoff, continue west. Turn left immediately after the second cattle guard. Follow the road to a Y and stay left. You will come to a gate that can be opened with a key. Continue down the hill and around a curve to the actual site. If the ground is wet, it's a good idea to park at the top of the hill and walk to the site.

Outlaw Trail Ride

To participate or obtain further information, contact: Outlaw Trail, Inc., Box 1046, Thermopolis, WY 82443. ☎ **307/864-2287.** Occurs annually in mid-August.

Begun in 1990 as a part of Wyoming's centennial celebration, the Outlaw Trail Ride takes 100 riders along 100 miles of trail made famous by the West's most notorious characters—Butch Cassidy and his infamous Wild Bunch. The weeklong event, held each year in mid-August, consists of camping and riding between Thermopolis and Cassidy's Hole-in-the-Wall country, outside of Casper. Forget about cowboy coffee: The food and entertainment are top-notch. Definitely not a dude ride, each participant is responsible for his or her own horse, tack, and gear. The ride usually fills up quickly, so make your reservations well in advance.

WHERE TO STAY

Holiday Inn of the Waters

Hot Springs State Park, Thermopolis, WY 82443. ☎ **307/864-3131** or 800/HOLIDAY. 80 rms. A/C TV TEL. $60–$90 double. AE, DC, DISC, MC, V.

This particular Holiday Inn has a prime, albeit unusual, location in the heart of Hot Springs State Park in Thermopolis, giving it a distinct advantage over many of its counterparts elsewhere in the state. It has all of the amenities you'd expect from a Holiday Inn, with the added bonus of being close to kids' attractions—the Star Plunge comes to mind—and parental preferences: How about a subdued soak in one of the mineral pools sans screams and squeals? The hotel periodically runs a "Hot Water Holiday" package, which gives you two nights' lodging, a prime rib dinner for two along with a bottle of champagne, and free use of the steam rooms, all for $119. The hotel's hot mineral-water Jacuzzi is complimentary (some of their amenities are not) and is open daily from 7am–10pm; it is also possible to complement your soak with a relaxing massage from the staff massage therapist.

The Safari Club Restaurant is a favorite dining spot among locals, though the mounted big-game trophies that preside over the dining room, lobby, and lounge may make some lose their appetite: The interior decorator didn't seem to realize that a little big game goes a long way. The hotel does a fine job in providing opportunities for fitness enthusiasts to keep in shape—from racquetball courts to weight training machines to bike rentals.

Roundtop Mountain Motel

412 N. 6th, Thermopolis, WY 82443. ☎ **307/864-3126** or 800/584-9126. 12 rms. TV TEL. $35–$50 double. MC, V.

The Roundtop is the budget alternative in Thermopolis, with lodging in either a motel or log cabins. Patios and kitchenettes outfit some of the units, making the Roundtop a bargain when compared to its competition. Though not directly adjacent to the hot springs, the motel is located downtown and within a short drive or walk to the mineral baths.

CAMPING

The **Fountain of Youth RV Park** (☎ 307/864-3265) has tent and RV sites available almost year-round (they're closed in December and January) and is located 1.5 miles north of town on U.S. Hwy. 20. The campground features a large mineral pool of its own with RV supplies, barbecue grills, and other sundries available at the camp store. Facilities are wheelchair-accessible and an EMT is on site. The **Latchstring Campground** (☎ 307/864-5262) is a similar facility with almost identical amenities and is located on U.S. Hwy. 20 south of Thermopolis.

WHERE TO EAT

Legion Supper Club

At the Legion Golf Club. ☎ **307/864-3918.** Lunch $5–$10; main dinner courses $8–$15. AE, DISC, MC, V. Mon–Sat lunch 11am–2pm, Mon–Thurs dinner 5–9pm, Fri–Sat dinner 5–10pm, Sun brunch 10am–2pm, dinner 4–9pm. AMERICAN.

The Legion is the place for fine dining in Thermopolis, with 360-degree views from the dining room of the golf course that surrounds it. Lunch is a festive affair, with a Mexican menu that includes smothered burritos and a taco salad as well as standard sandwich fare—the crab-and-cheese melt and shrimp salad are local favorites. The cheerful ambience during lunch becomes decidedly more polished and romantic at dinner, when linen tablecloths, flowers, and candles grace the tables and entrées of prime cuts of beef and seafood are served. Although more distinctive dining experiences can be found elsewhere in the state, you'll not find another place in Thermopolis to rival the Legion. The restaurant also has a full-service bar.

⑤ Pumpernick's

512 Broadway. ☎ **307/864-5151.** Breakfast items $2–$6; lunch $3–$6; main dinner courses $7–$16. AE, DISC, MC, V. Mon–Sat 7am–9pm. AMERICAN.

This busy Thermopolis restaurant claims a following known as the Local Yokel Club, proof of its enduring popularity among the town's residents. Open throughout the day, Pumpernick's serves breakfast, lunch, and dinner on every day of the week save Sunday. Their three-room dining area has a rustic ambience that agrees well with the friendly staff and hearty meals. Three-egg omelets are the breakfast order of the day, while crepes and specialty sandwiches monopolize the lunch menu. Dinner features generous portions of T-bone steaks and seafood—sautéed scallops, rainbow trout, and steamed shrimp are but a few of their offerings.

A full bar serves wine, beer, and mixed drinks. Pumpernick's best feature is its freshly baked breads, which appear throughout the day in various forms: hoagie buns, bread bowls (for their equally scrumptious soups), and mini dinner loaves. Try the Strawberry Kiss cheesecake for a melt-in-your-mouth treat. The open-air patio is an especially nice place to enjoy your meal during summer.

Spatol's Deli

500 Broadway. ☎ **307/864-3960.** Reservations not accepted. Most items $3–$5. No credit cards. Mon–Fri 10am–5pm, Sat 10am–3pm. DELI.

East Coast–style hoagies are the specialty at this small, made-to-order downtown delicatessen. Homemade cheesecake and salads are tasty accompaniments to their sandwiches, all of which are available for take-out. Enjoy a glass of iced tea or lemonade on their outdoor patio tables during the summer. Spatol's is an unbeatable choice if you're in a hurry or if you're planning a day trip and want to pack a lunch along.

5 A Side Trip to the Wind River Valley

The snow-capped peaks of the Wind River Mountain range follow the Continental Divide from Jackson to Lander to form this stunning valley along with the Owl Creeks to their east. It's home to a blended heritage rich in both Native American and ranching traditions. One of Wyoming's more fascinating spots to visit, here you'll find the larger towns of Riverton and Lander, along with the smaller communities of Dubois, Shoshoni, and South Pass City.

The big bend of Wind River marks **Riverton,** a friendly Wyoming town nestled in the heart of the Wind River Reservation, though not on reservation land. A sleepy small town throughout most of the year, Riverton comes alive each summer with the annual **Riverton Rendezvous and Balloon Rally,** held during the third week in July.

A spectacular high-flying adventure with colorful balloons set against the majestic backdrop of the Wind River range, the Balloon Rally gathers hot air balloonists from all over the Rocky Mountains for a week of arts and crafts and vaudeville performances. Rendezvous events include a rodeo, a pig-wrestling competition, and stock car races. Wyoming's largest **cowboy poetry gathering** is held here in October. Memorial Day's **Wind River Muzzleloaders Black Powder Shoot** also honors Riverton's heritage as a frontier trading center with events that include a run, a father-and-son tomahawk throw, and a primitive shoot.

If you're only in town for a few hours, consider fishing for walleye pike at nearby **Boysen Reservoir** or go for a hike or bike ride along one of the city's interlocking trails. Golf the Riverton Country Club's 18-hole course for a diversion from stereotypical Western activities, but watch out for the third hole, a 595-footer with lots of sand and water.

Shoshoni, which translates as "Little Snow," is located 22 miles from Riverton, and is a place where you can collect rocks at abandoned copper mines on Copper Mountain or hunt for arrowheads and other Native American relics. Visit during Memorial Day weekend and you'll be treated to the state's premier **Old Time Fiddlers' Contest.** Drive through the scenic Wind River Canyon toward Thermopolis— north on Hwy. 20 from the junction of Hwys. 26 and 20, at the center of Shoshoni—to experience the dramatic beauty of the Wind River and its opposing sharply jagged cliffs.

If you plan to stay overnight in Riverton, your best bet is the **Holiday Inn** (☎ 307/856-8100 or 800/HOLIDAY). Located at N. Federal and Sunset, it has 121 rooms that usually rent for a very affordable $48 to $53 double. The **Super 8** (☎ 307/857-2400 or 800/800-8000) is comparable in price, but it is a much smaller facility with only 32 rooms. It is located at 1040 N. Federal.

For more information on Riverton, contact the **Riverton Chamber of Commerce,** Depot Bldg., 1st and Main, Riverton, WY 82501 (☎ 307/856-4801). The **Shoshoni Chamber,** Box 324, Shoshoni, WY 82649 (☎ 307/876-2221) will be happy to provide you with information on activities in their area.

While you're in the vicinity of Riverton, you may also want to check out **Lander,** 25 miles to the southwest. Each year in early June, Wyoming honors a long-standing mountain man tradition here with the **Popo Agie Rendezvous.** The re-creation of the state's first rendezvous, held in 1829, includes horse- and mountain-man races, an art auction, demonstrations of gold panning, and more. Contact the Fremont County Pioneer Museum at 630 Lincoln St., Lander, WY 82520 (☎ 307/332-4137) for more information.

Another Lander event sure to become bigger and better with each passing year is their **International Climber's Festival.** Begun in 1994, it is the only gathering specifically geared for climbers in the country and features informative sessions with climbing greats and hands-on climbing at nearby Wild Iris Cliffs and Sinks Canyon. Contact Heidi Badaracco or Paul Piana at the Gravity Club (☎ 307/332-6339) in Lander for more information on this annual event.

Learn to responsibly enjoy wild places through a **National Outdoor Leadership School** (NOLS) course. The school's Lander office at 288 Main St., Lander, WY 82520 (☎ 307/332-6973) can give you more specific details on programs that help participants to develop common sense and good judgment while in the wilderness. If a less intense outdoor adventure is what you crave, then make a date with a llama with the **Lander Llama Company,** 2024 Mortimore Land, Lander, WY 82520 (☎ 307/332-5624). Their naturalist-led Red Desert trip is as enlightening as it is enjoyable, incorporating ancient Native American history and fossil viewing with stunning Wyoming scenery. If you'd prefer to horse around, check out **Allen's Diamond Four Ranch,** P.O. Box 243, Lander, WY 82520 (☎ 307/332-2995) for guided horseback tours in the Popo Agie Wilderness and Wind River Mountains. Although the ranch takes in guests for overnight stays, accommodations are in barebones guest cabins: no electricity, just wood stoves and propane lights, *and* you have to bring your own bedding (although mattresses are supplied). If you're looking for a remote, pristine, and simple lifestyle—if only for a few days—then this is the place for you.

Winter transforms this country into a snowmobiler's playground, with 250 miles of the **Continental Divide Trail** reaching from Lander all the way to Yellowstone.

Call the **Wind River Visitors Council** at 800/645-6233 for information on this and other snowmobile trails in the area. The **Lander Area Chamber of Commerce,** 160 N. First Street, Lander, WY 82520 (☎ 307/332-3892) can also provide you with information on the area.

History also comes alive daily in nearby **South Pass City** a state historic site that was once at the center of the fight to pass women's suffrage during the territory's early days.The epitome of an Old West ghost town, many of South Pass City's buildings were restored in 1995 and visitors can wander through them during the summer for a glance at authentic artifacts. Host to a festive Fourth of July celebration with old-fashioned fun and activities, contact the **South Pass Historic Site,** 125 South Pass Main, South Pass City, WY 82520 (☎ 307/332-3684) for additional information on this visible remnant of Wyoming's past.

6 Wind River Indian Reservation

Over two million acres of the Wind River Indian Reservation surround the town of Riverton, encompassing an area that stretches 70 miles east to west and 55 miles north to south. Wyoming's sole reservation, it is home to over 2,800 Eastern Shoshone and 3,700 Northern Arapaho tribal members and is governed by a joint council made up of representatives from both tribes.

Established by the Fort Bridger Treaty of July 2, 1863, the Shoshone reservation originally included portions of four other Western states. An amended treaty, signed nearly five years to the date later, established the reservation in its present location, drastically reducing reservation lands. With the advent of irrigation (in an area that later became Riverton) and the discovery of gold in the region, even more of the land was ceded to the government.

The Northern Arapaho came to the reservation in the late 1870s for what they thought was a temporary placement before being given their own reservation. However, federal administrations changed soon after their arrival and promises were forgotten or ignored: The two tribes have shared the reservation ever since, though they remain two distinct tribes and have little to do with each other.

A source of great pride to the people of the Wind River Reservation is Shoshone Chief Washakie. Greatly revered by his people, he was instrumental in helping to bridge the cultural gap between Native Americans and the whites who were settling the West. A friend of mountain man Jim Bridger, Washakie was the only Native American chief to be buried with full military honors—at the age of 102. One of his most lasting legacies, and one which visitors to Wyoming can certainly appreciate, is his insistence that a portion of the mineral hot springs at Thermopolis (once reservation land), always be available to people free of charge.

Rich in agricultural resources, the Wind River Reservation today provides ranching opportunities for its residents, along with monthly royalties from oil and gas leases. Though rich in heritage and scenic splendor, the reservation remains a troubled place, with high rates of alcoholism, domestic abuse, and unemployment.

There are several sites on the reservation well worth visiting, that are open to the public. The **St. Stephen's Mission and North American Indian Heritage Center** sit next to each other and provide a glimpse of reservation life, past and present. The mission, which was built in 1884 and educated children for a hundred years, now houses the offices for the St. Stephen's Mission Heritage Center, and exhibits photographs that illustrate the mission's history. Next door at the newly constructed Heritage Center, contemporary Indian art as well as historical photographs are featured.

St. Michael's Mission was established by Sherman Coolidge, an Arapaho who was adopted by a Fort Washakie military officer after his parents were killed, and later returned to the reservation after being educated and ordained an Episcopal minister in the East. A strong proponent of preserving Native American culture, Coolidge encouraged students to dress and speak according to native traditions. Last used as a school in the late 1950s, the mission is now utilized for church events and local activities. A cultural center of Arapaho relics is open during the summer from 8am–5pm, Mon–Fri; 10am–3pm on Sat.

The graves of expedition scout **Sacajawea** and **Chief Washakie** are located on the reservation. Sacajawea is buried at the cemetery of the same name; Chief Washakie is buried in the Fort Washakie Cemetery, just outside of the town of Fort Washakie, current tribal headquarters. The military post at the old Fort Washakie compound is now used by the Bureau of Indian Affairs' Wind River Agency; there was never a stockaded fort.

In late June, Native Americans from around the country converge at Fort Washakie for **Shoshone Treaty Days,** a celebration of Native American tradition and culture. The **Eastern Shoshone Powwow and Indian Days** follows a week later, with one of the West's largest powwows and all-Indian rodeos. For information on these events, call 307/433-0662.

Non-Indians are welcomed to both sundances and powwows, but visitors should remember that sundances are deeply religious ceremonies and no photographs or recordings of any kind are allowed. Powwows, on the other hand, encourage visitors to join in the many aspects of the celebration and photos can be taken.

If you plan to spend enough time here that you'll need overnight lodging, drive to **Lander** or **Riverton** (also good places for a meal or a snack).

14 Eastern Wyoming

Eastern Wyoming is an expansive land characterized by plains, farmland, an enormous number of protected forests, and large amounts of mineral wealth. The region's farthest reaching protected area is the 1.8-million-acre Thunder Basin National Grassland; and the state's greatest reserves of oil and coal are found in its largest cities, Casper and Gillette. But by far the most compelling reason to visit this part of the state is to see a rather remarkable natural attraction: the stump–shaped, 1280-foot Devils Tower, a flat-topped rock tower that was featured in the 1977 film *Close Encounters of the Third Kind*. Some think this otherworldly geological formation looks, particularly when viewed from a distance, as if it were clawed by a gigantic wild beast, since it appears to have wide gouges running up its sides. On closer inspection, however, it's clear that these gashes are actually separate columns of rock carved into different-sided shapes: four-, five- and six-sided, to be precise. In addition to being a noteworthy natural attraction, Devils Tower is a well-regarded rockclimbing and volksmarching (group walking) destination. More than 100 different routes have been climbed here since the first technical ascent in the late 1930s, and thousands of climbers add their names to the growing list each year.

The Big Horns west of Sheridan are a mountain biker's playground, with countless opportunities for exploring the wilderness and rolling prairies. Trout streams and glacial lakes, along with unique alpine flora and fauna, accentuate a series of marked trails, which can usually be toured from May to November. While you won't find wicked whitewater in this part of Wyoming, you can enjoy a scenic float from a raft or a canoe in the North Platte River near Casper. And the Keyhole Reservoir, north of I-90 between Gillette and Sundance, is one of this area's most popular multiuse facilities with opportunities for fishing, boating, waterskiing, camping, and hiking.

For a more leisurely paced outdoor vacation, try hiking one of the moderate trails on Casper Mountain, relaxing on a pontoon boat while you cruise the Alcova Reservoir just west of downtown Casper, or spending a sunny Sunday afternoon at a polo match at Big Horn's Equestrian Center.

1 Scenic Drives

Eastern Wyoming's line of demarcation is Interstate 25, which heads south from I-90 at Buffalo in the north and winds southeast all the way into neighboring Colorado, just south of Cheyenne. Wyoming's only other interstate, I-90, cuts a swath from the midpoint of the state on its northern border to a point in the east near Devils Tower. Wyoming's state highway 59 and U.S. Hwys. 18 and 85 also run through much of this part of the state, providing access to smaller towns across the region.

This chapter approaches this region as travelers might drive it: starting in the northwest in the town of Sheridan, moving south along I-90 to Buffalo, then continuing east along the Interstate to Gillette, and on to Devils Tower farther east and north on U.S. Hwy. 14 to Devils Tower Jct., where you pick up WYO 24 to go by the monument. The chapter finishes with a section on Casper, Wyoming's second largest city, which travelers can reach either by backtracking to Gillette, picking up I-90 east to Buffalo, then heading south on I-87; or by returning to Gillette, picking up WYO 59 into Reno Jct., then driving west on WYO 387 to Midwest, to rejoin I-87 and take it south into Casper. Below follows a scenic and enjoyable ride from Sundance through the Black Hills and back which includes an optional loop by Devils Tower.

DRIVING TOUR #1: BLACK HILLS LOOP

This half-day loop tour begins and ends in Sundance, a town long associated with Butch Cassidy's sidekick, the Sundance Kid. Although the town wasn't named for him (it takes its name from the nearby mountain on which Sioux ceremonies were held) many might guess that the county in which it's located—Crook County—was. But they'd be wrong: Crook County actually takes its name from an infamous Indian fighter, General George Crook.

Enough background. After you've toured the local museum in Sundance that has preserved the very courtroom in which the town's most famous outlaw was tried, take to the road. From here, it's a short and scenic 28-mile drive to Devils Tower (21 miles north on Hwy. 14, then 7 miles on WYO 24 to the monument). From Devils Tower, continue north toward Hulett, a 9-mile drive. You will drive by scenic vistas that include the Bearlodge Mountains, sandstone formations, and red hills. At Hulett, drive east on WYO 24 to Alva and Aladdin, which hug the border of South Dakota and provide easy access to that state's Black Hills. In Aladdin, drive south along WYO 111 to Beulah and U.S. Hwy. 14, then back to Sundance.

You can extend this driving tour by adding on an additional loop: from Sundance to Upton on WYO 116 for 30 miles, then on to Moorcraft on Hwy. 16 for 20 miles, to Devils Tower Junction on Hwy. 14 for 26 miles, then back to Sundance (21 miles). Look for antelope and deer in this thickly forested area or enjoy water sports at the Keyhole Reservoir. Take in some Old West traditions at the ranching community of Moorcroft, which makes its home along the Belle Fourche River, bordered by purple sage and blue skies.

2 Sheridan

The Big Horn Mountain region epitomizes the Wyoming travelers seek when they come in search of a remote ranch vacation. Simple, scenic, and wild, these mountains overlook some of Wyoming's best guest ranches and provide a wonderfully untamed playground in which to enjoy a vacation rooted in a peaceful respect for some of our country's most beautiful, and fast disappearing, wild places. Sheridan, whose Main Street has Wyoming's largest collection of original, turn-of-the-century buildings, is the area's most gracious host for this sort of vacation.

Named after the feisty Civil War general Phil Sheridan by a devoted soldier, this vibrant Wyoming city—the state's lowest in elevation—has a population that hovers just under 14,000. Sunday polo matches and an annual polka festival are testaments to the enduring legacy left behind by the city's founding fathers, an eclectic mix of British and Polish immigrants.

The city's proximity to the Big Horn Mountains draws outdoor enthusiasts like a magnet, with opportunities for mountain biking, hiking, fly-fishing, rock climbing, snowmobiling, and cross-country skiing. Walk around downtown and you'll see how the city has responded to the influx of Generation Xers all these opportunities for outdoor recreation have wrought: The historic Cady building now houses a microbrewery that serves excellent Cajun food. And while you won't see Buffalo Bill regally conducting auditions for his Wild West Show from the verandah of the historic Sheridan Inn, visit in the spring and you may observe a grand march of high school prom-goers as they saunter across the inn's wide porch.

Although it has always enjoyed a fair share of the state's tourist trade, Sheridan's fortune has been largely determined by the nation's need for coal during the last century, an industry that has become less and less significant. Farming and ranching continue to contribute much to the local economy and these pursuits, along with tourism, keep the people of Sheridan occupied today.

ESSENTIALS

GETTING THERE   The **Sheridan County Airport,** just southwest of town on **Airport Rd.** (take exit 25 off I-90), has daily service from Denver on **United Express** (☎ 307/674-8455 or 800/241-6522).

Powder River Transportation (☎ 307/674-6188) provides regional bus service from their terminal at 580 E. Fifth. There are two daily buses from Billings, Montana, just over a two-hour ride away.

Located on the north end of I-25 in Wyoming, Sheridan is easily reached by the other cities along the interstate to its south: Casper, 147 miles; and Cheyenne, 325 miles. To reach Sheridan from Jackson, drive north to Yellowstone National Park, then east along the park's southern boundary on U.S. Hwy. 14-16-20 to Cody. From Cody, follow Hwy. 14 to Ranchester, pick up I-25, and drive 15 miles south to Sheridan. For road and travel information, call 307/674-9966 or 307/672-6454.

VISITOR INFORMATION   The **Sheridan Chamber of Commerce** (☎ 307/ 672-2485) is located at the State Information Center, off I-90 at exit 23. They have brochures that cover local attractions as well as things to see and do across the state. (Incidentally, if you look west from the information center, the Big Horns are in full view.) The **Wyoming Game and Fish Visitors Center** (☎ 307/672-7418), just across the road, has exhibits of big-game habitat and interactive displays that deal with the preservation of our wild things and places. They are open Mon–Fri 8am–5pm. A brochure they distribute, "Campbell County Wildlife and Natural History Loop Tours," contains scenic driving tours of the region that include opportunities for wildlife viewing.

GETTING AROUND   You can rent a car from **Avis** (☎ 800/331-1212) or **Enterprise** (☎ 800/325-8007) at Sheridan's airport.

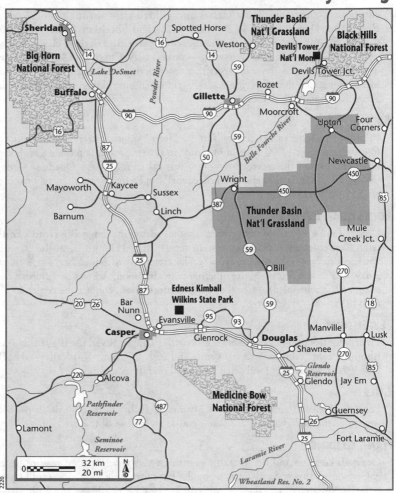

GETTING OUTSIDE

Regardless of the season, the **Big Horns** are the place to partake in outdoor recreation in the Sheridan area. See below for listings of the various sports you can practice in this national forest. In downtown Sheridan, **Kendrick Park** is ideal for a midday picnic. With a resident herd of elk and bison, a swimming pool (complete with waterslide) and tennis courts that are open 24 hours, Kendrick Park is sure to please even the grumpiest of kids. Look for small fish in the creek that runs through the park or enjoy the big band that plays free concerts every summer on Tuesday nights at 7pm.

Ritz Sporting Goods, 135 N. Main (☎ 307/674-4101), stocks a good selection of camping and backpacking gear as well as the latest in fly-fishing equipment and supplies. For topographical maps and advice on local hot spots for hiking and fishing, check with **Big Horn Mountain Sports,** 334 N. Main (☎ 307/672-6866). In addition to extensive lines of fly-fishing, backpacking, camping, and skiing equipment, they coordinate classes and guided trips through the **Sheridan Recreation Department** (☎ 307/674-6421) and **Sheridan College** (☎ 307/674-6446). Although visitors are encouraged to participate in these classes, reservations—usually three months in advance—are necessary. Check with Big Horn Sports or the agencies listed above for specific course offerings and dates. Past classes have included instruction in fly-tying, kayaking, cross-country skiing, and rock climbing at nearby Tongue River Canyon.

BIKING

In summer, a series of marked trails in Big Horn National Forest allow fat-tire fans to experience over 1,000 miles of moderate to extreme mountain biking, with some downhill canyon rides exceeding 4,000 vertical feet. Stop by **Outdoor Groove** (☎ 307/672-8186) in Sheridan for bike rentals and a free area trail map. Trail bikes are $15 per day, $84 per week.

EQUESTRIAN EVENTS

Dressage and steeplechase competitions are the order of the day at **Big Horn's Equestrian Center** (south of Sheridan toward Big Horn at 351 Bird Farm Road), where you can also view polo matches every Sunday from May to September. There are two a day, one in late morning, the other in early afternoon. Admission (unless a benefit match is scheduled) is free. For further information, contact the center at 307/674-4812.

FLY-FISHING

Fly-fish for trout up to 20 inches long along the Tongue River, the Big Horns' blue-ribbon stream. Inquire with the Game and Fish Division, 700 Valley View Dr. (☎ 307/672-7418) for local catch limits and permit requirements.

GOLF

For the golf enthusiast, the **Kendrick Municipal Golf Course** (☎ 307/674-8148), west of Sheridan, has a par-72, 18-hole course with views of the Big Horns.

HANG GLIDING

Great air currents and breathtaking mountain views are just two reasons people enjoy hang gliding at Sand Turn, a popular Big Horn peak located west of Dayton, a small community just 20 miles north of Sheridan on U.S Hwy. 14. With a paved runway and twice-yearly competitions, Sand Turn is making quite a name for itself in the hang gliding community, luring pilots from all over the world. **Eagle Air,** located in Dayton at 312 Main St. (☎ 307/655-2562), has been taking people up for 15 years and is the local authority on the sport. With a staff that includes a member of the U.S. Women's Hang Gliding Team, Eagle Air provides lessons for all levels of experience: A four-hour morning session and a four-hour afternoon session run around $50. Rentals are available only to certified pilots. If the weather isn't condusive to gliding or for a change of pace, ask them for their specialized **spelunking** tour of nearby Tongue River Canyon.

HIKING

The Cloud Peak Wilderness Area, a federally designated land to the southwest of Sheridan, is managed by the Forest Service and is a popular destination with hikers and backpackers. Call the Big Horn district of the National Forest Service, 1969 S. Sheridan Ave., Sheridan, WY (☎ 307/672-0751) for the locations of trailheads and other information about this wilderness area.

WINTER SPORTS

Snow brings snowmobiling and cross-country skiing to the Big Horns, with a groomed trail near **Sibley Lake.** To get there, take exit 9 north of Sheridan and drive 25 miles on Hwy. 14 to the Sibley Lake turnoff, in plain view on your left. Contact the Big Horn district of the National Forest Service, 1969 S. Sheridan Ave., Sheridan, WY (☎ 307/672-0751) for information on local trails and conditions. **Big Horn Safari,** 303 S. Main, Suite 207, Sheridan WY (☎ 307/674-6842), and **Home on the Range Travel,** Box 976, Sheridan WY (☎ 307/674-9442), can arrange a guided winter adventure for you, including sled rentals and guided forays into the Big Horns.

SEEING THE SIGHTS

✪ Trail End State Historic Site

400 Clarendon Ave, Sheridan, WY 82801. ☎ **307/674-4589** or 307/672-1729. Free admission. Daily during summer (June through August) 9am–6pm; call for off-season hours.

The city's most famous attraction, this historic site is the home of former Wyoming governor and U.S. Senator John B. Kendrick. Raised as an orphan in Texas, Kendrick came to Wyoming as a ranchhand in the late 1800s and immediately fell in love with the land. Over the years, he worked his way up to foreman, acquiring more than 200,000 acres of land in Wyoming and Montana. As his fortunes increased, so did his interest in politics. He served as governor from 1915 to 1917, exactly one decade before Wyoming would elect its first female governor, and later as a U.S. senator until his death in 1933. Prior to his term as governor, Kendrick began construction on this Sheridan mansion, a project that spanned five years and cost a then extravagant $165,000 to build.

Trail End, located on nearly four acres of groomed grounds that also include a sunken rose garden and English sundial, was designed by Kendrick to reflect the Flemish Revival style, utilizing arts and crafts from around the country: Kansas brick, Indiana limestone, Missouri roofing tiles, and Wyoming granite. The carriage house, which sits to the east of the main house, was occupied by the Kendricks during the construction of Trail End and today serves as the home of the Sheridan Civic Theater Guild, the local venue for community theater. The Mandel Cabin, which sits on the property but is not original to it, was reconstructed from its original logs and moved to Trail End in 1976. Built in 1879, it served as the area's first post office.

✪ The Sheridan Inn

Broadway and Fifth, Sheridan, WY 82801. ☎ **307/674-5440.** Admission $3 adults, children 12 and younger free, $2 seniors. Memorial Day through Labor Day, daily 9am–8pm; call for off-season days and hours.

Once considered the finest hotel between Chicago and San Francisco, the Sheridan Inn was built in 1893 and today maintains a discreet distance from downtown Sheridan. Nicknamed "The House of 69 Gables" for its distinctive dormer windows, an important component of its Scottish hunting-lodge design, it is perhaps better known for its expansive front verandah, where Buffalo Bill Cody once auditioned riders for his Wild West Show. Inside, hand-hewn wood beams and three impressive river rock fireplaces showcase distinctly Western raw materials on a grand scale with elegant touches that include an imported back bar from England and the town's first electric lights.

Since its grand opening just six years after Custer's Battle at Little Bighorn, the Sheridan Inn has hosted a variety of visiting celebrities and dignitaries, including

Calamity Jane, Teddy Roosevelt, and Ernest Hemingway. Although it hasn't operated as a hotel since 1965, tours of the National Historic Landmark are included in the price of admission.

Bradford Brinton Memorial Ranch

239 Brinton Rd. Big Horn, WY 82833. ☎ **307/672-3173.** Admission $3 per person, $5 per family. Memorial Day to Labor Day, daily 9am–5pm.

This 20-room ranch house illustrates the English influence on this region of Wyoming through its furnishings and appointments, and features an impressive Western art collection of Remington and Russell paintings. There is also an extensive collection of regional Native American artifacts and Western memorabilia.

King's Saddlery Museum

184 N. Main, Sheridan, WY 82801. ☎ **307/672-2702** or 307/672-2755. Free admission. Mon–Sat 8am–5pm.

An extensive collection of Western tack and cowboy memorabilia is displayed at this museum, located behind a store of the same name. If you want to know what a Western movie smells like, amble into King's Saddlery, internationally renowned for its high-quality saddles and leather goods.

WYO Theater

42 N. Main, Sheridan, WY 82801. ☎ **307/672-9083.** Summer performances held at 7:30pm nightly.

The oldest operating vaudeville theater in the state, the WYO Theater features a variety of entertainment. From nightly summer vaudeville to year-round dramatic performances and concerts—jazz, classical, and blues music—the WYO is synonymous with first-rate entertainment. Recent performers have included cowboy poet Baxter Black, Michael Martin Murphey, and the Bellamy Brothers.

WHERE TO STAY
GUEST RANCHES

✪ HF Bar Ranch

Saddlestring, WY 82840. ☎ **307/684-2487.** 26 cabins. $140 per person, per day; one-week minimum stay required (mid-June to mid-September). Rates include all meals and ranch activities. Round-trip transfers from Sheridan airport can be arranged for an additional $10 per person. No credit cards. Reserve at least six months in advance. Take I-90 35 miles south of Sheridan to exit 47. Turn west on Shell Creek Road for 7 miles to ranch.

The second oldest dude ranch in Wyoming, the HF Bar is one of the West's premier guest ranches, and one to which families return year after year. Set on 10,000 acres against the Big Horn Mountains just 35 miles southwest of Sheridan, this ranch classic has held strong to its old-time Western traditions: Ice is delivered daily to a wooden box on each of the cabin's front porches and hearty family-style meals are served in the main lodge. The daily horse rides are led by experienced wranglers, though guests who demonstrate adequate "horse sense" are allowed to ride alone. In summer, guests enjoy incredible fly-fishing for trout along the North and South Forks of Rock Creek and fall brings a drove of deer and elk hunters. Other activities include pheasant and chukar shooting on a private bird reserve or taking an overnight pack trip to the ranch's mountain camp, 15 miles distant in the Big Horns. The cabins are comfortably rustic and come equipped with private baths. There are lots of children's activities, as well as a babysitting service, although guests are encouraged to bring nannies along (they receive a 50% discount on their daily rate).

✪ Eaton Ranch

270 Eaton Ranch Rd., Wolf, WY 82844. ☎ **307/655-9285** or 307/655-9552. 50 cabins. $950 per person, per week; one-week minimum stay required, June through September. Rates include all meals and ranch activities and roundtrip airport transfers. MC, V.

This 7,000-acre working cattle ranch, adjacent to the Bighorn National Forest, may well be the oldest dude ranch in the country. Started by three brothers in North Dakota who couldn't seem to keep their friends back East away, the Eatons moved to their present location around the turn of the century and their ranch business has continued nonstop ever since. This is the kind of ranch that enables you to lose yourself in another time and place. Life here really *does* seem simpler, and the natural world somehow easier to appreciate. Although horseback riding is the primary activity, guests can fish and hike in the surrounding national forest.

✪ Paradise Guest Ranch

Box 790, Buffalo, WY 82845. ☎ **307/684-7876**. 18 cabins. $2,180 double per week (Sunday to Sunday), late May to October. Rate includes all meals and ranch activities and round-trip airport transfers. No credit cards.

This luxurious guest ranch 45 miles south of Sheridan is aptly named: It has the ambience and all the activities you'd expect from a dude ranch, along with many of the modern conveniences you *wouldn't:* how many log structures come equipped with their own washer and dryer? Another especially enjoyable amenity of the cabins is their private decks, each with its own spectacular view of the surrounding valley, mountains, or streams. As with most premier guest ranches in the West, horseback riding is the predominant activity, with several rides departing daily for riders at all levels of ability. Most meals are served family-style, but don't be surprised to be served a chuckwagon lunch along the trail if you happen to be riding at lunchtime. There are ample after-dark activities for the entire family, with evening entertainment in the ranch's French Creek Saloon and recreation center.

A BED-AND-BREAKFAST

✪ Spahn's Big Horn Mountain B&B

70 Upper Hideaway Lane, Big Horn, WY 82833. ☎ **307/674-8150**. 4 rms, all with private baths. $65–$115 double. All rates include a full breakfast. MC, V. Reservations should be made 3–6 months in advance. 15 miles southwest of Sheridan at edge of Bighorn National Forest.

Start with a view of the Big Horn Mountains that stretches 100 miles away in the distance. Add a secluded mountain hideaway, a few curious wildlife specimens, and a family dedicated to sharing all of this scenic wealth with visitors, and you have the perfect formula for an award-winning bed-and-breakfast. Spahn's Big Horn Mountain B&B prides itself on being the oldest B&B in Wyoming, and it's certainly one of the best. Though guests will enjoy the comforts of the massive home, which features a three-story common room decorated with country quilts and lodgepole furniture, the real appeal is the solitude and beauty this mountain retreat affords those who stay here. Nightly wildlife safaris to Teepee Creek yield glimpses of moose, elk, or ever-present deer. Kids love exploring the secret trail underneath nearby Little Goose Falls. There's even a secluded guest cabin called the Eagle's Nest that's just perfect for honeymooners.

CAMPING

The **Big Horn Mountain KOA Campground,** 63 Decker Rd. (☎ 307/674-8766), is located one-half mile north of Sheridan at the Port of Entry exit. Tent and RV sites are available from May to October. The **Bramble RV Park** is at exit #20 off I-90 (2366 N. Main, ☎ 307/674-4902) with seven RV sites available for $12 from April to November. Near Buffalo, check out the **Deer Park Campground** (☎ 800/ 222-9960) on U.S. Hwy. 16. Open from May through early October, expect it to be busiest during the summer because of its close proximity to two interstates. It's located one-half mile west of I-90 off exit 58 and three-quarters of a mile east of I-25 off exit 299. There are both tent and RV sites available. In addition, several **Forest Service campgrounds** can be found near Dayton in the Bighorn National Forest, all located at points southwest of Dayton along U.S. Hwy. 14. Contact the Big Horn District of the National Forest Service for information on the following (mileage given is from Dayton): **North Tongue** (29 mi.); **Owen Creek** (34 mi.); **Prune Creek** (26 mi.); and **Sibley Lake** (25 mi.). All have tent and RV sites and are open from June through October with a $7 fee.

WHERE TO EAT

Golden Steer

2071 N. Main. ☎ **307/674-9334.** Lunch $4–$8; main dinner courses $10–$20. AE, DISC, MC, V. Lunch Mon–Fri 11am–2pm; dinner daily 4–9pm. STEAK/SEAFOOD.

This very good steakhouse is located on the north end of town and is recommended by almost anyone you run into in Sheridan. The menu seldom strays from the norm, even though other dinner items are offered in addition to their steak and seafood specialties. If you're craving a big old rib-eye or a plateful of fried shrimp, head on over to the Golden Steer.

✪ Sanford's Grub, Pub & Brewery

1 E. Alger and N. Main. ☎ **307/674-1722.** Reservations not accepted. Lunch $5–$7; main dinner courses $9–$16. MC, V. Daily 11am–10pm. CAJUN.

Four specialty microbrews are on tap at this funky Sheridan brewery/restaurant that specializes in Cajun food. You almost have to see the place to believe it. Decorated junkyard style, Sanford's (as in the seventies sitcom "Sanford and Son") invites you to sit and stay a while: You can pull up a chair in the den, put up your feet in the living room, or take a breather in the garage before heading upstairs to the bar. There are 125 different bottled beers available and 37 on tap, including the restaurant's very own Cloud's Peak Raspberry Wheat and Cady House Stout, named for the 1907 historic Sheridan building in which the microbrewery is located. Numerous Cajun specialties and nightly specials are served in addition to a midnight appetizer menu, available for night owls after 10pm, that features Cajun quesadillas and calamari.

3　Buffalo: A Stop on the Drive from Sheridan to Gillette

A small, friendly town of less than 4,000 year-round residents, Buffalo is a short drive south from Sheridan along I-90. It's a fun day trip for history buffs interested in touring battlegrounds where Native American and white settlers fought, hideouts of local outlaws (including a cave with Indian pictographs sketched on its walls), and other sites of Western historical note (including the site of the Johnson County War and an old hotel believed to be commemorated in Owen Wister's *Virginian*).

In the late 1800s, this area—what the Sioux called Powder River country for the river of the same name that runs through it—was the site chosen for several U.S.

Army forts, erected to protect Western settlers and gold seekers from the native populations of Sioux, Cheyenne, and Arapaho. The largest of these was **Fort Phil Kearny,** which enclosed 17 acres and was established at the forks of Big and Little Piney Creeks in 1866. Although none of the fort's original buildings still stand today, the National Historic Site includes a visitor center and portions of two battle sites within its boundaries: the location of the Fetterman Fight of 1866 and the setting for the following summer's Wagon Box Fight. These two fights exemplified the regional struggle, both real and imagined, between the army and the area's native populations. While army soldiers labored to make the region safe for travelers passing through Wyoming, Native Americans—under Sioux chiefs Red Cloud and Crazy Horse—fought equally hard to keep them out of country that they vowed would remain theirs forever. As a result of this constant struggle, every army soldier in the Fetterman Fight perished, while an overwhelming percentage of Native Americans died in the following summer's Wagon Box Fight.

The museum and visitor center is open daily 8am–6pm from mid-May through the end of September and is closed from December to March. There is a $1 gate fee for adults 18 and over during the summer season. Call 307/684-7629 to arrange a guided tour of the fort area and battle sites.

If you drive 46 miles south along the interstate to the town of Kaycee, you'll be close to **Hole-in-the-Wall,** which may be most famous as the hangout of Butch Cassidy's Wild Bunch, but is also the site of the Dull Knife Battle between the U.S. Army and Cheyenne warriors in the fall of 1876. Most of this area is located on private land: Be sure to check with the Buffalo Chamber of Commerce (see below) before exploring on your own. Ask for information about the **Outlaw Cave,** a day hike that takes you to a prehistoric rock shelter with Indian pictographs, and views of the canyon of the Middle Fork of the Powder River, and the Dull Knife Battlefield area.

The historic **TA Guest Ranch,** Box 313, Buffalo, WY 82834 (☎ 307/684-7002) is located on the site of one of Wyoming's biggest battles—the Johnson County War—about 30 miles south of Buffalo on WYO 196. The war was fought over land rights between absentee cattle ranchers and homesteaders, and it culminated in a battle between the locals and the hired guns of the cattle barons. Several of the ranch's buildings are riddled with bullet holes from the historic confrontation. The conflict between these two groups was immortalized in the novel and motion picture *Shane* (although the mountains you see in the film are the Tetons of Wyoming's western side).

Another literary landmark is historic downtown Buffalo's **Occidental Hotel,** 10 N. Main St., reputed to be the place where novelist Owen Wister's *Virginian* "got his man." No longer open for business, the hotel is open for self-guided tours during daylight hours in summer. There's no charge for admission. While in town, check out the **Jim Gatchell Museum** for a look at local Native American relics and other Western memorabilia. This expansive collection is located on Main and Fort Streets and is open 9am–5pm from mid-May to mid-October. There is a $2 admission fee for adults (kids enter for free).

Just a few miles northwest of Buffalo along I-90 is **Lake De Smet,** an excellent fishing and boating destination, with opportunities for picnicking and camping. The **Buffalo Chamber of Commerce,** 55 N. Main St., Buffalo, WY 82834 (☎ 307/684-5544 or 800/227-5122) can provide additional information on the lake area and all of the above attractions.

4 Gillette

Between the scenic peaks of the Big Horns and the Black Hills of South Dakota lies the largest coal producer in the entire United States. Energy Capital of the Nation, Gillette doesn't have much to recommend it to travelers in search of conventional attractions, but it is a logical place to stop on your way from Sheridan or points farther west to Devils Tower (see Section 5 later in this chapter).

ESSENTIALS

GETTING THERE   The airport is 5 miles north of Gillette. **United Express** (☎ 800/241-6522) has daily commuter flights from Denver and Sheridan.

If you're driving, Gillette is 90 miles east from Sheridan along I-90 and approximately 46 miles from Devils Tower National Monument. From Cheyenne, take I-25 north to Buffalo (approximately 100 miles); at Buffalo, turn east on I-90 for 54 miles.

VISITOR INFORMATION   Call the **Gillette Convention and Visitors Bureau,** located at 314 S. Gillette Ave., Gillette WY 82716 (☎ 307/686-0040 or 800/ 544-6136) for a schedule of local events and/or more detailed listings of local accommodations.

GETTING AROUND   You can rent cars from **Avis** (☎ 307/682-8588) or **Hertz** (307/686-0550). Call **Yellow Checker Cab** (☎ 307/686-4090) for a taxi.

WHAT TO SEE & DO

The Wyodak Overlook, 5 miles east of Gillette off Hwy. 14-16, gives visitors a unique opportunity to view one of the city's working mines. Opened in 1922, the **Wyodak Mine** is one of the oldest in the area, with an annual production that exceeds two million tons of coal annually. About half of that amount is burned next door at the Wyodak Power Plant, a 330-megawatt power plant that burns coal to create steam that in turn produces electricity. Tours are given at the power plant (☎ 307/686-1248) from 9am–3pm, Mon–Fri year-round. Call 307/682-3673 for information on other coal-related tours in the area.

If you want to hit the links, the local **golf courses** in Gillette are found at the **Gillette Country Club,** 1800 Country Club Rd. (☎ 307/682-4774) and the **Bell Nob Golf Course,** 1316 Overdale (☎ 307/686-7069). The country club has a nine-hole course; Bell Nob has 18.

McManamen Park, near the corner of Gurley St. and Warlow Drive, simulates a waterfowl habitat and is an excellent spot for bird-watching.

Gillette is situated in Campbell County, a prime locale for big-game hunting; fall brings hunters in search of deer, antelope, and other wildlife. To obtain an out-of-state hunting license, you must file with the **Wyoming Game and Fish Department** in Cheyenne (☎ 307/777-4601) by March 15; any leftover licenses can be obtained after August 1. The "Stop Poaching" hotline can be reached at 800/331-9834.

If you're rather arrange a guided hunting trip, contact **Sagebrush Outfitters,** 22-A Lewis Rd., Gillette, WY 82716 (☎ 307/682-4394) or see the listing for **P Cross Bar Ranch** under "Where to Stay" below.

WHERE TO STAY

Best Western Tower West Lodge

109 N. U.S. Hwy 14-16, Gillette, WY 82716. ☎ **307/686-2210** or 800/762-PERK. 190 rms. A/C TV TEL. $50–$70 double. AE, DC, DISC, MC, V.

This Best Western property is considered by some to be the nicest place to stay in town. It's certainly the largest, and it features the most amenities. Guests can enjoy a heated indoor pool, weight room, and sauna as well as a lounge and restaurant on the premises. Located near exit 124 just off I-90, the Tower West Lodge is a short drive south from the airport and is also convenient to the Bell Nob Golf Course.

Days Inn

910 E. Boxelder Rd., Gillette, WY 82716. ☎ **307/682-3999** or 800/325-2525. 138 rms. A/C TV TEL. $45–$70 double. AE, DISC, MC, V.

A continental breakfast is included in the price of your stay at this Gillette motel, located behind the Holiday Inn and just off the interstate. Short on amenities, the Days Inn good-naturedly sends people next door to the Holiday Inn's restaurant. If you don't mind the walk and enjoy saving a few dollars, this very basic accommodation is fine. The Gillette Country Club and the Campbell County Recreation Center are within easy walking distance.

Holiday Inn

2009 S. Douglas Hwy., Gillette, WY 82716. ☎ **307/686-3000** or 800/HOLIDAY. 158 rms. A/C TV TEL. $62–$93 double. AE, DC, DISC, MC, V.

This Holiday Inn has been a Gillette fixture for decades and is conveniently located just off exit 126 on I-90. A brand-new heated indoor pool was installed in 1995 and a sauna and Jacuzzi are also available to guests. When making your reservation, ask where your room is in relation to the lounge: The hotel features live music every night of the week that just might rock your world a little too much.

A WORKING RANCH

P Cross Bar Ranch

8586 N. U.S. Hwy. 14-16, Gillette, WY 82716. ☎ **307/682-3994.** 2 rms, shared bath. $40 double. All rates include a full breakfast and roundtrip airport transfers. No credit cards.

Marion and Mary Scott's family-owned-and-operated cattle ranch has been hosting visitors for 40 years. A hunting and outfitting operation first and foremost, the P Cross Bar Ranch also serves as a bed-and-breakfast alternative, especially for those who are traveling with horses. Their "Horse Motel" will put up your steed in style, although the $12 nightly fee doesn't include the $5 bale of hay. The P Cross Bar Ranch is ideal for visitors who want to see first-hand the goings-on of a real working ranch. Hunters are especially prevalent during the fall, when trophy buffalo, mule deer, pronghorn, sage grouse, and Hungarian partridges are in season. A six-day guided trophy mule deer and pronghorn hunt (one hunter per guide) starts at $5,000 and includes ranch accommodations and family-style meals. A two-day trophy antelope hunt with two hunters per guide starts at $1,100 per person.

CAMPING

There are three choices for campers in Gillette. The **Circle G Shooting Park,** 32 Shooting Park Dr. (☎ 307/682-3003), has RV sites for $20 and is open from April through September. The **Greentrees Crazy Woman Campground,** 1001 W. Second St. (☎ 307/682-3665), is off exit 124, 1 mile from I-90, with tent and RV sites. It is open from mid-April through October, with a Jacuzzi, pool, and bike rentals. **High Plains Campground,** 1600 Garner Lake Rd. S. (☎ 307/687-7339), is located one mile south of I-90 at exit 129. Tent and RV sites start at $9, from May through September.

WHERE TO EAT

If you're just passing through, or none of the places listed below sounds enticing, a good place for a picnic is **McManamen Park,** located near the corner of Gurley St. and Warlow Drive. If you need to pick up supplies, just stop at one of the supermarkets or convenience stores located downtown.

Bazel's

408 S. Douglas Hwy. ☎ **307/686-5149.** Reservations not accepted. Breakfast items $2.88–$5; lunch $4–$6; main dinner courses $7–$16. DISC, MC, V. Mon–Sat 6am–8pm, Sun 7am–6pm. AMERICAN.

Perhaps the most popular restaurant in town, Bazel's is a fifties-style diner. Their all-day breakfast menu features the Bazel, a deal for $2.88: two eggs, two patties, and two pancakes. Belgian waffles and veggie omelettes (made with Egg Beaters and alfalfa sprouts) are two of the most popular breakfast items. Dinners are a little less frenzied, with snow crab making an unlikely appearance along with such old-time menu standards as chicken strips, spaghetti, and meatloaf.

The Prime Rib

1205 S. Douglas Hwy. ☎ **307/682-2944.** Reservations recommended. Lunch $4–$9; main dinner courses $7–$18 ($22 16-oz. prime rib, $35 lobster tail). AE, DISC, MC, V. Mon–Fri 11am–11pm, Sat–Sun 5–11pm. STEAK/SEAFOOD.

One of Gillette's finer dining establishments, the Prime Rib features a menu predictably heavy on red meat, except during lunch, when a wide variety of salads are represented: Cobb, Taco, and Caesar are just a few. This is where locals choose to celebrate birthdays, anniversaries, and promotions. A slightly more upbeat mood is noticeable mid-week, when the restaurant's keyboard lounge features live piano music on Wednesday nights.

5 Devils Tower National Monument

In *Close Encounters of the Third Kind,* Richard Dreyfuss nearly goes berserk trying to figure out what that stumplike shape that keeps invading his thoughts is. In the movie, it turns out to be a landing pad for aliens, but in real life, it's Devils Tower National Monument. If you've never seen the movie, the first glimpse of this massive formation can be unearthly.

Far away from the Wyoming plains, Devils Tower rises 1,280 feet in a striated flat-topped tower, the only structure higher than 20 feet for miles around. Believed to be of volcanic origin, the rock formation augments the hills bordering the Belle Fourche River and is especially popular with technical climbers, whose numbers seem to increase exponentially each year.

The National Park Service maintains the monument and charges a nominal $4 fee to enter the facility ($1 if you're hiking or biking). The most impressive views are from the surrounding countryside; most of the photographs you see of Devils Tower are from outside the park service's jurisdiction. A number of hiking trails lead around the monument and camping facilities are available.

From mid-June to Labor Day, the visitor center is open daily from 8am–8pm and from 8am–5pm the rest of the year. In addition to a small selection of books, the center features interpretive displays on the geology and history of the area. All climbers are required to register here before attempting an ascent. If you're an experienced climber, it's worth purchasing *Devils Tower National Monument—A Climber's Guide* by Steve Gardiner and Dick Guilmette (The Mountaineers, 1986) before attempting a climb.

If you prefer to be led, sign on with **Exum Mountain Guides** (☎ 307/
733-2297) or **Jackson Hole Mountain Guides** (☎ 307/733-4979), two Jackson-
based climbing outfitters that offer guided climbs of Devils Tower for all ability levels.
Especially popular is the four-pitch Durrance Route.

Nearby cities worth an extra look are **Sundance,** and the Black Hills gateway
communities of **Upton, Osage,** and **Newcastle.** The Keyhole Reservoir provides the
area with outstanding water-based recreation. Contact the Black Hills National
Forest, P.O. Box 680, Sundance, WY 82729 (☎ 307/283-1361) for information on
local forest service trails and campsites.

6 Casper

Wyoming's second largest city has flourished over the years because of its massive oil
reserves, but also because of its location at the point of convergence for several
prominent Western trails—the Oregon, the California, and the Mormon, among
others. Largely an unattractive industrial city today, Casper's history evolved during
the westward expansion of the 1800s, and can be interpreted through the visibly
rutted trails that run throughout the region. Its economy once thrived on vast reserves
of oil and uranium. While it's no longer considered the "energy hub of the Rockies,"
Casper continues to busy itself with mineral exploration and production, manufacturing, and tourism.

ESSENTIALS

GETTING THERE   Casper's **Natrona County Airport,** 8500 Airport Parkway
(☎ 307/472-6688), 10 miles northwest of Casper on U.S. Hwy. 20-26, provides
daily service on **Sky West** (☎ 800/453-9417) from Salt Lake City, and **Mesa
Airlines** (☎ 800/241-6522) from Denver.

Powder River Transportation (☎ 307/266-1094 or 800/442-3682) provides
limited local intrastate **Greyhound** bus service from Gillette, Douglas, Wheatland,
and Cheyenne.

To reach Casper from Sheridan, drive 153 miles south on I-25. From Cheyenne,
take I-25 north for 180 miles. From Jackson, take U.S Hwy. 191 to the Moran
Junction, then drive 255 miles east on Hwy. 26/287. For road and travel information, call 307/237-8411 or 800/442-2565.

VISITOR INFORMATION   The **visitors center** in Casper is located at 500 N.
Center St. and is open from Memorial Day to Labor Day, Mon–Fri 8am–6pm, Sat–
Sun 10am–6pm; in spring, fall, and winter, Mon–Fri 8am–5pm. For printed information on this area, contact the **Casper Area Convention & Visitors Bureau,** P.O.
Box 399, Casper, WY 82602 (☎ 307/234-5311 or 800/852-1889). Wyoming's
statewide newspaper, the *Casper Star-Tribune,* also happens to be one of the West's
only online newspapers; savvy surfers can find it at http://www.trib.com.

GETTING AROUND   Rent a car with **Avis** (☎ 800/331-1212), **Budget** (☎ 800/
527-0700), or **Hertz** (☎ 800/654-3131) at the airport. **RC Cab** (☎ 307/235-5203)
and **Rapid Cab** (☎ 307/235-1903) both provide taxi service; there is no city bus
in Casper.

ORGANIZED TOURS

"Your Ride" Tours (☎ 307/577-1226) provides customized sightseeing tours across
the state year-round. Participants choose their preferred mode of transportation.
Although the company fleet consists mainly of charter buses and vans, past clients
have requested horse-drawn wagons and mountain bikes. Customized educational

tours—the ecology of Yellowstone or the history of the Oregon Trail, for example—
are specialties. Reservations are required two to six months in advance, depending on
the mode of transportation desired.

GETTING OUTSIDE

Over 75% of the world's pronghorn antelope live within a 150-mile radius of Casper,
making the area an ideal spot for **wildlife-watching.** Look for mule deer, fox, sage
grouse, moose, bighorn sheep, wild birds, and elk in addition to the lively and
graceful antelope near Hells' Half Acre, located midway between Shoshoni and
Casper on U.S. Hwy. 20-26.

Casper Mountain is a popular spot for mountain biking and hiking in summer and
skiing and other winter sports in the colder months. **Edness Kimball Wilkins State
Park** is a nice day-use park just 6 miles east of Casper off I-25. Its walking path,
canoe launch, picnic tables, and river access appeal to a variety of interests.

BIKING

The best mountain biking trails are on **Casper Mountain,** but you'll have to bring
your own bike to enjoy them as nobody in town rents bikes. Check with the folks
at **Backcountry Mountain Works,** 4120 S. Poplar at Sunrise Center (☎ 307/234-
5330) or **Mountain Sports,** 543 S. Center (☎ 800/426-1136) for where to pick up
the best trails. **"Your Ride" Tours** (☎ 307/577-1226) and **Over the Hill Mountain Bike Tours** (☎ 307/237-5106 or 234-3757) can help you plan an extreme
outing or a leisurely ride.

FISHING

For the local skinny on where to fish, hook up with Wyoming's **Choice River
Runners** at 513 N. Lennox (☎ 307/234-3870) for guided trips on local rivers. For
equipment, flies, and rod building, locals recommend **Dean's Sporting Goods,**
260 S. Center (☎ 307/234-2788) and **Platte River Flyshop,** 7400 Alcova Hwy 200
(☎ 307/237-5997).

GOLF

The Municipal Golf Course, south of downtown on Casper Mountain Rd. (☎ 307/
234-1037) is the city's only public course and has 18 holes. The **Casper Country
Club,** 4149 E. Country Club Rd. (☎ 307/265-0767), and **Paradise Valley Golf
Club,** 70 Magnolia (☎ 307/237-3673), are both private 18-hole courses; call them
for eligibility requirements. Both have reciprocal privileges with other U.S. country
clubs.

HIKING

Day hikers should head over to Casper Mountain for the area's best trails. The
mountain's Braille Trail is a great way for visually impaired visitors to enjoy the
beauty of Beartrap Meadow, with interpretive Braille markers describing the area's
ecology. The **Casper Area Convention and Visitors Bureau** (☎ 307/234-5311 or
800/852-1889) can assist you with maps detailing this and other hiking trails on the
mountain.

SKIING

Hogadon Ski Area (☎ 307/235-8499) is situated atop Casper Mountain and is the
closest downhill ski area, although it pales in comparison to other resorts in the state.
Two double chairs and a Poma lift cover its 60 acres of groomed trails with on-site
equipment rentals available through **Mountain Sports** (☎ 800/426-1136).

There is also a ski school. A series of cross-country ski trails (tickets $4 per person) are groomed for skating and track skiing. The ski area generally opens around the first of December and closes sometime in April. Lift tickets are $20 for adults, $17 for students, and $14 for children. Call for information on seasonal discounts.

SNOWMOBILING

There are over 60 miles of groomed snowmobile trails on and around Casper Mountain. The **Medicine Bow National Forest,** 2468 Jackson St., Laramie, WY 82070-6535 (☎ 307/745-8971) will gladly assist you in planning a local outing on maintained forest service trails.

WATERSPORTS

The local spots for wet summer fun are **Alcova and Pathfinder Reservoirs,** where you can sail, fish, jet-ski, or windsurf. These major recreational areas of the North Platte, formed as a result of the construction of dams by the same names, are located 30 miles southwest of Casper on WYO 220. Rental boats are available at **Alcova Lakeside Marina** (☎ 307/472-6666).

WHITEWATER RAFTING

For watered-down whitewater junkets along the North Platte, call **AJ Outfitters** (☎ 307/473-1196), **RNR** (☎ 307/235-8017), or **Wyoming's Choice** (☎ 307/234-3870). **Alcova** (☎ 307/472-6666) and **Pathfinder** (☎ 307/267-1800) marinas can set you up with a pontoon for a relaxing boat-float.

WHAT TO SEE & DO

Fort Caspar Museum and Historic Site
4001 Fort Caspar Rd. ☎ **307/235-8462.** Free admission. Museum open year-round, Mon–Fri 8am–5pm, Sun 1–4pm; historic site open May through September.

The story behind this historic site encapsulates much of the history of the West during the turbulent 1800s, when land was being settled. Built from the remnants of Louis Guinard's Platte Bridge, which was constructed in 1859 to aid travelers in crossing the dangerous Platte, the fort was aptly named Platte Bridge Station. After a skirmish with the united tribes of Sioux and Cheyenne in the 1860s, in which a valiant Caspar Collins died defending the fort, the site was renamed in honor of him. A few years later, it was burned by the Sioux and now the site is marked with a collection of reconstructed fort buildings that illustrate the cultural and natural history of central Wyoming. Although visitors may tour the site and interpretive center at any time during the year, the actual buildings are only open from May through September. During the summer there are living history festivals and lectures. *A footnote:* Casper is actually named after Caspar Collins as well. But it's the city, not the fort, whose name is misspelled. When a telegraph operator sent word back East of Collins' courageousness, the operator typed a dot rather than a dot-dash when spelling the lieutenant's name and Caspar became Casper.

✪ Nicolaysen Art Museum
400 E. Collins Dr. (Collins and Kimball). ☎ **307/235-5247.** Admission $2 adults, $1 children 2–16. 10% discount for groups of 10 or more. Tues, Wed, Fri–Sun 10am–5pm, Thurs 10am–8pm; 1st and 3rd Thurs of every month free admission between 4–8pm.

This first-class facility is somewhat unique, not so much for its collections, but for its attempts to coax the artist out of each person who visits. Their Discovery Center enhances current exhibits by encouraging individuals to tap into their own creativity through workshops and hands-on experimentation with various art materials. There are traveling exhibits from world-famous museums as well as permanent works by local artists. Recent exhibits have included *Gerry Spence Photographs* (a collection of Wyoming landscapes and places photographed by the famed Wyoming attorney) and *Nineteenth Century Mexican Tin Retablos* (religious folk paintings on loan from New Mexico State University). Lectures, slide shows, films, tours, and concerts also aid in increasing an appreciation for art, regardless of the medium, among its visitors. Just look for the big red building.

Tate Mineralogical Museum

Tate Earth Science Center, Casper Mountain Rd. ☎ **307/268-2447.** Free admission. Mon–Fri 9am–5pm, Sat 10am–3pm.

Located in Tate Earth Science Center at Casper College, this museum brings prehistory into the world of modems and e-mail. Although the museum houses an extensive collection of jade and other natural materials found in and around Casper, the real treats here are actual dinosaur excavations from the Natrona County area. An ongoing paleontological work viewing area enables kids to see actual dinosaur fossils. Throughout the year there are various free programs, aimed at kids aged 6–14, that feature lectures from visiting paleontologists, archaeologists, or geologists.

Central Wyoming Fair and Rodeo

1700 Fairgrounds Rd. ☎ **307/235-5775.** Admission $6 gate and rodeo, $2 gate only, box and chute seats $12–$15, badge $25 (gate and rodeo grandstand for the week). Mid-July.

Casper draws its largest crowds during this five-day rodeo held each year in mid-July. A seven-day carnival of midway madness and hundreds of exhibits—from incredible home-baked goodies to 4-H prize winning heifers—round out the festivities.

Casper Planetarium

904 N. Poplar. ☎ **307/577-0310.** Admission $2 person, $5 family. Two showings daily from Memorial Day to Labor Day at 7pm and 8pm; Thurs 8pm during school year.

Travel through space at the Casper Planetarium for a unique look at the world of the stars. There are public showings throughout the year and summer programs every night from June through August. This is one of only two planetariums in the state.

✪ Wagon Rides

Historic Trails Expeditions, P.O. Box 428, Mills, WY 82644. ☎ **307/266-4868.**

Re-create a part of history by traveling the same routes taken by those who settled West by horse and covered wagon on one of the many trail rides offered by Historic Trails Expeditions. Trips range in length from three hours to six days and include a morning historic wagon train excursion to nearby Fort Caspar via the Oregon, California, and Mormon trails, as well as a six-day Warrior Trail Ride through the trails and canyons of the Sioux and Cheyenne.

Historic Trails Expeditions also offers a weeklong Wild West Cattle Drive, an Outlaw Trail Expedition to the Hole-in-the-Wall, a two-day re-creation of the Battle of Red Butte, and a Pony Express Ride. There are Oregon Trail rides of various lengths, but none as long as the one Carter himself took during the summer of 1993: He and his four daughters traveled the trail for six months, covering 2,600 miles by wagon. Participants sleep in tepees or tents and may be required to assist in preparing meals and tending to the horses. Travel is by horse or Conestoga wagon. Although dates are tentative and subject to change, most trips are scheduled for June through mid-September and advance reservations are required at least six months in advance.

WHERE TO STAY

Casper Hilton Inn

I-25 and N. Poplar, Casper, WY 82602. ☎ **307/266-6000** or 800/HILTONS. 229 rms. A/C TV TEL. $60–$70 double. AE, DC, DISC, MC, V.

Don't expect too much from this Hilton property at first sight. Though the rooms are adequate, you'll choose this hotel for its name, not its looks. The dingy white building just off I-25 isn't so much out of place in this industrial part of town as the Hilton's trademark *H* on the side is. An indoor pool, Jacuzzi, gift shop, and hair salon make up for the less-than-appealing location, and proximity to the interstate makes getting downtown fast and convenient. A restaurant, lounge, and recreation center round out the property's amenities.

✪ Holiday Inn

300 W. F St., Casper, WY 82602. ☎ **307/235-2531** or 800/HOLIDAY. 200 rms, 6 suites. A/C TV TEL. $65–$75 double, $150 suites. AE, DC, DISC, MC, V.

This Holiday Inn property is by far the nicest lodging in town. Recently renovated rooms and a new indoor pool area called a Holidome have improved its looks and value dramatically, but it's friendly service and an attention to detail that set it apart. The Holidome area features an indoor pool surrounded by foliage and skylights that will have you believing you're outside. A sauna, weight room, and Jacuzzi are nearby, as is a recreation center with a pool table, Ping-Pong table, and a basketball court. If that's not enough to keep the kids occupied, a game library is available for over-night check-outs. First floor rooms convenient to the Holidome are a little more expensive but a lot noisier; your money would be better spent on one of the two Jacuzzi suites far from this bustling center of activity. Located just past the interstate, the Holiday Inn is convenient to downtown Casper.

✪ Hotel Higgins

416 West Birch St., Glenrock, WY 82637. ☎ **307/436-9212** or 800/458-0144. 4 rms, 2 suites, each with private bath. $50 single, $60 double, $55–$70 suites. All rates include full breakfast. MC, V.

Built by area oil tycoon John Higgins in 1916, the Hotel Higgins is located in Glenrock, a small town 24 miles east of Casper. Listed on the National Register of Historic Places, the inn's exterior vinyl siding belies the treasures found within: ornate mahogany and oak woodwork with distinctive decorative touches that include alabaster chandeliers, beveled glass doors, and terrazzo tile floors. Each of the six guest rooms are decorated with old-fashioned charm. Chenille bedspreads and antique cu-rios are reminders of the guest inn's grander days. The excellent Paisley Shawl restaurant occupies the former ballroom and is one of the best places to eat near Casper (see "Where to Eat" below).

Royal Inn

440 E. A St., Casper, WY 82602. ☎ **307/234-3501** or 800/96-ROYAL. 40 rms, 3 kitchenettes. A/C TV TEL. Standard room $30–35 double, room with kitchenette $35–$45 double. AE, DISC, MC, V.

The Royal Inn is Casper's budget alternative to the Hilton. Located downtown off Center St. on E. A St., the Royal is a 20-year-old hotel with two levels. Upstairs rooms are $3 cheaper than their downstairs counterparts, which come with a cable TV with HBO, a microwave, and a mini-refrigerator. The only drawback to this lodging is the outdoor pool: it isn't heated. A definite plus is the complimentary air-port shuttle; cars can be rented at the hotel.

CAMPING

The Natrona County Parks Department maintains five campgrounds in the Casper area, including **Alcova Lake, Pathfinder Lake, Gray Reef Reservoir, Beartrap Meadow,** and **Casper Mountain.** All are open from April through mid-October and have tent and RV sites for a $5 fee. The Alcova, Pathfinder, and Gray Reef campgrounds are each roughly 30 miles west of downtown; Beartrap Meadow and Casper Mountain are both 7 miles south of town. For specific directions or additional information, contact the **Parks Department** at 307/234-6821. The **Fort Caspar Campground,** 4205 Fort Caspar Rd. (☎ 307/234-3260), is situated near the North Platte River and historic Fort Caspar with tent and RV sites available year-round for $10 and $15, respectively. The **Casper KOA,** 2800 E. Yellowstone (☎ 800/423-5155), is open all year with $11 tent sites and full RV hookups for $16. The Bureau of Land Management has two campgrounds each approximately 9 miles south of Casper on Muddy Mountain: **Lodgepole** and **Rim.** Both of these are open from mid-June through October with tent sites for $4. Contact the BLM at 307/261-7600 for specific directions.

WHERE TO EAT

Armour's

3422 Energy Lane. ☎ **307/235-3000.** Reservations recommended. Main dinner courses $10–$20. AE, DISC, MC, V. Sun–Thur 5–9pm, Fri–Sat 5–10pm. AMERICAN.

Blackened beef and chicken entrées are the local specialties at this Casper eatery, one of the city's larger restaurants with seating for more than 100 diners. The menu features typical beef and seafood entrées—prime rib, scampi alfredo—along with a decent wine list.

El Jarros

500 W. F St. ☎ **307/577-0538.** Lunch $4–$7; main dinner courses $5–$10. MC, V. Mon–Sat lunch 11am–2pm, dinner 5–9pm. MEXICAN.

This is the most popular of Casper's Mexican restaurants. Located downtown, El Jarros consistently packs in crowds for daily specials that are the best value in town. Don't load up on chips and salsa: Although the entrées are mostly mediocre, the sopapillas are a tasty way to finish up a satisfying meal and come in large portions.

✪The Paisley Shawl

Hotel Higgins, Glenrock. ☎ **800/458-0144.** Reservations recommended on weekends. Lunch $3–$9; main dinner courses $12–$25. DISC, MC, V. Lunch 11:30am–1:30pm, dinner 6–9:30pm, daily from June through August; Tues–Sat the rest of the year. CONTINENTAL.

Only 24 miles separate Casper from the smaller town of Glenrock and the Paisley Shawl, the area's best fine dining establishment. Set inside the grand Hotel Higgins, the Paisley Shawl is the dining complement to an unbeatable guest inn/restaurant combination. Specialties include shrimp scampi, veal Florentine, and the ever-popular Paisley Shawl chicken breast, lauded by locals and *Bon Appetit.* The restaurant is expansive, with seating for 60 in an atmosphere of sheer indulgence. There aren't many restaurants in Wyoming that make you feel as if you're indulging yourself by dining there. This is one of them. A full gourmet breakfast is served to overnight guests of the inn, and the restaurant is not open to the public until lunchtime.

CASPER AFTER DARK

The **Wyoming Symphony Orchestra,** 511 E. 2nd St., is based in Casper and performs throughout the year. Call 307/266-1478 for a current schedule of upcoming performances.

Collegiate theater is staged at the Gertrude Krampert Theatre at Casper College (☎ 307/268-2365) and the **Stage III Community Theatre** (☎ 307/234-0946) features the area's amateur thespians. Call for dates and times of productions.

Call 307/235-8441 to find out what's happening at the **Casper Events Center,** the city's largest venue for concerts and cultural events. Recent headline acts have included Reba McIntire, Brooks and Dunn, and Pearl Jam, as well as Disney on Ice, the annual PRCA Season Finals Rodeo, and Phantom of the Opera.

7 Also Worth a Look: Ft. Laramie National Historic Site

This fort, situated on the south bank of the North Platte River near its confluence with the Laramie River 123 miles from Casper, played an important part during the settlement of the West, both for emigrants and Native Americans alike. Originally established to serve the needs of travelers along the Oregon, Mormon, and California Trails, the stockaded fort later became an important military post and the site at which the Treaty of 1868 was signed. The treaty—which was shortly thereafter broken—assured the Sioux rights to the Black Hills and Powder River country "as long as the grass shall grow and the buffalo shall roam." The fort was designated a national historic site by Franklin Roosevelt in 1938 and visitors today can ramble through many of the site's 22 original structures.

Stop by the visitor center before touring the grounds for an in-depth look at life at the fort. From mid-May through mid-September, it is open daily 8am–7pm and daily from 8am–4:30pm the rest of the year. The visitor center screens videos about the fort and its role in the settlement of the West, and has an extensive collection of historic photographs. A gift shop sells a wide selection of Western-theme books and gift items. Pick up a copy of the self-guiding tour of the fort's historic buildings before you leave.

Some of the more notable (and restored) buildings you'll see are the **cavalry barracks,** where dozens of soldiers slept, crowded into a single room; **Old Bedlam,** the post's headquarters, which later served as housing for officers, bachelors and married couples alike; the **guardhouse,** a stone structure that housed the fort's prisoners; and the **bakery,** where the freshest component of the soldiers' daily meals was baked.

You can sample this bread along with a cup of cider or root beer during the fort's **living history programs.** Each summer, from June to mid-August, employees dress in period costumes, wandering around the fort and answering any questions visitors may have. On any given day, you may see a laundress, a baker, or cavalryman. But by far the most eagerly anticipated Fort Laramie event is its **Old-Fashioned Fourth of July celebration.** Past festivals have included a traveling medicine show, cannon salutes, a baseball game as it would have been played in 1886, and an authentic fashion show. And if you don't mind doing a little homework, bone up on what would have been included in an 1880s picnic lunch, and enter the historic picnic lunch competition.

Before leaving the fort, consider driving to the **Old Bedlam Ruts** (ask for a map from the visitor center), two miles northwest of the fort. The bumpy gravel road allows you to view the rutted trail marks left by the wagon trains of early Western settlers. Look for Laramie Peak and the grave of Mary Homsley, one of the many who died along the trail.

To get there, take I-90 south for 93 miles to exit 92. From here, drive east for 28 miles to the town of Ft. Laramie, then 2 miles south over the N. Platte River to the site. For more information, contact **Fort Laramie National Historic Site,** National Park Service, P.O. Box 218, Fort Laramie, WY 82212 (☎ 307/837-2221).

Southern Wyoming

15

Crossing southern Wyoming, you might think that the settlers who originally traversed this seemingly interminable stretch of prairie hardly tackled impressive terrain. Few mountains, plenty of water— what's the big deal? Of course, it's easy to reach this conclusion while ensconced in the air-conditioned comfort of a car whizzing along the 400 miles of interstate this region comprises in under eight hours. But if you get out of a car here when the mid-summer sun heats these plains to sweltering temperatures, or during the mid-winter when wind-chill temperatures can be measured in degrees above *absolute* zero, southern Wyoming doesn't seem particularly well suited for cross-country migration. Nevertheless, this part of Wyoming saw more travelers in the mid-1800s than any other part of the continental United States when more than 400,000 people used the Oregon and Overland Trails to travel from the Midwest to the Pacific Northwest, and points in between.

One hundred years later, the eastern part of southern Wyoming is anchored by Cheyenne, the state capital. Situated on Crow Creek, Cheyenne is the commercial hub for the state's cattle- and sheep-raising industries. And though the age-old occupations of farming and herding cattle are ingrained into the souls of the residents who live here, petroleum refineries and fertilizer and chemical plants are just as important to the local economy these days.

Wyomingans work hard, but they also play hard, and the one sport all of southern Wyoming embraces wholeheartedly, passionately, and unconditionally is the rodeo. Sure, in Laramie, the University of Wyoming's NCAA Division I sports teams enjoy a certain amount of support, especially when they garner national recognition, but nothing can take the place of the Cheyenne Frontier Days rodeo that takes place every summer. People from all over the country come to celebrate it because it's the biggest outdoor rodeo in the world.

In the central part of this region, the plains that host the rodeo give way to the spectacular Medicine Bow range, rising unexpectedly like a phoenix emerging from the southern Wyoming desert. Here, the summits soar above 10,000 feet (Medicine Bow Peak is an astounding 12,013 ft.) and aspen and pine tree–lined mountainsides transform the barren wasteland from above.

On the western side of the region, things return to earth. Rock Springs, a town of 20,000, was one of the unfortunate towns to be left virtually empty by the energy bust of the 1980s. Though it has yet to rebound, it still has a few delightful surprises up its sleeve—from its fine arts center that displays early paintings by Grandma Moses and Norman Rockwell to its proximity to the hauntingly beautiful natural statues of rock in the nearby Vedauwoo Recreation Area, and the yawning red canyon of the Flaming Gorge National Recreation Area that straddles the Utah border.

1   Scenic Drives

Though I-80 runs the length of southern Wyoming, it's not the most spectacular route through the region. It is, however, convenient, and if you drive it, you'll notice the inordinate number of 18-wheelers that will become your companions. The road runs a relatively straight course through the Laramie Plains region and parallels the historic Overland Trail as well as the route of the first transcontinental railroad.

The most concrete evidence of the Overland Trail can be found in the community of Arlington, 41 miles west of Laramie off exit 272. There you'll find the remnants of an old stage station used by travelers along the trail and, barely visible through the trees, one of Wyoming's oldest standing structures, an old log cabin built in the mid-1800s.

The monotonous straightaways of southern Wyoming's roads can be tiresome. If you stick to the interstate, you'll be driving the plains, which creep along. If you plan to spend any time at all in this region, driving will become a way of life.

There are really only two roads that offer anything in the way of scenery (and varied topography). Located in the central part of this region just west of Laramie, they are Wyoming State Highways 130 and 230, which offer views of the Medicine Bow Mountains south of the interstate.

DRIVING TOUR #1: THE SNOWY RANGE SCENIC BYWAY— FROM LARAMIE TO SARATOGA

Despite the cozy-sounding name, the Snowy Range Scenic Byway (Wyoming State Highway 130) can be a rather terrifying ride—at least for acrophobics. It's a twisting road that traverses high mountain passes in the Medicine Bow range, a series of peaks in southcentral Wyoming and northern Colorado known to Wyoming natives as the Snowy Range, hence the road's name.

What's so amazing about the road is the altitude it reaches at its highest point, Snowy Range Pass (just west of Centennial, Wyoming). While the pass doesn't have the tallest elevation in the Northern Rockies (the Beartooth Pass in the northwestern part of the state holds this distinction at 10,947 feet), it comes in a close second at 10,847 feet. Like the Beartooth National Scenic Byway, the Snowy range is so high that early snowfalls force the state to close it in the fall.

You can expect to see snow, sometimes lots of it, year-round. There's also a wealth of pine trees in the Medicine Bow National Forest, but clear-cutting practices have created a few eyesores along the way. Browns Peak, Sugarloaf Mountain, and Medicine Bow Peak are all visible from the roadside. Medicine Bow Peak is perhaps the most notable since, at 12,013 feet, it is the highest peak in the range. The most spectacular view from the road is of Lake Marie (you'll know it when you see it). The road runs along the lake providing views of the looming granite peaks reflected in the water.

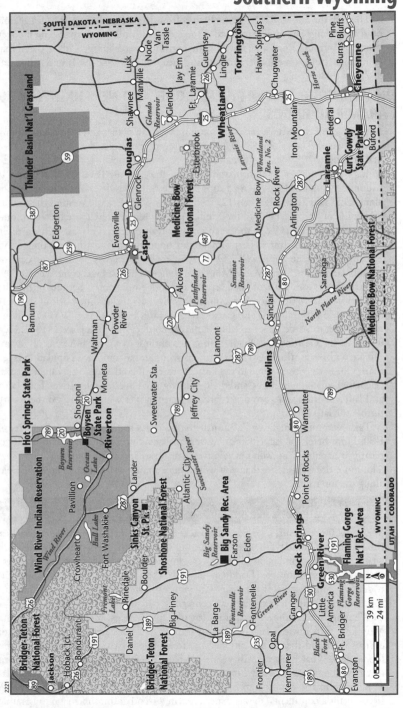

To reach the Snowy Range Scenic Byway from Laramie, take exit 311 off I-80 and head west along Snowy Range Road. Due to the altitude of the roads you'll cover, contact **Wyoming Road and Travel Information** services for regularly updated road conditions. In Laramie and its surrounding area, call 307/742-8981; in Rawlins, call 307/324-9966.

DRIVING TOUR #2: THE RIVERS ROAD AND NEW HIGHWAY 70: LARAMIE TO BAGGS

Another scenic drive travelers in the Laramie area can take is this tour from Laramie to the town of Baggs along WYO 230 and a recently completed stretch of Wyoming State Highway 70. Wyoming State Highway 230 (also known as "The Rivers Road") winds its way southwest from Laramie along the Laramie River until the town of Mountain Home, where the road dips south into Colorado. Here it makes a loop along Colorado State Highways 127 and 125 for 18 miles, and reenters the state of Wyoming on the other side of the Medicine Bow Range. The route then continues northwest along WYO 230 to the town of Encampment. This last portion offers plenty of beautiful river scenery and lots of opportunities for trout fishing. From Encampment, take the new WYO 70 west to Baggs across 58 miles of Carbon County land in the Sierra Madre Mountain Range. The road was completed in 1994 and the views from it are of filled aspens and lodge pole pines. Because of the altitude, views can stretch for miles around this virtually uninhabited belt of southern Wyoming. But the altitude also causes road closures in the winter. WYO 70 climbs to 9,955 feet to Battle Pass, named for a nearby conflict that took place in 1841. Here it crosses the Continental Divide before descending to the small towns of Savery, Dixon, and Baggs, three agricultural towns whose total combined population is less than 500. Early settlers came to the area in search of gold and silver. Butch Cassidy celebrated robberies in Baggs, and the quick-triggered livestock detectives Tom Horn and Bill Meldrum were two other famous personalities who frequented these parts during the late 1800s.

Take Wyoming Highway 789 north for 51 miles to Creston Junction to rejoin I-80. From here, you can either drive west to Rock Springs and the Utah border or return to Laramie. You won't have traveled as far as you think, but you'll have seen a lot more along this route than you would have staring at the back of an 18-wheeler along the interstate.

2　Cheyenne

With 50,000 residents, Cheyenne sits tucked into the state's southeast corner near the Idaho and Nebraska borders. Wyoming's largest city, it comes alive each July when cowboy hats and boots fill the streets, the hotels, the restaurants, and of course, the rodeo grounds, for the "Daddy of 'em All," the annual Cheyenne Frontier Days rodeo. At other times of the year, Cheyenne presides as the state's capital and southeastern Wyoming's agricultural center.

What separates Cheyenne from a lot of capital cities, most notably, Helena, Montana, is its obvious lack of cultural trappings. There aren't espresso stands on every corner and there aren't any quaint streets filled with boutiques and gourmet food stores. What you see in Cheyenne is what you get. While there are places to eat in Cheyenne, there's not anything even remotely resembling a restaurant scene: It's as if those in the position to establish one have decided there's no use trying. If you want a continental dining experience in a trendy atmosphere, go to Laramie. If you want meat and potatoes, Cheyenne satisfies.

There's plenty to see and do in Cheyenne if you're interested in state legislative buildings, old governor's mansions, or rodeos (if you happen to be passing through in July). But those who choose to visit during Frontier Days, beware: That's when a $35 hotel room goes for $150 a night.

ESSENTIALS

GETTING THERE   The **Cheyenne Municipal Airport** is on E. 8th Ave., off Yellowstone Rd. **United Express** (☎ 307/635-6623 or 800/241-6522) has daily flights from Denver, but most people choose to fly directly in and out of **Denver International Airport** (☎ 800/247-2336), 101 miles south of Cheyenne in Colorado on I-25, and rent a car to drive into Wyoming from there.

The bus terminal for **Greyhound** (☎ 307/634-7744) and **Powder River Transportation** (☎ 307/635-1327) is at 120 N. Greeley Hwy. Buses arrive and depart for Denver and Billings, Montana, on a regular basis.

Driving to Cheyenne is relatively simple from any direction. I-80 runs east and west through town and intersects with I-25, which runs north and south through town. To get to Cheyenne from **Casper,** take I-25 south for 180 miles. From **Rock Springs** in the southwest part of the state, take I-80 east for 258 miles.

VISITOR INFORMATION   Virtually any question you have about your Wyoming vacation can be answered at the **Wyoming Information Center** at Wyoming Division of Tourism, I-25 at College Drive. If they don't have what you're looking for, they can get it for you. The **Cheyenne Area Convention and Visitors Bureau** at 309 W. Lincolnway, P.O. Box 765, Cheyenne WY 82003 (☎ 307/778-3133 or 800/426-5009 outside Wyoming), has a variety of local maps and brochures on what to see and do in the Cheyenne area.

GETTING AROUND   **Dollar** (☎ 307/632-2422 or 800/800-4000) and **Hertz** (☎ 307/634-2131 or 800/654-3131) both maintain counters at the Cheyenne airport. Should you need a taxi, **Yellow Cab** can be reached at 307/635-5555. There is no taxi stand at the airport.

✪ CHEYENNE FRONTIER DAYS

The Cheyenne Frontier Days celebration, which runs for two weeks in late July each year, has been bringing folks from all over the world to see rodeos, parades, and other celebrations of the Western lifestyle since 1897.

Teddy Roosevelt once headed the Frontier Days parade, and another year Buffalo Bill brought his famous show to town. It has survived the Great Depression, two world wars, and thrived in years when even major league baseball bailed out. Made up of cowboys who work hard in a dangerous sport for little or no pay, the rodeo is definitely worth a look if you've never seen it. Beware: Everything during Frontier Days is expensive, and parking can be a challenge, at best. But if you've made plans well in advance and realize just how crowded Cheyenne can get, Frontier Days can be a great Western experience.

Though the rodeo lasts for a full 10 days, picking and choosing activities carefully could save you a lot of time and money. Rodeo ticket prices range anywhere from $8 to $17 per person and nightly shows featuring popular country music acts cost $14 to $18. But you can get a discount by ordering a one-day package for $26 per person. It includes a ticket to the afternoon's rodeo and the evening concert at less than what you'd pay if you purchased your tickets separately. It's only good between Monday and Thursday, and you need to order it six months in advance. Parking is provided at Frontier Park for $4 per vehicle, assuming you can get a spot. If you plan on seeing the rodeo at all during the weekend, you'd better get to the park several hours before the first rider is scheduled to come out of the chute. Shuttle parking is also available and makes much more sense. It's a lot less expensive and it's much easier to park at the area set up for shuttle parking than at the actual rodeo grounds. The shuttle is $3 round-trip per car load. In addition, during Frontier Days the city runs a special bus service to the park from downtown Cheyenne that also stops at nearby campgrounds. **Contact the Cheyenne Area Convention and Visitors Bureau** (☎ 307/778-3133) for bus stop locations and scheduled pickups.

Contact the **Cheyenne Frontier Days Committee** for brochures, ticket forms, and information on all shows and activities during upcoming Frontier Days celebrations. Cheyenne Frontier Days, P.O. Box 2477, Cheyenne, WY 82003-2477 (☎ 307/778-7222 or 800/227-6336).

The Parade
Starts at Capitol Ave. and 24th Street, runs down Capitol Ave. to 16th Ave., and up Carey Ave. to the finish at Carey Ave. and 24th St. Saturday, Tuesday, and Thursday, commencing at 9:30am during Frontier Days. Free.

With the exception of Buffalo Bill's somewhat tame walk through the streets of Cheyenne in 1898 and the rather docile march led by Teddy Roosevelt in 1910, the pageantry of Cheyenne's Frontier Days Parade was similar to that of a stagecoach holdup in its early days. From its start in 1897, guns blazed as cowboys rode through the streets with little regard to form or style. In 1925 things made a turn toward civility when the "Evolution of Transportation" theme was introduced. Today, many horse-drawn vehicles make their way through the streets of Cheyenne as part of the Old-Time Carriage section of the parade. In addition to the carriages and antique cars, marching bands, local clubs, and Plains Indians' groups march. It ain't Mardi Gras, but it's definitely a notch or two above your average homecoming parade. Anywhere along the parade route is fine for viewing, but you'll want to get into position 45 minutes before the start for a place curbside.

The Pancake Breakfast
Cheyenne City Center parking lot, corner of Lincolnway and Carey. Mon, Wed, Fri 7–9am during Frontier Days. Free.

Each year this event becomes increasingly popular. On Monday, Wednesday, and Friday from 7 to 9am, a cement mixer moves in to mix enough pancake batter to cook more than 100,000 flapjacks for 30,000 people. Started in 1952, these free breakfasts have grown steadily over the years with the annual help of the local Kiwanis Club and Boy and Girl Scout troops. The breakfasts are held downtown at the Cheyenne City Center parking lot on the corner of Lincolnway and Carey.

The Rodeo
Frontier Park, exit 12 off I-80. ☎ **307/778-7222** or **800/227-6336**. Tickets $8–$17. Daily at 1:15pm during Cheyenne Frontier Days.

Every afternoon during Frontier Days, the grandstand at the rodeo grounds looks like a major college football stadium. Crowds pack the stadium around 1pm to get a look at the nation's best cowboys in bronc riding, steer wrestling, bull riding, and calf roping. Participants from across the United States compete for nearly a half-million dollars in prize money. Daily tickets start at $8 for end bleachers and run to $17 for 50-yard-line seats. After the rodeo each night, Frontier Days sponsors a country music concert. Past performers have included John Michael Montgomery and Pam Tillis. Concert tickets run from $14 to $18.

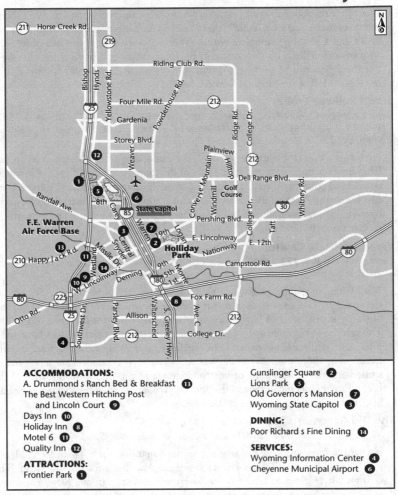

ACCOMMODATIONS:
A. Drummond s Ranch Bed & Breakfast **13**
The Best Western Hitching Post
   and Lincoln Court **9**
Days Inn **10**
Holiday Inn **8**
Motel 6 **11**
Quality Inn **12**

ATTRACTIONS:
Frontier Park **1**

Gunslinger Square **2**
Lions Park **5**
Old Governor s Mansion **7**
Wyoming State Capitol **3**

DINING:
Poor Richard s Fine Dining **14**

SERVICES:
Wyoming Information Center **4**
Cheyenne Municipal Airport **6**

SEEING THE SIGHTS

Frontier Days Old West Museum

Carey Ave., Frontier Park, Cheyenne, WY 82003. ☎ **307/778-7290**. Admission $4 adults, $3 children, $7 families. Mon–Fri 9am–5pm; Sat–Sun 11am–4pm (longer hours in summer and during Frontier Days).

Founded in 1978, this is a spin-off from the Frontier Days rodeo. The collection of carriages in the museum is worth the price of admission, but the history of the rodeo and the Cheyenne exhibit are also noteworthy. An hourlong video recaps the history of Cheyenne's most famous annual event.

Cheyenne Gunslingers

Gunslinger Square, 16th and Carey. ☎ **307/635-1028**. Free admission. Shows held nightly at 6pm, Saturdays at noon. During Frontier Days, the show runs twice daily at noon and 6pm.

From June through July every year, this nonprofit group puts on an Old West shoot-out downtown. The show, which takes place in Gunslinger Square, dramatizes a jail-break and a hanging, complete with a replica of a gallows, a sheriff's office, and cowboys in full dress. It's not necessarily the most accurate portrayal of the Old West, but these guys will be the first to admit it. This is a great place for families during the rodeos, full of stereotypical Western fun.

Street Railway Trolley

Departs from the Cheyenne Area Convention and Visitors Bureau, 309 W. Lincolnway. ☎ 307/778-3133. Tour prices adults $6.50, children $4. Summer, 2-hour tours at 10:30am and 2:30pm. Dec 15–30, special holiday tours at 6pm and 8pm.

No longer used as a mode of mass transit, the local trolley offers visitors a look around Cheyenne's historic areas as well as some of the more recent additions to the town's culture and economy. Every day throughout the summer, the Visitor's Bureau offers two-hour tours on the trolley at 10:30am and 2:30pm. In the winter, the trolley only operates during the holidays, but this is when it is at its untouristed best, riding quietly through the snow.

Wyoming State Capitol

Capitol Ave. ☎ 307/777-7220. Tours are given free of charge during the summer months, Mon–Fri 8am–5pm; Sat 9am–4pm.

With Cheyenne's flat topography, it's hard to miss the gold-leaf dome perched on Capitol Ave. Designed to look much like the capitol in Washington, D.C., this building in the heart of downtown was originally built for less than $200,000. Though the Wyoming capitol isn't architecturally spectacular, it does have some interesting attributes. For one, it hasn't undergone any major changes since its construction in 1886, when Wyoming was still a territory. Second, the inside is full of stuffed animals. Two statues of note outside are of the first woman justice of the peace, Esther Hobart Morris, and the Spirit of Wyoming, the wild bucking horse emblazoned on every license plate in the state.

The Old Governor's Mansion

300 E. 21st St. ☎ 307/777-7878. Free admission. Tues–Sat 9am–5pm.

It's hard to imagine a state building a governor's mansion for less than $35,000, but this structure, the governor's former residence, was built for just that sum. The Georgian-style structure served as the governor's residence from 1905–76 and over the years has housed more interesting personalities than it has accumulated lavish furnishings and worldly antiques. The building itself, with its four Corinthian columns, looks more like an old fraternity or sorority house in the south than a governor's mansion, but the video and tour provide a worthwhile look into the political past of Wyoming's governors.

SHOPPING

If you're in the market for ranchwear, Cheyenne has enough outfitters to transform your appearance instantly. Start off downtown at the **Wrangler,** 1518 Capitol Ave. What you don't find there you'll most likely discover at **Cheyenne Outfitters,** 210 W. 16th. For the rest of your needs, head over to the **Frontier Mall** along Dell Range Blvd. where stores include branches of **Foot Locker, Sears,** and **J.C. Penney**. There's also a sports bar where you can order a cold beer and get a bite to eat.

WHERE TO STAY
A HOTEL

Holiday Inn

204 W. Fox Farm Rd., Cheyenne, WY 82007. ☎ **307/638-4466** or 800/465-4329. 244 rms, 4 suites. A/C TV TEL. $49 double; $95 suites. AE, DC, DISC, MC, V.

Located just off I-80 on the south side of town (take exit 364 and make a left off S. Greeley to reach W. Fox Farm Road), this six-story Holiday Inn is Cheyenne's only hotel. A fairly typical Holiday Inn, it has more amenities than one can generally expect in Cheyenne: an indoor pool, a whirlpool, a sauna, a video game room, and an exercise room. John Q's Steakhouse is the restaurant on the premises and offers up typical chain restaurant food. For winter travelers, outlets for block heaters are available.

MOTELS

Best Western Hitching Post Inn and Lincoln Court

1700 W. Lincolnway, Cheyenne, WY 82001. ☎ **307/638-3301** or 307/638-3302 or 800/ 221-0125. 236 rms. A/C TV TEL. Best Western Hitching Post: May–Sept, $64 double; Oct–Apr, $90 double; during Frontier Days, $200 double. Lincoln Court: May–Sept, $31 double; Oct– Apr, $45 double; during Frontier Days, $140 double. AE, DC, DISC, MC, V.

These two adjoining properties are located along Cheyenne's motel strip and are under the same ownership. By far the larger of the two is the Best Western, with an indoor pool, three dining rooms, and better, newer rooms.

Lincoln Court is straight out of the fifties. Its rooms have been only casually updated with phone jacks and cable TV; there are no other amenities.

If you visit Cheyenne during Frontier Days and haven't reserved your lodging in advance, Lincoln Court may be where you'll have to stay since the Best Western, somewhat understandably, fills up faster.

Days Inn

2360 W. Lincolnway, Cheyenne, WY 82001. ☎ **307/778-8877** or 800/325-2525. 72 rms, 2 suites. A/C TV TEL. $52 double, $59 suite. AE, DC, DISC, MC, V.

Also located on the strip is the Days Inn, a comfortable motel with reasonable rates. If you plan to visit Cheyenne during Frontier Days, you must book at least two weeks in advance to get a room here. There's no pool, but there is a hot tub and a sauna. A suite for $7 more a night gets you a table and a couch, no more, no less. Free continental breakfast is served every morning and complimentary coffee is available 24 hours a day.

Motel 6

1735 Westland Rd., Cheyenne, WY 82001. ☎ **307/635-6806** or 800/466-8356. 108 rms. A/C TV TEL. $33 double. AE, DC, DISC, MC, V.

Located just off I-25, this Motel 6 offers a basic room at a cheap price. For a family in search of a room at the last minute, this place can be just the ticket. There's an outdoor swimming pool, but otherwise amenities are nonexistent. If you've got something a bit fancier in mind, head farther down Lincolnway to Days Inn and the Best Western Hitching Post.

Quality Inn

5401 Walker Rd., Cheyenne, WY 82001. ☎ **307/632-8901** or 800/876-8901. 105 rms. A/C TV TEL. $32–$44 double. AE, DC, DISC, MC, V.

Right off exit 12 and just a few blocks from the rodeo grounds, the Quality Inn is conveniently located for those planning to take in a rodeo during their stay. Travelers who roll into Cheyenne without reservations during Frontier Days may be alarmed to discover that room rates here can jump to over $100 a night. Located on the grounds is the Central Cafe and Lounge; there's a liquor store as well.

A BED-AND-BREAKFAST

✪ A. Drummond's Ranch Bed and Breakfast

399 Happy Jack Rd., Cheyenne/Laramie, WY 82007. ☎ **307/634-6042.** 4 rms. $65–$85 second-story room, $75–$100 garden room, $125–$150 carriage house room. All rates include breakfast. MC, V.

To give you an idea how special this place is, consider what happens in Cheyenne during Frontier Days. When other places are gouging tourists $150 for a $35 room, this remote mini-resort-style bed-and-breakfast charges only $25 extra for the best room in the house. And the owner, Taydie Drummond, feels guilty about it. She'd prefer to leave the prices as they are at other times of the year, but at $80 for a room with two beds, she doesn't want people to think this is a cheap motel. She needn't worry.

This four-room home was constructed in an earth berm to shield it from the wind. But wind or no wind, the hot tubs on the private deck of the Carriage House Loft and the deck of the Garden Room warm things up. The second-story rooms share a bath, and each has two beds. One of these rooms, aptly named Second Story View, looks out over Colorado's Rocky Mountain National Park, 75 miles away. Breakfast, which is included in the room rate, is a full meal, complete with fresh fruit. Throughout the day, snacks are available. Full lunches ($7 per person) and dinners ($15 per person) are served with advance notice. Located a mile and a half from Curt Gowdy State Park.

CAMPING

The **Greenway Trailer Park,** 3829 Greenway St. (☎ 307/634-6696), isn't exactly remote but does offer paved RV pads and cable TV hookups for $15. The biggest nearby campground is the **Restway Travel Park** off Whitney Rd., 2 miles east of Cheyenne (☎ 307/634-3811 or 800/443-2751). Here RV and tent campers alike will find a heated swimming pool, miniature golf, and a store stocked with basic supplies. The **Wyoming Campground** (there's a mobile home park here, too) is just 15 miles east of town at the Hillsdale exit (#377, off I-80). It has a swimming pool, laundry facilities, and a 24-hour convenience store. Hookups are $10.

WHERE TO EAT

Despite a great rodeo tradition and a colorful history, Cheyenne's culinary destiny looks bleak. It's not that there's a shortage of restaurants, just a limited supply of good ones.

The Albany

1506 Capitol Ave. ☎ **307/638-3507.** Lunch $3–$6; main dinner courses $8–$12. AE, DISC, DC, MC, V. Mon–Sat 11am–9pm, closed Sun. AMERICAN.

Though the locals seem to go crazy over this place, it's nothing to go crazy over. Around here it's considered fine dining, but the lunches are pretty basic, a cut above chain restaurants, and the dinner menu offers up prime rib, steaks, and the occasional chicken platter. The decor isn't any more exciting: historic black-and-white photos of the area. Its only redeeming quality is that it's the only place to eat downtown.

The Oregon Trail & the Overland Stage Route

Two of the most important routes in our nation's history run through the southern and central parts of Wyoming. Pioneers crossing the Oregon Trail endured great hardships in their crossing of the continent. Giving up their security and homes they set out for unknown lands in the Pacific Northwest that were said to be a veritable Eden. However, before they reached this Eden, they had to cross 2,000 miles of rugged country, and it was the last few miles near Baker City, Oregon, that were the hardest, since they were battling tremendous fatigue, sagebrush, and dust.

The first wagon train to complete the route was led by the Elijah White, a pioneer physician, who reached Oregon in 1842. In the early days of the trail, it took wagon trains six months to make the journey to Oregon, burdened by horrible equipment, illness, Indian attacks, and the near-constant threat of death. The route was as wide as the valleys over which the network of trails went, beginning in Missouri and cutting through Wyoming for a large portion, before reaching the Columbia River and the early terminus near Astoria, Oregon. In later years, travelers ended their journey in the Willamette Valley.

Perhaps the most famous Wyoming landmark is Independence Rock (now a state park 50 miles west of Casper). The rock served as a rest stop for travelers heading west and south along the trail. The names of more than 5,000 people who traveled along the Oregon Trail are etched into this massive rock.

The Overland Stage Route (which runs almost exactly parallel to I-80) was a rough road for stagecoaches and covered wagons heading west over the Laramie Plains that became popular after the Oregon Trail had been discredited amid rumors of Indian attacks. Folks heading west now undertook their western migration on a slightly more southern course near present-day Laramie. Stage stations were positioned along the route for weary travelers to stop, dine, and spend the night in some rather shabby accommodations.

Along Rock Creek in the small town of Arlington (west of Laramie, exit 272 off I-80) you can still see the remains of the old Rock Creek stage station that served as a relay point in the early 1860s. You can also visit the remnants of a partially hidden cabin from the same era.

The Medicine Bow Brewing Company

115 E. 17th St., ☎ **307/778–2739.** Lunch $3–$5; main dinner courses $4–$8. MC, V. Daily 11am–12am. AMERICAN.

This old-fashioned brick restaurant on 17th Street may seem like a somewhat fashionable brew pub, but the Louisiana backcountry has seeped into it like a swamp critter. At a glance the menu seems tame enough, then you start getting into the blackened side of things: blackened grouper and blackened catfish, for example. Still not interested? Stick around, as the chef so eloquently states, "We'll blacken damn near anything." Burgers, steaks, and broiled and fried seafood are other great complements to the brewpub's signature ales.

Poor Richard's Fine Dining

2233 Lincolnway ☎ **307/635-5114.** Lunch $4–$7; main dinner courses $6–$19. AE, DC, DISC, MC, V. Sun 5–10pm; Mon–Thurs 11am–2:30pm, 5–10pm; Fri–Sat 11am–2:30pm, 5–11pm. AMERICAN.

Poor Richard's decor goes a long way to summon up the spirit of Ben Franklin with tons of memorabilia bearing his likeness on the walls, but the fact is, by local standards, Poor Richard's is hardly for the budget-minded. The closest thing to fine dining in Cheyenne, its menu has numerous steak entreés, all served at sturdy oak tables. The clientele is a mixture of local politicians and tourists.

CHEYENNE AFTER DARK

Cheyenne's performing arts scene leaves much to be desired for a capital city, but every summer the **Little Theater Players** do their level best by performing well-known musicals and plays in the Atlas Theater at 211 W. 16th St. For shows, times, and ticket information, contact the Players at 307/635-0199. Recent performances have included *South Pacific* and *Oleanna*. The **Cheyenne Symphony Orchestra,** 1902 Thomes Ave., (☎ 307/778-8561) gives limited concert performances throughout the year.

Nightlife in Cheyenne can also be a mellow affair. During Frontier Days, however, the town comes alive with country music. Big stars usually headline at the fairgrounds, but local bands can be a treat, too. At the **Hitching Post Lounge** at 1700 Lincolnway, the same band, Ricky & the Redstreaks, has been playing rock 'n' roll covers during Frontier Days for the last 20 years. The **Mayflower,** 112 W. 17th, is a popular after-hours rodeo haunt as well.

3 Laramie

In the thick of the arid lands that plague southern Wyoming, Laramie sits on a high plateau just east of the Snowy Mountains and west of Cheyenne at an elevation of 7,165 feet.

Though the political capital is 40 miles to the east, Laramie is the capital of culture and erudition for Wyoming. It's home to the state's only university, public or private, and it's a place to get an espresso, buy a book, or take in a traveling troupe of performers. Unlike Jackson, which has a prefabricated feel designed to appeal to visitors, Laramie has an earnest charm it seems to have developed by accident. And Laramie has been this way for nearly a century. All along the downtown streets are attractive new, as well as second-hand, bookstores, and though Wild West bars are pervasive enough, they don't overwhelm Laramie's cultural bent. Wyoming's best planetarium is also located in town.

ESSENTIALS

GETTING THERE The **Laramie Regional Airport** or General Brees Field, 555 General Brees Rd. (☎ 307/742-4164), is situated west of town along WYO 130. It services daily flights on **United Express** (☎ 800/241-6522) from Denver.

The southern part of the state has reliable intrastate bus services. **Greyhound** (☎ 307/742-9663) offers east-west bus service that stops in Laramie at **Tumbleweed Express,** 4700 Bluebird Lane (☎ 307/721-7405). The bus stops at several Wyoming cities along I-80, including Rock Springs and Cheyenne.

The refurbished **Laramie Amtrak Depot** is at 1st Ave. The Pioneer line (Chicago–Seattle) stops here on Sunday, Tuesday, and Thursday. Call **Amtrak** (☎ 800/872-7245) for further information.

Laramie is situated 47 miles east of Cheyenne on I-80. The simplest route to Laramie from Casper is on WYO 220, which runs along the N. Platte River for 18 miles before joining with WYO 487. This highway winds for 71 miles down to

Medicine Bow, where it picks up U.S. 30/287. Head east from Medicine Bow for 55 miles to get to Laramie. From Rock Springs, Laramie is 211 miles west on I-80. From Moran Junction in Grand Teton National Park, take U.S. 287 south for 259 miles to Riverton and take I-80 east for 101 miles to Laramie. For information on road conditions in Laramie, call 307/742-8981.

VISITOR INFORMATION   The **Laramie Area Chamber of Commerce** (800 S. 3rd, 307/745-7339) provides brochures, city maps, and area maps that cover outdoor activities, shopping, dining, and tours not just for Laramie, but the surrounding area as well.

GETTING AROUND   Several rental car agencies, including **Avis** (☎ 800/ 331-1212), **Budget** (☎ 406/543-7001), **Hertz** (☎ 800/654-3131), and **National** (☎ 800/227-7368) maintain counters at Laramie Regional Airport.

Taxi service is available through **Laramie Taxi Service** (☎ 307/745-8294).

GETTING OUTSIDE

Curt Gowdy State Park, named for the television sportscaster who hails from Wyoming, is pleasant, if not spectacularly beautiful. Just outside Laramie, and 1,645 acres in size, it's a great spot for a picnic after driving all day along I-80. It's also possible to camp here. There are five campsites, all available for $5 per night. While there are two lakes here, no swimming is allowed (they provide part of Cheyenne's water supply), but boating is possible. Call 307/632-7946 for further information. To get to the park, take I-80 east until you see the exit for WYO 210, the scenic backroad to Cheyenne. Take this road to the park.

Southeast of Laramie, on the edge of the Medicine Bow National Forest, is **Pole Mountain** and the **Vedauwoo Recreation Area.** Vedauwoo and the Happy Jack Trailhead near the Summit exit of I-80 has some excellent summer and winter recreational opportunities.

No, the name has nothing to do with sticking pins in dolls, but Veduawoo (pronounced "VEE-duh-voo") has enough oddities of its own to warrant a visit. The recreation area is covered with strange formations that make for serious rock climbing or just interesting viewing for those who enjoy staring at unusual shapes. To get there, take I-80 east toward Cheyenne, past the second biggest Abe Lincoln head in these parts (10 miles outside town) to the Vedauwoo turnoff.

Sports that are popular in and around this college town include the following.

GOLF

The only golf course in town is the **Jacoby Park Golf Course,** an 18-hole public course on N. 30th (☎ 307/ 745-3111).

WINDSURFING

There's awfully good windsurfing on Lake Hattie, a lake 20 miles outside of town on Wyoming 230. For classes, call **Adventure Is,** 209 S. 2nd (☎ 307/742-3191), a local outfitter.

SEEING THE SIGHTS

The **Wyoming Territorial Park** (☎ 307/745-6161 or 800/845-2287) offers a fascinating look at Laramie's frontier history and its penal past. Formerly a penitentiary, it transmogrified into an experimental livestock station before becoming the park it is today. Almost everything having to do with frontier life before the turn of the 20th century can be found here. **The Horse Barn Theater** makes the trip a full-day event. Admission to the park only is $10; dinner theater tickets for the Horse Barn Dinner Theater show are $30; this price includes park admission. The Horse Barn show is an original music revue called "Raising the Roof." Dinner is served in the theater's restored loft.

The **Wyoming/Colorado Excursion Train** (☎ 307/742-9162 or 800/ 582-7245), offers a look at the Snowy Mountains from the comfort of a passenger train. A first-class ticket is $50. The **Laramie River Rodeo** (☎ 800/ 582-7245 or 307/745-7339) is a summer bonus. Shows are Thursday and Friday from June through August at the fairgrounds. **Jubilee Days** (☎ 307/745-7339) is another Western party that runs around the time Frontier Days begins calming down in Cheyenne. If you didn't get enough of what they had to offer in the capital city, then slide west to keep celebrating Wyoming. The **Plains Museum,** 603 Ivinson (☎ 307/742-4448), is an old Victorian home turned into a bizarre bazaar. The eclectic mix of furnishings seems to have no rhyme or reason, but for $5 you can see it all. **The Wyoming Children's Museum and Nature Center,** 710 Garfield (☎ 307/745-6332), is a treat for kids. It has enough things to keep them busy without having to keep quiet. Admission is $2.

The University of Wyoming
1408 Ivinson Ave., Laramie, WY 82070. ☎ **307/766-4075.**

It all began in 1887 with the funding of Old Main, the university's first building. At that time, there were five professors, two tutors, and 42 students on the 20-acre campus, which also included Prexy's Pasture, where the school's first president kept his cows. Today, the University of Wyoming has more than 2,000 faculty and staff members and an enrollment of 12,000 drawn from across the United States and 65 countries. *Money Guide* rated the University of Wyoming the seventh-best value in public education in the United States, and *Rugg's Recommendations on the Colleges* recommended more undergraduate programs at the University of Wyoming than at any other university in the Rocky Mountain area.

In 1993–94 the university received more than $30 million in grants and contracts for basic and applied research. Some of the research facilities headed by university departments include the Red Buttes Environmental Biology Laboratory in the northeast corner of the state, the Elk Mountain Atmospheric Science Lab atop 11,156-ft. Elk Mountain 60 miles west of Laramie, and the Atmospheric Science Flight Facility at Brees Field (Laramie Regional Airport).

To catch a glimpse of student life in Laramie, stop in at any of the downtown restaurants (their wait staffs are all almost entirely student-run), or swing by Prexy's Pasture, where students hang out in droves, especially in fall. Those visiting during the school year may also want to check out the **performing arts calendar**, by calling 307/766-5000.

In the fall, **Wyoming Cowboy** sports are the hottest thing around. The football and basketball teams, though certainly not perennial powerhouses, have been known to slip into the national limelight occasionally.

Several university museums are open year-round to the public free of charge. They include: the **Geological Museum** (☎ 307/766-4218), with plenty of dinosaur fossils, open Mon–Fri 8am–5pm, Sat–Sun 10am–3pm; the **Rocky Mountain Herbarium** (☎ 307/766-2236), open Mon–Fri 8am–5pm; and the **Insect Museum** (☎ 307/766-2298), which is more or less a research facility and therefore fairly uninteresting to the average visitor, but is open to the public Mon–Fri 8am–5pm year-round. The **Planetarium** (☎ 307/766-6150), the better of Wyoming's two planetariums, has stellar programming throughout the school year. Call for programs or to schedule a private group showing.

Laramie

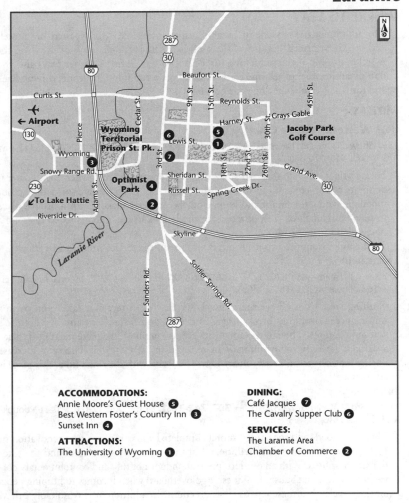

ACCOMMODATIONS:
Annie Moore's Guest House ❺
Best Western Foster's Country Inn ❸
Sunset Inn ❹

ATTRACTIONS:
The University of Wyoming ❶

DINING:
Café Jacques ❼
The Cavalry Supper Club ❻

SERVICES:
The Laramie Area
Chamber of Commerce ❷

SHOPPING

Any university town without a bevy of worthwhile bookstores is odd indeed. Thankfully, Laramie is no exception. **2nd Story Books** and **Personally Recommended Books,** both located at 107 Ivinson, have everything you could want in the way of popular fiction and literature. **Chickering Books** at 307 S. 2nd and Ivinson has a smaller selection of books, but is a worthy member of the scene, for its selection of classics and literature. **High Country Books,** across the street at 306 S. 2nd St., carries books, but also magazines you'll likely be missing while on the road.

　　The French Creek Gallery at 152 N. 2nd St. is an art gallery and framing shop that also sells pottery. **Earth, Wind, and Fire,** just a few doors down at 220 S. 2nd St., is *not* the place for low cut lamé, sequined boots, and disco music, but rather a pottery lover's dream come true. Another art gallery, **Gallery West,** 121 Ivinson Ave., distinguishes itself as a great frame shop. **Green Gold** at 215 S. 1st St. has all the Wyoming jade and most of the silver you'll need. To admire your purchases or to peruse your new copy of *On the Road,* head to the **Coal Creek Coffee Company** at 110 E. Grand, the best coffee shop in town for beats and nonbeats alike.

WHERE TO STAY

The accommodations scene in Laramie isn't remarkable. Mostly, there are motels and those few places that define themselves otherwise don't stray too far from the motel mold. But if you're looking for a place to stay during Frontier Days and you don't want to have to sell one of the kids to get a room in Cheyenne, driving back and forth to Laramie may be your best bet.

MOTELS

Best Western Foster's Country Inn

1561 Snowy Range Dr., Laramie, WY 82070. ☎ 307/742-8371 or 800/526-5145. 112 rms. A/C TV TEL. $55–$70 double. AE, DC, DISC, MC, V.

Located right off I-80, this two-story Best Western named for owner Dick Foster is doing its best to come up to speed in the hospitality game. An indoor pool and hot tub along with a restaurant and lounge on the property make it a comfortable place to stay, but compared with other accommodations in Laramie, its room rates are a touch high.

Five miles from the airport, it offers airport shuttle service from 7am–11pm.

Laramie Inn

421 Boswell, Laramie, WY 82070. ☎ 307/742-3721 or 800/642-4212. 80 rms. A/C TV TEL. $32–$68 double. AE, DC, DISC, MC, V.

Coming west from Cheyenne along I-80, the 3rd Street exit takes you to this hunter green and gray brick motel that is as comfortable as any of Laramie's accommodations. Though the amenities are few (a pool), the price makes this place a bargain. Twenty rooms underwent renovation in late 1995. The rates increase during football season and Frontier Days, but even with the small hike, this place is affordable.

Sunset Inn

1104 S. 3rd St., Laramie, WY 82070. ☎ 307/742-3741. 51 rms. A/C TV TEL. $40–$65 double. AE, DC, DISC, MC, V.

This little wood- and rock-sided motel completed a massive, two-year renovation in 1995. All of the rooms were redone, all of the carpets were replaced, and the exterior was repainted. With an outdoor pool, an indoor hot tub, and complimentary coffee in the office, the Sunset Inn doesn't go overboard when it comes to heaping perks on the traveler, but these few touches do count. In addition, it is reasonably priced and convenient to the the interstate. Despite the fact that you can see the highway from the office window, the rooms are far enough removed for noise to be an issue.

A BED & BREAKFAST

✪ Annie Moore's Guest House

819 University Ave., Laramie, WY 82070. ☎ 307/721-4177 or 800/552-8992. 6 rms (all with shared bath). $60 double, including continental breakfast. AE, DISC, MC, V.

In a town full of prosaic if not downright dull choices, this house across the street from the Old Main, the University of Wyoming's first building, stands out as a great place to stay. Guarded faithfully by Archina, a cat who is over 14 years old, Annie Moore's is a six-bedroom bed-and-breakfast with 50 windows and a simple decor. Thankfully, new owners Joe Bundy and Ann Acuff (they purchased it in 1992) haven't changed much.

The two downstairs garden level rooms—the Sunrise, a cheerful room with plenty of light and a queen-size bed, and the Green Room, with a queen- and a twin-size bed—look out onto the terrace. Annie's Room is in the basement, with one single bed, but it's well-lit. The main floor is devoted entirely to the Sun Room, a great place to read or watch passersby. It's not uncommon to find guests sipping tea and juice from the fridge there.

The upstairs rooms are all named for colors: the Blue Room, with a white iron queen-size bed, has a private sundeck; the Yellow Room, with a queen-size bed, has a writing desk; and the regal Purple Room, with a king-size bed and a bay window, overlooks the campus. It's hard to find this much charm for the price elsewhere in Wyoming.

CAMPING

N&H Trailer Ranch, open year-round, is near the University of Wyoming campus at 1360 N. 3rd (☎ 307/742-3158), and offers laundry facilities and full hookups for $11. The **Laramie KOA** is off I-80 at 1271 Baker St. (☎ 307/742-6553) and is open from March through November. Hookups are $10. The **Riverside Campground** is a smaller site near I-80 at the corner of Curtis and McCue Sts. (☎ 307/721-7405). This campground is open all year and has tent sites near the Laramie River. RV hookups are $10.

WHERE TO EAT

Café Jacques
216 Grand Ave. ☎ **307/742-5522.** Lunch $5–$7; main dinner courses $13–$17. AE, DC, DISC, MC, V. Mon–Fri 11am–2pm, 5–10pm; Sat 5–10pm, closed Sunday. STEAK/SEAFOOD.

This cafe celebrated its 10th anniversary in 1995, and it's no accident these guys have been around this long. The seafood is excellent and the steaks superb. This is the fanciest of the downtown restaurants (a cafe it isn't), but for a more casual dinner, the bar at Café Jacques is always an option. The dining room is big and elegant, with black napkins on white linens, and the service is excellent. Weekly chef's specials change every Thursday and often include the fish of the week.

The Cavalry Supper Club
4425 S. 3rd St. ☎ **307/745-5551.** Main dinner courses $15–$28. AE, DC, DISC, MC, V. Daily 4:30pm-10pm. STEAK/SEAFOOD.

A restaurant for those with large appetites, with admittedly high prices and an unusual atmosphere and decor, the Cavalry Supper Club is located a couple of miles south of town. It pays tribute to the 7th Cavalry that once used this site as a post on their famous march north to the Battle of the Little Bighorn with walls of taxidermy and waitresses dressed in uniforms that resemble those worn by the cavalry. Previously a schoolhouse and at one time, a brothel, we guess you could say that this is a restaurant with a colorful past. All meals come with complimentary appetizers (sautéed mushrooms), tea, coffee, and dessert. There are always at least eight entrées to choose from, including lobster, prime rib, and lasagna. Unless quantity is just as important to you as quality, you may be disappointed.

El Conquistador
110 Ivinson Ave. ☎ **307/742-2377.** Lunch $3–$5; main dinner courses $5–$11. DISC, MC, V. Mon–Sat 11am–9pm. MEXICAN.

This is the only Mexican restaurant in Laramie, and it's a good one. What started out as a snack bar in the Laramie bowling alley in 1973 has grown into an institution. Known among locals for exquisite Mexican food never smothered in sauce (as the cook told us, "We like you to see the food"), it's the chili, especially the green chili, that keeps people coming back. The delicious daily specials are also worth serious consideration.

✪ Jeffrey's Bistro

123 Ivinson Ave. ☎ **307/742-7046.** Lunch $4–$10; main dinner courses $4–$10. AE, DISC, MC, V. Mon–Sat 11am–9pm; Sun 9am–2pm. CREATIVE AMERICAN.

This is the best restaurant in town: It's inexpensive, good, and has a few dishes on the lighter side. The hardwood floors and brick walls give the Bistro a great downtown charm that makes it an appealing place for lunch and a calm place for dinner. We enjoyed the Siamese Chicken, a Thai dish of chicken, broccoli, and peanuts sautéed and served in a creamy curry sauce with brown rice, and the frozen pie, a cross between a cream pie and ice cream, on our last visit. The Chocolate Sin Cheesecake wasn't bad, either.

LARAMIE AFTER DARK

As far as the performing arts go, Laramie's options are limited. However, the only game in town does a pretty good job. The **University of Wyoming** hosts a year-round schedule of concerts, theater performances, and art exhibits that simply can't be seen elsewhere in the state. For a schedule of events, contact the **Department of Theater and Dance** (☎ 307/766-2198).

For a less formal evening, head downtown to **Bowman's Brewery,** the town's first brewpub. It serves typical pub food, but it's the home-grown beer that keeps locals returning. The **Buckhorn Bar** next door to El Conquistador on Ivinson is where all of Laramie mixes after hours. The **Cowboy Bar** offers up Laramie's contribution to the country-and-Western music scene.

4　A Side Trip for the Outdoor Enthusiast: Carbon County & the Snowy Mountains

Heading west from the high plateau of Laramie, there isn't a more desolate stretch to be found in Wyoming. There seems to be nothing significant for miles. The high plains get higher and just as you're about to curse the highway and the almost blindingly bright sun that reflects off the windshield of your car, something unexpected happens when you reach the 20-mile marker or so. Mountains rise, forests emerge, and suddenly, you find yourself in what is truly an undiscovered part of Wyoming: a part of the Medicine Bow National Forest called the Snowy Range. Numerous outdoor activities can be enjoyed here, a few highlights of which follow. Perhaps the best way to get a sense of the vastness of Carbon County and the great Snowy Mountains that stretch through this region is by driving the **Snowy Range National Scenic Byway.** To reach the road from Laramie, take exit 311 off I-80 and head west along Snowy Range Road (see Section 1 above for a driving tour).

EXPLORING THE SNOWY RANGE ON FOOT

There are three different districts in the Medicine Bow National Forest, and each can be explored by hikers of moderate ability. Our favorite is in the Brush Creek District. The **Medicine Bow Peak Trail,** is a 4.4-mile trek that at first glance seems to be a short and easy hike. Don't be fooled: At the end of the trail is the summit of 12,013-foot Medicine Bow Peak, the tallest mountain in the Medicine Bow range.

Other trails in the national forest range in length from 1 to 16 miles and in difficulty from moderate to extremely difficult. For **detailed trail maps** of the Medicine Bow National Forest, contact the **Medicine Bow National Forest Service** in Laramie at 307/745-2300.

RV AND TENT CAMPING

If you have an RV and think you might have trouble finding a spot in this area, don't worry. There are more than 30 different public sites and most are open from June through September. The **Forest Service** (☎ 307/745-2300) provides specific directions and takes reservations. Some of the public campgrounds in the area (all offer sites for less than $8 per night) have tent sites, but most do not.

GUIDED EXPLORATIONS WITH OUTFITTERS

Several fishing and whitewater rafting guides are based here and lead trips along the North Platte River that runs through the region. The average cost of a full-day two-person drift fishing expedition is $250 including lunch, $175 for a half-day excursion with no meal. A full-day whitewater rafting expedition runs approximately $280 for two people, with lunch included.

The Orvis-endorsed outfitter in the area is **Great Rocky Mountain Outfitters** at 216 E. Walnut in Saratoga (☎ 307/326-8750). This firm has been guiding anglers along the Upper North Platte since 1981. **Platte Valley Anglers,** at the corner of 1st Ave. and Bride St. in Saratoga (☎ 307/326-5750), offers drift fishing, whitewater fishing, and whitewater float trips.

5 Rock Springs & Flaming Gorge National Recreation Area

Rock Springs is to Wyoming what Butte is to Montana, only worse. It's really amazing how similar the towns are in certain respects: Both had an active mining industry up through the 1950s, both experienced the depression that followed the demise of that industry, and both struggled with the environmental cleanup. But Rock Springs breaths new life into the horror of industrialized overkill. While Butte retains some notable examples of 19th-century Western architecture, Rock Springs has the unremarkable, anywheresville buildup of an interstate town. Even Richard Ford's contemporary collection of short stories titled after the city does little to endear this place to anyone.

It is, however, close to two notable natural attractions, Flaming Gorge National Recreation Area and Fossil Butte National Monument. Composed of more than 200,000 acres of badlands and lakes that stretch across the Wyoming border into northeastern Utah, **Flaming Gorge National Recreation Area** is a vast park of kaleidoscopic colors that bears an eerie resemblance to the Missouri breaks, the badlands of South Dakota, and Makoshika State Park in Glendive, Montana. Eventually discovered and named by the one-armed explorer, John Wesley Powell, the area was first used by Native Americans and therefore has a number of petroglyphs that can be seen by visitors. **Fossil Butte National Monument** is, as the name suggests, an area that was established by the National Park Service to protect a butte filled with prehistoric plant and insect fossils.

ESSENTIALS

GETTING THERE   **Continental Express** (☎ 800/525-0280) and **United Express** (☎ 800/241-6522) have flights into the **Rock Springs Airport,** 15 miles east of town on I-80.

The bus terminal for **Greyhound** is at 1665 Sunset Dr. (☎ 307/362-2931). Two buses run from Cheyenne daily.

The **Amtrak** station is at 501 S. Main St. and can be reached at 307/362-3876 or 800/872-7245 for schedules and information. Trains arrive every Monday, Wednesday, and Friday from points east and west along the Chicago to Seattle Pioneer line.

Rock Springs is located just northeast of the Flaming Gorge National Recreation Area at the intersection of U.S. 191 and I-80. To reach Rock Springs from Cheyenne by car, take I-80 west 258 miles. From Casper, take WYO 220 for 74 miles to its junction with U.S. 287 at Muddy Gap, then take U.S. 287 south for 45 miles to I-80 at Riverton and head west for 143 miles to reach Rock Springs. From Jackson, take U.S. 191 south for 178 miles. For information on road conditions in Rock Springs, call 307/382-9966.

VISITOR INFORMATION The **Rock Springs Chamber of Commerce,** 1897 Dewar Dr. (☎ 307/362-3771), can help put a positive spin on Rock Springs and its immediate area. For maps and information about **Flaming Gorge National Recreation Area,** contact the Green River, Wyoming National Forest Service office (☎ 307/875-2871).

GETTING AROUND If you're in need of a rental car, **Avis** (☎ 800/331-1212) and **Hertz** (☎ 800/654-3131) both maintain counters at the airport in Rock Springs. **Taxi service** is available through **Downtown Taxi Service** (☎ 307/382-6161).

EXPLORING FLAMING GORGE NATIONAL RECREATION AREA

Those interested in houseboating, hiking, mountain biking, fishing, and other watersports will enjoy a visit to **Flaming Gorge National Recreation Area,** which begins close to Rock Springs. Though most of this designated recreation area lies in the northeast corner of Utah, it is possible to enjoy it from the Wyoming side.

The region is named for the impressive canyon John Wesley Powell first saw in his famous 1869 expedition down the Green River, near where the river enters the mountains. **Flaming Gorge Reservoir** is located in Wyoming, though it is backed up by a 500-foot-high concrete dam that was completed in 1964 and is located 15 miles south of the border in Utah. The reservoir is popular with boaters, waterskiers, and anglers.

Admission to the recreation area is free. Administered by the U.S. Forest Service, regulations here are mostly common sense, aimed at preserving water quality and protecting the forest and historic sites. In addition, Wyoming and Utah fishing and boating regulations apply in those states' sections of the recreation area. Dogs are not permitted in buildings and should be leashed at all times, but are permitted on hiking trails.

To get there, take I-80 west from Rock Springs for 15 miles to the town of Green River at the junction of WYO 530. Here, you can stop at the U.S. Forest Service-run **visitor center** in **Green River** at 1450 Uinta Drive, Green River WY 82935 (☎ 307/875-2871) and pick up maps and brochures, including detailed information about hiking and mountain biking trails if you've got your boots and/or bike along. As you drive south on WYO 530, the cactus and sagebrush-filled **Devils Playground** badlands and the humpbacked rock formations of **Haystack Buttes** will be to your right. WYO 530 runs the length of the recreation area's west side and provides access to the Flaming Gorge Reservoir at the **Buckboard Crossing Area** 20 miles south, where a full-service marina is in operation during the summer.

At the **Buckboard Marina** (☎ 307/875-6927) a 14-foot boat can be yours for 12 hours for only $30. (For $150, you can rent a waterskiing boat for the same amount of time.) From Buckboard, it's another 25 miles to Lucerne Valley and the **Lucerne Marina** across the border in Utah (☎ 801/784-3483). Here, you can rent a houseboat from mid-May to mid-September for two nights for $314 (it's cheaper the longer you rent; seven nights is $745).

From WYO 530, pick up Utah 44 just across the state line in Manila, Utah. Utah 44 runs south then east for 27 miles to pick up U.S. Hwy. 191. Along this route you'll catch glimpses of Utah's Uinta Mountains to the west and may see bighorn sheep in nearby **Sheep Creek Canyon,** which has been designated a special geological area by the forest service because of its dramatically twisted and upturned rocks. A mostly paved 11-mile loop road cuts off from Utah 44, offering a ¹/₂-hour tour of this beautiful, narrow canyon, with its lavish display of rocks that have eroded into intricate patterns, a process that began with the uplifting of the Uinta Mountains millions of years ago. This loop may be closed in winter; check at the visitor center in Green River, Wyoming, before heading out if you're visiting during winter.

Eventually, you'll come to the **Red Canyon Overlook** on the southern edge of the gorge, where a rainbow of colors adorns 1,000-foot-tall cliffs. In Wyoming, highways are farther from the rim, offering fewer opportunities to see the river and its canyons than in Utah. Here, you'll be able to drink them in. The **Red Canyon Visitors Center** (open 9:30am–5pm in summer) is nearby, as is **Flaming Gorge Dam.**

To head back to Wyoming, take U.S. Hwy. 191 north and south away from the eastern edge of the gorge. From the junction of Utah 44 and U.S. Hwy. 191, it's 16 miles to the border. Once you're at the state line, it's 30 miles to the turnoff for **Firehole Canyon,** an access to the gorge that offers views of the magnificent spires known as **Chimney Rocks.**

Camping sites are maintained by the National Forest Service (there are close to 20 in the area) and maps to the sites are available in Wyoming at the Green River, Wyoming, U.S. Forest Service Office or the Green River Chamber of Commerce at the same location (see above).

Fishing guides are available from the **Good Life** led by Cliff Redmon (☎ 307/786-2132 in winter or ☎ 801/784-3121 in summer) and from **Creative Fishing Adventures** led by Jim Williams (☎ 801/784-3301). An eight-hour excursion for two is just under $300 and includes all equipment, but no meals.

Although summer is the busiest time of year, this remains a relatively undiscovered destination, and you shouldn't have any trouble finding campsites, lodging, or boat rentals. Hikers enjoy the area in fall, and during the cold, snowy winter, it's popular with cross-country skiers and ice fishers.

For more information about the Utah portion of Flaming Gorge National Recreation Area, including additional outdoor recreational activities and outfitters, lodging options, and other nearby sites of interest, see *Frommer's Utah* by Don and Barbara Laine.

GALLERIES & MUSEUMS IN ROCK SPRINGS

Before you leave the Rock Springs area, there are a few sights worth taking the time to see. The **Community Fine Arts Center** at the Sweetwater County Library, 400 C St., contains a few original paintings by **Grandma Moses** and **Norman Rockwell.** Though not their most famous pieces by any stretch, these are early works that admirers may find notable. The Fine Arts Center was started by Rock Springs high school students in the 1930s. The **Rock Springs Historical Museum,** at 201 B St., is a great piece of Romanesque architecture. Formerly City Hall, the building now houses exhibits covering the city's mining history. The **Western Wyoming**

Community College Dinosaur Skeleton Collection at WWCC, 2500 College Dr., is also worth a stop. It has more than 10 dinosaur displays and a few fish and plant fossils. All of these museums are free.

WHERE TO STAY
MOTELS

American Family Inn

1635 N. Elk, Rock Springs, WY 82901. ☎ **307/382-4217** or 800/548-6621. 96 rms. A/C TV TEL. $40–$45 double. All rates inlcude continental breakfast. AE, DC, DISC, MC, V.

It's comfortable and clean and right off the interstate, but other than that, this cherry wood and brick motel doesn't have an incredible number of amenities. A laundry room, pool, and outdoor hot tub are available to guests and continental breakfast is served daily (it's included in the room rate). Also on the premises is a marginal restaurant called the Santa Fe Trail.

Days Inn

1545 Elk St., Rock Springs, WY 82901. ☎ **307/362-5646** or 800/343-6767. 105 rms. A/C TV TEL. $45–$65 double. All rates inlcude continental breakfast. AE, DC, DISC, MC, V.

It's hard to miss this Days Inn; just look for the giant sign that stares at you from the interstate. Amenities are few, but thoughtful for a chain motel: There's an outdoor pool, free continental breakfast, and every room comes with its own refrigerator and microwave oven. For economizing families, it's a good choice.

La Quinta

2717 Dewar Dr., Rock Springs, WY 82901. ☎ **307/362-1770** or 800/531-5900. 130 rms. A/C TV TEL. $44–$51 double. All rates inlcude continental breakfast. AE, DC, DISC, MC, V.

This particular La Quinta seems to have been passed over in the chain's recent effort to soundproof all of its rooms nationwide, but if all you seek is a clean, inexpensive place (and you're a heavy sleeper), this motel will do just fine. To get here, take exit 102 from the interstate and turn north. There's a heated pool and the continental breakfast of bagels, cereal, fruit, and coffee is better than what is offered by other nearby accommodations, even though it, too, is included.

CAMPING

See "Exploring the Flaming Gorge National Recreation Area" for places to camp in this region of Wyoming.

WHERE TO EAT

Killpepper's

1030 Dewar Dr. ☎ **307/382-8012.** Lunch $5–$7; main dinner courses $10–$14. AE, DC, DISC, MC, V. Daily 11am–9pm. AMERICAN.

A favorite among locals for over a decade for its fine dining atmosphere, Killpepper's recently repackaged itself as a somewhat trendy bar and grill. You can still get a highfalutin' steak, but most of the menu is now more simply prepared and moderately priced. The change was subtle, the linens were swept away quietly, but Rock Springs now has its first fern bar.

Sands Café

1549 9th St. ☎ **307/362-5633.** Breakfast items $4–$7; lunch $3–$15; main dinner courses $3–$15. AE, DISC, MC, V. Daily 7am–10pm. CHINESE.

If you're hankering for Chinese while in Rock Springs, then head for the Buddha statue. More like a coffee shop than a Chinese restaurant (one side looks like

Anywhere, U.S.A., the other like a Beijing storefront), the food is actually pretty good. We recommend the Singapore Chow Mien.

White Mountain Mining Company

240 Clearview. ☎ **307/382-5265.** Main dinner courses $10–$22. AE, DISC, MC, V. Mon–Sat 5–10pm; closed Sunday. STEAK/SEAFOOD.

This place got overhauled in 1995 and now is one of the nicer supper clubs in Southern Wyoming. The dining room tables are covered with mauve linens and the barn-style walls give the place the feel of, well, a barn (the bar and lounge had to settle for wallpaper during the renovation). Like any other supper club, this one serves a mean prime rib, of which they are very proud, but the deep-fried shrimp is a close second. Romantic candles grace the tables, which explains the local couples and celebrating families that frequent the place. Though White Mountain may not be a special place for tourists, it's a favorite in Rock Springs.

6 Also Worth a Look: Fossil Butte National Monument & the Killpecker Dunes

As far as Wyoming natural monuments go, Devils Tower may get most of the press, but Fossil Butte is well worth a side trip if you're exploring the southwestern part of the state. Located 86 miles northwest of Rock Springs in Kemmerer, Fossil Butte shares the local spotlight with the town's most famous son, J.C. Penney. Take an hour to visit the original **Penney home** and **mother store** in Kemmerer at 107 J.C. Penney Drive, and then head out to Fossil Butte for a picnic lunch.

Operated by the National Park Service, Fossil Butte's major attraction is a 1,000-foot-high escarpment that rises above the surrounding plains. Within this butte are millions of ancient fossils of insects, fish, turtles, plants, and snails. One of the few places in the world where fossilized birds and bats have been found, the site was not discovered until the railroad was laid in this area in the late 1800s.

To get there, take U.S. Hwy. 30 to Kemmerer. No fee is charged to enter the monument. The relatively new **Fossil Butte Visitor Center** (☎ 307/877-4455) is 3¹/₂ miles off U.S. 30 (just follow the signs). It's open daily 8am–7pm from Memorial Day to Labor Day and from 8am–4:30pm the rest of the year and houses displays on the area's geology, paleontology, and natural history. Two videos are available for viewing, and the shop sells several books on natural history. Officials are on hand to interpret the area for visitors, who can hike along trails leading to fossil beds over 50 million years old. Contact the **National Park Service** for maps and further information at P.O. Box 592, Kemmerer, WY 83101 (☎ 307/877-4455).

The **Killpecker Sand Dunes** are, no joke, east of Eden, a tiny town north of Rock Springs. The fastest way to get to them is via Hwy. 191 out of Rock Springs. If you plan on seeing them up close, it's best to be in a four-wheel-drive vehicle, since the last 20-odd miles of the journey is along a gravel road. The entrance to this unpaved road, Tri-Territory Road, is 10 miles north of Rock Springs on U.S. Hwy. 191 and the dunes are 22 miles east along it. (To get to the dunes from Fossil Butte, take U.S. Hwy. 189 to WYO 28 to the town of Farson. At Farson, take U.S. Hwy 191 to Eden, just 4 miles south. At this point, follow the directions given above.)

A great day-trip for the off-road enthusiast and wildlife watcher, this road also leads to the **White Mountain Petroglyphs,** and **Boar's Tusk,** the unusual remains of an ancient volcano. To reach the Native American rock carvings near White Mountain, head left at the marker. Approximately 4 miles down a very rough road, the track deadends at a low sandstone cliff. Many of the carvings depict hunting scenes and have horses in them, suggesting that they are of a more recent origin. It's best to avoid this road in spring or after a heavy downpour. Return to the road and turn left. Six miles to the east, turn right at the split to visit the dunes or left to visit Boar's Tusk or parts of the dunes where vehicles are not allowed. If you choose to bear left, you'll drive approximately 1 1/2 miles to an unmarked road that leads to the base of Boar's Tusk, a volcanic rock. A side road to Boar's Tusk (2 1/2 miles in length) can be driven with a four-wheel-drive vehicle, but is not recommended to those in cars. You may see rock-climbers in the area, since this is a popular place to practice the sport locally.

Index

WYOMING

FROMMER'S BEST BEACH VACATIONS

(The top places to sun, stroll, shop, stay, play, party, and swim, with each beach rated for beauty, swimming, sand, and amenities)

California
Carolinas/Georgia
Florida
Hawaii

Mid-Atlantic from New York to
Washington, D.C.
New England

FROMMER'S BED & BREAKFAST GUIDES

(Selective guides with four-color photos and full description of the best inns in each region)

California
Caribbean
Great American Cities
Hawaii
Mid-Atlantic

New England
Pacific Northwest
Rockies
Southeast States
Southwest

FROMMER'S IRREVERENT GUIDES

(Wickedly honest guides for sophisticated travelers and those who want to be)

Amsterdam
Chicago
London

Manhattan
New Orleans
San Francisco

FROMMER'S DRIVING TOURS

(Four-color photos and detailed maps outlining spectacular scenic driving routes)

Australia
Austria
Britain
Florida
France
Germany
Ireland

Italy
Scandinavia
Scotland
Spain
Switzerland
U.S.A.

FROMMER'S BORN TO SHOP

(The ultimate travel guides for discriminating shoppers from cut-rate to couture)

Great Britain
Hong Kong

London
New York

FROMMER'S FOOD LOVER'S COMPANIONS

(Lavishly illustrated guides to regional specialties, restaurants, gourmet shops, markets, local wines, and more)

France
Italy

Chicago '96
Denver/Boulder/Colorado Springs, 2nd Ed.
Disney World/Orlando '96
Dublin, 2nd Ed.
Hong Kong, 4th Ed.
Las Vegas '96
London '96
Los Angeles '96
Madrid/Costa del Sol, 2nd Ed.
Mexico City, 1st Ed.
Miami '95-'96
Minneapolis/St. Paul, 4th Ed.
Montreal/Quebec City, 8th Ed.
Nashville/Memphis, 2nd Ed.
New Orleans '96
New York City '96

Paris '96
Philadelphia, 8th Ed.
Rome, 10th Ed.
St. Louis/Kansas City, 2nd Ed.
San Antonio/Austin, 1st Ed.
San Diego, 4th Ed.
San Francisco '96
Santa Fe/Taos/Albuquerque '96
Seattle/Portland, 4th Ed.
Sydney, 4th Ed.
Tampa/St. Petersburg, 3rd Ed.
Tokyo, 4th Ed.
Toronto, 3rd Ed.
Vancouver/Victoria, 3rd Ed.
Washington, D.C. '96

FROMMER'S FAMILY GUIDES

(Guides to family-friendly hotels, restaurants, activities, and attractions)

California with Kids
Los Angeles with Kids
New York City with Kids

San Francisco with Kids
Washington, D.C. with Kids

FROMMER'S WALKING TOURS

(Memorable strolls through colorful and historic neighborhoods, accompanied by detailed directions and maps)

Berlin
Chicago
England's Favorite Cities
London, 2nd Ed.
Montreal/Quebec City
New York, 2nd Ed.

Paris, 2nd Ed.
San Francisco, 2nd Ed.
Spain's Favorite Cities
Tokyo
Venice
Washington, D.C., 2nd Ed.

FROMMER'S AMERICA ON WHEELS

(Guides for travelers who are exploring the USA by car, featuring a brand-new rating system for accommodations and full-color road maps)

Arizona and New Mexico
California and Nevada

Florida
Mid-Atlantic

FROMMER'S SPECIAL-INTEREST TITLES

Arthur Frommer's Branson!
Arthur Frommer's New World of Travel, 5th Ed.
Frommer's America's 100 Best-Loved State Parks
Frommer's Caribbean Hideaways, 7th Ed.
Frommer's Complete Hostel Vacation Guide to England, Scotland & Wales

Frommer's National Park Guide, 29th Ed.
USA Sports Traveler's and TV Viewer's Golf Tournament Guide
USA Sports Minor League Baseball Book
USA Today Golf Atlas

FROMMER'S COMPLETE TRAVEL GUIDES

(Comprehensive guides to sightseeing, dining, and accommodations, with selections in all price ranges from deluxe to budget)

Acapulco/Ixtapa/Taxco, 2nd Ed.
Alaska, 4th Ed.
Arizona '96
Australia, 4th Ed.
Austria, 6th Ed.
Bahamas '96
Belgium/Holland/Luxembourg, 4th Ed.
Bermuda '96
Budapest & the Best of Hungary, 1st Ed.
California '96
Canada, 9th Ed.
Caribbean '96
Carolinas/Georgia, 3rd Ed.
Colorado, 3rd Ed.
Costa Rica, 1st Ed.
Cruises '95-'96
Delaware/Maryland, 2nd Ed.
England '96
Florida '96
France '96
Germany '96
Greece, 1st Ed.
Honolulu/Waikiki/Oahu, 4th Ed.
Ireland, 1st Ed.
Italy '96
Jamaica/Barbados, 2nd Ed.
Japan, 3rd Ed.

Maui, 1st Ed.
Mexico '96
Montana/Wyoming, 1st Ed.
Nepal, 3rd Ed.
New England '96
New Mexico, 3rd Ed.
New York State '94-'95
Nova Scotia/New Brunswick/Prince Edward Island, 1st Ed.
Portugal, 14th Ed.
Prague & the Best of the Czech Republic, 1st Ed.
Puerto Rico '95-'96
Puerto Vallarta/Manzanillo/Guadalajara, 3rd Ed.
Scandinavia, 16th Ed.
Scotland, 3rd Ed.
South Pacific, 5th Ed.
Spain, 16th Ed.
Switzerland, 7th Ed.
Thailand, 2nd Ed.
U.S.A., 4th Ed.
Utah, 1st Ed.
Virgin Islands, 3rd Ed.
Virginia, 3rd Ed.
Washington/Oregon, 6th Ed.
Yucatan '95-'96

FROMMER'S FRUGAL TRAVELER'S GUIDES

(Dream vacations at down-to-earth prices)

Australia on $45 '95-'96
Berlin from $50, 3rd Ed.
Caribbean from $60, 1st Ed.
Costa Rica/Guatemala/Belize on $35, 3rd Ed.
Eastern Europe on $30, 5th Ed.
England from $50, 21st Ed.
Europe from $50 '96
Greece from $45, 6th Ed.
Hawaii from $60, 30th Ed.

Ireland from $45, 16th Ed.
Israel from $45, 16th Ed.
London from $60 '96
Mexico from $35 '96
New York on $70 '94-'95
New Zealand from $45, 6th Ed.
Paris from $65 '96
South America on $40, 16th Ed.
Washington, D.C. from $50 '96

FROMMER'S COMPLETE CITY GUIDES

(Comprehensive guides to sightseeing, dining, and accommodations in all price ranges)

Amsterdam, 8th Ed.
Athens, 10th Ed.
Atlanta & the Summer Olympic Games '96

Bangkok, 2nd Ed.
Berlin, 3rd Ed.
Boston '96